CURRENT
ISSUES IN
FINANCE

FIXED INCOME MARKETS AND THEIR DERIVATIVES

SURESH M. SUNDARESAN

Professor of Finance and Economics
Columbia Business School
Columbia University

SOUTH-WESTERN College Publishing

An International Thomson Publishing Company

Acquisitions Editor: Christopher Will
Team Director: Jack C. Calhoun
Developmental Editor: Lois Boggs-Leavens
Production Editors: Rebecca Roby and Sharon L. Smith
Production House: Omegatype Typography, Inc.
Verification: Angela Bansal
Cover Design: Paul Neff Design
Marketing Manager: Scott D. Person

Library of Congress Cataloging-in-Publication Data

Sundaresan, Suresh M.
   Fixed income markets and their derivatives / Suresh M. Sundaresan.
      p.   cm.
   Includes bibliographical references and index.
   ISBN 0–538–84005–6
   1. Fixed-income securities.   I. Title.
  HG4650.S86   1996
  332.63'2044—dc20   96-26325
                                        CIP

ISBN: 0-538-84005-6

3 4 5 6 7 8 MT 3 2 1 0 9 8

Printed in the United States of America

I ⓣ P
International Thomson Publishing
South-Western College Publishing is an ITP Company. The ITP trademark is used under license.

Dedicated to Raji, Savitar, and Sriya

Brief Contents

Contents

Preface

Fixed-income markets and their derivatives have grown tremendously in the last two decades. Nearly two thirds of the market value of all outstanding securities (including equity) are fixed-income securities. Fixed-income derivatives in the dealer market are estimated at a national value of over 11 trillion dollars.

This book provides an integrated, self-contained analysis of the market institutions, theory, and empirical evidence in the important area of fixed-income markets and their derivatives. The book is divided into two parts. Part I consists of 11 chapters. Nine chapters are devoted to the study of fixed-income markets and two are devoted to the development of the theory of term structure and options pricing. Part II is devoted to the study of fixed-income derivatives markets.

The subject of fixed-income markets and their derivatives is extraordinarily rich in market institutions and theories of valuation. In addition, a great deal of empirical evidence on the behavior of interest rates, inflation, default rates, financial distress, prepayments, etc., further bridges the gap between the richness of the market institutions and the relative sophistication of the theory of valuation. Empirical work has guided the development of valuation. The book attempts to capture this interplay.

The unique features of the book include the following:

- An analysis of the Treasury markets, including the auction mechanisms covering discriminatory auctions and the Treasury's experiment with uniform price auctions, is presented. The May 1991 auction of the two-year notes and the role played by Salomon Brothers is fully discussed and analyzed.

- A description and analysis of when-issued markets, interdealer broker markets, auctions, and the secondary markets is provided. Extensive treatment of repo markets and how they are used to finance dealer positions is included. The concepts of general collateral and special repo rates are also discussed.

- A comprehensive treatment of bond mathematics with over twenty examples using real-life prices and yields is offered. Difficult concepts such as PVBP (DV01), duration, and convexity are illustrated with simple examples. Applications of bond mathematics to trading (bond swaps, spreads, and butterfly trades) are illustrated. The concepts of forward rates, implied spot rates, strip rates, and par bond yield curves are developed in detail. The economics of stripping and reconstitutions is also addressed.

- An accessible treatment of the arbitrage-free models of the term structure, including the concept of state prices and no-arbitrage, is provided. We develop the concept of mean-reversion in interest rates and the idea of calibrating the model to market data.

Full discussion is provided for several single-factor models including the Black, Derman, and Toy model and the Ho and Lee model.

- A self-contained treatment of options pricing theory is provided in Part I in order to enable the reader to apply these concepts to value options on bonds and options on futures contracts. The pricing of options by Monte Carlo simulation is developed in detail. This also lays the pedagogical foundation for the valuation of corporate debt and mortgage-backed securities. Over a dozen examples are worked out to illustrate the key concepts.

- The theory and empirical work in the area of corporate debt pricing and corporate financial distress is presented in detail. Options pricing theory is applied to value default premia. Strategic debt service, deviations from absolute priority, and hybrid debt securities are also presented. Agency markets are analyzed.

- Primary mortgage markets (fixed and adjustable-rate mortgages) and the concept of securitization are described in detail. The prepayments risk in this market is discussed comprehensively. Factors determining prepayments, measures of prepayments and the integration of prepayments with a single-factor model of interest rates are presented. The concept of Option Adjusted Spreads (OAS) is described.

- Portfolio management techniques such as dedicated portfolios (matched funding), indexation, immunization and portfolio insurance are developed.

- An overview of the dealer and listed derivatives markets, their growth, breadth and applications is offered.

- A detailed analysis of the Treasury bond futures contracts is presented. Concepts such as basis, basis after carry, delivery options, coupon bias, and the determination of the cheapest deliverable bond are described in detail. Real-life prices and delivery strategies are used to integrate theory with practice.

- The Eurodollar cash and futures markets are described. The settlement of Eurodollar futures to LIBOR and the use of Eurodollar strips are illustrated with examples. The interest rate swaps markets and their pricing using the par bond curve as well as using the zeroes extracted from the Eurodollar futures are explored. The effect of credit risk on the swap dealer's bid-offer spreads is analyzed.

- Risk management techniques such as Value-at-Risk (VAR) and the concept of risk measurement are examined. The roles of holding period, correlation, liquidity and credit risk are addressed in designing risk management systems.

- Each chapter has several questions which test the reader on the concepts developed in the chapter as well as other issues of general interest related to the chapter. Some questions are designed based on historical data.

An instructor's manual provides solutions to the end-of-chapter questions.

The development of this book covered several years and I owe a debt of gratitude to many people. Several classes of MBA students at Columbia Business School (in my Debt Markets course and Advanced Derivatives course) offered critical comments and suggestions on the class notes which formed the basis for the book. Parts of the manuscript were also used in the training programs at Bankers Trust, Goldman Sachs, Credit Suisse and Morgan Stanley. I am grateful to many participants in these programs for their comments and suggestions.

The book uses results from published research co-authored with a number of my colleagues. In this context my thanks are due to Ron Anderson, Mark Broadie, In Joon Kim, Bruno Montalvo, Kjell Nyborg, Krishna Ramaswamy, Scott Richard, Tong-sheng Sun, Ching Wang, and Fernando Zapatero.

Several of my students have assisted me in the collection and analysis of the data. In particular, I want to thank Quing Du, Rao Aisola, Geoff Zin, G. R. K. Reddy, Tom Gill, Scott McDermott, and Wen-ching Wang for their help. The book has benefitted from a critical review by many colleagues who offered valuable insights. I thank the following reviewers:

Stanley M. Atkinson
University of Central Florida

Pierluigi Balduzzi
New York University

Bradford Cornell
University of California, Los Angeles
Director, Bank of America Research Center

Mark R. Eaker
University of Virginia Darden School

Michael Gibbons
Wharton School
University of Pennsylvania

Peter Knez
University of Wisconsin

James T. Lindley
University of Southern Mississippi

Ehud Ronn
University of Texas, Austin

Anthony B. Sanders
The Ohio State University

Chester Spatt
Carnegie Mellon University

Rajiv Sant
Mankato State University

Paul J. Swanson, Jr.
University of Cincinnati

The professional staff at South-Western Publishing made the task of writing this book as salubrious as possible. I thank Christopher Will who originated the idea and saw it through to its completion and Lois Boggs-Leavens who helped in the earlier stages. Sharon Smith gently nudged me along the final stages and I owe much to her help and encouragement. Mary Young and the staff at Omegatype Typography, Inc. did a splendid job in preparing the galleys and proofing. Finally, I thank my wife, Raji Ayer, for her understanding throughout this project and also for preparing many of the tables, figures and solutions to the problem sets.

Despite careful scrutiny by all involved, a few errors may have gone undetected. I retain responsibility for them. I will be grateful if any remaining errors are brought to my attention so that they can be corrected in the next printing.

Suresh Sundaresan

Part I

Fixed-Income Securities

Chapter 1

An Overview of Fixed-Income Securities

Chapter Objectives

The purpose of this chapter is to introduce and describe fixed-income securities and the markets in which they are issued and traded. Chapter 1 will help the reader understand and answer the following questions.

- What are fixed-income securities?
- What are the key categories of players in debt markets and what are their objectives? In this context, we will examine the following players:
  1. Issuers
  2. Investors
  3. Intermediaries
- What are the sources of risk and return in debt securities? The following sources of risk will be defined and addressed:
  1. Market risk
  2. Credit risk
  3. Liquidity risk
  4. Timing risk
- How are debt securities classified?

In addition, Chapter 1 will provide an overview of each segment of the debt markets in the United States and other leading capital markets in the world. In this overview the terminology used in each segment will also be defined.

INTRODUCTION

An overview of fixed-income securities markets is useful for many reasons. First, nearly two-thirds of the market value of all the securities that are outstanding in the world are classified as fixed-income securities. This means that a substantial amount of savings are invested in fixed-income securities. Second, most participants in corporate and financial sectors participate in the fixed-income securities market to varying degrees. For example, corporate Treasurers must decide on the types of securities to issue; frequently corporations issue debt securities, such as commercial paper, corporate bonds, and medium term notes. These securities are part of fixed-income securities markets. While corporations have the choice between the issuance of equity and fixed-income securities, federal government, state governments and municipalities do not have that choice; they issue only debt securities. Such securities form the core of the fixed-income securities markets. For these reasons, it is important to get a good understanding of the fixed-income markets.

This chapter provides an overview of debt securities, issuers, intermediaries and buyers and illustrates their diversity. We will provide a simple framework for comparing the risks and rewards of fixed-income securities. In subsequent chapters, we will develop in detail each segment of the fixed-income markets and their derivatives. The pricing of such securities and their risk-return trade-offs will be examined in detail. In addition to providing an overview of these markets, this chapter also introduces the vocabulary and some basic terminology that is frequently used by professionals in the fixed-income markets.

DEBT SECURITIES

Fixed-income securities are financial claims issued by governments (e.g., the U.S. Treasury, the German Treasury, etc.), government agencies (e.g., the Federal Home Loan Bank [FHLB]), state governments, corporations (e.g., Exxon, GM, etc.), municipalities (e.g., New York City), and banks (e.g., Citibank, Barclays, etc.) and other financial intermediaries. The cash flows promised to the buyers of fixed-income securities represent contractual obligations of the respective issuers. Typically, when such contractual obligations are not met, the buyers of fixed-income securities will have the right to take control of the firm which issued such debt securities. Fixed-income securities (or debt securities) are issued, traded and invested in markets that are called fixed-income markets (or debt markets).

Figure 1-1 gives a perspective of the debt markets. The sellers of fixed-income securities (governments, agencies, corporations, banks, etc.) share certain common objectives. For example, sellers of securities would like to receive fair value for their securities. In addition, they would like to be able to issue securities that best fit their needs. Some would like to issue simple noncallable debt securities with a fixed maturity date

FIGURE 1-1   *A Schematic Representation of Debt Markets*

Issuer of Debt Securities	Financial Intermediaries	Institutional and Retail Investors

Issuers:

1. Governments and their agencies
2. Corporations
3. Commercial Banks
4. States and municipalities
5. Special purpose vehicles
6. Foreign institutions

Intermediaries:

1. Primary dealers
2. Other dealers
3. Investment banks
4. Credit rating agencies
5. Credit and liquidity enhancers

Investors:

1. Governments
2. Pension funds
3. Insurance companies
4. Mutual funds
5. Commercial banks
6. Foreign institutions
7. Households

Objectives:

1. To sell securities at a fair market price.
2. To have orderly and liquid secondary markets in their securities.
3. To be able to reverse and modify earlier issuance decisions in response to market conditions efficiently.
4. To design and issue debt securities that best suit their needs.

Objectives:

1. To provide primary market making services such as bidding in the, auction underwriting, and distribution.
2. To provide orderly market making in the secondary market.
3. To provide risk management and asset liability management services.
4. To provide proprietary trading activities.

Objectives:

1. To buy securities of different risk-return profiles at a fair price.
2. To obtain diversification at a low cost.
3. To reverse previous decisions at a low cost.
4. To have access to risk management services such as derivatives.
5. To get information on credit ratings, etc., at a low cost.

and a fixed coupon; such securities are referred to as **bullet securities.** Others would like to issue securities that are callable, and some would like to issue debt that is convertible. For example, issuers who anticipate that their future credit ratings will improve might put in call features in their debt issue if the market does not share their optimism about the future potential for improved credit reputation. In Figure 1-1, we list some of the objectives of issuers in this market.

The buyers of fixed-income securities are typically large institutions such as pension funds, insurance companies, commercial banks, corporations, mutual funds, and central banks. In addition, smaller institutions and individual investors also participate in this market. Their objectives might include buying and selling at a fair price and at a narrow bid offer spread, for example. **Bid** is the price at which someone is willing to buy and **offer** is the price at which someone is willing to sell. Some of the key objectives of the buyers are listed in Figure 1-1.

Fixed-income securities are traded in secondary markets which are typically organized as dealer markets or over-the-counter (OTC) markets known as fixed-income markets that are spread all over the world. The intermediaries in these markets are many. They provide a variety of different functions for a fee. They help issuers in the initial offering of the security, assist in the pricing and distribution of the security, make a secondary market, provide liquidity, and engage in proprietary trading activities. In addition, intermediaries such as Moody's or Standard and Poor produce information about the credit quality of different issuers. This information, made available for a fee, is an important service provided by intermediaries in the corporate debt market. Other intermediaries exist who provide liquidity and credit enhancements for a fee. Such activities by intermediaries tend to promote a more liquid and efficient debt market. Some of the objectives of financial intermediaries are shown in Figure 1-1.

Debt Securities and Their Risks

Contractual cash flows. As noted earlier, debt contracts typically specify explicit rules of compensation to the buyer (investor) during their stated term which is prespecified at the time of issuance. Usually, payments are contractual. The examples of fixed-income securities provided here illustrate the diversity of the issuers as well as the diversity of the debt contracts traded in these markets.

Example 1-1:

> 7.25%, 5-15-2016 non-callable U.S. T-bond
> This debt contract has a compensation of 7.25% (payable semi-annually on May 15 and on November 15) of the face amount of the Treasury bond until its maturity date. On the maturity date, in addition to the interest payment, the face amount is also payable. The periodic compensation is referred to as the **coupon** and the remaining life of the claim is referred to as the **time to maturity.**

This is an example of a bullet debt security which is **default-free** as there is no doubt that the promised payments will be made. Thus investors face no **credit risk.** This is not to say that such an instrument has no risk. Indeed, investors who take a position in this Treasury bond are exposed to a significant **interest rate risk.** For example, the price of this T-bond fluctuated within a period of 18 months (from May 1986 to December 1987) from a minimum of 71.78% of the par amount to a maximum of 101.72% of par. This vividly brings home the interest rate risk of T-bonds. As Figure 1-2 clearly illustrates, the percentage price changes in this T-bond were rather high, reaching a 7% change within a day. An investor who bought a million dollar par value of this T-bond at par was exposed to a great deal of price risk; the value fell as low as $717,800 and went as high as $1,017,200. We will develop and illustrate later the different quantitative measures of interest rate and price risk that are used in practice.

The size of this specific T-bond outstanding in the market is on the order of $10 billion. This rather large size coupled with the fact that there are hundreds of dealers who stand ready to participate in a two-way market indicates that such a security is **liquid.** High liquidity means that investors can buy or sell large amounts easily at a narrow bid-offer spread without an adverse price reaction. The average bid-offer spread for this T-bond during this period was 1.1 basis points. The maximum was 4.31 basis points. This illustrates that the T-bond had a very low liquidity risk. The fact that this T-bond was not

FIGURE 1-2   *Interest Rate Risk of a 7.25%, 5/15/2016 T-bond*

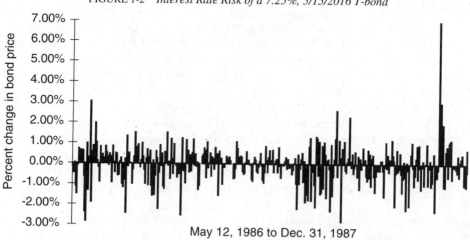

May 12, 1986 to Dec. 31, 1987

callable by the Treasury means that the investor has no uncertainty about the timing of the cash flows. Thus the security has no **timing risk.** Some securities are subject to **event risk.** This risk arises if the issuer's credit risk suddenly deteriorates or a major recapitalization (such as a leveraged buy out) occurs, adversely affecting the risk of the bond. Note that the T-bond in Example 1-1 has no event risk.

It is useful to classify this security along the dimensions of risk and return as in Table 1-1. The dimensions of risk enumerated in Table 1-1 are generally of great interest to investors in the fixed-income securities markets. (We have not explicitly identified reinvestment risk as a separate risk factor—it may be thought of as part of the interest rate risk dimension.)

Dimension of Risk & Return	*Level of Risk Present in the Security 7.25%, 5-15-2016 U.S. T-bond*
Credit risk	Not present
Interest rate risk	High
Liquidity risk	Generally very liquid; bid-offer spreads are small
Timing risk	No uncertainty of timing of cash flows
Taxation	Taxable only at federal level
Foreign exchange (FX) risk	None for domestic investor
Inflation risk	Present
Future cashflows	Known—no risk
Event risk	Not present

TABLE 1-1
Example 1-1, U.S. Treasury Bond

Example 1-2:

A $200 million par amount of floating rate notes was issued by Citicorp on June 26, 1978. The coupon of the floater is indexed to the six-month T-bill rates, that is, to the arithmetic average of the weekly market rate for the six-month U.S. Treasury bills as published by the Federal Reserve during the 14 calendar days immediately prior to the last 10 days of February and August. The actual coupon will be this average plus 120 basis points during the period 1979–1983 subject to a minimum of $7\frac{1}{2}$%. For the period 1984–1988 the spread over the average will be 100 basis points subject to a minimum of 7%, and for the period 1989–1998 the spread will be 75 basis points subject to a minimum of $6\frac{1}{2}$%. At the time of issue Citicorp was rated AAA/AA+. The note will mature on September 1, 1998. The floater did not have conversion features but was callable after September 1, 1988, at declining call prices.

The buyer of this floating rate note is subject to very different sources and degrees of risk than the buyer of the U.S. T-bond in Example 1-1. The Citicorp floater has credit risk. In addition, the future cash flows are uncertain as the coupons are indexed to the future path of six-month T-bill yields. As Example 1-2 shows, the coupon of debt securities need not always be fixed. The time to maturity is also not necessarily fixed. In Example 1-1, the life was known at the time of issuance. In Example 1-2, the life cannot be predicted; it depends on when the issuer calls or declares financial distress. Table 1-2 summarizes the risks of the Citicorp floater.

When the issuer of a debt claim has a probability of going bankrupt, the debt securities may only be issued with several additional features. We now turn to some of these contractual provisions.

Priority of Cash Flows. This issue is moot for government debt. The power of taxation virtually guarantees promised cash flows. For other issuers of debt securities, debt con-

Dimension of Risk & Return	Level of Risk Present in the Security: Citicorp Floater	
Credit risk	Present—spreads vary depending on issuer's credit reputation	TABLE 1-2 *Example 1-2, Citicorp Floater*
Interest rate risk	Relatively low since the coupons are indexed to short rates	
Liquidity risk	Generally not liquid; bid-offer spreads are relatively high	
Timing risk	Callability after 10 years introduces timing risk	
Taxation	Taxable at all (federal, state and local) levels	
FX risk	None for domestic investor	
Inflation risk	Present	
Future cashflows	Not known	
Event risk	Present	

tracts typically have precedence over residual claims such as equity. When there are multiple issues of debt securities by the same entity (as is typical), priorities and relative seniorities are clearly stated by the issuer in **bond covenants.** This leads to some important variations in debt contracts.

Secured and Unsecured Debt. Secured debt such as **mortgage bonds** are backed by tangible assets of the issuing company. In the event of financial distress, such assets may be sold to satisfy the obligations of debt holders. Unsecured debt, known as **debentures** in the U.S., are not secured by any assets.

Contingency Provisions. Debt securities sold by issuers that are subject to a positive probability of default typically contain two important contingency provisions.

First, debt contracts specify events that precipitate bankruptcy. In the debt pricing literature, this is known as the **lower reorganization boundary.** An example of such an event will be the nonpayment of promised coupon payments. Another example is the failure to make balloon payments. Such events give the debt holders the right to take over the firm. Often, the debt holders may not exercise the right to take over the issuing firm if they feel that they could do better by renegotiating with the managers. The lower reorganization boundary is also the point where debtholders may decide whether to enter into a process of workouts and renegotiations or force the firm into formal liquidation. Alternatives such as Chapter 7 or Chapter 11 of the Federal Bankruptcy Act must be considered by the debtholders at this stage. A detailed treatment of these issues is provided in Chapter 8.

Second, debt contracts also specify the rules by which debtholders will be compensated upon bankruptcy and transfer of control. Quite often, the actual payments may differ from the specified payments. Naturally, the value of debt issues is affected in important ways by such provisions and deviations. Often, renegotiations and workouts lead to deviations from the **absolute priority rules** whereby senior claim holders must be paid before any payments are made to junior claim holders. A fuller discussion of the empirical evidence is provided in Chapter 8.

Most corporate debt issues are **callable** at predetermined prices, which gives the issuer the right to buy back the debt issue at prespecified future times. Most are issued with **sinking fund provisions** which require that the debt issue be periodically retired in predetermined amounts. Some are **puttable** at the option of the buyer and some are **convertible** into a prespecified number of shares of common stock of the issuing company. Most convertible debt securities are also callable. Debt securities in different markets also have some idiosyncratic features; many municipal bonds are **serial issues.** In such issues, stated amounts mature at different points in time and bear different coupons. To understand some of these features, we provide the following additional examples of debt securities.

Example 1-3   Corporate bond:

On June 22, 1993, Anheuser Busch issued $200 million par amount of long-term bonds bearing a coupon of 7.375% and maturing in 2023. The bond was rated A1 and was callable after 10 years. Note that this bond is subject to credit risk, interest rate risk, timing risk, etc. Since this is just one of the several debt issues that have been made by the issuer in the past, and since the issuer has a positive probability of defaulting, all the contractual provisions that we outlined earlier will have an impact on the pricing of the security.

Example 1-4   Municipal bond:

In October 1993, nearly $200 million worth of bonds were issued by the Detroit municipality. This was a **revenue bond** for the water supply system which is backed by the revenues generated by the system. The debt had serial issues maturing from 1995 to 2023. The 1995 serial unit was priced to yield 3.40% and the 2023 unit was priced to yield 5.43%. The issue was tax-exempt and was insured by the Federal Guaranty Insurance Company. The issue was rated AAA by the rating agencies. Unlike the previous examples of debt securities, this municipal issue is tax-exempt in the sense that the interest payments are not taxed at the level of buyers (investors).

Example 1-5   Mortgage-Backed:

In October 1993, the Federal Home Loan Bank (FHLB) issued $750 million of real-estate mortgage-investment conduit securities. The thirty-year, 6.5% mortgage securities were offered by Salomon Brothers and backed by the Government National Mortgage Association (GNMA). The collateral has a weighted average coupon of 7% and a weighted average maturity of 358 months. This debt security is part of a securitized transaction which will be discussed in detail later in the chapter.

Example 1-6   Euro Bond:

Fujitec Co. (Japan) issued $60 million of Eurobonds with a coupon of 0.875%. The issue was sold with equity warrants that are due to mature on November 10, 1997. Each bond had two warrants attached to it. The warrants should be exercised by October 1997. This is an example of a hybrid debt security, discussed further in Chapter 8. This debt security provides some equity exposure to the investor. Other hybrids such as convertible bonds are also popular in the marketplace.

These examples should give the reader a taste of the richness and diversity present in debt securities. We provide a classification of debt securities next.

CLASSIFICATION OF DEBT SECURITIES

Usually debt securities are classified by issuers and, within each issuer class, they are further classified by maturity sectors.

Treasury (Sovereign) securities comprise U.S. Treasury securities, U.K. Gilts, German government bonds (Bunds), Japanese government bonds (JGBs), French government bonds (OATs), etc.

Agency securities are debt securities issued by government agencies, such as the Federal Home Loan Bank (FHLB), and Tennessee Valley Authority (TVA).

Corporate securities are debt securities issued by corporations. They may be further classified into investment grade corporates and noninvestment grade or high-yield securities.

Mortgage-backed securities are debt securities backed by pools of mortgages.

Municipal issues are debt securities issued by state governments and municipalities.

Emerging market securities are debt securities issued by less developed and developing countries.

Figure 1-3 presents a perspective of the domestic (U.S.) debt market.

Note that equity markets only account for 36% of the domestic capital markets. While most of the activity in the stock market tends to be in the secondary markets, where the ownership changes hands from one investor to another, the trading in fixed-income markets has a greater proportion of participation by the issuers as well as investors. The breakdown of the international sovereign bond markets along different issuers is shown in Figure 1-4. As is evident from the figure, the U.S. and the Japanese government bond (JGB) account for a substantial percentage of the global debt markets. The size of the world debt market (including the U.S) is $14.80 trillion. (Salomon Brothers 1993). As a consequence, it is a huge market for institutional investors in addition to the international equity markets.

FIGURE 1-3   *Composition of Domestic Capital Markets*

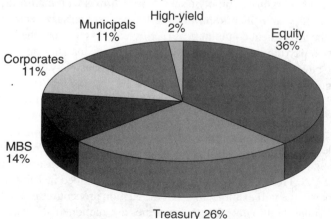

Compiled from J. P. Morgan and Salomon Brothers Reports

FIGURE 1-4   *Composition of Global Debt Markets*

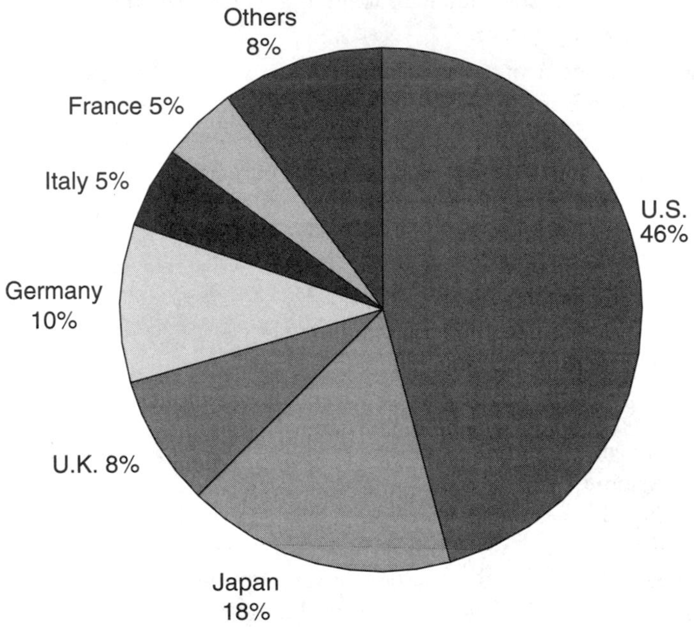

Source: Salomon Brothers, International Bond Market Analysis, 1993

Next, we provide an overview of each important segment of the debt market.

U.S. Treasury Market

The United States Treasury regularly issues debt securities with maturities ranging from a few days to 30 years. Such securities are known as Treasury securities. These are regarded by the investment community as risk-free. This is because the U.S. government stands ready to pay the necessary obligations (i.e., coupons and face amounts) to any investor who buys these securities. These securities are backed by the full faith and credit of the U.S. government. The economic power of the U.S., and the power of the government to levy taxes are obviously two of the important factors in the investor's perception that these securities are default-free. Recent increases in the budget deficit have led to an increased amount of these securities becoming outstanding in the market. Since a large amount of debt securities are issued by the U.S. government, the Treasury has to schedule regular and frequent auctions to sell these securities. The Treasury securities are auctioned by the U.S. Treasury according to the schedule provided in Table 1-3.

In Chapter 3, we will examine in detail the auction procedures of the U.S. Treasury. For now, it is important to note that the securities are auctioned at **benchmark maturities,** shown in Table 1-3. Recently, the Treasury has discontinued the auction of seven-

TABLE 1-3   *U.S. Treasury Auctions Schedule*

Issue Maturity	Frequency of Auction	Auction Day	Auction Method
3 months	Weekly	Every Monday	Discriminatory pricing
6 months	Weekly	Every Monday	Discriminatory pricing
1 year	Monthly	Every fourth Thursday	Discriminatory pricing
2 years	Monthly	Last day of the month	Uniform pricing
3 years	Quarterly	Feb., May, Aug., Nov. (Tuesday of second week)	Discriminatory pricing
5 years	Monthly	Last day of the month	Uniform pricing
10 years	Quarterly	Feb., May, Aug., Nov. (Wednesday of second week)	Discriminatory pricing
30 years	Semi-annually	Feb., Aug., (Wednesday of second week)	Discriminatory pricing

year Treasury securities and will auction thirty-year Treasury securities once every six months instead of the current quarterly auctions. Newly auctioned securities are known as **on-the-run issues.** The yields of on-the-run Treasury issues are shown in Table 1-4. The yield of a security is its internal rate of return, that is, the discount rate at which its present value of all its future cash flows is exactly equal to its market price. We will describe this concept in detail in Chapter 4.

The investor base for Treasury securities is truly global. Foreign central banks, domestic and foreign banks, pension funds, mutual funds, thrifts, etc., are major buyers of Treasury securities. The extent of participation by foreign investors in the domestic debt securities market is significant.

Issue	Yield	Coupon	Maturity
3 months	3.16%	—	
6 months	3.29%	—	
1 year	3.50%	—	
2 years	4.15%	4.125%	6/30/95
3 years	4.44%	4.250%	5/15/96
5 years	5.17%	4.250%	6/30/98
7 years	5.51%	5.500%	4/15/00
10 years	5.86%	6.250%	2/15/03
30 years	6.74%	7.125%	2/15/23

TABLE 1-4

On-the-Run Issues, as of June 24, 1993

Source: Salomon Brothers, *Bond Market Roundup*

Securities issued by the Treasury with a maturity of less than or equal to one year at the time of issuance by the Treasury are called **Treasury bills** or **T-bills**. Such securities do not pay any coupons and may be purchased in auctions at a discount to their face value which is typically $1,000,000. Treasury bills are thus U.S. Treasury discount obligations which promise the payment of face amount on a predetermined date. T-bills are auctioned by the U.S. Treasury at periodic intervals in the following maturities: 91 days (three months), 182 days (six months) and 364 days (one year). T-bills are perhaps among the most liquid and nominally riskless securities. The bid-offer spreads on newly issued (or the on-the-run issues) are rather small (in the neighborhood of 1 to 2 basis points). A basis point is $\frac{1}{100}$ of 1%. Transaction sizes may range from $5 to $100 million. As T-bills become more seasoned and approach their maturity date, their liquidity falls and investors typically pay a lower price as they require a liquidity premium in yields to buy such seasoned bills.

Treasury securities that pay coupons and that have maturities in the range of 1 to 10 years at the time of issuance are called **Treasury notes (T-notes)**. Treasury securities that have maturities in excess of 10 years are called **Treasury bonds (T-bonds)**. Maturities of Treasury bonds generally extend to 30 years. The thirty-year T-bond is known as the **long bond.** The Treasury regularly schedules auctions of such securities in the market. U.S. Treasury notes and bonds pay periodic (usually semi-annual) coupons in addition to the face amount at maturity. Their prices are quoted in fractions of $\frac{1}{32}$, $\frac{1}{64}$ and sometimes even in $\frac{1}{128}$. Price quotations do not include the accrued interest (discussed later in Chapter 4). U.S. Treasury coupon obligations may be bought or sold only with accrued interest. This is the amount of the next coupon that the current owner has earned by virtue of ownership of the Treasury note or bond. The buyer will have to pay the quoted price **(flat price)** plus the accrued interest. The flat price plus the accrued interest is known as the **full price** or the **invoice price.** About 20 outstanding Treasury issues are callable at par after the **call protection period,** which extends until 5 years before maturity. During the call protection period, the Treasury will not call the bonds back. Much of the active trading is usually concentrated in on-the-run issues. For liquid on-the-run issues, the bid-offer spreads are typically $\frac{1}{32}$ to $\frac{2}{32}$. Transaction sizes usually range from $5 million face amount to about $50 million or more. Seasoned issues (those issued in previous auctions) are known as **off-the-run issues.** For off-the-run issues, the spreads may be much higher. Transaction sizes and bid-offer spreads for off-the-run issues are difficult to predict. Generally the liquidity of off-the-run issues is poor compared to on-the-run issues. In a similar manner, practitioners refer to more seasoned issues as off-off-the-run issues.

In Figures 1-5, 1-6 and 1-7 we provide the frequency distribution of the transaction sizes in on-the-run, off-the-run and off-off-the-run two-year Treasury notes during the first half of 1992. This is based on the transactions executed by Garban, one of the major interdealer brokers in the Treasury market. These **interdealer brokers** make it possible for other dealers to trade anonymously. The next chapter discusses the interdealer brokers and other dealers in the debt markets.

FIGURE 1-5   *Frequency Distribution of Volume of Trading, On-the-run Issue*

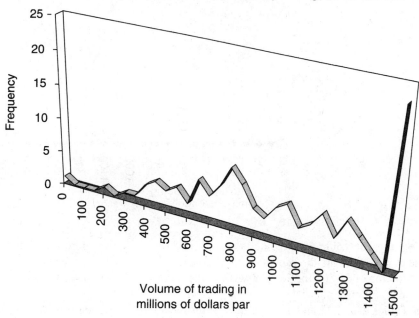

FIGURE 1-6   *Frequency Distribution of Volume of Trading, Off-the-run Issue*

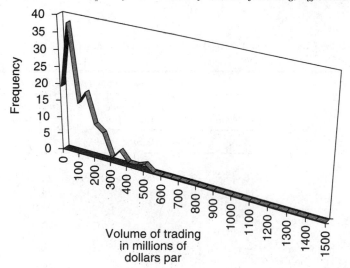

FIGURE 1-7   *Frequency Distribution of Volume of Trading, Off-off-the-run Issue*

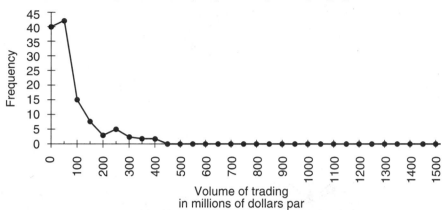

Note that the volume of trading in on-the-run issues is much more active than the volume of trading in off-the-run issues. The most frequent trade in on-the-run issues had a daily volume of $1,500 million par whereas the corresponding number for off-the-run was a mere $50 million par.

In Tables 1-5, 1-6, and 1-7, we have summarized the key measures of liquidity. Table 1-5 contains the summary evidence for three-month and six-month Treasury bills which are auctioned every week. Table 1-6 provides the corresponding information for one-year Treasury bills, two-year Treasury notes and five-year Treasury notes which are auctioned every month. Finally, Table 1-7 contains the results for three-year, ten-year and thirty-year quarterly refunding.

TABLE 1-5   *Summary Statistics for the Daily Transactions of Weekly-Auctioned Three-Month and Six-Month Treasury Bills between December 1992 and August 1993*

| | | | *Statistics for Daily Transactions* | | | | | |
| | | | *Number* | | *Volume (in millions)* | | *Time between Trades (in minutes)* | |
Maturity	*Number of Transactions*	*Number of Days*	*Mean*	*SD*	*Mean*	*SD*	*Mean*	*SD*
Three-month bills								
When-issued	3,757	223	16.9	12.4	496	539	28.2	22.3
On-the-runs	2,396	207	11.6	9.1	289	331	34.3	41.3
Off-the-runs	506	131	3.9	3.3	91	135	33.0	49.0
Off-off-the-runs	350	109	3.2	3.2	69	71	32.3	52.8
Six-month bills								
When-issued	5,043	229	22.0	13.3	591	418	23.7	31.7
On-the-runs	2,566	204	12.6	9.3	276	237	31.3	39.5
Off-the-runs	526	131	4.0	2.9	86	94	31.4	46.8
Off-off-the-runs	268	90	3.0	3.0	72	120	26.3	47.0

Compiled from the data provided by Garban

TABLE 1-6   *Summary Statistics for the Daily Transactions of Monthly-Auctioned One-Year Treasury Bills, and Two-Year and Five-Year Treasury Notes between December 1992 and August 1993*

| | | | Statistics for Daily Transactions | | | | | |
| | | | Number | | Volume (in millions) | | Time between Trades (in minutes) | |
Maturity	*Number of Transactions*	*Number of Days*	*Mean*	*SD*	*Mean*	*SD*	*Mean*	*SD*
One-year bills								
When-issued	5,541	129	43.0	26.6	894	677	14.3	11.2
On-the-runs	5,260	187	28.1	22.8	513	469	23.3	19.5
Off-the-runs	548	106	5.2	4.3	90	102	30.0	28.8
Off-off-the-runs	253	65	3.9	2.7	64	48	31.4	39.1
Two-year notes								
When-issued	9,074	87	104.3	87.9	1079	1071	10.4	12.9
On-the-runs	15,671	179	87.6	50.0	827	531	13.6	18.4
Off-the-runs	1,968	123	16.0	11.4	106	97	28.4	35.6
Off-off-the-runs	1,337	106	12.6	12.7	89	122	31.0	38.2
Five-year notes								
When-issued	13,416	87	154.2	123.9	1252	1054	8.0	9.2
On-the-runs	39,664	179	221.6	117.7	1591	946	6.9	10.1
Off-the-runs	3,305	127	26.0	14.1	160	117	24.2	29.3
Off-off-the-runs	1,403	111	12.6	9.9	58	48	33.6	38.8

Compiled from the data provided by Garban

TABLE 1-7   *Summary Statistics for the Daily Transactions of Quarterly-Auctioned Three-Year and Ten-Year Treasury Notes, and Thirty-Year Treasury Bonds between December 1992 and August 1993*

| | | | Statistics for Daily Transactions | | | | | |
| | | | Number | | Volume (in millions) | | Time between Trades (in minutes) | |
Maturity	*Number of Transactions*	*Number of Days*	*Mean*	*SD*	*Mean*	*SD*	*Mean*	*SD*
Three-year notes								
When-issued	3,625	39	93.0	66.5	885	835	10.6	11.7
On-the-runs	16,065	204	78.8	41.2	576	365	15.0	17.0
Off-the-runs	1,815	175	10.4	11.6	55	73	35.5	45.1
Off-off-the-runs	1,011	124	8.2	6.8	45	51	34.7	47.3
Ten-year notes								
When-issued	8,501	42	202.4	170.5	1091	924	8.8	11.5
On-the-runs	40,459	186	217.5	96.3	1099	536	6.4	8.6
Off-the-runs	1,589	71	22.4	12.0	98	70	26.9	30.2
Off-off-the-runs	458	59	7.8	5.9	28	28	49.4	62.2
Thirty-year bonds								
When-issued	2,933	33	88.9	102.9	412	497	20.1	26.3
On-the-runs	16,635	173	96.2	51.6	415	254	14.9	18.7
Off-the-runs	446	48	9.3	12.0	46	60	42.3	69.4
Off-off-the-runs	48	20	2.4	2.0	12	13	39.0	92.0

Compiled from the data provided by Garban

In these tables there are four categories of securities: the when-issued market, on-the-run, off-the-run and off-off-the-run securities. When-issued securities trade prior to the auction and are trades in the security that is yet to be auctioned. These trades are essentially forward commitments made by one dealer to another dealer or a customer.

The when-issued market is described in detail in Chapter 3. Note from Table 1-5 that the when-issued segment is the most liquid for three-month and six-month T-bills. In the case of three- month T-bills, the when-issued average size was 496 million, nearly twice the average size of on-the-run trades. The average number of transactions and the frequency of transactions indicate that the when-issued segment is the most liquid segment of the three-month T-bills. As one would expect, the on-the-run segment is much more liquid than both the off-the-run segment and the off-off-the-run segment. Note that the standard deviations (SD) of the volume fall rapidly for the off-the-run and the off-off-the-run segments, indicating small trade sizes and fewer transactions in general. An interesting fact is that the average time between trades has a very narrow range, varying from 28 to 35 minutes across these segments. This variation is not great, although the standard errors are far greater for the less liquid segments. The results for six-month T-bills are qualitatively very similar.

The results for monthly auctions reported in Table 1-6 are qualitatively very similar with some important exceptions. First, the five-year T-notes on-the-run segment is uniformly more liquid along all the three dimensions than any other segment. Second, the average time between trades has a much wider range for two-year and five-year T-notes; for the two-year T-notes the range is 9.9 to 31 minutes, and for the five-year T-notes the range is 4.9 to 33.6 minutes. Another important difference is the average volume of trades in the when-issued and on-the-run segments: they are far bigger than the corresponding values for three-month and six-month T-bills.

In Table 1-7, we have reported the basic results for quarterly refunding. The most striking result here is the very high liquidity of the ten-year T-note. In this benchmark maturity, the on-the-run segment has on average, a transaction every 6.4 minutes, the average size of the transaction is nearly 1,100 million and the average number of transactions per day is 217. A quick comparison with other benchmark maturities indicates that the five-year benchmark maturity is the only one that comes close to this level of liquidity along all dimensions. Based on these numbers, there is a case that the T-bills are not necessarily the most liquid segment of the Treasury markets.

To summarize, it is clear that the most recently auctioned securities (on-the-run) and the to-be-auctioned securities (when-issued) have considerably more depth than seasoned issues (off-the-run and off-off-the-run), along all dimensions of liquidity. Ten-year T-notes and five-year T-notes appear to have the most liquidity of all benchmark maturities. It appears that T-bills are not necessarily the most liquid segment of the Treasury market.

In Table 1-8 we provide the dollar value of T-bills, T-notes and T-bonds that were held by private investors and institutions as of December 1994. The total value of Treasury securities in private hands was $2,754 billion.

The prices of Treasury securities fluctuate a good deal in response to economic and political news. This, in turn, affects the return performance of Treasury securities. In

Description	Dollar Value	Percentage
T-bills	$657.70 bn	24.01%
T-notes	$1,608.90 bn	58.74%
T-bonds	$472.50 bn	17.25%

TABLE 1-8
Value of Treasury Debt

Source: Treasury Bulletin, Dec 1994

Table 1-9, the yield performance of Treasury thirty-year bonds are shown for the period 1977–1991.

Notice that the yields have ranged from a low of 5.78% in 1993 to a high of 14.88% in 1981. The variability can be severe even within one year; in 1982, the yields dropped from a level of 14.22% in January to a level of 10.54% in December. Such yield volatility coupled with the level of Treasury securities outstanding in the private sector poses very serious risks to portfolio managers and bond dealers. This emphasizes the fact that the absence of default risk does not necessarily imply that such securities are riskless. The plot of the yield (internal rate of return) and the maturity is referred to as the **yield curve.** Typically, as the maturity increases, yield increases. This is referred to as the **"normal"** or **"upward-sloping"** yield curve. Table 1-9 shows that

Year	High	Low	Spread of Thirty-Year T-bond Yields over Three-Month T-bill Yields
1977	7.94%	7.64%	NA
1978	8.85%	8.18%	82
1979	10.12%	8.94%	-114
1980	12.40%	9.81%	-51
1981	14.88%	12.14%	-106
1982	14.22%	10.54%	243
1983	11.88%	10.63%	241
1984	13.44%	11.52%	269
1985	11.81%	9.54%	306
1986	9.40%	7.27%	166
1987	10.26%	7.39%	279
1988	9.46%	8.30%	200
1989	9.32%	7.82%	-40
1990	9.17%	8.00%	116
1991	8.55%	7.41%	282
1992	8.10%	7.23%	425
1993	7.47%	5.78%	355
1994	8.16%	6.21%	308
1995	7.93%	5.96%	135

TABLE 1-9
Thirty-Year T-bond Yields & Yield Spreads

Source: *U.S. Treasury Bulletin* and Data Stream

there may be an overall relationship between the levels of the yields and the shape of the yield curve. This is seen by looking at the average spreads of thirty-year T-bond yields over the three-month T-bill yields. Note that the spread was negative from 1979 to 1981, when the rates rose to very high levels. This implies an **inverted yield curve** during this period. Then the spread became positive again in the period from 1982 to 1988. During 1989 the yield curve was inverted again.

Foreign Sovereign Bond Market

There is a large international government securities market. Most of the large bond dealers in the U.S. also make a market in these securities. These securities have several idiosyncratic features worthy of note. Table 1-10 provides a perspective of the Foreign Sovereign bond market.

Canadian Debt Market. Canadian bonds have a range of maturities from two to 30 years. Typically, the issues are noncallable bullet bonds, although index-linked debt has also been issued recently. As in the U.S. Treasury market, three-month and six-month T-bills are auctioned every week. In 1992 the size of total outstanding debt issue made by the Canadian government, its agencies, and provinces totaled 453 billion Canadian dollars. Of this, the marketable Canadian government debt accounted for 172 billion Canadian dollars.

Gilts. Gilt-edged stock or gilts are British government debt securities. Standard gilts carry fixed, annual coupons and pay the face amount at maturity date. In addition to the standard gilts, the British government issues

- index-linked gilts, which have coupon and face amounts indexed to the U.K. retail price index
- convertible gilts, which may be converted into one or more other gilts at specific dates and conversion ratios
- "irredeemable gilts," which are perpetuals callable at par. **Perpetuals** are securities with no maturity dates.

Coupon payments on gilts are called **dividends.** Typically, withholding taxes are applied to dividends from gilts, although there are gilts which are exempt from this rule. The flat price of a gilt is called the "clean price" and its full price is called the "dirty price." Gilts may be bought or sold cum dividend until 37 days before the next coupon date. The gilt goes ex-dividend at that point. Some highlights of the gilt markets are shown in Table 1-10. The total publicly issued debt in the U.K. market stood at 223.3 billion British pounds in 1992. Of these, the government gilt market accounted for 138.8 billion British pounds.

JGBs. The Japanese Government Bond (JGB) market is a large one with a market value at about $1.4 trillion (U.S.). JGBs are typically issued with a fixed maturity date, carry a fixed annual coupon (payable semi-annually) and are quoted on a simple yield basis. These conventions are analyzed in Chapter 4. Discount bonds are also issued and they

TABLE 1-10   *Foreign Sovereign Bond Market*

Sovereign Market	Highlights
Canadian Bond Market	Maturity range—2 to 25 years. 5 to 10 years most liquid. Market organization—OTC dealer network. Benchmarks—3, 5 and 10 years. Issue procedure—subscription offerings and yield auction. Coupon—semi-annual, actual/365 basis.
U.K. government bonds	Market organization—OTC dealer market very active. Issue procedure—multiple price auctions for T-bills. Issue procedure—single price auctions for Gilts; "tap issues" also used. Coupon—annual, actual/actual basis.
Japanese Government Bond Market (JGB)	Issued by Government of Japan. Classified into Construction bonds, Deficit Financing bonds and Refinancing bonds. Maturity—10 years is most common. Issues are referred to by their issue number. Coupon bonds are issued with original maturities of 2, 10 and 20 years. Discount bonds are issued with 5 years maturity. Market organization—Trades in Tokyo Stock Exchange. Cash JBG trading occurs on OTC markets. Issue procedure—A part is underwritten by a syndicate of banks, insurance companies and securities firms. Remaining is issued by auctions. Yield—Simple yield to maturity calculations.

German government bonds
  Federal government (Bunds)
  Federal railways (Bundesbahn)
  Federal post office
    (Bundespost)
	Maturity—10 years.
	Market organization—stock exchanges and OTC dealer markets.
	Benchmarks—most recent issues.
	Issue procedure—combination of Dutch auction and fixed allocation to a pool of institutions.
	Coupon—annual basis.

French government bonds Obligations Assimilable du Trésor (OATs)	Accounts for 70% of the market. Maturity range—10 to 30 years. New tranch of 10-year bonds reopened monthly; new tranch of long bonds reopened every two months, and additional issues. Market organization—listed on Paris Stock Exchange, OTC dealer market very active. Benchmarks—10 and 30 years. Issue procedure—Dutch auctions. Coupon—semi-annual, actual/actual basis. Special features—some OATs are convertible, some have warrants and some are indexed to short or long term rates.
French government notes Bons à Taux Annuel Normalisé (BTANs)	Accounts for 30% of the market. Maturity range—1 to 7 years. Typically issued in 2 and 5 years maturities. Market organization—OTC dealer market very active. Benchmarks—2 and 5 years. Issue procedure—Dutch auctions. Coupon—annual, actual/actual basis.

are quoted differently depending on whether they have less than or more than a year to maturity. JGBs are callable at any time by the Ministry of Finance. Maturities range from a few years to 20 years. Liquidity tends to be concentrated on a benchmark bond. Often the benchmark bond trades at several basis points below comparable JGBs. High coupon bonds are valued in Japan and therefore they trade at a lower yield. This coupon effect is distinct from the coupon effects that one sees in other international bond markets where high coupon bonds often sell for a higher yield.

German Debt Market. The German debt market has grown recently, due at least in part to the mounting deficits. The long-term government bonds are known as Bunds. They typically have a maturity of 10 years. Five-year notes are also issued by the government. The public debt is held in book-entry form. (This system will be described in Chapter 2.) The total publicly issued debt outstanding in 1992 was valued at 2,270 billion deutsche marks. Of these, Bunds (see Table 1-10) accounted for 662 billion deutsche marks.

French Government Debt. The most important bond issue in the French government market is the Obligations Assimilable du Trésor or OAT (see Table 1-10), which matures in the range of 10 to 30 years. This bond is issued in tranches to increase the supply as needed. Two-year and five-year debt securities are also auctioned. The total outstanding publicly issued debt was valued at 3,764 billion French francs in 1992. Of these, the government debt accounted for 1,516 French francs. The breakdown of this debt into short-term and long-term debt is shown in Table 1-10.

Agency Securities

The Federal Home Loan Bank, the Federal National Mortgage Association and the Federal Home Loan Mortgage Corporation are examples of agencies that routinely issue debt securities. Federal agencies such as the Tennessee Valley Authority (TVA) and Export-Import Bank also issue large amounts of debt securities. Federal agencies are, for the most part, privately owned, but are sponsored and backed by the federal government. Table 1-11 lists some characteristics of the issuing federal agencies.

The composition of the agency securities market is shown in Figure 1-8.

Agency securities are not direct obligations of the federal government. Even though the probability of default is very small, they trade at a spread to comparable Treasuries. Agency securities are issued in relatively smaller sizes compared with Treasuries and as a result are not as liquid. This factor may also contribute to the spread between Treasuries and agencies. Table 1-12 illustrates the spreads on agency securities issued by FNMA (Fannie Mae). Agency securities operate on a 30-day month and 360-day year convention.

Agency securities, by and large, have a very high credit reputation. The pressure from the U.S. Congress to examine the implicit and explicit guarantees issued by the government to agencies will sooner or later cause the agencies to acquire a high stand alone credit reputation. Until then, potential buyers will take into account both the stand alone quality and the explicit and implicit guarantees in valuing agency securities.

TABLE 1-11 *Federal Agencies*

Agency	Highlights
Federal Home Loan Bank	FHLB is well capitalized and it issues debt up to 15 years maturity. FHLB has also issued short-term notes and zero coupon bonds.
Federal National Mortgage Association (FNMA) & Federal Home Loan Mortgage Corporation	Fannie Mae and Freddie Mac were created to promote a liquid secondary market for mortgages. Fannie Mae is a publicly traded corporation. Freddie Mac is smaller than Fannie Mae. These agencies issue debentures, MBS, etc.
Refcorp	This agency was set up to bail out the savings and loans and thrifts. It has issued 40-year bonds.
Tennessee Valley Authority	TVA was created to promote the Tennessee River region.
Student Loan Marketing Association	Sallie Mae promotes a liquid secondary market for government-guaranteed student loans. Loans bought by Sallie Mae are insured. Its advances are collateralized; hence its credit is very good.
Farm Credit System	FCS provides low cost credit to agriculture and fisheries. It has considerable political support.

FIGURE 1-8 *Composition of Agency Debt Market*

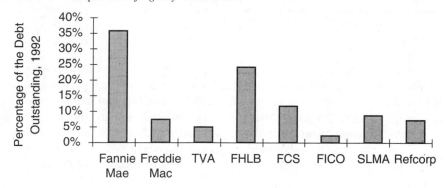

TABLE 1-12
Agency (FNMA) as of June 24, 1993

Issue	Yield	Coupon	Maturity	Spread over Treasury (in basis points)
Three-year	4.74%	7.700%	9/10/96	30
Four-year	4.95%	6.750%	4/22/97	15
Five-year	5.22%	5.250%	3/25/98	5
Seven-year	5.62%	6.100%	2/10/00	11
Ten-year	6.06%	6.800%	1/10/03	20
Thirty-year	7.01%	8.100%	8/12/19	27

Source: Salomon Brothers, *Bond Market Roundup*

The relative supply of agency securities also could influence their valuation. While agency securities generally are noncallable bullet bonds, some issues are quite innovative; Refco has issued forty-year bonds that are eligible for stripping, some agencies have issued zero coupon bonds and some have optional redemption features. These provisions require sophisticated techniques for their valuation. About a third of the agency issues tend to have call features. Sallie Mae has issued floaters and Fannie Mae has issued sinking fund debentures. Many of the Fannie Mae issues have call features.

Corporate Securities

The corporate fixed-income securities market has been the dominant way of raising capital for U.S. corporations in the last few years. Table 1-13 vividly illustrates the importance of this market for corporate funding.

Source	1990	1991	1992
All issues	340,149	465,243	559,444
All bonds	299,884	389,822	471,125
Public issues in U.S.A.	188,848	286,930	377,681
Private placements	86,982	74,930	65,853
Sold abroad	23,054	27,962	27,591
All stocks	40,175	75,424	88,324

TABLE 1-13
Corporate New Security Issues, in Millions of Dollars

Source: Federal Reserve Sep 1993 and Dec 1993

It is clear that the corporate debt market has been used to raise capital five to seven times more than the equity market during the last three years. Falling interest rates may have been the major motivation for this trend. Unlike the Treasury markets which are characterized by about 200 to 300 issues, each of which has a relatively large size outstanding, the corporate debt market is characterized by thousands of issues, each of which accounts for a small size. A typical corporate issue is of the order of $100 million to $200 million whereas a typical Treasury auction is of the order of $10 billion to $12 billion.

Much like the Treasury market, newly syndicated corporate issues are actively traded. The seasoned issues, which have been issued a few months earlier, tend to be illiquid and trade at wider bid offer spreads. Unlike the Treasury issues, most corporate issues tend to have call features or sinking fund features. We alluded earlier in this chapter to the question of why such contractual features are present in the corporate debt market. Call features also permit managers to eliminate debt, if necessary. Debt holders might place restrictive covenants that may not allow managers to undertake certain investments or may prohibit certain types of mergers and acquisitions. By having a call feature, managers give themselves the right to take such actions at a predetermined (call) price.

TABLE 1-14   *Seasoned Investment Grade Corporate Issues, as of June 24, 1993*

Issuer	Yield	Coupon	Maturity	Rating	Size (in millions)	Spread over Treasury
Chase Manhattan	3.97%	7.375%	1994	Baa2/A-	250	46
South Bell T & T	7.78%	8.50%	2029	Aaa/AAA	300	104

The presence of credit risk, the relative lack of liquidity compared to the Treasuries and the call features cause the investors to demand a higher yield on corporate issues than on other similar Treasuries. Table 1-14 shows that this is generally the case.

Along the maturity spectrum, the corporate debt issues fall into three groups:

- Short maturities under a year are in the *money markets sector*. The key corporate debt here is the commercial paper.
- In the 1 to 5-year sector are the *medium term notes*. Floaters also fall in this group.
- Finally, longer maturities come under the **corporate bonds** classification.

We will discuss these instruments briefly in this chapter and postpone to Chapter 8 a fuller account of the corporate debt.

Commercial Paper. Short-term corporate debt is known as **commercial paper** (CP). The maturity of commercial paper varies anywhere from 30 days to 270 days. CPs, like T-bills, are discount instruments. Maturities less than 270 days may be offered for sale to the public without registration with the Securities and Exchange Commission (SEC).

CPs are quoted on a discount basis. The discount yield of CPs, however, is measured a bit differently from that of a T-bill. Typically, CPs are priced off the London Interbank Offered Rates (LIBOR) of comparable maturities. For example, it is usual for a CP trader to say that IBM's ninety-day CP trades at 50 basis points below ninety-day LIBOR. Many corporations, by virtue of their strong credit reputations, are able to borrow directly from the public at rates that are lower than what they could get at banks. A good CP program provides the issuing corporation with yet another borrowing strategy. The Federal Reserve produces an index of CP rates by averaging across CP quotes from a randomly selected sample from a roster of CP dealers. This index, known as the Fed AA index, also is a barometer of the CP market. Highly rated CPs trade at rates well below comparable LIBOR, and poorly rated CPs trade well above LIBOR.

Medium-Term Notes (MTNs). This sector starts at maturities exceeding three months and extends out to several years. The MTNs can be issued through shelf registration, which provides a great deal of flexibility to the issuer. In a **shelf registration,** the issuer gets blanket approval from the SEC for an amount of debt that may then be issued over a prespecified period of time. This gives the issuer the ability to respond quickly to any rapid changes in interest rates. The structure of the MTNs indexes the issuance cost to the short-term interest rates.

Corporate Coupon Issues. Corporate debt is largely composed of coupon-bearing debt. These coupon obligations are contractual obligations; nonpayment of a coupon payment will provide an option to the debt holders to take control of the firm.

Corporate debt is rated by rating agencies such as Moodys and Standard and Poor. Depending on the ratings, corporate debt may be either investment grade or non-investment grade ("junk"). Moody's ratings go from Aaa to C. Standard and Poors go from AAA to D. Generally a bond with a rating of B or less has a high default risk. Investors require a high premium to hold those securities. Corporate bonds typically have a **mandatory sinking fund** provision. This provision calls for an orderly retirement of debt in scheduled installments. Sometimes issuers also provide an **optional sinking fund** feature whereby they could retire additional amounts. Contractual provisions of corporate bonds typically also have call features. After a call protection period (typically 5–10 years from the issue date) the issuer will have the option to call the bonds at face amount plus a predetermined premium schedule. Each corporate issuer may have several layers of debt and each layer might differ with respect to seniority and security. Debentures in the U.S. are unsecured debt. On the other hand, mortgage bonds are secured by a lien on specific tangible assets of the issuing firm. Senior debt holders have a prior claim on the assets of the firm in the event of bankruptcy. Subordinated (junior) debt holders will have the residual claim followed by equity holders. All these factors have to be carefully considered in valuing corporate debt securities.

High-Yield Debt. As pointed out earlier, high-yield bonds are those issued by entities that are rated as less than investment grade. Such issues were made in conjunction with leveraged buyout activities, although more recent issues have been made for raising capital to fund capital projects. This source of capital is important for issuers with poor credit rating as an alternative to bank debt.

High-yield securities come in varied forms. Since the issuers of high-yield bonds tend to have a large amount of debt in their capital structure, their ability to service debt payments is critical to their survival. Hence most high-yield debt securities are structured so that they carry very low coupons during early years. Hence they tend to sell at a discount. One of the most common structures is referred to as **deferred-interest bonds.** In these bonds, no coupons are paid for an initial period lasting for several years. This structure gives a chance for the firm to generate sufficient cash flow to be able to service the interest payments later. Similarly **payment-in-kind (PIK) bonds** provide the issuers with the option either to pay cash coupon or offer similar bonds instead of the coupon payments. These structures are discussed in Chapter 8.

Securitized Assets—Mortgage-backed Securities

In the fixed-income markets, the concept of securitization has led to the development of liquid markets, notably the mortgage-backed securities (MBS) markets. The mortgage market is one of the largest segments in the securities markets. **Securitization** is a process by which illiquid assets are transformed into very liquid financial instruments. Figure 1-9 highlights the key steps involved in the securitization process.

This process requires several distinct players and steps, outlined below.

1.   **Originator:** Securitization begins with an institution playing the role of the originator. The originator, which can be a private institution such as an S&L or a federal agency, creates individual mortgages or receivables.

2.   **Pooling and standardization:** The assets (loans) are then pooled. Such pools may be created using more than one originator. The pooling activity is performed to create a large enough loan portfolio to interest large institutional investors. The individual loans are standardized along several dimensions: the maturity, the interest rate (fixed or adjustable, levels and indices), the amount of the loan, the geographical location, etc. This standardization makes the cash flows from the pool easier to predict.

3.   **Guarantees and credit enhancement:** For a fee, a standardized portfolio is then guaranteed by a federal agency (or a private entity of sufficiently high credit reputation) against default. Such defaults may occur at the level of individual units in the pool (such as a particular home owner in a pool of mortgages or an account in a pool

FIGURE 1-9   *Concept of Securitization—Example from Mortgage-backed Securities*

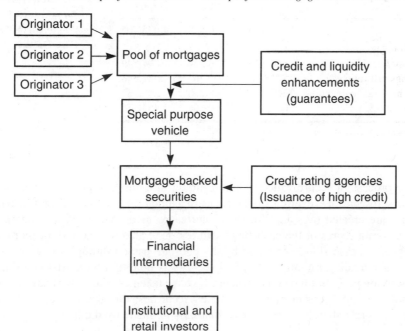

of credit card receivables) or at the level of issuers. Both classes of default are covered by guarantees. Together, standardization and the guarantee enhance the marketability of the securities that are then issued as claims to the guaranteed cash flows from the pool of assets.

4. **Special purpose vehicle (SPV):** The SPV is created solely to construct the pool of financial assets and then issue the asset-backed securities. The key idea here is to put some distance between the originators and the pool of assets. For instance, the SPV is structured such that the bankruptcy of the originator(s) will not affect the pool of financial assets held by the SPV. This separation is critical in obtaining the necessary credit enhancements which usually lead to a high credit rating.

This process of pooling, standardizing, and selling claims on guaranteed loans has the effect of improving the liquidity of what might otherwise be illiquid assets. It improves the allocation of risk and resources across different geographical locations. Hopefully, it also reduces the cost of mortgage loans in the mortgage-backed securities markets. Table 1-15 gives a perspective on the size of the mortgage market and the extent to which this market has been pooled and securitized. Note that the size of the pooled mortgage market is quite large—it is about $1.5 trillion. The potential for growth in this area is even greater. The process of securitization has transformed this market into a major segment of the fixed-income securities market.

	1990	1991	1992
Total	3,751,476	3,890,830	4,035,405
Institutional holders			
Commerical banks	844,826	876,284	894,549
Savings institutions	801,628	705,367	682,338
Life insurance companies	267,861	265,258	246,537
Pooled mortgages	1,079,103	1,250,666	1,452,546

TABLE 1-15
Mortgage Debt Outstanding in Millions of Dollars

Source: Federal Reserve Sep 1993

The process of securitization, while resulting in a highly liquid market for mortgage-backed securities, exposes the investors to a unique set of risks. Mortgage-backed securities are created by using a pool of mortgages as the underlying collateral and selling pro-rata shares of the cash flows that are generated by the pool of mortgages. In essence, the cash flows generated by the pool are passed through to the investors. The investor holding a mortgage-backed security is holding a proportionate share in the underlying pool. But the homeowners who have taken out mortgages have the right to prepay. For investors in mortgage-backed securities, this leads to the risk of receiving a pro-rata share of prepayments that may be made by the homeowners of the pool.

Prepayments occur because homeowners rarely hold mortgages to the stated maturities, which range up to 30 years. They have the option to prepay the loans and do so for many reasons. The following affect prepayments:

- **Drop in interest rates.** When the perceived benefits of low interest rates outweigh the costs of refinancing, refinancing is more attractive.
- **Labor market turnover.** When homeowners move from one job to another, they close out existing mortgage loans and take new ones.
- **Seasonal changes.** Families tend to move in summer and early fall, causing seasonal effects in prepayments.
- **Family circumstances.** Events such as divorces, deaths and other changes in the family size often lead to refinancing.
- **Housing prices.** When house prices fall, the incentive to prepay is reduced as the homeowners are trapped. When the house prices drop to a very low level, homeowners have a "walk away" option by which they can surrender the house to the bank and walk away from the loan. Clearly, this affects the prepayments during periods when the real estate market is falling.
- **Defaults.** In a pool, when defaults occur, the guarantees go into effect, resulting in additional payments.

MBSs have been structured to handle payments (scheduled and unscheduled) in different ways to suit the preferences of a wide spectrum of investors. One popular class of MBSs is that of **pass-through securities** which provide the investor with a pro-rated share of all payments made by the pool, including prepayments. Examples of such securities are GNMAs and FNMAs. Another type of MBS partitions prepayments according to stated rules. These securities, called collateralized mortgage obligations (CMOs), are typically backed (or collateralized) by pools of mortgages or pass-through securities such as GNMAs. Each partition will receive prepayments according to set rules. In Chapter 9, we undertake a detailed treatment of this market.

Municipal Issues

Municipalities (state and local governments) issue debt securities regularly. Broadly, such issues may be grouped into:

- **General obligation bonds,** which are backed by the full faith, credit, and taxing power of the issuer; and
- **Revenue bonds,** which derive their cash flows from specific project revenues.

Municipal issues maturing in one year or less are known as municipal notes and longer term issues are referred to as municipal bonds. The composition of the municipal bond market is provided in Table 1-16.

Municipal issues are smaller in size than those of other securities. In addition, typically they are issued as serial bonds. In serial issues, scheduled parts of the principal (balloon) payments are retired at prespecified maturities. Each specified maturity will carry a distinct coupon. These factors contribute to their low liquidity.

By Type of Issue		TABLE 1-16
General obligation	78,611	*Composition of the*
Revenue bonds	136,580	*Municipal Bond (Tax-*
		exempt Debt) Market,
By Type of Issuer		*in Millions of Dollars*
States	25,295	*(1992)*
Special district & statutory authority	127,618	
Municipality, county, township	60,210	
By Use of Proceeds		
Education	22,071	
Transportation	17,334	
Utilities & conservation	20,058	
Social welfare	21,796	
Industrial aid	5,424	
Others	33,589	

Source: Federal Reserve Sep 1993

Until very recently, the most distinctive feature of municipal securities was that the interest payments made by municipal securities were exempt from federal taxes (as well as from state and local taxes for local residents) and this caused their yields to be lower, *ceteris paribus.* The Tax Reform Act of 1986 has placed a number of restrictions on the tax exemption status of municipal securities. In effect, the reform has significantly eroded the tax-exempt status of municipal securities. Bonds issued for activities such as road construction and capital projects qualify for tax-exempt status. All other issues in which 10% or more of the proceeds are used to finance a project that will be used by a private entity are regarded as private activity bonds. Only qualified private activity bonds are eligible for tax-exempt status and to be considered a qualified private activity bond, the issuer has to meet a number of requirements and fall into certain categories of activities, such as the construction of airports or sewer systems, and student development.

In addition, the Tax Reform Law has placed other restrictions on municipals. States are now limited on the amount of partially tax-exempt private activity bonds they can issue every year. Also, prior to the 1986 law, financial institutions (especially commercial banks) were permitted to deduct the interest cost (for tax purposes) incurred in carrying the municipal securities, providing double tax benefits. This was eliminated by the Tax Reform Law of 1986.

The tax treatment of municipal securities results in municipals being priced to provide a lower yield compared to very similar Treasury or corporate securities. The market yields of these three fixed-income securities is plotted in Figure 1-10. The possibility that tax benefits may be reduced is a serious risk faced by municipal-bond investors. Note that the spreads of municipals have changed a great deal over time. In Chapter 10 we explore the determinants of such spreads. The tax status of municipal bonds tend to attract households, commercial banks, and property and casualty insurance firms to hold most of the municipal debt.

The following *Wall Street Journal* article will help the reader appreciate the effect of the tax risk on municipal bonds.

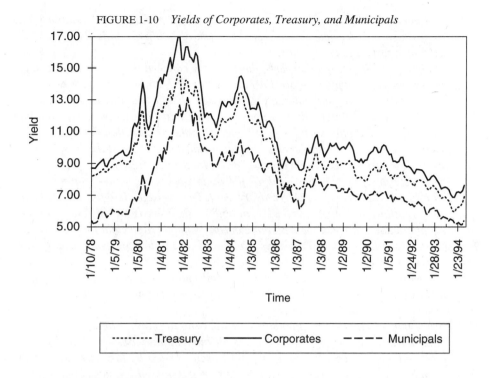

FIGURE 1-10   *Yields of Corporates, Treasury, and Municipals*

- - - - - - - Treasury   ———— Corporates   – – – – Municipals

Flat-Tax Cloud Unlikely to Rain on Munis

By NANCY ANN JEFFREY
Staff Reporter of *The Wall Street Journal*

NEW YORK — Municipal-bond investors have grown queasy in recent weeks at all the Washington talk of tax-overhaul plans that could clobber the muni market if enacted.

But reports of impending doom for municipals are greatly exaggerated, many financial advisers say. Sit tight for now, they urge. And consider buying long-term issues when flat-tax talk picks up as the 1996 election approaches. "Stay the course," says Ian MacKinnon, senior vice president and head of the fixed-income group at the Vanguard Group. "But stay tuned."

No one knows what any tax overhaul, if enacted, would look like. But various plans being discussed would exempt other types of investment income and thus make low-yielding munis less competitive.

Tax buzz has played a role in the muni market's languid response amid a spectacular rally in Treasurys in recent weeks. While the yield on the 30-year benchmark Treasury bond plunged to a 14-month low of 6.86% earlier this week, yields on municipals haven't fallen nearly as quickly. The gap is narrowing between Treasury and municipal yields, making munis look increasingly attractive.

Muni bonds typically lag behind Treasurys in a rally. And today's relatively low muni prices also reflect some of the increased risk of holding bonds that would get whacked under certain tax proposals.

But among municipal-bond experts, there is little concern that any radical change in the tax system could happen before 1997 and plenty of doubt that any such revolution will happen at all. It is a good bet that any proposed change that had a real chance of becoming law, would provoke fierce opposition from muni-bond investors, state and local governments and others with a vested interest in the $1.2 trillion muni market.

"There are enough constituencies . . . that would have some stake in seeing the incentives in the current tax system prevail," Mr. MacKinnon says.

As of yesterday, the average yield for the Bond Buyer's revenue-bond index was 6.15%, or 89.1% of the comparable Treasury yield. The average yield for a Bond Buyer general-obligation bond index was 5.92%, or 85.8% of the Treasury yield, according to the trade publication. Back at the beginning of April, the average yield for the revenue-bond index was only 84.6% of Treasurys' yield, while the figure for general-obligation munis was only 82%.

If premature fears continue to cloud the muni market's horizon, smart investors may find buying opportunities in bonds maturing in 15 years or more, especially 30-year bonds, some financial advisers say.

For the most part, however, they say these opportunities aren't here yet.

While soaring Treasury prices have made the muni market look relatively inexpensive compared with Treasurys, municipals still aren't cheap by historical standards, financial advisers say. And even if tax-reform never gets passed, rhetoric about the flat tax and other proposals is bound to heat up in an election year. The political hot air and news stories may well depress muni prices significantly below today's levels, some financial advisers say.

"Markets often react on news, not on actualities," says James Cooner, senior vice president and head of the tax-exempt bond management division for Bank of New York. "The publicity that's going to be given to these questions is what's going to move the market. At that time there might be some extremely interesting buying opportunities."

Advisers offer two strategies for different types of investors. The bold may want to increase cash or move into very short-term munis or Treasurys—with maturities of one year or less—to best position themselves to lock in fat long-term yields some months down the road, advisers say.

But for the many small investors in muni bonds who usually hold to maturity, this in-and-out game isn't recommended. These people are worrying about whether they should bail out in light of the chilling talk about tax changes.

At this early point in the debate, the best strategy is to take a wait-and-see approach, advisers say. The worst mistake investors could make, they say, is to let the rhetoric frighten them into selling bonds in a weak market.

"I don't think people should be focusing on a vague possibility two years from now," says Joseph Deane, managing director of tax-exempt fixed-income management at Greenwich Street Advisors, a subsidiary of Smith Barney Inc.

Mr. Deane says municipal investors should stay in double-A and triple-A rated bonds in maturities of seven to 10 years. If, however, they wish to invest in the longer-

term end of the market, they might consider a well-managed bond fund, Mr. Deane advises.

For investors convinced that "tax reform" is down the road, however, some caution is in order.

Lisa Hess, a senior vice president and portfolio manager of municipal and mortgage-backed securities for Loews Corp., believes that a major tax overhaul is likely. She suggests nervous investors "stay away from munis unless they feel confident they'll be holding them to maturity."

Emerging Markets

A number of developing countries have entered the fixed-income markets recently. Countries such as Argentina, Brazil, and Mexico have an active market for their debt securities. Here we present an overview of this growing segment of the fixed-income securities market. Since the middle of the 1980s, the emerging markets in debt securities have developed considerable liquidity.

As Table 1-17 shows, the emerging market's debt is sufficiently large for institutional investors to take an active part in it. Current estimates of the annual volume of trading in Argentinean debt is $90 billion. The yield spreads of Argentinean debt over similar U.S. Treasury has dropped from over 500 basis points in 1991 to about 300 basis points in 1993.

Recently, the Brady Plan has enabled these countries to securitize their debt issues and thereby attract a much broader pool of institutional buyers. The role of this plan in increasing the size of the emerging debt market is readily seen from Table 1-18.

Country	1987	1992
Argentina	9.53	36.65
Brazil	1.52	13.95
Mexico	2.85	40.81
Venezuela	0.97	21.18

TABLE 1-17
Emerging Markets Debt Outstanding, in Billions of Dollars

Source: First Boston (1993 Report on emerging markets)

Country	Bank Debt under Brady Plan	Debt Converted to Bonds
Argentina	26.40	16.60
Brazil	42.10	NA
Mexico	47.90	35.80
Venezuela	19.30	17.20

TABLE 1-18
Emerging Markets and Brady Plan Bonds, in Billions of Dollars

Source: First Boston (1993)

A FRAMEWORK FOR PRICING FIXED-INCOME SECURITIES

Our overview of fixed-income markets highlights the fact that fixed-income securities are exposed to various dimensions of risk. Depending on who the marginal investor is in any specific fixed-income security market and depending on the compensation required by the investor for bearing the risks, the pricing of the security will be affected. To assist the reader in developing some intuition about the relative pricing of fixed-income securities, we provide a simple framework in Table 1-19.

The general approach to pricing fixed-income securities proceeds logically. First, the Treasury securities, which are the most liquid securities and which are free from credit and timing risk, will be priced. Almost every other sector of the fixed-income securities market is then priced relative to the Treasury benchmark. This requires a theory of risk and return of the Treasury securities. But the valuation of Treasury securities can proceed without a theory of credit risk. To this end, many of the valuation procedures that will be described in detail in this text are for Treasury securities. The pricing of other securities, such as corporate and mortgage-backed securities, requires in addition a theory for pricing default risk and prepayments. In general, the pricing relationship will assume the following form. Let us say that we have been able to determine that the required rate of return on a Treasury security with a certain coupon and maturity is π_t. Then, a similar corporate security with credit risk will have a required return of the form, $\pi_t + \epsilon_t$ where ϵ_t is the compensation for credit risk. In reality, the premium in the required return (as measured by the yields) includes not only a compensation for credit risk but also a compensation for liquidity risk and for any contractual provisions that may be present in the corporate security. Such contractual provisions might include call

TABLE 1-19 *Relative Risk Exposures of Fixed-Income Securities*

Dimension of Risk & Return	Treasury	Agencies	Corporates	MBS	Municipals	Emerging Markets
Credit risk	Absent	Very low	Varies	Very low	Varies	High
Interest risk	Varies	Varies	Varies	Varies	Varies	Varies
Liquidity risk	Very low	Low/ moderate	Varies	Low	Varies	High
Timing risk	None	Low	High	Very High	High	Varies
Tax	Only federal taxes	Fully taxable	Fully taxable	Fully taxable	Tax-exempt	Fully taxable
FX risk	None	None	None	None	None	Present
Inflation	Present	Present	Present	Present	Present	Present

features, for example. By developing models of credit risk and prepayments, and super-imposing those models on the basic Treasury model, we will be able to value corporate and mortgage-backed securities.

In Figure 1-11, we provide a framework for the pricing of debt securities and the logical sequence of steps that are involved in the process.

As shown in Figure 1-10, the relationship between the yields in the Treasury, corporate, and municipal markets over the last two decades shows that the spread's ϵ_t has fluctuated a great deal over time. This suggests that the factors that determine the premium over the Treasury rates can be quite variable over time.

Note that the relative valuation of securities as reflected in the yield spreads has fluctuated a good deal. The pricing of debt securities focuses on the valuation of Treasury securities and on the determination of the spreads at which securities in the other segments of the fixed-income securities markets trade relative to comparable Treasury securities. These issues are taken up in detail in later chapters.

FIGURE 1-11   *Pricing of Debt Securities*

	Interest Rate Risk	*Default Risk*	*Contractual Provisions (Options)*	*Other Sources of Risk*	*Required Rate of Return*
Noncallable Treasury	Interest rate risk is critical and must be modelled.	Not relevant	New issues since 1985 are non-callable. There are about 20 callable issues outstanding.	Off-the-run issues may be illiquid.	Compensation for interest rate risk only.
Callable Treasury	Interest rate risk is critical and must be modelled.	Not relevant	The call option held by the Treasury has to be modelled.	Many of them are illiquid.	Compensation for interest rate risk plus a compensation for the timing uncertainty.
Corporate Securities	Interest rate risk is critical and must be modelled.	Issuer's credit reputation is critical. Credit risk must be modelled.	Sinking funds & calls may be present. Investors may have the right to put the bond back to the issuer. Call features may be present.	With the exception of new issues, liquidity is poor in this market	Compensation for interest rate risk plus a compensation for the timing uncertainty plus a compensation for credit risk minus the value of options held by the investor.

(Continued)

FIGURE 1-11   *Continued*

	Interest Rate Risk	*Default Risk*	*Contractual Provisions (Options)*	*Other Sources of Risk*	*Required Rate of Return*
Mortgage-backed Securities	Interest rate risk is critical and must be modelled.	When housing prices fall, home-owners can "walk away" from the loan and this affects the cash flows. Credit standing of the pool.	The home-owners have the option to prepay and this must be modelled.	Housing prices, seasonal factors, etc.	Compensation for interest rate risk plus a compensation for the timing uncertainty. Additional compensation for lack of liquidity and the credit standing of the structure.
Municipal securities	Interest rate risk is critical and must be modelled.	Issuer's credit reputation is critical. Credit risk must be modelled.	Sinking funds & calls may be present. Investors may have the right to put the bond back to the issuer.	Tax status is critical and must be modelled.	Compensation for interest rate risk plus a compensation for the timing uncertainty plus a compensation for credit risk minus the value of tax benefits held by the investor. Tax risks are present.
Emerging market securities	Interest rate risk is critical and must be modelled.	Issuer's credit reputation is critical. Credit risk must be modelled.	Sinking funds & calls may be present. Investors may have the right to put the bond back to the issuer.	Political risk, exchange rate risk and tax consider-ations must be modelled.	Compensation for interest rate risk plus a compensation for the timing uncertainty plus a compensation for credit risk plus a compensation for exchange rate and political risks.
Hybrids	Interest rate risk is critical and must be modelled.	Issuer's credit reputation is critical. Credit risk must be modelled.	Sinking funds & calls may be present. Investors may have the right to convert the bond into shares of common stock.	Equity risk is important.	Compensation for interest rate risk plus a compensation for the timing uncertainty plus a compensation for credit risk minus the value of the conversion option held by the investor.

FURTHER READING

Several texts with an emphasis on market institutions in fixed-income markets are available. Notable texts are Fabozzi (1993) and Ray (1993). In addition, there are texts that address topics relating to interest rates, such as Van Horne (1994). Many specialized texts are available, each dealing with one or two segments of fixed-income markets. Ray (1993) provides a detailed account of the Treasury market. Several anthologies edited by Fabozzi (1986, 1991, 1993) contain articles by professionals in different sectors of the fixed-income markets; Fabozzi (1991) provides an analysis of the fixed-income markets. These handbooks provide a more detailed description of instruments and market institutions in each segment of the fixed-income market. Several excellent texts are available on government securities markets. These include Bollenbacher (1988), Garbade (1982), and Scott (1965). Despite the fact that these books are somewhat dated, their treatment of the material is still of considerable value.

Specialized journals are available dealing with each segment of the fixed-income markets. The *Journal of Fixed-Income* publishes papers on topics spanning all segments of the fixed-income markets. Articles in this journal tend to be oriented more towards the practitioners. Other journals such as the *Journal of Portfolio Management* also contain articles of general interest to practitioners in the fixed-income area. Other academic journals such as the *Journal of Finance, Review of Financial Studies, Journal of Financial Economics, Journal of Financial and Quantitative Analysis,* and *Journal of Business,* carry academic papers with an emphasis on theoretical and empirical work in finance. Many influential papers on fixed-income securities have appeared in these journals. Some influential papers on interest rates and term structure theory have also appeared in the *Journal of Political Economy, Econometrica* and other journals of economics. Real estate and mortgage-backed securities have several academic and practitioner-oriented journals. Two prominent journals are the *Journal of AREUEA* and the *Journal of Real Estate Finance and Economics.* A number of journals, such as *Financial Analysts Journal, Journal of Portfolio Management,* and *Financial Management,* also carry many papers on fixed-income markets.

PROBLEMS

1.1   In the market, highly-rated corporate bonds are providing a 2% higher return than comparable Treasury securities. Does this mean that these corporate securities are better investments than Treasury securities? Discuss.

1.2   What types of institutional investors will value liquidity more? Why?

1.3   The fixed-income sector of the U.S. market consists of Treasuries, corporates, mortgage-backed securities and municipals.

  (a) Provide a brief analysis of each of these segments along each dimension of risk.

(b) Provide a pecking order among these segments for (i) pension funds, (ii) central banks, and (iii) hedge funds. Explain your conclusions. How would the tax status of these securities affect the pecking order?

1.4 Distinguish the terms T-bills, T-notes, and T-bonds.

1.5 What are the on-the-run, off-the-run, and off-off-the-run issues in the Treasury market? Why is such a distinction important?

1.6 Many corporate bonds have call features or sinking fund features: The issuer has the right to call these bonds at prespecified call prices on prespecified dates. Only a small percentage of Treasury bonds (of late, no Treasuries) have call features. What might be the reasons for this difference? Explain.

1.7 Explain why Treasuries of the same risk tend to sell for a lower yield than corporates of the same risk. Explain why municipals of the same risk tend to sell for a lower yield than either corporates or Treasuries. Using the data in the *Treasury Bulletin,* plot the spreads between long-term corporates, Treasuries and municipals for the last 20 years. Explain the spread behavior as a function of

    (a) the level of the yields,

    (b) the shape of the Treasury yield curve,

    (c) changes in the tax environment, and

    (d) credit risk.

1.8 Consider an investor with a marginal tax rate of 30%. If municipal securities yield 6% and a comparable corporate yields 7.5%, which is the better investment? Why? Provide a discussion of other factors that will affect the choice between these investments.

1.9 What are special purpose vehicles? Describe their functions in securitization.

1.10 Describe the process of securitization. How does this process help in the overall resource allocation of the economy?

1.11 What are revenue bonds? How do they differ from general obligation bonds?

1.12 Some floating-rate bonds are issued with a put feature which gives the investor the right to put the floater back to the issuer on preset dates at par. Discuss whether this put is a protection against interest rate risk or credit risk.

1.13 Briefly describe each of the following debt securities and the motivation behind the issuing of such securities. What might be the motivation for investors to invest in these securities?

    (a) Convertible bonds

    (b) Inverse floater

    (c) Pay-in kind (PIK) bonds

    (d) Zero coupon bonds

    (e) Yankee bonds

1.14 Describe the sectors of fixed-income markets in which institutional investors such as pension funds should not be investing their funds. Why?

1.15 What are the reasons for issuers to raise capital by issuing floating rate securities as opposed to fixed-rate securities?

1.16 Review the publication *Bond Week* by Salomon Brothers for this week. Using the information presented in this publication, write a summary report not exceeding one page highlighting the activities in the fixed-income securities market.

1.17 Bonds in the corporate sector are usually issued with sinking fund provisions. Supply the rationale for this contractual feature. Will it be beneficial to the bondholders? Why?

1.18 You have bought two securities from the same issuer. The first security is a bullet corporate bond with a maturity of 30 years and a coupon (semi-annual) of 10%. The second security is a floating-rate bond with a maturity of 30 years. The floater will pay a coupon (semi-annual) equal to the prevailing six-month T-bill rate plus 100 basis points. Assume that the floater has no additional contractual provisions and that the ex-coupon dates for the two securities are the same. Explain how you will assess the risks of these two securities.

1.19   Discuss the importance of the emerging market in the fixed-income markets. What is the Brady Plan? How has it affected the emerging market?

REFERENCES

Bollenbacher, G. 1988. *The Professional's Guide to the U.S. Government Securities Markets: Treasuries, Agencies, Mortgage-backed Instruments.* New York Institute of Finance, 1988.

Fabozzi, F. (ed.) 1987. *Mortgage Backed Securities: New Strategies Applications and Research.* Chicago: Probus.

Fabozzi, F. 1993. *Bond Markets, Analysis and Strategies.* 2nd ed. Englewood Cliffs, NJ: Prentice-Hall.

Fabozzi, F. (ed.). 1994. *Handbook of Fixed Income Securities.* Homewood, IL: Irwin Professional Publishing.

Garbade, K. D. 1982. *Securities Markets.* New York: McGraw Hill.

Jeffrey, N. A. 1995. "Flat-Tax Cloud Unlikely to Rain on Munis." *Wall Street Journal* (May 19): C1, C15.

Ray, C. 1993. *The Bond Market. Trading and Risk Management.* Homewood, IL: Business One Irwin.

Scott, I. 1965. Government Securities Market. New York: McGraw Hill.

Stigum, M. 1983. *The Money Market.* Homewood, IL: Dow-Jones Irwin.

Sun, T., and S. Sundaresan 1994. "Liquidity in Bond Markets," Working paper, Columbia University.

Sundaresan, S. 1991–1993. Debt Markets. Columbia University MBA B8308 course binders.

Van Horne, James C. 1994. *Financial Markets Rates and Flows.* 4th ed. Englewood Cliffs, N.J.: Prentice-Hall.

Chapter 2

Organization and Conduct of Debt Markets

Chapter Objectives

The purpose of this chapter is to describe the organization of debt markets. Chapter 2 will help the reader to understand and answer the following questions.

- What are different forms of market organizations?
- What is adverse selection?
- Who are the key players in debt markets? In this context, we will describe the following players:
  1. Treasury
  2. Federal Reserve
  3. Government agencies
  4. Primary dealers
  5. Interdealer brokers
  6. Investors
- What are the options that the Fed can use in implementing its monetary policies?
- What are repo markets? How are they used for financing Treasury securities?
- What happened in the May 1991 two-year auctions? What are short squeezes? What was the role played by Salomon Brothers in that auction?
- What are some of the regulatory issues in debt markets?
- What is transparency in securities markets?

INTRODUCTION

This chapter begins by briefly describing certain market organizations that are relevant to the study of fixed-income markets. We then discuss the salient properties of market organizations that participants take into account in their trading and pricing decisions. Next, we discuss the key players in the Treasury markets and the Treasury market organization. Other segments of the fixed-income markets are then taken up. The regulatory aspects of fixed-income markets in general are addressed in the final section of the chapter. We discuss in particular the scandal in the Treasury markets involving Salomon Brothers and explore its consequences for the future conduct of Treasury auctions and the regulation of the Treasury markets.

MARKET ORGANIZATION

The organization of markets or the market structure refers to the institutional arrangement by which buyers of securities are matched with sellers. Chapter 1 noted that most fixed-income securities markets around the world are organized as over-the-counter (OTC) or dealer markets. We provide below some basic market structures which will serve as a frame of reference for our analysis. The classification that follows is suggested in Garbade (1982), who also provides a more detailed treatment of some of these market organizations.

   Direct search is an arrangement in which buyers directly search and identify matching sellers without the benefit of one or more intermediaries. For this structure to come about, the frequency of transactions must be so low that no intermediary finds it economical to provide any service. The costs of search, location, and negotiation are fully borne by the individual transactor (buyer or the seller). As a result, this market structure may frequently lead to trades away from the best possible price. This type of market structure is not of interest in the context of fixed-income security markets and probably is descriptive only of primitive markets with very few buyers and sellers, which are extremely illiquid.

   When trading becomes more and more frequent, brokers may find it economical to intermediate (for a fee) and match buyers and sellers at mutually agreed-upon terms. For a **brokered market** to come about the trading volume in securities must be heavy and there must be significant economies of scale in the search costs to locate counterparties, so that a direct search is a more costly alternative to buyers and sellers. In addition, transactions away from the best possible price must not be too costly for the buyer and seller. The last condition is necessary because the broker may not be able to execute the order instantaneously. Note that the broker acts as an agent to buyers and sellers. Brokered markets are quite common in securities industry.

   The secondary market for U.S. Treasury is organized as a **dealer market.** Over 1,500 dealers stand ready to buy and sell Treasury securities at bid and offer prices that are widely disseminated to investors either through electronic screens or through telephones. (Bid and offer prices are defined in Chapter 1.) The dealer market structure reduces the time of search compared to brokered markets. Dealers may quote different bid-offer prices for the same security and hence a limited search for the best price may still be necessary. Dealers, unlike brokers, also take outright positions in securities. Thus, they are also exposed to the market risk on their inventories. Depending on the securities, their profits will depend on the market risks as well as the depth and breadth of their sales force and customer base.

Centralized markets in which all market participants interact simultaneously are known as **auction markets.** These reduce further the cost of search and provide better bid-offer spreads. The centralized open outcry markets, such as the futures and options exchanges, may be thought of as prototypical examples of auction markets. The seller of securities is concerned with designing the mechanism that enables the expected revenues to be maximized. In addition, if the issuer intends to be a repeat seller (such as the U.S. Treasury), then there is an incentive to ensure that the market is free from manipulations. We discuss some of the auction mechanisms used in the Treasury market in Chapter 3.

Properties of Market Organizations

An important trait of a well-functioning market organization is **transparency.** This, loosely interpreted, is the extent to which information about trades, quotes, and other market information such as volume of trading and open interest are available to all players in the market. The cost of obtaining such information is also critical. Hence, in a well-functioning market organization, transparency should be present at a sufficiently low cost.

When intermediaries attempt to match potential buyers with potential sellers in a market, they face the risk of trading with either buyers or sellers who have more information than the others about the security or the deal that is about to be transacted. This is referred to as the **adverse selection** problem. A common example is the used-car market. In such markets, the seller of the used car presumably knows a good deal more about the true condition (and the true value) of the car than potential buyers. In order to protect themselves against such trades, the intermediaries will then charge a wider bid-offer spread to all participants in the market. This can be a serious factor in the determination of the bid-offer spread when the availability of relevant information to all participants is not symmetric and the cost of obtaining additional relevant information is significant.

In addition to the adverse selection problem, the intermediaries routinely take large inventory positions in securities and absorb the risk of price fluctuations before such inventories are sold to customers. The risk of the security in a market, the ability to offload that risk in other markets, and the uncertainty in the cost of financing such inventories will all contribute both to the bid-offer spreads and to the depth of the market.

There is a growing body of literature on what is called the market microstructure that deals with these and other related questions. This literature examines the properties of different market arrangements on factors such as price formation and bid-offer spreads.

Generally, the form of the market organization (OTC or dealer markets, auctions, etc.) has a significant impact on the resulting price processes and bid-offer spreads. In addition, the informational disclosure requirements, the regulatory rules, and the effectiveness of their enforcement also affect the outcome significantly.

Several influential papers, notably Glosten and Milgrom (1985) and Glosten (1987), contain valuable models for the components of bid-offer spreads. One model is that the bid-offer spread consists of two components. The first component is the compensation that the market maker gets due to possible monopoly power, inventory carrying costs, etc. The second component is compensation due to the adverse selection component. When market makers realize that the counterparties with superior information will buy when the price is low relative to the true value and will sell when the price is high relative to the true value, this causes an upward revision of the true price after a buy and a downward revision of the true price after a sell. While most of the available theoretical models are interpreted in the context of equity markets, the basic insights apply to fixed-income markets as well.

The adverse selection component of the bid-offer spread will be less significant if the informational differences between the participants are negligible. Cornell (1993) examines the Treasury market for the presence of private information and adverse selection and concludes that the adverse selection problems are not severe. At the end of this chapter, we briefly review some of the regulatory aspects of fixed-income securities markets which bear on these properties of market organization.

PLAYERS IN GOVERNMENT SECURITIES MARKETS

In this section, the focus will first be on the government securities market. Later, we will describe the organization of other sectors of the fixed-income securities markets.

The government securities market in the U.S. has seven major participants.

The **U.S. Treasury** is the fulcrum of the government securities market. It is the issuer of short-term and long-term debt securities on a regular basis.

The **Federal Reserve System** acts as the agent of U.S. Treasury in issuing U.S. Treasury debt through a computerized book-entry system. Both the initial sale of securities and subsequent transfers are handled by the Federal Reserve System. The conduct of monetary policy, including the open market operations, is also carried out by the Fed.

Agencies of the U.S. government also issue securities of varying maturities. These are collectively known as agency debt issues. An overview of this market is in Chapter 1.

Primary dealers are those banks, bank subsidiaries, diversified investment banks, and specialty firms that are approved to transact directly with the Fed in its market operations. Currently, there are nearly 40 primary dealers.

Other dealers routinely trade in U.S. government securities but are not primary dealers. These include depository institutions, securities firms, and specialist firms.

Interdealer brokers are important players in the government securities market. They conceal the identities of the ultimate sellers and buyers, and act as principals to both sides of the trade.

Investors throughout the world hold U.S. government securities because they are, perhaps, the most liquid and nominally riskless securities. The investment community in this sector includes central banks, pension funds, insurance companies, commercial banks, corporations, and state and local governments. The Fed itself transacts heavily in government securities but it does not directly buy securities from the Treasury. It conducts its transactions through primary dealers.

U.S. Treasury

The United States Treasury is responsible for borrowing money in capital markets to meet government expenditures. In addition, it is also vested with the responsibility of tax collection. One of the key tasks connected with these responsibilities is determining the amount and type of debt that must be sold. The U.S. Treasury issues marketable debt securities such as T-bills, T-notes, and T-bonds. It also issues nonmarketable securities such as savings bonds, and special issues called cash management bills and foreign-targeted securities. Obviously, the composition of these securities is an important decision. The U.S. Treasury also decides on the time schedule of issuing debt and, given the large amount of debt that is issued, the Treasury decides on the maturity composition of debt. Lately, the U.S. Treasury has significantly reduced the average maturity by suspending the seven-year benchmark auction and making the thirty-year auction twice a year instead of quarterly refunding. Figure 2-1 shows the average length of Treasury debt over the last few years. The average maturity of U.S. Treasury debt reached a peak of ten years and five months in June 1947 and then followed generally a declining trend until December 1975, when it reached an all-time low of two years and five months. The current average maturity is six years. Decisions about maturity composition affect the supply of Treasury securities in an important way, influencing the pricing of Treasury yield curve across the maturity spectrum.

FIGURE 2-1   *Average Maturity of U.S. Treasury Debt*

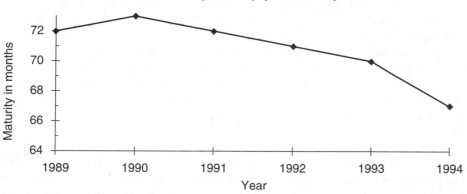

As a third major task, the Treasury must decide on the mechanism for selling Treasury securities to the public. Currently the Treasury is using the sealed-bid discriminating auction procedure for selling in the three-month, six-month, one-year, three-year, ten-year, and thirty-year auctions and is currently experimenting with the sealed-bid uniform-price Dutch auction for the monthly two-year and five-year auctions. The next chapter will discuss in detail these auctions, the theory behind them, and the empirical evidence. The schedule of Treasury auctions is provided in Chapter 1.

Federal Reserve

The Federal Reserve (Fed) is vested with the responsibility of conducting monetary policies. These policies control the money in the economy, and the level and the course of interest rates of different maturities. In addition, as the equivalent of central bank of the country, the Fed is the "lender of last resort." It also acts as an agent of the Treasury in conducting auctions and in handling payments and collections via electronic transfer systems. Finally, it plays the role of regulator in matters concerning commercial banks, Treasury securities, and derivative assets on interest rates.

The Fed consists of the Board of Governors and the Federal Reserve District Banks. Currently there are 12 district banks, each with its own branches. The Federal Reserve Board has seven members, one of the members serving as the Chairman. The members are appointed by the President of the United States.

The Federal Reserve System is also responsible for implementing monetary policies. Several policy options are available to the Fed.

1. The Fed can cut or raise the discount rate.
2. The Fed can change the reserve requirements.
3. The Fed can undertake outright transactions in Treasury and federal agency securities in the open market (at market prices) with securities dealers, and official foreign and international accounts maintained at the Federal Reserve Bank of New York.
4. The Fed also can enter into repurchase agreements (repos or RPs) for different terms to maturity.

The Federal Reserve has a committee known as the Federal Open Market Committee (FOMC) which authorizes the tools by which it conducts monetary policies.

One of these monetary policy tools is the reserve requirement. The reserves that depository institutions must place with the Fed depend on the level of the transaction balances and the composition of the liabilities. It is worth noting that Fed funds, repurchase agreements, and foreign deposits do not require any reserves. (The Fed funds market and the market for repurchase agreements are described later in this chapter.) The reserves are held in cash. Therefore, when the Fed decreases the reserve requirements, it increases the money supply in the economy. This potentially increases the money available for lending and provides a spurt to economic activity. A second monetary tool is the Fed's discount window.

Fed Funds Market. The Fed funds market is the market for the reserve balances at the Fed that depository institutions maintain to meet the reserve requirements. The Fed does not pay interest on these reserves and, as a consequence, the depository institutions try to maintain the minimum amount of reserves necessary to conduct their activities. A depository institution that is short of reserves will borrow reserves from a bank that has a surplus in the Fed funds market. Such borrowing and lending can be done either directly by the banks or through brokers. Usually, brokered transactions are of larger average size. Typically, big banks borrow reserves from smaller ones that have surplus reserves. Many of the depository institutions that have a surplus of reserves view the Fed funds market as a means of obtaining liquidity. The daily volume of Fed funds transactions arranged by the brokers exceeds $50 billion.

Fed funds transactions typically take place overnight. Sometimes the Fed funds transactions extend over a term of a few days. It must be recognized that the Fed funds transactions are unsecured lending and borrowing between depository institutions. The term Fed funds market is a lot less liquid than the overnight market.

A typical Fed funds transaction is shown in Figure 2-2. The bank with surplus reserves offers the reserves (typically through a Fed fund broker) to the bank that has a need for such reserves. The selling bank also informs the Federal Reserve Bank in its district, which arranges for the transfer.

The Fed funds rate is a barometer of the activities of the depository institutions. The rates go up when the demand for reserves is great and goes down when the demand is sluggish. The behavior of the Fed funds rates over the past five years is shown in Figure 2-3. From time to time, especially around the end of the calendar year, the Fed fund rates go up resulting in the spikes evident in Figure 2-3. This may be due to the fact that many big depository institutions drive up the Fed funds rates seasonally.

FIGURE 2-2   *Fed Funds Market Transaction*

FIGURE 2-3   *Federal Funds Rates During 1986–1993*

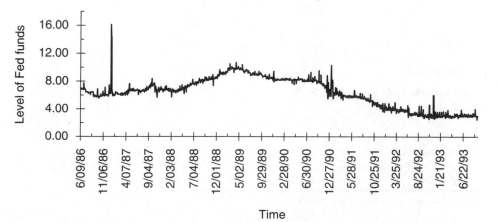

Open Market Operations. The Fed's discount window is an important monetary policy tool. Under this scheme, the Fed provides credit when there is a shortage; the discount rate is the rate at which the Fed acts as a lender of last resort to the depository institutions. The loans made by the Fed can be directed towards short-term scarcity, seasonal peak loads (as in agriculture) for credit, or distress credit to help depository institutions that are in serious financial trouble.

When the Fed changes its holdings of Treasury securities, it does so in this secondary market. The directives of the Federal Open Market Committee are implemented by the trading desk of New York Fed. Since its transactions influence the pace of monetary expansion, the Fed is only allowed to participate in outright transactions in the secondary market where Treasury and Federal agency securities are already outstanding. It is not allowed to bid directly in the auctions. The Fed has a wide choice in the type of securities to buy or sell (maturity, coupon, discount, etc.), as well as in the choice of the counterparties. The timing of the Fed's actions is dictated by the forecasts of the reserve demands, the larger the anticipated demand, the greater the purchases of securities. The Fed's portfolio has a diversified maturity composition, as Table 2-1 illustrates. How-

Type of Holdings & Maturity	April 1993	May 1993	June 1993
Total issues	84	129	1,534
< 15 days	54	82	1,447
15 > and < 90 days	30	47	87
90 > and < 365 days	0	0	0
Total acceptances	0	0	0
< 15 days	0	0	0
15 > and < 90 days	0	0	0
90 > and < 365 days	0	0	0
Total U.S. Treasury	305,381	304,494	328,199
< 15 days	11,295	8,196	29,971
15 > and < 90 days	74,524	79,097	74,113
90 > and < 365 days	95,254	94,431	101,750
1 year > and < 5 years	72,915	71,065	70,660
5 years > and < 10 years	21,471	21,606	21,606
> 10 years	29,922	30,099	30,099
Total Federal Agency	5,095	5,054	5,981
< 15 days	115	301	1,179
15 > and < 90 days	643	527	612
90 > and < 365 days	1,177	1,136	1,132
1 year > and < 5 years	2,307	2,237	2,181
5 years > and < 10 years	711	711	736
> 10 years	142	142	142

TABLE 2-1

Federal Reserve Bank's Holdings (in Millions of Dollars)

Source: *Federal Reserve Bulletin* September 1993

ever, the bulk of the Fed's holdings are in U.S. Treasury securities. Nearly 60% of the Treasury holdings are under a maturity of one year.

In addition to outright transactions, the Fed routinely undertakes temporary transactions in which reserves are either injected or drained for a day or two. If, for example, a shortage of reserves is anticipated, the Fed can either buy securities outright, as explained earlier, or temporarily buy the securities with an agreement to sell them back within a day or two. Usually, much larger operations are carried out using the temporary transactions. One strategy used by the Fed in this context is the **matched sale-purchase transactions** (MSP) in which the Fed sells T-bills for immediate delivery through dealers and simultaneously buys them back for delivery in a day or two. These are viewed as two separate transactions.

The Fed also uses repurchase agreements to effect temporary transactions. Reverse repos (explained later) are used by the Fed to either provide or absorb bank reserves. The aggregate repurchase agreement transactions by the Fed in 1990–1992 exceeded $200 billion, as shown in Table 2-2. In addition, the Fed transacts on behalf of foreign central banks and official institutions.

TABLE 2-2   *Federal Reserve Open Market Operations (in Millions of Dollars)*

Policy Dimension	Activity	1990	1991	1992
Outright transactions	Gross purchases	25,414	31,439	34,079
	Gross sales	7,591	120	1,628
	Redemptions	4,400	1,000	1,600
Matched transactions	Gross purchases	1,363,434	1,571,534	1,480,140
	Gross sales	1,369,052	1,570,456	1,482,467
Repurchase agreements	Gross purchases	219,632	310,084	378,374
	Gross sales	202,551	311,752	386,257

Source: *Federal Reserve Bulletin* September 1993

Many foreign accounts place a percentage of their U.S. dollar holdings with the Fed in an overnight repo facility. If such holdings are placed in repo using an MSP with the Fed's portfolio, then the reserves will be drained—this is because the funds received by the foreign account stay with the Fed. This is referred to as a **system RP.** When the foreign order can be routed through the market it is referred to as a **customer RP.** Usually, customer RPs signal a modest addition to the reserves, limited by the funds in the foreign accounts. On the other hand, system RPs signal a larger magnitude of reserve adjustments. For a more detailed treatment of the repo transactions by the Federal Reserve, see Meulendyke (1989). As Table 2-2 indicates, the matched transactions account for a large percentage of the Federal Reserve's Open market operations. This is closely followed by the repo transactions.

The monetary policies followed by the Fed underwent a major change in October 1979 when Paul Volcker became Chairman. The growth rates in money measures were targeted and the emphasis of the Fed funds rates was diminished. Figures 2-4 and 2-5 illustrate the wild fluctuations in the levels of interest rates and their volatilities from

FIGURE 2-4   *Level of Interest Rates*

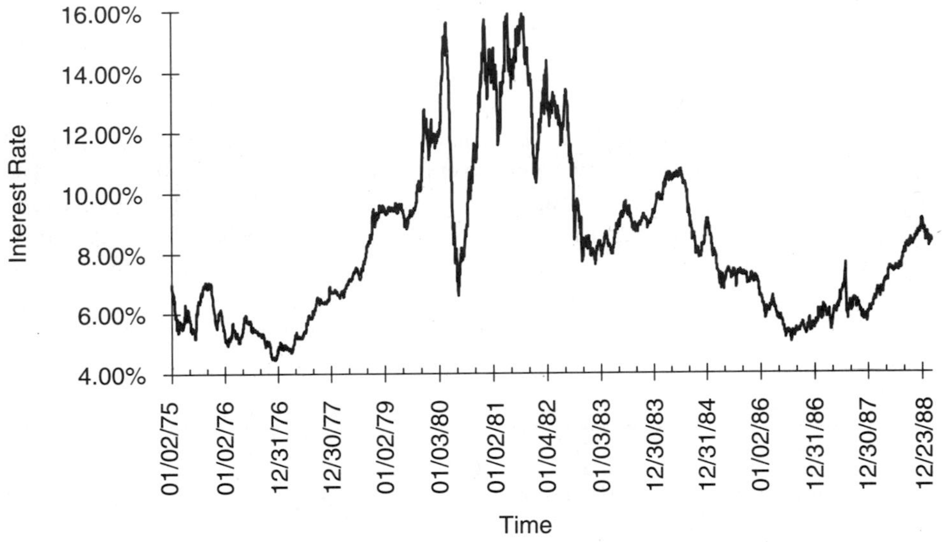

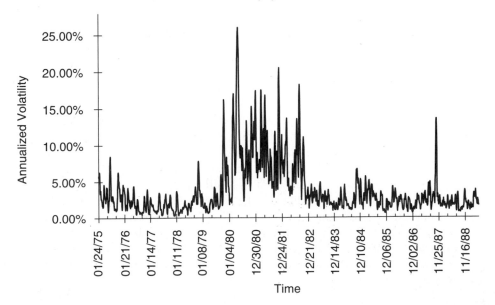

FIGURE 2-5   *Volatility of Interest Rates*

1975 to 1989. Note that the period 1980–1983 witnessed very high levels of interest rates and very high volatilities as market participants came to grips with the new monetary policy. In addition, the yield curve was inverted for an extended period of time. This is also evident in Table 1-9, where we found that the spreads were negative in 1979–1981.

The Fed, acting as a fiscal agent for the Treasury, conducts the auctions of new Treasury securities. This entails collecting and processing competitive and noncompetitive bids from dealers. These auctions are considered in detail in Chapter 3. T-bills, T-notes, and T-bonds are issued in **book-entry** form. This is a **tiered custodial system.** This system records the ownership of securities in entries on the books of a series of custodians. This system begins with the Treasury and extends through the Federal Reserve Banks, depository institutions, brokers, and dealers to the ultimate owner. The tiered system operates as follows. The Treasury's book-entry will establish the total amount of each issue that is outstanding and the share of each that is held by each Federal Reserve Bank. Each Federal Reserve Bank will record how much of each issue is held by the depository institutions in its district that maintain book-entry accounts with it. The record of each depository institution will establish the amount that is held in its Reserve Bank for other depository institutions that do not maintain accounts at the Fed and for others.

Interest payments, as well as principal payments at maturity, are made by the Treasury, crediting the funds down the custodial tiers just described. Only certain depository institutions may have book-entry accounts at Federal Reserve Banks. Others must have their holdings reflected on the books of a depository institution that in turn has holdings through a depository institution. Transfers are made by making appropriate entries. If the transfer of a security takes place within the jurisdiction of a Federal Reserve Bank, no entries will be made at the Fed level or above. All entries will take place below the level of that Federal Reserve Bank.

Here we have only sketched the role of the Federal Reserve. A more comprehensive analysis appears in Hubbard (1991).

Government Securities Dealers

Currently there are nearly 40 primary dealers in the government securities markets. In addition to the nearly 40 primary dealers, there are more than 1,500 other dealers who perform a variety of trading and market-making functions in the Treasury market. The primary dealer system was established by the Federal Reserve. The basic advantage of such a system is that the Fed is in a position to conduct its monetary policies efficiently with a small number of well-capitalized dealers. Primary dealers are expected to participate in Treasury auctions and distribute Treasury securities, and to stand ready to buy or sell securities for customers, that is, act as "market makers." Fed has an approved list of primary dealers. The Fed takes into account factors such as the capital base (financial strength), the customer base, the volume of activity, the commitment to making a market under varied market conditions, and the ability to meet the needs of Fed when approving a dealer to be one of its primary dealers. Government securities dealers perform several tasks. They make markets for customers, providing relevant information, analysis, and advice to customers; maintain a sales force to accomplish this, do transactions, and win customer loyalty; maintain an inventory of government securities to meet customer needs; absorb and distribute a large chunk of U.S. government securities when securities are sold at auction; and buy and sell securities in the secondary market. The price at which the dealer is willing to buy is called a bid. The price at which a dealer is willing to sell is called an offer.

Trading Activities. The volume of daily trading activity by government dealers is large. This is illustrated in Table 2-3, where the transactions in the underlying cash market are reported. These are classified first according to the type of securities and then according to the type of counterparties engaged in the transactions. These statistics reveal some interesting patterns. First, a major percentage of the transactions occurs in the Treasury securities. Mortgage-backed securities form a distant second, followed by the Federal

	March 1993	April 1993	May 1993
By type of securities			
U.S. Treasury securities			
T-bills	43,300	41,403	42,349
Coupon sector			
< 3.5 years maturity	47,300	36,975	53,322
3.5 to 7.5 years maturity	45,252	42,812	44,104
7.5 to 15 years maturity	23,269	19,229	21,228
> 15 years maturity	17,592	16,963	16,527
Federal agency securities			
< 3.5 years maturity	5790	5715	6108
3.5 to 7.5 years maturity	788	640	572
> 7.5 years maturity	1125	578	350
Mortgage-backed securities			
Pass-throughs	14,705	17,293	18,294
All others	4,059	3,336	3,262
By type of counterparties			
Primary dealers and brokers			
U.S. Treasury securities	110,173	97,491	111,243
Federal agencies			
Debt	1,771	1,155	1,019
Mortgage-backed	7,388	8,855	9,484
Customers			
U.S. Treasury securities	66,539	59,531	66,289
Federal agencies			
Debt	5,931	5,778	6,011
Mortgage-backed	11,378	11,775	12,072

TABLE 2-3

Cash Market Transactions of U.S. Government Securities Dealers (Daily Averages in Millions of Dollars)

Source: *Federal Reserve Bulletin* September 1993

agency securities. This sheds further light on the depth and liquidity of Treasury markets. The classification of trades by counterparties shows a rather interesting pattern—nearly 60% of Treasury transactions occur between dealers and brokers, and only 40% occur between customers and dealers. In sharp contrast, more than 56% of the transactions in mortgage-backed securities occur between customers and dealers. For the Federal agency debt, the customer-driven transactions are even higher at 85%.

These patterns reveal that the dealers take positions in Treasury and other securities not only to make a market in these securities but also to take principal positions. This latter activity is referred to as **proprietary trading** and has been increasingly responsible for a large percentage of dealers' profits and risks. As we shall see later in Chapter 15 on risk management, some significant losses have occurred as a result of these proprietary trading activities.

Table 2-4 provides a summary of the transactions undertaken by dealers in **derivative markets** such as futures, forwards and options. A detailed account of these markets is presented in Part II. For now, it is important to note that these markets enable dealers to manage the risk in market-making.

Futures and Forward Transactions	March 1993	April 1993	May 1993
By type of deliverable securities			
U.S. Treasury securities			
T-bills	2,205	2,378	2,586
Coupon sector			
< 3.5 years maturity	2,348	1,942	1,937
3.5 to 7.5 years maturity	2,287	1,384	1,799
7.5 to 15 years maturity	3,542	2,377	3,067
> 15 years maturity	11,335	9,025	10,406
Federal agency securities			
< 3.5 years maturity	92	102	153
3.5 to 7.5 years maturity	103	128	73
> 7.5 years maturity	32	33	15
Mortgage-backed securities			
Pass-throughs	22,141	21,378	19,462
All others	1,471	1,463	1,743
Options transactions by type of underlying securities			
U.S. Treasury securities			
< 3.5 years maturity	1,662	1,611	1,108
3.5 to 7.5 years maturity	431	564	667
7.5 to 15 years maturity	687	507	521
> 15 years maturity	972	1,084	1,183
Federal agency & mortgage-backed securities	586	664	465

TABLE 2-4

Derivatives Transactions of U.S. Government Securities Dealers (Daily Averages in Millions of Dollars)

Source: *Federal Reserve Bulletin* September 1993

In addition, these markets enable dealers to leverage their positions significantly in their proprietary trading activities. Two patterns are evident in the data presented in Table 2-4. First, note that in the Treasury securities area, the bulk of the derivatives positions are in the maturity sectors exceeding 15 years. The Treasury bond futures contract, which is the most actively traded futures contract, accounts for this. Second, note that the forwards and futures transactions on mortgage-backed securities form the single most actively traded sector. As the organized futures exchanges do not have great liquidity in this area, presumably the dealer market forward transactions account for this extensive trading activity. Finally, the options are mostly on shorter maturity instruments. In Part II, we examine in detail how such derivative products are used in the fixed-income markets.

Position Management. The composition and management of inventory is structured to permit the dealer to sell at a price higher than the cost of acquiring the securities. (The bid-offer spread is the profit if the price risk of inventory is eliminated.) This calls for the management of the interest rate risk—a primary source of price fluctuations in the government securities market. Dealers manage their own positions, that is, speculate with a view to profit from interest rate fluctuations. Thus, dealers position securities to reflect their assessment of future interest rates. A dealer may take "a long position," anticipating a fall in interest rates, or "go short," anticipating a rise in interest rates. Most of the positions are highly leveraged or supported by borrowed funds. Hence, as noted earlier position management is often the dominant source of variation in profit and capital for securities firms.

The daily average positions of dealers are given in Table 2-5, classified by type of securities. It is of interest to note that the dealers had established significant short positions in the maturity sectors 3.5 years to 15 years in the Treasury cash market. In addition, they were holding significant short positions in the forward contracts on mortgage-backed securities market. This, however, might have been a hedge against the significant long positions that they were holding in the underlying mortgage-backed securities markets. In a similar way, the dealers were short in T-bills forwards and futures, as well as on forwards on CDs. This was probably to compensate for their significant long positions in T-bills, CPs, CDs and BAs.

The positions shown in Tables 2-3 and 2-4 are huge. How do dealers finance such huge positions? Surely, the capital base of the dealers is not sufficient to support such large positions. The answer is in the market for repurchase agreements or repo markets.

Repo Markets. The single most important source of financing for government dealers is the repo markets. Government securities are liquid and default-free. Hence they are excellent collateral. Dealers can borrow money on a collateralized basis to buy such securities. This enables dealers with limited capital to take positions in securities worth billions of dollars. Table 2-6 gives an idea of the financing of a dealer's position.

The repo market is very large—exceeding $600 billion. Repurchase agreements (repos or RPs) are transactions in which one party (say, Party A) sells securities to another (Party B) while agreeing to repurchase those securities at a later date. Reverse

	March 1993	April 1993	May 1993
By type of securities			
U.S. Treasury securities			
T-bills	13,550	18,483	7,999
Coupon sector			
< 3.5 years maturity	1,628	2,928	10,275
3.5 to 7.5 years maturity	−14,104	−17,023	−19,900
7.5 to 15 years maturity	−10,240	−12,805	−10,222
> 15 years maturity	9,342	9,248	8,228
Federal agency securities			
< 3.5 years maturity	6,451	6,342	5,389
3.5 to 7.5 years maturity	3,332	3,178	2,798
> 7.5 years maturity	4,896	3,958	2,957
Mortgage-backed securities			
Pass-throughs	33,009	34,056	29,356
All others	25,734	25,886	27,158
Money market instruments			
CDs	3,212	3,203	3,681
CPs	6,237	5,145	6,066
BAs	1,138	972	862
Futures and forward positions by type of deliverable securities			
U.S. Treasury securities			
T-bills	−5,103	−7,951	−5,222
Coupon sector			
< 3.5 years maturity	−568	−1,433	−1,556
3.5 to 7.5 years maturity	4,333	4,857	4,626
7.5 to 15 years maturity	2,954	4,385	4,410
> 15 years maturity	−5,119	−5,103	−4,613
Federal agency securities			
< 3.5 years maturity	−194	−285	−209
3.5 to 7.5 years maturity	−39	−50	−111
> 7.5 years maturity	33	−74	−85
Mortgage-backed securities			
Pass-throughs	−13,086	−12,900	−6,758
All others	3,376	4,770	1,773
CDs	−156,617	−160,960	−155,044

TABLE 2-5

Positions of U.S. Government Securities Dealers (Daily Averages in Millions of Dollars)

Source: *Federal Reserve Bulletin* September 1993

repurchase agreements (or reverse repos) are transactions in which Party A buys securities from Party B while agreeing to resell those securities at a later date.

Repos and reverse repos may be done on an overnight basis or on a term basis for a specified number of days, ranging from a few days to over 30 days. Many of the repo and

	March 1993	April 1993	May 1993
Reverse repurchase agreements			
Overnight and continuing	233,038	223,214	223,931
Term	360,955	393,238	373,495
Repurchase agreements			
Overnight and continuing	403,942	406,560	399,943
Term	349,516	369,281	346,717
Securities borrowed			
Overnight and continuing	115,244	117,774	123,353
Term	40,753	44,365	42,805
Securities loaned			
Overnight and continuing	3,504	4,762	5,055
Term	482	587	938
Collateralized loans			
Overnight and continuing	14,209	14,434	14,538
Matched book			
Reverse repurchase agreements			
Overnight and continuing	156,399	148,137	146,741
Term	313,182	341,856	321,698
Repurchase agreements			
Overnight and continuing	214,034	204,658	210,160
Term	266,309	283,791	257,391

TABLE 2-6
Financing of Positions of U.S. Government Securities Dealers (Daily Averages in Millions of Dollars)

Source: *Federal Reserve Bulletin* September 1993

reverse repo transactions are done on an overnight basis or for a very short term not exceeding a few weeks at most.

A repo transaction may be viewed conceptually as **secured lending.** There are two parties to any repo transaction. Party A is the owner of the security or the collateral. For example, in a repo transaction Party A may need the money to pay for the securities he is selling to Party B. Party B, who has the cash, will charge interest for agreeing to this transaction. Party A will still retain the rights to any cash flows from the security (i.e., coupons or accrued interest) that he has used to collateralize the loan.

Securities used in repo transactions are referred to as **collaterals,** signifying the secured loan nature of the transaction. The buyer of the collateral does not deliver funds equal to the market value of the collateral; a **hair cut** will be taken from the market value and only the remainder is delivered to the seller. This is one of the several ways in which credit risk is handled in repo transactions. Important considerations in any repo transaction include the term of the repo transaction (this may be overnight, a week, another specified term, or open), the amount of cash borrowed, and the rate of interest upon which the two parties have agreed. Overnight and open repo trades have to be renewed every day, possibly at new rates.

Most Treasury securities may be secured at a rate known as the **general collateral rate.** Thus, from the standpoint of obtaining secured credit, most of the Treasury securities may be close substitutes. Some of the securities may be in demand from time to time owing to a short squeeze or the deliverability in futures market. Such securities may trade at rates that are much lower than the general collateral rate. Such rates are called **special repo rates.** Generally, repo markets involve large transfers of funds, extend for short terms, and are characterized by small earnings relative to potential changes in the value of the underlying securities or collaterals.

Interest rates in repo markets (repo rates) are generally lower than those on Federal funds due to the collateralized nature of transactions. The Fed funds rates reflect the fact that they are uncollateralized transactions. Repo markets are used by a large number of institutions—corporations, financial institutions, pension funds, commercial banks, etc. In contrast, the Fed funds market is open only to depository institutions. Figure 2-6 provides the historical spreads between the Fed funds rates and the repo rates. Although the Fed fund rates are typically higher than the general collateral repo rates, if the supply of Treasury securities increases and the need to finance the inventory position becomes critical, the repo rates will go up. This sometimes causes the repo rates to become higher than the Fed fund rates. During the first half of 1993, the repo rates often exceeded the general collateral rates.

Repo markets are used extensively by dealers to leverage their business activity; this is a natural outcome as government securities dealers regularly transact in securities that qualify as collaterals. Often, a dealer's capital is an extremely small fraction of the securities holdings; most of the securities are financed in the repo markets. Repo trades

FIGURE 2-6   *Fed Funds Rate Minus Overnight Repo Rates, March 1987 to December 1990*

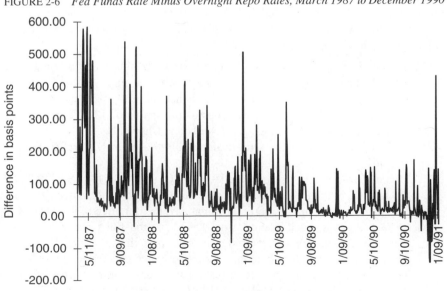

are simple to execute and provide the dealers with flexibility. The main alternative to repo financing for dealers is a bank loan, which would be relatively more expensive and less flexible. Dealers with good credit reputations may also use commercial paper to finance some of their activities.

The example of a simple repo transaction below clarifies the mechanics of RPs, as well as the risks that are involved. Throughout the text, we will treat repo transactions as conceptually equivalent to secured lending and borrowing.

Example 2-1   Repo Transaction

On June 10, 1986, dealer X wished to finance $10 million par amount of a 7.25%, 5/15/2016 T-bond. He wished to carry the position until June 13, 1986. Let us examine this trade. Table 2-7 gives the bid and ask prices in the market during the relevant period.

Date	Ask Price	Bid Price
6/10/86	94.16	94.03
6/11/86	94.97	94.84
6/12/86	95.03	94.91
6/13/86	96.91	96.78

TABLE 2-7
Repo Transactions to Finance Positions, 7.25%, 5/15/2016, T-Bond

On June 10, 1986, dealer X bought the T-bond and delivered it to the repo dealer. (See Figure 2-7.) The repo dealer accepted the T-bond as a collateral and lent cash at the repo rate. Typically a repo dealer would not lend cash equal to the market price of the T-bond. He would take a hair cut to protect himself against adverse price movements. Let us say that he charged a hair cut of 0.5% of the market price. Then, the following transactions occurred.

1. The dealer bought the T-bond. Since the dealer bought the bond on June 10, 1986, he paid 94.16 plus accrued interest. The flat price of the T-bond was 94.16, the accrued interest was 0.5122; hence the full price was 94.6722. On $10 million par, the full price was approximately $9,467,220. (The mechanics of calculating accrued interest are described in Chapter 4.)

2. The hair cut taken by the repo dealer was 0.5% of market value: $0.5 \times \frac{1}{100} \times 9,467,220 = \$47,336.10$.

3. Hence, the amount borrowed was: $9,467,220 - \$47,336.10 = \$9,419,883.90$.

4. On June 13, 1986, the dealer took possession of the T-bond, and sold it for the full (invoice) price in the market. On that day, the flat price of the T-bond was 96.78 and the accrued interest was 0.5713, so the full price was 97.3513. Hence, on $10 million par, the full price was approximately $9,735,130.

5. The repo dealer would be paid the amount borrowed plus the repo rate interest. The interest paid at a repo rate of 6% for three days on the borrowed money was: $9,419,884 \times \left(0.06 \times \frac{3}{360}\right) = \$4710$. Hence, the amount paid for finaning at a repo rate of 6% was: $9,419,884 \times \left(1 + 0.06 \times \frac{3}{360}\right) = 9,424,594$.

6. Also, during this period the bond dealer earned from the T-bond an accrued interest of: $(0.5713 - 0.5122) \times 100,000 = \$5,910$. This is reflected in the transaction prices.

The repo transaction itself is shown in Figure 2-7.

Repo trades generally settle on the trade day itself; this is in contrast to Treasury securities in the cash market, which normally settle a day after the trade day.

Note that in Example 2-1, the financing costs are lower than the accrued interest earned over the same period. This is referred to as **positive carry,** reflecting the fact that every day that the bond dealer carries his position in the repo markets, his interest income provides a cushion exceeding the financing costs. This is typical in a normal or positively sloped yield curve, where the coupons reflect medium-term and long-term yields and the financing costs reflect the short-term yields. On the other hand, when the yield curve is inverted, the yields of the Treasury securities are less than the repo rates, which are short-term relative to Treasury securities. This is referred to as **negative carry.** In day-to-day operations, carry can be significant for dealers.

As pointed out earlier, from time to time the repo rates of some securities trade special. In Figure 2-8, we plot the difference between the general collateral rates and the

FIGURE 2-7   *Repo Transaction*

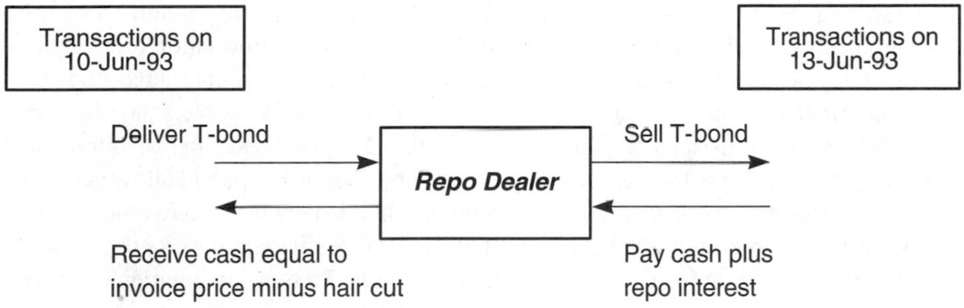

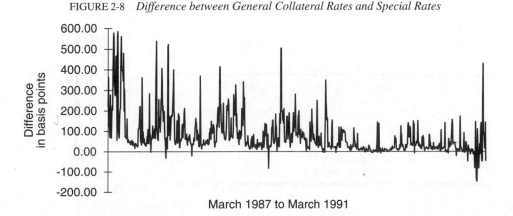

FIGURE 2-8   *Difference between General Collateral Rates and Special Rates*

special rates for on-the-run three-month Treasury bills. Note that on-the-run bills have been extremely expensive to borrow in the repo markets. Conversely, the owner of these bills could have borrowed at attractive rates using these bills as collateral—on some days, the repo rates are 500 basis points cheaper than the general collateral rates. We show that there are systematic auction effects in repo rates in Chapter 3. Duffie (1992) and Sundaresan (1994) explore the reasons for these special repos.

Dealers may have a significant repo position (on the order of several billion dollars) which is exactly matched with reverse repo positions. In such situations, the dealer is earning a spread, provided there is no credit risk. The counterparty, who has loaned cash in exchange for the collateral, faces the risk that the other party may not repay the cash plus the repo interest. This risk is mitigated by the fact that the collateral can be sold in the market. If the market value of the collateral drops significantly in relation to the cash loaned plus the interest owed, the credit risk becomes significant. In such situations, the positions may be marked to market, obliging the borrower of the cash to post additional collateral or cash.

Interdealer Brokers

The **inner market** in the government securities market comprises the interdealer brokers. The primary dealers rely on the interdealer brokers for a significant percentage of their trades, as noted in Table 2-3. Interdealer brokers aggregate information about the bids and offers posted by various dealers and disseminate that information on computer screens. They do so without revealing the identities of the dealers. This enables the dealers to undertake their proprietary trading activities anonymously. Dealers pay the interdealer brokers commissions for this service. Table 2-8 provides a list of interdealer brokers in the U.S. Treasury market. Of these brokers, Cantor Fitzgerald allow access to their screens not only to all primary dealers and to other dealers but also to other institutions such as pension funds and banks. In addition, Cantor Fitzgerald make their quotes available through Telerate. Their market share is nearly 25% of the interdealer broker market. Other brokers provide access only to primary dealers. There is a real-time price and quote distribution system known as GOVPX that disseminates information about the Treasury market round the clock. It also shows all the executed trades, best bids, and offers.

Cantor Fitzgerald
Garban Ltd.
EJV Brokerage Inc.
Fundamental Brokers Inc.
Liberty Brokerage Inc.
RMJ Securities Corp.
Hilliard Farber & Co.

TABLE 2-8
*Interdealer Brokers,
U.S. Treasury Market*

Note that the trading volume is huge in the government securities market (about $90 billion per day, on average). In comparison, the equity market's average trading volume is about $6 billion to $6.5 billion a day. The number of transactions per day in the government market, however, is rather small compared to those in the equity market. GOVPX reports that only 2,000 trades occur in the Treasury market per day. In contrast, more than 100,000 trades per day occur in the equity market. The coverage of GOVPX is much poorer compared to the interdealer broker system that is in place. This raises some questions about the transparency of the market. Table 2-9 illustrates the trades executed during a 90-minute window by Garban, one of the interdealer brokers.

Several aspects of Table 2-9 are worthy of note. Note that each transaction is either a "hit" or a "take". If the offer to sell is accepted, it is considered a take. If a dealer's bid to buy is accepted it is considered a hit. Some of the securities are traded on a yield basis. Note, for example, that at 8:34:49 AM, a six-month when-issued (WI) T-bill was traded at a yield of 3.23%. The size of the transaction was $100 million par. Of course, bills always trade in terms of yields. All when-issued transactions trade on a yield basis until the day after the auction. In the last transaction shown in Table 2-9, note that a 6% coupon note maturing on October 15, 1999, was taken at a price of 97.78125. The size of this transaction was $3 million par.

The interdealer broker market has become quite competitive over the last few years. The interdealer brokers provide liquidity for dealers. For this service, they enjoy a commission and a spread. But with the entry of Liberty Brokerage, the profitability of interdealer brokers has fallen sharply.

Investors

As was pointed out in Chapter 1, the government securities markets command a rather large pool of institutional customers including large institutions abroad. Central banks, commercial banks, pension funds, mutual funds, and insurance companies are examples of investors in this market. A more recent addition to this impressive list is the group called hedge funds. A **hedge fund** is a private investment partnership which takes leveraged positions in various segments of the capital markets. A number of such hedge funds are well-capitalized, with assets exceeding more than a billion dollars. Such funds have been known to invest billions of dollars in just a single Treasury issue. The ramifications of such investments for the Treasury auction, secondary market prices, and repo rates are taken up in Chapter 3.

Investors tend to be classified according to their investment strategies. For example, some investors are passive, tending to run **indexed portfolios** in which the investor's portfolio is indexed to a broad market index such as the Lehman Brothers Fixed-Income Index. Other investors follow active portfolio policies. Still others are classified as current yield accounts, and so on.

The broad base of investors with varying investment objectives and strategies necessitates a reasonably large sales force. Most government dealers have a large sales force to cover their customers, providing research reports on interest rates, markets, and instruments; trade ideas and execution; asset-liability management services; etc.

TABLE 2-9   *Actual Transactions of an Interdealer Broker, November 2, 1992, from 7:12 AM to 8:42 AM*

Hit/ or Take	Time	Price or Yield	Coupon	Maturity	Price/Yield	Size
Take	7:12:41 AM	P	4	9/30/94	99.34375	1,000,000
Take	7:35:45 AM	P	6	10/15/99	98.00000	3,000,000
Hit	7:45:13 AM	P	$6\frac{3}{8}$	8/15/02	97.06250	1,000,000
Hit	8:01:16 AM	P	$6\frac{3}{8}$	8/15/02	97.03125	3,000,000
Hit	8:01:26 AM	P	6	10/15/99	97.98438	2,000,000
Hit	8:02:11 AM	P	$5\frac{3}{4}$	10/31/97	99.34375	1,000,000
Hit	8:05:20 AM	P	$5\frac{3}{4}$	10/31/97	99.32813	25,000,000
Take	8:07:02 AM	P	$6\frac{3}{8}$	8/15/02	97.03125	1,000,000
Hit	8:13:36 AM	P	$5\frac{3}{4}$	10/31/97	99.32813	2,000,000
Hit	8:13:59 AM	P	$5\frac{3}{4}$	10/31/97	99.32813	8,000,000
Hit	8:14:50 AM	P	4	9/30/94	99.35156	1,000,000
Hit	8:14:55 AM	P	$5\frac{3}{4}$	10/31/97	99.31250	5,000,000
Hit	8:14:59 AM	P	$4\frac{1}{4}$	10/31/94	99.71875	1,000,000
Hit	8:23:57 AM	P	$5\frac{1}{2}$	11/30/93	101.81250	5,000,000
Hit	8:24:42 AM	P	$6\frac{3}{8}$	8/15/02	96.81250	2,000,000
Hit	8:26:05 AM	P	$7\frac{1}{4}$	8/15/22	95.28125	1,000,000
Hit	8:26:39 AM	P	$7\frac{1}{4}$	8/15/22	95.28125	1,000,000
Hit	8:28:06 AM	P	$6\frac{3}{8}$	8/15/02	96.71875	1,000,000
Hit	8:28:17 AM	P	$5\frac{3}{4}$	10/31/97	99.21875	2,000,000
Hit	8:28:50 AM	P	$7\frac{1}{4}$	8/15/22	95.21875	5,000,000
Hit	8:29:05 AM	P	$5\frac{1}{2}$	11/30/93	101.81250	1,000,000
Hit	8:29:30 AM	P	$7\frac{1}{4}$	8/15/22	95.21875	7,000,000
Hit	8:29:59 AM	P	$7\frac{1}{4}$	8/15/22	95.20313	1,000,000
Hit	8:30:34 AM	P	$5\frac{3}{4}$	10/31/97	99.18750	6,000,000
Take	8:31:36 AM	P	$5\frac{3}{4}$	10/31/97	99.21875	1,000,000
Take	8:31:36 AM	P	$5\frac{3}{4}$	10/31/97	99.21875	8,000,000
Take	8:31:46 AM	P	$7\frac{1}{2}$	5/15/02	104.01560	1,000,000
Take	8:31:53 AM	P	$5\frac{1}{2}$	9/30/97	98.29688	1,000,000
Take	8:31:56 AM	P	$6\frac{3}{8}$	8/15/02	96.75000	1,000,000
Take	8:31:56 AM	P	$6\frac{3}{8}$	8/15/02	96.75000	1,000,000
Take	8:32:16 AM	P	$6\frac{3}{8}$	8/15/02	96.75000	1,000,000
Take	8:32:20 AM	P	$5\frac{3}{4}$	10/31/97	99.21875	1,000,000
Take	8:32:20 AM	P	$5\frac{3}{4}$	10/31/97	99.21875	10,000,000
Hit	8:34:49 AM	P	$4\frac{1}{4}$	10/31/94	99.68750	3,000,000
Hit	8:34:49 AM	P	6 WI	5/06/93	3.23000	100,000,000
Hit	8:35:03 AM	P	6	10/15/99	97.73438	1,000,000
Hit	8:35:08 AM	P	$4\frac{5}{8}$	8/15/95	99.29688	2,000,000
Hit	8:35:12 AM	P	$7\frac{1}{2}$	5/15/02	104.03130	10,000,000
Hit	8:35:20 AM	P	$6\frac{3}{8}$	8/15/02	96.71875	10,000,000
Hit	8:35:45 AM	P	$4\frac{5}{8}$	8/15/95	99.29688	1,000,000
Hit	8:35:47 AM	Y	$5\frac{3}{4}$	10/31/97	99.18750	10,000,000
Hit	8:35:49 AM	P	$7\frac{1}{2}$	5/15/02	104.03130	6,000,000
Hit	8:35:57 AM	P	$6\frac{3}{8}$	8/15/02	96.71875	8,000,000
Hit	8:36:17 AM	P	1 YR	10/21/93	3.44000	25,000,000

TABLE 2-9   *Continued*

Hit/ or Take	Time	Price or Yield	Coupon	Maturity	Price/Yield	Size
Hit	8:37:30 AM	P	6	10/31/93	102.23440	5,000,000
Hit	8:37:30 AM	P	6	10/31/93	102.23440	6,000,000
Take	8:37:31 AM	P	$7\frac{1}{2}$	5/15/02	104.04690	2,000,000
Take	8:37:33 AM	P	$5\frac{3}{4}$	10/31/97	99.21875	5,000,000
Hit	8:37:47 AM	P	$5\frac{1}{2}$	11/30/93	101.79690	11,000,000
Hit	8:38:15 AM	P	$5\frac{3}{4}$	3/31/94	102.29690	10,000,000
Take	8:38:45 AM	P	$7\frac{1}{2}$	5/15/02	104.09380	1,000,000
Hit	8:38:46 AM	P	$5\frac{1}{2}$	11/30/93	101.79690	2,000,000
Take	8:39:49 AM	P	$7\frac{1}{2}$	5/15/02	104.09380	1,000,000
Take	8:40:09 AM	P	$5\frac{3}{4}$	10/31/97	99.25000	10,000,000
Take	8:40:25 AM	P	$7\frac{1}{4}$	8/15/22	95.25000	1,000,000
Take	8:40:47 AM	P	$7\frac{1}{4}$	8/15/22	95.25000	1,000,000
Take	8:41:14 AM	P	6	10/15/99	97.78125	7,000,000
Take	8:41:14 AM	P	6	10/15/99	97.78125	3,000,000

Source: Garban

ORGANIZATION AND STRUCTURE OF OTHER MARKET SEGMENTS

In this section, we will summarize briefly the organization and structure of other segments of the fixed-income markets. Since the intermediaries are more or less the same players, the focus will be on the issuers and on regulatory matters, which differ significantly from the Treasury markets.

Corporate Debt Market

Two key differences between the Treasury and the corporate markets were noted earlier: there is credit risk in the corporate sector, and there are many more issuers with relatively smaller issues in the corporate market. The existence of credit risk means that there will be efforts to generate information about the credit-worthiness of issuers. This is the task performed by credit rating agencies such as Moody's, Standard & Poors, and Fitch. There are also organizations that provide credit and liquidity enhancements. For example, a letter of credit is typically issued by a highly rated financial institution to help issuers place commercial paper.

The major Treasury securities dealers, such as Goldman Sachs and Salomon Brothers, are also the key corporate securities dealers. Typically, such dealers work with corporations to price the new issues of corporate debt and arrange the distribution of the paper to various institutional and retail accounts. Although a small number of bonds are traded on New York Stock Exchange (NYSE), a substantial percentage of the corporate debt is traded in the dealer market.

In Figure 2-9, we provide an example of the trading activity in corporate bonds in NYSE as reported by the *Wall Street Journal.*

The Securities and Exchange Commission (SEC), which oversees this market, has permitted shelf registration, under which the issuing corporation is not required to disclose the amount of debt it plans to issue or the timing of issuance. By giving a blanket authority to issue debt that is valid for a three-year period, the SEC has significantly enhanced the flexibility of the corporation to issue debt at a short notice. This is known as **Rule 415.**

In addition, the market for privately placed corporate debt has expanded significantly in the last few years. The impetus for this growth is the ruling of SEC known as **Rule 144A,** which, among other things, permits the trading of privately placed debt amongst large institutions known as qualified institutional buyers (QIBs). This has enabled the development of a market for underwriting privately placed debt securities. A detailed treatment of this market is undertaken in Chapter 8.

Mortgage-backed Securities

Agency and mortgage-backed securities are also traded in the dealer market. Typically, the primary dealers and other major dealers in the Treasury market are also the major players in this market. Dealers work closely with Federal agencies such as FHLB and FHLMC (Freddie Mac) in underwriting new issues, pricing, and market-making. Much of the activity in this market is in the primary issuance and structuring. Secondary market trading is not as active as in the Treasury secondary market. Many players are involved in the securitization and creation of mortgage-backed securities besides the dealer and the Federal agency; in Chapter 1 we mentioned some of the other players involved in this process. This market is analyzed in detail in Chapter 9.

Municipal Debt Market

The municipal debt market is similar to the corporate debt market in the sense that there is credit risk, and hence there are rating agencies who produce information about the credit standing of various issuers. In addition, there are credit enhancers and insurers in this market; the American Municipal Bond Assurance Corporation (AMBAC), the Municipal Bond Investors Assurance Corporation (MBIAC), the Financial Guarantee Insurance Company (FGIC), and the Bond Investors Guaranty Insurance Company (BIG) are the insurers in this market.

General obligations bonds must be approved by the taxpayers but revenue bonds do not require the taxpayers' approval. Although municipal issuers are not subject to any issue disclosure requirements (as in the corporate market, where issues must be regis-

FIGURE 2-9 Wall Street Journal Securities Page

NEW YORK EXCHANGE BONDS

Quotations as of 4 p.m. Eastern Time
Thursday, May 18, 1995

Volume $32,851,000

SALES SINCE JANUARY 1
(000 omitted)
1995 $2,956,641
1994 $3,353,215
1993 $4,444,358

Issues traded	Domestic Thu.	Wed.	All issues Thu.	Wed.
Issues traded	370	378	380	387
Advances	121	131	124	135
Declines	185	191	191	152
Unchanged	64	56	65	80
New highs	8	7	8	8
New lows	1	2	1	0

Dow Jones Bond Averages

	1994 High	Low	1995 High	Low	1995 Close	Chg.	1994 Close	Chg.
20 Bonds			100.40	99.63	100.55	+0.27	97.85	+0.37
10 Utilities			96.26	94.21	95.15	+0.25	98.08	−0.45
10 Industrials			104.55	97.45	100.55	+0.29	98.00	−0.19

AMEX BONDS

Volume $3,980,000

SALES SINCE JANUARY 1
1995 $267,044,000
1994 $284,786,000
1993 $320,040,000

NASDAQ
Convertible Debentures
Thursday, May 18, 1995

FOREIGN BONDS
Volume $720,000

EXPLANATORY NOTES

CORPORATION BONDS
Volume $31,178,000

Source: *Wall Street Journal*, May 19, 1995. Reprinted by permission of *The Wall Street Journal* © 1995 Dow Jones & Company, Inc. All Rights Reserved Worldwide.

65

tered), the sellers of municipal securities are required to produce and disseminate information about the proposed issue. The SEC Rule 15c2-12 addresses this issue and will be discussed in Chapter 10. Both negotiated and competitive types of issues are used in the municipal debt market. Typically, the general obligations issues are sold by the competitive system and the revenue issues are sold by the negotiated system.

As in the Treasury markets, there are brokers' brokers who do not underwrite or carry inventories, or deal with public customers. Two of the biggest brokers' brokers in this market are J. J. Kenny and Chapdelaine. They assist dealers in secondary-market trading activity. In addition, the dealers also use services such as the blue list, blue list ticker, or munifacts; these are news and wire services in which dealers participate to conduct their secondary-market trading activities.

REGULATION OF FIXED-INCOME MARKETS

Fixed-income markets are largely self-regulated. Although powerful regulators such as the Federal Reserve and the Securities and Exchange Commission closely follow this market, by and large this market is left to function on its own.

The Treasury Department has the authority to issue Treasury securities and to set the conditions for their issuance and sale. The responsibility for compliance with and enforcement of the Treasury auction rules also rests with the Treasury. The Federal Reserve, which is the agent of the Treasury in conducting auctions, spot-checks customer bids in the Treasury auctions for their authenticity. In addition, the Federal Reserve has extensive market surveillance responsibility.

There are three major institutions that oversee the regulation of fixed-income securities markets: the U.S. Treasury, the Federal Reserve, and the Securities and Exchange Commission (SEC). These institutions set rules governing the sale of securities, underwriting practices, reporting requirements, audit trails, etc., that have far-reaching implications for the conduct of these markets and the outcomes of trades in these markets.

As part of market surveillance, information on the government securities market is generated and shared by these three regulatory institutions. Effective surveillance requires the timely collection and analysis of relevant information. The Fed currently gets data on market prices, trading volumes, and yields directly from automated computer systems. Telephone surveys of dealers are also used for collecting additional data. Much of the analysis on trading activity and positions of dealers reported in this chapter is based on the data gathered by the Fed for surveillance purposes.

The regulatory tool used to improve market transparency, discussed earlier in this chapter, is improved access to information. Thus, there is a focus on providing increased access to interdealer broker price and volume information. This is not very surprising given that the interdealer broker screen is possibly the best source on current bids and offers and transactions for government securities; timely access to such information allows customers to evaluate the execution quality and depth of current and illiquid issues. As mentioned earlier, GOVPX is the current system used to disseminate information.

In addition, large position reporting and audit trails help prevent manipulations and squeezes in government markets. However, unlike the equity markets, where positions exceeding 5% of a class of equity securities must be disclosed, in debt markets there are no such large positions reporting requirements.

We have already seen some of the rules affecting the issuance of securities. The auction mechanisms for the Treasury have been reviewed and tested by the U.S. Treasury and the Federal Reserve. The sale of corporate bonds comes under the registration requirements and other provisions of the SEC. The underwriting practices in the municipal debt markets are also regulated.

Salomon Brothers Treasury Scandal

As noted earlier, the U.S. Treasury market is generally self-regulated. But during the May 1991 two-year auction, Salomon Brothers Inc., one of the major primary dealers, was involved in violations of certain rules of the auction procedure. They submitted bids on behalf of customers without obtaining their authorization. In the process they ended up controlling a major fraction of the May 1991 two-year note supply, together with some hedge funds. During July and the first half of August 1991, government regulators launched a sweeping investigation of Salomon Brothers Inc., alleging that the firm might have controlled 85% of the two-year Treasury notes that were auctioned on May 22, 1991 (*Wall Street Journal,* August 12, 1991). The SEC broadened its investigation of the Treasury Market further by looking at the possibility of widespread collusion and price fixing by more than a dozen investment and commercial banks (*Wall Street Journal,* August 27, 1991). A written report from Salomon Brothers Inc. opened new areas of investigation for government regulators and the focus of the investigation widened to include investment firms, such as Paul Tudor Jones' Tudor Investment Corporation and Steinhardt Partners (*Wall Street Journal,* September 5, 1991).

One of the reports of the investigation that appeared in *Wall Street Journal* during this period follows.

Precise Role of Salomon Brothers in May Sale Probed

By CONSTANCE MITCHELL

NEW YORK—Government investigators—and angry bond dealers—are trying to find out exactly what role Salomon Brothers Inc. and others may have played in an effort to improperly control the market for new two-year Treasury notes in May.

That's one of the issues at the heart of the unfolding scandal that already has besmirched the reputation of Salomon Inc.'s big investment bank unit and the $2.3 trillion Treasury market.

For some time, bond traders had noticed that the price of two-year notes as well as many other shorter-term securities would often rise ahead of their auction date. That's due mainly to demand.

Because the two-year note is the shortest maturing Treasury security with a "coupon" that makes semiannual interest payments, it is highly popular with small and large investors around the world, who tend to buy it at the auction and hold it to maturity. But the price sometimes declines modestly right after the auction, when interest in the note sale fades.

In a strategy designed to profit on the two-year note's trading pattern, many traders and arbitragers would sell the two-year notes "short" ahead of the auction. In a short sale, speculators borrow securities and sell them in hopes of replacing what was borrowed with cheaper securities after the price has fallen. In this case, traders would operate in the "when-issued" market, in which securities are traded before they are actually issued.

But that strategy backfired with a vengeance when something unusual happened at the May 22 auction of $12.26 billion of two-year notes. Instead of declining, the price of the two-year notes jumped sharply and remained at lofty levels for more than a month, causing short sellers and others that needed the notes to be "squeezed" into paying premium prices to cover their positions. Squeezes only occur when securities are heavily concentrated in the hands of a few dealers.

On May 30, one week after the auction, the two-year notes were quoted at a price of 100 5/32 to yield 6.60%, up from an average auction price of 99 29/32 to yield 6.81%. In other words, the $12.26 billion of notes appreciated in value by $30.6 million in just one week.

To make matters worse, the two-year notes became so scarce that the dealers who owned the notes charged exorbitant fees and financing costs when lending them to short-sellers.

From small bond arbitrage operations in Chicago to the New York powerhouses, bond traders across America were badly burned.

"The arbs were hurt the worst; several of the smaller shops went out of business," said Barbara Kenworthy, a portfolio manager at Dreyfus Corp., a mutual fund company that manages about $16 billion of bonds, most of which are Treasurys. A financial firm in Chicago that trades bonds, commodities and foreign exchange said it recently hired two former bond traders who lost their jobs because of the two-year note squeeze.

The pain was so severe and the cries of foul play were so loud that the two-year note squeeze became the talk of the bond market for weeks. More significantly, the Securities and Exchange Commission and the Justice Department's antitrust division began an investigation.

Investigators say Salomon Brothers may have controlled as much as 85% of the notes sold at the auction. The most widespread theory among traders was that Salomon placed huge quantities of bids for itself and on behalf of big clients, rumored to be Michael Steinhardt and George Soros, investment managers that run aggressive "hedge" funds that usually speculate in the stock market.

Last week, Salomon admitted that it had acquired 44% of the notes at the auction, violating Treasury rules that bar anyone from buying more than 35% of a single issue at auction. Traders say Salomon may have controlled far more than that amount through so-called prearranged trades with big investors.

At the time, Mr. Steinhardt acknowledged that his firm owned some two-year notes sold at the May auction. Mr. Soros would not comment. The Securities and Exchange

Commission investigators have asked the Steinhardt firm for information about its role in the two-year auction.

When asked by The Wall Street Journal in late May to comment on these allegations, Salomon Brothers bond trading manager Paul Mozer became furious and ticked off a list of reasons why he would not comment. When asked for his opinion why the price of two-year notes had risen so sharply, Mr. Mozer said his views about the market were considered by Salomon's sales managers to be "too valuable" to be quoted in the U.S. financial press.

The accusation that somehow the auction was cornered by one dealer, perhaps in collusion with a few major investment firms, has far-reaching implications. The stakes for the U.S. government are obvious: the Treasury auctions in this market frequently and any questions about the integrity of the marketplace may easily increase the cost of public debt. U.S. Treasury securities have a reputation for safety and liquidity, and are held by major central banks and financial institutions for those reasons. The yields in the U.S. Treasury sector typically form the basis on which agencies, corporations and banks set their borrowing rates. It is reasonable to say that in each maturity sector Treasury yields represent the floor for the borrowing costs of other major institutions. As a result, it is imperative that the Treasury market be free from corners, squeezes, and manipulations.

The efficiency of the dealer market structure, organized around the primary dealers, has been called into question by many in the wake of the May two-year Treasury note auction. The conventional arguments for the primary-dealer system are essentially grounded on the financial strength of the primary dealers and their probity. Some have argued that with a primary-dealer system the Treasury does not have to worry about no shows in its auctions. However, this may not be so important given the default-free and liquid nature of the Treasury securities. The fact that Salomon Brothers were able to buy 44% of the May auction casts a shadow on the assumption of probity. Such events clearly point to some of the problems in the current market mechanisms for auctioning Treasury securities.

May Auction of Treasury Notes. To provide a perspective on auctions, we will first examine the results of monthly auctions of two-year Treasury notes during the first half of 1991. Table 2-10 provides a summary of these two-year Treasury note auctions. This not only gives a perspective on the two-year auctions, but also gives us a broader context in which to evaluate the May 1991 auction.

From Table 2-10 we see that the May auction differed in a qualitative way from the rest of the 1991 auctions in that only 14% of the accepted competitive tenders were filled at higher yields. The corresponding percentages for other auctions ranged from a low of 60% to a high of 90%. The unusually large percentage of the competitive bids that were accepted at a lower yield is consistent with aggressive bidding for the Treasury notes during the May auction.

The range of yields from 6.81% to 6.83% in the competitive bids led the Treasury to set a coupon of $6\frac{3}{4}\%$ for the May 1991 issue. This means that the Treasury issued the notes at 99.853% of par. Simon (1994) reports that the auction bid was 6.81%, as compared to the when-issued rates prior to the auction of around 6.84%. Figure 2-10

TABLE 2-10   *Auction of Two-Year Treasury Notes, 1991*

Auction Announcement Date	Jan. 16	Feb. 12	Mar. 20	Apr. 17	May 15	Jun. 19
Tender Date	Jan. 23	Feb. 20	Mar. 26	Apr. 24	May 22	Jun. 25
Maturity of Notes	1/31/1993	2/28/1993	3/31/1993	4/30/1993	5/31/1993	6/30/1993
Tender Time *(Non-competitive)*	12 noon EST Jan. 23	12 noon EST Feb. 20	12 noon EST Mar. 26	12 noon EST Apr. 24	12 noon EST May 22	12 noon EST Jun. 25
Tender Time *(Competitive)*	1 PM EST Jan. 23	1 PM EST Feb.20	1 PM EST Mar. 26	1 PM EST Apr. 24	1 PM EST May 22	1 PM EST Jun. 25
Amount Tender (In Millions) *(Non-competitive)*	$1,329	$917	$1,244	$1,317	$1,059	$1,080
Amount Tender (In Millions) *(Competitive)*	$40,135	$40,068	$29,556	$44,117	$33,801	$37,199
Amount Accepted *(Competitive)*	$12,619	$12,062	$11,529	$12,006	$13,560	$12,529
Range of Yields *(Competitive)*	7.08 to 7.09	6.85 to 6.87	7.13 to 7.15	6.99 to 7.00	6.81 to 6.83	7.03 to 7.06
Percent Accepted At Higher Yield (Competitive)	60%	61%	71%	96%	14%	64%

FIGURE 2-10   *Two-Year Treasury Note Auctioned May 22, 1991*

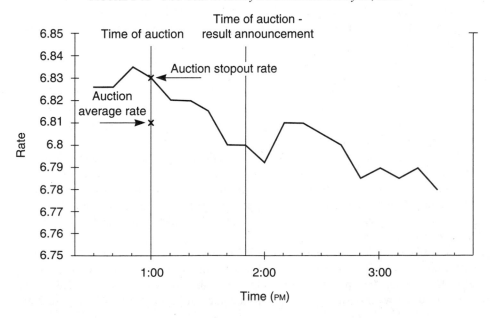

(reproduced from Simon 1994) shows the nature of the yield behavior surrounding the auction.

Post-Auction Prices. The post-auction prices (adjusted for overall movements in relevant interest rates) are an excellent indicator of whether the prices were artificially different from their economic values. To this end, we provide Tables 2-11, which documents the post-auction yields for a period of six days (including the auction date). The change in the yields between day 0 (the auction date) and day 5 is tabulated in Table 2-12 to give an indication of the post-auction price behavior.

A review of Tables 2-11 and 2-12 indicates that in the May 1991 auction, the yields of Treasury notes fell by 20 basis points in the five days following the auction. Taken in isolation, this means little. It is possible that the interest rates simply might have fallen during these five days. To account for this possibility, we need to look at the spread between the May Treasury note and the April Treasury note during this period. As Table 2-13 shows, this spread decreased from 4 to 0 basis points in the same period, suggesting

TABLE 2-11   *Yield Behavior after the 1991 Two-Year Treasury Notes Auctions*

Days after Auction Date	June Auction	May Auction	April Auction	March Auction	Feb Auction	Jan Auction
0	7.06%	6.81%	7.00%	7.15%	6.87%	7.09%
1	7.03%	6.75%	6.91%	7.07%	6.96%	7.04%
2	6.97%	6.68%	6.89%	7.03%	6.98%	7.08%
3	6.91%	6.69%	6.88%	7.04%	6.97%	7.11%
4	6.96%	6.66%	6.78%	7.01%	7.01%	7.09%
5	6.99%	6.61%	6.80%	6.96%	7.01%	7.07%

TABLE 2-12   *Yield Changes in the 1991 Post-Auction Period*

	June Auction	May Auction	April Auction	March Auction	Feb Auction	Jan Auction
Change in yield after auction date	−7	−20	−20	−19	+4	−2

Days after Auction Date	June Auction	May Auction	April Auction
0	16	4	5
1	19	6	−2
2	21	−1	−3
3	22	−1	−4
4	26	−2	−5
5	24	0	−5

TABLE 2-13

Spread* Behavior after the 1991 Two-Year 1991 Treasury Notes Auctions

*Spread = on-the-run − off-the-run

that the May note appreciated in value even after accounting for the overall changes in interest rates.

But as Table 2-13 also illustrates, the situation was worse in the April auction. The April note appreciated to the tune of 20 basis points in the five days following the auction and its spread relative to the March note decreased from 5 to −5 basis points in the same period. Thus, the April note prices were driven to a greater extent by idiosyncratic factors.

Since the on-the-run notes and off-the-run notes differ only by a month in their maturity and by little more than 50 basis points in coupons, we do not use duration or more precise measures of risk-adjusted spreads (developed later in chapters 4 and 9) in our calculations. Our suspicion is that adding those corrections would not introduce any qualitative changes in our conclusions.

Post-auction Financing Rates. The when-issued (WI) trades are settled on the issue date, which is typically the last business day of the month for two-year auctions. It is therefore instructive to look at the financing rates around this period to see if there is any evidence of tightness in the market. Traders noticed significant tightness on the last business day of the auction, as well as during the following weeks. The collateral-specific repo rates for the May two-year were about 75 to 200 basis points lower than the general collateral. When the available supply of a security is limited in relation to its demand, the owners of the security are in a position to squeeze the investors who demand that security. In a well-functioning capital market, close substitutes for that security typically will then become available to meet the excess demand. But there are situations where close substitutes will simply not do and only the specified security can meet the demand of the investors. An example of this situation is the short squeeze, in which short sellers of a security need to buy that security to cover their short positions, despite the fact that many close substitutes (from a cash-flow perspective) may be available. In a squeeze, the investors who are long observe that there is an excess demand for a security and they take advantage of it by extracting economic rents from the investors who are short, either via preposterously low repo rates or via prices that do not reflect the economic value of that security. So a necessary condition for establishing that a squeeze is present in the market is to show that the prices and repo rates are artificially different from their economic values.

In the May 1991 auction, aggressive bidding enabled Salomon Brothers to accumulate a dominant position in the security. The other dealers were obliged to buy back the security from Salomon Brothers at a very high price to cover their short positions that existed beyond their auction awards. This short squeeze is evident in the price of the May 1991 T-note, as well as in the spread relationship between the May 1991 T-note and the previously auctioned April 1991 T-note, as shown in Table 2-13.

Regulatory Implications. Salomon Brothers was fined nearly $300 million. But, more importantly, in response to these problems major changes have been introduced in the Treasury markets. (See U.S. Department of the Treasury et al. 1992 for more details.) The Treasury has reserved the right to address the squeeze problem by increasing the supply of newly auctioned securities via reopening. In addition, it may release more collateral into the repo market to minimize the squeeze potential there. The bidding process may also be automated. The possibility of allowing some iterative bidding schemes has also been discussed. Finally, the Treasury has also been experimenting since September 1992 with uniform-price auctions in the monthly two-year and five-year benchmark maturities as a possible alternative to the discriminatory auction that is currently in use in all benchmark maturities. (We take up these Treasury auctions in detail in Chapter 3.) In addition, the Federal Reserve is likely to tighten surveillance regarding the authenticity of bids placed by dealers in the auctions.

FURTHER READING

The theoretical literature on market organization is vast. Directly relevant to the subject of market microstructure are the academic journals cited in Chapter 1. The profitability of dealers has been analyzed in a relatively old, but still valuable, study by Meltzer and Gert von der Linde (1960). Another useful source is Meulendyke (1989), which focuses more on the Federal Reserve and open market policies. Several economics journals, notably the *Journal of Monetary Economics,* and *Journal of Money, Credit and Banking,* provide a prominent forum for academic research in this area.

A number of authors have explored the issue of liquidity in fixed-income markets. One paper of special interest in this area is Amihud and Mendelson (1986), examining the bid-ask spread in an asset-pricing framework. Garbade and Silber (1979) investigates the frequency of market clearing in the dealer market as one of the measures of liquidity. Kamara (1987, 1991) explore liquidity of Treasury bills and the effect of market organization on liquidity. Sarig and Warga (1989) and Warga (1992) examine the effect of liquidity on the pricing of bonds.

Squeezes in Treasury auctions and specialness in repo rates have been explored by a number of researchers. Jegadeesh (1993) has investigated this problem using data on secondary market prices. Cornell (1993) has investigated whether an adverse selection component is present in the bid-offer spreads and has concluded that this is a less serious issue in the Treasury markets. Cornell and Shapiro (1989) provide evidence of specialness in repo rates and Duffie (1992) provides a simple model for explaining this specialness. Sundaresan (1994) uses data on general collateral and special repo rates to show that there is a tendency for on-the-run issues to get very special as the next auction date approaches.

PROBLEMS

2.1 Compare the NYSE with the OTC fixed-income markets on the following dimensions:
   (a) Average size of trades per day,
   (b) Average number of trades per day, and
   (c) Total dollar volume traded per day.
   How would you go about comparing the liquidity of these two markets?

2.2   Look up the last full year (January to December) of Treasury auctions from the *Treasury Bulletin.* What is the total dollar amount borrowed by the Treasury? How is this amount distributed across different maturities? What is the rate at which the Treasury has borrowed in each maturity sector? What considerations are relevant in determining the maturity composition of Treasury debt?

2.3 (a)   Describe briefly: (i) brokered markets and (ii) dealer markets. Explain the key differences between them.

(b)   In two separate but simultaneous transactions, security XYZ was transferred at unit prices of $105 and $95. Under what types of market structure would the above transactions be possible and which is the most likely one? Explain your conclusions.

(c)   What will be your conclusion if unit prices were $102 and $101.85 in the above transactions? Why?

2.4   What are the key factors that determine the bid-offer spreads in U.S. Treasury market? Look up the Bloomberg screen for the Treasury market and document the bid-offer spreads in the Treasury market for all maturity sectors.

2.5   Briefly describe the role played by the Federal Reserve in the Treasury market. What methods are used by the Fed to implement its monetary policies?

2.6   What are Fed fund rates?

2.7   Describe repo markets. What is the relationship between repo rates and fed fund rates? Under what circumstances can the repo rate be higher than the fed fund rates?

2.8   Describe the role of primary dealers in the Treasury market.

2.9   What are the risks faced by the dealers in the Treasury market? What are the expected rewards?

2.10   What are the institutions responsible for the regulatory oversight of Treasury market? In which areas do you think there is a great need for regulatory oversight? Why?

REFERENCES

Amihud, Y., and H. Mendelson 1986. "Asset Pricing and the Bid-Ask Spread." *Journal of Financial Economics* 17:223–249.

Bollenbacher, G. 1988. *A Professional's Guide to the U.S. Government Securities Markets: Treasuries, Agencies and Mortgage-Backed Instruments.* New York Institute of Finance.

Cornell, B., and A. C. Shapiro 1989. "The Mispricing of U.S. Treasury Bonds: A Case Study," *Review of Financial Studies* 2(3):297–310.

Cornell, B. 1993. "Adverse Selection, Squeezes and the Bid-Ask Spreads on Treasury Securities," *Journal of Fixed Income* 3:39–47.

Duffie, D. 1992. Special Repo Rates. Stanford University Research Working Paper.

Garbade, K. D. 1982. *Securities Markets.* New York: McGraw Hill.

Garbade, K. D., and W. L. Silber 1979. "Structural Organization of Secondary Markets: Clearing Frequency, Dealer Activity and Liquidity Risk." *Journal of Finance* 34:577–593.

Glosten, L. R. 1987. "Components of the Bid-Ask Spread and the Statistical Properties of Transaction Prices," *Journal of Business* 42(5):1293–1307.

Glosten, L. R., and P. R. Milgrom 1985. "Bid, Ask and Transaction Prices in a Specialist Market with Heterogeneously Informed Traders." *Journal of Financial Economics* 14:71–100.

Hubbard, G. 1991. *Money the Financial System and the Economy.* Reading, MA: Addison-Wesley.

Jegadeesh, N. 1993. "Treasury Auction Bids and the Salomon Squeeze." *Journal of Finance* 48:1403–1419.

Kamara, A., 1987. "Market Trading Structures and Asset Pricing: Evidence from the Treasury-Bill Markets." *Review of Financial Studies* 1:357–375.

Kamara, A. 1991. Liquidity and Short-term Treasury Yields. University of Washington Working Paper.

Meltzer, A., and G. von der Linde 1960. A Study of the Dealer Market for Federal Securities. Materials prepared for the Joint Economic Committee, 86th Congress.

Meulendyke, A.-M. 1989. *U.S. Monetary Policy and Financial Markets.* Federal Reserve Bank of New York.

Sarig, O., and A. Warga 1989. "Bond Price Data and Bond Market Liquidity." *Journal of Financial and Quantitative Analysis* 24:367–378.

Scott, I. 1965. *Government Securities Market.* New York: McGraw Hill.

Simon, D. P. 1994. "Underwriting Premium and Informational Advantages at Treasury Coupon Auctions: Evidence from Intraday Quotes." *Journal of Financial Economics* 35:43–62.

Sundaresan, S. 1991–1993. Debt Markets. Columbia University MBA B8308 Course Binders.

Sundaresan, S. 1994. "An Empirical Analysis of U.S. Treasury Auctions: Implications for Auction and Term Structure Theories." *Journal of Fixed-Income* 4:35–50.

U.S. Department of the Treasury, Securities and Exchange Commission, and Board of Governors of the Federal Reserve System 1992. *Joint Report on the Government Securities Market.* Washington, D.C.

Warga, A. 1992. "Bond Returns, Liquidity and Missing Data." *Journal of Financial and Quantitative Analysis* 27:605–617

Chapter 3

Treasury Auctions and Selling Mechanisms

Chapter Objectives

This chapter describes the mechanisms used by the U.S. Treasury to sell its debt securities to investors and evaluates each mechanism. Chapter 3 will help the reader to understand and answer the following questions.

- What are discriminatory auctions?
- What are uniform price auctions?
- What is the when-issued market and what role does it play in the bidding of auctions?
- What are private-value auctions?
- What are common-value auctions?
- What is winner's curse?
- What are short squeezes in auctions?
- How should the U.S. Treasury sell debt to minimize the cost of public debt?

INTRODUCTION

U.S. Treasury securities have been sold to investors for over five decades using auction mechanisms. Unlike auctions of wines or works of art, U.S. Treasury auctions are preceded by forward trading among potential bidders in the auction. This forward market, known as the **when-issued market,** is an integral part of the Treasury bidding and distribution system that is currently in place. Such when-issued trading is not present in most auctions involving other commodities. In some foreign sovereign bond markets, Treasury auctions are preceded by some form of precommitments by way of when-issued trading. In when-issued trading, the bidders are liable to enter the auction and bid with prior short or long positions. Consequently, this affects their bidding strategies and the outcomes of the auction. In Chapter 2, we discussed an example of a when-issued trade transaction that was executed by an interdealer broker. In addition to the when-issued market, where a significant percentage of the to-be-auctioned securities are sold, there is a secondary market (the resale market) where participants are able to buy and sell the auctioned securities in "spot" trading. When spot trading occurs the trade usually is settled one day following the trade date. Therefore, strictly speaking, all transactions are forward transactions. Moreover, as explained in Chapter 2, investors are also able to borrow or lend their securities overnight or for specified terms in repo markets. The when-issued market, the primary auctions market, the repo markets, and the secondary markets compose the integrated mechanism by which Treasury securities are sold to the investing public. In this chapter, we will focus on Treasury auctions and the when-issued markets.

TREASURY AUCTIONS

Over the period 1929–1992, the amount of Treasury securities sold steadily increased. To get an idea of the size of this market, consider that in 1981, the Treasury sold $670 billion of marketable Treasury securities. In 1991, the corresponding figure was an astounding $1.70 trillion! (The material in this section is drawn extensively from the *Joint Report on the Government Securities Market* (U.S. Department of the Treasury et al. 1992).) The Treasury auction procedure has undergone important changes along the way. Prior to the 1970s, the U.S. Treasury used subscription offerings (in which the interest rate was preset and the security was sold at a fixed price), exchange offerings (which permitted investors to exchange maturing issues with new ones at fixed prices) and advanced refunding (which allowed outstanding securities to be exchanged prior to their maturities). These mechanisms are not covered in the text.

In 1970, the Treasury instituted an auction procedure in which the coupons were preset and investors were asked to bid on the basis of prices. This procedure continued until 1974 when the Treasury stopped setting the coupon prior to receiving bids and switched over to yield auctions. (During the period February 1973 to May 1974, Treasury conducted six uniform-price, sealed-bid auctions.) The auction procedure now used by the Treasury is very similar to the yield auction scheme that was set up in 1974. In this scheme, the U.S. Treasury offers Treasury bills, notes and bonds via a sealed-bid discriminating auction. The schedule of auction dates are set as per Treasury auction cycles. For example, all three-month and six-month Treasury bills are auctioned every Monday and issued the following Thursday. One-year T-bills are auctioned every four weeks; and two-year and five-year Treasury notes are auctioned every month, typically near the end of the month, for settlement on the last business day of the month. The three-year, ten-year, and thirty-year securities are issued via quarterly refunding and settled on February 15, May 15, August 15, and November 15. These scheduled auctions typically add up to about 150 auctions per year. The schedule is in Chapter 1. The quantities to be auctioned are posted at the time the auction is announced, typically a week prior to the auction date. The securities are issued one to five days following the auction.

The sequence of events in a typical auction may be best summarized in the context of an actual Treasury auction. Accordingly, we provide in Table 3-1 a typical auction announcement by the U.S. Treasury for three-year, ten-year, and thirty-year quarterly refunding auctions.

Note in Table 3-1 that the announcement of the auction was made on August 4, 1993. The auction date itself varied from August 10 to August 12, 1993, depending on the security being auctioned. On the announcement date, potential bidders know the size of the auction and the maturity, but they do not know the coupon, which is set by the Treasury after all the bids have been submitted on the auction day at 1:00 PM.

Note that the securities are not issued on the auction date; the issue date itself is August 16, 1993, four to six days after the auction, depending on the security. The when-issued trading commences on the announcement date (August 4, 1993) and continues until the securities are issued (August 16, 1993). Thus, the when-issued trading commences on the announcement date without the knowledge of the coupon of the issue.

In the case of ten-year T-notes, the when-issued trading commenced on August 4, 1993, and continued until the issue date of August 16, 1993. During the period between the announcement date (August 4, 1993) and the auction date (August 11, 1993), the when-issued trading will be done on the basis of yields as the coupon of the issue is not known until the auction results are posted on the auction date. On the auction date, sealed bids are received at 1:00 PM and the Treasury sets the coupon and announces the auction awards approximately one hour after the bids are received (2:00 PM). Subsequently, the when-issued trades are done on a price basis. In all when-issued trades, the settlement date is the issue date.

Note that the Treasury announcement reproduced in Table 3-1 indicates that the ten-year note and the thirty-year bond are eligible for the strips program. Chapter 5 contains a description and an analysis of the Treasury strips market. In brief, this is a market in which zero coupon Treasury securities are created by "stripping" coupon and principal payments. We discuss the need for such securities in Chapter 11 in the context of asset-liability management, and the risk properties of strips in Chapters 4 and 5.

Note that until the securities are issued no financing is necessary. Subsequent to the settlement of the issued securities, financing becomes necessary.

TABLE 3-1   *U.S. Treasury Auction Announcement*

Treasury August Quarterly Financing
August 4, 1993

The Treasury will auction $16,500 million of 3-year notes, $11,000 million of 10-year notes, and $11,000 million of 30-year bonds to refund $26,706 million of publicly held securities maturing August 15, 1993 and to raise about $11,800 million new cash.

In addition to the public holdings, Federal Reserve Banks hold $4,524 million of the maturing securities for their own accounts which may be refunded by issuing additional amounts of the new securities.

The maturing securities held by the public include $3,856 million held by the Federal Reserve Banks as agents for foreign and international monetary authorities. Amounts bid for these accounts by Federal Reserve Banks will be added to the offering.

The 10-year note and the 30-year bond being offered today are eligible for the STRIPS program.

Offering amount description	$16,500 mill.	$11,000 mill.	$11,000 mill.
Term & type	3-year notes	10-year notes	30-year bonds
CUSIP	912827 L7 5	912827 L8 3	912810 EQ 7
Auction date	Aug 10, 93	Aug 11, 93	Aug 12, 93
Issue date	Aug 16, 93	Aug 16, 93	Aug 16, 93
Dated date	Aug 15, 93	Aug 15, 93	Aug 15, 93
Maturity	Aug 15, 96	Aug 15, 2003	Aug 15, 2023
Interest rate	Set based on the average of accepted competitive bids.	Set based on the average of accepted competitive bids.	Set based on the average of accepted competitive bids.
Yield	set at auction	set at auction	set at auction
Coupon dates	Feb 15 & Aug 15	Feb 15 & Aug 15	Feb 15 & Aug 15

Notes: Non-competitive bids accepted up to $5 million at the average of accepted competitive yields. Competitive bids must be expressed as a yield in two decimals. Net long position for each bidder must be reported when the sum of the total bid amount at all yields, and the net long position is $2 billion or greater. Net long position must be determined as of one half-hour prior to the closing time for receipt of competitive tenders. Maximum recognized bid at a single yield is 35% of public offering. The maximum award is also 35% of public offering.

Source: U.S. Treasury August 4, 1993

The U.S. Treasury sells a vast amount of securities every year. It is also a repeat seller of securities in the market. By designing an optimal mechanism of sale, it can reduce the cost of public debt and ensure continued participation by a large number of well-capitalized dealers in the process of sale. Theoretical literature on appropriate mechanism design in general and on auctions in particular is vast. Broadly speaking, auctions have been classified into private-value auctions and common-value auctions. In **private-value auctions,** bidders (potential buyers) have their own idiosyncratic valuation of the object that is being auctioned. In **common-value auctions,** bidders have a shared, common value of the object that is being auctioned. Excellent survey papers on auctions theory are available. Milgrom (1989) and Engelbrecht-Wiggins (1990) are particularly relevant. In designing an appropriate auction, the Treasury should attempt to get the best possible price and also ensure that the scope for manipulation and squeezes is kept at a minimum to encourage the orderly conduct of auctions. The second objective is particularly relevant given the fact that the Treasury is a repeat seller in the market.

Discriminatory and Uniform-Price Auctions

Two types of auction mechanisms are currently used by the U.S. Treasury. The sealed-bid discriminatory auction has been in use for many decades. Since September 1992, the Treasury has been experimenting with the sealed-bid uniform price auctions for the monthly two-year and five-year auctions (as noted in Chapter 2).

Sealed-bid Discriminatory Auctions. Two types of bids are accepted by the Treasury, competitive and noncompetitive bids. In competitive bids, both prices and quantities are submitted by primary dealers and major institutional investors. Each competitive bidder is allowed to submit multiple bids. The competitive bidders (if successful) are assured of the prices they have bid for the security, although they may not get the entire quantity they bid for. Noncompetitive bids from the public are limited to no more than five million. The total quantity bid by the investors in the noncompetitive tender is subtracted from the aggregate amount of the security that the Treasury has to offer in the auction to determine the amount that will be sold via the competitive bids. The U.S. Treasury acts as a perfectly discriminating monopolist by awarding the security to the highest bidder and working its way down until the entire amount is sold. (This means that the Treasury starts at the lowest yield and works its way down to the higher yield. At the highest winning yield the allocation will be done on a pro-rata basis.) It is worth emphasizing that each successful competitive bidder pays the price that he bid for. The average of the successful auction prices in the competitive tender on a quantity-weighted basis is then applied to the bidders in the noncompetitive tender. The bidders on the noncompetitive tender are assured of the quantities that they bid for at the quantity-weighted average price established in the competitive tender. So, noncompetitive bidders face no quantity uncertainty but are unsure of the prices at which their orders will be filled. Since the Treasury restricts the bids in the noncompetitive sector to $5 million par amount of the auctioned security, only small investors and institutions tend to participate in this sector of the auctions. There is a limit on the maximum amount of securities awarded to a single bidder. Under the 35% rule, the bidder's net long position in the auction at any one yield inclusive of futures, forwards and when-issued markets may not exceed 35% of the amount of the security in the auction. When the issue is reopened, the net long position will include any position in the outstanding security as well. Once the bidding is completed, the 35% rule is lifted.

The auction awards of the discriminating sealed-bid auction announced in Table 3-1 is presented in Table 3-2 for the thirty-year bonds.

The lowest yield (most aggressive bid) was 6.32%, resulting in those bidders paying a price of 99.063 for the thirty-year bond. The quantity-weighted average of the

TABLE 3-2
*Result of the U.S.
Treasury Sealed-Bid
Discriminatory Auction*

**Results of Treasury's Auction of 30-year Bond
August 12, 1993**

Tenders for $11,002 million of 30-year bonds to be issued Aug 16, 1993 and to mature Aug 15, 2023 were accepted today. (CUSIP:912810EQ7). The interest rate on the bonds will be $6\frac{1}{4}\%$. The range of accepted bids and corresponding prices are as follows.

Bids	**Yield**	**Price**
Low	6.32%	99.063
High	6.35%	98.666
Average	6.33%	98.931

Tenders by (by location)	**Received** (in thousands)	**Accepted** (in thousands)
Boston	9,347	9,347
New York	22,150,499	10,747,399
Philadelphia	1,878	1,878
Cleveland	12,240	12,240
Richmond	38,138	38,138
Atlanta	3,306	3,306
Chicago	936,429	128,929
St. Louis	664	664
Minneapolis	2,394	2,391
Kansas City	8,613	8,613
Dallas	916	746
San Francisco	295,083	42,982
Treasury	5,197	5,197
Total:	23,464,704	11,001,830

The $11,002 million of accepted tenders includes $390 million of non competitive tenders and $10,612 million of competitive tenders from the public. In addition, $525 million of tenders were also accepted at the average price from Federal Reserve Banks for their own account in exchange for maturing securities.

Source: U.S. Treasury August 12, 1993

winning bids (the market consensus) was 6.33%, resulting in a price of 98.931. The Treasury sets the coupon in increments of $\frac{1}{8}$% and the process generally is such that the coupon is set slightly below the weighted average of the bids. This typically leads to the bonds selling at a slight discount at issue.

Note that the bids were processed by the twelve district branches of the Federal Reserve and the bulk of the bids were through the Federal Reserve Bank of New York; this is typical.

Metrics to Assess Auctions. Although only a little over $11 billion of the security was awarded, the Treasury received a total of nearly $23.5 billion worth of bids. The ratio of the bids received to the amount awarded is computed and is used as a metric of how well the auction went; the higher this ratio, the stronger the auction is, *ceteris paribus.* This ratio is called the **bid-cover ratio.** In this auction the bid-cover ratio was $\left(\frac{23,464,704}{11,001,830}\right) = 2.13$. The uncertainty about the auction outcome is sometimes summarized by the dispersion of the winning bids; in this auction, it is $6.35 - 6.32 = 0.03$ or 3 basis points. Another measure known as the **tail of the auction** is computed as the difference between the quantity-weighted average and the lowest bid. This equals $6.33 - 6.32 = 0.01$ or 1 basis point. Note that the percentage of the awards going to the noncompetitive bids is rather small; this is also typical. Recall that only retail accounts and small investors participate in this segment. The $5 million limit also discourages big institutions from actively bidding in this leg of the auction. The percentage of the awards that went to the noncompetitive tender is $\left(\frac{390}{11,002}\right) = 3.545\%$.

Later in this chapter, we will review the historical evidence as to how these measures of auctions have reacted to uncertainty and the levels of interest rates in discriminatory auctions.

Uniform Price Auctions. Since September 1992, the U.S. Treasury has been experimenting with the **uniform-price** or **Dutch auction** in the auction of monthly two-year and five-year T-notes. Under this system, dealers submit sealed bids and the Treasury awards the securities at the common market-clearing yield. Under this procedure there is also competitive and noncompetitive bidding. The bidders in the noncompetitive tenders are again restricted to $5 million par of the security. Unlike the bidders at the discriminatory auction, they will pay the same yield as the bidders in the competitive tender. The common yield is the highest winning yield. It is expected that the dealers' ability to pay the same yield irrespective of what the dealers bid at the auction will significantly minimize the possibility of short squeezes and will therefore promote more aggressive and active participation in the bidding process. This procedure is expected to ease the bidding process due to minimal investments in pre-auction information gathering. This should significantly increase the participation in the auction and the increased demand should more than offset the loss of discriminating power in the process.

We provide in Table 3-3 the results of the uniform-price Dutch auction for the five-year Treasury notes that were sold in September 1993.

Note that the **stop out yield** was 4.83%; bidders who bid at yields above the stop out yield did not win any security in the auction. All the other bidders (who bid more aggres-

TABLE 3-3   *Results of a U.S. Treasury Uniform-price Auction*

Results of Treasury's Auction of 5-year Note
September 22, 1993

Tenders for $11,015 million of 5-year notes to be issued Sep 30, 1993 and to mature Sep 30, 1998 were accepted today. (CUSIP:912827M41). The itnerest rate on the notes will be $4\frac{3}{4}\%$.

All competitive tenders at yields lower than 4.83% were accepted in full. Tenders at 4.83% were allotted 27%. All non-competitive and successful competitive bidders were allotted securities at the yield of 4.83%, with an equivalent price of 99.648. The median yield was 4.81%. The low yield was 4.75%–5% of the amount of the accepted competitive bids were tendered at or below that yield.

Tenders by (by location)	**Received** (in thousands)	**Accepted** (in thousands)
Boston	17,631	17,631
New York	29,109,098	10,543,848
Philadelphia	14,391	14,391
Cleveland	25,568	25,568
Richmond	37,645	30,345
Atlanta	32,753	7,751
Chicago	868,539	199,229
St. Louis	17,803	17,803
Minneapolis	6,343	6,343
Kansas City	17,167	17,167
Dallas	4,546	4,546
San Francisco	552,023	52,018
Treasury	78,497	78,497
Total:	30,782,004	11,015,137

The $11,015 million of accepted tenders includes $532 million of non-competitive tenders and $10,483 million of competitive tenders from the public. Also, $650 million of tenders was awarded at the high yield to Federal Reserve Banks as agents for foreign and international monetary authorities. In addition, $900 million of tenders were also accepted at the average price from Federal Reserve Banks for their own account in exchange for maturing securities.

Source: U.S. Treasury

sively in the auction) received the security at a common market clearing yield of 4.83%. Note again that the Treasury set the coupon to be a bit below the stop out yield and rounded it down to the nearest $\frac{1}{8}$ at 4.75%. The bid-cover ratio for this uniform price auction was $\left(\frac{30,782}{11,015}\right) = 2.795$. Note that the median yield of the bidders was 4.81% and the low yield was 4.75%. Remember that even the most aggressive bidder who bid at 4.75% paid only 4.83%. This has important implications for both the level of bidding in these auctions and for the possible dispersion of the bids. Note that the **tail** of the auction, defined as the median yield minus the lowest yield, is $4.81 - 4.75 = 0.06$ or 6 basis points. At least in the context of the auctions presented in Tables 3-2 and 3-3, the uniform-price auction appears to have a higher bid-cover ratio and a higher dispersion of winning bids. Traders familiar with the bidding process confirm that this is fairly typical in their experience. At first glance, it may appear that the Treasury is losing out: Bidders who bid at 4.75% only ended up paying 4.83%. But the reason for their aggressive bidding is precisely that the bids are not discriminated. Indeed, if lots of bidders bid aggressively, then the stop out yield will go down, reflecting the overall aggressiveness. This will increase the revenue of the Treasury and thus lower the cost of public debt.

In both auction mechanisms, bidders face quantity uncertainty. In the uniform-price auction presented in Table 3-3, bidders who bid most aggressively were allotted the security first and as the supply was depleted, the bidders who exactly bid at the stop out yield ended up receiving less than their total demand. The U.S. Treasury makes a pro-rata allocation for bidders at the stop out yield. So, if the demand by bidders who bid exactly at 4.83% was 2 billion, but the Treasury had only 1 billion left to allocate, then all these bidders receive 50% of their demand. Bidders in discriminatory auctions are subject to similar quantity uncertainty. This is a significant quantity risk which should encourage more aggressive bidding. In addition, bidders may also diversify their bids by submitting multiple price-quantity bids.

The foregoing discussion indicates that the choice of the auction mechanism is of great importance to the seller. In discriminatory auctions, the Treasury is able to act as a perfectly discriminating monopolist. But this action results in **winner's curse:** The winning bidder knows that he will pay a higher price than his competitor, with whom he has to compete in the secondary market. This creates an incentive to shade down the bids and possibly engage in pre-auction information sharing. On the other hand, uniform-price auctions significantly reduce winner's curse, but the Treasury gives up its ability to price discriminate. The trade-offs in this context are clear. Which auction is more prone to collusion and squeezes? We explore this question later in the chapter.

WHEN-ISSUED TRADING

One of the major features of the U.S. Treasury auction is the "when, as, and if issued" trading, known simply as when-issued (WI) trading. During the period between the auction announcement date and the issue date (which as we saw earlier varies from five to 10 days), when-issued trading occurs. This was officially sanctioned in August 1981, and was initiated to encourage trading in Treasury securities after the announcement of the auction but before the securities are actually issued. Prior to the Treasury's scheduled auction date for a given security, dealers and investors actively participate in the when-issued market. In this market, dealers and investors may either take long positions or short positions in the security (to be auctioned by the Treasury) for a future settlement on the issue date. Thus WI trades are forward contracts with a settlement date equal to the issue date. The trading in this market is done in terms of the yields at which the security is expected to be issued. The coupon of the issue is announced by the Treasury after all the bids are received. After the coupon is announced, the issue trades on a price basis one day after the auction. Typically the securities are issued about one to five days following the auction date.

As Table 3-4 illustrates, the WI trades can be significant in size; note that the first trade is 200 million. Trades on the order of several hundred million dollars may occur in the WI markets from time to time. The fact that it is a forward transaction allows investors to lock in a price and quantity in the WI market, which would be difficult to do in other markets. Furthermore, as positions in the WI market need not be financed, fairly large positions can be taken and offset in a manner similar to the futures markets. Note in Table 3-4 that eight transactions took place prior to the 1:00 PM auction time. During the period after bidding but prior to the announcement of the results at 2:00 PM a number of further transactions took place. We will focus on the trading in the windows 1:00–2:00 and after 2:00 to determine whether there is strategic post-auction buying in the WI market in which some bidders attempt to squeeze others.

The aggregate positions taken in the when-issued market may exceed the total amount of the security that the Treasury has scheduled to auction. As the auction date approaches, such positions are unwound and the positions approach the amount that is to be auctioned. Note that the yields varied from 3.02% in the first trade to 3.04% in the trade at 3:35 PM, after the auction. A dealer might have sold 100 million par in the WI market in the morning at 3.02% and, after bidding in the auction and finding out the awards, might have covered by buying back 100 million par around 3:00 PM at 3.04%, netting a profit of 2 basis points on 100 million without any delivery of securities.

Transaction Type	Time of Transaction	Yield	Size of Transaction	TABLE 3-4 *When-Issued Trading around Monday, November 2, 1992, Three-Month T-Bill Auction (Maturity date: February 4, 1993)*
Hit	09:03:24 AM	3.02000	200,000,000	
Hit	10:05:21 AM	3.03000	100,000,000	
Hit	11:38:13 AM	3.03000	15,000,000	
Hit	11:52:51 AM	3.03000	5,000,000	
Take	12:34:20 PM	3.04000	40,000,000	
Take	12:40:11 PM	3.04000	25,000,000	
Take	12:48:06 PM	3.04000	6,000,000	
Take	12:52:10 PM	3.04000	22,000,000	
Hit	01:00:54 PM	3.04000	5,000,000	
Take	01:04:23 PM	3.04000	14,000,000	
Take	01:06:53 PM	3.04000	6,000,000	
Hit	01:08:15 PM	3.03500	50,000,000	
Hit	01:58:11 PM	3.04500	40,000,000	
Take	02:32:02 PM	3.04000	5,000,000	
Take	03:12:08 PM	3.04000	25,000,000	
Take	03:35:08 PM	3.04000	49,000,000	

Source: Compiled from Garban

Short Squeeze

The term 'squeeze' is used by market participants to refer to a shortage of supply relative to demand for a particular security, as evidenced by a movement in its price to a level that is out of line with prices of comparable securities—either in outright trading quotations or in financing arrangements (U.S. Department of the Treasury et al. 1992).

A squeeze, which forces some traders to pay very high premiums to borrow the securities they want, is not necessarily illegal. But it is illegal if there is collusion in creating a shortage of securities.

It is possible that some investors might enter the auction (and the post-auction trading) with a short position. Such investors who are short have obviously borrowed securities (from other investors who are long) which they must buy eventually to cover their short positions. All trades in the when-issued market are settled for delivery and payment on the scheduled issue date. When dealers sell short in the when-issued market, they sell securities that they do not own on the assumption that they can acquire them, either through purchase or loan, in time for delivery.

Table 3-5 shows that the dealers typically enter the auction with significant short positions. This situation presents significant risk to the bidders. A bidder who is short and unable to get sufficient quantity of the security in the auction must cover the short position by the issue date by buying in the WI market after the auction. Or alternatively, he must borrow the security on the issue date in the repo market to fulfill his WI commitments; but in such a case, he is still short in the security and is exposed to the possibility of a short squeeze. Note in Table 3-5, that the short positions are particularly significant for the two-year and five-year auctions ranging from 46% to 48% of the dealer awards. The average short position is 38% of the auction awards. So, even if one or two dealers are relatively more aggressive in the auctions, there could be significant imbalances in dealer long positions relative to their prior short positions. This fact has rather important implications for both the price behavior and the repo-rate behavior

Benchmark Maturity	Primary Dealer Competitive Awards	Primary Dealer Net Position before Auction	Net Position as a Percentage of Awards
Two-year	$173,633	-$80,637	-46.40%
Three-year	$61,731	-$22,194	-36.00%
Four-year	$22,852	-$5,338	-23.40%
Five-year	$83,058	-$39,890	-48.00%
Seven-year	$46,654	-$11,221	-24.10%
Ten-year	$53,453	-$14,262	-26.70%
Thirty-year	$58,356	-$17,387	-29.80%
Total	$499,737	-$190,929	-38.20%

TABLE 3-5
Primary Dealer Net Position before Auctions, January 1990 to September 1991, in Millions of Dollars

Source: U.S. Department of the Treasury et al. (1992)

immediately following the auction, as will be shown later. In a short squeeze, one may expect the post-auction repo rates (especially during the issue date and the few days immediately following the issue date) to be much lower (later in the chapter, we provide evidence and an explanation as to why this must be the case) and the prices to be correspondingly higher.

The positions of dealers in the auction are substantial and this compounds the risk of a short squeeze. This is easily seen from the evidence on dealer positions presented in Chapter 2 and as presented here in Table 3-6.

TABLE 3-6   *Awards in Treasury Auctions, January 1990 to September 1991, in Percent of Private Awards*

Benchmark Maturity	Primary Dealer Competitive Awards	Primary Dealer Customer Competitive Awards	Other Competitive Awards	Non-competitive
Three-Month	67.6%	5.1%	4.2%	23.0%
Six-Month	73.0%	4.4%	2.5%	20.1%
One-Year	80.0%	5.7%	4.1%	10.2%
Total	71.5%	4.9%	3.5%	20.0%
Two-year	67.8%	12.8%	7.9%	11.4%
Three-year	72.1%	14.9%	2.3%	10.7%
Four-year	71.0%	15.2%	3.6%	10.3%
Five-year	74.7%	15.9%	2.0%	7.4%
Seven-year	80.7%	10.3%	3.1%	5.9%
Ten-year	69.7%	22.9%	2.0%	5.5%
Thirty-year	78.1%	15.9%	2.6%	3.4%
Total	72.0%	14.9%	4.4%	8.6%

Source: U.S. Department of the Treasury et al. (1992)

Note that the primary dealers dominate the competitive awards. In the money markets sector, they get 71.5% of the auction awards; in the T-note and T-bond sectors, they get 72% of all the awards. An interesting fact is that the noncompetitive allocation appears to be relatively more important for the T-bills sector.

Primary dealers, depository institutions, and government securities brokers and dealers registered with the SEC may submit competitive and noncompetitive bids for their own accounts as well as for their customers. Others wishing to bid may do so only for their own accounts. The possibility that one or two dealers could have a commanding position by capturing a major percent of the auction further accentuates the effect of a potential short squeeze. We saw evidence of this type of short squeeze in Treasury auctions in Chapter 2 in our discussion of the Salomon Brothers scandal.

Coupon Rolls

Dealers need to position themselves to bid in auctions. Given the size of the auctions (typically about 10 to 15 billion per auction), it is essential that dealers be in a position to ascertain the demand for the forthcoming auction and be able to hedge any exposure which may result from shortfalls. Such shortfalls may arise in a number of ways. First, dealers may be unable to determine with great precision the demand for the auction— they know only the demands that go through their sales desk and what they see on broker screens. It is possible that many investors will directly bid in the auction without participating in any pre-auction activities. In this context, a few big customer-driven trades passing through the sales desk of a single bidder could be very valuable private information to the dealer. Second, dealers may face significant uncertainty in the primary auction process as to the amount that they are likely to be awarded; the sealed-bid discriminating auction produces a great deal of uncertainty. But it also provides the dealer with a unique opportunity to incorporate private information into bidding. Finally, the only effective way to hedge a to-be-auctioned issue is to utilize the current on-the-run issue. Other alternatives, such as futures, have delivery requirements, basis risk, and delivery options that make them less attractive.

A trading mechanism that is an integral part of the Treasury new issues market is known as **coupon rolls** and **reverse rolls.** For example, after the announcement of the next auction but prior to the actual auction and issuance, coupon rolls are executed by dealers as follows. The dealer doing the roll buys the current on-the-run issue (which is outstanding) and sells the to-be-auctioned issue on a yield basis. Prior to the auction date and the issuance date, significant rolls transactions forecast a significant short position in the to-be-on-the-run issue and a corresponding long position in the outstanding issue. Often, prior to executing rolls, dealers short the outstanding on-the-run issues. One reason for this is the anticipation that the current on-the-run issue may become cheap once the new auction is held and new securities are issued. Moreover, the dealers may be hedging their commitments using the current on-the-run issue. On-the-run issues are also used to hedge securities in the mortgage-backed securities market, the corporate bond market, and the swaps market, so the demand for on-the-run issues is high.

This has implications for the repo rate behavior of the outstanding issue. Given that the rolls occur prior to the auction, the repo rates in the week prior to the auction date may be tight. (Later in this chapter, we provide evidence for this using repo rates data.) The information from the when-issued market can be of significant help for dealers and institutional investors assessing the depth of the forthcoming issue; the when-issued market permits the sharing of information. The need for financing does not arise in when-issued trading, but once the security is issued, financing becomes necessary. This financing takes place in the repo markets.

Implications for Repo Rates

As noted in Chapter 2, U.S. Treasury securities may be used as collaterals in the market for repurchase agreements to borrow cash at a repo rate. Also, the cash from the sale of such securities may be used to collateralize short positions. Such cash positions earn reverse repo rates. Bond dealers finance a substantial percentage of their inventory positions in this market. Recall that in a repo contract the security is sold with a simultaneous forward agreement to buy it back at a currently agreed upon price, and that, conversely, in a reverse repo transaction the security is purchased and at the termination of the contract (usually overnight) sold back.

It is possible that U.S. Treasury securities that are perfect substitutes in terms of their cash flow pattern will command significantly different repo rates because their collateral values may differ significantly in the repo market. Such differences arise due to the scarcity value of the security in the repo market to cover short positions. This scarcity may arise as a natural outcome of the ex-post-settling-up process by which dealers who are net short cover their positions by either buying or borrowing securities from the dealers who are net long.

When a security is in demand, the owners may be willing to lend that security for cash (as collateral), provided the interest cost on cash is low enough to reflect the demand for the security. The cash will then be used by the owner of the security to earn a spread over the interest cost. Typically, Fed funds or other short-term investments will serve this purpose. This suggests that in a short squeeze the repo rates must fall to induce the owners of securities to lend their securities (sometimes referred to as the special repo rate, see Chapter 2). Note that this process is unique for the on-the-run issues.

The Secondary Market

As detailed in Chapter 2, the Treasury market is a dealers' market with fewer than 40 primary dealers. Primary dealers have a direct line (known as the Fed wire) to the Open Market Trading Desk of the Federal Reserve. The primary dealers are obligated to bid regularly at Treasury auctions, for their own accounts as well as for their customers. This is part of their responsibility to maintain liquid markets in all government securities. The Federal Reserve deals directly only with the primary dealers, who form the core of the Treasury trading and the market-making activities. All primary dealers are subject to certain disclosure requirements. The breadth and the depth of the dealers' participation, as well as the bid-offer spreads under different market conditions, are reviewed constantly by the Federal Reserve.

The secondary market is an active market where the benchmark issues trade at a relatively narrow bid-offer spread ranging from $\frac{1}{64}$ to about $\frac{2}{32}$. In addition to primary dealers and other dealers, there are broker dealers who facilitate transactions between dealers anonymously. Trading in this market is based on electronic screens and the trades usually settle in one business day.

To sum up, the when-issued market, the primary auction, the secondary market, and the repo markets are all integrated. See Chapters 4 and 5 for a closer look at the secondary market.

Historical Evidence

From 1980 to 1991, the U.S. Treasury conducted nearly 2,000 auctions in which securities with benchmark maturities ranging from three months to 30 years were sold. Using the available data on these auctions, the following questions can be examined.

- How "strong" were these auctions? Some light on this question may be shed by looking at the bid-to-cover ratio, the ratio of the aggregate amount that the investors' bid to the amount that the Treasury auctioned. The higher this ratio, *ceteris paribus,* the stronger is the auction. The period 1980–1983 is an extraordinary period for students of fixed-income securities markets. In October 1979, the Federal Reserve effected a change in its monetary policy that led to significant fluctuations in interest rates.

- A review of Figures 2-4 and 2-5 illustrates that the three-year period 1980–1983 was one of the most volatile periods in the history of these markets. Only in the two-week period following the stock market crash of 1987 did volatilities of interest rates approaching such levels occur. During 1980–1983, the levels of interest rates were high and the yield curve was inverted for much of this period. How did the auction mechanism perform in this turbulent period? Stated differently, did the performance (results) of auctions during this period differ from the performance during the rest of the decade?

- Short-term interest rates are more volatile than long-term interest rates. (We will present evidence for this in Chapter 5.) How does this affect the auction outcome? Is the dispersion of winning bids greater for the auctions of T-bills (shorter term) compared with the auctions of T-bonds and T-notes (longer term)? Is there a systematic difference between the results of T-bill auctions (short term) and the long bond auction (long term)?

- Treasury securities may be obtained in the auction either via a competitive tender or via noncompetitive tender. The individual purchases in the noncompetitive tender are small and the buyers face price uncertainty but no quantity uncertainty. Is there any systematic relationship between the type of the security sold and the proportion of that security that gets allocated via competitive tender?

The data are from the *Treasury Bulletin,* for the period 1980–1986 for Treasury bills and for the period 1980–1991 for Treasury coupon issues. By the very nature of the auction schedule, the sample is dominated by the Treasury bills, especially the three-month and the six-month T-bills, which are auctioned every week. The full sample period 1980–1991 was punctuated by several important events that deserve special mention at the outset. As mentioned earlier, the policy switch that occurred in late 1979 might have been responsible for the extreme volatility and the high levels of interest rates during the 1980–1983 period. In the last part of 1981, when-issued trading was officially permitted as part of the bidding process in the Treasury markets. Two benchmark securities (four-year and twenty-year) were eliminated from the auction schedule by the Treasury. The stock market crash of October 1987 produced tremendous pressures on the financing rates in the Treasury market. During 1988, there was a significant debate about the debt ceiling levels in the U.S. Congress which led to delays in some auctions and the cancellation of at least one auction.

In each auction, two factors are exogenously specified: the size of the issue, and the maturity and timing of coupon and principal payments. After the bidding is completed, the coupon is announced. Note that for the T-bill auctions, there are no coupons and hence there is less uncertainty to the bidders. The auction process results in the following endogenous outcomes: the allocation of the security to competitive and noncompetitive sectors, the dispersion in winning bids, the amount tendered relative to the size of the issue, and the allocation within the competitive sector. The relationship between these endogenous variables and the exogenous factors is interesting. In addition, there is an active secondary market in which close substitutes are actively traded, and the interest rates prevailing on these close substitutes may affect the endogenous outcomes.

To get a perspective on these issues, compare Tables 3-7 and 3-8. They show how the results of the auctions during 1980–1983 have qualitatively differed from the corre-

Benchmark Maturity	Bid-to-Cover Ratio	Dispersion of Winning Bids	Percent Sold in Competitive Tender
Three-month	4.1429	4.8846	77.8028
Six-month	4.5758	3.4230	78.8750
Two-year	2.7613	3.3330	83.3200
Three-year	2.9045	2.6000	88.7500
Five-year	2.9120	2.5930	93.4400
Seven-year	2.6886	3.1785	93.4900
Ten-year	2.3450	3.7000	94.1970
Thirty-year	2.2870	3.6785	95.3500

TABLE 3-7

Mean Across All Auctions, Sample: 1984–1991

Source: Sundaresen (1994)

Benchmark Maturity	Bid-to-Cover Ratio	Dispersion of Winning Bids	Percent Sold in Competitive Tender
Three-month	2.9917	15.7726	72.1244
Six-month	3.2801	11.4000	75.4320
Two-year	2.2366	10.1914	76.3475
Three-year	2.4255	10.9375	72.3400
Five-year	2.2237	9.3750	83.9900
Seven-year	2.0994	10.3571	82.2300
Ten-year	2.2230	9.2000	81.3800
Thirty-year	2.0810	10.7860	87.0800

TABLE 3-8

Mean Across All Auctions, Sample: 1980–1983

Source: Sundaresen (1994)

sponding results of the auctions held during 1984–1991. During 1980–1983, the average bid-to-cover ratios were lower, the dispersion was higher and a lesser percentage got sold in the competitive tender.

When-Issued Trading and Repo Rate Behavior. All trades in the when-issued market are settled after the auction when the securities are actually issued. This fact has empirical implications for the behavior of market prices of the newly auctioned issue in the post-auction when-issued trading, and in the cash market prices and the repo rates on the issue date. To see why this is the case, we must remember that, at the end of when-issued trading just prior to the auction, some investors will be net short and some net long. Since each bidder has no private information about other bids, there is residual uncertainty about the bids of other participants in the auction. This fact, coupled with the auction mechanism which introduces quantity uncertainty, implies that it is impossible to guarantee that the short positions will be fully covered by the auction awards. As a consequence, any shortfall must be covered in the post-auction when-issued trading and must be settled up on the issue date either in the cash market or in the repo market.

To get an appreciation of these factors, examine Table 3-9, which shows the average of the difference between the general collateral rate and the special rates for all on-the-run issues from the issue date of the current on-the-run security to the issue date of the next on-the-run security.

The summary information in Table 3-9 serves as a useful benchmark. The general collateral rate is the rate applied to most Treasury securities for overnight collateralized lending and borrowing purposes. Dealers generally permit substitution of collaterals in such general collateral agreements. The special rates apply to collateralized transactions where no such substitutions are permitted. As a consequence, it is intuitive why the special rates must be below the general collateral: The owner of a security which is trading special is able to get a much lower rate on collateralized loan transactions. This rent can be substantial. In practice, 90% to 95% of the Treasury securities trade at the general collateral rate. The remaining few exceptions trade special.

As Table 3-9 demonstrates, on-the-run issues trade special as a rule and trade, on average, at 45 to 100 basis points below the general collateral rate. That the spreads are reliably positive is evident from the t-statistics.

TABLE 3-9   *Repo Rates (Overnight) Summary Statistics, General Collateral—Special Rate (in Basis Points), Sample: 1987–1991*

Statistic	Two-year	Three-year	Five-year	Seven-year	Ten-year	Thirty-year
Number of Auctions	57	19	23	18	19	16
Mean	56.57	47.20	67.39	56.22	96.94	69.47
Standard Deviation	107.42	82.90	110.31	87.13	130.68	105.82
t-statistic	18.25	19.51	21.03	21.90	25.42	22.22

Source: Sundaresan (1994)

The evidence presented in Table 3-10 clearly demonstrates that during the days prior to auctions, securities become very expensive to borrow and in some cases they continue to be expensive for days. This is consistent with the existence of periodic squeezes in Treasury markets over a long period of time. The "auction day effect" is clearly present in the repo rates data. The report from *New York Times* on short squeezes illustrates this point.

TABLE 3-10   *Repo Rates (Overnight) around Auctions, General Collateral—Special Rate (in Basis Points), Sample: 1987–1991*

Benchmark	-4	-3	-2	-1	0	+1	+2	+3	+4
Two-year	90.33	73.17	73.87	60.35	58.07	54.29	38.68	36.89	36.04
	(5.20)	(4.51)	(4.32)	(4.12)	(3.86)	(4.01)	(3.76)	(3.39)	(2.77)
Three-year	121.71	96.18	74.63	37.71	38.18	40.61	37.47	30.36	21.71
	(3.44)	(3.65)	(2.41)	(4.91)	(3.39)	(3.54)	(5.12)	(6.46)	(12.03)
Five-year	153.17	126.19	92.39	72.78	62.80	51.94	79.52	95.00	89.17
	(5.55)	(5.40)	(5.27)	(5.60)	(4.79)	(3.94)	(4.14)	(2.94)	(2.38)
Seven-year	119.11	113.44	93.72	102.64	103.56	50.22	51.05	59.64	24.16
	(4.04)	(4.55)	(4.59)	(4.00)	(3.12)	(5.04)	(3.31)	(2.94)	(3.38)
Ten-year	233.55	189.63	177.90	178.29	147.97	153.92	109.64	99.93	112.55
	(5.63)	(5.02)	(4.43)	(3.74)	(3.71)	(3.50)	(2.81)	(2.70)	(2.90)
Thirty-year	155.19	132.81	131.22	112.75	130.59	83.70	83.08	106.00	111.50
	(4.45)	(3.77)	(4.01)	(3.82)	(2.59)	(3.63)	(3.48)	(2.86)	(3.22)

1. The t-statistics are provided in parentheses.

2. The sample period is from April 1, 1987, to December 1991.

3. Auction date is denoted by 0. The spreads are computed for the 9-day window starting from four days prior to the auction (−4) and ending four days after the auction (+4).

Fed Looks Into "Squeeze" in Treasuries

By Jonathan Fuerbringer

The "squeeze" on the Treasury's seven- and 10-year notes has become tight enough to prompt the Federal Reserve Bank of New York to collect information on dealer positions and study the dynamics of the shortage of securities.

A squeeze, which forces some traders to pay very high premiums to borrow the securities they want, is not necessarily illegal. But it can be if there is collusion involved in creating a shortage of securities.

The Federal Reserve Bank, which is collecting the data as part of the broadened market surveillance effort that was started after the Treasury auction scandal involving Salomon Brothers in August 1991, confirmed the special request to dealers for information yesterday.

Hedging Operations

Several dealers said yesterday that they saw nothing happening beyond a normal squeeze on the 10-year note. There is a shortage of the securities because so many dealers have sold them, without actually owning them, as part of hedging operations against large holdings of corporate issues that have been difficult to sell to customers recently.

Two traders, who asked not to be identified, said Yamaichi International, a primary dealer, was at the center of the shortage of seven-year notes.

But Scott E. Pardee, co-chairman of Yamaichi, dismissed the accusations as finger-pointing. "There has been a tendency on the part of people in the center to point fingers at people who are not in the center, so I am not surprised that they are trying to point the finger at us," he said.

Mr. Pardee, a former Federal Reserve official, said traders had done similar finger-pointing at Yamaichi earlier this year in connection with a squeeze of 10-year notes, so his firm was being "scrupulously careful in this." He said the Federal Reserve Bank of New York, in earlier situations, "has done a good job in making sure that no one is sitting on the bonds."

The measure of a squeeze or shortage of notes or bonds is in the repurchase market, where these securities are borrowed. In normal circumstances, a dealer swaps cash for the securities. He lends the cash to the holder of the securities at daily market rates, which are around 3 percent.

But when there is a shortage, the dealer must "pay" by lending that cash at lower than market rates, a move that benefits the dealer who has the securities. Yesterday, the rate on 10-year notes was at zero, while the rate on seven-year notes was around $\frac{1}{8}$ of a percent.

Involvement of the Fed

The Federal Reserve Bank of New York has gathered such data on seven other issues this year, including the five-year note that was auctioned in July, said a spokesman, Peter Bakstansky. "We are trying to better understand the positions in the market and the market dynamics," he said.

In similar instances earlier this year, the information gathered has gone to the interagency working group for Treasury market surveillance, which includes the Treasury, the Fed and the Securities and Exchange Commission.

Under the changes made after the Salomon bidding scandal, the Treasury said it would use its power to make additional securities available to the market to end any acute shortage or squeeze in the market. Although this weapon has not been used, the increased surveillance is part of the first step that would lead to a decision on whether to break up a squeeze.

Table 3-10 also provides evidence on the tightness in repo rates surrounding the auction date. Note that the spreads prior to the auction date are considerably higher than the overall sample means reported in the previous table. The ten-year and thirty-year sectors clearly show that the current on-the-run issues have traded at significant spreads under general collateral rates in days prior to the auction.

WINNER'S CURSE

Winner's curse refers to the possibility that the aggressive bidder in a discriminatory auction will end up paying too much relative to the market consensus. Anticipating this possibility, bidders will tend to shade down their bids relative to the true value of the security, to minimize the winner's curse and invest considerable resources in pre-auction information gathering to learn more about the market consensus, so that their bids are not out of line from the market consensus. The Treasury loses money because of the winner's curse but is able to exercise the power of a discriminating monopolist by selling the same security by marching down the demand curve submitted by the bidders.

In the uniform price auction, the Treasury allocates the security at a common price; hence it gives up the power to discriminate. On the other hand, bidders can be more aggressive since they pay the same price irrespective of their bids. The incentive to gather pre-auction information is possibly less in this auction. Therefore, the winner's curse should be less of an issue in uniform price auctions.

In Table 3-11 we summarize the available evidence on the winner's curse. Note that the markup on Treasury bills has varied from four basis points to one basis point. For coupon issues, Simon (1994a) estimates a markup of about $\frac{3}{8}$ basis point. As shown in Table 3-11, researchers have employed several different methods to assess the success of a particular auction format in achieving a high selling price. Cammack (1991) uses the difference between the auction average and the average of WI quotes at the end of the auction day. The main reason for this is the fact that the true value of the security might be affected by the possibilities of short squeezes in the periods immediately

TABLE 3-11   *Markups in Auctions, a Summary of Evidence*

Source	Data and Sample	Measure of Markup	Size of Markup
Cammack (1991)	T-bills (1973–1984)	Auction average minus average of WI at close on auction date	4 basis points
Spindt and Stolz (1992)	T-bills (1982–1988)	Auction average minus bid of WI at 30 minutes before auction	1.5 basis points
Bikhchandani et. al. (1993)	T-bills (1986–1988)	Auction average minus bid of WI at 1:00 PM	1 basis point
Simon (1994)	Coupon (1990–1991)	Auction average minus bid of WI at 1:00 PM	$\frac{3}{8}$ basis point

surrounding the auction. The assumption is that by looking at the prices at the close of the auction day, one can abstract from those effects.

Simon (1994a) takes the yield difference using the quoted when-issued bid at the time of the auction. The motivation behind this measure comes from auction theory dealing with unit-good auctions. If the when-issued market aggregated information perfectly, the when-issued price just prior to bidding should ideally be equal to the auction price. In Treasury auctions, the bids and asks in the when-issued market are valid only for small quantities. To a potential bidder who has sold a total of 2 billion before 1:00 PM at a weighted average when-issued rate of 6.01%, the break-even bidding yield at the auction is 6.01%. The 1:00 PM when-issued quote (which is valid for a small amount) is important to the extent that it represents the new yield at which a large quantity (2 billion) may be purchased. Typically, the bidders bid for large quantities (on the order of several billion dollars) in the auction, so comparing the when-issued price at 1:00 PM with the auction average is not necessarily informative. In addition, Nyborg and Sundaresan (1994) show that a large proportion of the when-issued trading occurs well before the bidding time. In such situations, the when-issued prices at 1:00 PM, which are good for small amounts, do not convey much information about where the bids will be placed in the auctions. The critical issue, then, is whether the when-issued market is liquid around the bidding time.

Based on the transactions that flowed through Garban at 1:00 PM, Nyborg and Sundaresan (1994) show that the trading activity at 1:00 PM is rather sparse. They present evidence for both discriminatory- and uniform-price auction formats for the period 30 minutes prior to the bidding time in ten minutes intervals. This evidence is reproduced in Tables 3-12a and 3-12b.

They find that the markups for Treasury bills vary from 0 to $\frac{1}{2}$ basis point. This is lower than the evidence summarized for T-bills in Table 3-11. The weighted average markups for discriminatory auctions is $\frac{1}{3}$ basis point. As T-bills constitute the majority of the sample, the weighted average is very strongly influenced by the experience of

TABLE 3-12a   *Depth of When-Issued Market, Markups from 12:30 to 1:00 PM, Discriminatory-Price Auctions*

Maturity	Mean Markup	Standard Deviation of Markups	Maximum Markup	Minimum Markup	Number of Trades
Two-year					
12:30 to 12:40	0.0050	0.0000	0.0000	0.0000	1
12:40 to 12:50	0.00167	0.00183	0.0025	0.0000	7
12:50 to 1:00	No trade	No trade	No trade	No trade	
Five-year					
12:30 to 12:40	0.00250	0.0000	0.00250	0.00250	3
12:40 to 12:50	0.00550	0.0031	0.00750	0.0000	7
12:50 to 1:00	0.0050	0.0050	0.0100	0.000	4

Source: Nyborg and Sundaresan (1994)

TABLE 3-12b   *Depth of When-Issued Market, Markups from 12:30 to 1:00 PM,*
Uniform-Price Auctions

Maturity	Mean Markup	Standard Deviation of Markups	Maximum Markup	Minimum Markup	Number of Trades
Two-year					
12:30 to 12:40	0.00928	0.02241	0.0400	−0.01750	14
12:40 to 12:50	−0.004464	0.01963	0.0400	−0.01750	28
12:50 to 1:00	−0.004736	0.01777	0.0350	−0.01500	38
1:00 PM	0.03500				
Five-year					
12:30 to 12:40	0.00293	0.033969	0.0850	−0.02750	31
12:40 to 12:50	0.00711	0.032528	0.0800	−0.02500	39
12:50 to 1:00	0.00150	0.017676	0.0700	−0.03000	40
1:00 PM	0.010500				

Source: Nyborg and Sundaresan (1994)

Treasury bill auctions. In all other maturity sectors, as Table 3-11 shows, the markups are statistically significantly different from zero. In contrast, for the 15 uniform price auctions in Table 3-12b, the average markups from 12:50 to 1:00 PM are not significantly different from zero. This is due to the fact that the markups fluctuate a great deal in uniform-price auctions prior to bidding, indicating a greater liquidity in the when-issued market. In the two-year uniform-price auctions there were 80 trades in the 12:30 to 1:00 period with about 2.5 trades per minute. For the five-year notes, there were a total of 110 trades in the same period, averaging four trades per minute. Contrast the corresponding results from discriminatory auctions reported in Table 3-12a for two-year and five-year notes: The depth is poor and the markups are uniformly positive.

Auction theory says that the magnitude of the markups is a function of the auction mechanism. Friedman (1991) and Milgrom (1989) argue that uniform-price auctions should lead to better expected revenue for the Treasury. A recent contribution by Back and Zender (1993) points out that with more realistic modeling of Treasury auctions, it is possible to show that the single-price auction may actually increase the cost of borrowing. Nyborg and Sundaresan (1994) provide evidence that the discriminatory-price auctions have markups that are less volatile prior to bidding. In uniform-price auctions, markups are much more volatile prior to bidding and the depth of the when-issued trading is greater.

Auction Mechanism and WI Trading

What are the effects of the auction mechanism on when-issued trading? The when-issued trading, as noted earlier, provides a key mechanism for the price-discovery process. In addition, it provides quantity and price insurance to the participants.

Dealers use this market to learn about the demand for the security that is going to be auctioned. As the trading progresses towards the auction date, this market generates and aggregates more information about the depth of the auction (in terms of the strength of the demand) and about the diversity of the participants. This process of generating information about the demand for the forthcoming auction (or the price-discovery role) is clearly vital to the dealers bidding in the discriminatory auction. However, for the uniform-price auctions, this may not be critical. This suggests that the WI trading should be less for uniform-price auctions and more for discriminatory auctions.

On the other hand, if the when-issued market is viewed as a place where risk-averse investors buy quantity and price insurance, then the trading activity in the when-issued market should not diminish. If anything, the ability to pay the same price in the auction, irrespective of one's access to information, suggests that the informational advantages may be less important here and therefore the trading activity may actually increase.

Nyborg and Sundaresan (1994) examine when-issued trading activity under the two auction mechanisms using transactions data from Garban, an interdealer broker in the U.S. Treasury market. Their evidence suggests that when-issued trading is relatively more active under the uniform-price format. The data presented in Table 3-13 indicates that the uniform-price auctions in the two- and five-year maturities have much bigger trades; the average transaction volume in the two-year and five-year auctions is over $1300 million, well in excess of all the other benchmark maturities.

The breakdown of the overall number of trading days and the total number of trades is given in Table 3-14. The sample has a total of 30,979 trades, of which 14,695 transactions are drawn from discriminatory auctions and 16,284 trades are from uniform-price auctions. On a per-day basis, uniform-price auctions have about 148 transactions

TABLE 3-13   *When-Issued Transactions Volume Breakdown per Trading Day*
(in millions of par amount)

Benchmark Maturity	Mean	Maximum	Minimum	Standard Error
Three-month	427.16	4716.00	5.00	29.25
Six-month	473.05	2970.00	8.00	23.81
One-year	1149.94	4962.00	102.00	116.19
Two-year (UP)	1325.98	6078.00	117.00	195.04
Two-year (D)	472.36	1076.00	43.00	79.03
Three-year	1918.50	4318.00	248.00	453.49
Five-year (UP)	1330.52	5254.00	64.00	127.49
Five-year (D)	795.25	1598.00	73.00	128.22
Thirty-year	228.38	735.00	27.00	91.00

D indicates discriminatory auction

UP indicates uniform-price auction

Source: Nyborg and Sundaresen (1994)

TABLE 3-14   *When-Issued Days and Transactions*

Benchmark Maturity	Number of Trading Days	Number of Total Transactions	Mean Number of Transactions Per Day	Standard Error of Number of Transactions per Day
Three-month (D)	247	3,660	14.82	10.44
Six-month (D)	247	4,419	17.89	11.58
One-year (D)	50	2,665	53.30	30.12
Two-year (D)	14	738	52.71	29.61
Two-year (UP)	45	5,377	119.49	15.24
Three-year (D)	8	1,456	182.00	92.97
Five-year (UP)	65	10,907	167.80	15.85
Five-year (D)	14	1,464	104.57	59.65
Thirty-year (D)	8	293	36.63	31.11

D indicates discriminatory auction

UP indicates uniform-price auction

Source: Nyborg and Sundaresan (1994)

and the discriminatory auctions have about 25 transactions. It is quite clear that the when-issued trading is much more active in uniform-price auctions.

FURTHER READING

This chapter has presented an analysis of Treasury auctions, when-issued markets and repo markets. These topics are typically given short shrift in texts on fixed-income markets. Even in the academic literature, the when-issued markets and repo markets have been treated only recently. Auction theory and mechanism design are active research topics in the economics literature. An excellent survey of auction theory is provided in Milgrom (1989). More directly related to Treasury auctions are Bikchandani and Huang (1993) and Chari and Weber (1992). Academic papers addressing the effect of secondary markets on Treasury auctions, the vulnerability of auction mechanisms to manipulation, and a comparative analysis of uniform-price and discriminatory auctions are provided, respectively, in Bikchandani and Huang (1993), Back and Zender (1993), and Nyborg and Sundaresan (1994). In the chapter, we have already reviewed some papers dealing with winner's curse in auctions. Empirical studies in this area by Cammack (1991); Simon (1994a); and Spindt and Stolz (1992) have examined the presence and the magnitude of winner's curse in discriminatory auctions. Simon (1994b) and Nyborg and Sundaresan (1994) examine uniform-price auctions; the latter study provides explicit comparisons between the two auction formats. Repo markets have been described in detail in an excellent text by Stigum (1990). Academic research in this area includes Duffie (1992) and Sundaresan (1994). The when-issued market and its implications for auctions have been explored by Bickchandani, Edsparr and Huang (1994) and Nyborg and Sundaresan (1994).

PROBLEMS

3.1   Describe clearly the salient features of the discriminatory auction mechanism used by the U.S. Treasury to sell T-bills, and three-year and ten-year T-notes and thirty-year T-bonds.

3.2   Explain the meaning of the term "winner's curse." Why should the U.S. Treasury be concerned about the possibility of winner's curse being present in Treasury auctions?

3.3   Explain the role of the when-issued market in the context of Treasury auctions. What are the advantages and disadvantages of when-issued trading?

3.4   Describe clearly the salient features of the uniform-price auction mechanism used by the U.S. Treasury to sell two-year and five-year T-notes.

3.5   Which mechanism, the uniform-price auction or the discriminatory auction, is expected to have a greater degree of winner's curse? Why?

3.6 (a)   Briefly describe the role of primary dealers in Treasury auctions.

   (b)   These auctions are preceded by WI trading. Briefly describe the WI market.

   (c)   Discuss the advantages and disadvantages of WI trading for (i) the ultimate investor, (ii) primary dealers, (iii) the U.S. Treasury, and (iv) the price-discovery process.

3.7   Who are likely to be the buyers in the WI market and who are likely to be the sellers? What consequences does the WI market have for the auction prices and the secondary-market prices?

3.8 (a)   Briefly describe the repo markets.

   (b)   Describe and explain the differences between general collateral repo rates and special repo rates.

   (c)   Explain the difference between on-the-run and off-the-run issues.

   (d)   It appears that on-the-run issues tend to go special more often than off-the-run issues. What are the reasons for this pattern?

3.9   Is there a general association between the level of interest rates and the shape of the yield curve? Review the evidence presented in this chapter and in Chapter 1 in answering this question.

3.10   Is there a relationship between the levels of interest rates and their volatility? Discuss the evidence.

REFERENCES

Back, K., and J. Zender 1993. "Auctions of Divisible Goods: On the Rationale for the Treasury Experiment." *Review of Financial Studies* 6:733–764.

Bikchandani, S. 1988. "Reputation in Repeated Second-Price Auctions." *Journal of Economic Theory* 46:97–119.

Bikchandani, S., and C. Huang 1989. "Auction with Resale Markets: An Exploratory Model of Treasury Bill Markets." *The Review of Financial Studies* 2:311–339.

Bikchandani, S., and C. Huang 1993. "The Economics of Treasury Securities Markets." *Journal of Economic Perspectives* 7:117–134.

Bikchandani, S., P. L. Edsparr, and C. Huang 1994. The Treasury Bill Auction and the When-Issued Market: Some Evidence. M.I.T. Working Paper.

Cammack, E. 1991. "Evidence of Bidding Strategies and the Information in Treasury Bill Auctions." *Journal of Political Economy* 99:100–130.

Chari, V. V., and R. Weber 1992. "How the U.S. Treasury Should Auction Its Debt." Northwestern University Working Paper.

Duffie, D. 1992. Special Repo Rates. Stanford University Research Working Paper.

Engelbrecht-Wiggins, R. 1990. "Auctions and Bidding Models: A Survey." *Management Science* 26:119–142.

Friedman, M. 1991. "How to Sell Government Securities." *Wall Street Journal,* August 28.

Fuerbringer, J. 1992. "Fed Looks into 'Squeeze' in Treasuries." *New York Times* (Sept. 25): D,1:6,D11.

Jegadeesh, N. 1993. Treasury Auction Bids and the Salomon Squeeze. *Journal of Finance* 18: 1403–1419.

Maskin, E., and Riley, J. 1989. "Optimal Multi-Unit Auctions." In *The Economics of Missing Markets, Information, and Games,* F. Hahn, ed. Clarendon Press.

Milgrom, P., 1989. "Auctions and Bidding: A Primer." *Journal of Economic Perspectives* 3:3–22.

Nyborg, K., and S. Sundaresan 1994. Discriminatory versus Uniform Treasury Auctions—Evidence from When-Issued Transactions. Columbia University Working Paper.

Simon, D. P. 1994a.. "Markups, Quantity Risk and Bidding Strategies at Treasury Coupon Auctions." *Journal of Financial Economics* 35:43–62.

Simon, D. P. 1994b. "The Treasury's Experiment with Single-Price Auctions in the Mid-1970s: Winner's or Taxpayer's Curse?" *Review of Economics and Statistics* 76:754–760.

Spindt, P., and R. Stolz 1992. "Are U.S. T-bills Underpriced in the Primary Market?" *Journal of Banking and Finance* 16:891–908.

Stigum, M. L. 1989. *The Repo and Reverse Markets.* Homewood, IL: Dow Jones-Irwin.

Stigum, M. 1990. *The Money Market.* Homewood, IL: Dow Jones-Irwin.

Sundaresan, S. 1992. "Pre-Auction Markets and Post-Auction Efficiency: The Case for Cash Settled Futures on On-the-run Treasuries." Columbia University Working Paper.

Sundaresan, S. 1994. "An Empirical Analysis of U.S. Treasury Auctions: Implications for Auction and Term Structure Theories." *Journal of Fixed Income* 4:35–50.

U.S. Department of the Treasury, Securities and Exchange Commission, and Board of Governors of the Federal Reserve System 1992. *Joint Report on the Government Securities Market.* Washington, D.C.

Vickrey, W. 1961. "Counterspeculation, Auctions, and Competitive Sealed Tenders." *Journal of Finance* 16:8–37.

Chapter 4

Bond Mathematics

Chapter Objectives

The purpose of this chapter is to lay the mathematical foundations that are necessary for understanding the instruments and strategies in fixed-income markets. Chapter 4 will help the reader to understand and answer the following questions.

- What are the different methods used to compound cash flows? How do they affect the present and future values?
- What are annuities and perpetuities?
- What is the concept of yield? In particular,
  1. what is yield to maturity?
  2. what is yield to call?
  3. what is current yield?
  4. what is a yield curve?
- What are the different methods used to measure risk? In particular,
  1. what is the price value of a basis point (PVBP) or the dollar value of an 01 (DV01)?
  2. what is Macaulay duration?
  3. what is modified duration?
  4. how should duration be interpreted?
  5. what is convexity?
- How does one hedge interest rate risk?
- How does one apply bond mathematics to trading and risk management to perform
  1. spread trades?
  2. butterfly trades?

INTRODUCTION

The analysis of risk and return of fixed-income securities depends extensively on the concept of discounting, and therefore on the concept of the time value of money. Fixed-income securities are quoted in terms of their yields. The yield of a security is a concept that is closely related to its internal rate of return. There are many measures of yields discussed in this chapter.

Many risk measures have been developed for assessing the risk of fixed-income securities and portfolios. Such measures include the price value of a basis point (PVBP) or dollar value of an 01 (DV01), Macaulay duration, modified duration, and convexity. These measures are fully developed and illustrated in this chapter. In addition, the analysis of fixed-income securities requires a thorough understanding of the basics of yield curve. These include the concepts of the spot rates of interest, the forward rates of interest, and the par bond yield curve; these concepts will be discussed in Chapter 5.

It is customary in the fixed-income markets to quote values in terms of yields instead of prices. The relationship between prices and yields and the assumptions implicit in the price-yield relationship are very important. We develop these ideas in stages in this chapter.

DISCOUNTING

The rate at which money placed in interest-bearing accounts grows depends on the method used for computing the interest payments and reinvestment assumptions. There are two methods of interest calculation, simple interest and compound interest. Compound-interest calculations vary with respect to the number of compounding intervals used in any given period.

To illustrate, let y be the interest rate (annualized) in decimals, that is, 8% or 0.08, let N be the number of years from today, and let FV be the future value of an investment made today after N years. First, consider the case of **simple interest** calculations. Consider investing P (in dollars) today for x days at a simple interest rate of y. The amount that will be available from the account at the end of x days will be

$$P \times \left(1 + y \times \frac{x}{365}\right).$$

When $x = 365$, or when the money is placed in the account for one year, the future value will be $P \times (1 + y)$. Consider a simple interest calculation in which a bank agrees to pay 6% annual (simple) interest on a deposit of $1,000 placed in the bank for 90 days. At the end of 90 days, the total amount will be

$$1,000 \times \left(1 + 0.06 \times \frac{90}{365}\right) = \$1,014.795.$$

Simple interest is used in repo markets and in some money market instruments. Often, in simple interest calculations one year is assumed to have 360 days. If this market convention is used, then for the example illustrated above, the total amount will be

$$1{,}000 \times \left(1 + 0.06 \times \frac{90}{360}\right) = 1{,}015$$

It is also used in some government bond markets. However, most securities compound their interest payments.

The **future value** of investing P today for N years at an annual interest rate y (with annual interest payments) is

$$FV = P \times (1 + y)^N \qquad (4.1)$$

If the interest is **compounded semi-annually,** that is, we are paid interest at the end of a half year and we earn interest on that interest, then what will be the future value of our capital? At the end of a half year, we will have

$$P \times \left(1 + \frac{y}{2}\right).$$

We reinvest this for another half year and at the end of the year earn an amount equal to

$$P \times \left(1 + \frac{y}{2}\right) \times \left(1 + \frac{y}{2}\right) = P \times \left(1 + \frac{y}{2}\right)^2.$$

So, with semi-annual compounding, the terminal value is

$$FV = P \times \left(1 + \frac{y}{2}\right)^2.$$

The future value of setting aside P today for N years (with m compounding intervals per year) is

$$FV = P \times \left(1 + \frac{y}{m}\right)^{N \times m}. \qquad (4.2)$$

As we increase m to ∞ we get a future value with continuous compounding of

$$FV = P \times e^{yN}. \qquad (4.3)$$

Generally, we can convert from one method of compounding to another. If we are given the annually compounded interest rate $\hat{y}$, we can convert it to the semi-annually compounded interest rate y using

$$\left(1 + \frac{y}{2}\right)^2 = (1 + \hat{y}).$$

Table 4-1 records the future values of $100 at a 5% interest rate under annual, semi-annual, quarterly, and continuous compounding. Note that the value differences resulting from the number of compounding intervals per year are rather small for maturities of 1–10 years. At the end of one year, the simple interest earned is $5 whereas with

TABLE 4-1   *Future Value Table*

Years to Maturity	Annual Compounding	Semi-Annual Compounding	Quarterly Compounding	Continuous Compounding
1	105.00	105.06	105.09	105.13
2	110.25	110.38	110.45	110.52
3	115.76	115.97	116.08	116.18
4	121.55	121.84	121.99	122.14
5	127.63	128.01	128.20	128.40
6	134.01	134.49	134.74	134.99
7	140.71	141.30	141.60	141.91
8	147.75	148.45	148.81	149.18
9	155.13	155.97	156.39	156.83
10	162.89	163.86	164.36	164.87
11	171.03	172.16	172.74	173.33
12	179.59	180.87	181.54	182.21
13	188.56	190.03	190.78	191.55
14	197.99	199.65	200.50	201.38
15	207.89	209.76	210.72	211.70
16	218.29	220.38	221.45	222.55
17	229.20	231.53	232.74	233.96
18	240.66	243.25	244.59	245.96
19	252.70	255.57	257.05	258.57
20	265.33	268.51	270.15	271.83

We use an annual interest rate of 5%. Equation (4.1) has been used to calculate annual compounding, and equation (4.2) has been used to calculate semiannual compounding (with $m = 2$) and quarterly compounding (with $m = 4$). Equation (4.3) has been used to calculate continuous compounding.

continuous compounding the interest earned is $5.13. Clearly, the more frequent the compounding, the more interest is earned on interest.

A security that pays C (in dollars) per period for n periods is known as an **annuity.** We can determine the future value of an annuity that pays C for two years as follows. The first year's payment can be reinvested for one more year at a rate y to get, at the end of year two, an amount

$$C \times (1 + y).$$

This, added to the payment of C at the end of year two, gives a future value of

$$FV = C + C(1 + y).$$

Multiplying the previous equation by $(1 + y)$ gives

$$FV(1 + y) = C(1 + y) + C(1 + y)^2.$$

Subtracting the first equation from the second and simplifying gives

$$FV = \frac{C}{y}\{(1 + y)^2 - 1\}.$$

The future value of an annuity C for N years with an annual interest payment is

$$FV = C \times \left[\frac{(1+y)^N - 1}{y} \right].$$ (4.4)

We may rewrite the Equation (4.4) as

$$FV = \frac{C}{y} \times [(1+y)^N - 1].$$

Example 4-1 illustrates the use of this formula.

Example 4-1

Consider a loan in which a payment of $C = 100$ per annum has to be made for the next 10 years. Let the interest rate y be equal to 9%. Then, the future value of this loan is

$$FV = \frac{100}{0.09} \times [(1 + 0.09)^{10} - 1] = 1{,}519.29.$$ (4.5)

For holders of securities which promise cash flows at future dates, the concept of **present value** (PV) is important. What is the present value (PV) of one dollar to be received N years from today? The present value (with annual compounding) is

$$PV = 1 \times \frac{1}{(1+y)^N}.$$ (4.6)

Therefore, the PV of one dollar received after N years with m interest compounding intervals per year is

$$PV = \frac{1}{\left(1 + \frac{y}{m}\right)^{N \times m}}.$$ (4.7)

And as m approaches ∞ we get the present value corresponding to continuous compounding

$$PV = 1 \times e^{-yN}.$$ (4.8)

Example 4-2

Consider a case in which $100 will be paid 10 years from now and the interest rate is 5% compounded continuously. In this case, the present value is

$$PV = 100 \times e^{-0.05 \times 10} = 60.65.$$

In Table 4-2, we tabulate the present value of $100 to be paid at maturities ranging from one to 20 years at a discount rate of 5% under four different compounding methods.

TABLE 4-2   *Present Value Table*

Years to Maturity	*Annual Compounding*	*Semi-Annual Compounding*	*Quarterly Compounding*	*Continuous Compounding*
1	95.24	95.18	95.15	95.12
2	90.70	90.60	90.54	90.48
3	86.38	86.23	86.15	86.07
4	82.27	82.07	81.97	81.87
5	78.35	78.12	78.00	77.88
6	74.62	74.36	74.22	74.08
7	71.07	70.77	70.62	70.47
8	67.68	67.36	67.20	67.03
9	64.46	64.12	63.94	63.76
10	61.39	61.03	60.84	60.65
11	58.47	58.09	57.89	57.69
12	55.68	55.29	55.09	54.88
13	53.03	52.62	52.42	52.20
14	50.51	50.09	49.87	49.66
15	48.10	47.67	47.46	47.24
16	45.81	45.38	45.16	44.93
17	43.63	43.19	42.97	42.74
18	41.55	41.11	40.88	40.66
19	39.57	39.13	38.90	38.67
20	37.69	37.24	37.02	36.79

We use an annual interest rate of 5%. Equation (4.5) has been used to calculate annual compounding, and equation (4.6) has been used to calculate semiannual compounding (with $m = 2$) and quarterly compounding (with $m = 4$). Equation (4.7) has been used to calculate continuous compounding.

The present value of an annuity C for N years with annual compounding is

$$PV = C \times \left[\frac{1 - \frac{1}{(1 + y)^N}}{y} \right]. \tag{4.9}$$

This equation can be rewritten as

$$PV = \frac{C}{y} \times [1 - (1 + y)^{-N}].$$

Example 4-3

Consider an annuity of $100 per year for the next 10 years at an interest rate of 9%. What is the present value of this annuity?

$$PV = \frac{100}{0.09} \times [1 - (1 + 0.09)^{-10}] = 641.77$$

As N approaches ∞, we get the present value of a perpetuity,

$$PV = \frac{C}{y}.$$

Note that as y increases, P falls and that as y decreases, P increases. **This illustrates that the present value and the interest rate used for discounting are inversely related.**

YIELDS

The **internal rate of return** of a bond, denoted by y and sometimes referred to as the **yield to maturity,** is the rate of discount at which the present value of the promised future cash flows equals the price of the security.

In this section, we explore this concept assuming annual compounding, then semi-annual compounding, and finally continuous compounding.

Annual Compounding

The price P of a bond that pays annual dollar coupons of C for N years, per \$100 of face value, is

$$P = \frac{C}{1+y} + \frac{C}{(1+y)^2} + \frac{C}{(1+y)^3} + \cdots + \frac{C+100}{(1+y)^N} \qquad (4.10)$$

Assuming that there is no default, the price of a bond (in equilibrium) will equal the present value of promised future cash flows.

Let us define the percentage coupon c such that $C = c \times 100$. Then, an important result derived from Equation (4.10) is that when $c = y$, $P = 100$. In a similar way, we can verify that

$$c > y \quad \Rightarrow \quad P > 100$$

and

$$c < y \quad \Rightarrow \quad P < 100$$

where the symbol $\Rightarrow$ denotes "implies."

We therefore conclude: When the coupon of a security is set equal to its yield to maturity, the security will sell at par.

Thus we know that when the coupon of a security is greater than (less than) its yield to maturity, the security will sell at a premium (discount) to its par.

Note that Equation (4.10) can be written by recognizing that it is an N-year annuity paying C per period plus the terminal payment of 100. This enables us to write the price P as

$$P = \frac{c \times 100}{y} \times [1 - (1+y)^{-N}] + \frac{100}{(1+y)^N}.$$

The first term on the right hand side is the present value of an annuity that pays c per period for N years. The second term on the right hand side is the present value of the terminal balloon payment of 100.

In Table 4-3, we provide the prices and yields of three U.S. Treasury notes. The yields in this market vary from 8.47%–8.49%. The T-note with a coupon of 7.0% is selling at a considerable discount. The T-note with a coupon of 9.5% is selling at a premium and the T-note with a coupon of 8.5% is selling close to par. The prices are in $\frac{1}{32}$, as noted in Chapter 2.

Coupon	Maturity	Bid	Ask	Yield
8.5%	08/15/1995	100.01	100.03	8.47%
9.5%	05/15/1994	103.05	103.09	8.49%
7.0%	01/15/1994	95.13	95.17	8.48%

TABLE 4-3
*T-note Prices and Yields
on June 21, 1990,
Par, Premium, and
Discount*

Another measure known as the **current yield** is defined as the dollar coupon of the security divided by its price, or

$$y_c = \frac{C}{P}. \tag{4.11}$$

Note from example 4-3 that the present value of a perpetuity is $PV = \frac{C}{y}$. If we choose y to be the yield of perpetuity then the PV of perpetuity is also its price. If we denote the price by P, then $P = \frac{C}{y}$. Rearranging, we get $y = \frac{C}{P}$ which is precisely (4.11).

Note therefore that the current yield assumes that the bond is a perpetuity, an assumption that is more reasonable for long-term bonds.

Semi-Annual Compounding

The U.S. Treasury market uses semi-annual compounding. The price of a default-free bond which has a round number N of coupons remaining trading at a semi-annual yield y is given by

$$P = \frac{\frac{C}{2}}{1 + \frac{y}{2}} + \frac{\frac{C}{2}}{\left(1 + \frac{y}{2}\right)^2} + \frac{\frac{C}{2}}{\left(1 + \frac{y}{2}\right)^3} + \cdots + \frac{\frac{C}{2} + 100}{\left(1 + \frac{y}{2}\right)^N}. \tag{4.12}$$

Using summation notation, we can simplify Equation (4.12) as

$$P = \sum_{j=1}^{N} \frac{\frac{C}{2}}{\left(1 + \frac{y}{2}\right)^j} + \frac{100}{\left(1 + \frac{y}{2}\right)^N}. \tag{4.13}$$

The first term, with the summation sign, is the present value of all future semi-annual coupons and the second term is the present value of the balloon payment. For a bond with exactly N round coupon payments that matures in $\frac{N}{2}$ years, we can specify a simple analytical relationship between the price of the bond and its semi-annually compounded yield. This price-yield formula is represented as:

$$P = \frac{C}{y} + \frac{100 - \frac{C}{y}}{\left(1 + \frac{y}{2}\right)^N} \qquad (4.14)$$

C is the dollar coupon. As before, $C = c \times 100$, where the coupon rate c is in percent (i.e., if $c = 0.05$, the coupon rate is 5%), then Equation (4.14) becomes

$$P = \frac{c \times 100}{y} + \frac{100 - \frac{c \times 100}{y}}{\left(1 + \frac{y}{2}\right)^N}.$$

Example 4-4

Consider a bond with a dollar coupon of $C = 10$ per annum and with 10 round coupons remaining so that $N = 10$. For this bond, the price at a yield of 9% ($y = 0.09$) may be computed as

$$P = \frac{10}{0.09} + \frac{100 - \frac{10}{0.09}}{\left(1 + \frac{0.09}{2}\right)^{10}} = 103.9564 \qquad (4.15)$$

As before, from Equation (4.14) when the coupon rate c is equal to the yield to maturity y, $P = 100$. Also, when N approaches ∞

$$y = \frac{c \times 100}{P}.$$

We can see that the current yield $\frac{c \times 100}{P}$ is probably a better approximation for the yield to maturity when N is large.

To verify this intuition, we provide in Table 4-4 the semi-annual yields and the current yields of two U.S. Treasury securities with different maturities. The current yield of the long bond is its dollar coupon divided by its ask price at which it can be purchased. So, current yield is $\frac{8.75}{99 + 29/32} = 8.758\%$, which is close to its semi-annual yield. For the T-note maturing on August 15, 1998, the current yield is $\frac{9.125}{103 + 21/32} = 8.803\%$, which is 19.30 basis points higher than its yield to maturity.

Figure 4-1 shows the price-yield relationship for a 10% (annualized) coupon bond having 80 semi-annual coupon periods with round number of coupons. Notice that the

TABLE 4-4   *Comparison of Yields of Two U.S. Treasury Securities, Settlement on August 15, 1990*

Coupon	Maturity	Bid Price	Ask Price	Yield Semi-annual	Current Yield
8.75%	08/15/2020	99.27	99.29	8.76%	8.758%
9.125%	08/15/1998	103.17	103.21	8.61%	8.803%

FIGURE 4-1   *Price-Yield Relationship, Coupon = 10% and N = 80.*

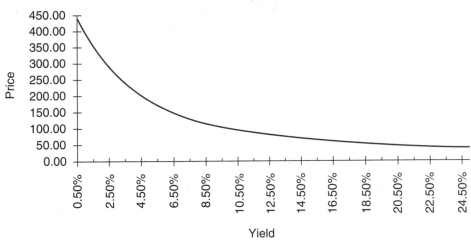

price-yield relation is convex to the origin. Figure 4-1 indicates that the bond is much more elastic at low interest rates than it is at higher interest rates.

Continuous Compounding

If we assume continuous compounding, then the price of a bond with continuously compounded yield to maturity y is

$$P = 100e^{-y \times N} + \int_0^N e^{-y \times t} C \, dt. \tag{4.16}$$

Example 4-5

Consider a bond with a continuously compounded yield of 9%. Let the dollar coupon $C = 10$. Let $N = 10$ years. For this bond, the price at a yield of 9% ($y = 0.09$) is

$$P = 100e^{-0.09 \times 10} + \int_0^{10} 10e^{-0.09t} dt = 106.59 \tag{4.17}$$

All these variations in yields are important. Eurobonds pay annual coupons, the U.S. Treasury pays semi-annual coupons, and GNMAs make monthly payments. As the coupons become more frequent, it becomes more accurate to assume continuous compounding. This is a very useful concept, as we will show later in the chapter.

COMPUTING YIELDS IN PRACTICE

In Figure 4-1 we use the price-yield formula with a round number of coupons; however, in practice, we rarely encounter securities with round coupon payments. Before discussing yield calculations in practice, let us first review the market conventions and terminology.

Debt contracts, such as Treasury bonds, corporate medium-term notes, and municipal bonds, promise to pay periodically a fixed-interest payment, known as the coupon of the security. For example, in Table 4-5 the first Treasury note has a coupon of 4.25%. T-notes have a fixed date, the maturity date, on which they expire; the T-note with the 4.25% coupon matured on August 31, 1994. On the maturity date, T-notes pay the principal amount plus the last coupon payment. The simplest of debt contracts (e.g., noncallable Treasury notes and bonds or noncallable corporate bonds) will only have a periodic fixed coupon plus the principal payment at maturity. But often debt contracts have explicit contractual provisions that render the timing of their cash flows uncertain. For example, some Treasury bonds and many corporate bonds are issued with call features that give the issuer the right to call the securities at prices that are set at issuance. Since the issuer has a greater incentive to call the issue when the interest rates go down, the timing of the cash flows of these securities cannot be predicted with certainty.

Table 4-5 lists the quotes from the Treasury market for selected Treasury securities. The settlement date is September 10, 1992. The price quotes for the T-bills are in decimals and the yields in basis points. (The quoted yields for T-bills are discount yields, which will be described shortly.) The table gives the prices and yields of three-month,

TABLE 4-5 *Fixed-Income Securities Quotes*

Description	Coupon	Maturity	Price	Yield
Three-month T-bill	NA	12/10/1992	99.267	2.900%
Six-month T-bill	NA	03/11/1993	98.521	2.925%
One-year T-bill	NA	08/26/1993	97.069	3.015%
Two-year T-note	4.25%	08/31/1994	$100\frac{27}{32}$	3.801%
Three-year T-note	4.625%	08/15/1995	$100\frac{31}{32}$	4.269%
Five-year T-note	5.625%	08/31/1997	$101\frac{28}{32}$	5.188%
Seven-year T-note	6.375%	07/15/1999	$103\frac{15}{32}$	5.753%
Ten-year T-note	6.375%	08/15/2002	$100\frac{20}{32}$	6.289%
Thirty-year T-bond	7.25%	08/15/2022	$100\frac{13}{32}$	7.216%
Nineteen-year T-bond	14.00%	11/15/2011	$164\frac{18}{32}$	7.565%

Source: Federal Reserve Bank of New York

six-month, and one-year T-bills; and the prices and yields of the most recently auctioned T-notes and T-bonds. The prices are quoted in $\frac{1}{32}$. The last entry provides the price and the yield of a callable Treasury bond that matures on November 15, 2011, but that can be called at par starting November 15, 2006, on any coupon date.

None of the securities in Table 4-5 has credit risk. They all carry inflation risk, as their payoffs are in nominal currency. With the exception of the 14% T-bond, none of the securities has timing risk. All the T-notes and T-bonds pay intermediate coupons, so the holder may face some risk of reinvestment; this risk arises because the buyer of the bond will not know the rate at which future coupons can be reinvested.

Price and Yields of Treasuries

In practice, the return measure used extensively is yield to maturity. Current yield and yield to call are also used. To provide a systematic account of these measures, we start with the concept of invoice price of a security.

Invoice price is the price that the buyer of a security has to pay.

Treasury bills are quoted on a discount yield basis. The procedure for obtaining the invoice price from discount quotes is illustrated in Example 4-6.

Example 4-6   Invoice price of a T-bill

The quotations for settlement on December 14, 1990, for U.S. Treasury bills maturing on May 23, 1991, are shown below.

Quote Date	Bid d	Ask d	Yield
12/14/90	6.78	6.76	7.06

A time line showing the settlement date (SD) and the maturity date (MD) is shown next.

$$
\begin{array}{ccc}
SD & & MD \\
|\leftarrow & n \text{ days} & \rightarrow|
\end{array}
$$

The invoice price, P, using the bid discount yield is then calculated as

$$P = 100 \times \left[1 - \frac{n \times d}{360} \right]$$

where the T-bill has n days remaining from the settlement date to maturity and has a discount yield d per \$100 face amount, or

$$P = 100 \times \left[1 - \frac{160 \times 0.0678}{360} \right] = 96.98667$$

$$P = 96.98667.$$

P is a percentage of the par amount of the Treasury bill. T-bills are traded in \$1 million par, so that the invoice price per million will be \$969,867.

For T-notes and T-bonds the quoted price or **flat price** is typically not the invoice price. To arrive at the invoice price we add the accrued interest to the flat price. The **accrued interest** is the coupon income that accrues from the last coupon date to the settlement date of the transaction. Example 4-7 illustrates this.

Example 4-7   Invoice price of a T-bond

The quotations for the December 17, 1991, settlement of a U.S. Treasury bond with an 8% coupon and a maturity date of November 15, 2021, are shown below. Recall that the price quotations are in $\frac{1}{32}$.

Quote Date	Bid	Ask	Yield
12/17/91	102.29	102.31	7.74

First, we compute the accrued interest. To do this, we determine the last coupon date (LCD), which in this case is November 15, 1991. The next coupon date (NCD) is May 15, 1992. So, the number of days between the NCD and the LCD is 182 days. The number of days between the last coupon date and the settlement date, December 17, 1991, is 32 days. The accrued interest is

$$ai_t = \frac{32}{182} \times \frac{1}{2} \times 8 = 0.7032967.$$

The quoted bid price is $102 + \frac{29}{32} = 102.90625$. Then the invoice price on the bid side is $102.90625 + 0.7032967 = 103.60955$. This is the price at which the owner of the security will be able to sell it. The purchase price will be the quoted ask price plus the accrued interest, $102.96875 + 0.7032967 = 103.6720467$.

Once again, these prices are a percentage of the principal amount, which is usually \$1 million. The purchase price per million is therefore \$1,036,720.47 and the selling price, \$1,036,095.47.

We could also have used the approximation of round number of coupons $N = 60$ to compute the price of the bond using equation (4.14) as

$$P = \sum_{j=1}^{60} \frac{\frac{8}{2}}{\left(1 + \frac{0.0774}{2}\right)^j} + \frac{100}{\left(1 + \frac{0.0774}{2}\right)^{60}}$$

$$= \frac{8}{0.0774} + \frac{\left(100 - \frac{8}{0.0774}\right)}{\left(1 + \frac{0.0774}{2}\right)^{60}} = 1{,}030{,}149.62.$$

The yield of a noncallable security is similar to the internal rate of return. The conventions used in the securities industry differ depending on the segment of the fixed-income securities market (Treasury, agencies, MBS, etc.) and on the country (in the U.S. or the markets abroad). We will illustrate the concept using the domestic Treasury market. First, we consider Treasury bills.

Example 4-8   Yield of a T-bill with $n < 182$ days

Consider the same T-bill as in Example 4-6. The **discount yield** is

$$d = \frac{(100 - P)}{100} \times \frac{360}{n}$$

where the T-bill has n days remaining from the settlement date to maturity and sells at a price of P per \$100 face amount. Note that the discount yield has two shortcomings. It uses 360 days per year and it divides the dollar gain (or discount), $100 - P$, by 100. The **bond equivalent yield** or BEY corrects these two shortcomings. For a T-bill with a maturity of less than 182 days the BEY is calculated as

$$\text{BEY} = \frac{(100 - P)}{P} \times \frac{365}{n}. \tag{4.18}$$

Using this formula, we can identify a simple relation between the discount yield d that traders quote and the BEY,

$$\text{BEY} = \frac{365d}{360 - dn}.$$

Thus, using the bid discount quote of 6.78% we get a BEY of 7.0877%, and using the ask discount quote of 6.76% we get a BEY of 7.0662%.

Note that the BEY is always greater than d. This is hardly surprising given that we obtain BEY by dividing the dollar discount by P (which is less than 100) and multiplying the result by 365 (which is more than 360). The reported BEY is based on the ask discount quotes. In measuring the return of a T-bill, it is more meaningful to use the BEY than d.

Equation (4.18) gives the formula for the BEY of a T-bill maturing in fewer than 182 days. When a T-bill has more than six months to maturity, the calculation must reflect the fact that a T-bill does not pay interest, whereas a T-note or T-bond will pay a semi-annual interest. The industry convention is to assume that an interest y is paid after six months and that it is possible to reinvest this interest, that is,

$$P\left(1 + \frac{y}{2}\right) + \frac{y}{365}\left(n - \frac{365}{2}\right)\left(1 + \frac{y}{2}\right)P = 100.$$

Solving for y gives the BEY for T-bills with a maturity of more than 182 days as

$$\text{BEY} = \frac{\frac{-2 \times n}{365} + 2\sqrt{\left(\frac{n}{365}\right)^2 - \left(\frac{2 \times n}{365} - 1\right) \times \left(1 - \frac{100}{P}\right)}}{\frac{2 \times n}{365} - 1}. \tag{4.19}$$

Example 4-9   Yield of a T-bill with $n > 182$ days

The quotations for the April 18, 1991, settlement of a U.S. Treasury bill maturing on April 9, 1992, are shown below.

Quote Date	Bid d	Ask d	Yield
4/18/91	5.94	5.92	6.29

Note that $n = 357$ days and the ask discount yield is $d = 0.0592$. First we calculate the price P as

$$P = 100 \times \left[1 - \frac{357 \times 0.0592}{360}\right] = 94.1293.$$

Substituting this price in Equation (4.19), the formula for the BEY, gives

$$\text{BEY} = \frac{\frac{-2 \times 357}{365} + 2\sqrt{\left(\frac{357}{365}\right)^2 - \left(\frac{2 \times 357}{365} - 1\right) \times \left(1 - \frac{100}{94.1293}\right)}}{\frac{2 \times 357}{365} - 1}.$$

$$\text{BEY} = 6.2802\%.$$

In Figure 4-2, we provide both the discount yields and the bond equivalent yields of a Treasury bill with a May 10, 1993 settlement. Notice that the BEY is always higher than the discount yield and that the difference between these two measures increases with maturity. Table 4-6 provides the T-bill discount yields and BEYs. The on-the-run

FIGURE 4-2   *T-bill Discount Yield and BEY*

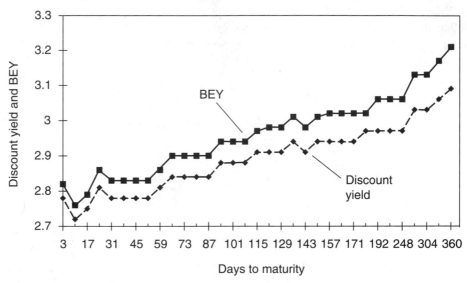

(benchmark issues) issues are in bold for ready reference. Note that the bid-offer spreads for the bills vary from 2 to 4 basis points.

We now turn to Treasury coupon issues that are in their final coupon period. Such Treasury issues are known as **short governments** in the industry. As we showed in Example 4-7, the accrued interest is computed using the number of days x between the last coupon date (LCD) and the next coupon date (NCD). Let z be the number of days between the settlement date (SD) t and the next coupon date, and C be the annual dollar coupon.

LCD	*SD*	*NCD*
	$\mid \leftarrow$	z days $\rightarrow \mid$
$\mid \leftarrow$	x days	$\rightarrow \mid$

Then the accrued interest at the settlement date ai_t is

$$ai_t = C \times \frac{x-z}{2x} \tag{4.20}$$

The invoice price P_t equals the flat price (quoted price) FP_t plus the accrued interest.

The total wealth obtained by selling this security at maturity is $100 + \frac{C}{2}$. The initial investment in the security is the full price paid at the settlement date t, P_t. Hence the rate of return is $\frac{100 + C/2}{P_t} - 1$. Note that this return is earned over a period of z days, so, we could annualize the return as

$$\left(\frac{100 + \frac{C}{2}}{P_t} - 1 \right) \times \frac{365}{z}.$$

TABLE 4–6   *T-bill Yield Curve for Settlement on May 10, 1993*

Maturity Date	Days to Maturity	Bid Yield	Ask Yield	BEY	Bid-Ask Spread (Basis points)
05/13/93	3	2.82	2.78	2.82	4
05/20/93	10	2.74	2.72	2.76	2
05/27/93	17	2.79	2.75	2.79	4
06/03/93	24	2.83	2.81	2.86	2
06/10/93	31	2.8	2.78	2.83	2
06/17/93	38	2.82	2.78	2.83	4
06/24/93	45	2.81	2.78	2.83	3
07/01/93	52	2.82	2.78	2.83	4
07/08/93	59	2.85	2.81	2.86	4
07/15/93	66	2.87	2.84	2.9	3
07/22/93	73	2.88	2.84	2.9	4
07/29/93	80	2.87	2.84	2.9	3
08/05/93	**87**	**2.88**	**2.84**	**2.9**	**4**
08/12/93	94	2.9	2.88	2.94	2
08/19/93	101	2.91	2.88	2.94	3
08/26/93	108	2.92	2.88	2.94	4
09/02/93	115	2.93	2.91	2.97	2
09/09/93	122	2.94	2.91	2.98	3
09/16/93	129	2.95	2.91	2.98	4
09/23/93	136	2.96	2.94	3.01	2
09/30/93	143	2.94	2.91	2.98	3
10/07/93	150	2.97	2.94	3.01	3
10/14/93	157	2.97	2.94	3.02	3
10/21/93	164	2.98	2.94	3.02	4
10/28/93	171	2.97	2.94	3.02	3
11/04/93	**176**	**2.99**	**2.97**	**3.02**	**2**
11/18/93	192	3.01	2.97	3.06	4
12/16/93	220	3.01	2.97	3.06	4
01/13/94	248	3.01	2.97	3.06	4
02/10/94	276	3.05	3.03	3.13	2
03/10/94	304	3.06	3.03	3.13	3
04/07/94	332	3.09	3.06	3.17	3
05/05/94	**360**	**3.11**	**3.09**	**3.21**	**2**

Source: Bloomberg

However, in practice the yield to maturity of short governments is annualized as

$$y = \left(\frac{100 + \frac{C}{2}}{P_t} - 1\right) \times \frac{2x}{z}. \tag{4.21}$$

Similarly, the invoice price is computed using the yield to maturity as

$$P_t = \left(\frac{100 + \frac{C}{2}}{1 + y\frac{z}{2x}}\right). \tag{4.22}$$

Example 4-10 illustrates how these formulae are applied to debt securities.

Example 4-10   Yield of a Short Government

The quotations for the July 18, 1991, settlement of a U.S. Treasury note with a coupon of 7.75% and a maturity date of November 15, 1991, are shown below.

Quote Date	Bid	Ask	Yield
07/18/91	100.19	100.21	5.81

In this example, $c = 7.75$, $x = 184$, $z = 120$, $x - z = (SD - LCD) = 64$, and $FP = 100\frac{19}{32}$. The accrued interest $ai_t = 7.75\frac{64}{2 \times 184} = 1.3478$. Thus the invoice price $P_t = 100\frac{19}{32} + 1.3478 = 101.9415$. Using these in Equation (4.21) gives the yield to maturity

$$y = \left(\frac{100 + \frac{7.75}{2}}{101.9415} - 1 \right) \times \frac{2 \times 184}{120} = 5.816\%. \tag{4.23}$$

The concept of yield to maturity that we have used so far can be extended to Treasury coupon issues with more than one coupon date remaining before the maturity date. Consider a Treasury bond that matures at date T. Let us assume that the settlement date is $t < T$ and that there are N coupon dates remaining. Let z be the number of days between the settlement date and the next coupon date, and x be the number of days between the last coupon date and the next coupon date. Then, given the invoice price P_t, the relation between P_t and y is

$$P_t = \left(\frac{100}{\left(1 + \frac{y}{2}\right)^{N-1+\frac{z}{x}}} \right) + \sum_{j=0}^{j=N-1} \frac{\frac{c}{2}}{\left(1 + \frac{y}{2}\right)^{j+\frac{z}{x}}} \tag{4.24}$$

We can use this formula to find the price P_t given the yield to maturity y or we can solve for y given the price P_t. Equation (4.14) is the price-yield relation for the special case of a round number of coupon payments remaining. Equation (4.24) pertains to the more frequently occurring case. Example 4-11 illustrates its application in determining the yield to maturity of a Treasury bond. As in Example 4-7, this example shows a situation in which the settlement date falls between two coupon dates.

Example 4-11   Yield of a Treasury Bond

The quotations for the January 9, 1992, settlement of a U.S. Treasury bond with a coupon of 8.00% and a maturity date of November 15, 2021, are shown below.

Quote Date	Bid	Ask	Yield
01/09/92	106.30	107.00	7.41

Typically, bond calculators such as the HP-12C are available to handle problems of this sort. Using the bid price, we calculate the invoice price as $P_t = 106\frac{30}{32} + 1.20879 = 108.1463$. Then using Equation (4.24), $y = 7.418\%$. Using the ask price, we calculate the invoice price as $P_t = 107 + 1.20879 = 108.20879$. The yield corresponding to this price is $y = 7.413\%$. Standard spreadsheet packages such as EXCEL have functions that calculate yield to maturity once all the other information has been provided.

Earlier, in Table 4-4 using Equation 4.11, we computed the current yield y_c for different Treasury securities. This can also be expressed as

$$y_c = \frac{c \times 100}{P_t} \tag{4.25}$$

As we noted in Example 4-4, loosely speaking, the current yield measures the immediate cash-flow yield and is equivalent to the yield to maturity only if the security is a perpetuity. We can compute the current yield of the bond in Example 4-11 as

$$y_c = \frac{8}{108.1463} = 7.397\%. \tag{4.26}$$

Some bonds are callable. For such bonds, it is customary to also calculate **yield to call.** Consider the callable bond in Table 4-5 which has a coupon of 14%, matures on November 15, 2011, but is callable on November 15, 2006 for the first time. After the first call date, the bond is callable on every coupon date. The call price is 100. The yield to call is calculated assuming that the bond is callable on the first call date. We report in Table 4-5 the yield to maturity of the bond to be 7.565%. For this bond, using the flat price $= 164\frac{18}{32}$, coupon $= 14\%$, settlement date of September 10, 1992, and the first call date November 15, 2006, as the maturity date we get yield to call to be 6.821%.

In practice, when market yields are below the coupon rate, it is customary to report the yield to call. The reasoning is that the bond is likely to be called as the yields are relatively low. On the other hand, when the market yields are above the coupon rate, typically yield to maturity is reported since the likelihood of a call is low.

The T-note and T-bond prices and yields are shown in Tables 4-7 and 4-8, respectively. We now introduce **yield curve,** a concept used extensively in the industry. Yield curve is the plot of yield to maturity (along the y-axis) against the time to maturity shown as the maturity date (along the x-axis). The T-note and T-bond yield curves for the data in Tables 4-7 and 4-8, as well as the overall yield curves, are shown in Figures 4-3, 4-4, and 4-5.

Table 4-7 highlights all the on-the-run issues in the T-notes sector of the yield curve. The bid-offer spreads are in $\frac{1}{32}$. The yield increases from 3.25% at the lowest maturity to 5.87% at the highest maturity. As Figure 4-3 attests, the T-note yield curve is steeper than the bill sector of the yield curve shown in Figure 4-2.

TABLE 4-7   *T-note Prices and Yields, for Settlement on May 10, 1993*

Maturity Date	Coupon Rate	Bid Price	Ask Price	BEY	Bid-Ask Spread (in $\frac{1}{32}$)
06/30/94	8.50000	105.68750	105.81250	3.25	4
09/30/94	8.50000	106.71875	106.84375	3.41	4
12/31/94	7.62500	106.28125	106.40625	3.56	4
04/15/95	8.37500	108.50000	108.62500	3.70	4
04/30/95	**3.87500**	**100.15625**	**100.25000**	**3.74**	**3**
05/30/95	5.87500	103.96875	104.09375	3.74	4
07/15/95	8.87500	110.37500	110.50000	3.80	4
10/15/95	8.62500	110.68750	110.81250	3.91	4
01/31/96	**7.50000**	**108.59375**	**108.71875**	**4.08**	**4**
02/15/96	4.62500	101.25000	101.34375	4.10	3
03/31/96	7.75000	109.43750	109.56250	4.20	4
05/31/96	7.62500	109.37500	109.50000	4.27	4
09/30/96	7.00000	107.90625	108.03125	4.42	4
12/31/96	6.12500	105.40625	105.53125	4.46	4
05/15/97	8.50000	113.65625	113.78125	4.69	4
10/15/97	8.75000	115.28125	115.40625	4.84	4
01/15/98	7.87500	112.00000	112.12500	4.94	4
04/30/98	**5.12500**	**100.46875**	**100.56250**	**5.00**	**3**
10/15/98	7.12500	109.21875	109.34375	5.13	4
01/15/99	6.37500	105.50000	105.62500	5.22	4
05/15/99	9.12500	119.31250	119.43570	5.31	4
11/15/99	7.87500	113.09375	113.21875	5.44	4
02/15/00	8.50000	116.62500	116.75000	5.50	4
04/15/00	**5.50000**	**99.87500**	**99.96875**	**5.50**	**3**
08/15/00	8.75000	118.43750	118.56250	5.60	4
11/15/00	8.50000	117.15625	117.28125	5.65	4
02/15/01	7.75000	112.62500	112.75000	5.69	4
05/15/01	8.00000	114.31250	114.43750	5.73	4
08/15/01	7.87500	113.56250	113.68750	5.77	4
11/13/01	7.50000	111.06250	111.18750	5.81	4
02/15/03	**6.25000**	**102.71875**	**102.81250**	**5.87**	**3**

Source: Bloomberg

TABLE 4-8   *T-bond Prices and Yields for Settlement on May 10, 1993*

Maturity Date	Coupon Rate	Bid Price	Ask Price	BEY	Bid-Ask Spread (in $\frac{1}{32}$)	Callable(C)/ Noncallable(NC)
05/15/2005	12.000	148.96875	149.15625	6.15	6	NC
08/15/2005	10.750	138.81250	139.00000	6.17	6	NC
02/15/2006	9.375	127.43750	127.62500	6.21	6	NC
02/15/2007	7.625	109.81250	110.00000	6.13	6	C
11/15/2007	7.875	111.78125	111.96875	6.19	6	C
08/15/2008	8.375	115.93750	116.12500	6.22	6	C
11/15/2008	8.750	119.06250	119.25000	6.23	6	C
05/15/2009	9.125	122.50000	122.68750	6.24	6	C
11/15/2009	10.375	133.40625	133.59375	6.24	6	C
02/15/2010	11.750	145.06250	145.25000	6.26	6	C
05/15/2010	10.000	131.00000	131.18750	6.27	6	C
11/15/2010	12.750	155.43750	155.56250	6.27	4	C
05/15/2011	13.875	166.59375	166.78125	6.28	6	C
11/15/2011	14.000	169.21875	169.40625	6.30	6	C
11/15/2012	10.375	135.93750	136.06250	6.50	4	C
08/15/2013	12.000	152.68750	152.81250	6.49	4	C
05/15/2014	13.250	166.09375	166.28125	6.52	6	C
08/15/2014	12.500	159.06250	159.18750	6.53	4	C
11/15/2015	11.750	151.78125	151.90625	6.56	4	C
02/15/2015	11.250	150.21875	150.40625	6.78	6	NC
08/15/2015	10.625	143.31250	143.43750	6.81	4	NC
11/15/2015	9.875	134.75000	134.87500	6.82	4	NC
02/15/2016	9.250	127.46875	127.59375	6.84	4	NC
05/15/2016	7.250	104.40625	104.53125	6.86	4	NC
11/15/2016	7.500	107.15625	107.28125	6.87	4	NC
05/15/2017	8.750	121.90625	122.03125	6.86	4	NC
08/15/2017	8.875	123.43750	123.56250	6.87	4	NC
05/15/2018	9.125	126.75000	126.87500	6.86	4	NC
11/15/2018	9.000	125.34375	125.46875	6.87	4	NC
02/15/2019	8.875	123.87500	124.00000	6.87	4	NC
08/15/2019	8.215	114.81250	114.93750	6.89	4	NC
02/15/2020	8.500	119.56250	119.68750	6.88	4	NC
05/15/2020	8.750	122.75000	122.87500	6.88	4	NC
05/15/2020	8.750	122.78125	122.90625	6.88	4	NC
02/15/2021	7.875	112.09375	112.21875	6.88	4	NC
05/15/2021	8.125	115.31250	115.43750	6.88	4	NC
08/15/2021	8.125	115.31250	115.43750	6.88	4	NC
11/15/2021	8.000	114.00000	114.12500	6.86	4	NC
08/15/2022	7.250	104.71875	104.81250	6.87	3	NC
11/15/2022	7.6250	109.65625	109.78125	6.85	4	NC
02/15/2023	**7.1250**	**104.00000**	**104.09375**	**6.80**	**3**	**NC**

Source: Bloomberg

FIGURE 4-3   *T-note Yield Curve (See Table 4-7)*

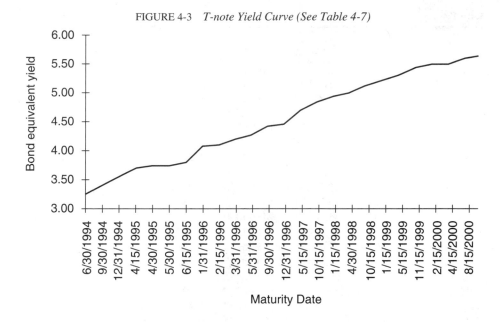

FIGURE 4-4   *T-bond Yield Curve (See Table 4-8)*

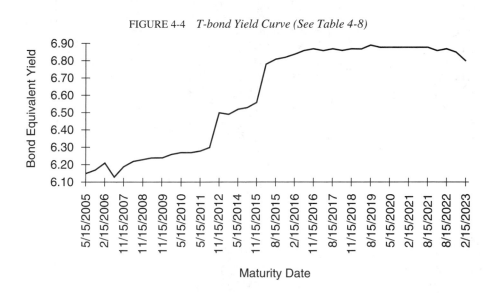

Price-Yield Relationship. Price and yield have an inverse relationship, as was shown earlier in the chapter; as the price increases, the yield falls, and vice versa. We can see this relationship clearly by varying the yield in Equation (4.24) and computing the prices associated with each yield. For the Treasury bond in Example 4-11, this process results in Table 4-9.

FIGURE 4-5   *Overall Yield Curve (Settlement on May 10, 1993)*

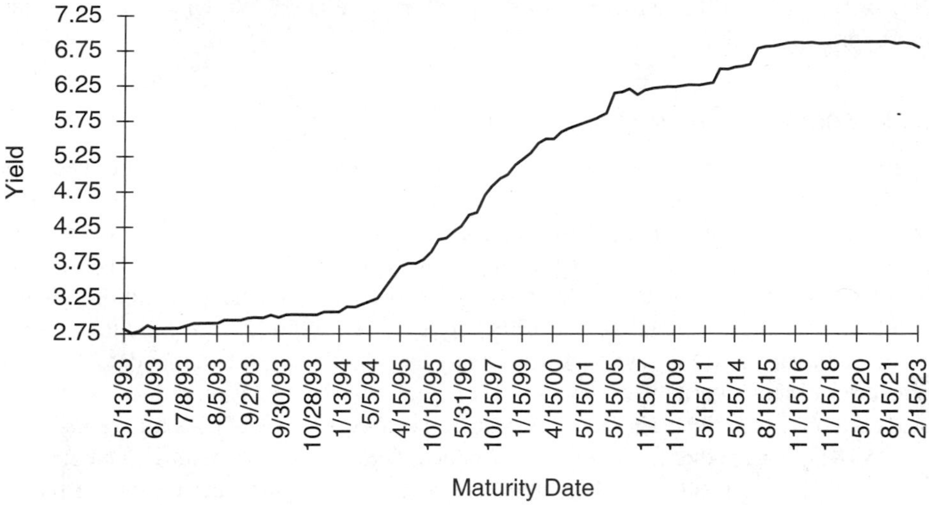

	Yield	Price
	10.00%	81.0625
	9.50%	85.1875
	9.00%	89.6875
	8.50%	94.5938
	8.00%	100.0000
	7.50%	105.9063
	7.41%	**107.0000**
	7.00%	112.4375
	6.50%	119.6563
	6.00%	127.6250

TABLE 4-9
*Price Versus Yield
to Maturity of a T-bond*

Settlement date: January 9, 1992
Maturity date: November 15, 2021
Coupon: 8.00%

The price column reports the flat prices. The bold row represents the price and
the yield to maturity on January 9, 1992.

The actual price of the T-bond and its actual yield to maturity for the settlement date
are indicated in boldface. Note that as the yield increases from 7.41% to 10%, the price
falls from 107.00 to 81.0625. Note that the rate of change in price for a given change in
yield depends on the level of the yield; the price change is greater at low levels of yield
and lower at high levels of yield. For a 50-basis-point drop from 6.50% to 6.00% in
yield, the price increases by almost 8 full points. However, for the 50-basis-point drop

from 10.00% to 9.50% in yield, the price increases by only about 4.2 points. This property is referred to as the **convexity** of the price-yield relation. We will investigate this more formally later.

Observations on Yields

The yield to maturity is based on the internal rate of return, but the industry conventions about its calculation change depending on the market segment and the security. For example, the day-count methods differ from market to market. The Treasury market convention is based on actual day counts, while the corporate market convention is based on 30/360 day counts. In the Treasury market, the industry convention ignores holidays. If the maturity date of a security happens to be a holiday, the yield to maturity is still calculated as if the cash flow at maturity date would be paid on that date. In addition, the yield to maturity uses the number of days between the last coupon date and the next coupon date as the basis for its computation (see equation 4.24). As this varies from 181 to 184 days, another inaccuracy is introduced into the yield to maturity calculation.

A more fundamental problem arises from the fact that the internal rate of return implicitly assumes a reinvestment rate equal to the currently prevailing (on the settlement date) internal rate of return throughout the life of the security. To see that this is the case, let us consider the price-yield relationship in a simplified setting in which t is the settlement date, T is the maturity date and the coupons are paid at intervals of six months. Assuming that there are N round semicoupon payments remaining, $N = 2T$. The price is then

$$P_t = \frac{C}{\left(1 + \frac{y}{2}\right)} + \frac{C}{\left(1 + \frac{y}{2}\right)^2} + \frac{C}{\left(1 + \frac{y}{2}\right)^3} + \cdots + \frac{C + 100}{\left(1 + \frac{y}{2}\right)^{2T}}. \qquad (4.27)$$

Cross multiplication results in

$$P_t \times \left(1 + \frac{y}{2}\right)^{2T} = C \times \left(1 + \frac{y}{2}\right)^{2T-1} + C \times \left(1 + \frac{y}{2}\right)^{2T-2} + \cdots + C + 100. \qquad (4.28)$$

The left-hand side of Equation (4.28) represents the cash flow that may be obtained by investing the price for a period of T years at a yield to maturity of y. On the right-hand side, we find that all coupons are assumed to be reinvested at y. This is a serious shortcoming in the use of the yield to maturity as a measure of return. Nevertheless, as explained at the outset, associated with every price is a yield. In this sense, the yield to maturity is best thought of as a way to convey the price or the value of the security.

RISK AND DEBT SECURITIES

In this section, we define several measures of price risk. First, we derive analytical expressions that assume a round number of coupons. Then, we consider applications to Treasuries that do not have a round number of coupons.

Price Risk

Given a bond with a round number of coupon payments remaining, the price risk can be calculated exactly. We define the price risk as $-\frac{\partial P}{\partial y}$, where the negative sign denotes that the price decreases as the yield increases. Differentiating Equation (4.14) with respect to y and simplifying, we get the price-risk formula,

$$-\frac{\partial P}{\partial y} = \frac{C}{y^2}\left[1 - \frac{1}{\left(1 + \frac{y}{2}\right)^N}\right] + \frac{N\left(100 - \frac{C}{y}\right)}{2\left(1 + \frac{y}{2}\right)^{N+1}}. \tag{4.29}$$

Typically, the price risk is scaled by a factor of 100 to reflect a change in price for a percentage change in yield. We denote this measure of price risk as Δ_p and write it as

$$\Delta_p = \frac{-\frac{\partial P}{\partial y}}{100} = \frac{1}{100}\left(\frac{C}{y^2}\left[1 - \frac{1}{\left(1 + \frac{y}{2}\right)^N}\right] + \frac{N\left(100 - \frac{C}{y}\right)}{2\left(1 + \frac{y}{2}\right)^{N+1}}\right). \tag{4.30}$$

This price-risk measure is the slope of the tangent to the price-yield curve at yield y.

Example 4-12

Consider a bond with a dollar coupon of $C = 10$ per annum paid semi-annually and with 80 round coupons remaining ($N = 80$). For this forty-year bond, the price risk at a yield of 9% ($y = 0.09$) is computed as

$$\Delta_p = \frac{-\frac{\partial P}{\partial y}}{100} = \frac{1}{100}\left(\frac{10}{0.09^2}\left[1 - \frac{1}{\left(1 + \frac{0.09}{2}\right)^{80}}\right] + \frac{80\left(100 - \frac{10}{0.09}\right)}{2\left(1 + \frac{0.09}{2}\right)^{81}}\right) \tag{4.31}$$

$$\Delta_p = 11.86.$$

In the same way we can compute the price risk for each yield level and plot the result, as shown in Figure 4-6. Notice that the price risk is higher at lower yield levels and progressively falls as the yield increases.

This is most easily seen when N approaches ∞ and

$$\Delta_p = \frac{1}{100} \times \frac{C}{y^2}.$$

When $C = 10$ and $y = 0.09$, the price risk of the perpetuity is $\Delta_p = \frac{1}{100} \times \frac{10}{0.09^2} = 12.346$. Note that this price risk is not significantly different from that of the bond with 40 years maturity. Figure 4-7 compares the price risks of a 10%, forty-year bond and of a perpetuity. Note that at yields near the coupon, the price risks are indistinguishable. Only at very low-level yields do we find that the perpetuity becomes much more convex than the forty-year bond.

FIGURE 4-6   *Price Risk Versus Yield*

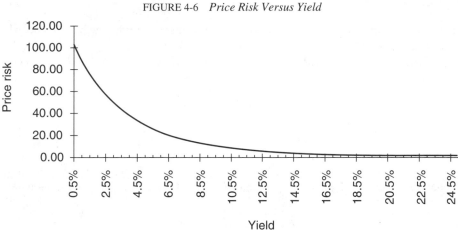

FIGURE 4-7   *Price Risks of a Forty-Year Bond and of a Perpetuity*

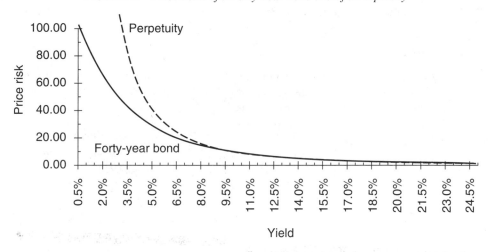

PVBP or Dollar Value of 0.01

The measure of price risk Δ_p is useful. In the industry, several related measures are used; one of these is the **price value of a basis point** (PVBP), defined as the change in the price of a bond per basis point change in its yield. Given the definition of Δ_p, it is clear that

$$\text{PVBP (per 100\% of par)} = \frac{\Delta_p}{100}.$$

Sometimes PVBP is expressed in dollars per million. In such cases,

$$\text{PVBP (per \$1 million par)} = \Delta_p \times 100. \tag{4.32}$$

Example 4-13

Consider the bond in Example 4-12, with a dollar coupon of $C = 10$ per annum paid semi-annually and with 80 round coupons remaining ($N = 80$). For this bond, the price risk at a yield of 9% ($y = 0.09$) was found in Example 4-12 to be 11.86. By using the relationship between PVBP and Δ_p in Equation (4.32) we can compute

$$\text{PVBP (per \$1 million par)} = 11.86 \times 100 = \$1{,}186 \text{ per million.}$$

PVBP is also referred to as the dollar value of 0.01 or DV01.

Example 4-14

Consider the T-bond in Example 4-11. Its price P_1 at yield $y_1 = 7.4138\%$ is 106.9914. Then the price P_2 is 106.8651 when the yield is $y_2 = 7.4238\%$ (one basis point over y_1). Let $\Delta P = P_1 - P_2$ and $\Delta y = y_1 - y_2$. Then the PVBP is defined as

$$\text{PVBP} = -\frac{\Delta P}{\Delta y} \times 10{,}000. \tag{4.33}$$

We multiply by 10,000 to express this in dollars per million dollar par. The negative sign simply reflects the fact that prices and yields move in opposite direction.

For this example, 0.1262865 is the change in price for a one basis-point change in yield, which is one one-hundredth of one percent and the PVBP = 1262.865.

By Taylor series approximation, we can write the change in price as

$$\Delta P = \frac{\partial P}{\partial y} \times \Delta y + \frac{1}{2}\frac{\partial^2 P}{\partial y^2} \times \Delta y^2 + o(3).$$

where $o(3)$ refers to terms in Δy raised to an exponent of 3 or more. If we were to ignore quadratic terms and beyond, then we get the useful approximation that

$$\Delta P \approx \frac{\partial P}{\partial y} \times \Delta y. \tag{4.34}$$

In terms of Example 4-14, $P_2 \approx P_1 - (\text{PVBP} \times \frac{1}{10{,}000})$ or $P_2 = 106.9914 - 0.1262865 = 106.8651$.

Example 4-15   PVBP of Treasury Bills

The PVBP of Treasury bills is computed in practice as (remembering that a basic point is $\frac{1}{100}$th of 1%)

$$\text{PVBP} = \frac{z}{360} \times 1{,}000{,}000 \times \frac{1}{100 \times 100}.$$

Recall that z is the number of days between the settlement date and the next coupon date (or the maturity date, in the case of T-bills), or $PVBP = \frac{z}{360} \times 100$. Hence, a ninety-day T-bill will have a PVBP of $25 per million par of the security.

Duration

Another concept widely used to measure risk is duration. Two related measures are used in the industry, **Macaulay duration** and **modified duration.** Macaulay duration has several interpretations:

*   Duration is the **discounted time-weighted cash flow of the security divided by the price** of the security. In this sense, the duration measures the average time taken by the security, on a discounted basis, to pay back the original investment; the longer the duration, the greater the risk.
*   Duration is the **price elasticity,** which is the percentage change in price for a percentage change in yield; in this sense, the greater the duration of a security, the greater the risk of the security.
*   Duration is the **fulcrum in the timeline of security's life,** where the reinvested cash flows exactly balance out the present value of the remaining future cash flows.

We will consider all these interpretations in detail in the context of an example in Table 4-10.

Duration as Discounted Time-weighted Cash Flows. Consider a zero-coupon bond with a maturity of three years yielding 5% (yield to maturity). Consider also a three-year bond paying a coupon of 5% per annum also yielding 5% yield to maturity. These two bonds are represented in Table 4-10 below. For simplicity we assume annual coupons.

The price of the three-year zero is $\frac{100}{1.05^3} = 86.3838$. The discount factors for the first three years are:

$$\frac{1}{1.05} = 0.952381,$$

$$\frac{1}{1.05^2} = 0.907029,$$

and

$$\frac{1}{1.05^3} = 0.863838.$$

The discounted time-weighted cash flow definition of duration works as follows for the zero coupon bond. Each cash flow is multiplied by the number of years elapsed before it is paid. Then the time-weighted cash flow is discounted back. For year 1, this approach produces

$$0 \times 1 \times 0.952381.$$

This is due to the fact that at year 1, no cash flow is paid.

TABLE 4-10   *Understanding Duration and Its Interpretations*

Duration and Its Interpretation

(Duration as a measure of time to cash flows)				(Duration as a measure of time to cash flows)			
Coupon = 0% **Price =** 86.3838		**Yield =**	5%	**Coupon =** 5% **Price =** 100.00		**Yield =**	5%
Year	0	1	2	3	Year	0	1	2	3

Year	0	1	2	3	Year	0	1	2	3
Cash flows	−86.38	0	0	100	Cash flows −100.00		5	5	105
Time-weighted cash flows		0	0	300	Time-weighted cash flows		5	10	315
Discount factor		0.952381	0.907029478	0.863838	Discount factor		0.952381	0.907029478	0.863838
Discounted Time-weighted cash flows		0	0	259.1513	Discounted Time-weighted cash flows		4.761905	9.070294785	272.1088
Sum of Discounted Time-weighted cash flows				259.1513	Sum of Discounted Time-weighted cash flows				285.941
Duration				3	Duration				2.85941

Duration as Price Elasticity

Price at 4.99%	86.4084		Price at 4.99%	100.02724
PVBP	(86.4084 − 86.3838) · 10,000 = **246.00**		PVBP	(100.02724 − 100) · 10,000 = **272.38**
Duration $\frac{\text{PVBP}}{\text{P}} \cdot (1 + y)$	2.9901		Duration $\frac{\text{PVBP}}{\text{P}} \cdot (1 + y)$	2.8599

Duration as a Fulcrum Balancing the Present Value of Cash Flows

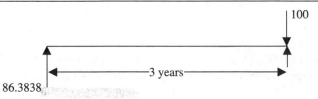

(1) The price P = 86.3838 exerts a force equal to   86.3838 × 3 =   259.1514
(2) The present value of 100 exerts a force equal to   86.3838 × 3 =   259.1514

Duration as a Fulcrum Balancing the Present Value of Cash Flows

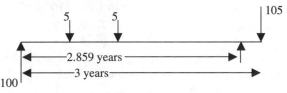

(1) The price P = 100 exerts a force equal to   100 × 2.859   285.9
(2) The present value of all cash inflows
        exert a force equal to   PV(5) · 1 + PV(5) · 2 + PV(105) · 3 =   285.9

For year 2, this approach produces

$$0 \times 2 \times 0.907029,$$

Again, this is due to the fact that at year 2, no cash flow is paid.
For year 3, this approach produces

$$100 \times 3 \times 0.863838.$$

This is because at year 3, the zero coupon bond pays 100.
The total of all these discounted time-weighted cash flows divided by the price of the bond is the duration of the bond:

$$D = \frac{0 \times 1 \times 0.952381 + 0 \times 2 \times 0.907029 + 100 \times 3 \times 0.863838}{86.3838}$$

$$= 3 \text{ years for the three-year zero-coupon bond.}$$

We can produce similar calculations for the coupon bond. Its duration can be computed as

$$D = \frac{5 \times 1 \times 0.952381 + 5 \times 2 \times 0.907029 + 105 \times 3 \times 0.863838.}{100}.$$

This can be simplified as

$$D = \frac{4.761905 + 9.07029478 + 272.1088}{100} = \frac{285.941}{100} = 2.859.$$

Note that the coupon bond has a duration which is less than the zero-coupon bond even though both bonds have the same maturity of three years and the same yield. This is because a coupon bond pays its interest payments well before maturity, leading to a lower duration.

Duration as Elasticity of Interest Rates. **Duration is also the price elasticity, which is the percentage change in price for a percentage change in yield.** Formally, the elasticity measure of duration is referred to as the Macaulay duration and is represented by

$$D = -\frac{\partial P}{\partial y} \frac{1 + y}{P}. \qquad (4.35)$$

Another related measure is **modified duration** (MD). **Modified duration is the percentage change in price for a change in yield.** Modified duration is denoted as

$$MD = -\frac{\partial P}{\partial y} \frac{1}{P}. \qquad (4.36)$$

For the example in Table 4-10, we can use these equations to compute the Macaulay and modified durations. Note that the duration in Equation (4.35) can be represented as

$$\frac{PVBP \times (1 + y)}{P}.$$

For the zero-coupon bond, PVBP is 246.86 per million dollars par amount. Dividing this by its price and multiplying the result by $(1 + y)$ we get the duration as

$$D = \frac{246.86 \times 1.05}{86.3838} = 3$$

In the same manner, we can compute the duration of the coupon bond. The PVBP of the coupon bond is 272.38. Its duration is

$$D = \frac{272.38 \times 1.05}{100} = 2.85.$$

The modified duration for the zero-coupon bond is

$$MD = \frac{246.86}{86.3838} = 2.857$$

and the modified duration of the coupon bond is

$$MD = \frac{272.38}{100} = 2.72.$$

Duration as a Fulcrum of Cash Flows. Consider in Table 4-10 the investment of $86.3838 in the zero coupon bond. It provides a cash flow of 100 after three years and nothing in between. After how many years from the date of investment will the investment in the zero (net of any reinvested cash inflows) be exactly equal to the present value of the *remaining* future cash inflows? In the case of zero coupon bond, this question is easy to answer. The only future cash inflow is $100 after three years. The current investment of $86.3838 will exactly grow to $100 after three years. The cash price of the zero and the present value of the future cash flows exert exactly the same force at three years which is the duration of the zero. To see this note that

$$86.3838 \times 3 = PV(100) \times 3$$

Hence the fulcrum is after three years. This is pictured in Table 4-10.

For the coupon bond, this is a bit trickier. As we consider any future date as a possible fulcrum, there may be some cash inflows from the security before that future date. These cash inflows have to be reinvested. Note that in Table 4-10, we have the fulcrum at 2.859 years. This is arrived at by balancing two sets of cash flows as shown below: Investment carried forward at 5% *net* of all the coupon cash flows carried forward:

$$100 \times (1.05)^{2.859} - 5 \times (1.05)^{1.859} - 5 \times (1.05)^{0.859} = 104.285$$

Present value of the terminal cash flows:

$$\frac{105}{1.05^{3-2.859}} = 104.285$$

Of course, this equality will hold at any other point as well. But a comparison of the forces exerted indicated that duration is the fulcrum as is evident from the equation next.

$$100 \times 2.859 = PV(5) \times 1 + PV(5) \times 2 + PV(105) \times 3$$

Generalizations—Price-Yield and Duration

It is useful to represent the price-yield relationship in Equation (4.27) in a compact form using the summation sign as in Equation (4.37), where C is the dollar coupon in each coupon period and $2T$ is the number of coupon periods.

$$P_t = \sum_{j=1}^{2T-1} \frac{C}{\left(1 + \frac{y}{2}\right)^j} + \frac{C + 100}{\left(1 + \frac{y}{2}\right)^{2T}} \tag{4.37}$$

Differentiating Equation (4.37) with respect to y produces

$$\frac{\partial P_t}{\partial y} = \sum_{j=1}^{2T-1} \frac{-C \times \frac{j}{2}}{\left(1 + \frac{y}{2}\right)^{j+1}} - \frac{(C + 100) \times \frac{2T}{2}}{\left(1 + \frac{y}{2}\right)^{2T+1}}.$$

Dropping the time subscript, we can write the price sensitivity as

$$\frac{\partial P}{\partial y} = -\frac{1}{2\left(1 + \frac{y}{2}\right)} \left[\sum_{j=1}^{2T-1} \frac{Cj}{\left(1 + \frac{y}{2}\right)^j} + \frac{(C + 100)2T}{\left(1 + \frac{y}{2}\right)^{2T}} \right]. \tag{4.38}$$

Macaulay duration with semi-annual compounding is given by

$$D = -\frac{\partial P}{\partial y} \frac{\left(1 + \frac{y}{2}\right)}{P}.$$

Recall that duration (D) can be considered to be the discounted average time to the security's future cash flows. Equation (4.38) can be rewritten as

$$\frac{\partial P}{\partial y} \frac{1}{P} = -\frac{1}{2\left(1 + \frac{y}{2}\right)P} \left[\sum_{j=1}^{2T-1} \frac{Cj}{\left(1 + \frac{y}{2}\right)^j} + \frac{(C + 100)2T}{\left(1 + \frac{y}{2}\right)^{2T}} \right].$$

Rearranging, we get

$$-\frac{\partial P}{\partial y} \frac{\left(1 + \frac{y}{2}\right)}{P} = \frac{1}{2P} \left[\sum_{j=1}^{2T-1} \frac{Cj}{\left(1 + \frac{y}{2}\right)^j} + \frac{(C + 100)2T}{\left(1 + \frac{y}{2}\right)^{2T}} \right] \tag{4.39}$$

or,

$$D = \frac{1}{2P} \left[\sum_{j=1}^{2T-1} \frac{Cj}{\left(1 + \frac{y}{2}\right)^j} + \frac{(C + 100)2T}{\left(1 + \frac{y}{2}\right)^{2T}} \right]. \tag{4.40}$$

Note that the right-hand side is the time-weighted discounted cash flows expressed as a fraction of the price of the security. We can express duration in units of years by rewriting Equation (4.40) slightly as

$$D = \frac{1}{2P}\left[\sum_{j=1}^{2T}\frac{C_j j}{\left(1+\frac{y}{2}\right)^j}\right] \tag{4.41}$$

where $C_j = C$ for $j = 1, 2, \cdots, 2T - 1$ and $C_{2T} = C + 100$. Let us set $x_j = \frac{1}{P}\left[\frac{C_j}{(1+y/2)^j}\right]$ so that

$$D = \frac{1}{2}\sum_{j=1}^{2T}(x_j \times j) \tag{4.42}$$

It is easy to verify that $\sum_{j=1}^{2T}x_j = 1$ and that therefore we can interpret duration as the weighted average time to future cash flows. The units will be years. Example 4-16 illustrates how to use Equation (4.42) to calculate duration.

Example 4-16   Macaulay duration

Examine Table 4-11. Column 3 lists the timing of the cash flows in days from the settlement date. Column 4 expresses this in semi-annual periods by dividing the

TABLE 4-11   *Macaulay Duration of a T-note*

(1) Coupon Dates	(2) Cash Flows, C	(3) Number of Days from Settlement	(4) Semi-annual Periods from Settlement, j	(5) Time-weighted Cashflows, $C \times j$	(6) Discount Factor, $\frac{1}{\left(1+\frac{y}{2}\right)^j}$	(7) x_j
2/28/93	21250	171	0.9448	20076	0.9824	0.02068
8/31/93	21250	355	1.9613	41678	0.9637	0.02028
2/28/94	21250	536	2.9613	62928	0.9458	0.01991
8/31/94	1021250	720	3.9779	4062431	0.9278	0.93849

Settlement date: September 10, 1992
Maturity date: August 31, 1994
Coupon: 4.25%
Yield to maturity: 3.801%
Flat price: 100.84375
Accrued interest: 0.1174

days by 181 to find the current basis. The time-weighted cash flows are shown in column 5. The discount factors are shown in column 6. The weights x_j are presented in column 7. Given this data, the present value of the time-weighted cash flows is computed as

$$20,076 \times 0.9824 + 41,678 \times 0.9637 + 62,928 \times 0.9458 + 4,062,431 \times 0.9278$$
$$= 3,888,528.$$

The invoice price (per million dollars par) of the bond is $1,009,612.

The Macaulay duration can be then obtained by dividing the present value of the time-weighted cash flows by the invoice price

$$D = -0.5 \times \frac{3888528}{1009612} = 1.93 \text{ years.}$$

Note that we can get the same results by applying Equation (4.42):

$$D = \frac{1}{2}[0.9448 \times 0.02068 + 1.9613 \times 0.02028 + 2.9613 \times 0.01991$$
$$+ 3.9779 \times 0.93849]$$
$$= 1.926.$$

Turning to modified duration, it is easy to verify that

$$MD = \frac{D}{\left(1 + \frac{y}{2}\right)}.$$

Referring back to the Taylor series approximation in Equation (4.34), ignoring the quadratic terms and beyond, we can see that

$$\frac{\Delta P}{P} \approx \frac{\partial P}{\partial y} \times \frac{1}{P}\Delta y.$$

Using Equation (4.36), this is the same as

$$\frac{\Delta P}{P} \approx -MD\Delta y. \tag{4.43}$$

For Example 4-16, we can compute the modified duration as $MD = \frac{1.926}{1 + 0.03801/2}$ $= 1.89$.

For the special case with N round semi-annual coupons remaining, the analytical formulae for Macaulay and modified durations are obtained using Equation (4.30) in

$$D = \frac{PVBP}{P} \times \left(1 + \frac{y}{2}\right) = \frac{\Delta_p \times 100}{P} \times \left(1 + \frac{y}{2}\right)$$

$$MD = \frac{PVBP}{P} = \frac{\Delta_p \times 100}{P}.$$

Example 4-17   Duration of Treasury Securities

The quotations for the September 10, 1992, settlement of on-the-run U.S. Treasury notes and bonds are provided in Table 4-12. For each security, we also indicate the MD and the PVBP.

TABLE 4-12   *PVBP and Modified Duration*

Security	Coupon	Maturity	Yield to Maturity	MD	PVBP
T-note	4.25%	8/31/1994	3.801%	1.88	189
T-note	4.625%	8/15/1995	4.269%	2.71	274
T-note	5.625%	8/31/1997	5.188%	4.29	438
T-note	6.375%	7/15/1999	5.753%	5.47	571
T-note	6.375%	8/15/2002	6.289%	7.25	733
T-bond	7.25%	8/15/2022	7.216%	12.12	1223

PVBPs are calculated by using the yields. First, the price is calculated. Then the yield is increased by 1 basis point and the price is recalculated at the new yield. The price difference is multiplied by 10,000 to get PVBP.

Note that,
$$MD = \frac{PVBP}{P}.$$

This can be easily verified from the Table 4-12. Consider the T-bond. The accrued interest is 0.5122, so the invoice price is $100\frac{13}{32} + 0.5122 = 100.91845$. The PVBP per million dollars face is 1,223. Hence the modified duration is $\frac{1,223}{100.91845} = 12.12$.

Consider Equation (4.40), which is the definition of Macaulay duration. Set $C = 0$ in Equation (4.40). Recall that for a zero coupon bond, the price is given by

$$P = \frac{100}{\left(1 + \frac{y}{2}\right)^{2T}}.$$

Substituting this in Equation (4.40), we note that for a zero coupon bond $D = T$.

The fact that the duration of zero coupon bonds is equal to their maturity is very important. Thirty-year zeroes are available in the market; they will have a duration of 30 years. If a company (such as an insurance company) has liabilities with a long duration, then by buying thirty-year zero coupon bonds, it can match the duration of the liabilities to the duration of assets. Stated differently, the interest-rate sensitivity of the assets will be matched to the interest rate sensitivity of the liabilities. This is known as asset-liability management and we will explore this concept in detail in Chapter 11.

Coupon Effect on Duration

The duration measure that we have developed is extensively used in the industry. A feature of this measure is that the duration undergoes discrete changes when coupons are paid. This is shown in Figure 4-8.

FIGURE 4-8   *Effect of Coupon Payments on Duration, Coupon Dates: 5/15/94, 11/15/94, and 5/15/95*

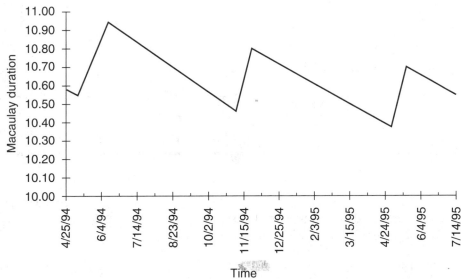

Using the third interpretation of duration from Table 4-10, it is easy to see that when a coupon is paid, the fulcrum has to move more to the right to balance the present value of cash flows. This increases the duration. As time passes, the maturity of the bond declines, leading to a decrease in duration. These observations explain why we observe a sawtooth pattern in the duration of bonds over time.

Properties of Duration and PVBP

The finding that the duration of a zero-coupon bond is equal to its maturity means that the zero-coupon bond is the most interest-rate-elastic security for a given maturity class. It is easy to verify that duration is generally increasing in maturity, decreasing in coupons and yield to maturity as shown earlier. The duration of coupon bonds will be less than their maturity. Clearly, as time passes, duration will change. This requires some attention in portfolios of assets and liabilities whose durations are held the same. Note in Table 4-12 that the security with the highest duration (or PVBP) also had the highest yield to maturity.

Portfolio Risk Measures

So far, we have looked at the risk measures of a single security. It is important to see whether these concepts can be generalized to many securities. Consider a portfolio consisting of n_1 units of security 1, n_2 of security 2, ... , and n_m of security m. Let P_i be the invoice price of security $i = 1, 2, \ldots , m$. The value of the portfolio V_p can be written as

$$V_p = n_1 P_1 + n_2 P_2 + n_3 P_3 + \cdots + n_m P_m \qquad (4.44)$$

In our notation $n_1 = 100$ indicates a par value of \$100 million of bond 1. The yield to maturity of a single security was defined earlier. It is natural to extend this concept to a portfolio of securities. Let us define C_{l_j} as the lth cash flow from security j. Assume also that security j expires at T_j, paying its last cash flow. Then,

$$P_j = \sum_{l=1}^{T_j} \frac{C_{l_j}}{\left(1 + \frac{y_j}{2}\right)^{l_j}}.$$

The portfolio value is

$$V_p = \sum_{j=1}^{m} n_j P_j = \sum_{j=1}^{m} \sum_{l=1}^{T_j} \frac{C_{l_j} n_j}{\left(1 + \frac{y_p}{2}\right)^{l_j}}$$

where the yield to maturity of the portfolio is y_p and is the internal rate of return of the cash flows of the entire portfolio.

From Equation (4.44) we get

$$\frac{\Delta V_p}{\Delta y} = n_1 \frac{\Delta P_1}{\Delta y} + n_2 \frac{\Delta P_2}{\Delta y} + n_3 \frac{\Delta P_3}{\Delta y} + \cdots + n_m \frac{\Delta P_m}{\Delta y}. \qquad (4.45)$$

Here we have assumed that the yield curve is flat, or, $y_j = y$ for all j. In addition, we assume that the changes $\Delta y_j = \Delta y$ for all j. This is called a parallel shift in the yield curve.

From this we get

$$\mathrm{PVBV}_p = n_1 \mathrm{PVBP}_1 + n_2 \mathrm{PVBP}_2 + n_3 \mathrm{PVBP}_3 + \cdots + n_m \mathrm{PVBP}_m. \qquad (4.46)$$

In deriving this result, we have assumed that the shifts in the yields are parallel; in other words, that the yields of all securities increase by one basis point.

Example 4-18   PVBP of a Treasury Portfolio

The quotations for the September 10, 1992, settlement of on-the-run U.S. Treasury notes and bonds are provided in Table 4-12. Consider a portfolio which has a \$200 million par amount of the 7.25% T-bond and a \$100 million par amount of the 4.25% T-note. What is the PVBP of this portfolio?

Let $n_1 = 200$ and $n_2 = 100$. Then $PVBP_1 = 1{,}223$ and $PVBP_2 = 189$. Then,

$$PVBP_p = 200 \times 1{,}223 + 100 \times 189 = 263{,}500.$$

The portfolio will lose \$263,500 per basis point increase in the yield.

Reconsider the equation that describes the portfolio value V_p. Let $D(p)$ be the Macaulay duration of the portfolio. Then,

$$D(p) = -\frac{dV_p}{\partial y} \times \frac{\left(1 + \frac{y}{2}\right)}{V_p}.$$

Using Equation (4.45) for the value of the portfolio, we may write this as

$$D(p) = -\frac{\left(1 + \frac{y}{2}\right)}{V_p}\left[n_1 \times \frac{\partial P_1}{\partial y} + n_2 \times \frac{\partial P_2}{\partial y} + \cdots + n_m \times \frac{\partial P_m}{\partial y} \right].$$

This can be rewritten as

$$D(p) = -\frac{\left(1 + \frac{y}{2}\right)}{V_p}\left[n_1 V_1 \times \frac{\partial P_1}{\partial y}\frac{1}{V_1} + n_2 V_2 \times \frac{\partial P_2}{\partial y}\frac{1}{V_2} + \cdots + n_m V_m \times \frac{\partial P_m}{\partial y}\frac{1}{V_m} \right].$$

Simplifying, we get

$$D(p) = \left[-\frac{\left(1 + \frac{y}{2}\right)}{P_1}\frac{n_1 P_1}{V_p}\frac{\partial P_1}{\partial y} - \frac{\left(1 + \frac{y}{2}\right)}{P_2}\frac{n_2 P_2}{V_p}\frac{\partial P_2}{\partial y} - \cdots - \frac{\left(1 + \frac{y}{2}\right)}{P_m}\frac{n_m P_m}{V_m}\frac{\partial P_m}{\partial y} \right]$$

Let $x_i = \frac{n_i P_i}{V_p}$ be the fraction of the portfolio held in security i. Define $D(i)$ to be the Macauley duration of security i. Obviously, $x_1 + x_2 + \cdots + x_m = 1$. It then follows that

$$D(p) = [x_1 D(1) + x_2 D(2) + \cdots + x_m D(m)]. \tag{4.47}$$

In a similar way, we can derive the corresponding result for modified duration of a portfolio as

$$MD(p) = [x_1 MD(1) + x_2 MD(2) + \cdots + x_m MD(m)] \tag{4.48}$$

Once again, it is important to note that we have assumed a parallel shift in the yields of all the securities in the portfolio. In addition, we are assuming that the securities have no default risk and that they are bullet securities with no call or sinking-fund features.

A comparison of the expressions for portfolio durations in Equations (4.47) and (4.48) with the portfolio PVBP in Equation (4.46) highlights one important difference. **To calculate the portfolio PVBP we use par values. On the other hand, to compute portfolio durations we use proportions of market values.**

Example 4-19   Duration of a Treasury Portfolio

Let us reconsider the portfolio that has a $200 million par amount of the 7.25% T-bond and a $100 million par amount of the 4.25% T-note. What is the duration of this portfolio?

The invoice prices are $P_1 = 100\frac{13}{32} + 0.5122 = 100.91845$ and $P_2 = 100\frac{27}{32} + 0.1174 = 100.96115$. The market value of the portfolio (in millions) is $200 \times 1.0091845 + 100 \times 1.0096115 = 302.79805$. Hence, $x_1 = \frac{200 \times 1.0091845}{302.79805} = 0.6666$ and $x_2 = \frac{100 \times 1.0096115}{302.79805} = 0.3334$. As given in Table 4-12, $MD_1 = 12.12$ and $MD_2 = 1.88$; then the portfolio duration is $0.6666 \times 12.12 + 0.3334 \times 1.88 = 8.71$.

APPLICATIONS OF PVBP AND DURATION CONCEPTS

We showed in the previous sections how to compute the PVBP and duration of single security and a portfolio of many securities. In this section, we provide some applications using these concepts. To make the applications concrete, we present Table 4-13, which gives the prices and yields of two Treasury securities.

Let us say that a dealer is long on January 2, 1992, in $100 million par amount of the T-bond, which has a coupon 8% and a maturity date of November 15, 2021. The dealer decides to set up a neutral hedge using a T-note, which has a coupon of 7.5% and a maturity date of November 15, 2001. A **neutral hedge** is one in which movements in market interest rates leave the portfolio value (including the hedge instrument) unchanged.

Hedging under the Parallel-Shift Assumption

We will first approach the hedging problem ignoring the fact that the shifts in the yields of these securities are actually not parallel. Later, we will provide a framework which takes into account the fact that the shifts are not parallel. Recall that parallel shifts mean that there is a perfect correlation of changes in yields of the two securities.

Let the 8%, 11-15-2021 T-bond be security 1 and the 7.5%, 11-15-2001 T-note be security 2. Obviously $n_1 = 100$ and we need to determine n_2 such that

$$PVBP_p = n_1 \times PVBP_1 + n_2 \times PVBP_2 = 0.$$

That is, for parallel shifts in the yields, the portfolio will have a zero change in its value; hence the hedge produced by choosing n_2 this way is called a neutral hedge. Solving the equation above, we get

$$n_2 = -n_1 \times \frac{PVBP_1}{PVBP_2}. \tag{4.49}$$

TABLE 4-13   *Price and Yield Histories of Two Treasury Securities*

Date	T-Bond, 8%, 11-15-2021			T-note, 7.5%, 11-15-2001		
	Bid	Ask	Yield	Bid	Ask	Yield
11/20/91	100.31	101.01	7.91	100.27	100.29	7.37
11/21/91	100.15	100.17	7.95	100.24	100.26	7.38
11/22/91	100.04	100.06	7.98	100.14	100.16	7.43
11/25/91	100.05	100.07	7.98	100.11	100.13	7.44
11/26/91	100.19	100.21	7.94	100.19	100.21	7.41
11/27/91	100.12	100.14	7.96	100.19	100.21	7.41
11/29/91	100.21	100.23	7.94	100.27	100.29	7.37
12/2/91	100.31	101.01	7.91	101.08	101.10	7.31
12/3/91	101.05	101.07	7.89	101.18	101.20	7.27
12/4/91	101.26	101.28	7.84	102.10	102.12	7.16
12/5/91	101.18	101.20	7.86	102.01	102.03	7.20
12/6/91	102.17	102.19	7.78	101.22	101.24	7.25
12/9/91	102.17	102.19	7.78	101.31	102.01	7.21
12/10/91	102.15	102.17	7.78	102.01	102.03	7.20
12/11/91	102.06	102.08	7.80	102.00	102.02	7.21
12/12/91	102.22	102.24	7.76	102.07	102.09	7.17
12/13/91	102.15	102.17	7.78	101.31	102.01	7.21
12/16/91	102.21	102.23	7.76	102.01	102.03	7.20
12/17/91	102.29	102.31	7.74	102.08	102.10	7.17
12/18/91	102.26	102.28	7.75	102.06	102.08	7.18
12/19/91	103.25	103.27	7.67	102.25	102.27	7.10
12/20/91	104.28	104.30	7.58	103.24	103.26	6.96
12/23/91	105.17	105.19	7.53	104.13	104.15	6.87
12/24/91	105.19	105.21	7.52	104.14	104.16	6.87
12/26/91	105.26	105.28	7.50	104.20	104.22	6.84
12/27/91	105.23	105.25	7.51	104.27	104.29	6.81
12/30/91	106.16	106.18	7.45	105.10	105.12	6.75
12/31/91	107.01	107.03	7.41	105.22	105.24	6.69
1/2/92	106.13	106.15	7.46	105.04	105.06	6.77
1/3/92	106.04	106.06	7.48	104.21	104.23	6.83
1/6/92	106.23	106.25	7.43	104.28	104.30	6.80
1/7/92	107.09	107.11	7.39	105.10	105.12	6.74
1/8/92	107.03	107.05	7.40	105.06	105.08	6.76
1/9/92	106.30	107.00	7.41	105.03	105.05	6.77

The negative sign merely indicates that the dealer should short security 2 to set up a neutral hedge for security 1 (which is being held long). On January 2, 1992, the $PVBP_1 = 1,255.36$ per million dollars par. Similarly, $PVBP_2 = 735.29$ per million dollars par. So, the neutral hedge ratio is $n_2 = -100 \times \frac{1,255.36}{735.29} = -170.72$. We will round out the decimals and use $170 million par amount of the T-note to hedge $100 million par amount of the T-bond.

The resulting positions are tracked in Table 4-14 for the period January 2, 1992, through January 9, 1992, when the hedge is lifted. Bid prices have been used in the analysis. Column (1) gives the dates on which the hedge was in place and column (2) gives the daily changes in T-bond position in percentage per million par. For example, the change on January 2, 1992, relative to the previous trading day was $\frac{20}{32} \times 10{,}000 \times 100 = -625{,}000$. This is shown in Column (2). Column (3) provides the changes in the value of short position in the T-note. This is obtained by multiplying the change in price on January 2, 1992, which is $\frac{18}{32}$ by $10{,}000 \times 170 = 956{,}250$. Note that the short position made more money than was lost by the dealer in the long position during the period December 31, 1991, to January 2, 1992. Column (4) provides the combined position. As this column demonstrates, changes in the hedged position are much less variable.

(1)	(2)	(3)	(4)	(5)
				Changes
	Changes	Changes	Changes	in Hedged
	in T-bond	in T-note	in Hedged	Value
Date	Value	Value	Value	(with $\hat{\beta}$)
1/2/92	-625,000	956,250	331,250	-2,673
1/3/92	-281,250	796,875	515,625	237,356
1/6/92	593,750	-371,875	221,875	351,733
1/7/92	562,500	-743,750	-181,250	78,467
1/8/92	-187,500	212,500	25,000	-49,205
1/9/92	-156,250	159,375	3,125	-52,528
Range			696,875	404,262

TABLE 4-14
Hedging T-bonds
with T-notes

In formulating this hedging problem, we made the assumption that the yields of the T-bond and the T-note move in parallel. As we see from Table 4-13, this assumption is clearly violated. For example, between January 2, 1992, and January 9, 1992, the T-bond yields fell by 5 basis points whereas the T-note yields during the same period were unchanged. The actual correlation is positive but not perfect.

Hedging under Imperfect Correlation

Using the data on daily yields from November 20, 1991 to December 31, 1991, in Table 4-13 we can compute the daily yield changes and estimate the correlation between the yield changes of the T-bond and the T-note by computing the regression:

$$\Delta y_{1t} = \alpha + \beta \Delta y_{2t} + \epsilon_t$$

where Δy_{1t} is the change in the yield of T-bond between date t and date $t - 1$ and Δy_{2t} is the change in the yield of T-note between date t and date $t - 1$. We estimate that the constant term $\alpha = 0.0253$ and the slope coefficient $\beta = 0.6508$. The correlation coefficient $R^2 = 0.548$.

Since the correlation is less than perfect, our hedge must be modified to reflect this fact. To obtain the optimal hedge under these conditions, we need to specify an objective for the hedge policy; we will assume that it is to minimize the variance of the changes in the value of the hedged portfolio.

From Equation (4.46), for the two-security case here, we can write,

$$\Delta V_p = n_1 PVBP_1 \Delta y_1 + n_2 PVBP_2 \Delta y_2. \tag{4.50}$$

We are now ready to explicitly recognize that the two securities have changes in yields that are less than perfectly correlated. We compute the variance of the change in the portfolio value as

$$Var(\Delta V_p) = n_1^2 PVBP_1^2 Var(\Delta y_1) + n_2^2 PVBP_2^2 Var(\Delta y_2) \tag{4.51}$$
$$+ 2n_1 n_2 PVBP_1 PVBP_2 Cov(\Delta y_1, \Delta y_2)$$

where Var denotes variance and Cov denotes covariance.

We choose an n_2 that will minimize the variance of the changes in the portfolio value. Differentiating $Var(\Delta V_p)$ with respect to n_2, and setting the derivative to zero, and solving for n_2 gives

$$n_2^* = -n_1 \frac{PVBP_1}{PVBP_2} \frac{Cov(\Delta y_1, \Delta y_2)}{Var(\Delta y_2)}. \tag{4.52}$$

As the regression slope coefficient $\hat{\beta}$ is an estimate of $\frac{Cov(\Delta y_1, \Delta y_2)}{Var(\Delta y_2)}$, the optimal hedge can be written as

$$n_2^* = -n_1 \frac{PVBP_1}{PVBP_2} \hat{\beta} = -110 \tag{4.53}$$

The hedge is now modified by using the β estimate and the performance of the modified hedge is tracked from January 2, 1992, in column (5) of Table 4-14. The performance of the two hedges relative to the unhedged position is also shown in Table 4-14.

Note that the hedges that we calculated using the PVBP can be calculated using modified duration as well. Indeed, recall from Equation (4.43) that

$$\frac{\Delta P}{P} \approx -MD\Delta y.$$

From this relation we can write $\Delta P \approx -MDP\Delta y$. By reasoning as we did before, we can construct the optimal hedge using the modified durations of the two securities:

$$n_2^* = -n_1 \frac{P_1 MD_1}{P_2 MD_2} \hat{\beta} \tag{4.54}$$

Spread Trades

This section illustrates how the theoretical concepts that have been developed are applied to set up trading strategies. Consider the data in Tables 4-15a and 4-15b.

A trader is evaluating the shape of the yield curve for settlement on December 2, 1991. The yield spread between the thirty-year T-bond and the two-year T-note stands at 266 basis points. The trader is expecting this spread to significantly increase in a few

Bid	Ask	Yield	Settlement Date	Accrued Interest	PVBP
108.8405	108.903	7.96%	12/2/1991	0.408654	1200.643
109.0806	109.1431	7.94%	12/3/1991	0.432692	1204.999
109.8076	109.8701	7.88%	12/4/1991	0.456731	1218.246

TABLE 4-15a

Thirty-year T-bond, Coupon 8.75%, Maturity 5/15/2020

Bid	Ask	Yield	Settlement Date	Accrued Interest	PVBP
100.3735	100.4360	5.30%	12/2/1991	0.03022	187.3602
100.4664	100.5289	5.25%	12/3/1991	0.04533	187.34
100.5967	100.6592	5.18%	12/4/1991	0.06044	187.4086

TABLE 4-15b

Two-year T-note, Coupon 5.50%, Maturity 11/30/1993

days; in other words, the trader is expecting the yield curve to get steeper. He wants to set up a trade that will break even if the spread stays at 266 basis points and make money if the spread widens. Of course, he is willing to accept the risk that there will be a loss if the yield curve were to flatten; that is, if the spread actually decreases.

How can the trader implement the trade reflecting his view about the yield curve? The overall yields may either go down or go up, but it is the spread that the trader is betting on. Let us consider two scenarios, presented in Table 4-15c, in which the trader's expectations come true. In scenario 1, two-year yields fall by 20 basis points but the 30-year yields fall only by 10 basis points. This leads to a steepening of the yield curve. In scenario 2 precisely the opposite happens. The two-year yields increase by 20 basis points and the 30-year by 30 basis points, resulting in a steeper curve.

First, the trader recognizes that for the spreads to increase in a bullish market, the two-year yields must drop by much more than the thirty-year yields. Similarly, in a bearish market, the two-year yields must increase by much less than the thirty-year yields. This calls for a long position in the two-year T-note and a short position in the thirty-year T-bond.

Second, the trader must determine the amount of the two-year T-note to buy and the amount of the thirty-year T-bond to short. This is where the concepts that we have developed come in handy. The trader will want to set up the trade such that

$$n_2 \times \text{PVBP}_2 = n_{30} \times \text{PVBP}_{30}$$

where n_2 is the number of two-year T-notes and n_{30} is the number of thirty-year T-bonds.

	Yield Two-year T-note	Yield Thirty-year T-bond	Spread
Scenario 1	5.1	7.86	276
Scenario 2	5.5	8.36	286

TABLE 4-15c

Possible Scenarios

If $n_{30} = 100$ million par amount, then we can compute n_2

$$n_2 = n_{30}\frac{\text{PVBP}_{30}}{\text{PVBP}_2}.$$

$$n_2 = 100 \times \frac{1200.6435}{187.3642} = 641.$$

So, the trader will go long in 641 million par amount of the two-year T-note and go short in 100 million par amount of the thirty-year T-bond.

Precisely how are these transactions arranged? Let us review the repo diagram in Figure 4-9. The trader posts 641 million par amount of the two-year T-note as collateral and borrows the cash. Ignoring the hair cut (margin), the trader will borrow the entire market value at a repo rate of 5%. This way he is long in the two-year T-note and is entitled to its coupon. In addition, the trader will borrow and sell 100 million par amount of the thirty-year T-bond and post the cash proceeds as collateral. Ignoring the hair cut (margin), the trader will earn, on the entire cash proceeds, an interest income at a repo rate of 4.90%. This way he is short in the thirty-year T-bond and is obliged to make restitution for any coupon payments. We summarize the key transactions related to this trade in Table 4-16.

The profitability of the spread trade depends on a number of factors, including:

- The bid-offer spreads. The trader buys at the offer price and sells at the bid price. The wider the bid-offer spread, the less profitable the trade.
- The repo rates. If the repo rates are low, the trader pays less to borrow, but also receives less on the cash collateral.

FIGURE 4-9   *Repo Diagram*

Transactions on December 2, 1991

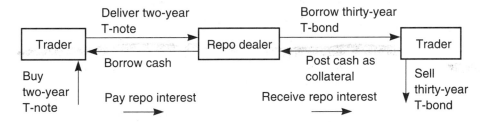

Transactions on December 4, 1991

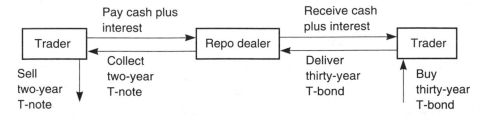

TABLE 4-16 *Summary of Transactions in Spread Trade*

Date	Transactions	Cash Flows
12/2/91	Borrow cash and pay for the two-year T-note. Post two-year T-note as collateral. $(100.4360 + 0.03022) \times 10{,}000 \times 641 =$	(643,988,470)
	Borrow thirty-year T-bond and sell. Post cash as collateral. $(108.8405 + 0.408654) \times 10{,}000 \times 100 =$	109,249,154
12/4/91	Sell two-year T-note. Per 641 million par, this becomes	
$\boxed{1}$	$(100.5967 + 0.0604) \times 10{,}000 \times 641 =$	645,212,011
	Repay the amount borrowed plus repo interest. Per 641 million par, this becomes	
$\boxed{2}$	$643{,}988{,}470 \times \left(1 + 2 \times \frac{0.05}{360}\right) =$	(644,167,356)
	Collect the cash plus interest.	
$\boxed{3}$	$109{,}249{,}154 \times \left(1 + 0.049 \times \frac{2}{360}\right) =$	109,278,894
	Buy the thirty-year T-bond to cover the short position.	
$\boxed{4}$	$(109.8701 + 0.4567) \times 10{,}000 \times 100 =$	(110,326,800)
	Profits (Losses): $\boxed{1} + \boxed{2} + \boxed{3} + \boxed{4}$	(3,251)

- Special rates. If the security that is long goes special (see Chapter 3), then the trader makes more money, as it is possible to borrow cheap by using that collateral. Conversely, if the security that is short goes special, the trader will lose money.
- Hair cut (margin). The trader will have to post some margin and this will reduce the profitability as well.

The exposure is high: the trader is long 641 million of the two-year T-note and short in 100 million of the long bond. Being wrong about the spread expectations, could lose the trader money. The credit risk also has to be factored in. Margins (hair cuts), mark-to-market provisions, and other policies should be considered in this context.

The concepts that we have developed thus far ignored the fact that duration changes with yield. We take up this issue next.

CONVEXITY

Recall that we have ignored second-order effects of yield changes on price changes by focusing on measures such as PVBP and D or MD, which are essentially related to the first derivative of the price with respect to the yield. Recall also that

$$Var(\Delta V_p) = n_1^2 \text{PVBP}_1^2 Var(\Delta y_1) + n_2^2 \text{PVBP}_2^2 Var(\Delta y_2)$$
$$+ 2n_1 n_2 \text{PVBP}_1 \text{PVBP}_2 Cov(\Delta y_1, \Delta y_2) \tag{4.55}$$

We now want to recognize the presence of the quadratic term $\frac{1}{2}\frac{\partial^2 P}{\partial y^2} \times \Delta y^2$. Differentiate Equation (4.39) with respect to y and simplify to get

$$\frac{\partial^2 P}{\partial y^2} = \frac{1}{4(1+\frac{y}{2})^2}\left[\sum_{j=1}^{2T-1}\frac{Cj(j+1)}{(1+\frac{y}{2})^j} + \frac{(C+100)2T(2T+1)}{(1+\frac{y}{2})^{2T}}\right] \tag{4.56}$$

The convexity Cx is defined as

$$Cx = \frac{1}{2}\frac{\partial^2 P}{\partial y^2}\frac{1}{P} \tag{4.57}$$

Note that convexity of a security is always positive. Another measure, known as **dollar convexity,** DCx is obtained by multiplying Cx by the price P.

For bonds with exactly N round coupons remaining, the second derivative can be written as

$$\frac{\partial^2 P}{\partial y^2} = \left[\frac{N(N+1)(100-\frac{C}{y})}{4(1+\frac{y}{2})^{N+2}} - \frac{CN}{y^2(1+\frac{y}{2})^{N+1}} - \frac{2C}{y^3}\left[\frac{1}{(1+\frac{y}{2})^N}-1\right]\right]$$

Example 4-20   Convexity of a T-note

Reconsider the T-note in Example 4-16 and Table 4-11. The calculations pertaining to convexity are shown in Table 4-17.

To obtain the second derivative, we first evaluate the sum $3.835 + 11.895 + 23.576 + 1,876.323 = 1,915.630$. We then divide the sum by $(1+\frac{y}{2})^2$. The result is $1,844.841$. We divide this quantity by 4 to get the second derivative. This is 461.21. The convexity is then obtained by dividing this by the invoice price and then by 2. The result is $Cx = 2.28$.

TABLE 4-17   *Convexity of a T-note*

Coupon Dates	Cash Flows, C	Number of Days from Settlement	Semi-annual Periods from Settlement, j	Time-weighted Cashflows, $C \times j(j+1)$	Discount Factor $\dfrac{C \times j(j+1)}{(1+\frac{y}{2})^j}$
2/28/93	2.1250	171	0.9448	3.9043	3.835
8/31/93	2.1250	355	1.9613	12.3423	11.895
2/28/94	2.1250	536	2.9613	24.9479	23.576
8/31/94	102.1250	720	3.9779	2,022.2377	1,876.323

Settlement date: September 10, 1992, Maturity date: August 31, 1994
Coupon: 4.25%, Yield to maturity: 3.801%
Flat price: 100.84375, Accrued interest: 0.1174

From Equations (4.36), (4.55), and (4.57) we get

$$\frac{\Delta P}{P} = -\text{MD} \times \Delta y + Cx \times \Delta y^2 + o(3). \qquad (4.58)$$

We find that the convexity contributes to the price change favorably. The gain from convexity is $Cx \times P \times \Delta y^2$. In the example the gain from convexity is $2.28 \times 100.84375 \times (0.01)^2 = 0.023$.

Holding maturity and yield to maturity fixed, the convexity decreases as the coupon increases. Convexity increases with duration.

Portfolio Construction Strategies

Let us consider Table 4-18 which provides the statistics for three zero-coupon bonds or Treasury strips. Using the concepts we have developed, we can easily verify the table entries corresponding to modified duration, gain from convexity and PVBP. Let us consider a portfolio which has $100 million par amount of the strip maturing on August 15, 2002. Is it possible to replace this strip with a portfolio of the other two strips, which mature on August 15, 1997 and August 15, 2012, respectively, such that there is no cash outlay and the PVBP remains the same?

Let n_i be the number of strip i; we require that the cash proceeds from the sale of strip 2 be sufficient to buy the requisite amounts of strip 1 and strip 3.

$$n_2 P_2 = n_1 P_1 + n_3 P_3 = V_p \qquad (4.59)$$

We further require that the modified duration of the strip that is sold is equal to the modified duration of the portfolio that is purchased.

$$\text{MD}_2 = \frac{n_1 P_1}{V_p} \text{MD}_1 + \frac{n_3 P_3}{V_p} \text{MD}_3 \qquad (4.60)$$

From the table, we substitute $n_2 = 100$, $\text{MD}_1 = 4.7995$, $\text{MD}_2 = 9.5982$, $\text{MD}_3 = 19.1776$, $P_1 = 76.86$, $P_2 = 50.99$, and $P_3 = 21.60$. So the two conditions are

$$100 \times 50.99 = n_1 \times 76.86 + n_3 \times 21.60$$

and

$$9.5982 = \frac{n_1 \times 76.86 \times 4.7995 + n_3 \times 21.60 \times 19.1776}{100 \times 50.99}.$$

TABLE 4-18   *Treasury Strips, Settlement Date: September 9, 1992*

Security (Strips)	Maturity Date	Price	Yield	Modified Duration	Gain from Convexity	PVBP
1	8/15/1997	76.86	5.41	4.8	0.1270	369
2	8/15/2002	50.99	6.90	9.6	0.4838	489
3	8/15/2012	21.60	7.84	19.2	1.8838	414

Solving, we get $n_1 = 44.20$ and $n_3 = 78.79$. The portfolio we have created by selling strip 2 is very similar but not identical to the strip 2 that we sold. To see why this is the case, we need to analyze the effects of changes in yields on strip 2 and on the portfolio we have created.

Note that by construction, at the prevailing market yields (underlined in Table 4-19) the market value of the strip 2 and its PVBP are exactly matched by those of the barbell portfolio. When there is a parallel shift in the yields, the value of the barbell portfolio dominates the value of the bullet (strip 2) security. Consider what happens to the portfolio when the yields drop. The PVBP of the barbell portfolio, given in the last column, exceeds the PVBP of strip 2. This indicates that the barbell portfolio will benefit more from the reduction in yields. On the other hand, as the yields go up, the PVBP of the barbell portfolio is always lower than that of strip 2. As a consequence, the barbell portfolio will lose less value as compared to strip 2.

Trades of this sort, in which an intermediate maturity security is sold (bought) and two securities whose maturities straddle the intermediate maturity are bought (sold) are

TABLE 4-19

Convexity Effect, Bullet vs Barbell

y_2	P_2	PVBP$_2$	y_1	y_3	V_p Barbell	PVBP Barbell
5.00%	61.23	5.936	3.51%	5.94%	61.76	6.559
5.10%	60.64	5.876	3.61%	6.04%	61.11	6.456
5.20%	60.06	5.817	3.71%	6.14%	60.47	6.355
5.30%	59.48	5.758	3.81%	6.24%	59.84	6.255
5.40%	58.91	5.700	3.91%	6.34%	59.22	6.158
5.50%	58.34	5.642	4.01%	6.44%	58.61	6.063
5.60%	57.78	5.585	4.11%	6.54%	58.01	5.969
5.70%	57.22	5.529	4.21%	6.64%	57.42	5.877
5.80%	56.67	5.473	4.31%	6.74%	56.84	5.787
5.90%	56.13	5.418	4.41%	6.84%	56.26	5.698
6.00%	55.59	5.363	4.51%	6.94%	55.70	5.611
6.10%	55.06	5.309	4.61%	7.04%	55.14	5.526
6.20%	54.53	5.256	4.71%	7.14%	54.59	5.442
6.30%	54.01	5.203	4.81%	7.24%	54.05	5.360
6.40%	53.49	5.150	4.91%	7.34%	53.52	5.279
6.50%	52.98	5.099	5.01%	7.44%	53.00	5.200
6.60%	52.47	5.047	5.11%	7.54%	52.48	5.123
6.70%	51.97	4.997	5.21%	7.64%	51.97	5.046
6.80%	51.47	4.947	5.31%	7.74%	51.47	4.971
6.90%	50.98	4.897	5.41%	7.84%	50.98	4.898
7.00%	50.49	4.848	5.51%	7.94%	50.50	4.826
7.10%	50.01	4.799	5.61%	8.04%	50.02	4.755
7.20%	49.53	4.751	5.71%	8.14%	49.54	4.685
7.30%	49.06	4.703	5.81%	8.24%	49.08	4.617
7.40%	48.59	4.656	5.91%	8.34%	48.62	4.550
7.50%	48.13	4.610	6.01%	8.44%	48.17	4.484

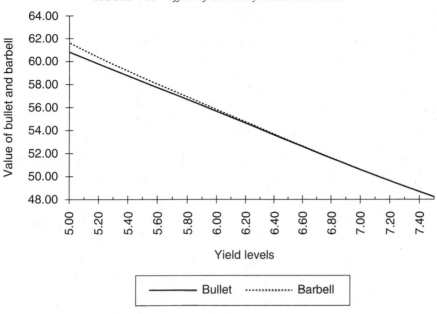

FIGURE 4-10   *Effect of Convexity: Bullet vs Barbell*

known as **butterfly trades.** To get a better perspective, we have plotted in Figure 4-10 the amount by which the barbell portfolio exceeds the strip 2 at different levels of yields.

Note that the convexity effect really kicks in only at very high or very low yield levels. In fact, for ±100 basis points change in yields, the effect of convexity is hardly evident. A critical assumption which we have maintained throughout this discussion is that the shift in yields is parallel. This assumption is especially suspect when there is a large change in the levels of the yields. Hence the analysis presented above should not be construed to mean that convexity is necessarily a desirable attribute.

FURTHER READING

A number of papers have explored the concepts of duration and convexity. A lucid analysis of duration appears in Ingersoll, Skelton, and Weil (1978). The problem of computing duration when interest rates are uncertain is addressed in Cox, Ingersoll, and Ross (1979) in the context of a specific model of term structure. Using duration to "immunize" portfolios is considered by Bierwag (1977). In immunization strategy, the duration of assets is set equal to that of liabilities, through careful choice of asset-liability mix. Since duration measures interest-rate sensitivity, in such portfolios assets and liabilities will have the same interest-rate sensitivity and hence will be well-hedged with respect to interest-rate movements. The issue of convexity is addressed in Klotz (1985) and Yawitz (1986).

PROBLEMS

4.1   An investor buys a face amount $1 million of a six-month (182 days) Treasury bill at a discount yield of 9.25%. What is the cost of purchasing these bills? Calculate the bond equivalent yield. Indicate clearly the formula you used and show all the steps in your calculations. Recalculate the bond equivalent yield if the T-bill has a maturity of 275 days.

4.2   On November 18, 1987, a $7\frac{7}{8}$% T-bond maturing on May 15, 1990, was quoted at $99\frac{29}{32}$ for settlement on November 20, 1987. The last coupon was paid on November 15, 1987.

    (a)   What is the invoice price of the T-bond?

    (b)   What is the yield on the T-bond?

4.3   What is the price of a ten-year zero-coupon bond priced to yield 10% under each of the following assumptions?

    (a)   Annual yield.

    (b)   Semi-annual yield.

    (c)   Monthly yield.

    (d)   Daily yield

Explain the differences you found. What is the continuous limit?

4.4   In the table below, fill in the indicated blanks. Show all the steps in your calculations in separate sheets. Duration is denoted by D, coupon by C, and yield by Y. The settlement date is February 15, 1986.

Bond Mathematics

C	Y	Maturity Date	Price	D	Value of 0.01.	Y Value of $\frac{1}{32}$
9%	9.00%	5/15/xx	100.00	5.0	xxxx	xxxx
0%	9.00%	2/15/92	xxx.xx	x.x *6.0*	xxxx *0.0339*	xxxx *0.0032*
10%	9.00%	2/15/96	106.50	6.66	xxxx *0.069*	xxxx *0.046 106.44*

4.5   Using the information in the following table, construct a $100 million portfolio with a Macaulay duration of 5.0. Supply the missing information in the table. The settlement date is February 15, 1986.

Duration of Portfolios

C	Y	Maturity Date	Price	D
0%	9.12%	2/15/90	70.00	xx.xx
9%	x.xx%	2/15/xx	110.00	6.00

4.6   On November 15, 1986, you bought $10 million (face amount) of a 7.50% T-bond maturing on November 11, 2016, at a yield of 7.60%. All coupons were reinvested at 5% yield. The bond was sold on June 20, 1987, at a yield of 7.50%. Calculate the annualized rate of return from this transaction. Show all the key steps.

4.7 (a) Assuming that the settlement date is August 15, 1986, determine the duration of the T-bond from the next table. From the duration formula, estimate the price of the T-bond for a yield change of +10 basis points.

(b) Repeat the analysis at yield levels of 5%, 6%, 7%, 8%, 10%, 11%, and 12%.

(c) For these yield levels determine the actual price from price-yield formula.

(d) Compare the estimated price with the actual price. Explain the deviations. (Use a spreadsheet program such as EXCEL or Lotus 123 to handle this problem.

Duration of a T-bond

C	Y	Maturity Date	Price	D
10%	9.00%	11/15/98	107.3043	xx.xx

4.8 Reconsider Problem 4.7. You may now estimate the prices at different yield levels by using both duration and convexity. Compare the estimated prices with the actual price and explain the deviations.

4.9 An investor expects a strong market rally. Assume that the yield-curve shifts will be parallel (i.e., all yields change by the same amount irrespective of maturities). In order to get the highest return over the rally, which of the following securities should be chosen by the investor: (i) the security with the highest duration, (ii) the security with the lowest yield value of $\frac{1}{32}$, or (iii) the security with the highest dollar value of 0.01? Explain your answer.

4.10 Spreadsheet Problem. Use *Wall Street Journal* quotes to solve this problem. Compute the spread between the current five-year T-note and the current thirty-year T-bond. Anticipate that this spread will narrow significantly in a month's time. Structure a spread trade using these two securities. The trade must be positioned in the market for a repurchase agreement using weekly term repo rates. Assume that the one-week term repo rates are 3.00%–3.05%. One leg of the trade will have 100 million par amount of the long bond. Set up the trade as of today and carry the position for five days. Unwind the trade at the end of five days and report the details of your trade and your position market-to-market using the *Wall Street Journal* prices.

4.11 Spreadsheet Problem. Use *Wall Street Journal* quotes to solve this problem. Determine the invoice prices, PVBP, yield value of $\frac{1}{32}$, and the modified duration of all on-the-run securities. Explain your findings.

4.12 Spreadsheet Problem. Use *Wall Street Journal* quotes to solve this problem. You are a pension-fund manager with 100 million par amount of the current seven-year T-note. You would like to swap out of this seven-year T-note and replace it with a portfolio of the current five-year T-note and the current ten-year T-note. But the trade should be self-financing: The proceeds from the sale of the seven-year T-note should exactly cover the cost of the portfolio of the five-year and ten-year T-notes. In addition, the PVBP of the seven-year T-note must be equal to the PVBP of the portfolio you plan to purchase.

(a) Determine the amount of five-year and ten-year T-notes you must buy.

(b) Is the new portfolio identical to the security you sold? Explain.

REFERENCES

Bierwag, G. 1977. "Immunization, Duration and the Term Structure of Interest Rates." *Journal of Financial and Quantitative Analysis* 12:725–743.

Chance, D. M. 1990. "Default, Risk and the Duration of the Zero Coupon Bonds." *Journal of Finance* 55:265-274.

Cox, J., J. Ingersoll, and S. Ross 1979. "Duration and the Measurement of Basis Risk." *Journal of Business* 52:51–61.

Ingersoll, J. E., J. Skelton, and R. L. Weil 1978. "Duration Forty Years Later." *Journal of Financial and Quantitative Analysis* 13:627–650.

Kidder, Peabody, and Co. 1987. Applications of Duration and Convexity for the Analysis of Callable Bonds. Fixed-Income Group.

Klotz, R. 1985. Convexity of Fixed-Income Securities. Salomon Brothers.

Yawitz, J. 1986. Convexity: An Introduction. Financial Strategies Group, Goldman Sachs.

Chapter 5

Yield-Curve And Term-Structure Analysis

Chapter Objectives

This chapter provides the building blocks for the analysis of the yield curve and the concept of the term structure of interest rates. Chapter 5 will help the reader to understand and answer the following questions.

- What is meant by the volatility of interest rates? How does it differ across yields of different maturities?
- What is the term structure of interest rates?
- How can coupon bonds be built as a portfolio of zero coupon bonds?
- What are the concepts of the term structure of interest rates? In particular,
    1. what are spot rates of interest?
    2. what are forward rates of interest?
    3. what does it mean to extract spot rates from the coupon-bond prices?
    4. What is par bond yield curve?
- What are strips? What is meant by reconstitutions?
- What economic considerations are involved in stripping and reconstituting bonds?

INTRODUCTION

In this chapter, our focus will be on yield-curve and term-structure analysis. In Chapter 4, we developed some basic measures of risk and return that are used in fixed-income markets. The measures of return which we considered there included yield to maturity and current yield. The measures of risk included the dollar value of an 0.01 (PVBP), duration (Macaulay and modified), and convexity. Several applications of these measures in portfolio management and bond-trading strategies were illustrated. The concepts of duration and convexity, as noted in the previous chapter, were based on the premise that the shifts in the yield curve are parallel. In this chapter, we first provide an illustration of parallel shifts in yield curve, and then some empirical evidence on the movements that the default-free yield curve has experienced in the past. We show that non-parallel movements occur frequently enough for us to develop concepts that are robust with respect to such movements.

Critical to the development of such concepts that do not depend on the assumption of parallel shifts in yield curve is the pricing of zero coupon securities. One of the underpinnings to the understanding of the pricing of fixed-income securities is the fact that most coupon-bearing fixed-income securities may be properly viewed as a portfolio of zero coupon securities. This interpretation is valid so long as there is no credit risk, and no options are held by issuers to call the issue or by the investors to put the issue. We provide a simple illustration of this idea in this chapter to underscore the importance of pricing zero coupon securities in yield-curve analysis. In addition, we develop concepts such as the spot rate of interest, forward rate of interest, and par bond yield curve, which are central to the analysis of yield curve. We then introduce the strips markets and discuss the relationship between strip rates and spot rates. Finally, some practical issues that are relevant in the estimation of zero coupon bond prices from the yield curve are presented.

YIELD-CURVE ANALYSIS

Yield curve is a term used to describe the plot of yield to maturity against time to maturity or against a risk measure, such as the modified duration of debt securities in a certain market segment (such as Treasury). By incorporating the expectations of diverse participants in the marketplace, the shape of the yield curve succinctly captures and summarizes the cost of credit for loans of various maturities. The shape of the default-free yield curve is therefore of considerable interest to practitioners in the financial markets.

Recall that the concepts of duration and convexity are strictly valid only when the movements in the yield curve are parallel. To remind yourself what we mean by parallel shifts in yield curve, examine Table 5-1 and Figure 5-1 which illustrate parallel shifts: all the yields go up or go down by precisely the same amount. Note that when the yield to maturity of the three-month T-bill goes up from 4.5% to 5.5%, the yield to maturity on the thirty-year T-bond also increases from 13% to 14%. Both securities experience an increase of 100 basis points in their yields.

Maturity in Years	Current Level of Yields	Parallel Shift by +100 Basis Points	Parallel Shift by -100 Basis Points
0.25	4.5%	5.5%	3.5%
0.5	5.0%	6.0%	4.0%
1	6.0%	7.0%	5.0%
2	7.2%	8.2%	6.2%
3	8.0%	9.0%	7.0%
5	9.5%	10.5%	8.5%
7	11.0%	12.0%	10.0%
10	12.0%	13.0%	11.0%
30	13.0%	14.0%	12.0%

TABLE 5-1
Parallel Shifts in Yields of Securities

FIGURE 5-1   *Parallel Shifts in Yield Curve*

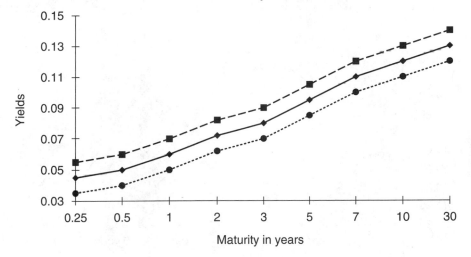

How realistic is the parallel shift assumption? To examine this question, we begin by presenting first the shape of the yield curve at selected points in time and noting the shifts in the shape of the yield curve over time.

Over the last several decades, the Treasury yield curve has assumed different shapes. We review briefly some sample periods to illustrate this richness over time. In Figure 5-2, we provide the shape of the default-free yield curve during June 1981. Figure 5-3 provides the shape as of April 1982, and Figure 5-4 as of December 1982. Figure 5-2 shows that the yield curve was steeply inverted during June 1981. That is to say that the short-term yields were at around 15.50%, which is a level much higher than the long-term yields, which were around 13.00%. Note that the overall levels of interest rates were quite high all across the maturity spectrum.

FIGURE 5-2   *Inverted Yield Curve (June 1981)*

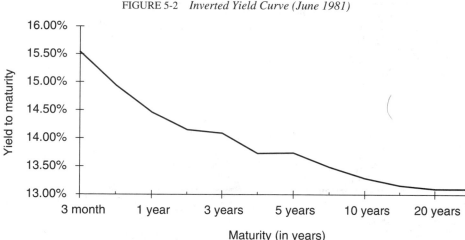

FIGURE 5-3   *Humped Yield Curve (April 1982)*

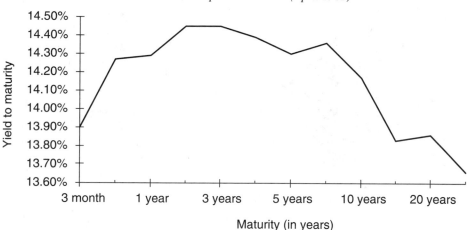

Source: Salomon Brothers, *Analytical Record of Yields*

   In Figure 5-3, we note that within a year's time the yield curve has become humped. Compared to June 1981, short-term interest rates have fallen but the long-term interest rates have increased. The yields start at around 13.90% and increase to about 14.50% at a maturity of two years (hump at two years) and then drop to about 13.70% at 30 years. At the end of 1982 (just eight months after April 1982) the yield curve becomes normal or upward sloping as shown in Figure 5-4. But the levels of interest rates have fallen significantly. Short-term rates begin at 8.50% and long-term rates end at around 11.00%. While Figures 5-2 to 5-4 represent a particularly volatile period, such nonparallel shifts in the yield curve are encountered from time to time.

FIGURE 5-4   *Normal Yield Curve (Dec 1982)*

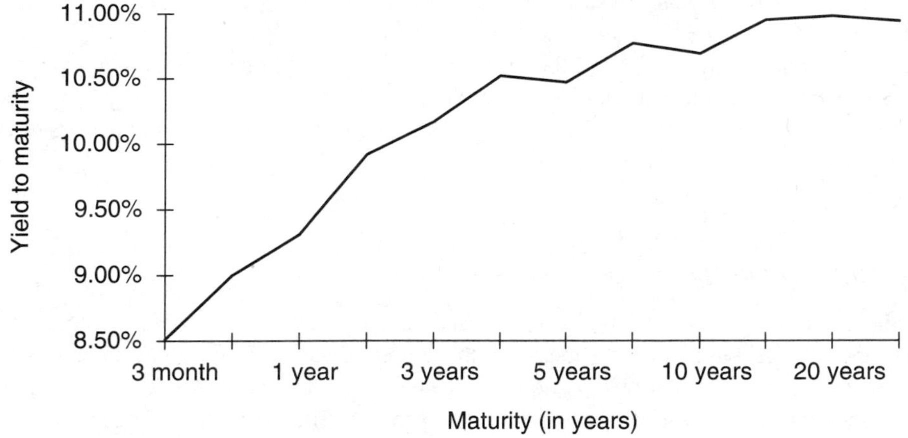

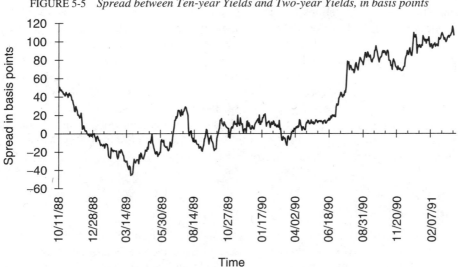

Source: Salomon Brothers, *Analytical Record of Yields*

To get an idea of the risk associated with nonparallel shifts in the yield curve, examine Figure 5-5 where the spread between the ten-year yields and two-year yields are plotted for the period November 1988 to March 1991. Note that the spread started at about 50 basis points in late 1988 and reached a low of -42 basis points in early 1989, leading to an inverted yield curve during the first half of 1989. Later, the spread became positive and reached a high of 110 basis points towards the beginning of 1991. Note that periodically the yield curve becomes inverted and that nonparallel shifts appear to be pervasive.

FIGURE 5-5   *Spread between Ten-year Yields and Two-year Yields, in basis points*

In this discussion we have chosen to work with data for specific maturities: 3 months, 6 months, 1 year, 2 years, 3 years, 4 years, 5 years, 7 years, 10 years, 15 years, 20 years, and 30 years. In reality, as we will illustrate later, there are over 200 Treasury securities that are outstanding in the marketplace, ranging in maturity from a few days to 30 years. In order to get additional insights into the shape of the yield curve and the pattern of its changes, we need to examine the volatility of short-term and long-term interest rates.

Volatility of Short and Long Rates

Volatility measures the variability of interest rates relative to their expected average levels. Loosely speaking, volatility measures the degree of variation of any variable around its mean. Given historical observations, we can estimate the volatility. It stands to reason that the degree of variation as well as the mean of the interest rates change with time as the economic determinants of interest rates change. For example, the short rates of interest changed significantly between 1978 and 1983. As we saw in Chapter 2, this was, in part, due to a change in the monetary policy that was effected by the Fed. (This is an extreme example in the sense that the entire structure underlying interest rates was affected.) The levels of interest rates and their volatility might systematically incorporate the changes in the factors that affect them. As a consequence, the time series of interest rates might exhibit a systematic clustering effect. The estimation procedures used for volatility vary significantly in their levels of sophistication. Some do not explicitly account for the fact that the volatilities exhibit clustering effects; others do.

The traditional approach to estimating volatility looks at a predetermined amount of historical information of a certain frequency (daily, weekly, monthly, etc.) and then computes the standard deviation of that series. This is then annualized and reported as the volatility estimate. The next level of sophistication assigns different weights to different historical observations. For example, more recent observation can be given greater importance. In markets where the liquidity is high and where many transactions occur in any given day, intraday prices or the high-low prices may be used for the purposes of estimating volatility. Later in the book, we will introduce the concept of implied volatilities whereby volatility estimates are obtained by using the prices of a derivative assets and a pricing framework for the derivative asset. Finally, the GARCH (generalized autoregressive and conditional heteroskedastic) models postulate specific relationships between the level of current volatility and their historical levels in their estimation procedures. The interested reader is referred to Bollerslev and Engle (1993). We present the traditional approach to estimating later in this chapter.

Price-based vs. Yield-based Volatility

It is useful to distinguish between price-based and yield-based volatilities in the context of fixed-income securities markets. The prices of fixed-income securities tend to par as their maturity dates approach. The price-yield relation that we developed earlier can be used to derive one volatility given the other. For example, we showed that the modified duration is given by

$$MD = -\frac{dP}{dy}\frac{1}{P}$$ (5.1)

where P is the price and y is the yield of the fixed-income security. Price-based volatility is the standard deviation of the rate of change in prices. Let us denote the price-based volatility as $\sigma_P = \sigma(\frac{dP}{P})$. The yield-based volatility is the standard deviation of the percentage change in yields. Denote the yield-based volatility as $\sigma_y = \sigma(\frac{dy}{y})$. Then from the expression for the modified duration, we can derive the relationship between price-based volatility and yield-based volatility as follows.

From Equation (5.1) we get

$$\frac{dP}{P} = -MD \times dy.$$

From the above expression, we can derive

$$\sigma_P = \sigma_y \times y \times MD.$$ (5.2)

We can use Equation (5.2) to transform price-based volatility into yield-based volatility and vice versa. Thus, the procedures for estimating the price-based volatility can easily be used to compute the yield-based volatility. We illustrate the traditional approach to estimating volatility in Example 5-1.

Example 5-1

To provide a concrete illustration, consider the 7.25%, 05152016 Treasury bond. Table 5-2a shows the prices and yields of the 7.25%, 05152016 Treasury bond over the period May 9, 1986 to June 20, 1986.

Let P_t denote the price at date t and y_t denote the yield at date t. Then, the traditional volatility measure is computed as follows.

1. Compute the natural log of the price ratio $R_t = \ln\left(\frac{P_{t+1}}{P_t}\right)$ for each date t in the sample, where $t = 0,1,\ldots N$. Note that this is the same as the difference in the log of the prices, $[\ln P_{t+1} - \ln P_t]$, at dates $t+1$ and t.
2. Compute the mean $\mu = \frac{\sum_{t=0}^{N} R_t}{N}$ of the natural log of the price ratio.
3. Calculate the squared deviations for each t as $x_t = (R_t - \mu)^2$.
4. Then, the traditional daily volatility estimate is

$$\sqrt{\frac{\sum_{i=1}^{N-1}(x_i)}{N-1}}.$$

5. And the traditional *annual* volatility estimate σ_P is

$$\sigma_P = \sqrt{\frac{\sum_{i=1}^{N-1}(x_i) \times 252}{N-1}}.$$

This recognizes that there are 252 trading days per year.

The results of these calculations appear in Table 5-2a. For example, the data from May 9, 1986, ($t = 0$) to June 23, 1986, ($t = N$) are used to estimate the price-based volatility on June 24, 1986. This turns out to be 19.36%.

Using the relationship between price-based volatility and yield-based volatility, we can compute the yield volatility as well. In the financial markets both price

TABLE 5-2a   *Price-based Volatility Estimation from 7.25%, 05/15/2016 T-bond Prices*

	Date	Price	Yield	Price Ratio	Natural Log of Price Ratio	Deviation from the Average	Squared Deviation from the Average
1	5/9/86	98.4375	7.3800				
2	5/12/86	98.2813	7.3930	0.9984	-0.0016	-0.0015	0.0000
3	5/13/86	97.8438	7.4300	0.9955	-0.0045	-0.0044	0.0000
4	5/14/86	97.8750	7.4280	1.0003	0.0003	0.0004	0.0000
5	5/15/86	96.7813	7.5220	0.9888	-0.0112	-0.0112	0.0001
6	5/16/86	95.3438	7.6480	0.9851	-0.0150	-0.0149	0.0002
7	5/19/86	95.2500	7.6560	0.9990	-0.0010	-0.0009	0.0000
8	5/20/86	95.9375	7.5950	1.0072	0.0072	0.0072	0.0001
9	5/21/86	96.3125	7.5620	1.0039	0.0039	0.0039	0.0000
10	5/22/86	96.9375	9.5080	1.0065	0.0065	0.0065	0.0000
11	5/23/86	97.5625	7.4540	1.0064	0.0064	0.0065	0.0000
12	5/27/86	98.1563	7.4040	1.0061	0.0061	0.0061	0.0000
13	5/28/86	97.5313	7.4570	0.9936	-0.0064	-0.0063	0.0000
14	5/29/86	95.2188	7.6590	0.9763	-0.0240	-0.0240	0.0006
15	6/2/86	92.5313	7.9040	0.9718	-0.0286	-0.0286	0.0008
16	6/3/86	93.4375	7.8200	1.0098	0.0097	0.0098	0.0001
17	6/4/86	92.2188	7.9330	0.9870	-0.0131	-0.0131	0.0002
18	6/5/86	92.5000	7.9070	1.0030	0.0030	0.0031	0.0000
19	6/6/86	95.3125	7.6500	1.0304	0.0300	0.0300	0.0009
20	6/9/86	93.5000	7.8140	0.9810	-0.0192	-0.0192	0.0004
21	6/10/86	94.0313	7.7660	1.0057	0.0057	0.0057	0.0000
22	6/11/86	94.8438	7.6920	1.0086	0.0086	0.0086	0.0001
23	6/12/86	94.9063	7.6870	1.0007	0.0007	0.0007	0.0000
24	6/13/86	96.7813	7.5210	1.0198	0.0196	0.0196	0.0004
25	6/16/86	97.7813	7.4350	1.0103	0.0103	0.0103	0.0001
26	6/17/86	97.9063	7.4240	1.0013	0.0013	0.0013	0.0000
27	6/18/86	97.7188	7.4400	0.9981	-0.0019	-0.0019	0.0000
28	6/19/86	96.8438	7.5160	0.9910	-0.0090	-0.0090	0.0001
29	6/20/86	97.6250	7.4480	1.0081	0.0080	0.0081	0.0001
30	6/23/86	97.8750	7.4270	1.0026	0.0026	0.0026	0.0000
31	6/24/86	98.3125	7.3900	1.0045	0.0045	0.0045	0.0000

Average (annualized)   -0.01067
Volatility (annualized) **19.36%**

and yield volatilities are used. In Table 5-2b, we illustrate the estimation of yield-based volatility. The volatility of the yield for the period is 21.44%.

Using Equation (5.2), we can also estimate the price-based volatility from the yield-based volatility that we estimated in Table 5-2b. As can be seen from Figure 5-6, these two estimates appear to differ just by a scaling factor.

TABLE 5-2b   *Yield-based Volatility Estimation from 7.25%, 05/15/2016 T-bond Prices*

Date	Price	Yield	Yield Ratio	Natural Log of Yield Ratio	Deviation from the Average	Squared Deviation from the Average
5/9/86	98.4375	7.3800				
5/12/86	98.2813	7.3930	1.0018	0.0018	0.0017	0.0000
5/13/86	97.8438	7.4300	1.0050	0.0050	0.0049	0.0000
5/14/86	97.8750	7.4280	0.9997	−0.0003	−0.0003	0.0000
5/15/86	96.7813	7.5220	1.0127	0.0126	0.0125	0.0002
5/16/86	95.3438	7.6480	1.0168	0.0166	0.0166	0.0003
5/19/86	95.2500	7.6560	1.0010	0.0010	0.0010	0.0000
5/20/86	95.9375	7.5950	0.9920	−0.0080	−0.0080	0.0001
5/21/86	96.3125	7.5620	0.9957	−0.0044	−0.0044	0.0000
5/22/86	96.9375	7.5080	0.9929	−0.0072	−0.0072	0.0001
5/23/86	97.5625	7.4540	0.9928	−0.0072	−0.0073	0.0001
5/27/86	98.1563	7.4040	0.9933	−0.0067	−0.0068	0.0000
5/28/86	97.5313	7.4570	1.0072	0.0071	0.0071	0.0001
5/29/86	95.2188	7.6590	1.0271	0.0267	0.0267	0.0007
6/2/86	92.5313	7.9040	1.0320	0.0315	0.0314	0.0010
6/3/86	93.4375	7.8200	0.9894	−0.0107	−0.0107	0.0001
6/4/86	92.2188	7.9330	1.0145	0.0143	0.0143	0.0002
6/5/86	92.5000	7.9070	0.9967	−0.0033	−0.0033	0.0000
6/6/86	95.3125	7.6500	0.9675	−0.0330	−0.0331	0.0011
6/9/86	93.5000	7.8140	1.0214	0.0212	0.0212	0.0004
6/10/86	94.0313	7.7660	0.9939	−0.0062	−0.0062	0.0000
6/11/86	94.8438	7.6920	0.9905	−0.0096	−0.0096	0.0001
6/12/86	94.9063	7.6870	0.9993	−0.0007	−0.0007	0.0000
6/13/86	96.7813	7.5210	0.9784	−0.0218	−0.0219	0.0005
6/16/86	97.7813	7.4350	0.9886	−0.0115	−0.0115	0.0001
6/17/86	97.9063	7.4240	0.9985	−0.0015	−0.0015	0.0000
6/18/86	97.7188	7.4400	1.0022	0.0022	0.0021	0.0000
6/19/86	96.8438	7.5160	1.0102	0.0102	0.0101	0.0001
6/20/86	97.6250	7.4480	0.9910	−0.0091	−0.0091	0.0001
6/23/86	97.8750	7.4270	0.9972	−0.0028	−0.0029	0.0000
6/24/86	98.3125	7.3900	0.9950	−0.0050	−0.0050	0.0000

Average	0.000045
Volatility	21.44%

FIGURE 5-6   *Price-based Volatility and Yield-based Volatility*

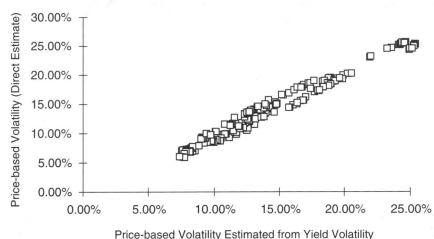

Evidence on Volatility

When we examine the volatility of interest rates of different maturities, we note that the short-term rates are much more volatile than long-term rates. A clue to this pattern is present in Figures 5-2 through 5-4. Note how the short-term rates changed much more dramatically than long-term rates between June 1981 and April 1982. In addition, as the yield curve moved from a humped shape in April 1982 to an upward-sloping shape in December 1982, the short rates fell by over 500 basis points whereas the long rates fell by under 250 basis points. Using the data on the Treasury markets, we document in Table 5-3a the short-rate volatilities and long-rate volatilities for various monthly subperiods from November 1988 to March 1991.

The volatilities display two discernible patterns. First, short-term volatilities are generally higher than long-term volatilities, although there are some exceptions in the sample period. Second, the volatility appears to be related to the level of the interest rates and the shape as captured by the average spread between ten-year and two-year T-notes. Note from Table 5-3b that short-term rates (two-year) have varied from a minimum of 6.87% to a high of 9.67%, a range of 280 basis points. In contrast, long-term rates (ten-year) have varied from a minimum of 7.83% to a maximum of 9.35%, a range of 152 basis points. Thus, the range of the short-term rate is nearly twice that of the long-term rate. This pattern is consistent with what we saw in Figures 5-2 through 5-4 earlier. Out of the 29 months from November 1988 to March 1991, during 20 months the volatility of the short-rate exceeded the volatility of the long-rate.

TABLE 5-3a   *Rate Volatility from November 1988 to March 1991*

	Two-year	Three-year	Four-year	Five-year	Seven-year	Ten-year
11/1988	23.31%	21.92%	21.56%	21.20%	17.50%	14.79%
12/1988	11.90%	11.16%	10.76%	10.28%	9.16%	7.26%
1/1989	7.81%	9.15%	10.27%	10.80%	12.18%	11.46%
2/1989	16.22%	12.21%	14.92%	15.97%	15.12%	14.83%
3/1989	15.44%	16.73%	14.42%	12.74%	10.83%	8.64%
4/1989	12.27%	12.35%	12.85%	12.13%	10.18%	8.36%
5/1989	15.24%	15.37%	15.79%	17.36%	18.65%	19.11%
6/1989	12.73%	11.77%	12.44%	11.36%	10.23%	10.02%
7/1989	13.24%	11.40%	11.85%	11.39%	10.83%	7.58%
9/1989	20.89%	19.46%	19.70%	17.01%	16.29%	12.95%
10/1989	11.38%	12.31%	10.63%	10.18%	9.39%	7.67%
11/1989	19.54%	16.47%	15.63%	13.80%	12.24%	10.12%
12/1989	9.78%	9.98%	7.66%	6.91%	5.24%	4.39%
1/1990	7.84%	6.69%	6.73%	6.50%	6.26%	4.97%
2/1990	15.89%	17.96%	18.08%	18.32%	17.35%	18.77%
3/1990	7.63%	8.21%	8.19%	7.53%	8.31%	8.56%
4/1990	7.05%	6.21%	7.21%	6.23%	5.55%	5.95%
5/1990	16.87%	17.73%	17.94%	18.17%	18.18%	18.85%
6/1990	11.97%	12.71%	11.87%	12.05%	10.81%	10.90%
7/1990	5.35%	5.43%	5.36%	5.30%	5.14%	5.07%
8/1990	13.66%	12.16%	11.59%	9.78%	8.34%	6.46%
9/1990	13.25%	13.55%	13.83%	14.58%	14.10%	13.81%
10/1990	5.25%	5.83%	5.86%	5.89%	6.24%	6.81%
11/1990	6.37%	7.61%	8.69%	8.81%	9.21%	8.79%
12/1990	6.36%	6.82%	8.31%	9.38%	10.11%	11.40%
1/1991	10.13%	8.49%	8.29%	8.41%	8.97%	9.11%
2/1991	4.92%	5.30%	6.82%	7.82%	8.35%	8.90%
3/1991	10.00%	10.74%	9.87%	9.51%	7.87%	7.85%
4/1991	6.92%	7.01%	7.12%	6.69%	5.96%	5.86%

In Figure 5-7, we provide the association between the level of interest rates and the volatility. Note that there is a general positive association between the level of the short-rate and its volatility. In other words, the volatility of rates appears to be level dependent and tends to increase with the levels. As Figure 5-8 shows, during periods of inverted yield curves, the volatility levels are very high and short-rate volatility more often exceeds long-rate volatility.

These considerations are important for several reasons. First, in the specification of a satisfactory model of the term structure (discussed in Chapter 6), it is necessary to

TABLE 5-3b   *Average Interest Rates from November 1988 to March 1991*

	Two-year	Three-year	Four-year	Five-year	Seven-year	Ten-year	Overall Spread in Basis Points
11/1988	8.65%	8.72%	8.75%	8.77%	8.87%	8.95%	29.88
12/1988	9.07%	9.08%	9.09%	9.08%	9.12%	9.10%	3.10
1/1989	9.18%	9.19%	9.18%	9.14%	9.15%	9.09%	−8.17
2/1989	9.36%	9.31%	9.29%	9.24%	9.22%	9.16%	−20.10
3/1989	9.67%	9.60%	9.57%	9.50%	9.42%	9.35%	−31.72
4/1989	9.44%	9.39%	9.35%	9.28%	9.24%	9.17%	−26.54
5/1989	8.97%	8.93%	8.90%	8.86%	8.85%	8.82%	−15.15
6/1989	8.36%	8.33%	8.31%	8.26%	8.28%	8.25%	−11.24
7/1989	7.80%	7.82%	7.82%	7.82%	7.92%	8.01%	20.50
9/1989	8.19%	8.17%	8.14%	8.11%	8.14%	8.13%	−5.65
10/1989	8.26%	8.23%	8.22%	8.17%	8.22%	8.18%	−7.93
11/1989	7.95%	8.00%	7.98%	7.94%	8.01%	7.99%	4.00
12/1989	7.78%	7.80%	7.81%	7.79%	7.85%	7.87%	8.24
1/1990	7.75%	7.76%	7.77%	7.74%	7.84%	7.83%	7.96
2/1990	8.08%	8.13%	8.12%	8.12%	8.20%	8.21%	13.89
3/1990	8.35%	8.38%	8.41%	8.40%	8.47%	8.46%	11.28
4/1990	8.62%	8.62%	8.65%	8.60%	8.64%	8.58%	−3.42
5/1990	8.72%	8.77%	8.78%	8.76%	8.80%	8.78%	6.11
6/1990	8.60%	8.64%	8.69%	8.68%	8.75%	8.72%	11.96
7/1990	8.34%	8.38%	8.44%	8.43%	8.51%	8.48%	13.88
8/1990	8.14%	8.23%	8.30%	8.32%	8.44%	8.46%	32.87
9/1990	8.06%	8.23%	8.37%	8.45%	8.67%	8.79%	72.41
10/1990	8.06%	8.24%	8.42%	8.52%	8.76%	8.88%	82.06
11/1990	7.86%	8.02%	8.21%	8.32%	8.58%	8.71%	85.07
12/1990	7.58%	7.72%	7.89%	8.01%	8.26%	8.39%	80.41
1/1991	7.30%	7.44%	7.63%	7.73%	7.99%	8.07%	77.07
2/1991	7.13%	7.34%	7.56%	7.70%	7.97%	8.09%	95.89
3/1991	6.87%	7.08%	7.29%	7.48%	7.73%	7.86%	99.12
4/1991	7.08%	7.32%	7.56%	7.76%	7.98%	8.10%	101.61

incorporate this feature of interest-rate volatility. Second, the pricing and hedging of many interest-rate derivative products are significantly influenced by the volatility and it is important to incorporate the differential volatility of short-term and long-term interest rates in their valuation.

Yield vs. Maturity and Duration

The yield curve, as mentioned earlier, is the plot of yield to maturity as a function of time to maturity or of modified duration. In Figure 5-9, we depict the yield curve on

FIGURE 5-7   *Volatility and the Level of Interest Rates*

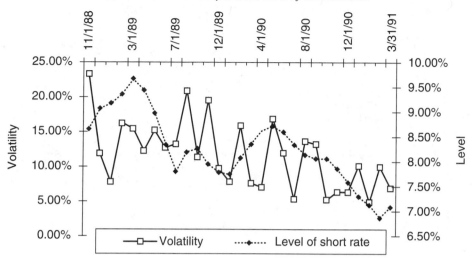

FIGURE 5-8   *Volatility and the Shape of Yield Curve*

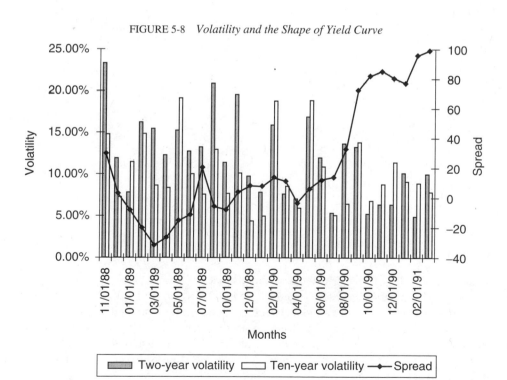

FIGURE 5-9   *Yield Curve on January 15, 1991, First Plot*

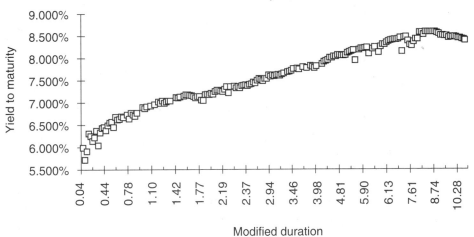

FIGURE 5-10   *Yield Curve on January 15, 1991, Second Plot*

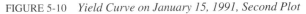

January 15, 1991. All Treasury notes and bonds that were outstanding on that day (for settlement on January 17, 1991) are represented in the figure. In Figure 5-10, we have represented the yield curve as a plot between yield to maturity and modified duration.

To illustrate the problems of drawing sensible inferences from this yield curve, note first that on that day over 200 Treasury notes and bonds were outstanding in the market. In Table 5-4, we present a list of all Treasury notes and bonds that were outstanding on that day. Over 20 outstanding bonds are callable by the Treasury at par on any coupon day during the last five years of the bond's stated life. These issues are identified in Table 5-4 with their respective first call dates shown in a separate column. Some of the issues are on-the-run and most are off-the-run.

TABLE 5-4   *Treasury Notes and Bonds Prices and Yields Quoted on January 15, 1991. Settled on: January 17, 1991*

Coupon (rounded)	Maturity or First Call Date	Maturity Date of Callable Issues	Price (in $\frac{1}{32}$)	Modified Duration	Maturity (in years)	Yield
9.00000%	1/31/91		100.03	0.04	0.04	4.69%
7.37500%	2/15/91		100.01	0.08	0.08	5.99%
9.12500%	2/15/91		100.06	0.08	0.08	5.72%
9.37500%	2/28/91		100.10	0.11	0.12	5.91%
6.75000%	3/31/91		100.00	0.19	0.20	6.31%
9.75000%	3/31/91		100.19	0.19	0.20	6.25%
12.37500%	4/15/91		101.12	0.23	0.24	6.14%
9.25000%	4/30/91		100.24	0.28	0.28	6.22%
8.12500%	5/15/91		100.15	0.32	0.32	6.37%
4.50000%	5/15/91		102.17	0.32	0.32	6.04%
8.75000%	5/31/91		100.25	0.36	0.37	6.33%
7.87500%	6/30/91		100.18	0.44	0.45	6.43%
8.25000%	6/30/91		100.23	0.44	0.45	6.45%
13.75000%	7/15/91		103.15	0.48	0.49	6.38%
7.75000%	7/31/91		100.19	0.04	0.53	6.49%
7.50000%	8/15/91		100.15	0.54	0.58	6.55%
8.75000%	8/15/91		101.05	0.54	0.58	6.57%
14.87500%	8/15/91		104.19	0.53	0.58	6.45%
8.25000%	8/31/91		100.28	0.58	0.62	6.68%
8.37500%	9/30/91		101.04	0.66	0.70	6.62%
9.12500%	9/30/91		101.20	0.66	0.70	6.63%
12.25000%	10/15/91		103.29	0.69	0.74	6.69%
7.62500%	10/31/91		100.21	0.74	0.79	6.67%
6.50000%	11/15/91		99.24	0.78	0.83	6.74%
8.50000%	11/15/91		101.11	0.78	0.83	6.73%
14.25000%	11/15/91		105.29	0.77	0.83	6.64%
7.75000%	11/30/91		100.24	0.82	0.87	6.77%
7.62500%	12/31/91		100.24	0.90	0.95	6.73%
8.25000%	12/31/91		101.11	0.90	0.95	6.70%
11.62500%	1/15/92		104.17	0.94	0.99	6.77%
8.12500%	1/31/92		101.08	0.50	1.04	6.79%
6.62500%	2/15/92		99.22	1.00	1.08	6.87%
9.12500%	2/15/92		102.07	0.98	1.08	6.90%
14.62500%	2/15/92		107.26	0.95	1.08	6.87%
8.50000%	2/29/92		101.20	1.02	1.12	6.91%
7.87500%	3/31/92		101.01	1.11	1.20	6.91%
8.50000%	3/31/92		101.23	1.10	1.20	6.93%
11.75000%	4/15/92		105.16	1.12	1.24	7.00%
8.87500%	4/30/92		102.08	1.18	1.28	6.96%
6.62500%	5/15/92		99.17	1.24	1.33	6.95%
9.00000%	5/15/92		102.13	1.22	1.33	7.02%
13.75000%	5/15/92		108.12	1.19	1.33	6.99%
8.50000%	5/31/92		101.26	1.26	1.37	7.04%
8.25000%	6/30/92		101.21	1.35	1.45	6.99%
8.37500%	6/30/92		101.25	1.35	1.45	7.02%
10.37500%	7/15/92		104.19	1.38	1.49	7.04%
8.00000%	7/31/92		101.10	0.95	1.54	7.04%
7.25000%	8/15/92		100.08	1.43	1.58	7.00%
7.87500%	8/15/92		101.02	1.42	1.58	7.11%
8.25000%	8/15/92		101.19	1.41	1.58	7.12%
8.12500%	8/31/92		101.15	1.45	1.62	7.11%
8.12500%	9/30/92		101.16	1.53	1.70	7.13%

(Continued)

TABLE 5-4   *(Continued)*

Coupon (rounded)	Maturity or First Call Date	Maturity Date of Callable Issues	Price (in $\frac{1}{32}$)	Modified Duration	Maturity (in years)	Yield
8.75000%	9/30/92		102.16	1.53	1.70	7.13%
9.75000%	10/15/92		104.04	1.55	1.75	7.15%
7.75000%	10/31/92		100.28	1.62	1.79	7.18%
7.75000%	11/15/92		100.29	1.66	1.83	7.18%
8.37500%	11/15/92		101.31	1.65	1.83	7.17%
10.50000%	11/15/92		105.18	1.63	1.83	7.16%
7.37500%	11/30/92		100.11	1.70	1.87	7.14%
7.25000%	12/31/92		100.06	1.79	1.96	7.11%
9.12500%	12/31/92		103.16	1.77	1.96	7.14%
8.75000%	1/15/93		102.28	1.81	2.00	7.14%
6.75000%	2/15/93		99.05	1.85	2.08	7.06%
7.87500%	2/15/93		101.10	1.83	2.08	7.05%
8.25000%	2/15/93		101.31	1.83	2.08	7.18%
8.37500%	2/15/93		102.06	1.82	2.08	7.19%
10.87500%	2/15/93		106.29	1.78	2.08	7.18%
9.62500%	3/31/93		104.23	1.92	2.20	7.21%
7.37500%	4/15/93		100.08	2.00	2.24	7.19%
7.62500%	5/15/93		100.21	2.07	2.33	7.25%
8.62500%	5/15/93		102.25	2.06	2.33	7.28%
10.12500%	5/15/93		105.28	2.03	2.33	7.28%
8.12500%	6/30/93		101.25	2.19	2.45	7.26%
7.25000%	7/15/93		99.28	2.24	2.49	7.25%
7.50000%	8/15/88	8/15/93	100.07	2.24	2.58	7.30%
8.00000%	8/15/93		101.13	2.23	2.58	7.36%
8.62500%	8/15/93		103.00	2.31	2.58	7.22%
8.75000%	8/15/93		103.05	2.31	2.58	7.36%
1.87500%	8/15/93		110.10	2.41	2.58	7.36%
8.25000%	9/30/93		102.02	2.34	2.70	7.37%
7.12500%	10/15/93		99.12	2.41	2.75	7.33%
7.75000%	11/15/93		100.29	2.47	2.83	7.36%
8.62500%	11/15/93		103.04	2.45	2.83	7.33%
9.00000%	11/15/93		104.00	2.44	2.83	7.38%
11.75000%	11/15/93		110.26	2.37	2.83	7.39%
7.62500%	12/31/93		100.17	2.60	2.96	7.40%
7.00000%	1/15/94		98.28	2.65	3.00	7.38%
8.87500%	2/15/94		103.27	2.58	3.08	7.41%
9.00000%	2/15/94		104.05	2.57	3.08	7.42%
8.50000%	3/31/94		102.27	2.71	3.20	7.46%
7.00000%	4/15/94		98.20	2.80	3.24	7.44%
9.50000%	5/15/94		105.21	2.79	3.33	7.50%
13.12500%	5/15/94		116.02	2.69	3.33	7.54%
8.50000%	6/30/94		102.28	2.95	3.45	7.52%
8.00000%	7/15/94		101.13	3.01	3.49	7.49%
8.62500%	8/15/94		103.07	2.95	3.58	7.54%
8.75000%	8/15/94		103.20	2.94	3.58	7.54%
12.62500%	8/15/94		115.10	2.80	3.58	7.62%
8.50000%	9/30/94		102.27	3.07	3.70	7.59%
9.50000%	10/15/94		105.29	3.07	3.75	7.62%
8.25000%	11/15/94		102.00	3.20	3.83	7.60%
11.12500%	11/15/94		108.02	3.09	3.83	7.62%

TABLE 5-4   *(Continued)*

Coupon (rounded)	Maturity or First Call Date	Maturity Date of Callable Issues	Price (in $\frac{1}{32}$)	Modified Duration	Maturity (in years)	Yield
11.62500%	11/15/94		112.30	3.07	3.83	7.63%
7.62500%	12/31/94		100.00	3.35	3.96	7.61%
8.62500%	1/15/95		103.07	3.34	4.00	7.64%
7.75000%	2/15/95		100.08	3.34	4.08	7.66%
10.50000%	2/15/95		109.19	3.20	4.08	7.68%
11.25000%	2/15/95		112.04	3.17	4.08	7.69%
8.37500%	4/15/95		102.09	3.46	4.24	7.70%
8.50000%	5/15/95		102.24	3.53	4.33	7.72%
10.37500%	5/15/95		109.11	3.44	4.33	7.76%
11.25000%	5/15/95		112.16	3.40	4.33	7.76%
12.62500%	5/15/95		117.14	3.35	4.33	7.77%
8.87500%	7/15/95		104.02	3.67	4.49	7.75%
8.50000%	8/15/95		102.23	3.63	4.58	7.76%
10.50000%	8/15/95		110.03	3.51	4.58	7.80%
8.62500%	10/15/95		103.05	3.78	4.75	7.78%
8.50000%	11/15/95		102.22	3.87	4.83	7.78%
9.50000%	11/15/95		106.18	3.81	4.83	7.81%
11.50000%	11/15/95		114.13	3.70	4.83	7.83%
9.25000%	1/15/96		105.23	3.98	5.00	7.81%
7.87500%	2/15/96		100.10	3.99	5.08	7.78%
8.87500%	2/15/96		104.07	3.92	5.08	7.82%
9.37500%	4/15/96		106.09	4.04	5.25	7.86%
7.37500%	5/15/96		97.25	4.27	5.33	7.86%
7.87500%	7/15/96		99.28	4.39	5.50	7.87%
8.00000%	10/15/96		100.08	4.45	5.75	7.92%
7.25000%	11/15/96		96.23	4.59	5.83	7.94%
8.00000%	1/15/97		100.02	4.69	6.00	7.96%
8.50000%	4/15/97		102.08	4.70	6.25	8.01%
8.50000%	5/15/97		102.08	4.78	6.33	8.01%
8.50000%	7/15/97		102.07	4.94	6.50	8.04%
8.62500%	8/15/97		102.26	4.81	6.58	8.04%
8.75000%	10/15/97		103.13	4.95	6.75	8.07%
8.87500%	11/15/97		104.02	5.02	6.83	8.07%
7.87500%	1/15/98	5/15/98	98.31	5.29	7.00	8.06%
8.12500%	2/15/98		100.07	5.14	7.08	8.06%
7.00000%	5/15/93		93.29	5.51	7.33	8.07%
9.00000%	5/15/98		104.21	5.27	7.33	8.12%
9.25000%	8/15/98		106.02	5.26	7.58	8.14%
8.87500%	11/15/98	5/15/99	103.30	5.54	7.83	8.16%
8.87500%	2/15/98		103.29	5.55	8.08	8.18%
8.50000%	5/15/94		101.11	5.86	8.33	7.95%
9.12500%	5/15/99		105.10	5.75	8.33	8.21%
8.00000%	8/15/99	2/15/00	98.24	5.90	8.58	8.19%
7.87500%	11/15/99		97.24	6.16	8.83	8.22%
7.87500%	2/15/95		97.23	6.16	9.08	8.22%
8.50000%	2/15/00	8/15/00	101.18	6.06	9.08	8.23%
8.87500%	5/15/00		103.30	6.24	9.33	8.24%
8.37500%	8/15/95		100.29	6.32	9.58	8.10%
8.75000%	8/15/00		103.07	6.24	9.58	8.25%
8.50000%	11/15/00		101.28	6.52	9.84	8.21%

(Continued)

TABLE 5-4   *(Continued)*

Coupon (rounded)	Maturity or First Call Date	Maturity Date of Callable Issues	Price $(in \frac{1}{32})$	Modified Duration	Maturity (in years)	Yield
11.75000%	2/15/01	8/15/01	123.12	6.07	10.09	8.25%
13.12500%	5/15/01		133.05	6.17	10.33	8.26%
8.00000%	8/15/96		98.26	6.80	10.58	8.13%
13.37500%	8/15/01		135.12	6.09	10.58	8.26%
15.75000%	11/15/01		152.06	6.13	10.84	8.31%
14.25000%	2/15/02		142.06	6.18	11.09	8.31%
11.62500%	11/15/02		124.01	6.85	11.84	8.35%
10.75000%	2/15/03		117.17	6.88	12.09	8.38%
10.75000%	5/15/03		117.19	7.11	12.33	8.40%
11.12500%	8/15/03		120.19	6.99	12.58	8.41%
11.87500%	11/15/03		126.16	7.13	12.84	8.42%
12.37500%	5/15/04		131.03	7.22	13.33	8.42%
13.75000%	8/15/04	5/15/05	142.09	6.99	13.59	8.43%
11.62500%	11/15/04		125.12	7.45	13.84	8.46%
8.25000%	5/15/00		100.16	8.23	14.33	8.15%
12.00000%	5/15/05		128.28	7.55	14.33	8.47%
10.75000%	8/15/05	2/15/07	118.20	7.61	14.59	8.48%
9.37500%	2/15/06	11/15/07	108.06	7.99	15.09	8.39%
7.62500%	2/15/02	8/15/08	93.30	8.65	16.09	8.30%
7.87500%	11/15/02	11/15/08	96.08	8.96	16.84	8.28%
8.37500%	8/15/03	5/15/09	99.29	8.81	17.59	8.37%
8.75000%	11/15/03	11/15/09	102.12	8.94	17.84	8.43%
9.12500%	5/15/04	2/15/10	105.13	8.98	18.34	8.43%
10.37500%	11/15/04	5/15/10	114.08	8.80	18.84	8.58%
11.75000%	2/15/05	11/15/10	125.17	8.47	19.09	8.58%
10.00000%	5/15/05	5/15/11	111.28	8.98	19.34	8.53%
12.75000%	11/15/05	11/15/11	134.13	8.68	19.84	8.59%
13.87500%	5/15/06	11/15/12	144.16	8.66	20.34	8.59%
14.00000%	11/15/06	8/15/13	146.07	8.74	20.84	8.59%
10.37500%	11/15/07	5/15/14	115.21	9.33	21.84	8.59%
12.00000%	8/15/08	8/15/14	130.17	9.04	22.59	8.59%
13.25000%	5/15/09	11/15/14	142.17	9.22	23.34	8.59%
12.50000%	8/15/09		136.01	9.14	23.59	8.57%
11.75000%	11/15/09		129.17	9.47	23.84	8.55%
11.25000%	2/15/15		127.25	9.39	24.10	8.51%
10.62500%	8/15/15		121.17	9.54	24.59	8.51%
9.87500%	11/15/15		113.31	9.89	24.84	8.50%
9.25000%	2/15/16		107.19	9.81	25.10	8.50%
7.25000%	5/15/16		87.09	10.50	25.34	8.46%
7.50000%	11/15/16		89.23	10.48	25.85	8.48%
8.75000%	5/15/17		102.25	10.28	26.34	8.47%
8.87500%	8/15/17		104.01	10.06	26.59	8.48%
9.12500%	5/15/18		106.27	10.32	27.34	8.47%
9.00000%	11/15/18		105.23	10.40	27.85	8.45%
8.87500%	2/15/19		104.13	10.24	28.10	8.45%
8.12500%	8/15/19		96.19	10.43	28.59	8.43%
8.50000%	2/15/20		100.24	10.42	29.10	8.42%
8.75000%	5/15/20		103.21	10.63	29.35	8.40%
8.75000%	8/15/20		103.22	10.43	29.60	8.40%

Source: Federal Reserve Bank, New York

Coupon Effect

In each maturity sector there are clusters of Treasury securities of varying vintages, coupons, and contractual provisions. For example, as noted in Table 5-4, there are five Treasury securities maturing on February 15, 1993, ranging in coupons from 6.75% to 10.875%. The modified durations of these five securities were practically identical. Yet, their yield to maturity varied from a low of 7.05% to a high of 7.19%. Note that high-coupon securities generally yield higher. This pattern is by no means an accident: Three securities were maturing on May 15, 1993, and the security with a coupon of 10.125% was yielding 7.28%, whereas the security with a coupon of 7.625% was yielding 7.25%. This difference of 3 basis points is well outside the bid-offer spread and hence is of economic significance. Similar situations can be noted in the long end of the yield curve. The 8.5% coupon T-bond maturing on February 15, 2020, has a modified duration of 10.42 years and has a yield to maturity of 8.42%. In comparison, the 9% coupon T-bond maturing on November 15, 2018, with a modified duration of 10.41 years, has a yield to maturity of 8.45%, which is higher by 3 basis points.

What are the reasons for high-coupon securities to trade at a slightly higher yield even though the duration is the same? Many institutional investors with long-dated liabilities might prefer low-coupon securities, which tend to have a longer duration. As noted in Chapter 4, higher duration means a higher sensitivity to interest rates. Such assets may be ideal to match the interest-rate sensitivity of long-dated liabilities. Pension funds and insurance companies are examples of such institutional investors. They may drive up the price of low-coupon securities, thereby bringing down their yields.

The process of auctions may also contribute to this pattern. The Treasury attempts to sell the security close to par; this means that as the rates decrease, the newly issued security will tend to have a lower coupon, and a number of issues that were issued in the recent past will become high coupons. Thus, the relative supply of high coupons will be larger. This tends to lower their price and hence increase their yield. Of course, exactly the reverse will occur when the rates increase. There may be tax considerations as well. High-coupon bonds that pay higher interest may subject certain investors to a greater tax exposure. If such investors are the marginal holders of these bonds, they may demand a higher yield. Conversely, low-coupon bonds may be accepted at a lower yield.

The regulatory restrictions faced by institutions may also play a part. In Japan, certain institutions are not permitted to pay dividends from capital gains; they are permitted to pay dividends only from interest income. They prefer high-coupon bonds. As a result, high-coupon bonds in Japan have tended to exhibit lower yield in many periods. In Chapter 10 we explore further the effect of taxes on the pricing of fixed-income securities.

Liquidity Effect

The newly issued securities (the on-the-run issues) tend to be more liquid; we showed evidence of this in Chapter 1. As such, they will sell at a higher price. In other words, they command a liquidity premium while off-the-run issues will be cheaper, *ceteris pari-bus,* because of their illiquidity. This pattern is obvious for the thirty-year T-bonds in the last section. Recall that the on-the-run T-bond (8.75% coupon, maturing on August 15, 2020) was trading at a yield of 8.40%, whereas the old thirty-year T-bond (8.50% coupon, maturing on February 15, 2020) was trading at a higher yield of 8.42%.

The liquidity effect is probably best seen by comparing Treasury bills with Treasury notes and bonds that have the same maturity. In Table 5-5, we present all the T-bills that were traded on January 15, 1991, for settlement on January 17, 1991. Consider the bill maturing on May 16, 1991, trading at a yield of 6.31%. Compare this with the old T-notes maturing on May 15, 1991, from Table 5-3; the T-note with a coupon 8.125% maturing on May 15, 1991, was yielding 6.37%. Although both are riskless and are virtually identical, the T-note is cheaper than the T-bill by six basis points.

TABLE 5-5   *U.S. Treasury Bills Quoted: January 15, 1991. Settlement: January 17, 1991.*

Maturity	Bid	Ask	Yield	Maturity	Bid	Ask	Yield
01/24/1991	5.09	5.05	5.13	05/23/1991	6.13	6.11	6.33
01/31/1991	5.36	5.32	5.41	05/30/1991	6.13	6.11	6.34
02/07/1991	5.46	5.38	5.47	06/06/1991	6.11	6.09	6.32
02/14/1991	5.60	5.58	5.68	06/13/1991	6.13	6.11	6.35
02/21/1991	5.82	5.80	5.91	06/20/1991	6.15	6.13	6.38
02/28/1991	5.83	5.79	5.91	06/27/1991	6.09	6.07	6.33
03/07/1991	5.99	5.97	6.10	07/05/1991	6.19	6.17	6.44
03/14/1991	6.00	5.98	6.12	07/11/1991	6.17	6.15	6.43
03/21/0991	6.00	5.98	6.13	07/18/1991	6.16	6.14	6.42
03/28/1991	5.99	5.97	6.12	08/01/1991	6.21	6.19	6.48
04/04/1991	6.03	6.01	6.17	08/29/1991	6.21	6.19	6.49
04/11/1991	6.02	6.00	6.17	09/26/1991	6.18	6.16	6.47
04/18/1991	6.05	6.03	6.21	10/24/1991	6.27	6 .25	6.59
04/25/1991	6.12	6.10	6.29	11/21/1991	6.27	6.25	6.61
05/02/1991	6.11	6.09	6.29	12/19/1991	6.20	6.18	6.55
05/09/1991	6.11	6.09	6.29	01/16/1992	6.20	6.18	6.58
05/16/1991	6.12	6.10	6.31				

Generally T-bills are more expensive than off-the-run T-notes and T-bonds is borne out in Figure 5-11.

Warga (1992) shows that recently issued bonds (on-the-run) are priced to reflect a premium of about 55 basis points per annum compared to otherwise identical bonds. Table 5-6, taken from Warga's paper, vividly illustrates that off-the-run issues are priced at a discount relative to on-the-run issues across a duration range of 20 to 84 months.

FIGURE 5-11   *Liquidity Effects in Yield Curve*

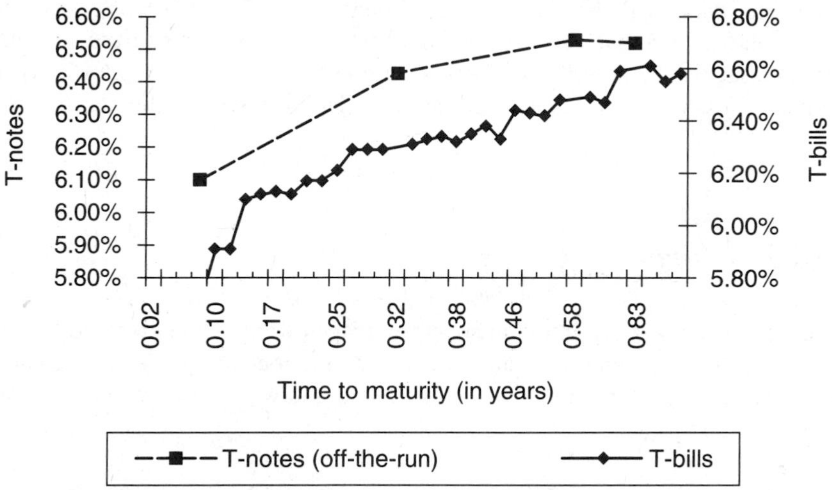

Time to maturity (in years)

- –■– T-notes (off-the-run)   –♦– T-bills

Duration Range (Months)		Mean Difference*
20–24	Portfolio 1	47.6
	t-stat	3.5
28–32	Portfolio 3	40.6
	t-stat	2.4
36–40	Portfolio 5	55.9
	t-stat	4.1
40–44	Portfolio 6	38.5
	t-stat	1.6
44–48	Portfolio 7	65.2
	t-stat	3.5
48–52	Portfolio 8	131
	t-stat	5.3
56–60	Portfolio 10	7.16
	t-stat	0.25
60–64	Portfolio 11	101
	t-stat	3.1
64–72	Portfolio 12	56.5
	t-stat	1.9
72–84	Portfolio 13	8.67
	t-stat	0.2

TABLE 5-6
EM-Based Mean Differences—All Bonds Minus "On the Run" (figures are in basis points per annum)

*Measured in basis points per annum.

Source: Warga, 1992

With so many issues outstanding, it is very difficult to estimate the correct yield at any given maturity date. We need a good benchmark at each maturity date clearly indicating the yield at that maturity date. In addition, there are some maturity dates for which no issues are present in the market. In order to develop estimates of yields at those maturities, we need a benchmark as well. This leads us to the concept of term structure.

TERM-STRUCTURE ANALYSIS

In order to develop a sharp intuition about the shape of the yield curve and the factors that underlie the levels and the shape, we need a more parsimonious representation of the yield curve than Figure 5-9. It is in this context that we define the term structure of interest rates.

Term structure of interest rates refers to the relationship between the yield to maturity of default-free zero coupon securities and their maturities.

Often, the yield to maturity on a default-free zero coupon (pure discount) bond is termed the **spot rate of interest.** The relationship between the spot rate of a pure discount bond and its maturity is referred to as the **spot curve.** In order to get a better handle on the pricing of zero coupon bonds, we first develop the pricing principles for a default-free pure discount bond.

Pure Discount Bonds

The concept of term structure is best developed in terms of pure discount bonds or zero coupon bonds. We define the notation for the price of a zero, suggested earlier, more formally as $b(t, T)$, the price at date $t \leq T$ of a pure discount bond which pays \$1 at date T. We assume that the discount bonds are free from default risk. (The treatment of credit risk requires the modeling of economic factors that lead to financial distress and of the negotiations between creditors and borrowers in times of financial distress. In addition, factors such as liquidation costs, cash-flow generating capacity of the borrower, etc. become relevant. We consider such factors in Chapter 8 in the context of corporate debt.) Examples of default-free zero coupon securities are T-bills (considered in Chapter 4) and zero coupon securities obtained by stripping U.S. Treasury securities. The analysis of strips is taken up later in this chapter.

Bootstrapping Procedure. Spot rates are associated with specific maturities. Thus, the spot rate y_j for a pure discount bond maturing j years from now may be defined as the discount rate at which the present value of the promised terminal cash flow of the pure discount bond is equal to its price. If $b(t, j)$ is the price at date t of a pure discount bond paying \$100 in j years from date t, then

$$b(t, j) = \frac{100}{(1 + y_j)^{j-t}} \qquad (5.3)$$

where y_j is the spot rate of interest on a zero coupon bond with a time to maturity of $j - t$.

Often, we are confronted with situations where the prices of coupon bonds are readily available, but zero coupon prices are difficult to get. So, it is necessary to try to estimate zero coupon bond prices based on the prices of coupon bond prices. A procedure known as boot strapping is used for this purpose. This procedure is illustrated in Example 5-2.

Example 5-2

Consider the problem of finding the pure discount bond prices from the coupon bond prices that are available. Table 5-7 gives data for three bonds for a period of three years. Note that Bond 1, which matures in a year's time, has a coupon of 5% (annual) and is selling at a price of 99.50. Bond 2, which matures two years from now, pays a coupon of 6% (annual) and is selling at a price of 101.25. Finally, Bond 3, which pays a coupon of 7%, matures three years from now and is selling at a price of 100.25.

Bond	Price	Year 1	Year 2	Year 3
1	99.50	105	0	0
2	101.25	6	106	0
3	100.25	7	7	107

TABLE 5-7
Prices, Coupons, and Maturities

Let P_i be the price of bond i. Let c_i denote the dollar coupon associated with bond i. Then, we can denote the price of the first bond as

$$P_1 = \frac{100 + C_1}{(1 + y_1)}. \qquad (5.4)$$

$P_1 = 99.50$ and $C_1 = 5$. Thus, Equation (5.4) becomes

$$99.50 = \frac{100 + 5}{(1 + y_1)}. \qquad (5.5)$$

Solving for y_1, we get a one-year spot rate of interest of 5.53%. The one-year implied zero, $b(0, 1)$ is defined as

$$b(0, 1) = \frac{1}{1 + y_1}. \qquad (5.6)$$

Substituting $y_1 = 5.53\%$ in the equation and solving, we get $b(0, 1) = 0.9476$. More generally, we can use Equation (5.4) to solve for the one year zero price as follows:

$$b(0, 1) = \frac{1}{1 + y_1} = \frac{P_1}{100 + C_1}$$

Once the price P_1 and the coupon C_1 of the one-year coupon bond are known, we can solve for $b(0, 1)$, the zero coupon bond price.

Armed with the knowledge of y_1, we can determine y_2. To do this, recognize that the price of Bond 2 can be written in terms of the two spot rates of interest as

$$P_2 = \frac{C_2}{1 + y_1} + \frac{100 + C_2}{(1 + y_2)^2}. \tag{5.7}$$

Note that the first coupon C_2, which will be paid at year 1, is discounted at the one-year spot rate of interest. The final payment $100 + C_2$, paid in year 2, is discounted at the second-year spot rate of interest. Substituting $P_2 = 101.25$, $C_2 = 6$, and $y_1 = 5.53\%$, we get

$$101.25 = \frac{6}{1 + 0.0553} + \frac{100 + 6}{(1 + y_2)^2} \tag{5.8}$$

Solving for y_2, we get $y_2 = 5.32\%$. The implied zero for two-year maturity may be found by

$$b(0, 2) = \frac{1}{(1 + y_2)^2} \tag{5.9}$$

$$b(0, 2) = 0.9015.$$

As before, using Equation (5.7), we can solve in a general way for $b(0, 2)$ as follows:

$$b(0, 2) = \frac{1}{(1 + y_2)^2} = \frac{P_2 - C_2 b(0, 1)}{100 + C_2}$$

The computed values for $b(0, 1)$, P_2 and C_2 are used to solve for $b(0, 2)$.

Proceeding in this way, we can determine y_3 and $b(0, 3)$ as well. The price of Bond 3 may be written as

$$P_3 = \frac{C_3}{1 + y_1} + \frac{C_3}{(1 + y_2)^2} + \frac{100 + C_3}{(1 + y_3)^3}. \tag{5.10}$$

Note that in the above equation, the only unknown quantity is y_3, the three-year spot rate of interest. Substituting for the values of P_3, C_3, y_1, and y_2, we get

$$100.25 = \frac{7}{1 + 0.0553} + \frac{7}{(1 + 0.0532)^2} + \frac{100 + 7}{(1 + y_3)^3}. \tag{5.11}$$

Solving for y_3, we obtain $y_3 = 7.02\%$. Then

$$b(0, 3) = \frac{1}{(1 + y_3)^3} \tag{5.12}$$

$$b(0, 3) = 0.8159.$$

The results are presented in Table 5-8.

Maturity (years)	Implied Zero	Spot Rate
1	0.9476	5.53%
2	0.9015	5.32%
3	0.8159	7.02%

TABLE 5-8
*Implied Zeroes
and Spot Rates*

Note that this example is hypothetical and is intended just to illustrate the concept of building the spot curve from coupon bonds. In this and earlier examples, we have used premium and discount coupon bonds which in a real transaction have coupon effects discussed earlier. In addition, bonds may not be available at every maturity sector. Some maturity ranges are spanned by bonds that are callable. In Table 5-4, we note that callable bonds dominate the maturity range 2002 to 2009. So, the problem of building implied zeroes is far from being as simple as suggested by the examples so far.

Before proceeding to address this important estimation problem, we briefly state the general relationship between coupon bond prices and spot rates of interest.

In Example 5-2, we used the information on coupon bond prices as input to derive the zero coupon bond prices. Let us denote the information about coupon bonds as Matrix **A**:

$$\mathbf{A} = \begin{bmatrix} 105 & 0 & 0 \\ 6 & 106 & 0 \\ 7 & 7 & 107 \end{bmatrix}.$$

Let us denote by

$$\mathbf{p} = [99.50, 101.25, 100.25]'$$

the vector of bond prices, and let

$$\mathbf{b} = [b(0, 1), b(0, 2), b(0, 3)]'$$

be the vector of zeroes. Then, the zero bond prices and the coupon bond prices satisfy the relation

$$\mathbf{p} = \mathbf{Ab}.$$

We then solve for the zero prices by inverting matrix **A**:

$$\mathbf{b} = \mathbf{A}^{-1}\mathbf{p}.$$

While in Example 5-2 this process worked well, in practice this will be problematic. The reason is that matrix **A** is sparse in many maturity sectors; there may not be any liquid coupon bonds available in certain maturity sectors. However, the approach, with suitable modifications, can be used in situations where there is a large number of bonds (here **A** is only a 3 × 3 matrix). Generally, the price (at date 0) P_n, of a bond maturing in n years and paying an annual coupon of C dollars per year may be represented as

$$P_n = \frac{C}{1 + y_1} + \frac{C}{(1 + y_2)^2} + \dots + \frac{100 + C}{(1 + y_n)^n}.$$

Using the relationship in Equation (5.3) that the zero prices $b(0, j) = \frac{1}{(1 + y_j)^j}$, we can write

$$P_n = Cb(0, 1) + Cb(0, 2) + \ldots + Cb(0, n) + 100b(0, n).$$

The bootstrapping procedure then uses the above relationship recursively:

1. First, we compute $b(0, 1)$ as

$$b(0, 1) = \frac{P_1}{100 + C_1}$$

   where C_1 is the coupon of the one-year bond and P_1 its price.
2. With the knowledge of $b(0, 1)$, we next proceed to estimate $b(0, 2)$ as

$$b(0, 2) = \frac{P_2 - C_2 b(0, 1)}{(100 + C_2)}$$

   where C_2 is the coupon of the two-year bond and P_2 its price.
3. Proceeding this way, we can estimate the last zero bond price P_n as

$$b(0, n) = \frac{P_n - [C_n b(0, 1) + C_n b(0, 2) + \ldots + C_n b(0, n - 1)]}{(100 + C_n)}.$$

The bond is assumed to pay a coupon of C_n per year. When bonds pay semi-annual coupons, the same idea is used with minor modifications. For example, the price of a one-year bond with exactly two semi-annual coupons outstanding can be written as:

$$P = \frac{\frac{C}{2}}{\left(1 + \frac{y_1}{2}\right)} + \frac{100 + \frac{C}{2}}{\left(1 + \frac{y_2}{2}\right)^2}.$$

In general, we can write bond prices with semi-annual compoundings as

$$P = \frac{\frac{C}{2}}{\left(1 + \frac{y_1}{2}\right)} + \frac{\frac{C}{2}}{\left(1 + \frac{y_2}{2}\right)^2} + \ldots + \frac{\left(100 + \frac{C}{2}\right)}{\left(1 + \frac{y_N}{2}\right)^N}$$

where there are N coupon payments. Note that with exactly N coupon payments remaining, the time to maturity in years T will be $\frac{N}{2}$.

Par Bond Yield Curve. A concept that is used in the industry is the par bond yield curve. It is the relationship between the yield to maturity and time to maturity of bonds that sell at their par value. We illustrate this concept by looking again at Example 5-2. To obtain the par bond yield curve we begin with a one-year bond. If a one-year bond is issued to sell at par, what will be its coupon? The present value of the coupon and the balloon payment must equal 100. Or,

$$100 = \frac{100 + x_1}{1 + y_1}$$

where x_1 is the dollar coupon of the par bond. We conclude from this equation that $x_1 = 5.53$. We now turn attention to the two-year par bond. The present value of its coupons and balloon payments must equal the par amount. Or,

$$100 = \frac{x_2}{1 + y_1} + \frac{100 + x_2}{(1 + y_2)^2}$$

where x_2 is the two-year par bond coupon. Using $y_1 = 5.53\%$ and $y_2 = 5.32\%$, we get

$$100 = \frac{x_2}{1 + 0.0553} + \frac{100 + x_2}{(1 + 0.0532)^2}$$

or, $100 = 0.9476x_2 + (100 + x_2)0.9015.$

Solving, we get the two-year par bond coupon to be $x_2 = 5.327$.

Finally, the three-year par bond must satisfy the requirement that the price (100) should be equal to the present value of its cash flows. Or,

$$100 = \frac{x_3}{1 + y_1} + \frac{x_3}{(1 + y_2)^2} + \frac{100 + x_3}{(1 + y_3)^3}$$

or, $100 = 0.9476x_3 + 0.9015x_3 + 0.8159(100 + x_3).$

Solving, we get the three-year par bond coupon to be $x_3 = 6.908$.

Since for a par bond, yield to maturity must be equal to its coupon rate, we conclude that the par bond yield curve for the next three years must be:

Par Bond Yield Curve

Years to Maturity	Par Bond Yield
1	5.530%
2	5.327%
3	6.908%

The concept of par bond yield curve is extremely useful in real life. For example, a corporate treasurer wishing to issue a three-year AAA corporate note will wish to know the three-year par bond yield in the Treasury market since the yield of the corporate note will be at a spread over a similar Treasury.

So far, we considered annual and semi-annual compounding. Now we turn to continuous compounding.

Continuous Compounding. The yield to maturity y_T at date t of the pure discount bond maturing at date T is the continuously compounded rate at which the bond appreciates to the par amount at maturity date. It is defined as

$$b(t, T) \times e^{y_T \times (T-t)} \equiv 1 \tag{5.13}$$

Solving for the yield to maturity, we get

$$y_T = \frac{-\ln b(t, T)}{(T - t)} \tag{5.14}$$

A snapshot at date t of the yield to maturity y_T for various values of T is known as the term structure of interest rates in continuous-time framework. These rates are also known as the zero yields or the spot yields.

The par bond yield in continuous compounding can be defined in the following manner. The price of a bond with a maturity of N and paying a flow dollar coupon at a rate of C_N continuously may be expressed as the discounted value of all the coupons plus the discounted value of the balloon payment. This is stated as

$$P = 100b(t, N) + C_N \int_t^N b(t, s)\, ds.$$

As we show in Chapter 4, for par bonds the coupon should be equal to the yield to maturity. If we can identify a par bond, then $C_N = 100y_N$. Using this and the fact that $P = 100$ for par bonds, we get

$$100 = 100b(t, N) + 100y_N \int_t^N b(t, s)\, ds. \tag{5.15}$$

The equation above is very important in the sense that once we have the par bond information, the pure discount bond prices $b(t, s)$ can be extracted from the par bond curve.

If there is no uncertainty in interest rates, then to preclude riskless profits the instantaneous holding-period return on bonds of all maturities must be the same and equal to the instantaneous riskless spot rate $r(t)$. Formally, we can say that

$$\frac{db(t, T)}{b(t, T)} = r(t)\, dt. \tag{5.16}$$

The condition in equation (5.16) is simply a requirement that riskless profits do not exist in well-functioning capital markets. If this condition fails to hold, there will be profitable opportunities. For example, let us say that at a particular instant, a thirty-year bond provides a higher return than a two-year note. Then by buying the thirty-year bond and selling the two-year note, it should be possible to make riskless profits. To prevent such opportunities, in an efficient capital market securities must satisfy the condition in Equation (5.16).

In addition, since the pure discount bond must converge to par at maturity, we must require that

$$b(T, T) = 1. \tag{5.17}$$

We can solve Equation (5.16) subject to the convergence condition in Equation (5.17). The yield curve is then given by the solution shown in the Equation (5.18).

$$b(t, T) = e^{-\int_t^T r(s)\, ds} \tag{5.18}$$

The important implication of the equation above is that the knowledge of the instantaneously riskless spot rate completely specifies the term structure of interest rates. This becomes evident when we note that the right-hand side of Equation (5.18) depends only on the path of instantaneous spot rates of interest.

FORWARD RATES OF INTEREST

Given a set of pure discount bond prices $b(t, T)$, we can calculate a set of forward rates defined on date t as $f_t(T_1, T_2)$. This forward rate can be locked in on date t for a loan starting on date $T_1 \geq t$ and maturing at $T_2 \geq T_1$.

How do we determine the forward rate on date t, so that we can lock the rate in for a loan that begins on date T_1 and matures on date T_2 (naturally, $T_2 \geq T_1 \geq t$)? In Table 5-9, we consider the strategy of investing one dollar on date t at a rate of y_1 to get $(1 + y_1)^{T_1 - t}$ on date T_1. We then sell forward these proceeds on date T_1 at a forward rate of $f_t(T_1, T_2)$ to get $(1 + y_1)^{T_1 - t} \times [1 + f_t(T_1, T_2)]^{T_2 - T_1}$ on date T_2. Note that there is no risk in this transaction, since the forward rates are established on date t. (We ignore the credit risk that may arise from the nonperformance by any of the counterparties.) These are indicated in transactions 1 and 2 in Table 5-9. Of course, we can instead invest on date t at a rate y_2 to get $(1 + y_2)^{T_2 - t}$ on date T_2 (transaction 3).

Note that transactions 1 and 2 together require an investment of one dollar on date t, as does transaction 3. To prevent riskless profits, both strategies must produce the same cash flow at date T_2. Hence, we must have

$$(1 + y_1)^{T_1 - t} \times (1 + f_t(T_1, T_2))^{T_2 - T_1} = (1 + y_2)^{T_2 - t}.$$

Solving this equation, we get the forward rate

$$f_t(T_1, T_2) = \left[\frac{(1 + y_2)^{T_2 - t}}{(1 + y_1)^{T_1 - t}} \right]^{\frac{1}{T_2 - T_1}} - 1. \qquad (5.19)$$

This is illustrated in Example 5-3.

TABLE 5-9   *Forward Rate*

Transaction	Cast Flow on Date t	Yield on T_1	Yield on T_2
1. Invest \$1 on t at rate y_1, maturing on T_1	-1	$(1 + y_1)^{T_1 - t}$	
2. Sell forward the proceeds from transaction 1 on date T_1 at a forward rate $f_t(T_1, T_2)$, maturing on date T_2	0		$(1 + y_1)^{T_1 - t}[1 + f_t(T_1, T_2)]^{T_2 - T_1}$
Total	-1	0	$(1 + y_1)^{T_1 - t}[1 + f_t(T_1, T_2)]^{T_2 - T_1}$
3. Invest \$1 at rate y_2, maturing on T_2	-1		$(1 + y_2)^{T_2 - t}$

Example 5-3

Let $y_1 = 8\%$, $y_2 = 9\%$, $t = 0$, $T_1 = 1$, and $T_2 = 2$. Using Equation (5.19), the forward rate at date 0 for the period starting date 1 and ending date 2 is

$$f_0(1, 2) = \frac{1.09^2}{1.08} - 1 = 10.009\%.$$

The same concept also applies to pure discount bonds as trading instruments. This is shown in Table 5-10, where

$$f_t(T_1, T_2) = \frac{b(t, T_1)}{b(t, T_2)} - 1. \tag{5.20}$$

Table 5-10 shows how to lock in forward rates by trading in spot securities. Equations (5.19) and (5.20) illustrate that the current term structure $b(t, T)$ contains the relevant information for the forward rates of interest. We may synthesize forward contracts from the spot term structure as follows. We have seen that the current term structure thus defines a series of forward rates. A forward rate between two future dates k and l where $l \geq k$ is a currently agreed-upon rate at which one may borrow or lend on date k for maturity on date l. Let the spot rates on date t be y_k and y_l for dates k and l, respectively.

Transaction	Cash Flow on Date t	Yield on T_1	Yield on T_2
1. Long the discount bonds maturing on T_2	$-b(t, T_2)$		$+1$
2. Short $\dfrac{b(t, T_2)}{b(t, T_1)}$ discount bonds maturing on T_1	$+b(t, T_1) \times \dfrac{b(t, T_2)}{b(t, T_1)}$	$-1\dfrac{b(t, T_2)}{b(t, T_1)}$	
Net	0	$-\dfrac{b(t, T_2)}{b(t, T_1)}$	$+1$

TABLE 5-10
Forward Rate, Pure Discount Bonds

Then the forward rate, $f_t(k, l)$, must satisfy the condition:

$$(1 + y_l)^{l-t} = (1 + y_k)^{k-t} \times [1 + f_t(k, l)]^{l-k} \tag{5.21}$$

Setting $k = t + 1$ and $l = t + 2$, we get the one-period forward (one-period) rate

$$(1 + y_2)^2 = (1 + y_1)^1 \times [1 + f_t(t + 1, t + 2)]. \tag{5.22}$$

Solving, we find the forward rate

$$f_t(t + 1, t + 2) = \frac{(1 + y_2)^2}{(1 + y_1)^1} - 1.$$

The equation above is a special case of Equation (5.20) and was used in Example 5.3.

The difference between the forward rates and the spot rates is referred to as the **term premium.** Often, this term premium is thought to contain some information about the changes in the expected spot rate of interest. Some hypotheses about term structure have postulated relationships between forward rates (which can be computed today) and the expected future spot rates, allowing us to write the coupon bond prices in terms of the forward rates.

Our analysis makes it clear that the coupon bond prices incorporate information about the discount factors. We now provide a detailed example of computing forward rates.

Example 5-4

The prices of pure discount bonds are provided in Table 5-11 for four maturities. Using this as the basic data, we can compute all the applicable forward rates as well as the par bond yields.

Maturity Date	Price	Yield
1	0.9500	5.263%
2	0.9000	5.409%
3	0.8500	5.567%
4	0.7900	6.070%

TABLE 5-11
Pure Discount Bonds

Note that the forward rates at year 0 may be computed for the future periods 1 to 2, 1 to 3, 1 to 4, 2 to 3, 2 to 4, and 3 to 4. In effect, there are six forward rates that we can compute at year 0.

The forward rate at date 0 for the period 1 to 2 may be calculated as follows. We recognize that taking one dollar at date 0 and investing it in a one-period zero at 5.263%, and then rolling that forward at date 1 until date 2 at the currently-fixed forward rate of $f_0(1, 2)$ must yield the same dollar amount as investing at date 0 in a two-period loan at a rate of 5.409%. This leads to the equation:

$$1 \times (1 + 0.05263) \times [1 + f_0(1, 2)] = (1 + 0.05409)^2.$$

Solving, we get

$$[1 + f_0(1, 2)] = \frac{(1 + 0.05409)^2}{(1 + 0.05263)} = 1.0556$$

$$f_0(1, 2) = 5.56\%.$$

In a similar way, the forward rate at date 0 for the period 2 to 3 may be calculated as follows. We recognize that taking one dollar at date 0 and investing it in a two-period zero at 5.409%, and then rolling that forward at date 2 until date 3 at the currently-fixed forward rate of $f_0(2, 3)$ must yield the same dollar amount as investing at date 0 in a three-period loan at a rate of 5.567%. This leads to the equation:

$$1 \times (1 + 0.05409)^2 \times [1 + f_0(2, 3)] = (1 + 0.05567)^3.$$

Solving, we get

$$[1 + f_0(2, 3)] = \frac{(1 + 0.05567)^3}{(1 + 0.05409)^2} = 1.0588$$

$$f_0(2, 3) = 5.88\%.$$

The forward rate at date 0 for the period 3 to 4 may be calculated as follows. We recognize that taking one dollar at date 0 and investing it in a three-period zero at 5.567%, and then rolling that forward at date 3 until date 4 at the currently-fixed forward rate of $f_0(3, 4)$ must yield the same dollar amount as investing at date 0 in a four-period loan at a rate of 6.070%. This leads to the equation:

$$1 \times (1 + 0.05567)^3 \times [1 + f_0(3, 4)] = (1 + 0.06070)^4.$$

Solving, we get

$$[1 + f_0(3, 4)] = \frac{(1 + 0.06070)^4}{(1 + 0.05567)^3} = 1.0759$$

$$f_0(3, 4) = 7.59\%.$$

Now we compute the forward rates $f_0(1, 3), f_0(1, 4)$ and $f_0(2, 4)$.

The forward rate at date 0 for the period 1 to 3 may be calculated as follows. We recognize that taking one dollar at date 0 and investing it in a one-period zero at 5.263%, and then rolling that forward at date 1 until date 3 at the currently-fixed forward rate of $f_0(1, 3)$ must yield the same dollar amount as investing at date 0 in a three-period loan at a rate of 5.567%. This leads to the equation:

$$1 \times (1 + 0.05263) \times [1 + f_0(1, 3)]^2 = (1 + 0.05567)^3.$$

Solving, we get

$$[1 + f_0(1, 3)]^2 = \frac{(1 + 0.05567)^3}{(1 + 0.05263)} = 1.1177$$

$$f_0(1, 3) = 5.72\%.$$

The forward rate at date 0 for the period 1 to 4 may be calculated as follows. We recognize that taking one dollar at date 0 and investing it in a one-period zero at 5.263%, and then rolling that forward at date 1 until date 4 at the currently-fixed forward rate of $f_0(1, 4)$ must yield the same dollar amount as investing at date 0 in a four-period loan at a rate of 6.070%. This leads to the equation:

$$1 \times (1 + 0.05263) \times [1 + f_0(1, 4)]^3 = (1 + 0.0607)^4.$$

Solving, we get

$$[1 + f_0(1, 4)]^3 = \frac{(1 + 0.0607)^4}{(1 + 0.05263)} = 1.2025$$

$$f_0(1, 4) = 6.34\%.$$

The forward rate at date 0 for the period 2 to 4 may be calculated as follows. We recognize that taking one dollar at date 0 and investing it in a two-period zero at 5.409%, and then rolling that forward at date 2 until date 4 at the currently-fixed forward rate of $f_0(2, 4)$ must yield the same dollar amount as investing at date 0 in a four-period loan at a rate of 6.070%. This leads to the equation:

$$1 \times (1 + 0.05409)^2 \times (1 + f_0(2, 4))^2 = (1 + 0.0607)^4.$$

Solving, we get

$$[1 + f_0(2, 4)]^2 = \frac{(1 + 0.0607)^4}{(1 + 0.05409)^2} = 1.1392$$

$$f_0(1, 4) = 6.74\%.$$

Generally, we can compute forward rates in this manner for various forward dates in the future. What are the problems with these concepts in practice? The first difficulty arises from the fact that there are few benchmark maturities. As noted in Chapter 3, there are only eight benchmark maturities: 3 months, 6 months, 1 year, 2 years, 3 years, 5 years, 10 years, and 30 years. This means that there are significant gaps in the five-year to ten-year maturity sectors and in the ten-year to thirty-year maturity sectors. Secondly, the frequency of auctions is low in the thirty-year sector and in the quarterly refunding maturity sectors. This means that even the on-the-run issues may not trade at or near par on dates further away from the auction date. These complications not withstanding, we will show that it is possible to develop good spot-rate curves based on limited information about the par bond yield curve. We apply the bootstrapping principle to real-life data next.

PRACTICAL CONSIDERATIONS

We will apply the bootstrapping concepts to the data presented in Table 5-4. Consider the $11\frac{5}{8}\%$ Treasury security maturing January 15, 1992. We can write its price as

$$P = \frac{\frac{11.625}{2}}{1 + \frac{y}{2}} + \frac{105.8125}{\left(1 + \frac{y}{2}\right)^2}. \tag{5.23}$$

Since the settlement date is just two days after the coupon date, let us ignore the accrued interest and treat the full price as $P = 104.5313$. Solving Equation (5.23) we get $y = 6.859\%$. Recall that this procedure assumes a reinvestment rate equal to yield to maturity and that this assumption is unsatisfactory, especially for long-term bonds. A timeline for this security appears in Figure 5-12. When Equation (5.23) is applied to the full price of the bond (with two days accrued interest), we get a yield of 6.79%, which is closer to what is reported in Table 5-4.

FIGURE 5-12   *Timeline*

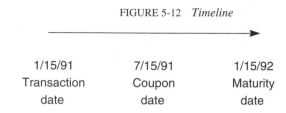

1/15/91	7/15/91	1/15/92
Transaction	Coupon	Maturity
date	date	date

What is the appropriate discount rate for discounting the first coupon that will be paid on July 15, 1991? Reviewing Table 5-4, we find that there is an off-the-run Treasury security maturing on July 15, 1991. It has a coupon of 13.75% and sells at $103\frac{15}{32}$. Its yield is found using the equation:

$$103.46875 = \frac{106.875}{1 + \frac{y_1}{2}}.$$

(5.24)

Thus, the yield y_1 by solving Equation (5.24) is 6.584%. (We are again ignoring the accrued interest for simplicity.) Therefore it seems reasonable to discount the first coupon of the Treasury security maturing on January 15, 1992, at 6.584%. Since we estimated y_1 by looking at a security that had no intermediate coupon but had only a balloon payment of 106.875, it is called an implied zero yield or the spot yield. How do we estimate the implied zero yield y_2 for the date January 15, 1992? Let us again use the price of the 11.625% bond maturing on January 15, 1992, as in Equation (5.23). Then,

$$104.53125 = \frac{\frac{11.625}{2}}{1 + \frac{y_1}{2}} + \frac{105.8125}{\left(1 + \frac{y_2}{2}\right)^2}.$$

(5.25)

Note that we are now using y_1 to discount the first coupon and y_2 to discount the second payment, which includes the balloon. Since everything in the equation except y_2 is known, we can solve for y_2, the implied zero yield for January 15, 1992. Using $y_1 = 6.584\%$ and solving, we get $y_2 = 6.867\%$. Generally the procedure that we have described uses a distinct discount rate for each maturity. Such a formulation has very different implications for the reinvestment rates of intermediate coupons. Consider the two-period security:

$$P = \frac{\frac{c}{2}}{1 + \frac{y_1}{2}} + \frac{100 + \frac{c}{2}}{\left(1 + \frac{y_2}{2}\right)^2}.$$

(5.26)

Multiplying through by $\left(1 + \frac{y_2}{2}\right)^2$ and simplifying, we get

$$P \times \left(1 + \frac{y_2}{2}\right)^2 = \frac{c}{2} \times \frac{\left(1 + \frac{y_2}{2}\right)^2}{1 + \frac{y_1}{2}} + \left(100 + \frac{c}{2}\right).$$

(5.27)

Note that the reinvestment rate for the first coupon is

$$\frac{\left(1 + \frac{y_2}{2}\right)^2}{1 + \frac{y_1}{2}}.$$

As seen earlier in this chapter, this is nothing more than the forward rate at date 0 for the forward period from date 1 to date 2. Recall from Table 5-10 that these rates can be locked in by trading in spot instruments that are available at the current time.

Notice how in our analysis of the yield curve, which is about coupon-paying securities, we have moved on to a discussion of zero coupon securities. To see this connection in a more transparent manner, consider the strategy of replicating the cash flows of the 11.625% security using T-bills that are zero coupon securities. This strategy is illustrated in Table 5-12. On January 15, 1991, we buy 100 million par of an 11.625% bond maturing on January 15, 1992. This is shown as transaction 1. To replicate this, we can buy 5.8125 million par amount of the T-bill maturing on July 11, 1991. (Note from Table 5-5 that there are no T-bills maturing exactly on July 15, 1991.) The T-bill matures on July 11, 1991, paying \$5.8125 million, which replicates the coupon cash flow from the bond. The ask price of the bill is easily calculated from the discount rate of 6.15% (given for this T-bill in Table 5-5) as 97.01, which is used in transaction 2 of Table 5-12. To replicate the last coupon and the balloon payment, we buy 105.8125 million par of the T-bills maturing on January 16, 1992 (as there are no bills maturing exactly on January 15, 1992). The ask discount rate is 6.18% (see Table 5-5, last entry) leading to a price of 93.7513. On maturity, these bills will match the cash flows from the bond. If the bills and the bond were equally liquid and the relevant maturity dates and coupon dates coincided, this strategy would have been perfect. If P is the price of the bond on January 15, 1991 (denoted by date 0), $b(0, 1)$ is the price of the T-bill on January 15, 1991, for maturity on July 11, 1991 (denoted by date 1) and $b(0, 2)$ is the price of the T-bill on

Transaction on 1/15/91	Cash on 1/15/91	Cash on 7/15/91	Cash on 1/15/92
1. Buy 100 million par of 11.625% T-bond	−104.53125	5.8125	105.8125
2. Buy 5.8125 million par of T-bill maturing on 7/11/91	−5.8125 × 0.9701 = (−5.6387)	5.8125 (July 11)	
3. Buy 105.8125 million par of T-bill maturing on 1/16/92	−105.8125 × 0.9375 = (−99.1992)		105.8125 (Jan 16)

TABLE 5-12

Coupon Bond as a Portfolio of Zeroes Quoted: January 15, 1991 Settlement: January 17, 1991

January 15, 1991, for maturity on January 16, 1992 (denoted by date 2), then we may write a no-arbitrage condition as

$$P = c \times b(0, 1) + (100 + c) \times b(0, 2).\qquad(5.28)$$

The foregoing equation says that the coupon bond is a portfolio of zero coupon securities. Of course in reality T-bills, as we have seen, are more expensive than bonds, so the replicating strategy is likely to be more expensive. Consider the cost of the replicating strategy. The total cost is

$$5.8125 \times 0.9701 + 105.8125 \times 0.9375 = 104.8379$$

which is well in excess of the cost of the bond, 104.5313, that we tried to replicate.

The accrued interest of the bond between January 15, 1991, and the settlement date January 17, 1991, is approximately:

$$\frac{2}{365} \times 0.11625 \times 100 = 0.0637$$

Adding this to the bond price, we get $104.5313 + 0.0637 = 104.595$. Note that the T-bill portfolio is still more expensive.

But this analysis does illustrate that the coupon bond prices contain information about the prices of pure discount bonds. If the prices of coupon bonds are out of alignment with those of pure discount bonds, after accounting for liquidity and coupon effects, there will be profitable trading opportunities without any risk. Ideally, to abstract from the liquidity effects that are present in bills, we would like to use coupon securities. Since there are coupon effects in these securities, we should use those coupon securities that sell close to or at par in constructing the implied zero coupon bond prices. We will illustrate this later in the chapter. More generally, this analysis indicates that the schedule of coupon bond prices and pure discount bond prices must stay in alignment to preclude profitable trading opportunities. Pure discount bonds are also traded in the market. We turn to these securities next.

STRIPS MARKETS

Through the Federal Reserve Book entry system, the Treasury permits certain securities to be stripped. These are called strips—Separate Trading of Registered Interest and Principal Securities. Under this program, Treasury securities may be maintained in the book-entry system operated by the Federal Reserve Banks in such a way that it is possible to trade, in book-entry form, interest and principal components as direct obligations of the U.S. Treasury. The Treasury first made eligible for strips the ten-year and thirty-year issues that were made as part of the quarterly refunding on February 15, 1985. Currently about $115 billion worth of U.S. Treasury issues have been stripped into coupon and principal components. Effective May 1, 1987, securities held in stripped form became eligible for **reconstituting,** as well. Only thirty-year (long) bonds and ten-year notes are eligible for stripping.

In Table 5-13, the stripping and reconstituting activities for 1987 to 1990 are provided on a monthly basis. Note that the stripping activity has progressively increased.

TABLE 5-13 *Summary of Strips Program, July 1987 to December 1990*

			Number	Coupon Range	Maturity Range			
		T-bonds	20	7.25%–12%	2000–2020			
		T-notes	23	7.25%–11.25%	1994–2000			

	Dollar Amount Issued	Coupon Issue Remaining	Strips Remaining	Reconstitutions	Percent as Coupons	Percent as Strips	Percent as Reconstitutions
12/90	4.74E+08	359,953,194	113,586,390	5,076,440	76.01%	23.99%	1.07%
11/90	4.74E+08	359,768,677	113,770,490	4,633,120	75.97%	24.03%	0.98%
10/90	4.51E+08	337,776,650	113,284,170	4,571,080	74.88%	25.12%	1.01%
9/90	4.51E+08	338,734,330	112,326,490	3,510,320	75.10%	24.90%	0.78%
8/90	4.51E+08	341,511,055	109,549,780	4,473,560	75.71%	24.29%	0.99%
7/90	4.3E+08	325,342,356	104,178,340	3,461,640	75.75%	24.25%	0.81%
6/90	4.3E+08	327,505,616	102,015,100	4,016,320	76.25%	23.75%	0.94%
5/90	4.3E+08	328,250,321	101,270,450	1,983,760	76.42%	23.58%	0.46%
4/90	4.09E+08	310,745,253	98,120,330	2,074,720	76.00%	24.00%	0.51%
3/90	4.09E+08	312,650,853	96,214,730	2,948,560	76.47%	23.53%	0.72%
2/90	4.09E+08	318,490,903	90,374,690	3,084,960	77.90%	22.10%	0.75%
1/90	3.88E+08	301,987,992	85,975,690	1,690,560	77.84%	22.16%	0.44%
12/89	3.88E+08	304,875,812	83,087,850	1,276,960	78.58%	21.42%	0.33%
11/89	3.88E+08	305,741,138	82,221,610	2,879,280	78.81%	21.19%	0.74%
10/89	3.67E+08	285,341,204	81,558,050	2,497,600	77.76%	22.23%	0.68%
9/89	3.67E+08	285,415,644	81,513,610	2,081,680	77.78%	22.22%	0.57%
8/89	3.67E+08	285,259,009	81,670,250	3,490,840	77.74%	22.26%	0.95%
7/89	3.47E+08	266,160,196	81,488,690	2,092,400	76.78%	23.51%	0.60%
6/89	3.47E+08	264,058,156	82,590,410	3,680,440	76.17%	23.83%	1.06%
5/89	3.47E+08	263,938,710	82,709,610	8,133,020	76.14%	23.86%	2.35%
4/89	3.27E+08	239,787,572	87,172,590	1,797,760	73.34%	26.66%	0.55%
3/89	3.27E+08	247,755,712	79,204,430	1,627,280	75.78%	24.22%	0.50%
2/89	3.27E+08	250,378,914	76,581,270	18,928,840	76.58%	23.42%	5.79%
1/89	3.08E+08	234,223,102	73,407,310	17,170,680	76.14%	23.86%	5.58%
12/88	3.08E+08	237,424,747	70,205,670	15,774,520	77.18%	22.82%	5.13%
11/88	3.08E+08	241,942,818	65,687,350	14,703,320	78.65%	21.35%	4.78%
10/88	2.89E+08	226,036,922	62,657,790	14,014,520	78.30%	21.70%	4.85%
9/88	2.89E+08	227,903,382	60,791,330	13,436,100	78.94%	21.06%	4.65%
8/88	2.88E+08	227,224,636	60,722,290	11,115,500	78.91%	21.09%	3.86%
7/88	2.77E+08	221,321,396	56,030,670	10,511,100	79.80%	20.20%	3.79%
6/88	2.77E+08	223,112,846	54,239,210	10,105,660	80.44%	19.56%	3.64%
5/88	2.77E+08	224,720,866	52,630,990	9,546,200	81.02%	18.98%	3.44%
4/88	2.59E+08	208,725,814	50,752,190	9,354,200	80.44%	19.56%	3.61%
3/88	2.59E+08	209,918,069	49,559,950	8,646,600	80.90%	19.10%	3.33%
2/88	2.59E+08	211,248,369	48,229,550	8,113,480	81.41%	18.59%	3.13%
1/88	2.41E+08	195,071,292	46,406,510	7,030,760	80.78%	19.22%	2.91%
12/87	2.41E+08	196,703,867	44,773,630	6,699,000	81.46%	18.54%	2.77%
11/87	2.41E+08	198,115,540	43,361,830	5,946,480	82.04%	17.96%	2.46%
10/87	2.27E+08	183,645,408	43,082,390	4,658,240	81.00%	19.00%	2.05%
9/87	2.27E+08	187,671,968	39,055,830	4,027,280	82.77%	17.23%	1.78%
8/87	2.27E+08	190,548,819	36,178,950	2,880,480	84.04%	15.96%	1.27%
7/87	2.08E+08	172,339,492	35,940,310	2,522,080	82.74%	17.26%	1.21%

The effect of the shape of the yield curve on the percentage of reconstituting is shown in Figure 5-13. The spread between the thirty-year and two-year yields is used as a proxy for the shape of the yield curve. Note that this proxy appears to have a strong correlation to the amount of reconstituting.

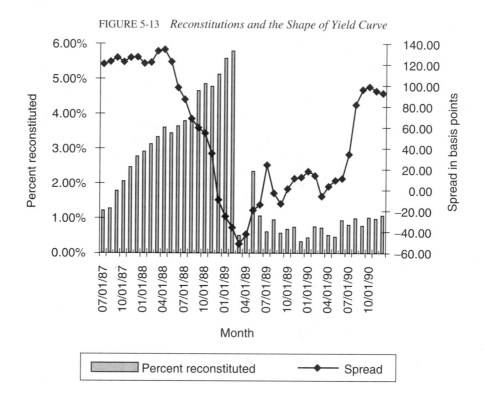

FIGURE 5-13   *Reconstitutions and the Shape of Yield Curve*

It should be stressed that strips are not implied zeroes. Strips are traded securities directly subject to demand and supply. Implied zeroes are estimated pure discount functions derived from the prices of coupon paying Treasury securities. Yet, as expected, implied zeroes provide a benchmark for assessing the relative richness or cheapness of Treasury securities.

Treasury strips are popular securities and they are traded in OTC markets by dealers. In addition, exchanges have also shown an interest in making a market in these securities. As shown in the *Wall Street Journal* article, AMEX has shown an interest in making a market in strips.

Amex Sells Zero-Coupon Strips

NEW YORK — The American Stock Exchange said it began trading zero-coupon bonds based on U.S. Treasury notes or bonds.

The securities, commonly referred to as strips, allow for separate trading of the interest and principal portions of U.S. Treasury notes and bonds. A zero-coupon security makes no periodic interest payments, but instead is sold at a deep discount to its face value, which the buyer receives at maturity.

Why would investors want to hold zero coupon securities? Several motivating factors are at work here. We saw in Chapter 4 that the duration of Treasury coupon securities change with interest rates and the passage of time. As a result, investors who buy Treasury coupon securities to hedge against their liabilities (by matching the duration of assets with liabilities) may have to frequently rebalance their positions. When a thirty-year zero coupon bond is purchased, its duration is always its time to maturity irrespective of interest rates. This may significantly reduce the need to rebalance positions. Furthermore, note from Table 5-4 that the maximum duration that may be achieved in the Treasury market using the current thirty-year T-bond maturing on August 15, 2020, is 10.44 years. There may be many institutional investors holding liabilities with a duration of 15 or more years and for these investors strips may be the only realistic alternative. A thirty-year strip has a duration of 30 years and may thus be preferred by investors with long-dated liabilities for hedging purposes. If there are many such investors, the strong demand for such securities may drive up the prices of long-dated strips and bring down their yields. Later we will present evidence supporting this.

Moreover, when a Treasury coupon bond is purchased, the investor is obliged to buy a bundle of cash flows; the thirty-year T-bond in Table 5-4, maturing on August 15, 2020, is a bundle of 60 coupon payments (8.75% payable on February 15 and August 15 of every year) and a balloon payment on August 15, 2020. This exposes the investor to reinvestment risks if cash flows are needed to fund liabilities only at selected points in time in future. Then the investor may be better off buying a few strips and customizing the cash flows to suit the profile of liabilities.

Strip Yields

The prices of Treasury coupon strips and principal-only strips as of January 15, 1991, are plotted in Figures 5-14 and 5-15, respectively. The prices themselves are shown in Tables 5-14 and 5-15, respectively, along with their yields.

FIGURE 5-14   *Price of Treasury Coupon-only Strips*

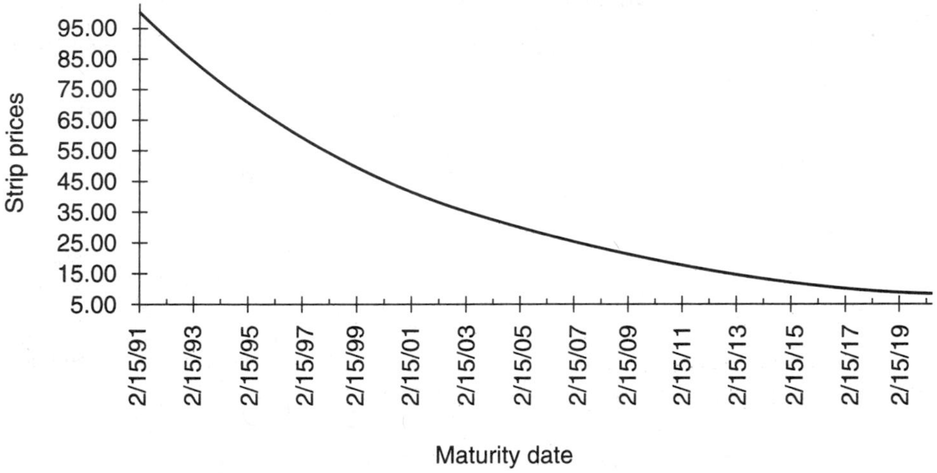

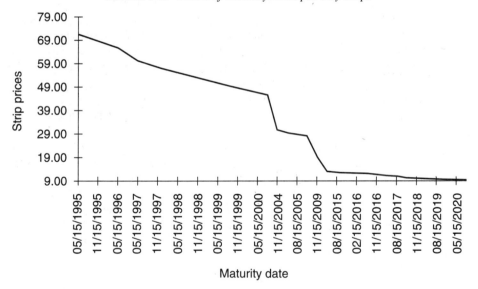

FIGURE 5-15   *Prices of Treasury Principal-only Strips*

Example 5-5

Let us illustrate the pricing of strips to get a better appreciation of zero coupon securities. Consider the strip maturing on November 15, 2000, in Table 5-14. Its price was 44.34 and its yield 8.45%. The convention in the strips market is semi-annual compounding. The price of the strip for settlement on January 17, 1991 (denoted by

t), and maturing on November 15, 2000 (denoted by j) is $b(t, j) = 44.34$. By semi-annual compounding,

$$b(t, j) = \frac{100}{\left(1 + \frac{y_j}{2}\right)^{j-t}}. \tag{5.29}$$

where y_j is the yield to maturity. Note that for this strip, $y_j = 0.0845$, $j = 11/15/2000$ and $t = 1/15/1991$. The time to maturity, $j - t$, in years is 9.8411. In semi-annual terms, the time to maturity, $j - t$, is 19.6822. If we substitute $y_j = 0.0845$, and $j - t = 19.6822$, we will get $b(t, j) = 44.29$, which is different from the market price of the strip. This difference is due to the market convention used for pricing strips. Similar to the pricing of Treasury coupon securities, discussed in Chapter 4, semi-annual periods are used in computing the maturity of the strip. For this strip, the next coupon date is May 15, 1991 and the last coupon date is November 15, 1990. So, the current coupon period is 181 days. Since the settlement date is January 17, 1991, the number of semiannual periods to the next coupon date is $\frac{[5/15/1991] - [1/17/1991]}{181} = 0.6519$. In addition, there are 19 whole semi-annual periods remaining until maturity, so there are 19.6519 semi-annual periods in all until maturity. Using this information, the price of the strip may be calculated as

$$\frac{100}{\left(1 + \frac{0.0845}{2}\right)^{19.6519}} = 44.34. \tag{5.30}$$

When the strip has a maturity which is less than the current coupon period, then the simple interest convention is used for pricing. Note that the yield of zeroes in Table 5-14 generally increases with maturity; but after the August 15, 2006, maturity, yields begin to decline, suggesting that long-dated strips are relatively more valued in the market by investors. The strip prices plotted in Figures 5-14 and 5-15 are downward-sloping functions.

To preclude riskless profits, the following restrictions must hold on the pure discount functions:

$$b(t, t + 1) \geq b(t, t + 2) \geq b(t, t + 3) \geq \ldots \geq b(t, t + n). \tag{5.31}$$

To see why this must be the case, let us consider the prices of strips in Table 5-14.

Example 5-6

Suppose the February 15, 1992, strip is priced at 92.96 as shown in Table 5-14, but the May 15, 1992, strip was priced at 93.00 (instead of 91.37 as shown in Table 5-14). Then the following arbitrage strategy can be put in place: Sell the more expensive strip (if necessary, short it) maturing on May 15, 1992, at a price of 93.00 and buy the cheaper strip maturing on February 15, 1992, at 92.96. This nets a cash flow of 0.24. On February 15, 1992, collect the par amount of 100.00 and earn interest on

TABLE 5-14   *Treasury Coupon-only Strip Yields and Prices*

Maturity Date	Yield	Price	Maturity Date	Yield	Price	Maturity Date	Yield	Price
2/15/91	6.10	99.52	5/15/01	8.55	42.13	8/15/11	8.70	17.33
5/15/91	6.48	97.93	8/15/01	8.55	41.24	11/15/11	8.70	16.97
8/15/91	6.60	96.31	11/15/01	8.57	40.31	2/15/12	8.70	16.61
11/15/91	6.60	94.78	2/15/02	8.62	39.26	5/15/12	8.70	16.27
2/15/92	6.88	92.96	5/15/02	8.64	38.37	8/15/12	8.70	15.92
5/15/92	6.92	91.37	8/15/02	8.64	37.55	11/15/12	8.70	15.59
8/15/92	7.06	89.62	11/15/02	8.64	36.78	2/15/13	8.69	15.29
11/15/92	7.09	88.05	2/15/03	8.65	35.96	5/15/13	8.69	14.97
2/15/93	7.29	86.17	5/15/03	8.68	35.09	8/15/13	8.69	14.65
5/15/93	7.37	84.51	8/15/03	8.67	34.38	11/15/13	8.68	14.38
8/15/93	7.43	82.85	11/15/03	8.67	33.67	2/15/14	8.67	14.10
11/15/93	7.35	81.55	2/15/04	8.69	32.87	5/15/14	8.67	13.81
2/15/94	7.59	79.50	5/15/04	8.70	32.15	8/15/14	8.66	13.55
5/15/94	7.64	77.93	8/15/04	8.70	31.46	11/15/14	8.65	13.30
8/15/94	7.70	76.31	11/15/04	8.70	30.81	2/15/15	8.65	13.02
11/15/94	7.68	74.95	2/15/05	8.71	30.11	5/15/15	8.65	12.75
2/15/95	7.85	73.05	5/15/05	8.71	29.48	8/15/15	8.65	12.48
5/15/95	7.88	71.58	8/15/05	8.71	28.85	11/15/15	8.63	12.28
8/15/95	7.91	70.10	11/15/05	8.65	28.49	2/15/16	8.62	12.05
11/15/95	7.83	69.03	2/15/06	8.72	27.61	5/15/16	8.61	11.83
2/15/96	8.01	67.11	5/15/06	8.72	27.03	8/15/16	8.60	11.60
5/15/96	8.06	65.65	8/15/06	8.72	26.46	11/15/16	8.59	11.39
8/15/96	8.10	64.21	11/15/06	8.71	25.94	2/15/17	8.57	11.21
11/15/96	8.11	62.93	2/15/07	8.72	25.35	5/15/17	8.56	11.01
2/15/97	8.21	61.32	5/15/07	8.72	24.82	8/15/17	8.55	10.80
5/15/97	8.26	59.93	8/15/07	8.72	24.29	11/15/17	8.54	10.61
8/15/97	8.29	58.60	11/15/07	8.72	23.78	2/15/18	8.52	10.44
11/15/97	8.31	57.36	2/15/08	8.72	23.28	5/15/18	8.51	10.26
2/15/98	8.35	56.04	5/15/08	8.72	22.79	8/15/18	8.49	10.10
5/15/98	8.37	54.84	8/15/08	8.72	22.30	11/15/18	8.48	9.92
8/15/98	8.39	53.64	11/15/08	8.72	21.84	2/15/19	8.43	9.84
11/15/98	8.39	52.56	2/15/09	8.71	21.41	5/15/19	8.42	9.67
2/15/99	8.45	51.24	5/15/09	8.71	20.96	8/15/19	8.38	9.57
5/15/99	8.46	50.16	8/15/09	8.71	20.52	11/15/19	8.34	9.49
8/15/99	8.47	49.08	11/15/09	8.71	20.09	2/15/20	8.29	9.42
11/15/99	8.47	48.09	2/15/10	8.70	19.70	5/15/20	8.24	9.37
2/15/00	8.49	47.01	5/15/10	8.70	19.29	8/15/20	8.23	9.20
5/15/00	8.49	46.05	8/15/10	8.70	18.87			
8/15/00	8.49	45.09	11/15/10	8.70	18.48			
11/15/00	8.45	44.34	2/15/11	8.70	18.09			
2/15/01	8.54	43.05	5/15/11	8.70	17.71			

Source: Bear Stearns

Maturity	Yield	Price
5/15/1995	7.89	71.55
8/15/1995	7.90	70.13
11/15/1995	7.91	68.77
2/15/1996	7.97	67.24
5/15/1996	8.03	65.75
11/15/1996	8.09	63.00
5/15/1997	8.22	60.07
8/15/1997	8.24	58.79
11/15/1997	8.27	57.51
2/15/1998	8.27	56.35
5/15/1998	8.31	55.07
8/15/1998	8.32	53.91
11/15/1998	8.32	52.84
2/15/1999	8.34	51.68
5/15/1999	8.34	50.65
8/15/1999	8.34	49.61
11/15/1999	8.35	48.58
2/15/2000	8.35	47.58
5/15/2000	8.36	46.59
8/15/2000	8.37	45.59
11/15/2004	8.72	30.73
5/15/2005	8.72	29.44
8/15/2005	8.72	28.81
2/15/2006	8.59	28.13
11/15/2009	8.87	19.52
2/15/2015	8.61	13.14
8/15/2015	8.61	12.59
11/15/2015	8.59	12.39
2/15/2016	8.54	12.28
5/15/2016	8.49	12.17
11/15/2016	8.49	11.68
5/15/2017	8.48	11.23
8/15/2017	8.46	11.05
5/15/2018	8.44	10.45
11/15/2018	8.38	10.18
2/15/2019	8.35	10.06
8/15/2019	8.28	9.84
2/15/2020	8.20	9.66
5/15/2020	8.18	9.53
8/15/2020	8.14	9.44

TABLE 5-15
*Treasury Principal-only
Strip Yields and Prices*

Source: Bear Stearns

it by placing it in overnight funds until May 15, 1992, when you will have more than enough money to cover the short position (by paying 100.00).

Therefore, the restriction in Equation (5.31) must hold.

EXTRACTING ZEROES IN PRACTICE

Recall from our bootstrapping procedure, that given a set of par bond coupons and maturities, it is possible for us to extract the spot rates of interest. And once we know the spot rates of interest, we can compute the relevant implied forward rates of interest. Let us consider the problem of building the spot curve based on the data that we have in Table 5-4 for January 15, 1991. The par bond data have to be gleaned from this table first. Note from Table 5-4 that the bonds and notes (presented in Table 5-16) were selling close to par on that date. Note that not all bonds are selling at precisely the par amount. The bonds also clearly vary with respect to their liquidity. Notwithstanding these facts, we will use this information to extract the implied zeroes and the spot curve.

Since the data are sparse, we need to develop a smooth curve-fitting procedure. A number of approaches have been used in the academic literature and in practice. We will briefly review some of these approaches and use a nonlinear curve-fitting scheme that has been suggested to illustrate the idea in the context of the market conditions on January 15, 1991.

Generally, the task of extracting zero prices from the yield curve is complicated by the following factors, as pointed out earlier.

1. There are few issues that sell at par at any point. In Table 5-4, we can only identify a handful of issues (listed in Table 5-16) that sell close to par out of more than 200 issues that are outstanding in the market.

Coupon	Maturity Date	Price	Yield to Maturity	Years to Maturity
$6\frac{5}{8}\%$	2/15/92	$99\frac{22}{32}$	6.87%	1.0795
$7\frac{1}{4}\%$	8/15/92	$100\frac{8}{32}$	7.00%	1.5781
$7\frac{1}{4}\%$	12/31/92	$100\frac{6}{32}$	7.11%	1.9836
$7\frac{5}{8}\%$	12/31/94	100	7.61%	3.9562
8%	1/15/97	$100\frac{2}{32}$	7.96%	6.0000
$8\frac{1}{8}\%$	2/15/98	$100\frac{7}{32}$	8.06%	7.0849
$8\frac{1}{2}\%$	2/15/20	$100\frac{24}{32}$	8.42%	29.0986

TABLE 5-16
Par Bond Data

2. To obtain zero prices for all future maturities, we just do not have enough information in the yield curve. We do not have coupon bonds selling close to par maturing at every point in the future.

The approach to this problem is to start by specifying a simple function that describes the zero function. For example, we may specify that

$$b(t, T) = F(T - t, \underline{x}) \tag{5.32}$$

where $\underline{x}$ is a vector of parameters that are to be estimated. We can then postulate that, under ideal conditions, the coupon bond prices are portfolios of zero coupon bond prices. For bond i that pays a dollar coupon of C_i at date j we can write

$$P_{\text{model}, i} = \sum_{j=t}^{T_i} C_i b(t, j) + 100 b(t, T_i) \tag{5.33}$$

where bond i matures at date T_i. According to the model, we expect the price of the coupon bond i to be given by $P_{\text{model}, i}$. Let P_i be the market price of bond i. Then, the zero extraction problem may be stated as

$$\min_{\underline{x}} (P_i - P_{\text{model}, i})^2$$

subject to Equations (5.32) and (5.33). Once this is done, we can use the estimated $\underline{x}$ in Equation (5.32) to determine all the zeroes as estimates from the model. Given the estimated zero prices, we can estimate the forward rates as shown earlier.

In a recent paper, Diament (1993) has suggested an approach which falls broadly into the framework that we just described. Diament assumes that the yield to maturity of *par bonds* be described by the functional form:

$$y(t, T) = \frac{a_1(T - t)^{a_2} + a_3}{a_4(T - t)^{a_2} + 1}. \tag{5.34}$$

In this functional form, there are four parameters (a_1, a_2, a_3, a_4) that need to be estimated using the data provided in Table 5-16. We will assume that all the bonds in Table 5-16 are selling at par for the purposes of estimation. Once this functional form is estimated, we get the values of (a_1, a_2, a_3, a_4). The results of the estimation lead to the following fitted equation for the par bond curve.

$$y(t, T) = \frac{0.06486(T - t)^{1.92727} + 0.06751}{0.7671(T - t)^{1.92727} + 1}. \tag{5.35}$$

The implied zeroes and the spot curve are then extracted in a manner similar to the procedures illustrated earlier. The resulting implied zeroes and the spot rates are provided in Table 5-17. To get an idea of how well they describe reality, we also present in Figure 5-16 the spot and the strip rates. We are using implied zeroes as a benchmark for

TABLE 5-17 Extracted Implied Spot Rates

Maturity in Years	Strip Rates	Implied Spot Rates	Maturity in years	Strip Rates	Implied Spot Rates	Maturity in Years	Strip Rates	Implied Spot Rates
0.08	6.10%		10.09	8.54%		20.09	8.70%	
0.32	6.48%		10.33	8.55%		20.34	8.70%	
0.58	6.60%		10.58	8.55%		20.59	8.70%	
0.83	6.60%		10.84	8.57%		20.84	8.70%	
1.00		6.99%	11.00		8.59%	21.00		8.76%
1.08	6.88%		11.09	8.62%		21.09	8.70%	
1.33	6.92%		11.33	8.64%		21.34	8.70%	
1.58	7.06%		11.58	8.64%		21.59	8.70%	
1.83	7.09%		11.84	8.64%		21.84	8.70%	
2.00		7.28%	12.00		8.63%	22.00		8.77%
2.08	7.29%		12.09	8.65%		22.10	8.69%	
2.33	7.37%		12.33	8.68%		22.34	8.69%	
2.58	7.43%		12.58	8.67%		22.59	8.69%	
2.83	7.35%		12.84	8.67%		22.84	8.68%	
3.00		7.59%	13.00		8.66%	23.00		8.78%
3.08	7.59%		13.09	8.69%		23.10	8.67%	
3.33	7.64%		13.33	8.70%		23.34	8.67%	
3.58	7.70%		13.59	8.70%		23.59	8.66%	
3.83	7.68%		13.84	8.70%		23.84	8.65%	
4.00		7.85%	14.00		8.68%	24.00		8.78%
4.08	7.85%		14.09	8.71%		24.10	8.65%	
4.33	7.88%		14.33	8.71%		24.34	8.65%	
4.58	7.91%		14.59	8.71%		24.59	8.65%	
4.83	7.83%		14.84	8.65%		24.84	8.63%	
5.00		8.06%	15.00		8.70%	25.00		8.79%
5.08	8.01%		15.09	8.72%		25.10	8.62%	
5.33	8.06%		15.33	8.72%		25.34	8.61%	
5.58	8.10%		15.59	8.72%		25.59	8.60%	
5.83	8.11%		15.84	8.71%		25.85	8.59%	
6.00		8.22%	16.00		8.71%	26.00		8.79%
6.08	8.21%		16.09	8.72%		26.10	8.57%	
6.33	8.26%		16.33	8.72%		26.34	8.56%	
6.58	8.29%		16.59	8.72%		26.59	8.55%	
6.83	8.31%		16.84	8.72%		26.85	8.54%	
7.00		8.34%	17.00		8.73%	27.00		8.80%
7.08	8.35%		17.09	8.72%		27.10	8.52%	
7.33	8.37%		17.34	8.72%		27.34	8.51%	
7.58	8.39%		17.59	8.72%		27.59	8.49%	
7.83	8.39%		17.84	8.72%		27.85	8.48%	
8.00		8.43%	18.00		8.74%	28.00		8.80%
8.08	8.45%		18.09	8.71%		28.10	8.43%	
8.33	8.46%		18.34	8.71%		28.34	8.42%	
8.58	8.47%		18.59	8.71%		28.59	8.38%	
8.83	8.47%		18.84	8.71%		28.85	8.34%	
9.00		8.50%	19.00		8.75%	29.00		8.80%
9.08	8.49%		19.09	8.70%		29.10	8.29%	
9.33	8.49%		19.34	8.70%		29.35	8.24%	
9.58	8.49%		19.59	8.70%		29.60	8.23%	
9.84	8.45%		19.84	8.70%		30.00		8.81%
10.00		8.55%	20.00		8.76%			

FIGURE 5-16   *Spot Rates versus Strip Rates on January 15, 1991*

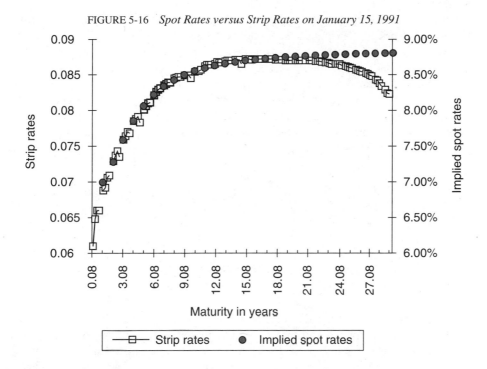

the strips market. If the implied zero prices and the strips prices are out of line, then there may be a lack of alignment between the coupon bond prices and the strips prices that can be exploited for profits. Note that in deciding whether to strip certain strippable Treasury securities, dealers must compare the price of the strippable security to the sum of the prices of each strip that will be obtained from that coupon security. Thus if a thirty-year bond is strippable, dealers will compare the price of the thirty-year bond with the sum of the prices of the 61 strips that they will get by stripping. Note that there are 60 (semi-annual) coupon payments and one principal payment, equaling 61 strips. It is possible that the dealer will sell some of the strips at a price below the implied zeroes of identical maturities. The dealer will sell other strips at a price higher than the implied zeroes of identical maturities.

The overall profitability of stripping is evaluated by the expression (where P_i is the price of a strip maturing at date i and P_{bond} is the price of the bond which has been stripped):

$$\pi = \sum_{i=1}^{61} P_i - P_{\text{bond}}.$$

If π is positive, then there is a potential for profits from stripping. Note that the dealer should use those strip prices at which he can actually sell all the strips in computing the profits π. If $\pi < 0$, then there is a potential for profits by reconstituting the bond; the dealer will buy all the strips and put the thirty-year bond back together.

It is clear that the Treasury coupon security prices contain a great deal of information about the prices of strips. The spot rates and the strip rates are very closely aligned at lower maturities. At intermediate maturities, the spot rates are a bit below strip rates. But at the long end, strip rates are well below the spot rates of interest.

We have illustrated the extraction of spot rates of interest from the par bond yield curve using a specific statistical (curve-fitting) approach. There have been many approaches presented in the academic literature for fitting a yield curve. In Nelson and Siegel (1987), it is suggested that the discount bond prices are a nonlinear function of time to maturity $T - t$ as shown by

$$b(t, T) = \left(\frac{1}{1 + r_s}\right)^{T-t}$$

and

$$r_s = \theta_0 + (\theta_1 + \theta_2)\frac{1 - e^{-\frac{T-t}{\lambda}}}{\frac{T-t}{\lambda}} + \theta_2 e^{\frac{T-t}{\lambda}}.$$

The parameters θ_1, θ_2 and λ will have to be estimated to get the pure discount factors. A simple curve-fitting approach of the sort presented here has been used by McCulloch (1975) and Litzenberger and Rolfo (1984). It should be emphasized that all these methods are curve-fitting procedures; as such they are statistical in their approach and generally do not have a sound economic foundation.

FURTHER READING

There is a large literature in the area of the term structure of interest rates. The behavior of short and long rates is explored in Campbell and Shiller (1984). A number of papers have examined the estimation of the term structure. Notable contributions in this area include Langtieg (1980), Roley (1981), and McCulloch (1971). The tax effect on term structure is examined by Jordon (1984), Litzenberger and Rolfo (1984), and Schaefer (1981). A number of books have addressed the problem of the term structure of interest rates; notable ones include Malkiel (1966), Meiselman (1962), and Roll (1972).

PROBLEMS

5.1   A ninety-day T-bill is trading at 8.25% and may be financed at a thirty-day term repo of 8%. What is the break-even rate on the future sixty-day T-bill created by this transaction? Show all steps in your analysis.

5.2   Assume the following spot rate (zero coupon) curve for this problem.

Years	0.5	1.0	1.5	2.0	2.5
Rate	7.50	7.75	8.00	8.00	8.00

Zero Curve

(a) If all bonds were priced consistently with this curve, what would be the price of a two-year semi-annual, 14% coupon security? Why?

(b) Under what circumstances will you expect the value of the total package (coupon bond) to differ from the sum of its component parts (strips)? Why?

5.3   Suppose that the one-year spot rate of interest at time 0 is 8% and the two-year spot rate is 8.50%. What is the one-year forward rate for year 2? Why?

5.4   Summarize different versions of the expectations hypothesis. What does the expectations theory of term structure say about the relationship between forward rates for one-year loans one year from now and the one-year spot rates one year from now?

5.5   The data in the next table reflects the conditions on October 8, 1985.

Coupon	Maturity	Price
9%	9-30-1987	$100-\frac{3}{32}$
$10\frac{5}{8}\%$	8-15-2015	100

Settlement on October 8, 1985

(a) Calculate the yield to maturity, PVBP, and yield value of $\frac{1}{32}$ of each security. What is the yield spread?

(b) You expect that the yield curve will flatten, but you have no clue as to whether the overall interest rates will rise or fall. Using the two securities suggest a spread trade that is consistent with your expectations.

5.6   Assume the following spot rate (zero coupon) curve for this problem.

Years	0.5	1.0	1.5	2.0	2.5
Rate	11.00	10.50	10.00	9.50	9.00

Spot Curve

Two-year bonds that are strippable and paying a coupon of 10.375% are selling at a yield of 10%. Is it worthwhile to strip them and sell the stripped pieces? Or is it better to sell them as a unit? (Assume that you own them and that the strips may be sold at spot yields.)

REFERENCES

Bollerslev, T., and R. Engle 1993. "Common Persistence in Conditional Variances." *Econometrica* 61:167–186.

Brown, S. J., and P. H. Dybvig 1986. "The Empirical Implications of the Cox, Ingersoll, Ross Theory of the Term Structure of Interest Rates." *Journal of Finance* 41:617–630.

Campbell, J. Y. and R. J. Shiller 1984. "A Simple Account of the Behavior of Long Term Interest Rates." *American Economic Review* 74:44–48.

Culbertson, J. M. 1957. "The Term Structure of Interest Rates." *Quarterly Journal of Economics* 71:489–504.

Diament, P. 1993. "Semi-empirical Smooth Fit to the Treasury Yield Curve." *Journal of Fixed Income* 3(1):55–70.

Dobson, S. W., R. Sutch, and D. Vanderford 1976. "An Evaluation of the Alternative Empirical Models of the Term Structure of Interest Rates." *Journal of Finance* 31:1035–1065.

Echols, M. E., and J. W. Elliott 1976. "A Quantitative Yield Curve Model for Estimating the Term Structure of Interest Rates." *Journal of Financial and Quantitative Analysis* 11:87–94.

Jordan, J. V. 1984. "Tax Effect in Term Structure Estimation." *Journal of Finance* 39:393–406.

Langetieg, T. C. 1980. "A Multivariate Model of the Term Structure." *Journal of Finance* 35:71–97.

Litzenberger, R. H., and J. Rolfo 1984. "An International Study of Tax Effects on Government Bonds." *Journal of Finance* 39:1–22.

Malkiel, B. 1966. *The Term Structure of Interest Rates.* Princeton, NJ: Princeton University Press.

McCallum, J. 1978. "The Expected Holding Period Return, Uncertainty and the Term Structure of Interest Rates." *Journal of Finance* 30:307–323.

McCulloch, J. 1971. "Measuring the Term Structure of Interest Rates." *Journal of Business* 44:19–31.

McCulloch, J. H. 1975. "The Tax-Adjusted Yield Curve." *Journal of Finance* 30:811–830.

McCulloch, J. 1987. "The Monotonocity of the Term Premium: A Closer Look." *Journal of Financial Economics* 18:185–192.

Meiselman, D. 1962. *The Term Structure of Interest Rates.* Englewood Cliffs, NJ: Prentice Hall.

Nelson, C. R., and A. F. Siegel 1987. "Parsimonious Modelling of Yield Curves." *Journal of Business* 60(4):473–489.

Roberts, G. S. 1980. "Term Premiums in the Term Structure of Interest Rates." *Journal of Money, Credit and Banking* 12:184–197.

Roley, V. V. 1981. "The Determinants of the Treasury Yield Curve." *Journal of Finance* 36:1103–1126.

Roll, R. 1972. *The Behavior of Interest Rates.* New York: Basic Books, Inc.

Sargent, T. J. 1972. "Rational Expectations and the Term Structure of Interest Rates." *Journal of Money, Credit and Banking* 4:74–97.

Sarig, O., and A. Warga 1989. "Bond Price Data and Bond Market Liquidity." *Journal of Financial and Quantitative Analysis* 24(3):367–378.

Schaefer, S. 1981. "Measuring a Tax Specific Term Structure of Interest Rates in the Market for British Government Securities." *Economic Journal* 91:415–438.

Shiller, R., and J. McCulloch 1987. The Term Structure of Interest Rates. National Bureau of Economic Research Working Paper 2341.

Stambaugh, R. 1988. "The Information in Forward Rates: Implications for Models of the Term Structure." *Journal of Financial Economics* 21:41–70.

Van Horne, J. C. 1965. "Interest Rate Risk and Term Structure of Interest Rates." *Journal of Political Economy* 73:344–351.

Van Horne, J. C. 1966a. "Interest Rate Expectations and the Shape of the Yield Curve and Monetary Policy." *Review of Economics and Statistics* XLVIII:211–215.

Van Horne, J. C. 1966b. "Reply." *Journal of Political Economy* 74:633–635.

Warga, A. 1992. "Bond Returns, Liquidity and Missing Data." *Journal of Financial and Quantitative Analysis* 27(4)605–617.

Wood, J. H. 1963. "Expectations, Error and the Term Structure of Interest Rates." *Journal of Political Economy* 71:160–171.

Chapter 6

No-Arbitrage Principle and the Term Structure

Chapter Objectives

This chapter develops the concept of no arbitrage and applies the concept to value fixed-income securities. Chapter 6 will help the reader to understand and answer the following questions.

- What are real rates of interest?
- What are nominal rates of interest?
- What is the relationship between nominal and real rates?
- What is the empirical evidence on inflation?

In addition, this chapter develops the different hypotheses of term structure of interest rates. The concept of state prices and their relationship to no arbitrage are developed in the context of bond pricing. Several models of term structure are then discussed. In particular, models such as Black, Derman, and Toy (1990), and Ho and Lee (1986) are discussed in detail to show how the models can be calibrated to market data. Several numerical examples are worked out to illustrate the models.

INTRODUCTION

In Chapter 4, we developed the basic mathematical tools that are used in the calculations of present values of cashflows, future values of cashflows, yield to maturity, forward rates, spot rates, and par bond yield calculations. In addition, Chapter 4 presented the concepts of value of 0.01, duration, convexity; and the applications of these concepts in trading and risk-management applications. In developing these concepts in Chapter 4, there was no need to specify a model of interest rates. The only assumptions that were needed in Chapter 4 were that the yield curve is flat and the shifts in the yield curve are parallel. The concepts of duration and convexity are extensively used in the industry, despite the simplifying assumptions on which they rest. In large part, the popularity of these concepts is due to the fact that they are relatively simple to construct and use in real-life applications. In addition, in many real-life applications, risk-management tools based on these concepts work reasonably well in spite of the simplifying assumptions. Chapter 5 developed several important tools that are central to the analysis of the yield curve and term structure. These tools comprise spot rates, forward rates, and the par bond yield curve. While these tools are quite central to the analysis of fixed-income securities, they do not address the factors which determine the yields. In addition, these tools are unable to provide a framework for valuing fixed-income securities such as corporate bonds and derivatives on fixed-income securities.

In this chapter, we will explore theories and models of term structure which are used in pricing fixed-income securities and their derivatives. The chapter begins by reviewing the empirical evidence on the behavior of interest rates. Recall that one important regularity that emerged in earlier chapters is that the volatility of interest rates has dramatically increased since the monetary policy shift in late 1979. Short-term interest rates exhibit much greater volatility compared to long-term interest rates. In addition, the evidence suggests that the shape of the yield curve shifts in response to the levels of interest rates. Another important fact readily apparent from the evidence presented earlier is that the yield curve is rarely flat. When interest rates are relatively low, the yield curve is normal or upward sloping. When rates are very high the shape of the yield curve is inverted. In this chapter, we first investigate the determinants of real and nominal interest rates; then we review the behavior of real and nominal interest rates in the U.S. economy.

These regularities serve as the backdrop for a review of hypotheses about the term structure of interest rates and the development of term-structure models. We then define and explain the concept of no arbitrage. In this context we show that the existence of certain primitive securities is central to the absence of arbitrage. In addition, we show that the absence of arbitrage requires that the market price of risk (which is the excess return divided by the risk) of all bonds has to be the same, irrespective of their maturity or coupon payments. We present several quantitative examples to illustrate these important concepts. The rest of the chapter introduces the reader to various models of the term structure of interest rates. We review several single-factor models of term structure; these models are then applied in a variety of practical applications to illustrate their uses.

In previous chapters, we have confined our attention mostly to U.S. Treasury securities which are noncallable (bullet) securities. Such securities provide no options or flexibility to either the seller or the buyer. We will soon begin the analysis of other sectors of the fixed-income markets. In these sectors (which include corporate debt securities, mortgage-backed securities, and municipal securities) either the issuer or the investor tends to have optional features. For example, many corporate bonds are issued with call features that give the issuer the option to call the bond at a prespecified price. The issuer is likely to exercise this option when the interest rates fall enough that the savings associated with the new issue at a lower coupon exceeds the costs of retiring the old, higher coupon bond. Many corporate bonds are also issued with sinking-fund features which may give the issuer some options concerning the amount that must be retired. Some bonds permit the investors to sell or put the bond back to the issuer at a predetermined price. Such bonds, known as putable bonds, give an option to the investor. Mortgage-backed securities are backed by pools of mortgages. These mortgages permit homeowners to prepay their loans. Homeowners will tend to exercise their prepayment options when refinancing rates fall significantly below their current loan rates.

Many debt securities have such options imbedded in them. In order to properly understand their valuation, it is necessary to develop the basic principles of options-pricing theory. Here, we develop some no-arbitrage principles which form the basis of options pricing. Options pricing, itself, is taken up in the next chapter.

DETERMINANTS OF INTEREST RATES

A number of factors determine interest rates. As a simple model, we can think of interest rates consisting of two parts. The first part is derived from the real sector of the economy. Important factors in this context include the propensity of investors to save, the productivity of the economy, and unemployment. The second part is driven by the monetary sector of the economy. Important factors in this sector will include the money supply in the economy, central bank policies, and inflationary aspects. We begin by examining briefly the real sector first. An important part of this sector is the investor's propensity to save and the set of opportunities facing the investors.

Risk Aversion of Investors

In economic models of the willingness of investors to accept risk, the concept of a **utility function** is used. In its simplest form, a risk-averse investor prefers more wealth to less, but every additional unit of wealth provides less incremental utility. A risk-neutral investor also prefers more wealth to less, but each incremental unit of wealth provides a constant incremental utility. A risk-loving investor prefers more wealth to less and each incremental unit of wealth provides more incremental utility. These functions are illustrated in Figure 6-1.

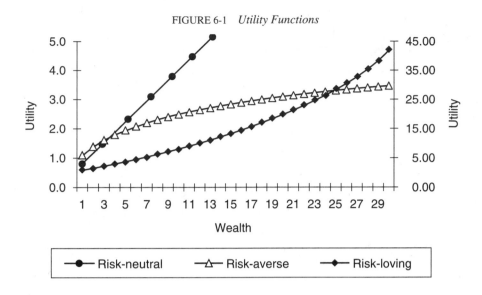

FIGURE 6-1   *Utility Functions*

The concept of utility functions enables us to formalize the relationship between risk and return. In particular, this is important in determining the risk premium. By buying securities, investors save. In so doing, they forego current consumption in the hope of increasing future consumption. This trade-off implies that future cash-flow distributions from securities are evaluated by consumers using their marginal utilities for current and future consumption.

Real Rate of Interest

First, let us focus on the determinants of the real rate of interest. In an economy with no opportunity for lending or borrowing, the real rate of interest is determined by the investment opportunities and the preferences of investors for savings or consumption.

To see this point, review Figure 6-2, which represents a stylized two-date setting (date 0 and date 1). The investor is assumed to have at date 0 a wealth of W_0. The preferences of the investor are represented by the indifference curves shown in the figure. By investing a part of the wealth, the investor is able to transform the current wealth into future wealth, and hence into future consumption. Thus, by allocating an investment of I, the investor consumes $W_0 - I$ at date 0 and is able to consume an amount equal to $f(I)$ at date 1, where $f(I)$ is the production associated with an investment of I units at date 0. The optimal level of investment is determined by the propensity of the investor to save; the higher the patience level of the investor, the more will be saved towards investment for future consumption. The indifference curves in Figure 6-2 illustrate that the point of tangency is the optimal level of investment. If $U(c_0, c_1)$ is the utility function for current

FIGURE 6-2   *Investment Opportunities and Investor Preference*

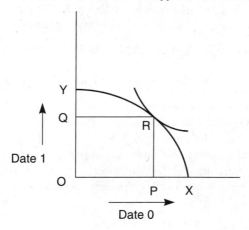

Notes:

    1. Initial endowment is represented by OX. In the absence of riskless lending and borrowing opportunities, an amount PX will be invested in the production-opportunity set. This produces an amount PR.

    2. The present value of the wealth is OX

    3. The consumption pattern is (OP, OQ)

and future consumption denoted by c_0 and c_1, respectively, then the optimal investment decision arises out:

$$\max_{c_0,\, c_1} U(c_0,\, c_1)$$

subject to

$$c_0 = W_0 - I$$

and

$$c_1 = f(I).$$

The optimal investment strategy I^* is given by

$$f'(I) = \frac{\frac{\partial U}{\partial c_0}}{\frac{\partial U}{\partial c_1}} = \frac{dc_1}{dc_2}. \tag{6.1}$$

Note that the marginal rate of return from investment $f'(I)$ is set equal to the marginal rate of substitution between current and future consumption. Thus, the investment opportunities and the propensity to save interact to determine the optimal level of investment. Under certainty, the marginal rate of return must also be the real rate of return $1 + R$. Two intuitive relationships emerge in this admittedly stylized setting:

- the higher the productivity of the investment-opportunity set, the higher will be the real rate of interest;
- the greater the propensity to save, the lower will be the real rate of interest.

One of the important features of this stylized analysis is that the investment decisions and consumption decisions are tightly aligned because investment in the production-opportunity set is the only way to save for the future.

What would happen if riskless lending and borrowing opportunities were provided in addition to the production-opportunity set? This situation is presented in Figure 6-3. Note that the welfare of the investor is improved in this new situation as consumption

FIGURE 6-3   *Investment Opportunities, Riskless Lending/Borrowing, and Investor Preference*

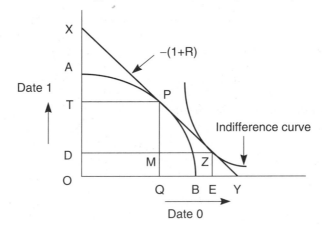

Notes:

1. Initial endowment is represented by OB. In the presence of riskless lending and borrowing opportunities, an amount QB will be invested in the production-opportunity set. This produces an amount PQ. Note that the optimal investment occurs at the tangency point, where the marginal return from production opportunity equals the riskless rate.

2. The present value of the wealth is OQ + PQ/(1 + R) = OQ + QY = OY

3. The present value of consumption is OE + ZE/(1 + R) = OE + EY = OY

4. Amount borrowed at date 0 is EQ

5. Amount repaid at date 1 is EQ(1 + R) = PM

can be transferred from one date to another in two ways. In addition to using the production technology, the investor is able to borrow or lend at a rate R. Borrowing against future wealth gives the investor important additional flexibility in this new situation. In a stylized way, the investor can be thought of as investing an amount I in the production technology such that

$$f'(I) = 1 + R. \tag{6.2}$$

With diminishing marginal returns to scale, the investment will be carried up to a level where the marginal return is exactly equal to the riskless rate. Then, the present value of the investor's endowments $\{W_0 - I, f(I)\}$ is given by

$$PV = W_0 - I + \frac{f(I)}{1 + R}. \tag{6.3}$$

Now, the investor is free to choose any consumption bundle (c_0, c_1) which satisfies the following condition:

$$PV = c_0 + \frac{c_1}{1 + R}.$$

In other words, any consumption bundle that has the same present value as the present value of the resources can be consumed by the investor. The precise consumption bundle will naturally depend on the preferences of the investor as shown in Figure 6-3.

One important implication of the foregoing analysis is that the optimal investment decision I^* is independent of the consumption decision. This result is known as the **Fisher separation result.** Another important implication is that the wealth of the consumer in the current situation has improved to the point given by the present value of the investor's resources in Equation (6.3).

Note that the real rate of return depends on a number of factors, such as the savings rate and the productivity (marginal rate of return) of the economy. In general, we may denote the real rate of interest as $R(\underline{x})$ where $\underline{x}$ is the vector of factors that may influence the real rate of interest. As an empirical matter, while the real rates of interest change over time depending on the evolution of the relevant factors, volatility of the real rates is generally low.

Nominal Interest Rates

While the real rate of interest is an important economic concept, in most markets the focus is on the nominal rate of interest. Due to the fact that most economic transactions occur in terms of the local currency, the nominal interest rate denominated in the local currency is of utmost importance to many players in the capital markets. The nominal rate of interest differs from the real rate due to inflation.

Inflation risk is primarily due to the fact that the future price of a typical consumption bundle denominated in the local currency could differ from the current price level of the same consumption bundle. Many factors, such as the demand for money and supply of money, influence inflation. Let us denote $p(\underline{y})$ as the price level where $\underline{y}$ is the vector of factors that may influence the price level. Then, the nominal rate of interest will typically depend on both factors $\{x, y\}$. In general, these factors may be correlated with each other and their correlation properties may be important in the determination of the nominal interest rate.

It is also possible that some of the factors in $\underline{x}$ may also be factors in y; factors that influence the real rate may have an effect on the nominal rate of interest, and vice versa. One such interaction was suggested by Mundell (1963), who argued that an increased inflation risk will make nominally denominated financial assets much less valuable, thereby forcing investors to save more to compensate for the loss in the value of their savings due to increased inflation. The real effect of increased savings, as discussed earlier, is to reduce the real interest rate. It has also been argued that the volatility (risk) of inflation will affect the real rate of interest. Intuitively, we expect the factors determining the price level to induce a lot more volatility in the nominal rate of interest than the factors determining the real rate of interest.

The relationship between nominal and real rates of interest is known as the **Fisher effect** and it has been at the core focus of much of the empirical work on interest rates. The basic premise behind this relation is the notion that investors will require a compensation for inflation risk in order to hold securities whose returns are in nominal terms. Thus, an investor holding a ninety-day Treasury bill will require a compensation for the possible loss in the purchasing power of dollars in 90 days. This compensation is the expected inflation rate.

Suppose that the price level at date t is p_t and at date $T > t$ is $\tilde{p}_T$. Then, the inflation rate $\tilde{\pi}_t$ between dates t and T is defined as

$$\tilde{\pi}_t = \frac{\tilde{p}_T}{p_t} - 1.$$

Note that the price level at date T is uncertain. As a consequence, the inflation rate $\tilde{\pi}_t$ is also uncertain. In Figure 6-4, we plot the realized inflation rates in the U.S. economy as given by the percentage change in the consumer price index over the last two decades. The fluctuations in the realized inflation rates vividly demonstrates the risk associated with financial assets. The holder of a T-bill at date t will get a nominal return

$$r_t = \frac{100}{b_t} - 1$$

where b_t is the nominal price of the Treasury bill at date t. The real price of the T-bill at date t is $\frac{b_t}{p_t}$ and the real value of par amount to be received at date T is $\frac{100}{p_T}$. Hence, the real rate of return $\tilde{R}_t$ is

$$\tilde{R}_t = \frac{\frac{100}{p_T}}{\frac{b_t}{p_t}} - 1.$$

Remembering that $1 + \tilde{\pi}_t = \frac{p_T}{p_t}$ and $1 + r_t = \frac{100}{b_t}$ we get the real rate of return as

$$1 + r_t = (1 + \tilde{R}_t) \times (1 + \tilde{\pi}_t). \tag{6.4}$$

FIGURE 6-4   *Monthly Inflation Rates (Annualized), 1972–1994*

Note that the nominal rate of return of the T-bill is known with certainty. The inflation rate, dependent on the uncertain price level at date T, introduces an element of uncertainty in the real rate of return. Let us rewrite Equation (6.4) and simplify it as

$$1 + r_t = 1 + \tilde{R}_t + \tilde{\pi}_t + \tilde{R}_t\tilde{\pi}_t.$$

Taking the expected value, we get the relationship between the nominal rate of interest and the expected real rate of interest:

$$r_t = E[\tilde{R}_t] + E[\tilde{\pi}_t] + E[\tilde{R}_t\tilde{\pi}_t].$$

Remember that the expectation of a product of two random variables is the sum of the product of the expectations and the covariance between the two random variables. Hence,

$$E[\tilde{R}_t\tilde{\pi}_t] = E[\tilde{R}_t]E[\tilde{\pi}_t] + \mathrm{Cov}[\tilde{R}_t,\ \tilde{\pi}_t]$$

Using this and simplifying we get,

$$E_t[R_t] = \frac{r_t - E_t[\pi_t] - \mathrm{Cov}[R_t,\ \pi_t]}{1 + E_t[\pi_t]}. \tag{6.5}$$

Note that the expected real rate of return associated with holding a nominal security such as a T-bill depends on the covariance between the real rate of return and the inflation rate.

Ignoring second-order effects, we can write

$$E_t[R_t] = r_t - E_t[\pi_t]. \tag{6.6}$$

This is the Fisher effect, linking nominal interest rates, expected real interest rates, and the expected rate of inflation. Note that if the real rates do not vary a lot, then changes in expected inflation rates are fully captured by the changes in the nominal rates of interest. But if the changes in expected inflation rates affect real activity such as investments, they may well affect the real rates as well. In such a case, nominal rates may not fully respond to the changes in inflation rates. In the development of the Fisher effect above we considered T-bills, which have a known nominal return. A similar relation holds for securities whose nominal return is uncertain due to the reinvestment risk of coupon income.

We have not considered the effect of taxes on Fisher relation. Darby (1975) has suggested that the effect of taxes (ignoring second-order effects) will be to modify the relation as follows:

$$E_t[R_t] = r_t \times (1 - \tau) - E_t[\pi_t]$$

where τ is the tax rate. The key implication of taxes, under the Darby formulation is that the nominal rate will be more elastic for a given change in the real rate. The real rate behavior in the U.S. economy is shown in Figure 6-5.

A number of authors have attempted to test the extent to which the Fisher effect holds in real life. Two papers that have been influential in this area are Fama (1975) and Fama and Gibbons (1982).

Fama (1975) tests for the presence of the Fisher effect by regressing the nominal rates of interest with the realized inflation rate. He uses the regression specification:

$$\pi_t = a_0 + a_1 r_t + \epsilon_t$$

where π_t is the realized inflation rate, r_t is the nominal rate of interest, and ϵ_t is the error term in the regression. Fama starts with the Fisher equation $E_t[R_t] = r_t - E_t[\pi_t]$, but makes the assumption that the real rates are constant. Then, the realized inflation rate π_t should be the expected inflation rate, $E_t[\pi_t]$ plus a level of random noise, ϵ_t. This leads

FIGURE 6-5   *Real Rate Fluctuations during 1975–1985*

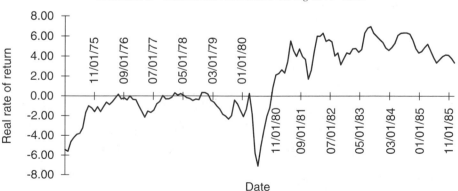

to the regression specification used by Fama. His approach avoids the estimation of the expected inflation rate. Fama uses one-month Treasury bills in his tests and his sample period covers 1953–1971. Note that under the Fisher effect, the coefficient of the nominal rate r_t, which is a_1, should be equal to 1. In addition, a_0 should be negative. Fama tests these hypotheses and finds that the Fisher effect cannot be rejected. He finds that in most of the sample period, a_1 was close to unity.

It has been argued that Fama's result is primarily due to the fact that the sample period he chose is one in which the volatility of interest rates was very low. As Table 6-1 indicates, there are other sample periods in which inflation rates showed a much greater variability. In these other sample periods with higher volatility, the nominal rates do not fully adjust to changes in inflation rate. This is not entirely surprising given that Fama was testing the joint hypothesis that the real rate is constant and that the Fisher effect is present in the data. During periods of higher volatility, one would expect the real rates also to display some variation. In fact in a later paper, Fama and Gibbons (1982) find evidence that the real rates fluctuate with the levels of real activity in the economy. They also find evidence that a_1 is close to unity.

TABLE 6-1
Inflation Rates

Period	Mean Rate of Inflation	Volatility of Inflation
1940–1989	4.58%	3.97%
1940–1949	5.56%	5.91%
1950–1959	2.22%	2.19%
1960–1969	2.53%	1.76%
1970–1979	7.42%	3.43%
1980–1989	5.13%	3.18%
1953–1971 (Fama)	2.31%	1.76%

Smith and Spudeck (1993)

HYPOTHESES OF TERM STRUCTURE

A number of hypotheses have been advanced concerning the term structure of interest rates. They attempt to relate interest rates on pure discount bonds of differing maturities with forward rates, expected spot rates, and so on. We provide a very brief overview of some of these hypotheses.

Expectations Hypothesis

One of the most popular hypotheses is the expectations hypothesis. There are many versions of this hypothesis, which was formally developed by Hicks (1946) and Lutz (1940).

One version of the expectations hypothesis says that current forward rates are unbiased predictors of future spot rates. Let $f_t(k, k + 1)$ be the forward rate at date t for a one-period loan between two future dates k and $k + 1$. Let R_k^* be the unknown one-period spot rate at date k. Then the expectations hypothesis says,

$$f_t(k, k + 1) = E_t[R_k^*] \qquad (6.7)$$

Thus, the forward rate $f_t(k, k + 1)$ is the expected value of the future one-period spot rate denoted by R_k^* at date k. This version is referred to as the **unbiased expectations hypothesis.**

Another version says that the guaranteed return that one gets during the interval $[t, T]$ by holding a $(T - t)$-period bond should be equal to the expected return from rolling over a series of single-period bonds. This may be formally stated as

$$\frac{1}{b(t, T)} = E_t[(1 + r_t)(1 + r_{t+1}) \cdots (1 + r_{T-1})]. \qquad (6.8)$$

The left-hand side of the equation above represents the return associated with holding a discount bond to its maturity. The right-hand side is the expected return associated with rolling over one dollar from date t to date T in a sequence of one-period maturity bonds at varying future one-period rates of return $\{r_s\}$.

Yet another version of this hypothesis states this in terms of yields. In this version, the yield to maturity of the discount bond at date t is specified in the left-hand side.

$$\left[\frac{1}{b(t, T)}\right]^{\frac{1}{T-t}} = E_t\left[\{(1 + r_t)(1 + r_{t+1}) \cdots (1 + r_{T-1})\}^{\frac{1}{T-t}}\right] \qquad (6.9)$$

Liquidity-Premium Hypothesis

The liquidity-premium hypothesis says that current forward rates differ from future spot rates by an amount known as the liquidity premium.

$$f_t(k, k + 1) = E_t[R_k^*] + \pi_t(k, k + 1) \qquad (6.10)$$

Thus, the forward rate $f_t(k, k + 1)$ is the expected value of the future one-period spot rate denoted by R_k^* at date k plus the liquidity premium which depends on the term of the loan. Hicks (1946) argues that there will be a "normal backwardation" whereby the forward spot rate will exceed the expected future spot rate by the amount of the liquidity premium. The idea here is that borrowers may prefer to borrow long-term to avoid future uncertainties in the supply of capital. On the other hand, lenders will prefer to lend short. Speculators will then bridge this gap by borrowing short and lending long, provided they are compensated by the liquidity premium.

Segmented-Markets Hypothesis

The segmented-markets hypothesis says that different maturity sectors represent distinct markets with their own demand and supply forces. Culberston (1957) argues that different investors may have strong maturity preferences. Sometimes such preferences are also driven by regulatory constraints. Modigliani and Sutch (1967) propose a preferred habitat theory in which investors have a preferred maturity and will only deviate from their preferred maturity if they are offered a premium. As Cox, Ingersoll, and Ross (1981) have suggested, preferred habitat theory may be viewed as a special case of the liquidity-preference hypothesis in which the preferred habitat is short-term bonds, and long-term bonds are held only if they offer liquidity premiums.

Local-Expectations Hypothesis

The local-expectations hypothesis (LEH) says that all bonds provide the same expected rate of return over very small holding periods. It turns out that the LEH is the only hypothesis that is free from arbitrage. Formally, this hypothesis is stated as

$$\frac{E_t[b(t + 1, T)]}{b(t, T)} = 1 + r_t. \tag{6.11}$$

The expected one-period return during the interval $[t, t + 1]$ on a bond maturing at date T is equal to the one-period return r_t on a bond at date t maturing at date $t + 1$.

It turns out that only the LEH is consistent with no-arbitrage. As a consequence, in the term-structure theory and models that follow, we will confine our attention to LEH.

CONCEPT OF NO ARBITRAGE

The **principle of no arbitrage** says that two perfect substitutes that are freely traded have to sell at the same price in the absence of frictions (such as transactions costs, short-sale constraints, taxes, etc.). This simple concept also has been referred to as the **absence of free lunch,** or the **law of one price.** In the context of fixed-income securities markets, this concept has tremendous relevance. In valuing bonds of different maturities and con-tractual provisions, we must ensure that there are no arbitrage opportunities. In other words, it should not be the case that some combination of bonds may be used to replicate the cash flows of some other bond at a lower cost. At a first glance, it may appear that there are no perfect substitutes that are simultaneously traded, and hence one might con-clude that this concept is of limited value. But, as we will show in this chapter, by using specific trading strategies it is possible to create perfect substitutes. We will show that it is possible to replicate the payoffs of options on bonds, by trading in the underlying bond, and either lending or borrowing money on an overnight basis. We will formalize these ideas next.

Concept of State Prices

Consider a simple setting in which, at date $t = 0$, a bond is selling at price P. At date $t = 1$, it can either sell at uP with a probability q or sell at dP with a probability $1 - q$.

We denote the bond price uP at date 1 as an "up state," and the bond price dP at date 1 as a "down state."

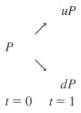

$$uP$$

$$P$$

$$dP$$

$$t = 0 \quad t = 1$$

We assume that $u > 1 + R > d$ where R is the riskless rate of interest (such as 4% or 0.04). Let us define $r = 1 + R$. The expected return on this bond defined by

$$E(\bar{R}) = \frac{quP + (1 - q)dP}{P} = qu + (1 - q)d.$$

In a similar manner, we can compute the variance of the return on the bond

$$\sigma^2(\tilde{R}) = [q\{u - E(\bar{R})\}^2 + (1 - q)\{d - E(\bar{R})\}^2].$$

This expression for the variance of the return on the bond can be simplified as

$$\sigma^2(\tilde{R}) = [q(1 - q)](u - d)^2.$$

The volatility of the return can then be obtained by taking the square root:

$$\sigma(\tilde{R}) = [q(1 - q)]^{\frac{1}{2}}(u - d).$$

Since we have assumed a riskless asset, this asset will produce a payoff distribution:

$$r$$

$$1$$

$$r$$

$$t = 0 \quad t = 1$$

Consider a security that pays one dollar at date $t = 1$ in the "up state" and nothing in the "down state." We will label this security **primitive security 1.** Let its price at date 0 be denoted by π_u. Consider another security that pays one dollar at date $t = 1$ in the "down state" and nothing in the "up state." Let its price at date 0 be denoted by π_d. We will call this security **primitive security 2.**

The payoffs of the bond can be replicated using the primitive securities by the strategy illustrated in Table 6-2.

We are able to exactly replicate the cash flows of the bond at day $t = 1$ in both the "up state" and the "down state" by buying uP of the primitive security 1 and dP of the primitive security 2. This portfolio of primitive security 1 and primitive security 2 cre-

Transaction at Date 0	Investment at Date 0	Cash Flows at Date 1 in "Up State"	Cash Flows at Date 1 in "Down State"	TABLE 6-2 Pricing Bonds
1. Buy the bond	P	uP	dP	
2. Buy uP units of the primitive security 1	$\pi_u uP$	uP	0	
3. Buy dP units of the primitive security 2	$\pi_d dP$	0	dP	

ates a perfect substitute for the bond. These substitutes must sell for the same price. Hence at date 0 we must have

$$P = \pi_u uP + \pi_d dP.$$

Cancelling out P and simplifying we get

$$\pi_u u + \pi_d d = 1. \tag{6.12}$$

Note that by buying one unit of primitive security 1 and one unit of security 2, we get one dollar at date 1, no matter which state occurs. The present value of this dollar at date 0 is $\frac{1}{r}$. Hence, we have

$$\pi_u + \pi_d = \frac{1}{r}. \tag{6.13}$$

Solving (6.12) and (6.13), we get the prices of primitive security 1 and primitive security 2 (also known as state prices):

$$\pi_u = \frac{r - d}{r(u - d)} \tag{6.14}$$

$$\pi_d = \frac{u - r}{r(u - d)} \tag{6.15}$$

Example 6-1 gives a concrete illustration.

Example 6-1   Computing State Prices

Let $P = 100$, $u = 1.07$, $R = 0.02$, and $d = 0.98$. This leads to the following evolution of bond prices.

$$\begin{array}{ccc}
 & & 107 \\
 & \nearrow & \\
100 & & \\
 & \searrow & \\
 & & 98 \\
\\
t = 0 & & t = 1
\end{array}$$

Let us further assume that the probability of an "up" move is $q = 0.5$ and the probability of a "down" move is $1 - q = 0.5$.

We can then compute the state prices π_u and π_d as shown in Equations (6.16) and (6.17), respectively.

$$\pi_u = \frac{1.02 - 0.98}{[1.02 \times (1.07 - 0.98)]} = 0.435730 \qquad (6.16)$$

$$\pi_d = \frac{1.07 - 1.02}{[1.02 \times (1.07 - 0.98)]} = 0.544662 \qquad (6.17)$$

Example 6-2   Pricing Bond 1

Table 6-3 illustrates how the primitive securities can be used to exactly replicate the cash flows of bond 1. Together the total value of the primitive securities that are needed to replicate the bond is

$$0.43573 \times 107 + 0.544662 \times 98 = 100$$

TABLE 6-3   *Pricing Bond 1*

Transaction at Date 0	Investment at Date 0	Cash Flows at Date 1 in "Up State"	Cash Flows at Date 1 in "Down State"
1. Buy the bond	P	107	98
2. Buy 107 units of the primitive security 1	0.435730×107	107	0
3. Buy dP units of the primitive security 2	0.544662×98	0	98

Note that this is precisely equal to the value of the bond. What do the prices of primitive security 1 and primitive security 2 represent? In effect, they represent the present values of receiving one dollar at date 1 contingent on the occurrence of a certain state. The prices of such securities (state prices) are fundamental in the valuation of other securities.

Example 6-3   Pricing Bond 2

We can use the prices of primitive securities to value any bond available for trading. Consider for example bond 2 with the following payoff distribution.

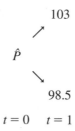

$$
\begin{array}{ccc}
 & & 103 \\
 & \nearrow & \\
\hat{P} & & \\
 & \searrow & \\
 & & 98.5 \\
t = 0 & t = 1 &
\end{array}
$$

What is the price $\hat{P}$ of this bond? The price of bond 2 is the sum of:

- the present value of $103 in the "up state"

$$\pi_u \times 103 = 0.43573 \times 103 = 44.88017$$

- the present value of $98.5 in the "down state"

$$\pi_d \times 98.5 = 0.544662 \times 98.5 = 53.64924$$

Adding these two present values together gives:

$$44.88017 + 53.64924 = 98.52941.$$

Hence bond 2 should sell at 98.52941 to be consistent with the pricing of bond 1.

No Arbitrage and Bond-Price Dynamics

If bond 1 and bond 2 are priced to preclude arbitrage possibilities, then the evolution of these bond prices must satisfy certain conditions.

The expected return on bond 1 is

$$\frac{q \times 107 + (1 - q) \times 98}{100} = 1.025000.$$

The expected return on bond 2 is

$$\frac{q \times 103 + (1 - q) \times 98.5}{98.52941} = 1.022537.$$

Note that the expected returns on bond 1 and bond 2 differ. Does this mean that the bonds are not fairly priced? To see that, even though the expected returns on these bonds differ, they are priced fairly, let us compute for each bond the market price of risk

$$\phi_b = \frac{E(R_b) - r}{\sigma_b}$$

where $E(R_b)$ is the expected return on bond b, and σ_b is the volatility of the returns on bond b.

Example 6-4   Market Price of Risk of Bond 1

Let us compute the market price of risk of bond 1. The expected return on bond 1 is

$$E(R_1) = \frac{[quP + (1 - q)dP]}{P} = qu + (1 - q)d = 1.025. \qquad (6.18)$$

The volatility of the returns of bond 1 is

$$\sigma_1 = [q(1 - q)(u - d)^2]^{\frac{1}{2}} = .045 \qquad (6.19)$$

The market price of risk for bond 1 is

$$\phi_1 = \frac{1.025 - 1.02}{0.045} = .111111. \tag{6.20}$$

Example 6-5   Market Price of Risk of Bond 2

Let us compute the market price of risk of bond 2. Note that in the "up state" the price of the bond is 103. Its price at date 0 is 98.52941. This means that the up move factor $\hat{u} = \frac{103}{98.52941} = 1.045373$. The price of the bond in the "down state" is 98.5. Therefore, the down move factor $\hat{d} = \frac{98.50}{98.52941} = .999702$. The expected return on bond 2 is

$$E(R_2) = \frac{[q\hat{u}\hat{P} + (1 - q)\hat{d}\hat{P}]}{\hat{P}} = q\hat{u} + (1 - q)\hat{d} = 1.022537. \tag{6.21}$$

The volatility of the returns of bond 2 is

$$\sigma_2 = [q(1 - q)(\hat{u} - \hat{d})^2]^{\frac{1}{2}} = 0.022836. \tag{6.22}$$

The market price of risk for bond 2 is

$$\phi_2 = \frac{1.022537 - 1.02}{0.022836} = 0.111. \tag{6.23}$$

We see from Equations (6.20) and (6.23) that the market prices of risk for bond 1 and bond 2 are the same. In other words, bond prices should evolve in such a way as to ensure that

$$\phi_1 = \frac{E(R_1) - r}{\sigma_1} = \phi_2 = \frac{E(R_2) - r}{\sigma_2}.$$

This is a general implication of no arbitrage in capital markets.

Relationship between State Prices and No Arbitrage

Using the state prices, the value of bond 2 is 98.52941. How do we know that there are no arbitrage opportunities between bond 1 and bond 2? To verify this, let us consider a simple replicating portfolio strategy in which we replicate the cash flows of bond 2 using bond 1 and the riskless asset which provides a return of 2%.

Example 6-6   Replicating Bond 2 with Bond 1

At date 0, we buy $\frac{1}{2}$ units of bond 1 and lend $\$\frac{49.5}{1.02}$ at 2% interest rate. (Precisely how we arrived at these numbers will be explained shortly.) The total investment in this portfolio is

$$\frac{1}{2} \times 100 + \frac{49.5}{1.02} = 98.52941. \tag{6.24}$$

Note that the cost of this portfolio is exactly equal to the price of bond 2, whose cash flows we are trying to replicate.

Let us consider the payoffs from this strategy next. In the "up state" at date $t = 1$, the value of this portfolio is

- $\frac{1}{2}$ units of bond 1 is worth: $\frac{1}{2} \times 107 = \$53.5$.
- The money that was lent is worth: $\frac{49.5}{1.02} \times 1.02 = \$49.5$.
- So the total amount in the up state is:

$$\frac{1}{2} \times 107 + \frac{49.5}{1.02} \times 1.02 = 103.$$

This is precisely the value of bond 2 in the "up state." In the "down state" at date $t = 1$, the value of this portfolio is:

- $\frac{1}{2}$ units of bond 1 is worth: $\frac{1}{2} \times 98 = \$49$.
- The money that was lent is worth: $\frac{49.5}{1.02} \times 1.02 = \$49.5$.
- So the total amount in the up state is:

$$\frac{1}{2} \times 98 + \frac{49.5}{1.02} \times 1.02 = 98.5.$$

Note that this is precisely the value of bond 2 in the down state.

Thus, this portfolio has exactly replicated the cash flows of bond 2 in date 2 both in the "up state" and in the "down state." Hence we have created a perfect substitute. This must sell for the same price as bond 2. The investment in this portfolio, as shown earlier, is equal to 98.52941. This is therefore the price of bond 2.

We have just verified a very important principle: **Whenever we can find state prices and value securities using state prices, then such a pricing procedure is free from arbitrage.** Duffie (1992) provides a general proof that there is no arbitrage if and only if there are state prices.

Precisely how did we compute the number of bonds 1 to buy and the amount of money to loan out at date $t = 0$? At date $t = 0$ let us buy Δ units of bond 1 and place B dollars in a bank account earning an interest rate of $1 + R$. The motivation for these transactions is simple; to replicate bond 2, it seems reasonable to take a long position in bond 1, as we expect the bond 1 price to go up when the bond 2 price goes up, and vice versa. Why do we lend money? Note that bond 2 is less volatile than bond 1. When bond 1's price goes up to 107, bond 2's price goes up only to 103. Similarly, when bond 1's price goes down to 98, bond 2's price goes down only to 98.5. To achieve this lowered fluctuation, we place some money in a safe bank account. The total investment, I, in this strategy is

$$I = \Delta \times 100 + B. \tag{6.25}$$

At date 1 in the "up state," this portfolio is worth

$$I_u = \Delta \times 107 + B \times 1.02. \tag{6.26}$$

We would like the value of this portfolio to exactly match the value of bond 2. Hence we set:

$$I_u = \Delta \times 107 + B \times 1.02 = 103. \qquad (6.27)$$

The value of this portfolio in date 1 in the "down state" is worth

$$I_d = \Delta \times 98 + B \times 1.02. \qquad (6.28)$$

This should exactly replicate the value of bond 2 in the "down state." Therefore, we have

$$I_d = \Delta \times 98 + B \times 1.02 = 98.5. \qquad (6.29)$$

We solve the two equations (6.27) and (6.29) to get the values of $\Delta = \frac{1}{2}$ and $B = \frac{49.5}{1.02}$. Using these values in Equation (6.25), we get the investment $I = 98.52941$.

Risk-Neutral Pricing

In a world where investors are risk neutral, they are satisfied with an expected return equal to the riskless rate of return. Is there a probability p under which bond 1 and bond 2 will provide just the riskless rate of return? For bond 1, this would mean:

$$\frac{uP \times p + dP \times (1 - p)}{P} = r.$$

Solving, we find that

$$p = \frac{r - d}{u - d}. \qquad (6.30)$$

Note that this risk-neutral probability p may be written in terms of the state price π_u as

$$p = \pi_u \times r.$$

In a similar manner, we may write,

$$1 - p = \pi_d \times r.$$

For bond 1, we get

$$p = \frac{1.02 - 0.98}{1.07 - 0.98} = .444444. \qquad (6.31)$$

and

$$1 - p = 0.555556. \qquad (6.32)$$

Note that if we use the risk-neutral probabilities to compute the expected return of bond 2, we get:

$$\frac{103 \times p + 98.5 \times (1 - p)}{98.52941} = 1.02.$$

This indicates that all bonds are priced to provide the riskless rate of return under the risk-neutral probability. We can also write the pricing derivation in the following manner:

1. Price of bond 1 is given by

$$P = \pi_u uP + \pi_d dP.$$

2. Using the relationship between π_u and p, and π_d and d we can write this as:

$$P = \frac{puP + (1 - p)dP}{r}.$$

3. But $puP + (1 - p)dP$ is the expected value of the bond price at date $t = 1$, where the expectation is taken with respect to the risk-neutral probability p. Thus, we can write the pricing formula as

$$P = \frac{E_p[\tilde{P}]}{r}. \qquad (6.33)$$

where $E_p[\cdot]$ is the expectations operator with respect to the risk-neutral probability measure p.

This gives us a very simple pricing procedure: First, we find the risk-neutral probability p. We then calculate the expected future cash flows under the risk-neutral probability. Finally, this expected value is discounted at the riskless rate to compute the price of the security. This pricing rule is especially convenient for valuing securities by Monte Carlo simulation techniques. We will illustrate these ideas in Chapter 7.

Note that in our analysis, the original probability q does not play a direct role in pricing the bonds. It is the risk-neutral probability that matters. We will develop these ideas further in this chapter in the context of the term structure of interest rates. All our analyses thus far have been conducted in a two-date setting. In order to provide a true setting for term-structure analysis, it is necessary to develop an intertemporal framework that extends beyond a two-date setting to a multiperiod setting. The next section analyzes the processes that can be used to describe the behavior of bond prices and interest rates through time.

DYNAMICS OF BOND PRICES AND INTEREST RATES

The bond-pricing process used in the previous sections can be easily generalized to a multiperiod setting. As a direct extension, consider a three-date version of the process that was specified earlier.

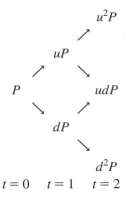

$$t = 0 \quad t = 1 \quad t = 2$$

Note that the set of possible bond prices increases linearly with time—at date 0, there is one price; at date 1, there are two possible prices (uP and dP); and at date 2, there are 3 possible prices (u^2P, udP and d^2P). This process is known as the **binomial process** and this has been studied extensively by Cox, Ross, and Rubinstein (1979).

Consider a bond at date t. Assume that we consider a horizon date $T > t$. We can subdivide the life of the bond into n time intervals. Define the length of each subinterval as $h = \frac{(T-t)}{n}$. Consider the annualized riskless rate of interest $1 + R$; its allocation to the subintervals will be governed by the relation:

$$(1 + \hat{R}) = (1 + R)^{\frac{T-t}{n}}.$$

Cox, Ross, and Rubinstein (1979) select

$$u = \frac{1}{d} = e^{\sigma\sqrt{\frac{T-t}{n}}} \tag{6.34}$$

where σ is the volatility of the underlying asset returns, $T - t$ is the time to the horizon date in years, n is the number of time intervals into which the time to maturity is divided, and e is the base of natural logarithm. They let the probability $q = 0.5 + 0.5\frac{\mu}{\sigma}\sqrt{\frac{T-t}{n}}$ where μ is the expected rate of return on the underlying asset. Then as $n \rightarrow \infty$, it can be shown that the underlying bond price P follows a process that can be described as

$$\frac{dP}{P} = \mu dt + \sigma dz \tag{6.35}$$

where dz is normally distributed with a mean equal to zero and a variance of dt. The bond price P_T at the horizon date is a random variable. Its properties are summarized by the mean and variance as

$$E\left[\ln\left(\frac{P_T}{P_t}\right)\right] = \mu(T - t).$$

and

$$\sigma^2\left[\ln\left(\frac{P_T}{P_t}\right)\right] = \sigma^2(T - t).$$

In other words, future bond prices are lognormally distributed. This is not a desirable feature; as bonds approach their maturity date, their price should converge to par. This simple requirement is not met by this process.

In practice, this process is used in the industry only in specific applications where convergence to par is not a serious problem. This would be the case if the bond has many years to maturity. There are processes in which convergence to par is satisfied. The process specified in Equation (6.35) is a continuous time limit of the discrete-time binomial process that we considered earlier. Similar processes have been specified for interest rates as well and we will review some of them.

The derivation of bond prices illuminates an important feature of pricing securities: The original probability distribution is not the relevant one. We can change the original probability measure with a risk-neutral probability measure. Then, using the risk-neutral probability measure, we can take the expected value of the option and discount this expected value at the riskless rate of interest. This insight was originally outlined by Cox and Ross (1976) and later formally developed as a broader implication of no arbitrage by Harrison and Kreps (1978) in an influential paper. This insight also allows us to use Monte Carlo simulation techniques to price certain types of options and contingent claims. (This is taken up in the next chapter to value options.)

VALUATION OF THE YIELD CURVE

The binomial process that we used for describing bond prices can be applied to interest rates as well. Rendelman and Bartter (1980) applied this idea to modeling interest rates behavior.

Binomial Process

We will illustrate the approach in the context of a single-factor model in which the nominal rates follow a binomial process. Consider a simple binomial process for the spot rate of interest.

$$
\begin{array}{ccccc}
& & & & u^2 r(t) \\
& & & \nearrow & \\
& & ur(t) & & \\
& \nearrow & & \searrow & \\
r(t) & & & & udr(t) \\
& \searrow & & \nearrow & \\
& & dr(t) & & \\
& & & \searrow & \\
& & & & d^2 r(t) \\
\end{array}
$$

$$t = 0 \quad t = 1 \quad t = 2$$

This process is shown in the discrete-time model of Rendelman and Bartter (1980). We will assume throughout that the probability of an up move is q and that of a down move is $1 - q$, irrespective of the level of the spot rate of interest. More satisfactory processes will be taken up later. Consider a pure discount bond paying a dollar at date 2.

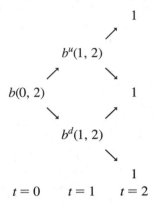

$$t = 0 \qquad t = 1 \qquad t = 2$$

Recall that LEH, described earlier in this chapter, says that the expected return over one period on any bond should be the same as the one-period rate prevailing at that time. Therefore, by LEH, at date $t = 1$ the following two conditions hold:

$$\frac{1}{b^u(1,\,2)} = 1 + ur(t)$$

and

$$\frac{1}{b^d(1,\,2)} = 1 + dr(t).$$

These conditions say that the return at date 1 from holding a one-period bond should be equal to the one-period rate at that node. As a consequence, we can rearrange these two equations to get the bond-price distributions

$$b^u(1,\,2) = \frac{1}{1 + ur(t)}$$

and

$$b^d(1,\,2) = \frac{1}{1 + dr(t)}.$$

Working with known cashflows at date $t = 2$, we determined the bond prices at date $t = 1$.

We now proceed in a recursive fashion to date $t = 0$. By LEH we have

$$\frac{q \times b^u(1,\,2) + (1 - q) \times b^d(1,\,2)}{b(0,\,2)} = 1 + r(t).$$

Rearranging the above equation and solving for the bond price at date $t = 0$ we get

$$b(0,\,2) = \frac{q \times b^u(1,\,2) + (1 - q) \times b^d(1,\,2)}{1 + r(t)}.$$

Note that we could expand the procedure to any arbitrary future date and compute the pure discount bond prices at date 0 as the sequence $b(0, 1), b(0, 2), b(0, 3), b(0, 4), \cdots$ $b(0, n)$. In addition, at each future date s in the spot rate tree, we can obtain the entire distribution of yield curve. The ability to get the entire distribution of zero coupon bond prices is important in the valuation of interest rate derivatives. We illustrate these ideas in Example 6-7.

Example 6-7

Given the current one-period rate is 10%, the up move factor $u = 1.25$, the down move factor $d = 0.80$, the probability of an up move is $q = 0.5$, and the evolution of the one-period rates given next.

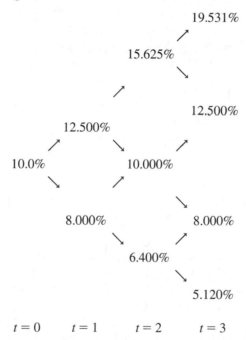

Determine the term structure of interest rates at date $t = 0$ for maturities $T = 1, 2, 3$, and 4.

We first begin by solving for the price of a single-period bond. This bond pays one dollar at date $t = 1$ no matter which state occurs. Therefore its price at date $t = 0$ is $b(0, 1) = \frac{1}{(1 + 0.10)} = 0.9091$. This is shown as:

$$
\begin{array}{ccc}
 & & 1 \\
 & \nearrow & \\
0.9091 & & \\
 & \searrow & \\
 & & 1 \\
t = 0 & & t = 1
\end{array}
$$

The yield of a one-period bond at date $t = 0$ is 10%.

We now determine the value of a two-period bond. At date $t = 1$, in the up node, the value of the bond is $\frac{1}{1+0.125} = 0.8889$. At date $t = 1$, in the down node, the value of the bond is $\frac{1}{1+0.08} = 0.9259$. Now that we have the prices of the bond at date $t = 1$, we can move back to date $t = 0$. At date $t = 0$, the expected value of the bond is $(0.8889 \times 0.5 + 0.9259 \times 0.5)$.

The discounted value of this expected price is

$$b(0, 2) = \frac{[0.8889 \times 0.5 + 0.9259 \times 0.5]}{1.10} = 0.8249.$$

The yield to maturity of the two-period bond is computed as

$$0.8249 = \frac{1}{(1 + y_2)^2} \Rightarrow y_2 = 10.10\%$$

The evolution of the two-period bond is given next.

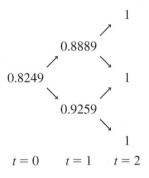

$$
\begin{array}{ccc}
 & & 1 \\
 & 0.8889 \nearrow & \\
0.8249 \nearrow & & 1 \\
 & 0.9259 \searrow \nearrow & \\
 & & 1 \\
t = 0 \quad t = 1 \quad t = 2
\end{array}
$$

We now proceed to value the three-period bond. At date $t = 2$, at the top node, the value of the bond is $b^{uu}(2, 3) = \frac{1}{1+0.15625} = 0.8649$. At date $t = 2$, at the intermediate node, the value of the bond is $b^{ud}(2, 3) = \frac{1}{1+0.1000} = 0.9091$. At date $t = 2$, at the lowermost node, the value of the bond is $b^{dd}(2, 3) = \frac{1}{1+0.0640} = 0.9398$.

Having determined the bond prices at date $t = 2$, we step back to date $t = 1$. At the top node in date 1, the value of the bond is the expected value of the bond in date 2, discounted by the one-period rate at the top node in date 1. This is given by

$$b^u(1, 3) = \frac{[0.5 \times 0.8649 + 0.5 \times 0.9091]}{1 + 0.1250} = 0.7884.$$

In a similar way, we can determine the price of the bond at date 1, at the lower node as

$$b^d(1, 3) = \frac{[0.5 \times 0.9091 + 0.5 \times 0.9398]}{1 + 0.0800} = 0.8560.$$

We now step back to date $t = 0$ and determine the value of the three-period bond as

$$b(0, 3) = \frac{[0.5 \times 0.7884 + 0.5 \times 0.8560]}{1 + 0.1000} = 0.7475.$$

The yield to maturity of the three-period bond is computed as

$$0.7475 = \frac{1}{(1 + y_3)^3} \Rightarrow y_3 = 10.19\%.$$

The evolution is shown by:

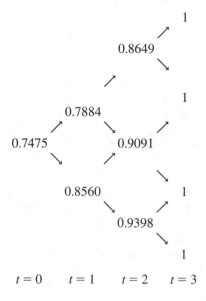

$$t = 0 \qquad t = 1 \qquad t = 2 \qquad t = 3$$

In a similar manner, we can determine the pricing of the four-period bond. The evolution of the four-period bond prices is

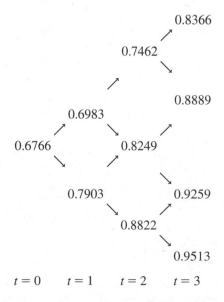

$$t = 0 \qquad t = 1 \qquad t = 2 \qquad t = 3$$

The yield to maturity of the four-period bond is computed as

$$0.6766 = \frac{1}{(1 + y_4)^4} \Rightarrow y_4 = 10.26\%.$$

The term structure of interest rates that we have calculated is recorded in Table 6-4.

TABLE 6-4

Term Structure

Bond Maturity (number of periods)	Bond Price	Yield to Maturity
1	0.9091	10.00%
2	0.8249	10.10%
3	0.7475	10.19%
4	0.6766	10.26%

In addition to determining the term structure, we also have information on the future yield distributions. For example, we can answer the question: What is the distribution of two-period yields on date 1 (one-period from now)? To address this question, we need to determine $b^u(1, 3)$ and $b^d(1, 3)$. Note that we already have this information from our analysis of the three-period bond pricing. We have determined that $b^u(1, 3) = 0.7884$ and $b^d(1, 3) = 0.8560$. The two-period yields at date 1 can be determined as follows:

$$0.7884 = \frac{1}{(1 + y_2^u)^2} \Rightarrow y_2^u = 12.623\%.$$

In a similar way,

$$0.8560 = \frac{1}{(1 + y_2^d)^2} \Rightarrow y_2^d = 8.084\%.$$

In a way similar to our analysis of bond-price dynamics, we can determine the continuous time limit of this binomial process for interest rates. It turns out to be the lognormal process

$$dr = r[\mu dt + \sigma dz].$$

The terminal distribution of the interest rate for any time T is lognormal. Its mean and variance are

$$E\left[\ln\left(\frac{r_T}{r_t}\right)\right] = \mu(T - t)$$

and

$$Var\left[\ln\left(\frac{r_T}{r_t}\right)\right] = \sigma^2(T - t).$$

While our model ensures that the bond prices converge to par at maturity, this process is still unsatisfactory as it assumes a lognormal distribution at any future date T.

This distribution means that some extremely high interest rates can occur in the future. Note that the probability of an up move or a down move is independent of the level of the interest rates. Empirically, interest rates appear to revert to a mean level (possibly a varying mean) of interest rates. This underscores the need to examine alternative processes for interest rates.

We illustrate a mean-reverting interest rate process next. In this process, the interest rate is pulled towards a central value but propagates randomly around the central value.

Mean-Reverting Interest Rate Process

We present a simple discrete-time process in which the probability of an up move and a down move depend on the level of the interest rates.

Let us assume that the short rate follows a stochastic process specified below:

Upper limit, $r = 2\mu$

$$r_{t+2} = r_t + 2\delta$$

$$r_{t+1} = r_t + \delta$$

$$r_t$$

$$r_{t+2} = r_t$$

$$r_{t+1} = r_t - \delta$$

$$r_{t+2} = r_t - 2\delta$$

$$t \qquad t+1 \qquad\qquad t+2$$

Lower limit, $r = 0$

The probabilities associated with each node are dependent on the interest rate at these nodes. These are specified as

$$q[r_t] = 1 - \frac{r_t}{2\mu},$$

and

$$1 - q[r_t] = \frac{r_t}{2\mu}.$$

When the interest rate reaches the upper limit, the probability of a down move is 1. Similarly, when the interest rates reach the lower limit, the probability of an up move is 1. The process has lower and upper limits at 0 and 2μ, respectively. The rates must evolve within these barriers. In the process specified above, δ represents the amount by which the short rate can go up or go down in the interval $(t, t+1)$. This time interval could be a day, a week, or several weeks. Depending on how the time intervals are divided, the choice of the parameter δ will vary. The process specified affords some flexibility. By choosing the parameter μ suitably, both increasing and decreasing interest rate scenarios can be modeled in an expectations context. When $r_t = \mu$, the probability of an up move is exactly equal to the probability of a down move. On the other hand, when $r_t < \mu$, the probability of an up move is greater than the probability of a down move, indicating that rates are expected to go up. In a similar manner, when $r_t > \mu$, the probability of an up move is less than the probability of a down move, indicating that rates are expected to go down. Viewed in this context, we may regard the parameter μ to be the long-run mean rate of interest. The location of the current value of the short rate relative to the long-run mean is therefore of interest in the bond-pricing problem. Another feature of interest is the speed with which the short rates are expected to approach the long-run mean value. The parameter δ can be interpreted as the speed of adjustment. When δ is large, the short rate r_t approaches the long-run mean interest rate rapidly. On the other hand, if δ is small, the short rate approaches the long-run mean rate sluggishly. The choice of δ, μ, and the current rate r_t provides flexibility in modeling different term-structure scenarios. The interest rate process we have chosen has a steady-state distribution. It can be shown that the mean and the variance of the process (as the number n of movements in the rates approaches infinity) are given by μ and $\frac{\delta\mu}{2}$, respectively. Therefore, by estimating the mean and variance of the interest-rate process using real-life data on interest rates, it is possible to identify the parameters μ and δ, which in turn may be used to generate the interest-rate tree. We provide a simple example to illustrate this model in Example 6-8.

Example 6-8

Given the current interest rate (one-period) is 10%, the parameter $\delta = 1\%$, and $\mu = 12\%$. Determine the term structure of interest rates at date $t = 0$. The evolution of the one-period interest rates is:

$t = 0 \quad t = 1 \quad t = 2 \quad t = 3$

Unlike in the binomial process, the probabilities change at each node of the lattice. Hence we need to keep track of the probabilities. The next lattice shows **the evolution of up move probabilities through time.**

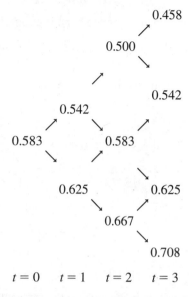

$$t=0 \quad t=1 \quad t=2 \quad t=3$$

Note that the probability is exactly 0.5 when the interest rate is equal to 12%, which is the long-run mean. If the rates are below 12%, the probability of an up move increases beyond 0.5; otherwise it decreases below 0.5.

As we did in the case of the binomial process, we first begin by solving for the price of a single-period bond. This bond pays one dollar at date $t=1$ no matter which state occurs. Therefore its price at date $t=0$ is $b(0,\ 1)=\frac{1}{(1+0.10)}=0.9091$ as shown below.

$$
\begin{array}{c}
1 \\
\nearrow \\
0.9091 \\
\searrow \\
1
\end{array}
$$

$$t=0 \quad t=1$$

The yield of one-period bond at date $t=0$ is 10%.

We now proceed to value a two-period bond. At date $t=1$, at the up node, the value of the bond is $\frac{1}{1+0.11}=0.9009$. At date $t=1$, at the down node, the value of the bond is $\frac{1}{1+0.09}=0.9174$. Now that we have the prices of the bond at date $t=1$, we can move back to date $t=0$ and solve for the price of the two-period bond at date $t=0$. At date $t=0$, the expected value of the bond is $(0.9009 \times 0.5830 + 0.9174 \times 0.4170)$.

The discounted value of this expected price is

$$b(0, 2) = \frac{[0.9009 \times 0.5830 + 0.9174 \times 0.4170]}{1.10} = 0.8253.$$

The yield to maturity of the two-period bond is computed as

$$0.8253 = \frac{1}{(1 + y_2)^2} \Rightarrow y_2 = 10.076\%.$$

The evolution of the two-period bond is given next.

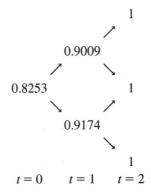

$$t = 0 \qquad t = 1 \qquad t = 2$$

The rest of the analysis is identical to that presented for the binomial process and therefore is not repeated here.

Cox, Ingersoll, and Ross Model

In a model proposed by Cox, Ingersoll, and Ross (1985) (CIR), interest rates follow a mean-reverting process much like the model that we presented in the previous section. However, the variance of the changes in interest rates is proportional to the level of the rates.

The interest rate process that they use is represented below:

$$dr = \kappa(\mu - r)dt + \sigma\sqrt{r}dz.$$

In this process there are three parameters: μ, the long-run mean of the short-term interest rate; σ^2, the variance parameter; and κ, the speed of adjustment of the short-term interest rate to the long-run mean. In addition, the parameter λ, which is related to the risk-averse behavior of investors, also affects the bond prices. These parameters must be estimated in order to implement the CIR model.

Prices of discount bonds are determined in the Cox, Ingersoll, and Ross (1985) model using a simple formula. Let the current time be denoted by t; then a bond paying $1 at time T should be priced as

$$b(t, T) = A(T - t)e^{-B(T-t)r_t} \tag{6.36}$$

Given the parameter τ, representing the time to maturity $T - t$ of a bond, then

$$A(\tau) = \left(\frac{2\gamma e^{(\kappa + \gamma + \lambda)\tau/2}}{2\gamma + (\kappa + \gamma + \lambda)(e^{\gamma\tau} - 1)} \right)^{2\kappa\mu/\sigma^2}$$

$$B(\tau) = \frac{2(e^{\gamma\tau} - 1)}{2\gamma + (\kappa + \gamma + \lambda)(e^{\gamma\tau} - 1)}$$

$$\gamma = \sqrt{(\kappa + \lambda)^2 + 2\sigma^2}.$$

This model can be used to generate different shapes of the yield curve. It is necessary that $2\kappa\mu \geq \sigma^2$ to ensure that the interest rate is positive. In the CIR model, when $r < \frac{2\kappa\mu}{\gamma + \kappa + \lambda}$, the term structure is upward-sloping, and when $r > \frac{\kappa\mu}{\kappa + \lambda}$ the term structure is downward-sloping. For intermediate values of r the term structure is humped.

Several authors have tested the Cox, Ingersoll, and Ross model. Brown and Dybvig (1986), Gibbons and Ramaswamy (1994), and Pearson and Sun (1994) have examined the model. The fact that the model is driven by only one factor (short rate) means that its ability to capture the richness in the yield curve is somewhat limited. Gibbons and Ramaswamy (1994) estimated the parameters of the model as $\mu = 1.54\%$, $\kappa = 12.43$, $\lambda = -6.08$, and $\sigma = 0.49$. They found that the CIR model that describes the behavior of real returns does a satisfactory job of explaining short-term T-bill returns. In much of the literature, there is a general agreement that single-factor models need to be generalized, perhaps to include three factors: short-term interest rates, the spread between short-term and long-term interest rates (which is a proxy for the slope of the yield curve), and the volatility of interest rates. In the industry, single-factor models are used with an important modification: Some free parameters are added to make the model fit the market data. In the CIR model, we can describe the long-run mean rate $\mu(t)$ as a function of time. Wang (1994) shows that by making $\mu(t)$ a step function, the CIR model can be made to fit the market data. We turn to this class of models next.

CALIBRATION OF MODELS

The models of interest rates that we have presented so far are not calibrated to market data. In other words, the parameters of the models are estimated, and using the estimated parameters, we compute zero prices. These zero prices may or may not correspond to the actual market prices of zeroes. If we believe there are liquid securities which are traded actively with narrow bid-offer spreads, then we would like a model that prices them close to their market values. There is a class of term-structure models that find the parameters from the market data much the same way implied volatilities are computed in equity options, using a process known as calibration. We present three such models of term structure next.

Black, Derman, and Toy Model

We will begin our treatment of the first of these, the Black, Derman, and Toy model, with an illustrative example.

Example 6-9

Consider a problem in which we want the term-structure model to be calibrated to the market data on one-period and two-period yields and to the volatilities presented in Table 6-5.

Term to Maturity	Yield to Maturity	Volatility
1	10.00%	
2	11.00%	19.00%
3	12.00%	18.00%

TABLE 6-5
Market Data on Yields

In calibrated models, the pricing procedure is turned on its head; normally term-structure models begin with the spot-rate evolution tree (based on the parameter estimates) and then solve for the term structure as an outcome of applying LEH to the spot-rate tree. This is what we did in the previous section. The outcome of such an exercise will be an output such as Table 6-5. **In the Black, Derman, and Toy model, however, the market data on yields is the input and the spot-rate tree is the output.**

To construct the spot-rate tree, we work from the root of the lattice and proceed forward.

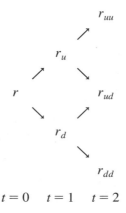

Given the data provided in Table 6-5, we can determine the prices of zeroes at date $t = 0$. Let $b(0, n)$ be the price of a zero with n years to maturity at date $t = 0$. At node 0, the following conditions exist for a zero that will mature at $t = 2$:

$$\frac{1}{2} \times \ln\left(\frac{r_u}{r_d}\right) = 0.19. \tag{6.37}$$

Equation (6.37) sets the volatility of the two-year rates (one period hence) equal to 19%.

$$\frac{\frac{1}{2} \times \left(\frac{1}{1 + r_u} + \frac{1}{1 + r_d}\right)}{1 + 0.10} = b(0, 2) \tag{6.38}$$

$$b(0, 2) = 0.8116$$

Equation (6.38) sets the price of a two-year zero equal to the one obtained by the LEH. We have assumed that $q = \frac{1}{2}$. Solving Equations (6.37) and (6.38) simultaneously, we get $r_u = 14.319\%$ and $r_d = 9.792\%$.

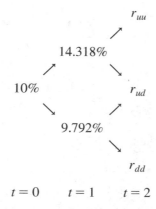

We can now construct the tree further forward. We solve for r_{uu}, r_{ud} and r_{dd} in such a way that when LEH is applied to the tree we get the market prices reflected in Table 6-5. Let $y_u(1, 3)$ be the two-year yield at date $t = 1$ in the "up state." Likewise, let $y_d(1, 3)$ be the two-year yield at date $t = 1$ in the "down state." Using these notations, we write the volatility condition:

$$\frac{1}{2} \times \ln\left[\frac{y_u(1, 3)}{y_d(1, 3)}\right] = 0.18. \tag{6.39}$$

Equation (6.39) sets the volatility of the three-year rates (one period hence) equal to 18%. In the "up state" at $t = 1$ the rate is $y_u(1, 3)$, and in the "down state" at date $t = 1$ the rate is $y_d(1, 3)$. Also, by no arbitrage, we must have

$$\frac{\frac{1}{2} \times \left\{\frac{1}{[1 + y_u(1, 3)]^2} + \frac{1}{[1 + y_d(1, 3)]^2}\right\}}{1 + 0.10} = b(0, 3) \tag{6.40}$$

where $b(0, 3)$ is the three-period zero price given by

$$b(0, 3) = \frac{1}{(1 + 0.12)^3}.$$

We solve the two equations above to get $y_u(1, 3) = 15.4159\%$ and $y_d(1, 3) = 10.7553\%$.

Note that at $t = 1$ the price of a zero maturing at $t = 3$ can be determined for both the "up state" and the "down state" as

$$b_u(1, 3) = \frac{1}{[1 + y_u(1, 3)]^2} = 0.750704$$

and

$$b_d(1, 3) = \frac{1}{[1 + y_d(1, 3)]^2} = 0.81521.$$

In addition, by the LEH, we must also have

$$b_u(1, 3) = \frac{\frac{1}{2} \times \left(\frac{1}{1 + r_{uu}} + \frac{1}{1 + r_{ud}} \right)}{1 + r_u} \tag{6.41}$$

and

$$b_d(1, 3) = \frac{\frac{1}{2} \times \left(\frac{1}{1 + r_{ud}} + \frac{1}{1 + r_{dd}} \right)}{1 + r_d}. \tag{6.42}$$

Also, assuming lognormality, we have

$$r_{ud} = \sqrt{r_{uu} \times r_{dd}}. \tag{6.43}$$

Solving the three equations above, we get $r_{uu} = 19.4187\%$, $r_{ud} = 13.7669\%$, and $r_{dd} = 9.076\%$. We can construct the yield curve at each node using the zero prices.

$$
\begin{array}{ccccc}
 & & & 19.4187\% & \\
 & & \nearrow & (j = 0) & \\
 & 14.318\% & & & \\
 & \nearrow \; (j = 0) & \searrow & & \\
10\% & & & 13.7669\% & \\
 & \searrow & \nearrow & (j = 1) & \\
 & 9.792\% & & & \\
 & (j = 1) & \searrow & & \\
 & & & 9.76\% & \\
 & & & (j = 2) & \\
t = 0 & t = 1 & & t = 2 &
\end{array}
$$

We proceed this way to get the entire tree. Once the tree is generated from selected market data, we can use the tree to value any derivative asset that is interest-rate related. A detailed treatment of the discrete-time version of this model in the context of pricing corporate bonds is found in Maloney (1992). We provide a brief description of the general implementation of the Black, Derman, and Toy model next.

Let $t = 0, 1, 2 \ldots, N$ be the time periods, and let $j = 0, 1, 2 \ldots, t$ be the nodes at any time node t. Let $b(t, j, T)$ be the price of a discount bond at date t at node j maturing at date T. Assume that the life of the bond is divided into n periods. Then the Black, Derman, and Toy model may be summarized formally as

$$b(t, j, T) = e^{-r(t, j, T)(T-t)}. \tag{6.44}$$

This equation simply says that the value of a zero is the discounted value of $1 to be received at date T. This is the price-yield relationship for the zero coupon bond at date t and state (node) j. The next relationship is the condition that the bonds are priced to eliminate arbitrage opportunities.

$$b(t, j, T) = \{0.5b(t + 1, j, T) + 0.5b(t + 1, j + 1, T)\}b(t, j, t + 1) \tag{6.45}$$

This condition is common to all models that are used in the industry to calibrate the model to the market data. In particular, the same condition is used in the Ho and Lee (1986) model and in the Heath, Jarrow, and Morton (1992) model. The Black, Derman, and Toy (1990) model also specifies conditions on the volatility structure,

$$b(t + 1, j + 1, T) = b(t + 1, j, T)^{v(t, T)} \tag{6.46}$$

where $v(t, T)$ is the volatility factor for a bond with a maturity date T in period $t + 1$ as of date t. The volatility factor is given by

$$v(t, T) = e^{[2\sigma(t, T)]} \tag{6.47}$$

where $\sigma(t, T)$ is the annualized volatility of the yield of a zero coupon bond maturing at date T as evaluated at date t. As shown earlier, the model takes as market data $y(0, j, T)$ and $\sigma(0, T)$ where $T = 1, 2, \ldots, N$. Note that at date $t = 0$ there is only one state, so $j = 0$.

When $t = 0$ in Equations (6.45) and (6.46) we first know the relation between $b(1, 0, T)$ and $b(1, 1, T)$ from the volatility structure. Using this in the no-arbitrage condition yields a single nonlinear equation in $b(1, 0, T)$ that can be solved by a univariate Newton-Ralphson iterative search procedure.

To see this clearly, let us rewrite Equations (6.45) and (6.46) for the case when $t = 0$. We get corresponding to Equation (6.45)

$$b(0, 0, T) = [0.5b(1, 0, T) + 0.5b(1, 1, T)]b(0, 0, 1).$$

Note that in this equation, $b(0, 0, T)$ is known for all T, and that hence the unknowns are $b(1, 0, T)$ and $b(1, 1, T)$. Corresponding to Equation (6.46) we get

$$b(1, 1, T) = b(1, 0, T)^{v(0, T)}.$$

In this equation $v(0, T)$ is known for all T. Substituting this equation into the previous equation we get

$$b(0, 0, T) = [0.5b(1, 0, T) + 0.5b(1, 0, T)^{v(0, T)}]b(0, 0, 1).$$

This nonlinear equation can be iteratively solved for $T = 1, \ldots, N$ for $b(1, 0, T)$. Once we determine $b(1, 0, T)$ we can utilize that information to determine $b(1, 1, T)$.

When $t \geq 1$ we have a system of two nonlinear equations that again can be solved by a bivariate Newton-Ralphson search procedure. This search is a bit more complicated because for each T we have two nonlinear equations to solve for $b(t, j, T)$. For each t we solve Equations (6.45) and (6.46) simultaneously. We illustrate the idea using the case when $t = 1$. Note that in this case, we get the following two conditions:

$$b(1, j, T) = [0.5b(2, j, T) + 0.5b(2, j + 1, T)]b(1, j, 2)$$

and

$$b(2, j + 1, T) = b(2, j, T)^{y(1, T)}.$$

For $j = 0$ and $j = 1$, the above system can be solved for $b(2, 0, T)$, $b(2, 1, T)$ and $b(2, 2, T)$. This allows us to get the term structure at $t = 2$ and so on.

Ho and Lee Model

The Ho and Lee (1986) model is developed in a discrete-state, discrete-time framework. The initial (current) term structure is exogenously specified based on market conditions. It is then assumed to be randomly perturbed. This perturbation is effected by allowing the entire term structure to evolve through time as a binomial process. Constraints on the perturbation function are then imposed to preclude pairwise arbitrage between any two bonds. It turns out that this condition alone is insufficient to rule out negative forward rates. As a result, the model still admits arbitrage.

The Ho and Lee model is a novel approach to dynamically modeling the term structure of interest rates. By construction, the model generates bond prices that are calibrated to market data. It also provides a unified preference-independent framework in which to price a wide variety of contingent claims, including futures contracts and options on both the cash instrument and futures contracts.

The price of a bond in state i at time t that pays \$1 at time T is represented by $b(t, i, T)$. The initial term structure $b(0, 0, T)$ is exogenously specified and is assumed to be randomly perturbed. This perturbation is reflected by allowing the entire term structure to evolve through time as a binomial process,

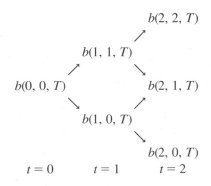

$$
\begin{array}{cccccc}
& & & & & b(2, 2, T) \\
& & & & \nearrow & \\
& & & b(1, 1, T) & & \\
& & \nearrow & & \searrow & \\
& b(0, 0, T) & & & & b(2, 1, T) \\
& & \searrow & & \nearrow & \\
& & & b(1, 0, T) & & \\
& & & & \searrow & \\
& & & & & b(2, 0, T) \\
t = 0 & & t = 1 & & t = 2 &
\end{array}
$$

where the perturbation functions $h(\tau)$ and $h^*(\tau)$ are defined as follows (where τ is the time to maturity remaining):

$$b(t+1, i+1, T) = \frac{b(t, i, T)}{b(t, i, t+1)} h(T - (t+1)) \tag{6.48}$$

$$b(t+1, i, T) = \frac{b(t, i, T)}{b(t, i, t+1)} h^*(T - (t+1)) \tag{6.49}$$

$$h(0) = h^*(0) = 1.$$

By dividing Equation (6.48) by Equation (6.49), we get

$$\frac{b(t+1, i+1, T)}{b(t+1, i, T)} = \frac{h(T - (t+1))}{h^*(T - (t+1))}. \tag{6.50}$$

Assume that the probability that the perturbation will be effected by $h(T)$ is q. Consequently, the probability that the perturbation will be effected by $h^*(T)$ is $1 - q$. The no-arbitrage condition that was used in the Black, Derman, and Toy model is also used here:

$$b(t, i, T) = \{(1 - q)b(t+1, i, T) + qb(t+1, i+1, T)\}b(t, i, t+1).$$

Combining the conditions above, we get the constraint on the perturbation functions to preclude arbitrage between any two pairs of bonds as

$$qh(\tau) + (1 - q)h^*(\tau) = 1 \text{ for } \tau, i > 0.$$

In addition, the following additional conditions are imposed by the Ho and Lee model:

$$h(\tau) = \frac{1}{q + (1 - q)\delta^\tau}$$

and

$$h^*(\tau) = \frac{\delta^\tau}{q + (1 - q)\delta^\tau}$$

for the constants $0 \geq q \geq 1$ and $0 \geq \delta \geq 1$. We illustrate the Ho and Lee model in Example 6-10.

Example 6-10

Let us consider the market data presented in Table 6-6. The evolution of the bond prices will be calibrated to this data. We will assume that $q = 0.5$ and that $\delta = 0.99$.

Term to Maturity	Yield to Maturity	Bond Price	TABLE 6-6 *Market Data on Yields*
1	8.00%	0.92593	
2	8.00%	0.85734	
3	8.00%	0.79383	

Note that we can solve for $h(\tau)$ and $h^*(\tau)$, for $\tau = 1, 2$, and 3. These values are shown in the table below.

τ	$h(\tau)$	$h^*(\tau)$
1	1.005	.995
2	1.010	.990
3	1.015	.985

The pricing procedure works as follows. The no-arbitrage condition

$$b(0, 0, 2) = [0.5b(1, 0, 2) + 0.5b(1, 1, 2)]b(0, 0, 1)$$

is combined with the perturbation requirement

$$\frac{b(1, 1, 2)}{b(1, 0, 2)} = \frac{h(1)}{h^*(1)}.$$

Solving these two equations, we get $b(1, 0, 2) = 0.92127$ and $b(1, 1, 2) = 0.93508$.

We can apply the same principles to solve for $b(1, 0, 3)$ and $b(1, 1, 3)$. The no-arbitrage condition

$$b(0, 0, 3) = \{0.5b(1, 0, 3) + 0.5b(1, 1, 3)\}b(0, 0, 1)$$

is combined with the perturbation requirement

$$\frac{b(1, 1, 3)}{b(1, 0, 3)} = \frac{h(2)}{h^*(2)}.$$

Solving these two equations, we get $b(1, 0, 3) = 0.848723$ and $b(1, 1, 3) = 0.865955$.

Having solved for the prices of discount bonds at date $t = 1$, we can move forward to value the prices of bonds at date $t = 2$ for different nodes. The no-arbitrage condition at date $t = 1$ is

$$b(1, 0, 3) = \{0.5b(2, 0, 3) + 0.5b(2, 1, 3)\}b(1, 0, 2).$$

This is combined with the perturbation requirement

$$\frac{b(2, 1, 3)}{b(2, 0, 3)} = \frac{h(1)}{h^*(1)}$$

Solving these two equations, we get $b(2, 0, 3) = 0.91662$ and $b(2, 1, 3) = 0.92588$. In this manner, the entire future distribution of bond prices can be obtained using the Ho and Lee approach.

	0	1	2	3	Ho-Lee Discount Factors
1-Year Zero	0.925926	1			
		1			
2-Year Zero	0.857339	0.930579	1		
		0.921273	1		
			1		
3-Year Zero	0.793832	0.865955	0.935231	1	
		0.848723	0.925879	1	
			0.916620	1	
				1	

Heath, Jarrow, and Morton Model

The Heath, Jarrow, and Morton (HJM) (1992) model, unlike other models, is based on the evolution of forward rates of interest. Conceptually, the insights of this paper are very similar to the Ho and Lee (1986) model. But, unlike the Ho and Lee model, the HJM model ensures that the interest rates are always positive. As in the Ho and Lee and the Black, Derman, and Toy models, this model enforces the no-arbitrage condition that

$$b(0, 0, j) = [0.5b(1, 0, j) + 0.5b(1, 1, j)]b(0, 0, 1).$$

The no-arbitrage condition means that the evolution of the forward rates are dictated by their volatility structure alone. Unlike the previous models, the HJM model is path dependent. With a path-dependent tree, even with a few steps many outcomes are possible. If we examine Figure 6-6, we note that after one period from the root of the tree, there are two possible forward rates. After two periods from the root of the tree, there are four possible forward rates: two consecutive up moves lead to f_{uu}, one up move followed by one down move leads to f_{ud}, one down move followed by one up move leads to f_{du} and two consecutive down moves lead to f_{dd}. In fact, in the HJM model, the number of nodes increases exponentially with time intervals. Thus, with four time intervals in the HJM model, we get $2^4 = 16$ nodes. With seven intervals, we get $2^7 = 128$ nodes. Computationally, the HJM model presents more of a challenge than the other models that we discussed in this chapter. Only a brief presentation of the Heath, Jarrow, and Morton model is given here. See Heath, Jarrow, and Morton (1992) for a detailed presentation. Hull and White (1990) offer another model to value the term structure.

FIGURE 6-6   *Heath Jarrow Morton (HJM) Model,*
Nonrecombining Tree of Forward Rates

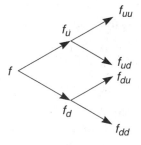

CONCLUSIONS AND FURTHER READING

In this chapter, we have examined the determinants of interest rates. Some evidence was presented on the presence of the Fisher effect in interest rates. Fama (1976, 1990) contains evidence concerning the ability of the term structure to predict future spot rates. He also presents the forecasting power of the term structure concerning inflation. Mishkin (1990a, 1991) has investigated these issues in international and domestic contexts. We also reviewed hypotheses on interest rates. A number of papers have addressed issues relating to hypotheses concerning term structure. Campbell (1986) contains a defense of the traditional models of the term structure. Other papers have been mentioned in our discussion. The conclusions of these papers differ depending on the sample periods chosen by the authors. Some models of term structure were also presented.

PROBLEMS

6.1   Distinguish real rates of interest and nominal rates of interest. Identify three factors that determine the real rate of interest.

6.2   Summarize the evidence provided by Fama (1975) and Fama and Gibbons (1982) on the effect of inflation on the real rate of return and investment.

6.3   What is the Fisher effect? How have the levels of interest rates in the economy and their volatility affected the presence of the Fisher effect?

6.4   **Spreadsheet Problem.** Use the market data on the yields and volatilities of yields provided in the table below for zeroes with maturities of one to five years.

(a)   Construct the lattice for this market data and derive the yield curve at each node of the lattice. In other words, determine $r_u, r_d, r_{uu}, r_{ud}, r_{dd}, r_{uuu}, r_{uud}, r_{udd}$ and r_{ddd}.

Market Data

Maturity	Yield	Volatility
1	9%	20%
2	9%	19%
3	9%	18%
4	9%	17%
5	9%	16%

(b)   Determine the yields of all securities with a maturity of five years or less as applicable in each node. Treat each period as one year. Assume that the probability $q = \frac{1}{2}$. Use the Black Derman, and Toy model for this problem.

(c)   Determine the par bond yield curve out to five years.

6.5   **Spreadsheet Problem.** Consider the lattice provided below.

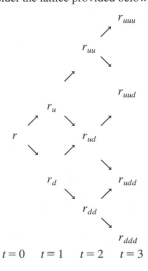

$t = 0 \quad t = 1 \quad t = 2 \quad t = 3$

Assume that at the root of the tree $r = 10\%$. Assume that the interest rates follow a binomial process, with $u = 1.1$ and $d = \frac{1}{u}$.

    (a) Determine all the short term interest rates in the lattice. (Recall that $r_u = ur, r_d = dr$, etc.)

    (b) Determine the yields of all securities with a maturity of five years or less as applicable in each node. Treat each period as one year. Assume that the probability $q = \frac{1}{2}$.

    (c) Compute the state prices. How would you use the state prices to value a two-year bond paying an annual coupon of 5% and a balloon payment of 100 at the end of two years?

REFERENCES

Black, F., E. Derman, and W. Toy 1990. "A One-Factor Model of Interest Rates and Its Application to Treasury Bond Options." *Financial Analysts Journal* 46(1):33–39.

Brennan, M. J., and E. S. Schwartz 1979. "A Continuous Time Approach to the Pricing of Bonds," *Journal of Banking and Finance* 3:133–155.

Brennan, M. J., and E. S. Schwartz 1980. *Savings Bonds: Theory and Empirical Evidence.* Monograph Series in Finance and Economics. New York: New York University.

Broadie, M., and S. Sundaresan 1987. "The Pricing of Timing and Quality Options: An Application to Treasury Bond Futures Markets." Unpublished paper presented at the EFA Meetings, Madrid, Spain.

Brown, S. J., and P. H. Dybvig 1986. "The Empirical Implications of Cox-Ingersoll-Ross Theory of the Term Structure of Interest Rates." *Journal of Finance* 41:617–630.

Campbell, J. Y. 1986. "A Defense of Traditional Hypotheses about the Term Structure of Interest Rates." *Journal of Finance* 41:183–193.

Courtadon, G. 1982. "The Pricing of Options on Default-Free Bonds." *Journal of Financial and Quantitative Analysis,* XVII(1):75–100.

Cox, J. C., and S. A. Ross 1976. "The Valuation of Options for Alternative Stochastic Processes." *Journal of Financial Economics* 3:145–166.

Cox, J. C., J. Ingersoll, and S. Ross 1979. "Duration and the Measurement of Basis Risk." *Journal of Business* 52:51–61.

Cox, J. C., S. A. Ross, and M. Rubinstein 1979. "Option Pricing: A Simplified Approach." *Journal of Financial Economics* 7:229–263.

Cox, J. C., J. Ingersoll, and S. Ross 1981. "A Re-examination of Traditional Hypotheses about the Term Structure of Interest Rates." *Journal of Finance* 36:769–799.

Cox, J. C., J. Ingersoll, and S. Ross 1985. "A Theory of the Term Structure of Interest Rates." *Econometrica* 53:385–407.

Culbertson, J. M. 1957. "The Term Structure of Interest Rates." *Quarterly Journal of Economics* LXXI:489–504.

Darby, M. R. 1975. "The Financial and Tax Effects of Monetary Policy on Interest Rates." *Economic Inquiry* 13:266–276.

Fama, E. 1975. "Short-Term Interest Rates as Predictors of Inflation." *American Economic Review* 65(3):269–282.

Fama, E. F. 1976. "Forward Rates as Predictors of Future Spot-Rates." *Journal of Financial Economics* 3:361–377.

Fama, E., and M. Gibbons 1982. "Inflation, Real Returns and Capital Investment." *Journal of Monetary Economics* 9(3):297–323.

Fama, E. F. 1990. "Term Structure Forecasts of Interest Rates, Inflation and Real Returns." *Journal of Monetary Economics* 25:59–76.

Fama, E. F., and K. French 1993. "Common Risk Factors in the Returns on Stocks and Bonds." *Journal of Financial Economics* 33:3–56.

Gibbons, M. R., and K. Ramaswamy 1994. "The Term Structure of Interest Rates: Empirical Evidence." *Review of Financial Studies.*

Harrison, J. M., and D. M. Kreps 1978. "Martingales and Arbitrage in Multiperiod Security Markets." *Journal of Economic Theory* 20:381–408.

Harvey, C. R. 1988. "The Real Term Structure and Consumption Growth." *Journal of Financial Economics* 22:305–333.

Heath, D., R. Jarrow, and A. Morton 1992. "Bond Pricing and the Term Structure of Interest Rates: A New Methodology for Contingent Claims Valuation." *Econometrics* 60(1):77–105.

Hicks, J. R. 1946. *Value and Capital.* 2nd ed. London: Oxford University Press.

Ho, T. S. Y., and S. Lee 1986. "Term Structure Movements and Pricing Interest Rate Contingent Claims." *The Journal of Finance* XLI(5):1011–1029.

Hull, J., and A. White 1990. "Pricing Interest-Rate Derivative Securities." *Review of Financial Studies* 3(4):573–592.

Jamshidian, F. 1987. Pricing of Contingent Claims in the One-Factor Term Structure Model. Trading Analysis Group, Merrill Lynch Capital Markets.

Lutz, F. A. 1940. "The Structure of Interest Rates." *Quarterly Journal of Economics* LV:36–63.

Maloney, K. J. 1992. A Contingent Claims Model of Corporate Security Valuation Using a Realistic Model of Financial Distress. Dartmouth University Working Paper.

Marsh, T. A., and E. R. Rosenfeld 1983. "Stochastic Processes for Interest Rates and Equilibrium Bond Prices." *The Journal of Finance* XXXVIII(2):635–646.

Mishkin, F. 1990a. "Can Futures Market Data Be Used to Understand the Behavior of Real Interest Rates?" *Journal of Finance* XLV:245-57.

Mishkin, F. 1990b. "What Does the Term Structure Tell Us about Future Inflation?" *Journal of Monetary Economics* 25:77–95.

Mishkin, F. 1991. "A Multicountry Study of the Information in the Term Structure about Future Inflation." *Journal of International Money and Finance.*

Modigliani, F., and R. Sutch 1967. "Debt Management and the Term Structure of Interest Rates: An Empirical Analysis of Recent Experience." *Journal of Political Economy* 75(Supplement): 569–589.

Mundell, R. 1963. "Inflation and Real Interest." *Journal of Political Economy* 71:280–283.

Nelson, C. R. 1972. *The Term Structure of Interest Rates.* New York: Basic Books.

Pearson, N. D., and T-S. Sun 1994. "Exploiting the Conditional Density in Estimating the Term Structure: An Application to the Cox, Ingersoll and Ross Model." *Journal of Finance* 49(4): 1279–1304.

Ramaswamy, K., and S. M. Sundaresan 1986. "The Valuation of Floating-Rate Instruments, Theory and Evidence." *Journal of Financial Economics* 17:251–272.

Rendleman, R. J., Jr., and B. J. Bartter 1980. "The Pricing of Options on Debt Securities." *Journal of Financial and Quantitative Analysis* XV(1):11–24.

Richard, S. F. 1978. "An Arbitrage Model of the Term Structure of Interest Rates." *Journal of Financial Economics* 6:33–57.

Smith, S. D., and R. E. Spudeck 1993. *Interest Rates: Principles and Applications.* Dryden Press, 1993 (The College Outline Series).

Wang, C. 1994. "Interest Rate Swaps." Unpublished doctoral dissertation, Columbia Business School, New York City, NY.

Chapter 7

Options Markets

Chapter Objectives

This chapter provides an overview of options contracts and options markets in the United States and abroad. Basic no-arbitrage propositions and put-call parity relationships are derived. Chapter 7 will help the reader to understand and answer the following questions.

- What are options on bonds and options on futures contracts?
- What are some commonly used option strategies?
- What are some of the key no-arbitrage relationships for options?
- Which factors determine the value of options?
- What are the put-call parity relationships for options on bonds, options on futures, etc.?
- How are Binomial and Black-Scholes formulas obtained and used?
- How can Monte-Carlo simulation techniques be used for valuing options?
- How are interest rate options priced?
- What are the ways in which the risks of options quantified? The concept of delta, gamma, vega and theta.

In addition, this chapter illustrates the central ideas using worked out examples. The results developed in this chapter are valuable for the valuation of corporate bonds and mortgage-backed securities which have option-like features. These securities are taken up in later chapters.

INTRODUCTION

In this chapter, a self-contained account of options in equity and fixed-income securities markets will be provided. First, the contracts will be defined and some institutional perspectives will be offered. Then the focus will shift to the no-arbitrage restrictions and the pricing procedures that have been developed for such options. In addition, examples will be provided showing how such options can be used in risk-management applications.

So far, we considered the analysis of Treasury securities that are mostly non-callable. But as we saw in Chapter 5, even in the Treasury market there are some callable issues. In order to analyze such issues it is essential to develop some key results in options pricing. This is because a callable Treasury bond provides a call option to the Treasury and this option will be exercised by the Treasury should the interest rates on similar bonds fall below that coupon. So, the investors would value such callable bonds as a portfolio of an otherwise identical non-callable bond minus the value of a call option that they have provided to the Treasury. As we move to the other sectors of fixed-income markets such as corporate bond markets and mortgage-backed securities markets later in the book, it will be noted that more option-like features are present in these markets. For example, many corporate bonds are callable, some provide a put option to the investor, etc. It will turn out that the default risk in corporate bonds can be modelled using option pricing techniques. We will show that the homeowners have the right to prepay their mortgage loan. This is nothing but a call option to "call away" their loan when mortgage rates fall. This option is at the center of pricing mortgage-backed securities.

For these reasons it is logical to develop the valuation of options and the terminology used in options literature at this stage. We proceed to do this next.

CONTRACT: DEFINITION AND TERMINOLOGY

Options are contracts that give the owner (buyer) the right but not the obligation to do something. For this right the buyer pays a fixed price which is referred to as the **option premium.** The sellers of options have a corresponding obligation to meet the financial responsibilities in the event the buyer decides to exercise or sell his right. Options that give the right to buy an underlying asset are known as **call options.** Options that give the right to sell an underlying asset are known as **put options.** When options may be exercised only at maturity, they are termed **European.** If they may be exercised at any time prior to (and including) maturity, they are called **American.**

Calls and Puts

A call option is a contract which gives its owner the right but not the obligation to buy a fixed number of a specified security at a fixed price at any time on or before a given date.

The following terminology are used in the context of options:

Exercise: the act of invoking the right.

Underlying security: the specified security on which the option exists.

Strike price: the fixed price at which the buyer has the right to buy.

Expiration date: the date on which the option (right) expires.

Premium: the market price of the option contract.

The buyer of the call can, at any time, exercise the option or retain the option or sell the option at the concurrent market price. On the expiration date, the buyer has to exercise it or sell it (these strategies are equivalent on expiry date) or let it expire.

In Figure 7-1 and Figure 7-2, we illustrate the transactions associated with call options and the alternatives that are available to the buyer and seller. Figure 7-1 illustrates the initial transaction. The buyer pays the call premium to the seller (writer) and receives the option. Upon exercise, (as Figure 7-2 shows) the buyer pays the strike price and surrenders the call option to the seller. In turn, the seller delivers the underlying security. This is an example of an option which settles by physical delivery. In options that are cash settled, instead of delivering the underlying security, the seller will pay the cash value of the underlying security.

FIGURE 7-1   *Initial Transaction*

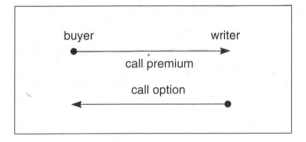

FIGURE 7-2   *Exchange at Option Exercise*

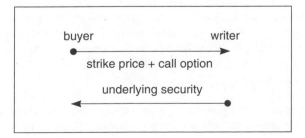

The market price of the option on the expiry date depends only on the underlying asset price and the strike price. Let K be the strike price and P^* be the market price of the underlying security on the expiration date. Then c^*, the value of the call (on the underlying security) on its expiration date, depends on whether the option will be exercised or will be allowed to expire. To exercise the option, the buyer of the option pays K, receives the underlying security, and sells the underlying security for P^*. This only makes sense when $P^* > K$. On the other hand, if $P^* \leq K$ it is better to let the option expire.

Thus, we can write the option's value on the expiry date succinctly as

$$c^* = \begin{cases} P^* - K & \text{if } P^* > K \\ 0 & \text{if } P^* \leq K \end{cases}$$

or more succinctly,

$$c^* = \max [0, P^* - K] \tag{7.1}$$

On the expiry date there is no difference between exercising and selling. If the exercise value is more than the market price, then it is possible to buy the option and exercise it immediately and make arbitrage profits. In a similar way, if the exercise value is less than the market price, then it is possible to sell the option, borrow the strike price, and buy the stock. If the option is exercised, then one delivers the stock and receives the strike price. This leads to riskless profits. If the option is not exercised, the position leaves a cash flow equal to the call premium.

Example 7-1 illustrates a dealer option on a Treasury bond.

Example 7-1   Dealer Option: Call on a T-bond

Pricing date: $t =$ May 6, 1993
Underlying security: $1 million par of 7.25%, 5/15/2016 T-bond
Price of underlying security: $P = 110\frac{10}{32}$
Strike price: $K = 110$
Expiration date: $T =$ June 6, 1993
Call premium: $c = 2.00$ ($20,000)
Style: European

The dealer here is offering a European call option to customers with a maturity of one month and the option is slightly in-the-money (i.e., $P > K$). Typically, there will be a bid-offer spread at which the dealer will stand ready to buy or sell the option. The quote is 2.00 but the dollar amount is $2 \times 10,000 = 20,000$, since the quotes are in percentages of a million-dollar par amount. (The price of the underlying bond, $110\frac{10}{32}$, is multiplied by 10,000 to get a dollar price of the bond as $110\frac{10}{32} \times 10,000 = 1,103,125$.)

A put option is a contract giving its owner the right, but not the obligation, to sell a fixed number of a specified security at a fixed price at any time on or before a given date.

The market price of the option on the expiry date depends only on the underlying asset price and the strike price. Let K be the strike price and P^* be the market price of the underlying security on the expiration date. Then, $p*$, the value of the put (on one of the underlying securities) on its expiration date, depends on whether the option will be exercised or will be allowed to expire. To exercise the option, the buyer of the option receives K and delivers the underlying security. It makes sense to exercise when $P* < K$. If $P* \geq K$ it makes sense to let the option expire.

Thus, we can write the option's value on the expiry date succinctly as

$$p* = \begin{cases} 0 & \text{if } P* \geq K \\ K - P* & \text{if } P* < K \end{cases}$$

or

$$p* = \max [0, K - P*] \tag{7.2}$$

At any time t prior to the maturity date of the option, let P be the value of the underlying asset. When $P \gg K$, call options are said to be **deep-in-the-money.** If $P > K$, then the calls are said to be **in-the-money.** When $P = K$, the calls are said to be **at-the-money.** Usually, when $P \approx K$, the calls are referred to as **near-the-money** options.

In Figure 7-3, we show what happens when the call option is exercised. We assume that the strike price of the option is $120 per share and that the option is on 100 shares. The buyer of the option pays the strike price ($120 per share) and surrenders the option. The writer of the option will deliver 100 shares of IBM. Figure 7-4 shows the initial transaction. The buyer pays the put premium to the writer and the writer delivers the put option to the buyer. Figure 7-5 shows transactions at maturity.

FIGURE 7-3   *If the Call Option is Exercised*

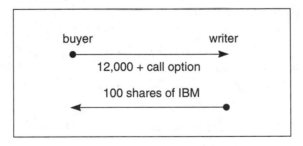

FIGURE 7-4   *Initial Transaction*

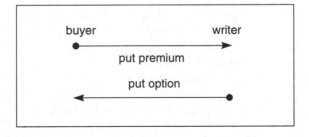

FIGURE 7-5 *Subsequent Exchange at Option Exercise*

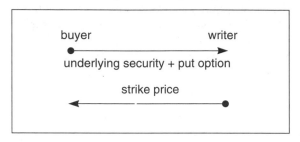

In a similar manner, when $P < K$, calls are referred to as **out-of-the-money** options. When $P \ll K$, calls are referred to as **deep-out-of-the-money options.** Corresponding terminology is used to describe put options.

The call and put premiums are also separated into intrinsic values and time values. The **intrinsic value of a call** is max $[0, P - K]$. If the call premium is c, then the **time value of a call** is $c - \max [0, P - K]$. In a similar way, the **intrinsic value of a put** is defined as max $[0, K - P]$. The **time value of a put** is $p - \max [0, K - P]$, where p is the put premium. Usually, the option premium is greater than the intrinsic value. The difference between the two represents the time value of the option.

Example 7-2   Dealer Option: Put on a T-bond

> **Pricing date:** $t =$ May 5, 1995
> **Underlying security:** $1 million par of 8.00%, 2/15/2023 T-bond
> **Price of underlying security:** $P = 100\frac{9}{32}$
> **Strike price:** $K = 101$
> **Expiration date:** $T =$ August 15, 1995
> **Put premium:** $p = 2.00$ ($20,000)
> **Style:** American

This put option is in-the-money (since $K > P$) by $\frac{23}{32}$. Its intrinsic value is $101 - 100\frac{9}{32} = \frac{23}{32}$. The time value of the option is $2.00 - \frac{23}{32} = 1\frac{9}{32}$.

MARKET OVERVIEW

An overview of the listed options markets in the fixed-income area in the U.S. is provided in Table 7-1. Note that the T-bond futures, T-note futures (ten-year and five-year maturities) and the municipal bond (index) futures have options contracts listed on them. These contracts pertain to the intermediate and long-term interest rates. In addition, options are also traded on futures contracts on Eurodollar deposits and Treasury bills (both with ninety-day maturity). All options listed in Table 7-1 are American and many of them are automatically exercised when the options reach a certain in-the-money status.

TABLE 7-1   *Listed Options on U.S. Fixed-Income Securities*

Underlying Asset/Exchange	Contract Details	Expiry Date	Position Limits
Thirty-year T-bond $100,000 par, minimum tick $\frac{1}{64}$, tick size 15.625, CBT	First 3 contracts, M, J, S, D. Two-point strike intervals.	Noon on the last Friday at least 5 business days prior to the first business day of the delivery month	3 points daily price limit. Exercise by 6:00 PM on the last trading day. Automatic exercise for intrinsic of 2 points or more.
Ten-year T-note $100,000 par, minimum tick $\frac{1}{64}$, tick size 15.625, CBT	First 3 contracts, M, J, S, D. Two-point strike intervals.	Noon on the last Friday at least 5 business days prior to the first business day of the delivery month	3 points daily price limit. Exercise by 6:00 PM on the last trading day. Automatic exercise for intrinsic of 2 points or more.
Five-year T-note $100,000 par, minimum tick $\frac{1}{64}$, tick size 15.625, FINEX	First 2 contracts, M, J, S, D. One-point strike intervals.	1:00 PM on the last Friday at least 5 business days prior to the first business day of the delivery month	No daily price limit. Exercise by 6:00 PM on the last trading day. Automatic exercise for intrinsic of 0.5 points or more.
Muni-bond index $100,000 par, minimum tick $\frac{1}{64}$, tick size 15.625, FINEX	First 3 contracts, M, J, S, D. One-point strike intervals.	1:00 PM on the last Friday at least 5 business days prior to the first business day of the delivery month	3 points daily price limit. Exercise by 6:00 PM on the last trading day. Automatic exercise for in-the-money options.
Ninety-day Eurodollar $1,000,000 par, minimum tick 0.01%, tick size 25.00, CME, LIFFE, SIMEX	First 8 contracts, M, J, S, D. Quarter-point strike intervals.	Simultaneously with the close of trading in the underlying futures (usually the third Monday of the contract month)	No daily limits. 500 futures equivalent position. Automatic exercise for in-the-money options.
Ninety-day T-bill $1,000,000 par, minimum tick 0.01%, tick size 25.00, CME	First 4 contracts, M, J, S, D. Quarter-point strike intervals.	Last business day of the week, preceding by at least 6 business days the first business day of the contract month	No daily limits. 5,000 futures equivalent position. No automatic exercise for in-the-money options.

In addition to these options, which are typically on futures contracts, there are interest-rate options which are European-style, settled by cash, and are backed by the Options Clearing Corporation (OCC). For example, Chicago Board of Exchange (CBOE) lists options on short-term interest rates (thirteen-week Treasury bills), medium-term interest rates (ten-year T-notes), and long-term interest rates (thirty-year T-bonds). Most of the activity in the options markets in the fixed-income sector listed here is concentrated in options on futures contracts.

In the international markets, fixed-income derivatives have acquired a dominant position. The derivatives in the international markets are summarized in Table 7-2.

TABLE 7-2   *Listed Options on International Fixed-Income Securities*

Underlying Asset/Exchange	*Contract Details*	*Expiry Date*	*Position Limits*
France			
MATIF ten-year FF500,000 par, minumum tick 0.01%, tick size FF50	First 4 contracts, M, J, S, D. One-point strike intervals.	4:00 PM on the last Friday of the month prior to the delivery month of the future	No daily limits. Automatic exercise for in-the-money options.
MATIF ninety-day FF500,000 par, minimum tick 0.01%, tick size FF125	First 3 contracts, M, J, S, D. 10-basis-point strike intervals.	3:30 PM on the last trading day of the underlying futures	No daily limits. Automatic exercise of in-the-money options.
Germany			
LIFFE ten-year DM250,000 par, minimum tick 0.01%, tick size DM25	First 3 contracts, M, J, S, D. One-point strike intervals.	4:00 PM six business days prior to the first business day of the delivery month	No daily limits. Automatic exercise of in-the-money options.
LIFFE ninety-day EuroDM DM1,000,000 par, minimum tick 0.01%, tick size DM25	First 2 contracts, M, J, S, D. Quarter-point strike intervals.	4:10 PM the second business day preceding the third Wednesday of the delivery month	No daily limits. Automatic exercise of in-the-money options.
MATIF ninety-day EuroDM DM1,000,000 par, minimum tick 0.01%, tick size DM25	First 4 contracts, M, J, S, D. Quarter-point strike intervals.	3:50 PM the second business day preceding the third Wednesday of the delivery month	No daily limits. Automatic exercise of in-the-money options.
United Kingdom			
LIFFE twenty-year Gilt Sterling 500,000 par, minimum tick $\frac{1}{64}$, tick size 7.8125	First 4 contracts, M, J, S, D. Two point strike intervals.	4:15 PM six business days prior to the first business day of the delivery month	No daily limits. Automatic exercise for in-the-money options.
LIFFE ninety-day Sterling 500,000 par, minimum tick 0.01%, tick size 12.5	First 3 contract, M, J, S, D. Quarter-point strike intervals.	3:30 PM on the last trading day of the underlying futures	No daily limits. Automatic exercise of 1 point plus in-the-money options.
Japan			
TSE ten-year bonds Yen 100,000,000 par, minimum tick 0.01%	First 2 contracts, M, J, S, D. One-point strike intervals.	3:00 PM the last business day of the month prior to the delivery month; trading is allowed till 4:30	No daily limits. No automatic exercise of in-the-money options.

International fixed-income derivatives have grown significantly in the last decade. The trading opportunities have significantly improved with multiple listings of the same (or similar) contracts.

Listed equity-options markets opened in 1973 at the CBOE. Currently, the equity-options markets span a wide variety of instruments and maturities, as is evident from Table 7-3.

TABLE 7-3   *Listed Options on Equities*

Underlying Asset/Exchange	Contract Details	Expiry Date
CBOE		
1. Common stocks, 100 shares	First 4 contracts, Jan., Feb., & Mar. cycle strike intervals depends on strike price	Saturday following third Friday of expiry month
2. Stock Index, S&P 100 size: 100 × index cash settled	4 monthly contracts	Last business day of the month
3. S&P 500 size: 500 × index, cash settled	4 monthly contracts	Third Friday of expiration month
4. LSE FTSE 100 10 × FTSE-100	First 4 contracts monthly	Last business day of the month
5. American Stock Exchange MMI 100 × MMI level	4 nearest months	Third Friday of expiration month

Although we have not shown this in Table 7-3, a number of stock-index options are traded, catering to the needs of different institutional investors. For example, in the American Stock Exchange, several industry indexes are used as underlying assets to trade options. Examples of these are the airline index and computer technology. In addition, the Philadelphia Stock Exchange, NASDAQ, and others also trade options on indexes of different capitalizations.

Institutional Arrangements

We now turn to the institutional arrangements designed to ensure the integrity of the contracts.

Listed options are supported by clearing houses. This arrangement delinks the seller of the option from the buyer. The **clearing house** interposes itself between the buyers and sellers and acts as sellers to the buyers and vice versa. The contract integrity therefore depends on the solvency and the credit worthiness of the clearing house and not on the individual buyers or sellers.

The options markets are organized in centralized exchanges where a number of competing floor traders or brokers and market makers participate. There is a separation of roles. Market makers are permitted to trade only for their own accounts and are not permitted to act on behalf of customers; they bring their own capital and provide liquidity to the exchange. Floor brokers, on the other hand, are only permitted to execute the orders of customers; in effect they act as the representative of the customer and are not permitted to trade for their own accounts. The floor brokers and market makers are members of the options exchanges. In addition to the floor brokers and market makers, there are order-book officials who are employees of the exchange and who handle the orders of public customers.

Classification of Options

Options may be classified along several dimensions. If options are classified based on who offers them, they are either OTC (over-the-counter) options or listed options. OTC options (also referred to as dealer options) are offered by dealer. It should be noted that OTC options are more customized, less liquid, and are driven by the dealer's capital that is assigned to the options business.

Options that are traded at the Chicago Board of Options Exchange (CBOE), the Chicago Board of Trade (CBT), and other centralized exchanges are known as listed options. Listed options are more standardized, more liquid, and are driven by the clearinghouse guarantees.

Options may also be classified according to the underlying assets: foreign exchange (FX) options, index options, equity options, options on futures contracts, options on bonds, options on interest rates, etc. Options may be explicit or implicit. Sellers of futures contracts have the option to choose which asset to deliver and when to deliver; these seller's options are reflected in the futures price, and such options are **implicit.** Similarly, in deciding to accept or reject a project, the corporate controller has the option of accepting the project now or later. Each project is in competition with itself postponed; by delaying the project, we give up the positive NPV today, but we may get a better draw on interest rates leading potentially to a lower cost of capital. In addition, we get more information about the project's cash flows and costs as the time passes. We could list other examples of options, but the point should be clear: Options are present in everyday choices.

Options are also present in most corporate contracts. Compensation packages typically include stock options, and corporate bonds are issued with call features, conversion options, sinking fund options and so on. Such options are called embedded options.

We need to understand

- the presence of such options,
- the motivation for such options, and
- how to value such options.

FACTORS DETERMINING AN OPTION'S VALUE

In this section, we will examine the determinants of an option's value. Recall that the intrinsic value of a call is max $[0, P - K]$ and that of a put is max $[0, K - P]$. Clearly, a call's intrinsic value increases in the underlying asset price and decreases in the strike price.

The option premium is, in general, greater than the intrinsic value. We enumerate the factors that influence the American and European options markets in Tables 7-4a and 7-4b. The effect of increasing each factor while holding all the other factors fixed is also shown as an arrow pointing in the direction of its impact on the option premium. Below we discuss each factor briefly.

P: The current market price of underlying security is clearly a major determinant of the option premium. As the market price increases, the value of a call option increases and that of the put decreases.

K: The strike price of an option clearly influences its value. The call's value decreases with the strike price and the put's value increases with the strike price.

Factor	Call	Put
Market price (P)	↑	↓
Strike price (K)	↓	↑
Volatility (σ)	↑	↑
Riskless interest rate (r)	↑	↓
Time to expiration (t)	↑	↑
Dividend yield (d)	↓	↑

TABLE 7-4a
Factors in American Options

Factor	Call	Put
Market price (P)	↑	↓
Strike price (K)	↓	↑
Volatility (σ)	↑	↑
Riskless interest rate (r)	↑	↓
Time to expiration (t)	?	?
Dividend yield (d)	↓	↑

TABLE 7-4b
Factors in European Options

σ: The volatility of the underlying security is another major factor. As the volatility increases, the probability of extreme outcomes increases. For a call option, extreme values on the upside places the option in-the-money and the holder benefits by either selling the option or exercising it; extreme outcomes on the downside are not of concern, since the loss on the downside is bounded by the call premium. Similar arguments show that a put also benefits from increased volatility.

r: The riskless interest rate is also an important factor in the determination of an option's value. The holder of a call option has to pay the strike price to exercise the option, and must set the present value of the strike price aside in the bank in order to make this payment at maturity. As the riskless rate increases, the holder of the call needs to set aside less money in the bank in order to pay the strike price at the maturity date of the option. Hence the call value increases with the riskless rate of interest. Conversely, the put value decreases with the riskless rate.

t: The time to maturity of the option plays two distinct roles. First, as the maturity increases, there is more time for the volatility effect to play out. This affects both calls and puts favorably. Second, as the maturity increases, the effect of the riskless rate takes on a bigger role; this favorably affects the call but adversely affects the put option. So, we can say that as the time to maturity increases, the call value increases. For puts, the direction depends on whether the put is European or American. For an American put, as the time to maturity increases, the value increases. We cannot be unequivocal about the value of European put options as the time to maturity increases. For European call options when dividends are paid by the underlying asset during the life of the option, we cannot be certain about the effect of time to maturity.

d: Coupon payments or dividends play a role in affecting the value of options. Loosely speaking, the payment of a coupon reduces the full price of the bond. The value of the call (put) depends on the design of the contract. Typically, the options on a bond are specified such that the holder will have to pay (receive) the strike price plus the accrued interest in order to receive (deliver) the underlying bond. This effectively means that the accrued interest or the coupon becomes a wash in computing the payoffs of the option. We will examine this in greater detail later in the chapter.

Note that the expected return on the underlying security is not a factor in determining option premium.

TRADING STRATEGIES

Options enable investors to obtain a variety of payoff distributions in future. Such risk-return patterns are not easy to create without options. In this section, we describe some of the trading strategies that are extensively used by practitioners in capital markets.

Cox and Rubinstein (1985) define four classes of options-trading strategies:

- Uncovered (naked) positions
- Covered or hedged positions

- Spreads
- Combinations

Uncovered Positions

First, we take up uncovered positions. There are four such positions: long call, long put, short call, and short put. (See Table 7-5.) The payoffs associated with each position on the maturity date of the option are shown in Figures 7-6 through 7-9. Note that in each figure, we show not only the payoffs at the maturity date of the option but also the pay-

TABLE 7-5 *Summary of Uncovered-Positions Strategies*

Classification	Features
Long call	Bullish view. Down side-limited call premium. Up side unlimited in principle. Break-even level is the premium paid plus the strike. (See Figure 7-6.)
Long put	Bearish view. Down side-limited put premium. Up side limited to the current underlying asset price at initiation. Break-even price is the strike minus the premium. (See Figure 7-7.)
Short call	Neutral to bearish view. Down side unlimited. Up side limited to the call premium. Break-even level is premium paid plus the strike. (See Figure 7-8.)
Short put	Neutral to bullish view. Down side limited to the underlying asset price (at initiation less the premium). Up side limited to the put premium. Break-even level is the strike minus the premium. (See Figure 7-9.)

FIGURE 7-6 *Long Position in a Call Option*

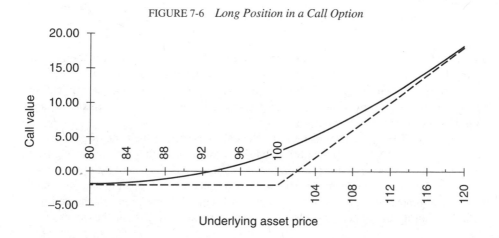

FIGURE 7-7   *Long Position in a Put Option*

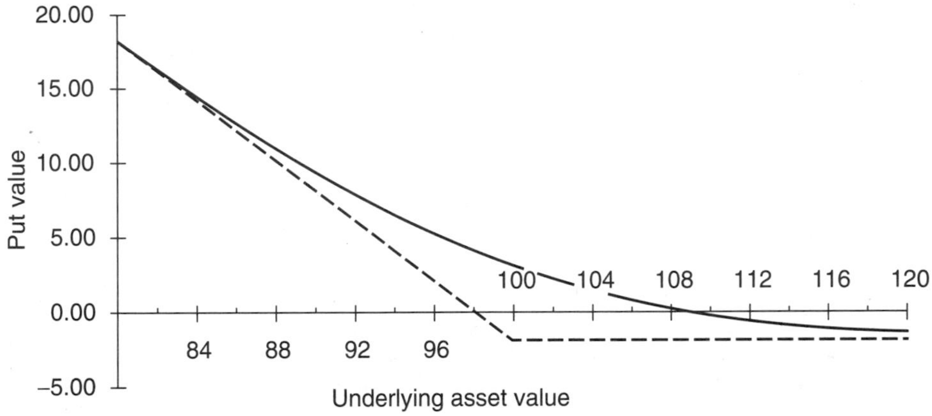

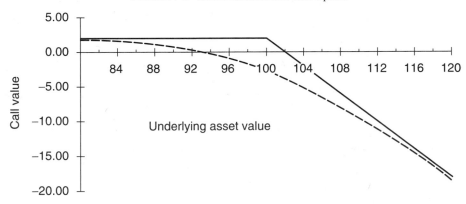

Position value at maturity and at three months prior to maturity.

Initial put premium = 1.80; strike = 100

FIGURE 7-8   *Short Position in a Call Option*

offs when the options have three months to maturity. This provides a useful contrast and also provides a distinction between the time value and intrinsic value.

Uncovered positions are essentially speculative positions. Using the replicating-portfolio concepts, it is possible to precisely characterize the nature of the risk associated with these positions as will be shown later.

In Figures 7-6 to 7-9, we assume that the call premium at the time of purchase or sale is 2.00 and that of the put is 1.80. In addition, we assume that the underlying asset price and the strike price of these options are the same at 100. In each of the options positions that are described, there are break-even points which separate the profitable regions from the other regions. For example, in Figure 7-6, the buyer of the call paid 2.00. At maturity the underlying asset price has to be at least 102 for the buyer of the

FIGURE 7-9   *Short Position in a Put Option*

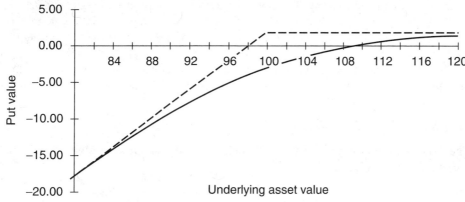

Call value at maturity and at three months prior to maturity.

Initial premium = 2.00; strike = 100

option to break even. It is easy to recognize that the option has no time value at maturity; all the value is represented by the intrinsic value. When the option has three months left to maturity, the option has both time value and intrinsic value.

The break-even price for a long position in the put option is 98.20. The underlying asset price will have to drop to this level for the put buyer to break even at maturity.

Covered (Hedged) Positions

The hedged positions (see Table 7-6) are frequently employed by professional portfolio managers in mutual funds, pension funds, and hedge funds. The strategy of buying the underlying asset and writing a call option is referred to as the buy-write strategy and is frequently employed in the industry; by writing a call at a strike of 102 and buying the asset at 100, the manager is able to take in the call premium and enjoy the up-side potential

TABLE 7-6   *Summary of Covered-Positions Strategies*

Classification	Features
Buy write (buy underlying and write call)	Neutral and low volatility view. Down side is cushioned by call premium. Up side is capped by the strike price. Break-even level is the strike price minus the premium received. (See Figure 7-10.)
Protective put (buy put and buy the underlying asset)	Insured position; underlying asset is insured at the strike less the premium paid. Up side potential is the same as the underlying asset less the put premium. Break-even price is the strike price plus the underlying asset price at initiation. (See Figure 7-11.)

up to 102. If the underlying asset price goes above 102, the call is in-the-money and the underlying asset is called away. The buy-write strategy is illustrated in Figure 7-10.

The strategy of buying the underlying asset and buying a put option on the underlying asset is an insurance strategy. This is illustrated in the payoff diagram in Figure 7-11.

Short positions in call and put options carry considerable risk; there is always the possibility that the buyer will exercise the option prior to the maturity date of the option.

Spreads and Combinations

The last two classes of options-trading strategies, spread positions and combinations, are presented in Tables 7-7 and 7-8.

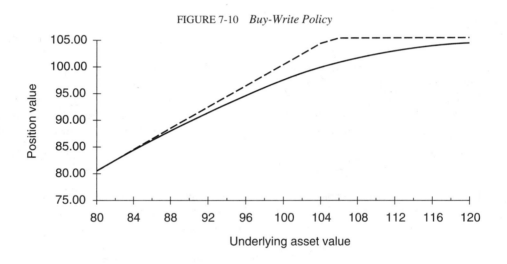

FIGURE 7-10   *Buy-Write Policy*

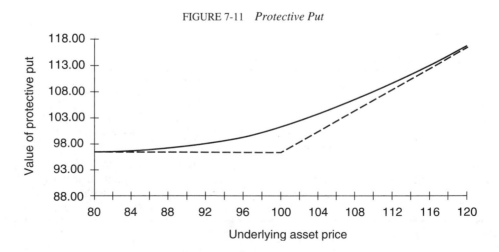

FIGURE 7-11   *Protective Put*

Classification	Features
Vertical spreads (VS)	
Bullish VS (buy $c(K_1)$ and write $c(K_2)$)	Position requires positive outlay. Moderately bullish. Break-even price is $K_1 + c(K_1) - c(K_2)$. Down side limited.
Bullish VS (buy $p(K_1)$ and write $p(K_2)$)	Same.
Bearish VS (buy $c(K_2)$ and write $c(K_1)$)	Position generates income. Mildly bearish.
Bearish VS (buy $p(K_2)$ and write $p(K_1)$)	Position generates income. Mildly bearish.
Time spreads (buy call $c(K_1)$ and sell call $c(K_1)$ with different maturities)	Position can be structured so as to generate a cash inflow or an outflow.

TABLE 7-7
Summary of Spread Strategies

Classification	Features
Straddle (buy call $c(K_1)$ and buy put $p(K_1)$ with same maturities ($S = K_1$))	Position requires a positive outlay. Makes money for a strong move on either side.
Strangle (buy call $c(K_3)$ and buy put $p(K_1)$ with same maturities ($S = K_2$))	Position requires a positive outlay. Makes money for a strong move on either side.

TABLE 7-8
Summary of Combinations

NO-ARBITRAGE RESTRICTIONS

The absence of riskless arbitrage means that the prices of options should satisfy certain relationships. These appear in Merton (1973), an important paper on options pricing.

Lower Bounds

Lower bounds specify levels below which no options may sell. If these bounds are violated, then there are riskless arbitrage opportunities. The lower bounds can be formulated as:

- $c \geq 0$ and $p \geq 0$. If the options premiums are negative, then the buyer of the option will be paid a positive sum. This is inconsistent with no arbitrage.
- $c \geq P - K$ (for American calls) and $p \geq K - P$ (for American puts), where P is the underlying asset price. If these restrictions are not met, then the optimal strategy is to buy the options and immediately exercise them.

Put-Call Parity

An important relation in options-pricing theory is known as the put-call parity relationship. In this section we state and prove the put-call parity results for options on bonds (stocks) and futures contracts.

In Table 7-9, we provide the basic recipe that may be used to verify that the calls on puts on stocks and bonds satisfy the parity relation. Note that transactions (2), (3) and (4) in Table 7-9 together exactly replicate transaction (1), which is a long position in call. To prevent arbitrage, then we must have

$$c = p + P - \frac{K}{(1 + R)^{T-t}} \tag{7.3}$$

Note that the put-call parity stated above means that an at-the-money call option on stock will be more expensive than an at-the-money put. To see why this is true, set $P = K$ and note that the put-call parity is

$$c = p + P - \frac{P}{(1 + R)^{T-t}} > p,$$

when $R > 0$. This relationship is modified when there are intermediate payments on the underlying security such as coupons or dividends. In interpreting the put-call parity for options on bonds, we must regard K as the strike price inclusive of accrued interest on the expiration date and P is the full price of the bond inclusive of accrued interest.

Transaction Today	Investment Today	$P^* \geq K$ Date T	$P^* < K$ Date T
1. Buy the call	$-c$	$P^* - K$	0
2. Buy the put	$-p$	0	$K - P^*$
3. Buy the bond	$-P$	P^*	P^*
4. Borrow the present value of the strike	$\dfrac{K}{(1 + R)^{T-t}}$	$-K$	$-K$
Total of (2) + (3) + (4)	$-p - P + \dfrac{K}{(1 + R)^{T-t}}$	$P^* - K$	0

TABLE 7-9
Put-Call Parity for Options on Stocks or Bonds

We illustrate the put-call parity with Example 7-3.

Example 7-3   Put-Call Parity for Options on T-bond

Pricing date: $t =$ February 15, 1995
Underlying security: $1 million par of 8.00%, 2/15/2023 T-bond
Price of underlying security: $P = 100\frac{9}{32}$
Strike price: $K = 100$

Expiration date: T = June 15, 1995

Call premium: c = 4.20 ($42,000)

Put premium: p = 2.00 ($20,000)

Style: European

Financing rate: r = 6%

Accrued interest: ai_t = 0

Let us set up the transactions which will replicate the call option by buying other securities, as shown next in Table 7-10. The maturity of the option is 120 days. The transactions indicate that the call's payoffs are exactly replicated by buying the put, buying the underlying bond, and borrowing the present value of the strike price. The difference between the price of the call, 4.20, and the value of the portfolio of put, bond, and the amount borrowed that replicates the call, 4.18, is negligible.

TABLE 7-10   *Put-Call Parity for Options on a T-bond (Example 7-3)*

Transaction Today	Investment Today	$P* \geq K$ Date T	$P* < K$ Date T
1. Buy the call	−4.20	$P* - 100$	0
2. Buy the put	−2.00	0	$100 - P*$
3. Buy the bond	$-100\frac{9}{32}$	$P*$	$P*$
4. Borrow the present value of the strike	$\dfrac{100}{(1 + 0.06)^{\frac{120}{365}}} = 98.1025$	−100	−100
Total of (2) + (3) + (4)	$-2 - 100.28125 + 98.1025 = -4.18$	$P* - 100$	0

Consider now a situation when at date s where $t \leq s \leq T$ there is a cash flow d from the underlying security. This might arise because the underlying bond pays a coupon during the life of the option. The put-call parity in such a case may be derived as shown in Table 7-11.

The put-call parity relationship is

$$c = p + P - \frac{K}{(1 + R)^{T-t}} - \frac{d}{(1 + R)^{s-t}} \tag{7.4}$$

For bond options, we regard d as coupon payments. Typically, for bond options, the buyer of the option pays the strike price plus accrued interest when the option is exercised. In turn, the underlying bond is delivered. Since the market convention is to work with the flat price B_t of the bond, we may write the put-call parity for bond options as

$$c = p + (B_t + a_t) - \frac{\hat{K} + a_T}{(1 + R)^{T-t}} - \frac{d}{(1 + R)^{s-t}} \tag{7.5}$$

TABLE 7-11   *Put-Call Parity for Options on Bonds with Coupons*

Transaction Today	Investment Today	Dividends Date s	$P^* \geq K$ Date T	$P^* < K$ Date T
1. Buy the call	$-c$		$P^* - K$	0
2. Buy the put	$-p$		0	$K - P^*$
3. Buy the bond	$-P$	d	P^*	P^*
4. Borrow the present value of strike	$\dfrac{K}{(1 + R)^{T-t}}$		$-K$	$-K$
5. Borrow the present value of dividend	$\dfrac{d}{(1 + R)^{s-t}}$	$-d$		
Total of (2) + (3) + (4) + (5)	$-p - P + \dfrac{K}{(1 + R)^{T-t}} + \dfrac{d}{(1 + R)^{s-t}}$		$P^* - K$	0

where the full price at t is P which equals the flat price B_t plus the accrued interest a_t. The option has a flat strike price of $\hat{K}$ and the person exercising the option at date T will pay the flat strike price plus the accrued interest at date T which is a_T.

Example 7-4   Put-Call Parity for Options on T-bond

In this example, we determine the price of a call given the price of a put, the underlying bond, and the financing rate, using the put-call parity relation.

Pricing date: $t =$ February 17, 1987
Underlying security: $1 million par of 7.50%, 11/15/2016 T-bond
Price of underlying security: $P = 98.625$
Strike price: $K = 100$
Expiration date: $T =$ June 15, 1987
Call premium: $c = $??
Put premium: $p = 5.00$ ($50,000)
Style: European
Financing rate: $(R =)$ 6%
Coupon date: $s =$ 5/15/1987
Accrued interest at t: (a_t) 1.95 $\left[\frac{94}{2 \times 181} \times 7.5 = 1.95\right]$
Accrued interest at T: (a_T) 0.64 $\left[\frac{31}{2 \times 181} \times 7.5 = 0.64\right]$

Note that the put-call parity shown in Table 7-12 produces the call price 3.12.

TABLE 7-12   *Put-Call Parity for Options on a T-bond with Coupons (Example 7-4)*

Transaction Today	Investment Today	Coupon Date s	$P^* \geq K$ Date T	$P^* < K$ Date T
1. Buy the call	$-c$		$P^* - K$	0
2. Buy the put	-5		0	$100.64 - P^*$
3. Buy the bond	-100.575	3.75	P^*	P^*
4. Borrow the present value of strike	$\dfrac{100 + 0.64}{(1.06)^{\frac{118}{365}}}$		-100.64	-100.64
5. Borrow the present value of coupons	$\dfrac{3.75}{(1.06)^{\frac{87}{365}}}$	-3.75		
Total of (2) + (3) + (4) + (5)	$-5 - 100.575 + 98.762$ $+ 3.698 = -3.12$		$P^* - 100.64$	0

If both the call and the put on the bond are at-the-money, so that $B_t = \hat{K}$, then we have

$$c = p + (B_t + a_t) - \frac{B_t + a_T}{(1 + R)^{T-t}} - \frac{d}{(1 + R)^{s-t}} \qquad (7.6)$$

Note that even if the bond does not pay any coupons during the life of the option (so that $d = 0$), the relation between the at-the-money call and put will depend on the shape of the yield curve. To see this, set $d = 0$ and write the put-call parity for at-the-money options as

$$c = p + (B_t + a_t) - \frac{B_t + a_T}{(1 + R)^{T-t}} \qquad (7.7)$$

The accrued interest of the bond reflects the coupons (yields) in the long end of the yield curve and R is the short-term financing rate. In a positively sloped yield curve, the increase in accrued interest $a_T - a_t$ far exceeds the financing costs:

$$(B_t + a_t) \times [(1 + R)^{T-t} - 1].$$

This may be rewritten as

$$c = p + \frac{(B_t + a_t) \times \{(1 + R)^{T-t} - 1\} - (a_T - a_t)}{(1 + R)^{T-t}} \qquad (7.8)$$

Clearly, **when the carry is positive, the at-the-money put option on a bond is more expensive than the at-the-money call option.**

For options on futures contracts, the put-call parity relationship may be derived as shown in Table 7-13.

Transaction Today	Investment Today	$H^* \geq K$ Date T	$H^* < K$ Date T
1. Buy the call	$-c$	$H^* - K$	0
2. Buy the put	$-p$	0	$K - H^*$
3. Buy the futures	0	$H^* - H$	$H^* - H$
4. Lend the present value of $(H - K)$	$-\dfrac{H - K}{(1 + R)^{T-t}}$	$H - K$	$H - K$
Total of (2) + (3) + (4)	$-p - \dfrac{H - K}{(1 + R)^{T-t}}$	$H^* - K$	0

TABLE 7-13

Put-Call Parity for Options on Futures

This leads to the put-call parity relation for options on futures,

$$c = p + \frac{H - K}{(1 + R)^{T-t}} \tag{7.9}$$

Note that an at-the-money call on futures is identical in price to an at-the-money put option. We illustrate the put-call parity relation for options on futures in Example 7-5.

Example 7-5 Put-Call Parity for Options on Futures

In this example, we determine the price of a put, given the price of a call, the underlying futures, and the financing rate, using the put-call parity relation.

  Pricing date: $t =$ February 17, 1987
  Underlying security: T-bond futures (March 1987)
  Futures Price: $H= 99.35$
  Strike price: $K = 100$
  Expiration date: $T = 06/15/1987$
  Call premium: $c = 5.00$
  Put premium: $p = $??
  Style: European
  Financing rate: $(R =) 6\%$

The steps are shown in Table 7-14. The put premium can be calculated from the equation:

$$p + \frac{99.35 - 100}{(1.06)^{\frac{118}{365}}} = 5.$$

Solving, we get $p = 5 + 0.64 = 5.64$.

TABLE 7-14   *Put-Call Parity for Options on Futures (Example 7-5)*

Transaction Today	Investment Today	$H^* \geq K$ Date T	$H^* < K$ Date T
1. Buy the call	-5	$H^* - 100$	0
2. Buy the put	$-p$	0	$100 - H^*$
3. Buy the futures	0	$H^* - 99.35$	$H^* - 99.35$
4. Lend the present value of $(99.35 - 100)$	$-\dfrac{99.35 - 100}{(1.06)^{T-t}}$	$99.35 - 100$	$99.35 - 100$
Total of (2) + (3) + (4)	$-p - \dfrac{99.35 - 100}{(1.06)^{T-t}}$	$H^* - 100$	0

It is important to note that the put-call parity relations hold only for European options. Further, in deriving the put-call parity relation for options on futures, we have assumed that the futures contracts are not marked to market every day.

Alternatively, we could have assumed that all future one-period interest rates are known. Then, as Cox, Ingersoll and Ross (1981) and Richard and Sundaresan (1981) have shown, forward and futures prices are the same and the put-call parity relation above goes through even when futures are marked to market. As a practical matter, the empirical effect of marking to market seems to be unimportant for short maturities.

Upper Bounds

Upper bounds specify levels above which no options may sell. If these bounds are violated, then there are riskless arbitrage opportunities.

- $c \leq P$ and $p \leq K$. The call premium must be less than the underlying asset price and the put premium must be below the strike price of the option. Note that $0 \leq c \leq P$. Hence, if $P = 0$, $c = 0$.
- The lower-boundary condition may be tightened as shown next.

$$c \geq P - \frac{K}{(1 + R)^{T-t}} - \frac{d}{(1 + R)^{s-t}} \tag{7.10}$$

This condition follows from the put-call parity relation and the fact that $p \geq 0$.

- $c(K_2) \leq c(K_1)$ and $c(t_2) \geq c(t_1)$ where $K_2 > K_1$ and $t_2 > t_1$. Note that if $c(K_2) > c(K_1)$, there is a riskless arbitrage; we will write the option $c(K_2)$ and buy the other, netting an income of $c(K_2) - c(K_1) > 0$. If the written call is exercised we can always exercise the call that we purchased. This action will net an additional income of $K_2 - K_1$. This condition holds for both American-style and European-style options. In a similar way, if $c(t_2) < c(t_1)$, there is an arbitrage opportunity; we will buy $c(t_2)$ and sell $c(t_1)$, netting an income of $c(t_1) - c(t_2) > 0$. If the options are

American, then any time the written option is exercised, we can either sell or exercise the option that we purchased to make money or break even.

We summarize in Table 7-15, the key no-arbitrage bounds that were developed originally in Merton (1973).

TABLE 7-15   *Summary of No-Arbitrage Bounds*

Underlying Asset	Bounds	Style (A or E)
Lower bounds	$c \geq 0$	A and E
	$c \geq P - K$	A
	$c \geq P - \dfrac{K}{(1+R)^{T-t}} - \dfrac{d}{(1+R)^{s-t}}$	A and E
	$p \geq 0$	A and E
	$p \geq K - P$	A
	$p \geq \dfrac{K}{(1+R)^{T-t}} + \dfrac{d}{(1+R)^{s-t}} - P$	A and E
Upper bounds	$c \leq P$	A and E
	$p \leq K$	A and E
	$p \leq \dfrac{K}{(1+R)^{T-t}}$	E
Other bounds	$c(K_1) \geq c(K_2) \text{ if } K_2 > K_1$	A and E
	$p(K_1) \leq p(K_2) \text{ if } K_2 > K_1$	A and E
	$c(K_1) - c(K_2) \leq K_2 - K_1$	A and E
	$c(K_1) - c(K_2) \leq \dfrac{K_2 - K_1}{(1+R)^{T-t}}$	E -
	$p(K_2) - p(K_1) \leq K_2 - K_1$	A and E
	$p(K_1) - p(K_2) \leq \dfrac{K_2 - K_1}{(1+R)^{T-t}}$	E
	$c(K_2) \leq \lambda c(K_1) + (1 - \lambda)c(K_3)$	A and E
	$p(K_2) \leq \lambda p(K_1) + (1 - \lambda)p(K_3)$	A and E
Early exercise rules	Never exercise the call if $PV(int) > PV(d)$ Never exercise the put if $PV(int) < PV(d)$	

Note: $\lambda = \frac{K_3 - K_2}{K_3 - K_1}$. (We derive the early exercise conditions in a later section of the chapter.) We assume that $K_3 > K_2 > K_1$.

Optimal Early Exercise

The flexibility of American options, permitting the holder to exercise at any time prior to the expiry date, make them more attractive than their European counterparts. In this section, we consider the optimal early exercise strategies for American calls and puts.

Early Exercise of American Calls. The optimal premature exercise of American call options is based on the trade-off between the present value of dividends achieved by exercising the call and the present value of the interest on the strike price given up by exercising it. Since any exercise strategy that calls for exercise prior to the payment of dividends results in foregone interest, it is by definition suboptimal. Hence the best time to exercise an option early is just prior to the ex-dividend date. Whenever the present value of dividends exceeds the present value of the interest on the strike price, you must exercise the option; otherwise, you should sell it.

To verify these claims, we can use the bounds that were developed earlier (see Table 7-15). The logic works as follows.

- The call is worth $c \geq (P - K)$, in general. (If $c < (P - K)$, then we will buy the call and immediately exercise it to make money.)
- If $c > P - K$, then it makes sense to sell the call and realize c rather than exercising and realizing just $P - K$.
- So, we need to identify the conditions under which $c = P - K$, so that the exercise value is the option value. To identify such circumstances, let us consider when $c = P - K$ will lead to possible riskless arbitrage.

  Suppose $c = P - K$. Then consider the following self-financing strategy: buy the call, short the underlying asset, and lend the strike price to earn interest. This position makes money, as long as the underlying asset does not make any cash payments.

  If a cash payment is made, then the short seller must make restitution.
- Hence we may conclude that $c > P - K$ on all days except on the ex-dividend dates and the expiration date.

A consequence of this logic is that if the underlying asset never pays any dividends during the life of the option, then $c > P - K$ and it is preferable to sell the option rather than to exercise it. Thus, we conclude that a call option on a stock not paying dividends during the option's life should never be exercised. A necessary condition for an American call to be exercised is that the underlying security must make some cash payments during the option's life. Note that even if dividends are paid, as long as the interest earned on the strike price is sufficient to make restitution of the dividends, it is still optimal to hold the option and not exercise it.

Define the present value of interest on the strike price as

$$PV(\text{int}) \equiv \frac{K \times (1 + R)^{T-t} - K}{(1 + R)^{T-t}}$$

Let the present value of dividends be defined as

$$PV(d) = \frac{d}{(1 + R)^{s-t}}$$

From the lower bound conditions in Table 7-15, we know that

$$c \geq P - \frac{K}{(1 + R)^{T-t}} - \frac{d}{(1 + R)^{s-t}}.$$

This may be rewritten as

$$c \geq P - K + PV(\text{int}) - PV(d).$$

Note that if $PV(\text{int}) - PV(d) > 0$, then $c > P - K$ and it is not optimal to exercise the call. For sufficiently large dividends, we will encounter cases in which $c = P - K$ and which call for optimal exercise of the call option.

Early Exercise of American Puts. An American put may be optimally exercised even in the absence of dividend payments. To see why this is the case, let us first note from the put-call parity relation that

$$p = c - P + \frac{K}{(1 + R)^{T-t}} + \frac{d}{(1 + R)^{s-t}}.$$

This holds for European options. We can rewrite the above equation as

$$p = c - P + K - PV(\text{int}) + PV(d).$$

Now consider an American put. For an American put, the following inequality must hold:

$$p \geq c - P + K - PV(\text{int}) + PV(d)$$

When early exercise is optimal, its value should be $p = K - P$. Using the condition above, if $c + PV(d) - PV(\text{int}) > 0$, then $p > K - P$ and hence early exercise is not optimal. Take the extreme case when $PV(d) = 0$. Then, if $c < PV(\text{int})$, it may be optimal to exercise the put option. Note that c in this context is a European call. As the strike price K increases, the value of a European call c will fall, but $PV(\text{int})$ will increase. This suggests that when K is sufficiently high, the put will be exercised.

In this section, we considered bounds that are the consequence of no arbitrage. To get a precise relationship between the value of an option and its determinants, we need to place additional structure on the valuation problem.

PRICING BY REPLICATION

Under certain assumptions, options-pricing theory shows that the payoffs distribution of options can be replicated by trading in a certain way in the underlying asset coupled with riskless lending or borrowing.

Are call options on T-bonds riskier than T-bonds? How can an asset which gives all the up side and limited down side be riskier than the underlying asset? We will show that the concept of replication gives us a much better framework in which to think about such questions.

Steps in Constructing Replicating Portfolios

Consider how we go about replicating a call option T-bond. First, we recognize that, however we construct the replicating portfolio, it must be the case that as the bond price goes up, the value of the portfolio goes up as well. This is because the call on the bond will appreciate in value as the bond price increases. This indicates that the replicating portfolio will have a long position in the T-bond.

We can refine this further. For a deep out-of-the-money call option, bond-price increases will hardly affect the call premium. Hence the replicating portfolio of a deep out-of-the-money call should have no bonds. By the same token, the premium of a deep in-the-money call option will increase by a dollar if the underlying bond price increases by a dollar. Hence the replicating portfolio for a deep in-the-money option should have one bond per each option. These observations indicate that the replicating portfolio has to constantly modify its exposure to the bond-price risk depending on whether the option is in-the-money or out-of-the-money. Further, when the option is at-the-money, the replicating portfolio should have one-half bond in it.

The number of underlying assets in the replicating portfolio for an option on a single unit of the underlying asset is known as the *delta* of the option and is denoted by Δ.

Consider the example in Figure 7-6. A three-month at-the-money call option on a bond had a premium of 2.00. To replicate this at-the-money option, we need to buy one-half bond, which will cost 50.00. Given that the replicating portfolio must exactly duplicate all the properties of the option, it is clear that its cost can be only 2.00. This means that 48.00 must be borrowed in addition to the out-of-pocket investment of 2.00 to buy the necessary bonds.

To summarize: To replicate a call option on a bond (stock), we borrow money to buy delta bonds (stocks). As the bond (stock) price increases and the option goes in-the-money, we borrow more money and buy more bonds (stocks), progressively increasing the number of bonds (stocks) to one when the option is deep in-the-money. As the bond (stock) price decreases and the option goes out-of-the-money, we sell bonds (stocks) progressively, decreasing the number of bonds (stocks) to zero when the option is deep out-of-the-money.

A Binomial Model for Bond Options

Let the full price (flat plus accrued) of the bond behave according to the binomial tree depicted below:

$$
\begin{array}{ccc}
 & & uP \\
 & \nearrow & \\
P & & \\
 & \searrow & \\
 & & dP \\
t = 0 & & t = 1
\end{array}
$$

We will assume throughout that the probability of an up move is q and that of a down move is $1 - q$, irrespective of the level of the underlying asset price.

Consider now a call option on this bond at a strike price of K. Let this option expire on date $t = 1$. We can observe P directly and we will estimate u and d from the volatility of the underlying bond as indicated later in this chapter.

The option value behaves according to the binomial tree depicted below:

$$c_u = \max(uP - K, 0)$$

$$c$$

$$c_d = \max(dP - K, 0)$$

$$t = 0 \qquad\qquad t = 1$$

Assume that the option expires at $t = 1$. In the up state, the option is worth $c_u = \max(uP - K, 0)$ and in the down state the option is worth $c_d = \max(dP - K, 0)$. We wish to determine what the option is worth, c, at date $t = 0$

Let us borrow $\$B$ at a rate $r = 1 + R$ and buy Δ of the underlying bond. Then this portfolio will have the following properties:

$$\Delta uP - Br$$

$$\Delta P - B$$

$$\Delta dP - Br$$

$$t = 0 \qquad t = 1$$

In the up state, the portfolio is worth $\Delta uP - Br$ and in the down state the portfolio is worth $\Delta dP - Br$. We want our portfolio to replicate the call at date $t = 1$ in both the states. Hence,

$$c_u = \Delta uP - Br$$

$$\Delta P - B$$

$$c_d = \Delta dP - Br$$

$$t = 0 \qquad\qquad t = 1$$

We thus have two conditions:

$$c_u = \Delta uP - Br$$
$$c_d = \Delta dP - Br.$$

Note that we know c_u and c_d, and can solve for Δ and B. We get

$$\Delta = \frac{c_u - c_d}{(u - d)P} \qquad\qquad (7.11)$$

and

$$B = \left[\frac{c_u d - c_d u}{u - d} \right] \times \frac{1}{r}. \qquad\qquad (7.12)$$

To preclude arbitrage, the replicating portfolio must sell for the same price as the call at date $t = 0$; hence,

$$c = \Delta P - B = \frac{pc_u + (1 - p)c_d}{r} \qquad (7.13)$$

where

$$p = \frac{r - d}{u - d}.$$

Equation (7.13) is the well-known binomial options-pricing formula. If the option is American, then we must check to see whether early exercise is optimal. We do this by comparing the value of c in Equation (7.13) with the exercise value $P - K$ and choosing the maximum of the two. The formula makes intuitive sense. We take the expected value of the option, using the probability factor p, and discount the resulting payoff at the riskless rate.

Consider now the expected return of the underlying bond under the probability p:

$$\frac{p \times uP + (1 - p) \times dP}{P}.$$

Substituting for p and simplifying we get the expected return equal to r, the riskless rate. **The probability parameter p, therefore, is known as the risk-neutral probability.**

Example 7-6

The full price of the bond at $t = 0$ is 100. On date $t = 1$, the price can either go to $100 \times 1.08 = 108.00$ in the up state or go down to $100 \times \frac{1}{1.08} = 92.593$ in the down state. Assume that the riskless rate is 5%. Assume that a call option on this bond is traded at date $t = 0$, maturing at date $t = 1$. It has a strike price of 100. Determine the replicating portfolio, risk-neutral probability p, and the option price c.

The bond price behaves as follows:

$$
\begin{array}{ccc}
 & & 108.00 \\
 & \nearrow & \\
P = 100 & & \\
 & \searrow & \\
 & & 92.593 \\
t = 0 & & t = 1
\end{array}
$$

The call option price distribution is

$$
\begin{array}{ccc}
 & & c_u = 8.000 \\
 & \nearrow & \\
c & & \\
 & \searrow & \\
 & & c_d = 0.000 \\
t = 0 & & t = 1
\end{array}
$$

Using Equation (7.11) gives

$$\Delta = \frac{c_u - c_d}{(u - d)P} = \frac{8.000 - 0.000}{(1.08 - 0.92593)100} = 0.5192.$$

In a similar way, using Equation (7.12) gives

$$B = \left[\frac{c_u d - c_d u}{u - d} \right] \times \frac{1}{r}$$

$$= \left[\frac{8.000 \times 0.92593 - 0.0000 \times 1.08}{1.08 - 0.92593} \right] \times \frac{1}{1.05}$$

$$= 45.789$$

Hence we borrow $45.7886 to buy 0.5192 shares to replicate the call option. Finally, using Equation (7.13) we get

$$c = \Delta P - B = 0.5192 \times 100 - 45.789 = 6.131.$$

The risk-neutral probability is

$$p = \frac{r - d}{u - d} = \frac{1.05 - 0.92593}{1.08 - 0.92593} = 0.805.$$

This strategy will also carry over many periods. Consider the options-pricing problem when the option expires at date $t = 2$.

The payoffs of the option on bond are:

First, we determine the value of the option c_u in the up state at date $t = 1$:

$$c_u = \frac{pc_{uu} + (1 - p)c_{ud}}{r}.$$

If early exercise is permitted (if the option is American), then

$$c_u = \max\left[uP - K, \frac{pc_{uu} + (1 - p)c_{ud}}{r} \right]. \qquad (7.14)$$

In a similar way,

$$c_d = \frac{pc_{ud} + (1 - p)c_{dd}}{r}.$$

Again, if early exercise is permitted, the value of the option in the down state is

$$c_d = \max\left(dP - K, \frac{pc_{ud} + (1 - p)c_{dd}}{r} \right). \qquad (7.15)$$

Once we have figured out the values at date $t = 1$ for the up state and the down state, we can determine the call premium at $t = 0$:

$$c = \max\left[P - K, \frac{pc_u + (1 - p)c_d}{r} \right] \qquad (7.16)$$

Example 7-7

We illustrate now the problem considered in Example 7-6 for two periods. The bond prices evolve as shown next.

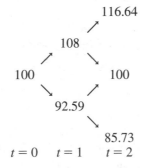

Then the payoffs of the option on the bond are:

The value of the option c_u in the up state at date $t = 1$ is

$$c_u = \frac{pc_{uu} + (1 - p)c_{ud}}{r} = \frac{0.805 \times 16.64 + 0.195 \times 0}{1.05} = 12.76.$$

In a similar way,

$$c_d = \frac{pc_{ud} + (1 - p)c_{dd}}{r} = 0.0.$$

Once we have figured out the values at date $t = 1$ for the up state and the down state, we can determine the call premium at $t = 0$:

$$c = \max\left(P - K, \frac{pc_u + (1 - p)c_d}{r}\right)$$

$$= \frac{0.805 \times 12.76 + 0.195 \times 0}{1.05}$$

$$= 9.78$$

The recursive structure of the formula allows us to determine the call premium for options which may have several periods to maturity. For European options, these recursive arguments lead to the simple formula:

$$c = P\Phi(a; n, p') - \frac{K}{r^n}\Phi(a; n, p) \tag{7.17}$$

where $p' = p \times \frac{u}{r}$ and a is the minimum number of up moves that the underlying asset price must make in order for the option to end in the money at maturity—it is the smallest integer greater than $(\ln\frac{K}{Pd^n})/(\ln\frac{u}{d})$. The function $\Phi(a; n, p)$ represents the cumulative binomial distribution function which denotes the cumulative probability of getting at least a upmoves in a total of n steps using the probability factor p or p'.

Options on Futures

Most listed options in the fixed-income markets are on futures contracts. It is therefore important to understand how these options are on future prices and in what ways they differ from OTC options, which are typically on underlying bonds or interest rates.

Let the futures price evolve according to the binomial tree depicted below:

Consider now a call option on this futures contract at a strike price of K. Let this option expire on date $t = 1$. We can observe H and we will estimate u and d from the volatility of the underlying futures contract.

The option value behaves according to the binomial tree depicted below:

$$c_u = \max (uH - K, 0)$$

$$c$$

$$c_d = \max (dH - K, 0)$$

$$t = 0 \qquad\qquad t = 1$$

We will assume that the option expires at $t = 1$. In the up state, the option is worth $c_u = \max (uH - K, 0)$ and in the down state the option is worth $c_d = \max (dH - K, 0)$. We wish to determine what the option is worth (C) at date $t = 0$.

The strategy that we developed in the context of bond options in the construction of a replicating portfolio needs to be modified. Let us consider how we will go about replicating a call option futures contract. First, we recognize that however we construct the replicating portfolio, it must be the case that as the futures price goes up, the value of the portfolio goes up. This is because the call on the futures will appreciate in value as the futures price increases. This indicates that the replicating portfolio will have a long position in the underlying futures contract.

We can refine this further. For a deep out-of-the-money call option, futures price increases will hardly affect the call premium. Hence the replicating portfolio of a deep out-of-the-money call should have no futures. By the same token, the premium of a deep in-the-money call option will increase by a dollar if the underlying futures price increases by a dollar. Hence, the replicating portfolio for a deep in-the-money option should have one futures per each option.

These observations indicate that the replicating portfolio has to constantly modify its exposure to the futures price risk depending on whether the option is in-the-money or out-of-the-money. Further, when the option is at-the-money, the replicating portfolio should have one-half futures in it. As before, the number of underlying assets in the replicating portfolio for an option on a single unit of the underlying asset is denoted by Δ.

Let us say that a three-month at-the-money call option on futures had a premium of 2.00. To replicate this at-the-money option, we need to buy one-half futures, which will be costless to initiate. Given that the replicating portfolio must exactly duplicate all the properties of the option, it is clear that it must cost only 2.00. This means that 2.00 must be set aside in Treasury bills (or lent) in order to replicate the futures option.

To summarize: To replicate a call option on a futures, we lend money to buy T-bills and also to buy Δ futures contracts. As the futures price increases and the option goes in-the-money, we buy more futures progressively and increase the number of futures to one when the option is deep in-the-money. Note that the initial futures position will throw off cash flows from mark to market, which will be swept into T-bills—we lend more money as the option gets deeper in-the-money. As the futures price decreases and the option goes out-of-the-money, we sell futures progressively decreasing the number of futures to zero when the option is deep out-of-the-money. We sell T-bills to meet the variation margin calls.

Let us lend $\$B$ at a rate $r = 1 + R$ and buy Δ of the underlying futures. Then this portfolio will have the following properties:

$$\Delta(uH - H) + Br$$
$$\nearrow$$
$$B$$
$$\searrow$$
$$\Delta(dH - H) + Br$$
$$t = 0 \qquad\qquad t = 1$$

In the up state, the portfolio is worth $\Delta(uH - H) + Br$ and in the down state the portfolio is worth $\Delta(dH - H) + Br$. We want our portfolio to replicate the call at date $t = 1$ in both the states. Hence,

$$c_u = \Delta(uH - H) + Br$$
$$\nearrow$$
$$B$$
$$\searrow$$
$$c_d = \Delta(dH - H) + Br$$
$$t = 0 \qquad\qquad t = 1$$

We thus have two conditions:

$$c_u = \Delta(uH - H) + Br$$
$$c_d = \Delta(dH - H) + Br.$$

Note that we know c_u and c_d, and can solve for Δ and B. We get

$$\Delta = \frac{c_u - c_d}{(u - d)H} \tag{7.18}$$

and

$$B = \frac{c_u(1 - d) + c_d(u - 1)}{(u - d)r}. \tag{7.19}$$

To preclude arbitrage, the replicating portfolio must sell for the same price as the call at date $t = 0$; hence,

$$c = B = \frac{pc_u + (1 - p)c_d}{r} \tag{7.20}$$

where

$$p = \frac{1 - d}{u - d}. \tag{7.21}$$

Equation (7.20) is the binomial futures options-pricing formula. If the option is American, then we must check to see whether early exercise is optimal. We do this by comparing the value of c in Equation (7.20) with the exercise value $H - K$ and choosing the maximum of the two.

$$c = \max\left[H - K, \frac{pc_u + (1 - p)c_d}{r}\right] \tag{7.22}$$

The formula makes intuitive sense. We take the expected value of the option, using the probability factor p, and discount the resulting payoff at the riskless rate.

We can verify this formula even for an option that has many periods to maturity. **Call options on futures may be optimally exercised prematurely even when it is suboptimal to exercise call options on the underlying spot asset.** This may be developed as follows.

Let us suppose that the option is in-the-money at date $t = 1$, no matter which state occurs. Then, $c_u = uH - K$ and $c_d = dH - K$. Substituting these values in the pricing formula, Equation (7.22), we get

$$c = \max\left[H - K, \frac{p(uH - K) + (1 - p)(dH - K)}{r} \right]$$

Note that when we substitute for $p = \frac{1-d}{u-d}$ in the above equation, we get

$$c = \max\left[H - K, \frac{H - K}{r} \right].$$

Clearly, the payoffs associated with early exercise at date $t = 0$ outweigh the value associated with waiting and exercising the option later. It is possible to verify this for put options on futures contracts as well.

We can now extend the analysis to cases in which the options have more than one period to their maturity date. To illustrate the idea, let us consider the options-pricing problem, when the option expires at date $t = 2$.

The payoffs of the option on the bond are:

First, we determine the value of the option c_u in the up state at date $t = 1$:

$$c_u = \frac{pc_{uu} + (1 - p)c_{ud}}{r}.$$

If early exercise is permitted (if the option is American), then

$$c_u = \max\left[uH - K, \frac{pc_{uu} + (1 - p)c_{ud}}{r}\right]$$ (7.23)

In a similar way,

$$c_d = \frac{pc_{ud} + (1 - p)c_{dd}}{r}.$$

Again, if early exercise is permitted, the value of the option in the down state is

$$c_d = \max\left[dH - K, \frac{pc_{ud} + (1 - p)c_{dd}}{r}\right].$$ (7.24)

Once we have figured out the values at date $t = 1$ for the up state and the down state, we can determine the call premium at $t = 0$:

$$c = \max\left[H - K, \frac{pc_u + (1 - p)c_d}{r}\right]$$ (7.25)

Example 7-8

Suppose that the futures price on a bond is at 100 now. The upmove factor is estimated to be 1.10 and the downmove factor is 0.909. A call option on a futures contract is traded now. The strike price of the option is 100 and the option will expire two periods from now. If the volatility of the futures prices is estimated at 12%, what is the value of the option now? (Assume that the one-period riskless rate is 5%).

The evolution of the futures price is given below:

```
                                            121.00
                                          ↗
                            110.00
                          ↗               ↘
              100                           100.00
                          ↘               ↗
                            90.91
                                          ↘
                                            82.64
              t = 1        t = 1            t = 2
```

The value of the call at maturity is shown below:

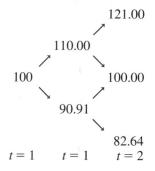

```
                                            21.00
                                          ↗
                            c_u
                          ↗               ↘
              c                             0.00
                          ↘               ↗
                            c_d
                                          ↘
                                            0.00
              t = 1        t = 1            t = 2
```

The risk-neutral probability is:

$$p = \frac{1 - 0.909}{1.1 - 0.909} = 0.47644$$

The value of the option at $t = 1$ in the up node is

$$c_u = \frac{0.47644 \times 21 + (1 - 0.47644) \times 0}{1.05} = 9.5288$$

Note that if the option is American, its immediate exercise value will be $110 - 100 = 10$. This exceeds the value of waiting and exercising at $t = 2$. Hence, $c_u = 10.00$. The value of the option at $t = 1$ in the down node is zero as the option ends worthless even if the futures price were to go up. So, $c_d = 0.00$.

The value of the option at $t = 0$ is

$$c = \frac{0.47644 \times 10 + (1 - 0.47644) \times 0}{1.05} = 4.537524$$

The value of the call over time is shown below:

```
                                           21.00
                                         ↗
                        c_u = 10.00
                      ↗              ↘
        c = 4.54                        0.00
                      ↘              ↗
                        c_d = 0.00
                                     ↘
                                           0.00
        t = 0         t = 1        t = 2
```

Note that the only thing that changes in the current formulation compared to the formulation of options on bonds is that the risk-neutral probability is given by Equation (7.21) as opposed to $p = \frac{r-d}{u-d}$. The recursive structure of the formula allows us to determine the call premium for options that have several periods to maturity. In fact, the binomial formula derived earlier applies to this case as well, once p has been redefined. Table 7-16 provides the appropriate risk-neutral probabilities for various underlying assets.

TABLE 7-16
Risk-Neutral Probabilities

Underlying Security	*Probability*	*Restrictions*
Common stock (no dividends)	$p = \dfrac{r - d}{u - d}$	$u > r > d$
Common stock (dividend yield δ)	$p = \dfrac{r(1 - \delta) - d}{u - d}$	$u > r(1 - \delta) > d$
Futures contract	$p = \dfrac{1 - d}{u - d}$	$u > 1 > d$
Spot currency (foreign interest rate r^*)	$p = \dfrac{\frac{r}{r^*} - d}{u - d}$	$u > \dfrac{r}{r^*} > d$

Risk-Neutral Pricing

Generally speaking, we can show that the no-arbitrage pricing is equivalent to finding the risk-neutral probabilities. Table 7-16 provides the risk-neutral pricing probabilities for some important options.

Note that in the application of the binomial options-pricing procedure, we are obliged to specify the number of time steps into which we have divided the life of the option. For example, we used two time steps and three time steps in our previous illustrations. At a pragmatic level, it could be argued that n, the number of time steps, should be such that we get sufficiently accurate answers. In an important paper, Cox, Ross, and Rubinstein (1979) show how to use the binomial approach to obtain the Black and Scholes (1973) options-pricing formula as a limiting case. Their arguments are summarized next.

Let $T - t$ be the life of the option in years. Subdivide the life of the option into n time steps. Define $h = \frac{T-t}{n}$. Consider the annualized riskless rate of interest $1 + R$. Its allocation to the subintervals will be governed by the relation:

$$(1 + \hat{R}) = (1 + R)^{\frac{T-t}{n}}.$$

Cox, Ross, and Rubinstein (1979) select

$$u = \frac{1}{d} = e^{\sigma\sqrt{\frac{T-t}{n}}}. \tag{7.26}$$

where σ is the volatility of the underlying asset returns, $T - t$ is the time to maturity of the option in years, n is the number of time steps into which the option is divided and e is the base of natural logarithm. They let the probability $q = 0.5 + 0.5\frac{\mu}{\sigma}\sqrt{\frac{T-t}{n}}$ where μ is the expected rate of return on the underlying asset. Then as $n \to \infty$ the options-pricing formula converges to the Black and Scholes formula:

$$c = PN(d_1) - Ke^{-r(T-t)}N(d_2)$$

where $N(d_1)$ is the cumulative normal density evaluated at d_1 and $N(d_2)$ is the cumulative normal density evaluated at d_2. Moreover,

$$d_1 = \frac{\ln\left(\frac{P}{K}\right) + \left(r + \frac{\sigma^2}{2}\right)(T - t)}{\sigma\sqrt{T - t}}$$

and

$$d_2 = d_1 - \sigma\sqrt{T - t}.$$

Example 7-9

Consider a bond with a price $P = 102$. A call option on this bond is available at a strike price of 101 with a maturity of six months. The financing rate is 5% and the volatility of the bond returns is estimated at 25%. Determine the value of the call option.

Note that $T - t = 0.5$ years. We can compute

$$d_1 = \frac{\ln\left(\frac{102}{101}\right) + \left(0.05 + \frac{0.25^2}{2}\right)0.5}{0.25\sqrt{0.5}} = 0.28554$$

and

$$d_2 = d_1 - \sigma\sqrt{T - t} = 0.28554 - 0.25\sqrt{0.5} = 0.10876.$$

Using the Black and Scholes options-pricing formula, we get

$$c = PN(d_1) - Ke^{-r(T-t)}N(d_2)$$
$$= 102N(0.28554) - 101e^{-0.05 \times 0.5}N(0.10876).$$

From the normal distribution tables, we note that $N(0.286) = 0.612386$ and $N(0.109) = 0.543306$. Then the call value is

$$c = 102 \times 0.612386 - 101e^{-0.05 \times 0.5} \times 0.543306 = 8.944.$$

Using the table of risk-neutral probabilities (Table 7-16) we can derive the Black and Scholes options-pricing formula for options on futures, foreign currencies, and so on. One of the most useful adjustments to the basic options-pricing formula of Black and Scholes is the Merton (1973) proportional-dividend model. The formula derived by Merton is shown.

$$c = Se^{-\delta(T-t)}N(d_1) - Ke^{-r(T-t)}N(d_2)$$

where δ is the proportional rate of dividend payout, $N(d_1)$ is the cumulative normal density evaluated at d_1, and $N(d_2)$ is the cumulative normal density evaluated at d_2. Moreover,

$$d_1 = \frac{\ln\left(\frac{S}{K}\right) + \left(r - \delta + \frac{\sigma^2}{2}\right)(T - t)}{\sigma\sqrt{T - t}}$$

and

$$d_2 = d_1 - \sigma\sqrt{T - t}.$$

Now let us consider an example in which the underlying asset pays dividends.

Example 7-10

Consider a stock with a price $P = 102$. A call option on this stock is available at a strike price of 101 with a maturity of six months. The financing rate is 5% and the volatility of the bond returns is estimated at 25%. Assume that the dividend yield of the stock is 4%. Determine the value of the call option.

Note that $T - t = 0.5$ years. We can compute

$$d_1 = \frac{\ln\left(\frac{102}{101}\right) + \left[0.05 - 0.04 + \frac{0.25^2}{2}\right](0.5)}{0.25\sqrt{0.5}} = 0.172406$$

and

$$d_2 = d_1 - \sigma\sqrt{T - t} = 0.172406 - 0.25\sqrt{0.5} = -0.00437.$$

From the normal distribution tables, we note that $N(0.172406) = 0.568441$ and $N(-0.00437) = 0.498256$. Then the call value is

$$c = 102e^{-0.04\times0.5} \times 0.568441 - 101e^{-0.05\times0.5} \times 0.498256 = 7.751475.$$

In a similar way, options on futures can be valued by using the formula

$$c = He^{-r(T-t)}N(d_1) - Ke^{-r(T-t)}N(d_2).$$

where $N(d_1)$ is the cumulative normal density evaluated at d_1 and $N(d_2)$ is the cumulative normal density evaluated at d_2. Moreover,

$$d_1 = \frac{\ln\left(\frac{H}{K}\right) + \frac{\sigma^2}{2}(T - t)}{\sigma\sqrt{T - t}}$$

and

$$d_2 = d_1 - \sigma\sqrt{T - t}.$$

Note that the Black-Scholes model is valid generally only for European options. Binomial model is valid for both European and American options.

Accuracy of Binomial Model. Let us examine how accurate the binomial options-pricing model is with respect to the parameter n. Note that when $n = 1$ at option's maturity, there are two possible outcomes for the underlying asset: uP and dP. When $n = 2$, there are three outcomes: u^2P, P, and d^2P. (Remember that $udP = P$.)

The values of the binomial model, theoretically, should converge to the Black and Scholes value as n approaches ∞. In Figure 7-12, we show the binomial values for $n = 10, 11, \cdots, 100$. The Black and Scholes value is also shown for reference.

Note that the binomial model provides a very good approximation of the Black and Scholes value for European options even with $n = 50$ or less. The pattern of the error also suggests that there may be efficient computational algorithms for implementing the binomial options-pricing model. Tables 17a and 7-17b provide illustrations of the Black and Scholes values and the binomial values for a set of options.

FIGURE 7-12   *Binomial Approximation to the Black and Scholes Value*

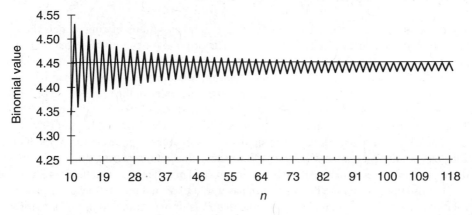

TABLE 7-17a   *Binomial Approximation of European Option Values*

Volatility		n = 10 Maturity (days)			n = 50 Maturity (days)			n = 100 Maturity (days)		
		30	60	90	30	60	90	30	60	90
0.20	95	5.90	6.76	7.68	5.88	6.83	7.66	5.88	6.82	7.67
	100	2.43	3.56	4.47	2.48	3.62	4.54	2.48	3.63	4.55
	105	0.75	1.57	2.46	0.72	1.62	2.44	0.73	1.62	2.44
0.25	95	6.24	7.48	8.56	6.27	7.46	8.50	6.26	7.47	8.47
	100	2.99	**4.34**	5.42	3.04	**4.42**	5.52	3.05	**4.43**	5.53
	105	1.15	2.41	3.49	1.20	2.39	3.41	1.19	2.38	3.38
0.30	95	6.65	8.22	9.46	6.69	8.16	9.34	6.69	8.13	9.34
	100	3.54	5.12	6.37	3.61	5.22	6.49	3.62	5.23	6.50
	105	1.66	3.24	4.50	1.67	3.17	4.36	1.68	3.13	4.37

TABLE 7.17b
Black and Scholes Option Values

Volatility	Price	Maturity (days)		
		30	60	90
0.20	95	5.88	6.84	7.68
	100	2.49	3.65	4.58
	105	0.73	1.64	2.45
0.25	95	6.27	7.47	8.49
	100	3.06	**4.45**	5.56
	105	1.19	2.38	3.40
0.30	95	6.70	8.15	9.35
	100	3.63	5.25	6.53
	105	1.69	3.15	4.37

MONTE CARLO SIMULATION

The derivation of the binomial and the Black and Scholes options-pricing models illuminates an important feature of options pricing: The original probability distribution is not the relevant one. We can exchange the original probability measure with a risk-neutral probability measure. Then, using the risk-neutral probability measure, we can take the expected value of the option and discount this expected value at the riskless rate of interest. This insight was originally formulated by Cox and Ross (1976), and later formally developed into the broader implication of no arbitrage by Harrison and Kreps (1978).

This allows us to use Monte Carlo simulation techniques to price certain types of options and contingent claims. Consider a European call option maturing on date T with a strike price of K. Let us denote the current time by 0. Thus the time to maturity is T years.

Let us suppose that the bond price P_t has a true expected return (mean) of μ and a volatility of σ^2. Furthermore, let us assume that P_t is drawn from a lognormal distribution. These assumptions are consistent with the ones employed in the binomial and the Black and Scholes models.

The life of the option $[0, T]$ is first divided into N steps as $\{0 \equiv t_0 < t_1 < \cdots < t_N \equiv T\}$. This means that $t_i - t_{i-1} \equiv \Delta t \equiv \frac{T}{N}$. In mathematical terms, the bond price at P_T at date T is given by

$$\ln P_T = \ln P_0 + \sum_{i=1}^{N}\left[\left(\mu - \frac{1}{2}\sigma^2\right)\Delta t + \sigma\sqrt{\Delta t}\tilde{z}\right] \tag{7.27}$$

In Equation (7.27) $\tilde{z}$ is a standard normal variable. Under the risk-neutral probability principle, we can change the probability measure and write the relevant pricing distribution as

$$\ln P_T = \ln P_0 + \sum_{i=1}^{N}\left[\left(r - \frac{1}{2}\sigma^2\right)\Delta t + \sigma\sqrt{\Delta t}\tilde{z}\right] \tag{7.28}$$

Note that Equation (7.27) differs from Equation (7.28); since we have replaced the expected return μ by the riskless rate r. Using a random number generator, we can now generate independent paths as follows. First, we generate N draws to determine P_T for path 1 from Equation (7.28). Note that this is done by generating N draws of $\tilde{z}$ (one for each time interval), which is a standard normal variable. We can write Equation (7.28) as

$$P_T = P_0 \times e^{\sum_{i=1}^{N}[(r - \frac{1}{2}\sigma^2)\Delta t + \sigma\sqrt{\Delta t}\tilde{z}]}$$

Next, we repeat this procedure to generate M paths. For each path we determine P_T. Then, we perform the calculations as shown in Table 7-18. The value of the option is

$$c = \frac{c^1 + c^2 + \cdots + c^M}{M}. \tag{7.29}$$

We illustrate this concept in Example 7-11.

Example 7-11

Consider a bond with a price $P = 102$. A call option on this bond is available at a strike price of 101 with a maturity of one month. The financing rate is 5% and the

Path Number	Terminal Bond Price	Option Value at Maturity
1	P_T^1	$c^1 = \max\left(0, P_T^1 - K\right) \times (1+r)^{-T}$
2	P_T^2	$c^2 = \max\left(0, P_T^2 - K\right) \times (1+r)^{-T}$
...	...	...
...	...	...
...	...	...
M	P_T^M	$c^M = \max\left(0, P_T^M - K\right) \times (1+r)^{-T}$

TABLE 7-18
Pricing Options by Simulation

volatility of the bond returns is estimated at 25%. Determine the value of the call option.

Any bond price path can be generated as

$$\ln P_T = \ln P_0 + \sum_{i=1}^{N}\left[\left(r - \tfrac{1}{2}\sigma^2\right)\Delta t + \sigma\sqrt{\Delta t}\tilde{z}\right]$$

Let us take the life of the option (1/12 years) and subdivide it into $N = 100$ intervals. Then, the formula for the price path becomes

$$\ln P_T = \ln 102 + \sum_{i=1}^{100}\left[\left(0.05 - \tfrac{1}{2}0.25^2\right)\Delta t + 0.25\sqrt{\Delta t}\tilde{z}\right].$$

Remember that $t_i - t_{i-1} \equiv \Delta t \equiv \frac{1/12}{100}$. We will generate many such paths. For each of those paths we will identify the payoffs of options. They will then be discounted back and averaged.

In Table 7-19a and 7-19b, we show several sample paths: along path 1 in Table 7-19a all realizations of $\tilde{z}$ are shown. The terminal bond price is 96.66 in path 1 as shown in Table 7-19b and therefore the option is out-of-the-money. Along path 3, the terminal stock price is 111.53 and the option is in-the-money and has a value of 10.53 at maturity. We take the discounted value of the option for each path and average them to get an option value of 4.06.

In the procedure presented here we have the value of the underlying asset at maturity for each path. This can be used to determine the value of option at maturity for each path. Using this information, we can construct a histogram or a frequency distribution of option values at maturity as shown in Figure 7-13. Note that in more than 50% of the paths the option ends up out-of-the-money at maturity. But in a few paths, the option ends up deep in-the-money at maturity. The average of the option values across all paths leads to a value of 4.06.

TABLE 7-19a   *Simulated Standard Normal Variable ($\bar{z}$)*

	Path 1	Path 2	Path 3	Path 4	Path 5	Path 6	Path 7	Path 8	Path 9	Path 10
$z1$	1.59	1.50	-0.19	-0.44	0.63	1.14	0.56	2.08	0.39	-0.85
$z2$	0.33	-1.48	0.07	-0.91	0.13	0.59	-2.16	-0.59	1.41	0.27
$z3$	0.15	-0.67	0.16	1.00	0.81	0.78	-1.05	1.63	0.34	0.07
$z4$	0.13	-1.07	0.47	1.17	-0.91	-1.35	1.17	0.31	0.21	-2.23
$z5$	-0.01	-0.74	-0.06	1.21	-0.48	-0.73	0.78	2.91	1.54	-0.54
$z6$	1.06	-0.14	0.52	-0.10	-0.39	-0.19	0.60	-0.03	1.31	1.27
$z7$	-0.10	1.19	0.63	1.27	0.05	-2.14	1.28	-0.65	-0.62	-1.05
$z8$	1.38	0.73	-0.32	-1.94	-0.48	-0.92	-0.17	0.06	-1.32	-0.82
$z9$	-0.40	-0.59	1.19	-1.60	0.03	1.14	-1.36	0.15	-0.43	-0.41
$z10$	0.88	-0.11	1.89	1.15	1.35	0.75	-1.22	-0.52	0.46	0.10
...	-1.05	0.86	0.26	0.54	-1.93	-0.49	0.65	1.50	-0.31	-1.10
...	0.07	0.64	-0.70	-0.05	0.10	-0.04	-0.21	-0.26	-0.37	0.32
...	-0.01	0.19	0.12	1.37	0.68	0.19	-0.82	-0.80	-0.37	-0.51
...	0.90	-0.93	-1.71	0.28	1.07	-0.08	0.00	0.07	-0.09	1.23
...	0.92	1.55	0.80	-1.05	-0.48	0.53	0.01	0.77	0.54	0.81
...	0.42	-0.66	0.27	0.14	-1.56	1.29	0.13	1.23	-1.39	-0.97
...	-1.13	-1.13	1.11	-1.55	1.23	0.72	0.65	-0.19	0.71	-0.09
...	-0.28	-1.38	-0.27	0.04	0.77	-0.64	-2.09	0.14	0.67	0.07
...	-0.21	-1.91	-0.03	-0.15	-0.26	-0.92	-1.29	-0.43	0.80	-1.92
...	-0.35	-0.73	0.32	-1.59	0.33	0.54	-0.23	-1.69	0.88	-0.67
...	0.54	-1.48	1.04	-0.72	-0.33	-0.97	-0.11	-0.81	0.38	-1.85
...	-0.33	0.48	-0.26	0.67	-0.34	0.26	0.62	2.18	-0.26	1.18
...	0.56	-0.68	0.18	0.68	-0.21	-0.42	0.39	0.00	-1.40	-2.06
...	0.14	1.47	-0.19	1.24	0.44	-0.94	0.17	1.41	-2.04	-0.10
...	-1.21	-0.59	-0.65	1.58	-0.45	-0.25	-0.33	0.71	0.27	0.82
...	-1.68	-1.03	-0.12	-0.29	0.12	-0.65	0.69	-0.71	0.81	1.00
...	-0.07	1.01	0.56	0.98	0.79	2.45	0.33	-0.99	-1.44	0.90
...	-0.97	0.20	-0.78	0.56	-0.29	-0.80	0.58	-0.79	-0.61	-0.99
...	0.74	-2.17	0.58	-1.38	0.58	0.33	1.40	-1.47	0.91	0.59
...	-0.58	1.50	-1.22	-1.59	0.24	1.45	-0.27	-0.85	1.58	-0.24
...	0.17	0.67	0.05	0.37	-0.57	0.85	1.71	0.91	-0.17	1.84
...	-0.62	-2.34	-0.20	0.08	1.31	1.93	0.85	1.27	-0.49	-1.14
...	0.75	0.11	1.05	0.19	-0.13	-0.95	-1.57	0.13	-0.85	0.25
...	0.32	-0.28	-0.83	0.14	-0.63	1.15	-0.68	0.93	0.32	-0.59
...	-1.36	-0.82	0.41	1.83	-0.77	1.27	-1.04	-0.81	-1.25	-1.03
...	-0.89	-0.62	0.84	-0.41	-0.28	-0.02	-1.16	0.94	-0.77	-0.98
...	-3.32	0.67	-0.26	2.04	-0.01	-1.18	-0.27	0.42	0.04	0.40
...	-0.09	-0.22	1.70	-0.03	1.37	0.15	-0.36	0.78	-0.01	0.06
...	-0.05	-0.24	2.08	-1.77	0.07	0.01	-0.15	1.46	-0.10	0.83
...	0.34	-0.68	0.20	0.68	-0.92	-0.51	-0.04	-0.30	0.04	0.64
...	-0.68	0.75	-0.40	-1.17	-1.85	2.20	-0.51	0.11	0.05	-0.93
...	-1.17	-1.57	-1.18	1.15	0.34	-0.68	-0.46	-1.47	-0.76	-0.96
...	0.46	-1.31	0.35	-0.90	1.29	0.18	1.22	-1.59	-0.25	0.56
...	0.97	-0.47	0.18	0.27	1.22	-1.45	-0.51	-1.37	-0.54	0.26
...	-0.38	0.35	-1.75	0.58	0.14	-0.49	-1.41	0.33	-1.55	-1.06
...	2.75	-1.01	-1.30	0.80	-0.36	0.40	-0.21	0.36	0.27	0.99
...	-0.82	-0.78	-0.81	-0.19	1.40	-0.29	0.07	0.80	0.02	0.53
...	0.36	1.50	-0.53	0.28	0.15	-0.81	0.68	-0.76	-0.40	-0.24
...	-0.46	1.06	-0.42	-2.27	-2.32	-0.53	-2.09	-0.59	-0.79	1.05
...	0.49	1.65	-1.48	1.92	-2.24	0.14	0.58	-2.02	0.56	-0.31

TABLE 7-19a *Continued*

	Path 1	Path 2	Path 3	Path 4	Path 5	Path 6	Path 7	Path 9	Path 9	Path 10
...	-0.45	0.07	1.01	-1.17	-0.95	-0.78	-0.07	-1.59	-1.06	-0.82
...	0.45	-0.59	-1.15	1.75	0.76	0.02	1.05	-0.06	-0.57	-0.41
...	-0.13	-1.43	0.53	-0.31	1.35	-0.18	0.21	-0.26	-0.21	0.08
...	-1.23	0.57	-1.21	-0.07	0.29	-0.24	-0.67	1.66	2.14	-0.06
...	-1.04	-0.78	-0.35	0.20	-0.30	1.40	-1.58	-1.04	0.23	1.33
...	-0.16	1.16	-0.31	1.70	0.77	0.69	0.36	0.11	0.45	0.70
...	-0.15	0.52	-0.41	1.90	-0.07	-1.35	0.02	-1.46	0.20	2.15
...	0.33	-0.28	-0.43	-0.65	-0.21	2.40	-1.40	2.79	-0.31	-0.54
...	0.73	0.13	-0.27	0.51	0.09	0.19	1.60	-0.39	-0.95	-0.31
...	-0.17	-0.74	-0.07	0.35	0.28	-0.31	-0.64	0.72	-1.07	0.79
...	0.14	-0.01	-0.41	-0.45	0.61	-0.81	1.41	-0.92	-0.80	-0.86
...	-0.88	-0.90	2.25	1.02	-1.93	-1.92	-0.10	-0.92	-0.03	-1.31
...	-0.33	-0.08	0.01	0.15	-3.52	-1.25	-0.62	0.10	-0.33	0.45
...	-0.48	-0.18	-1.83	-0.25	-0.78	-1.70	-1.26	0.68	0.07	1.82
...	0.55	-0.68	0.76	-3.40	0.43	1.11	-0.03	-1.98	0.16	1.79
...	-0.21	-0.74	0.26	1.46	0.06	0.83	1.68	0.25	0.43	1.04
...	-0.28	-0.71	-0.50	-1.28	0.40	1.34	0.66	1.03	1.92	2.77
...	2.30	0.79	-1.96	0.37	0.26	-0.51	1.47	-2.81	1.95	1.12
...	0.28	-0.36	0.97	-0.85	-0.42	1.48	0.03	1.75	0.60	0.08
...	0.76	-0.91	-1.24	2.41	0.24	0.73	0.12	-1.50	-1.06	1.21
...	0.23	-1.55	0.27	0.52	-2.25	-0.05	0.87	-0.62	-0.96	-0.56
...	0.65	-0.09	1.15	-0.36	1.38	-0.82	2.41	0.09	-1.35	0.60
...	1.18	-0.05	1.73	-0.30	2.57	0.45	-1.39	-2.20	0.77	-0.81
...	0.44	1.07	1.76	1.67	0.40	-0.74	0.82	0.57	-0.96	0.00
...	-0.71	0.53	0.01	0.90	-0.40	-1.94	0.59	-0.63	0.52	1.13
...	-0.31	-1.34	0.25	0.78	0.30	1.49	-0.97	0.04	-1.74	-1.60
...	-0.87	-1.03	1.68	1.38	-0.79	-0.25	-0.91	0.03	1.27	2.27
...	0.19	1.06	-0.62	0.75	1.96	1.33	1.42	0.35	-1.16	0.19
...	-0.89	-1.18	0.11	0.30	0.89	-1.24	0.60	-0.19	1.77	-1.49
...	-0.45	-0.27	1.46	-2.38	0.17	-0.23	-1.51	1.12	0.53	-0.61
...	-0.32	-0.24	-1.17	0.46	-2.15	-1.38	0.93	0.53	-0.02	-0.93
...	-0.98	-0.88	1.35	-1.35	0.84	0.23	1.83	0.02	0.37	-0.75
...	-1.99	-1.39	0.91	0.25	0.20	-0.67	-1.10	-1.47	-1.02	0.97
...	0.80	0.91	-0.19	0.31	-0.92	1.56	-0.91	1.38	0.71	-0.42
...	0.13	-0.25	-0.30	0.49	2.61	1.81	-0.98	-0.29	-0.46	-1.93
...	-0.16	1.25	0.44	0.98	-0.05	0.71	1.26	-0.84	0.70	-0.23
...	-0.89	0.84	-1.26	-0.79	1.67	0.22	-0.03	1.20	-0.30	-0.34
...	0.99	-1.01	0.30	-0.48	0.06	1.00	2.37	2.92	1.07	-0.36
...	-0.65	-1.60	-0.26	0.63	-0.14	-0.83	0.37	0.09	0.32	-0.39
z90	0.97	0.45	-0.37	1.14	0.24	-0.81	0.63	-0.20	-2.96	0.13
z91	-1.29	0.12	2.15	-0.01	-0.03	-0.12	0.38	0.08	0.83	0.67
z92	0.18	-0.94	-1.15	0.06	-0.07	-1.73	-1.30	-1.31	0.54	-0.70
z93	0.20	0.41	0.54	3.02	-0.06	-0.03	-1.29	1.39	-0.68	-1.05
z94	-0.32	0.02	1.44	0.27	-1.40	0.44	0.50	-0.42	0.10	-0.93
z95	-0.58	-0.56	1.94	0.45	-1.09	-1.70	1.66	-0.53	0.58	0.16
z96	-0.82	-0.74	0.77	-1.86	0.83	0.62	-0.41	-0.10	-0.79	-0.56
z97	-0.64	0.01	0.96	0.46	-1.03	0.43	1.22	0.62	0.70	-0.71
z98	0.74	-0.55	0.28	0.31	-0.40	-0.15	-0.60	-0.88	-0.50	0.07
z99	-0.04	-0.52	0.37	0.92	-0.37	-2.04	-0.46	0.52	0.67	0.05
z100	-0.74	1.28	0.66	0.31	-0.45	1.96	1.54	-0.75	0.29	0.96

TABLE 7-19b *Simulated Bond Prices and Option Values*

	1	2	3	4	5	6	7	8	9	10
P0	102	102	102	102	102	102	102	102	102	102
P1	103.17	103.10	101.86	101.68	102.46	102.84	102.41	103.53	102.28	101.38
P2	103.41	102.02	101.91	101.02	102.56	103.27	100.84	103.10	103.32	101.58
P3	103.53	101.53	102.03	101.75	103.16	103.85	100.09	104.31	103.57	101.63
P4	103.63	100.76	102.37	102.61	102.49	102.86	100.94	104.55	103.73	100.02
P5	103.63	100.23	102.32	103.50	102.14	102.32	101.50	106.75	104.88	99.63
P6	104.42	100.13	102.71	103.43	101.85	102.18	101.94	106.73	105.87	100.55
P7	104.35	100.98	103.17	104.37	101.89	100.63	102.88	106.23	105.40	99.79
P8	105.39	101.51	102.93	102.93	101.54	99.97	102.75	106.28	104.41	99.21
P9	105.09	101.08	103.82	101.76	101.57	100.79	101.75	106.40	104.09	98.92
P10	105.75	101.00	105.23	102.61	102.55	101.34	100.87	106.01	104.43	99.00
...	104.96	101.63	105.43	103.00	101.14	100.99	101.34	107.15	104.20	98.22
...	105.02	102.10	104.90	102.97	101.22	100.96	101.19	106.95	103.92	98.45
...	105.01	102.24	104.99	103.98	101.71	101.10	100.60	106.34	103.65	98.10
...	105.69	101.56	103.71	104.19	102.49	101.04	100.60	106.40	103.59	98.97
...	106.39	102.70	104.31	103.41	102.14	101.43	100.61	106.99	103.99	99.55
...	106.72	102.22	104.51	103.52	101.01	102.37	100.70	107.94	102.96	98.86
...	105.86	101.39	105.35	102.38	101.90	102.90	101.18	107.79	103.48	98.80
...	105.64	100.39	105.15	102.41	102.47	102.43	99.67	107.90	103.98	98.85
...	105.48	99.03	105.13	102.29	102.28	101.76	98.76	107.57	104.58	97.50
...	105.22	98.51	105.37	101.14	102.53	102.16	98.60	106.28	105.24	97.03
...	105.63	97.47	106.16	100.62	102.29	101.46	98.52	105.67	105.53	95.76
...	105.38	97.81	105.96	101.10	102.04	101.65	98.96	107.33	105.34	96.57
...	105.80	97.34	106.10	101.60	101.89	101.35	99.24	107.33	104.29	95.16
...	105.91	98.37	105.96	102.50	102.22	100.67	99.36	108.42	102.77	95.09
...	104.99	97.96	105.47	103.67	101.89	100.49	99.12	108.98	102.97	95.66
...	103.74	97.24	105.38	103.46	101.98	100.03	99.62	108.43	103.57	96.35
...	103.69	97.95	105.80	104.19	102.56	101.80	99.85	107.66	102.51	96.98
...	102.98	98.09	105.21	104.61	102.35	101.22	100.27	107.06	102.07	96.29
...	103.53	96.58	105.65	103.59	102.78	101.46	101.28	105.93	102.74	96.70
...	103.10	97.63	104.73	102.41	102.96	102.52	101.08	105.29	103.91	96.53
...	103.22	98.10	104.77	102.69	102.54	103.15	102.33	105.98	103.78	97.82
...	102.77	96.46	104.62	102.74	103.51	104.59	102.95	106.95	103.42	97.02
...	103.32	96.54	105.41	102.89	103.41	103.88	101.80	107.05	102.80	97.20
...	103.56	96.35	104.79	102.99	102.95	104.73	101.30	107.76	103.03	96.79
...	102.56	95.78	105.10	104.35	102.39	105.70	100.56	107.14	102.11	96.08
...	101.90	95.36	105.74	104.05	102.19	105.68	99.73	107.87	101.55	95.41
...	99.51	95.82	105.55	105.58	102.18	104.80	99.53	108.20	101.58	95.69
...	99.45	95.67	106.84	105.56	103.19	104.91	99.28	108.81	101.58	95.73
...	99.42	95.51	108.45	104.24	103.25	104.92	99.17	109.95	101.50	96.30
...	99.66	95.05	108.61	104.74	102.57	104.54	99.14	109.72	101.53	96.75
...	99.18	95.57	108.30	103.87	101.22	106.20	98.79	109.80	101.57	96.11
...	98.35	94.50	107.39	104.73	101.47	105.69	98.46	108.65	101.02	95.45
...	98.68	93.62	107.66	104.06	102.41	105.83	99.33	107.42	100.84	95.83
...	99.37	93.30	107.80	104.26	103.31	104.74	98.97	106.37	100.45	96.01
...	99.10	93.54	106.46	104.69	103.42	104.37	97.97	106.63	99.34	95.29
...	101.08	92.86	105.48	105.30	103.15	104.68	97.82	106.90	99.54	95.96
...	100.49	92.35	104.87	105.15	104.19	104.46	97.87	107.52	99.55	96.33
...	100.75	93.35	104.47	105.37	104.31	103.86	98.35	106.94	99.27	96.17
...	100.42	94.06	104.16	103.67	102.59	103.47	96.89	106.49	98.71	96.89
...	100.77	95.18	103.06	105.11	100.96	103.58	97.30	104.96	99.11	96.67

TABLE 7-19b   *Continued*

	1	2	3	4	5	6	7	8	9	10
...	100.45	95.23	103.81	104.23	100.28	103.00	97.25	103.77	98.36	96.11
...	100.78	94.83	102.96	105.55	100.82	103.01	97.99	103.72	97.96	95.83
...	100.68	93.87	103.35	105.32	101.81	102.88	98.14	103.54	97.82	95.88
...	99.80	94.25	102.46	105.27	102.02	102.71	97.67	104.78	99.33	95.84
...	99.06	93.73	102.21	105.42	101.80	103.74	96.57	104.00	99.49	96.77
...	98.95	94.52	101.98	106.72	102.37	104.26	96.83	104.08	99.81	97.25
...	98.84	94.87	101.69	108.18	102.32	103.26	96.84	103.00	99.96	98.76
...	99.08	94.68	101.38	107.68	102.17	105.06	95.87	105.09	99.74	98.39
...	99.60	94.77	101.19	108.08	102.24	105.20	96.98	104.79	99.06	98.17
...	99.48	94.27	101.14	108.35	102.45	104.97	96.53	105.34	98.31	98.73
...	99.58	94.26	100.85	108.00	102.90	104.36	97.52	104.65	97.75	98.12
...	98.96	93.66	102.49	108.79	101.49	102.94	97.45	103.97	97.73	97.21
...	98.73	93.61	102.50	108.91	98.96	102.02	97.02	104.04	97.50	97.52
...	98.39	93.49	101.16	108.72	98.41	100.79	96.15	104.55	97.55	98.81
...	98.78	93.04	101.71	106.10	98.72	101.59	96.13	103.08	97.66	100.08
...	98.63	92.54	101.90	107.22	98.76	102.20	97.29	103.27	97.96	100.83
...	98.43	92.08	101.53	106.24	99.05	103.19	97.76	104.04	99.32	102.86
...	100.07	92.60	100.12	106.53	99.23	102.81	98.79	101.97	100.72	103.69
...	100.27	92.36	100.82	105.88	98.93	103.91	98.82	103.26	101.16	103.75
...	100.82	91.76	99.93	107.72	99.10	104.46	98.90	102.15	100.39	104.66
...	100.99	90.75	100.12	108.13	97.52	104.42	99.52	101.70	99.71	104.25
...	101.47	90.69	100.96	107.85	98.49	103.81	101.25	101.77	98.75	104.70
...	102.33	90.66	102.22	107.62	100.32	104.15	100.25	100.18	99.29	104.10
...	102.66	91.36	103.52	108.92	100.61	103.60	100.85	100.59	98.62	104.10
...	102.14	91.71	103.53	109.62	100.33	102.17	101.28	100.13	98.99	104.95
...	101.91	90.83	103.72	110.24	100.54	103.27	100.57	100.16	97.76	103.75
...	101.28	90.17	104.98	111.33	99.97	103.09	99.92	100.19	98.66	105.45
...	101.42	90.86	104.52	111.93	101.39	104.08	100.94	100.44	97.84	105.59
...	100.77	90.10	104.61	112.18	102.03	103.16	101.38	100.31	99.09	104.47
...	100.45	89.92	105.71	110.28	102.16	102.99	100.29	101.12	99.47	104.02
...	100.23	89.77	104.83	110.65	100.60	101.98	100.96	101.50	99.45	103.34
...	99.53	89.20	105.85	109.59	101.21	102.15	102.29	101.52	99.72	102.78
...	98.11	88.32	106.54	109.79	101.36	101.67	101.50	100.45	98.99	103.50
...	98.68	88.89	106.40	110.04	100.69	102.82	100.84	101.45	99.50	103.19
...	98.77	88.74	106.17	110.43	102.59	104.16	100.13	101.25	99.17	101.77
...	98.66	89.54	106.51	111.20	102.56	104.70	101.04	100.64	99.67	101.60
...	98.03	90.08	105.56	110.58	103.79	104.86	101.02	101.50	99.46	101.36
...	98.74	89.43	105.78	110.21	103.84	105.62	102.75	103.65	100.23	101.10
...	98.28	88.41	105.59	110.70	103.74	104.99	103.03	103.72	100.46	100.82
P90	98.97	88.70	105.32	111.62	103.92	104.39	103.49	103.57	98.36	100.92
P91	98.06	88.78	106.96	111.61	103.90	104.30	103.77	103.64	98.95	101.41
P92	98.19	88.19	106.08	111.66	103.85	103.02	102.81	102.67	99.34	100.90
P93	98.33	88.45	106.50	114.10	103.81	102.99	101.87	103.70	98.85	100.15
P94	98.11	88.46	107.61	114.32	102.77	103.32	102.23	103.39	98.93	99.49
P95	97.70	88.11	109.12	114.70	101.98	102.07	103.46	103.00	99.34	99.61
P96	97.13	87.65	109.73	113.18	102.59	102.52	103.16	102.93	98.78	99.21
P97	96.69	87.65	110.49	113.56	101.84	102.84	104.06	103.38	99.28	98.71
P98	97.21	87.31	110.71	113.81	101.54	102.72	103.62	102.73	98.92	98.75
P99	97.18	86.99	111.01	114.57	101.28	101.24	103.28	103.11	99.40	98.79
P100	96.66	87.79	111.53	114.82	100.95	102.67	104.43	102.56	99.61	99.47

(Continued)

TABLE 7-19b *Continued*

	1	*2*	*3*	*4*	*5*	*6*	*7*	*8*	*9*	*10*
Min Price	96.66	86.99	99.93	100.62	97.52	99.97	95.87	100.13	97.50	95.09
C = Call Value	0.00	0.00	10.53	13.82	0.00	1.67	3.43	1.56	0.00	0.00
Discounted C	0.00	0.00	10.49	13.77	0.00	1.66	3.41	1.56	0.00	0.00
Average	4.06									
L = Lookback	0.00	0.80	11.60	14.21	3.44	2.70	8.56	2.43	2.10	4.38
Discounted L	0.00	0.80	11.55	14.15	3.42	2.69	8.52	2.42	2.09	4.36
Average	5.71									

FIGURE 7-13 *Histogram of Option Values in 100 Trials*

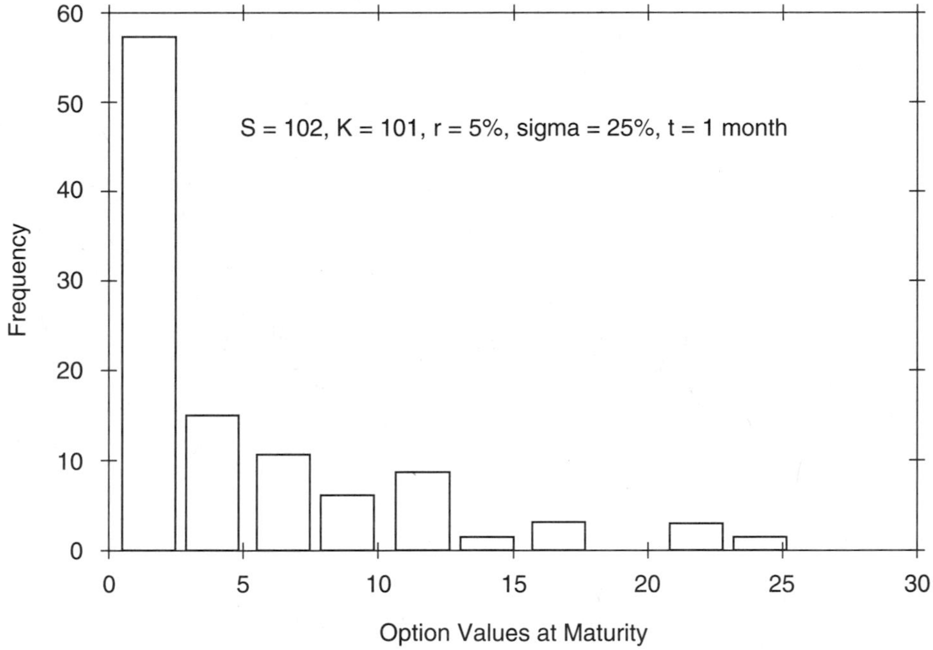

S = 102, K = 101, r = 5%, sigma = 25%, t = 1 month
Frequency
60
50
40
30
20
10
0
0
5
10
15
20
25
30
Option Values at Maturity

Variance-Reduction Procedures

The difficulty with the simulation procedure outlined in the preceding section is that the value we obtain tends to have a large variation from sample to sample. If we are trying to estimate the true value c of the call option through repeated samplings $\{c^1, c^2, \cdots, c^M\}$, then the sample mean of the option value is simply

$$\hat{c} = \frac{c^1 + c^2 + \cdots + c^M}{M} \qquad\qquad (7.30)$$

Note that variance of the estimated call price from the simulation procedure is inversely related to M. Increasing M beyond a certain number becomes computationally unattractive. To avoid this, some variance-reduction procedures are used.

Example 7-12

Using Example 7-11, we create another set of estimates $\{c^{1*}, c^{2*}, \cdots, c^{M*}\}$ by replacing $\bar{z}$ by $-\bar{z}$. This will lead to an option value of 3.54 in Example 7-11. We then take the average of the estimates

$$\bar{c}_i = \frac{c^i + c^{i*}}{2} = \frac{4.06 + 3.54}{2} = 3.80$$

The sample-mean estimate by this averaging rule is

$$\hat{\bar{c}} = \frac{\bar{c}_1 + \bar{c}_2 + \cdots + \bar{c}_M}{M}$$

The variance of this estimate of the call option is less than half of that of the first estimate $\hat{c}$. More sophisticated variance-reduction procedures have been developed in the literature which have not been addressed here. See Boyle (1977) and some of the references cited in that paper.

In Example 7-12, recall that the option value with variance reduction is 3.80. Had we used Black and Scholes model, we would have obtained an option price of 3.68. We are off by 12 pennies. By using more paths we can reduce the error even further. This is shown next. To illustrate how the simulation results behave as we increase the number of paths, we present Table 7-20. Throughout we have subdivided the life of the option into 100 intervals.

As we can see, the accuracy improves significantly at first and then tapers off quickly.

Table 7-19a also provides the value of the normal random variable in *each path* along *all* sub-intervals besides the maturity date. If our objective is just to value ordinary

Number of Paths	Option Value
100	3.800
200	3.782
500	3.687
1,000	3.708
10,000	3.664

TABLE 7-20
Ordinary Call Option on Bond

calls and puts, we do not need all this information. In fact there is no need to generate such information for valuing ordinary options. It is more efficient just to work with simulated prices just at maturity for each path.

Suppose, however, we are interested in valuing exotic options such as look-back options or Asean options. These are described in Chapter 12 in detail. A look-back option provides at maturity

$$\max\left[P_T - \min_i \{P_i\}, 0\right]$$

where $\min_i \{P_i\}$ is the minimum of the underlying asset price during the life of the option. In Table 7-19a note that for each path we can explicitly compute $\min_i \{P_i\}$. For example, in path 1 $\min_i \{P_i\} = 96.66$. Hence the payoff of the look-back option in path 1 is $P_T - \min_i \{P_i\} = 96.66 - 96.66 = 0$. For path 3, $P_T - \min_i \{P_i\} = 111.53 - 99.93 = 11.60$. Averaging across all paths and discounting we get the value of the look-back to be 5.71. We provide the results for look-back options for various simulation runs in Table 7-21 (after variance reduction).

Number of Paths	Option Value	TABLE 7-21
100	5.278	*Lookback Call Option*
200	5.727	*on Bond*
500	5.462	
1,000	5.347	
10,000	5.517	

Monte Carlo procedures are quite powerful in many applications; we will see later in Chapters 8 and 9 that a number of problems in corporate bonds and mortgage-backed securities can be solved using Monte Carlo simulation techniques. We now turn to the valuation of some interest rate derivatives.

Interest-Rate Derivatives

Interest-rate derivatives range from a simple call option on yields to a complicated structure involving yield-curve swaps in which yields with different maturities are swapped between counterparties. Other interest-rate derivatives include index-amortization swaps, caps, floors, and delivery options in Treasury bond futures contracts. We will illustrate the interest-rate derivatives pricing with an example of a call option on yields, and using the LEH that was developed in Chapter 6.

Consider the task of pricing a call option at date $t = 0$ on a two-period interest rate at a strike rate of $k\%$. Assume that the option is going to expire at date $t = 1$. Assume that the interest rate follows a multiplicative random walk as shown below. The probability of an up move is q and the probability of a down move is $1 - q$.

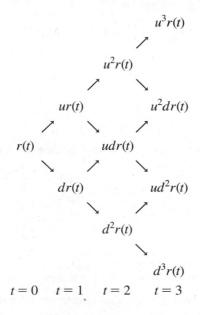

$$u^3r(t)$$
$$u^2r(t)$$
$$ur(t) \qquad u^2dr(t)$$
$$r(t) \qquad udr(t)$$
$$dr(t) \qquad ud^2r(t)$$
$$d^2r(t)$$
$$d^3r(t)$$

$t = 0 \quad t = 1 \quad t = 2 \quad t = 3$

At each node, we can compute the prices of a discount bond which matures at date $t = 3$. The price distribution is shown in the price tree below.

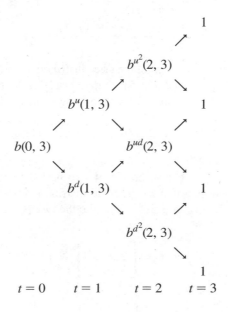

$$1$$
$$b^{u^2}(2, 3)$$
$$b^u(1, 3) \qquad 1$$
$$b(0, 3) \qquad b^{ud}(2, 3)$$
$$b^d(1, 3) \qquad 1$$
$$b^{d^2}(2, 3)$$
$$1$$

$t = 0 \qquad t = 1 \qquad t = 2 \qquad t = 3$

The price distribution (and hence the yield distribution) is obtained by applying the LEH recursively by beginning at $t = 3$, which is the maturity date of the bond, and working backwards. The pricing equations are:

$$\frac{1}{b^{u^2}(2,\ 3)} = 1 + u^2 r(t)$$

$$\frac{1}{b^{ud}(2,\ 3)} = 1 + udr(t)$$

and

$$\frac{1}{b^{d^2}(2,\ 3)} = 1 + d^2 r(t).$$

As a consequence, we can rearrange these three equations to get the bond-price distributions:

$$b^{u^2}(2,\ 3) = \frac{1}{1 + u^2 r(t)}$$

$$b^{ud}(2,\ 3) = \frac{1}{1 + udr(t)}$$

and

$$b^{dd}(2,\ 3) = \frac{1}{1 + d^2 r(t)}.$$

Having obtained the price distributions at date $t = 2$ for the one-period bonds, we step back to date $t = 1$ and obtain the following pricing relationship by using the LEH.

$$\frac{q \times b^{u^2}(2,\ 3) + (1 - q) \times b^{ud}(2,\ 3)}{b^u(1,\ 3)} = 1 + ur(t)$$

$$\frac{q \times b^{ud}(2,\ 3) + (1 - q) \times b^{d^2}(2,\ 3)}{b^d(1,\ 3)} = 1 + dr(t)$$

Solving the two equations above, we get the price distributions $b^u(1,\ 3)$ and $b^d(1,\ 3)$.

Having obtained the price distributions at date $t = 1$ for the two-period bonds, we step back to date $t = 0$ and obtain the following pricing relationship by using the LEH:

$$\frac{q \times b^u(1,\ 3) + (1 - q) \times b^d(1,\ 3)}{b(0,\ 3)} = 1 + r(t).$$

This enables us to solve for $b(0,\ 3)$.

Corresponding to the price distribution of two-period bond prices $b^u(1,\ 3)$ and $b^d(1,\ 3)$ at date $t = 1$ there is a two-period yield distribution. Let $y^u(1,\ 3)$ be the two-period yield at $t = 1$ in the up state and $y^d(1,\ 3)$ be the two-period yield at $t = 1$ in the down state. Note that

$$y^u(1,\ 3) = \left[\frac{1}{b^u(1,\ 3)} \right]^{\frac{1}{2}} - 1$$

and

$$y^d(1,\ 3) = \left[\frac{1}{b^d(1,\ 3)} \right]^{\frac{1}{2}} - 1.$$

In a similar way, we can start with a discount bond which matures at date $t = 2$ and solve for its price $b(0, 2)$ at date $t = 0$ and its price distribution at $t = 1$. At date $t = 0$, the two-period yield $y(0, 2)$ is given by

$$y(0, 2) = \left[\frac{1}{b(0, 2)}\right]^{\frac{1}{2}} - 1.$$

Having obtained the two-period yields, we can set up the two-period yield distribution as shown in the next tree.

$$
\begin{array}{ccc}
 & & y^u(1, 3) \\
 & \nearrow & \\
y(0, 2) & & \\
 & \searrow & \\
 & & y^d(1, 3) \\
t = 0 & & t = 1
\end{array}
$$

The payoffs of the call option at date $t = 1$ are:

$$
\begin{array}{ccc}
 & & C^u = \max\,[0,\, y^u(1, 3) - k] \\
 & \nearrow & \\
C & & \\
 & \searrow & \\
 & & C^d = \max\,[0,\, y^d(1, 3) - k] \\
t = 0 & & t = 1
\end{array}
$$

By the LEH, the value of call is

$$C = \max\left[y(0, 2) - k,\, \frac{qC^u + (1 - q)C^d}{1 + y(0, 1)} \right].$$

Example 7-13

Consider an interest-rate process in which the initial interest rate is 5%, $u = 1.06$, $d = \frac{1}{1.06}$ and $q = 0.5$. Assume that the strike rate on this yield option is 5%. The option is on two-period yields. The option expires at $t = 1$.

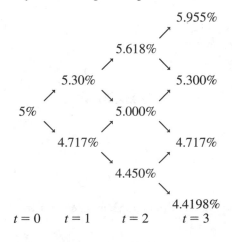

$$
\begin{array}{ccccccc}
 & & & & & & 5.955\% \\
 & & & & & \nearrow & \\
 & & & & 5.618\% & & \\
 & & & \nearrow & & \searrow & \\
 & & 5.30\% & & & & 5.300\% \\
 & \nearrow & & \searrow & & \nearrow & \\
5\% & & & & 5.000\% & & \\
 & \searrow & & \nearrow & & \searrow & \\
 & & 4.717\% & & & & 4.717\% \\
 & & & \searrow & & \nearrow & \\
 & & & & 4.450\% & & \\
 & & & & & \searrow & \\
 & & & & & & 4.4198\% \\
t = 0 & & t = 1 & & t = 2 & & t = 3
\end{array}
$$

Corresponding to this one-period interest rate process, we can compute the price of a four-period discount bond at date $t = 0$ maturing on date $t = 4$. Its evolution as it approaches maturity is shown next.

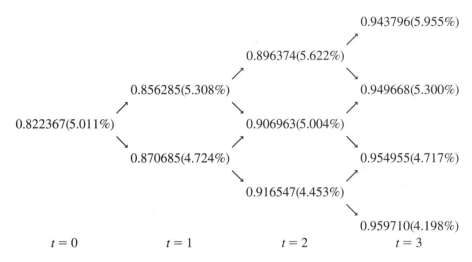

Note that each discount bond price can be converted to a yield, shown in the parentheses. For example, we now know that at date $t = 1$, the three-period yield can either be 5.302% or 4.719% with equal probabilities.

In this way, we can construct the lattice for a three-period bond at date $t = 0$. This leads to the following distribution.

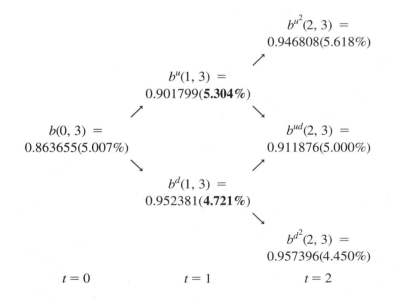

For the two-period discount bond, at date $t = 0$, the distribution is

$$b^u(1, 2) = 0.949668(5.300\%)$$

$$b(0, 2) = 0.906963(5.00\%)$$

$$b^d(1, 2) = 0.954955(4.717\%)$$

$$t = 0 \qquad\qquad\qquad\qquad t = 1$$

The payoffs of the option can now be determined as:

$$c^u = 5.304\% - 5\% = 0.304\%$$

$$c$$

$$c^d = 0.000\% = \max[4.717\% - 5\%, 0]$$

$$t = 0 \qquad\qquad\qquad\qquad t = 1$$

Thus, the value of the option is

$$\frac{0.304 \times 0.5 + 0.000 \times 0.5}{1.05} = 0.1447.$$

The option is worth 14.47 basis points.

We now examine the risk measures used in the options literature.

Option-Price Sensitivity

Delta Risk. As the underlying factors (such as the bond price, exchange rate, futures price, or spot-exchange rate) change, the value of the derivative asset changes as well. This exposure is called the **Delta risk** and is denoted by Δ_i. Using the options-pricing models, we can calculate these option-price sensitivities.

The first variable in the risk management of options is the option delta. It is formally defined as:

$$\Delta_C = \frac{\partial C}{\partial S}$$

$$\Delta_P = \frac{\partial P}{\partial S}.$$

The delta of an option (in a model of options pricing) measures the price change in an option for a small change in the value of the underlying asset (such as the spot rate). Intuitively, we expect the delta of a call to be positive and the delta of a put to be negative. Moreover, we expect the delta to change as the value of the underlying asset changes.

Note that the same derivative asset may have more than one delta. For example, a convertible bond may have a delta with respect to the underlying stock price and another with respect to the overall interest rates. In concrete terms, if the delta of a derivative asset is 0.5, then for a full-point change in the underlying factor, the derivative asset's value will change by one-half point. The behavior of delta as a function of the underlying asset's value is shown in Figure 7-14.

FIGURE 7-14   *Delta of a Call Option on a Futures Contract*

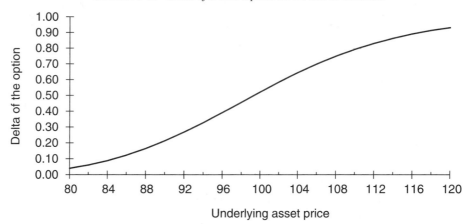

The delta risk is always measured in the context of a specific model. Hence the risk-management system is only as good as the models used to produce such risk measures.

The real-risk management problem in the derivatives area has less to do with the measurement of delta risk than with the fact that the deltas of derivative assets are, as a rule, constantly changing. This calls for a very dynamic and active risk or position management. Often, this is the biggest qualitative difference between other risk-management systems and derivative risk-management systems. In particular, the system requirements of a such a dynamic risk-management program are

- real time data and analytics from more than one market (underlying asset markets and derivative assets market),
- the ability to aggregate risks across different derivatives and report positions, and
- the ability to mark-to-market the book using several pricing models on real-time data.

The delta risk of the overall book in a certain derivative asset class (say, options on the OEX index) can be easily aggregated and reported. This turns out to be important in both risk measurement and management. For example, if Δ_i is the delta of option i (put or call, different strike prices, and different maturities) and the book has x_i such options, then the delta risk of the entire book (denoted by Δ_p) may be written

$$\Delta_p = \sum_{i=1}^{n} x_i \times \Delta_i \qquad (7.31)$$

Once the book's delta is measured by the aggregation scheme above, we find a suitable hedging instrument, such as MMI futures or S&P 500 futures and take an offsetting position so that the delta of the book is exactly offset by the delta of the hedging instrument. Such a policy is known as a **delta-neutral hedge policy.**

Note that some of the Δ_i will be positive and some will be negative, and thus the book is likely to contain some natural hedges. This raises a very important risk-management

question about how frequently each trade should be hedged. At one extreme, we can propose that each trade should be neutrally hedged as soon as the trade is executed. At the
other extreme, we can propose that the trades should be unhedged until the end of the day
and then the portfolio of trades should be hedged once neutrally. The fact of the matter is
that the optimal hedge policy lies between these two extremes and is dependent on the rate
of change of the delta risk. This leads us to the gamma risk measure.

Gamma Risk. The delta risk of derivative securities change as the market conditions in
the underlying factors change. The rate of change of delta is known as the **gamma risk**
of the derivative product. This is denoted by the symbol Γ.
    Formally,

$$\Gamma_C = \frac{\partial \Delta_C}{\partial S}$$

$$\Gamma_P = \frac{\partial \Delta_P}{\partial S}$$

The gamma of an option is the change in the delta of the option for a small change in the
value of the underlying asset.
    The Δs of derivative assets change constantly. The larger the Γ, more dramatic will
be the movements in the Δ of the derivative asset for a given change in the market conditions of the underlying factor. In mathematical terms, Δ is the first derivative of the
derivative asset's price function with respect to the underlying factor and Γ is the second
derivative. Stated differently, Γ is the Δ of the delta function.
    As with the delta risk, some derivative positions will have a positive gamma risk
and others will have a negative gamma risk. Intuitively, if an upward movement in the
underlying factor causes the delta (with respect to that factor) of the derivative asset to
increase and a downward movement causes the delta of the derivative asset to decrease,
then such a position has a positive gamma. On the other hand, if an upward movement
in the underlying factor causes the delta (with respect to that factor) of the derivative
asset to decrease and a downward movement causes the delta of the derivative asset to
increase, then such a position has a negative gamma. The behavior of gamma is shown
in Figure 7-15.
    In a way similar to the aggregation of delta risk, we can aggregate and measure the
overall gamma risk of a book within the same derivative asset class. For example, if Γ_i
is the gamma of option i (put or call, different strike prices, and different maturities) and
the book has x_i such options, then the gamma risk of the entire book (denoted by Γ_p) may
be written

$$\Gamma_p = \sum_{i=1}^{n} x_i \times \Gamma_i \qquad (7.32)$$

    It is worth pointing out that when the book has a positive gamma, the down-side risk
is bounded or limited. The profile of profits typically assumes a U shape, which approaches a V shape as the derivative positions approach maturity. On the other hand, if
the position has a negative gamma, the risk profile is such that the losses are not
bounded. Clearly, summarizing and measuring risk this way enables managers to understand and thus to respond to risks better.

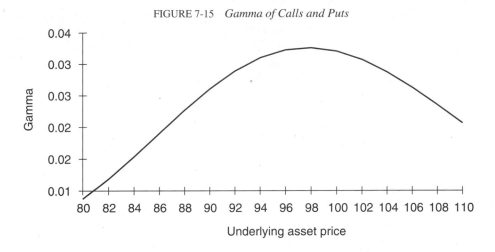

FIGURE 7-15   *Gamma of Calls and Puts*

Once the book's delta and its gamma are measured by the aggregation schemes given above, we find two suitable hedging instruments, such as MMI futures or Standard & Poor 500 futures, and listed options and take an offsetting position so that the delta of the book is exactly offset by the combined delta of the two hedging instruments and the gamma of the book is exactly offset by the combined gamma of the two hedging instruments. Such a policy is known as a **delta-and-gamma-neutral hedge policy.** The trade-offs associated with the frequency of hedging trades apply here as well. But, intuitively, it should be clear that a delta-and-gamma-neutral position is less vulnerable to infrequent hedging than a delta-neutral position.

Typically, all derivative positions have a limited term to maturity. For listed options and futures, it is typically of the order of a few days to a few weeks. For warrants and convertibles, the maturity period typically extends to several years. The book of derivatives typically tends to either appreciate in value or depreciate in value as the time passes even when the underlying factors do not change. This leads us to the next measure of risk.

Theta Risk. The rate of change in the value of a derivative asset as the time passes is known as the **theta risk** of the asset and is denoted by θ. Formally,

$$\theta_C = \frac{\partial C}{\partial t}$$

$$\theta_P = \frac{\partial P}{\partial t}$$

The theta of an option measures the change in the option value due to the passage of time. A positive theta position indicates that the book will lose value with time. The behavior of theta is graphed in Figure 7-16.

FIGURE 7-16   *Theta of a Call Option*

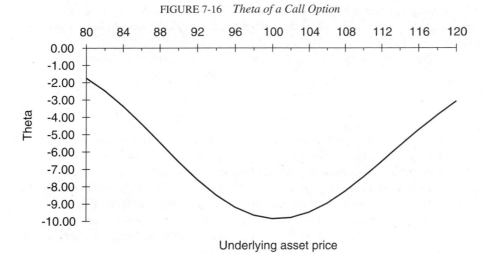

Once again, we can aggregate the overall theta of the book in a manner similar to delta and gamma risk. Define $\theta_i = \frac{\partial c_i}{\partial t}$. Then, we can aggregate the theta risk as

$$\theta_p = \sum_{i=1}^{n} x_i \times \theta_i. \tag{7.33}$$

Rho Risk. The sensitivity of the derivatives book to changes in the financing rates is called the **rho risk** and is denoted by ρ. This is an important policy measure in risk management.

Volatility Risk. By far the most important source of risk is the market volatility risk. There are two levels at which this risk is present.

First, the measures of volatility may be crude—sample unconditional standard deviations are often used in the industry. This measure, while simple, ignores time-series properties, such as volatility clustering, autoregression, and possible heteroscedasticity, that are present in various markets. More sophisticated estimation procedures such as ARCH (autoregressive and conditional heteroscedastic) and GARCH models are needed to minimize this source of risk, which I will call as the **estimation risk.** Using the listed options markets, it is possible to construct implied volatilities and aggregate those according to the "smile effect" or "the volatility skew." Usually, the weighting of such implied volatilities is obtained using measures such as the elasticity or vega of the options, which is the sensitivity of the option premiums with respect to the changes in the underlying volatilities.

The second source of risk arises when a constant volatility estimate is used in the pricing model, when in fact the market volatility is random. This is the **model misspecification risk.** This risk results from mispricing the options and using the incorrect hedge recipes that flow from such misspecifications.

The volatility factor is denoted by σ and the vega risk is dented by $\Omega_i = \frac{\partial c_i}{\partial \sigma}$. We can aggregate the volatility risk as before. Using an options pricing model allows these sensitivities to be calculated.

A full treatment of the risk management problem is presented in Chapter 15.

CONCLUSIONS

This chapter provided an overview of listed and OTC options markets. In addition to a survey of key contracts, we also developed basic propositions such as put-call parity relations, no-arbitrage restrictions, and basic pricing approaches. In addition, early exercise conditions were developed for American options. We also developed basic options strategies and their associated payoff diagrams. Valuation approaches such as Binomial, Black-Scholes and Monte Carlo simulation procedures were also developed. The price sensitivity of options, such as Δ, Γ, Θ and vega measures for individual options as well as portfolios of options, were obtained and interpreted.

PROBLEMS

7.1.   Evaluate the following statements. Explain each of your conclusions as precisely as possible. Provide, wherever possible, an analytical argument to support your answer.

(a) American options on futures should never be prematurely exercised.

(b) A call option on a portfolio of bonds is more valuable than a portfolio of call options on each of the bonds in the portfolio.

(c) An at-the-money six-month call option on a long bond that does not pay coupons during the life of the options should be at least as valuable as an at-the-money six-month put option on the same bond.

(d) In the absence of dividend payments during the life of the option, an American put should never be prematurely exercised.

7.2.   Solve this problem without using options-pricing software. A thirty-day call option (European-style) was offered by a dealer on 100 shares of IBM stock. The following terms apply:

- Stock price = 60.00
- Strike price = 58.00
- Financing rate = 5% per annum
- Volatility of IBM = 20% annualized

IBM was not expected to pay dividends over the next 30 days.

(a) Determine the value of this option.

(b) What is the probability that the option will end in-the-money when it expires?

(c) Determine the composition of the hedge portfolio. Show all the key steps.

7.3.   Spreadsheet Problem. The following data are available on Digital stock.

- Stock price = 40.00
- Volatility of Digital stock = 25% annualized

Digital never pays dividends. You are required to price a thirty-day at-the-money American put option on Digital stock. Assume that you are going to implement a binomial options-pricing model in which you intend to divide the life of the option into 30 steps. The annualized interest rate is 3%.

(a) Write a spreadsheet file (name the file `put.wk1` or `put.xls`) to value the binomial options-pricing model.

(b) Determine the value of the put option and its delta.

(c) Turn in the spreadsheet file with complete documentation.

7.4. The following table contains the book of options trades of a bank's equity-index trading desk. Determine the net exposure of this desk in terms of the underlying Standard & Poor 500 index and construct a delta-neutral hedge position. Assume that the market price of the options are fair so that the implied volatility of each option is the relevant volatility at which the option is priced. Assume a dividend yield of 3% and a financing rate of 3%.

Underlying Asset & Price (Standard & Poor 500 Index)	Option Type (Premium)	Long or Short Number	Strike Price	Maturity
462.35	Call (7.00)	Long 100	460	30 days
462.35	Call (10.50)	Long 200	460	60 days
462.35	Put $\left(9\frac{5}{8}\right)$	Long 300	460	90 days

REFERENCES

Black, F. 1976. "The Pricing of Commodity Contracts." *Journal of Financial Economics* 3:167–179.

Black, F., and M. Scholes 1973. "The Pricing of Options and Corporate Liabilities." *Journal of Political Economy* 81:637–659.

Boyle, P. P. 1977. "Options: A Monte Carlo Approach." *Journal of Financial Economics* 4:323–338.

Cox, J. C., and S. A. Ross 1976. "The Valuation of Options for Alternative Stochastic Processes." *Journal of Financial Economics* 3:145–166.

Cox, J. C., J. E. Ingersoll, and S. A. Ross 1981. "The Relation between Forward Prices and Futures Prices." *Journal of Financial Economics* 9:321–346.

Cox, J. C., S. A. Ross, and M. Rubinstein 1979. "Options Pricing: A Simplified Approach." *Journal of Financial Economics* 7:229–263.

Cox, J. C., and M. Rubinstein 1985. *Options Markets.* Englewood Cliffs, NJ: Prentice-Hall.

Goldman, M. B., H. Sosin, and M. Gatto 1979. "Path Dependent Options: 'Buy at the Low, Sell at the High.'" *Journal of Finance* 34(5):1111–1127.

Harrison, J. M., and D. M. Kreps 1978. "Martingales and Arbitrage in Multiperiod Security Markets." *Journal of Economic Theory* 20:381–408.

Hull, J. 1989. *Options, Futures and Other Derivative Securities.* Englewood, NJ: Prentice Hall.

Kemna, A. G. Z., and A. C. F. Vorst 1990. "A Pricing Method for Options on Averages Asset Values." *Journal of Banking and Finance* 14:113–129.

Merton, R. C. 1973. "Theory of Rational Options Pricing." *Bell Journal of Economics and Management Science* 4:141–183.

Parkinson, M. 1977. "Option Pricing: The American Put." *Journal of Business* 50:21–36.

Richard, S., and M. Sundaresan 1981. "A Continuous-Time Model of Forward and Futures Prices in a Multigood Economy." *Journal of Financial Economics* 9:347–372.

Chapter 8

Agency and Corporate Debt Securities

Chapter Objectives

This chapter describes agency, corporate, and hybrid securities. The theory of corporate debt pricing is also presented. Empirical evidence on financial distress and workouts is offered. The following questions are addressed in the chapter.

- What are Federal agencies and how do they raise capital?
- What is commercial paper (CP) and how is it rated?
- How is the corporate bond market classified?
- What are the contractual provisions in corporate bond market? In particular, what are
  1. sinking funds
  2. calls
  3. puts
- How big are the high-yield market and the private-placements market?
- What is the theory behind the valuation of corporate debt?
- What is the evidence on financial distress and reorganizations?

INTRODUCTION

U.S. government agencies, corporations, and financial institutions raise capital by issuing a variety of debt securities in the capital market. In this chapter, we will classify the agency and corporate debt securities, describe the market institutions and discuss the relevant attributes of each security from the standpoint of their risk and return. We will present some empirical evidence on the maturity composition, risk premiums, and contractual provisions that are used in agency and corporate debt based on all the issues that were made in the U.S. during the period January 1993 to August 1994. We will also summarize the available theories on the valuation of corporate debt securities. Empirical evidence on financial distress and restructuring will also be evaluated.

We begin by providing an overview of the agency securities markets. We examine in detail the contractual provisions of agency debt, the yield curve in the agency market, and the term structure of risk premiums in the agency market. We describe some of the key federal agencies and some recent developments in this market following the 1987 crisis in the Savings and Loan Association industry.

The corporate debt market is then analyzed. We present an overview of the corporate market based on the issues during 1993–1994 period. This enables us to compare this period with the evidence reported for the period 1980–1991 by Crabbe (1991). After documenting the credit risk distribution, default premiums, and contractual provisions in the corporate debt market, we review the evidence on financial distress, rate of defaults, and recoveries in the corporate debt market. Finally, we examine the hybrids market, where securities such as convertible bonds contain both equity and fixed-income exposures.

CLASSIFICATION OF AGENCY DEBT

In Chapter 1, we provided an overview of the U.S. Government agencies that actively participate in the debt markets. In this chapter, we provide a more detailed treatment of this important segment of the fixed-income markets. The agency market consists of a federally sponsored agency market which issues securities in the market and federal agencies which do not directly issue securities in the market—they tend to borrow from the Federal Financing Bank.

Federal Agencies

There are at present eight major federally sponsored agencies. Until 1987 there were only five such agency issuers: the Federal Farm Credit Board (FFCB), the Federal Home Loan Bank (FHLB), the Federal Home Loan Mortgage Corporation (FHLMC, also referred to as Freddie Mac), the Federal National Mortgage Association (FNMA, also referred to as Fannie Mae), and the Student Loan Marketing Association (SLMA, also referred to as Sallie Mae). The purpose of these agencies is to help promote credit availability in key sectors of the economy, such as the farm sector, housing sector, and education. In 1987, the Farm Credit Financial Assistance Corporation (FCFAC) was created. The problems in the savings and loan association led to the creation of the Financing Corporation (FICO) in 1987 and the Resolution Trust Corporation (RTC) in 1989. Although only the securities issued by FCFAC are backed by the full faith and credit of the U.S. government, generally agency securities are regarded as safe securities. The credit risk in agency securities is considered to be small. We will examine this in more detail later.

There are other agencies that do not directly issue securities but do so via the Federal Financing Bank such as the Tennessee Valley Authority (TVA), and the Government National Mortgage Association (GNMA).

Issuance Activity

Major agency issuers and their relative share of the issuance activity are reported in Table 8-1. We will be considering data from the period January 1993 to August 1994, unless otherwise indicated. During this period there was a total of 588 agency issues, amounting to a total of $74,384 million. As Table 8-1 shows, the most active issuer in the agency market is the Federal Home Loan Bank (FHLB) which made 341 issues netting over $25 billion during January 1993 to August 1994. During the same period, FHLMC raised over $13 billion by making nearly 100 issues and FNMA netted over $12.5 billion.

An interesting feature of the agency issues is that a large percentage of them are callable. These issues are priced relative to a Treasury security of similar maturity. Often, their yields are quoted as a spread over the benchmark Treasury security. The issues traded at a spread varying from 1 to 95 basis points, depending on the terms of the issue. All agency securities are regarded as virtually free from credit risk. They are rated AAA. When they are not rated, they are assumed to be of the highest quality. While this is generally the case, the financial strength of the agency is also a very important factor in determining the spread at which that agency's debt will trade relative to the Treasury.

Maturity Composition

Table 8-1 gives a bird's eye view of the agency market. We can get a sense of the maturity distribution of the agency market from Table 8-2, which considers only the issuers listed in Table 8-1. As Table 8-2 shows, the bulk of the agency debt is concentrated in the 2–10-year sector. This, coupled with the fact that a large percentage of the issues are

TABLE 8-1   *Agency Issues during January 1993–August 1994*

Issuer	Total Number of Issues	Dollar Amount (in millions)	Maturity Range	Call Feature	Spread to Treasury
FHLB	341	$25,349	1–20 years	205 callable	1–90 basis points
FHLMC	97	$13,155	1–15 years	85 callable	1–95 basis points
FNMA	60	$12,655	1–30 years	44 callable	1–93 basis points
FFCB	33	$4,709	1–20 years	16 callable	1–47 basis points
SLMA	26	$6,950	1–10 years	16 callable	NA basis points
TVA	20	$7,790	1–50 years	15 callable	4–8 basis points

Maturity Range	Total Number of Issues	Dollar Amount (in millions)
Less than 1 year	28	$7,878
1 year to less than 2 years	75	$7,293
2 years to less than 5 years	309	$34,670
5 years to less than 10 years	138	$18,292
10 years to less than 30 years	27	$1,571
30 years to less than 50 years	7	$2,550
50 years		

TABLE 8-2
*Maturity Distribution of
Agency Debt*

callable, indicates that the average maturity of this market is relatively small. Institutional investors wishing to invest in the 2–10-year maturity sector in debt securities with a very low credit risk will find the agency market particularly attractive, especially compared to the alternatives in the Treasury market. The investor will make a sacrifice in terms of lowered liquidity and increased call risk.

The article from *Euromoney* (Horwood 1995) indicates that, increasingly, agency securities are being sold in international markets. Note that the agencies tend to have call features since their loans are typically fixed-rate loans in which the borrower has the right to prepay when the rates fall. By issuing callable bonds, agencies can match the interest rate risk of their assets with the interest rate risk of their liabilities.

Global Bond Markets
Tough Call for US Agencies

By CLIVE HORWOOD

The competition for mandates from the US federal agencies is beginning to hot up. The agencies are tipped by many to become the heaviest issuers the international bond markets have ever seen. Domestic markets have become saturated with agency debt and new issue conditions have deteriorated, so the agencies have sought to diversify their funding sources. In recent months three have set up global debt facilities, including the $20 billion programme for the Federal National Mortgage Association (Fannie Mae), the largest the market has ever seen.

In the US, banks compete hard for agency mandates—after the government, they are the most frequent issuers of debt—and they rarely expect to make any money on the deals. Two deals from the Student Loan Marketing Association (Sallie Mae) in February led to fears of a fee-cutting war among London-based investment banks. Both were block trades—a $500 million deal via Nomura paid no fees, and a $750 million deal sole-managed by Merrill Lynch paid fees of just 12.5 basis points. Normally a lead manager would expect to receive fees of 18.75 bp on a three year deal.

Some syndicate managers say that this is unlikely to become a trend: "If the agencies want proper access to the markets they will have to pay proper fees," says one.

Source: *Euromoney* (March 1995) pp. 14, 16

Of more long-term relevance to the agencies in the international bond markets, however, is the development of a global market for callable bonds. Because much of the agencies' on-lending is in fixed-rate form, and the loans are generally repayable at any time, they like to issue callable bonds as a way to match their assets to liabilities. Over 60% of Fannie Mae's outstanding domestic debt is in callable form.

However there has traditionally been little demand for callables in the Euromarkets. Because of the call option, such bonds are difficult to price and quickly become illiquid. Callable bonds are usually issued purely for arbitrage reasons and are often aimed at retail investors who do not know how to value the cost of the embedded option. For these reasons there has never been a proper institutional market for callable bonds. Many bankers doubted that an international market could exist for callables.

There are three commonly used methods of valuing a call option. A yield-to-worst analysis is the lowest yield offered by the bond when the yield is calculated for each of the bond's possible call dates and prices. However this ignores the fact that the embedded option changes the behaviour and the value of a callable, not only from an actual change in interest rates, but also from an expected change. Break-even analysis compares callables to bullet bonds. By making forecasts on interest rates over different time horizons, the investor gets a reasonable idea how the bond might be influenced by movements in yield rates and volatility. The most accurate method, however, is the option adjusted spread (OAS). An OAS is a spread over the whole of the forward interest rate curve, rather than a nominal spread, which represents a spread at just one point on the curve. Analyzing the forward curve for interest rates and volatility helps to determine the likelihood of a bond's being called by establishing the possible path of underlying interest rates, the extent of each change, and the probability of each interest rate movement. It is, however, a complicated and time-consuming calculation.

Two deals in January showed the doubters that a market may exist. First was a $500 million two-year deal for Federal Home Loans Bank, which is callable at par after 12 months. Priced at 41 basis points over US treasuries, it sold out quickly and attracted strong non-US demand. Lead manager JP Morgan sold 95% of its bonds outside the US market. If the call option was exercised, the bonds would have paid a spread of 87bp over one-year treasury bills. That represented very good value for investors.

The deal, however, was at a much shorter maturity than the agencies usually issue at. Fannie Mae's $1 billion of 10-year global bonds, which have a five-year call protection period, is much more typical and presented the first real test for the market. Of Fannie Mae's callable bonds issued last year, over 50% were of 10-year duration, the majority of which had three years' call protection.

Lehman Brothers had begun discussions with Fannie Mae as long ago as last summer. According to Jonathan Hakim, a managing director at Lehman in London, they faced two main problems: a lack of secondary market liquidity in callable bonds, and the lack of transparency in option valuation. Investors also had to be convinced that this was not going to be an arbitrage-driven deal. "We had to convince the market that Fannie Mae was altogether differently motivated and that it had a natural need for the product," says Hakim.

To deal with the problems of liquidity and pricing, Lehman arranged Fannie Mae's $20 billion programme in October 1994. Lehman also arranged a facility via Bloomberg *by which dealers on the programme would post indicative bid/offer spreads and, for callable issues, would allow investors to conduct their own OAS analysis. A minimum size of $1 billion ensures a degree of secondary market liquidity.*

There was also a painstaking education process involving both Lehman's and joint lead Merrill Lynch's salesforces and potential investors. "The education process can be very theoretical," says Hakim. "We wanted to address the real issues, such as when do I start hedging a 10-year non-call five bond."

The leads wanted to place at least 25% of the bonds outside the US. They succeeded, with initial placement of 33% internationally, but Fannie Mae had to pay more for its funds than for equivalent domestic paper—80 basis points over 10-year US treasuries. Some rival syndicate officials say that the pricing was generous. Hakim says it was realistic: "We felt that the deal could have been done maybe one basis point inside this in the US," says Hakim. "But generous is too strong a word. Ten years was not exactly the ideal part of the curve at the time, and it was critical that the first issue was a success. Fannie Mae is now in good shape for its next issue."

Others remain unconvinced, saying that over time most of the paper has found its way back into the US. One head of syndicate says there is some way to go before a major market for callables exists internationally: "Until investors are forced to think more closely about callables, then they'll let them go by. There's plenty of plain vanilla paper out there."

The real test for the market will come if the agencies look to issue up to 50% of their international debt in callable form, as they do in the domestic markets. The three programmes set up so far envisage new issuance of $40 billion. The market appears to have digested the first $1.5 billion. Whether it has the appetite for $20 billion of agency callables remains to be seen.

Risk Premium in Agency Market

We examine next the risk premium in the agency debt market. The risk premium in this context is defined as the yield spread that investors demand (over and above a similar Treasury security) in order to hold these securities.

Table 8-3 provides the yield curve and the risk premiums in the agency market. The yield of agency securities under one year is slightly less than 5%. But it increases to

Maturity Range	At-Issue Yield	Spread over Treasury (basis points)	
Less than 1 year	4.93%	4.83	**TABLE 8-3**
1 year to less than 2 years	5.31%	8.92	*Risk Premium*
2 years to less than 5 years	6.17%	23.38	*of Agency Debt*
5 years to less than 10 years	7.00%	48.27	
10 years to less than 30 years	7.64%	79.00	
30 years to less than 50 years	7.79%	56.86	

nearly 8% for a maturity of 30 years or more. Note that the agency issues offer an increasing spread over Treasury benchmark issues as the maturity is extended. The risk premium jumps from 8.92 basis points for the maturity range 1–2 years to 23.38 basis points in the 2–5 years maturity range. The risk premium more than doubles to 48.27 basis points in the 5–10 year range. Call features might account for some of this behavior.

Market Conventions

A number of agency issues tend to have a maturity of six months or nine months. These agency securities tend to make interest payments at maturity (IAM). Agency yields are calculated on the assumption that all months have 30 days (even February, which actually has 28 or 29 days, and August, which actually has 31 days). We can write the yield of an IAM agency security as

$$P + ai = \frac{I + 100}{\left(1 + y\frac{n}{360}\right)} \tag{8.1}$$

where P is the quoted price of the agency security in $\frac{1}{32}$, I is the interest payable at maturity, ai is the accrued interest, and n is the number of days between the settlement date and the maturity date using the 30-day convention. The yield of the IAM agency is denoted by y.

Let $n = 200$ days, using the 30-day counting convention, and 6% be the stated interest for the agency. Let us also assume that the number of days between the issue date and the settlement date is 45, using the 30-day counting convention. Then we can compute $I = 6 \times \frac{245}{360} = 4.0833$. The accrued interest $ai = 6 \times \frac{45}{360} = 0.75$. If the quoted price of this agency security is 100, then we can write

$$100 + 0.75 = \frac{4.0833 + 100}{\left(1 + y\frac{200}{360}\right)}. \tag{8.2}$$

Solving, we get the yield of the agency equal to 5.955%.

The convention for agency securities with multiple interest payments is similar. If c is the rate of coupon, then the yield y is calculated as in Equation (8.3). Let us assume that the settlement date is $t < T$ and that there are N coupon dates remaining. Denote by z the number of days between the settlement date and the next coupon date, and by x the number of days between the last coupon date and the next coupon date. Then,

$$P_t + ai_t = \left(\frac{100}{\left(1 + \frac{y}{2}\right)^{N-1+\frac{z}{x}}}\right) + \sum_{j=1}^{j=N} \frac{\frac{c}{2}}{\left(1 + \frac{y}{2}\right)^{j-1+\frac{z}{x}}}. \tag{8.3}$$

The critical point to remember is that all days are counted using the 30-day conventions.

CORPORATE DEBT MARKET

There are six categories of corporate credit. By far the biggest of these is the corporate bond market, which accounts for nearly 40% of the market. This is followed by bank loans (25.8%) and the commercial paper market (22.8%). These three sources of credit account for more than 85% of the corporate credit market. The remainder is accounted for by medium-term notes, international bonds, and asset-backed securities.

While credit risk is perhaps the most important factor in the corporate debt market, it is useful to note that the issuance and refunding and call activities tend to occur in periods of relatively low interest rates. To underscore this point, we present Figure 8-1. Note how as AAA rates fell during the period 1990–1993, the corporate bond issuance activity picked up significantly. All corporations have a valuable timing option; they can issue debt now or wait and issue it later. The advantage of issuing now is to take advantage of the interest tax shield or capture the net present value of projects that can be financed using debt issuance. On the other hand, by waiting and issuing debt later, they may be able to take advantage of any drop in interest rates. At low enough interest rates, this waiting option is worth exercising and the corporation will issue debt or refund to take advantage of low rates.

FIGURE 8-1   *Total Corporate Bond Issuance and AAA Corporate Rates*

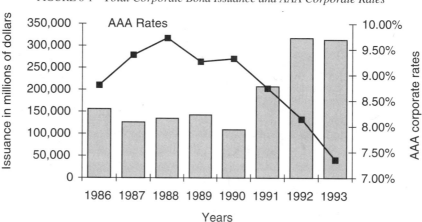

Credit Risk of Issuers

The most important dimension that distinguishes corporate debt from Treasury debt is the fact that the issuer in the corporate market is an institution which has some credit risk. Corporate debt securities are rated by various rating agencies such as Moody's and Standard and Poor. Table 8-4 provides the rating categories that are currently in use for long-term corporate debt. Corporate securities that are rated below Baa3 (Moody's) or BBB − (S&P) are considered "speculative" or "junk" or "noninvestment grade."

We begin our study of corporate debt market by examining the commercial paper market.

Description	Moody's	S&P	TABLE 8-4
Investment grade bonds			*Long-Term Credit*
Gilt-edge, prime maximum safety	Aaa	AAA	*Rating Categories for Corporate Debt*
Very high grade, high quality	Aa1	AA+	
	Aa2	AA	
	Aa3	AA-	
Upper medium grade	A1	A+	
	A2	A	
	A3	A-	
Lower medium grade	Baa1	BBB+	
	Baa2	BBB	
	Baa3	BBB-	
Junk bonds			
Low grade speculative	Ba1	BB+	
	Ba2	BB	
	Ba3	BB-	
Highly speculative	B1	B+	
	B2	B	
	B3	B-	

Commercial Paper

The commercial paper market is among the oldest of all the corporate credit markets in the United States. The market can be traced back to 1869 and its growth was fueled by the demand for corporate credit, which exceeded the supply of bank credit. Many companies directly accessed the lenders via the commercial paper market. Several new issuers also entered the market, as did new investors such as the money market mutual funds that primarily invest in commercial paper. Today, commercial paper is an important source of short-term credit for large, high-quality borrowers.

Commercial paper is a short-term corporate discount security. It is typically unsecured and the issuer is obligated to repay the principal amount to the holder of the commercial paper at maturity. Typically maturities are limited to 270 days or less. Commercial paper maturities can be customized to meet the needs of issuers and investors. Much of the liquidity in the market is concentrated in the maturity range of 30 to 45 days. Generally commercial paper is traded in denominations of $100,000 or more. The market is typically dominated by large borrowers with very high credit reputations. The largest commercial paper issuers tend to sell their commercial paper directly to investors. Such issuers are known as direct issuers. In 1991 there were about 75 such direct issuers. Other issuers, whose number is in excess of 1,500, sell their commercial paper through one or more dealers. Major commercial paper dealers are Goldman Sachs,

Merrill Lynch, Lehman Brothers, and First Boston. In 1991 these four dealers accounted for more than 90% of the dealer-placed commercial paper. It should be stressed that while the dealers make a secondary market in commercial paper, most commercial paper is held to maturity.

Under the Securities Act of 1933, corporations do not have to register with Securities and Exchange Commission (SEC) in order to issue CPs. This represents savings in time commitment and resources. This exemption is subject to the issuer meeting certain conditions, which vary with the type of the commercial paper program. These are described later. Further, by issuing CPs, corporations are able to directly access the capital market for short-term capital without having to rely on intermediaries such as commercial banks for their financing needs. For highly rated corporations, this is a real advantage as they are able to borrow at rates below the London interbank offered rates (LIBOR), or at "sub-LIBOR" rates. Most issuers in this market enjoy a rating of P-2/A-2 or better (Table 8-5 lists the rating categories.)

Description	Moody's	S&P
Prime	P-1+	A-1+
Prime-1	P-1+	A-1
Prime-2	P-2+	A-2
Prime-3	P-3+	A-3
Not Prime	N.P.	C

TABLE 8-5
Short-Term Credit Rating Categories for Commercial Paper

Commercial paper may be purchased by investors subject to the Investment Company Act of 1940. The investors tend to segment this market based on the issuer's credit reputation and origin (domestic or foreign). Investors of commercial paper are money market mutual funds, insurance companies, pension funds, corporations, and banks, among others.

A significant proportion of the commercial paper market is issued under section 3(a)(3) of the Securities Act of 1933. The exemption from registration under this section is derived provided the proceeds from the issuance of commercial paper are used to fund current transactions and the maturity is limited to under 270 days. Commercial paper under this program may be purchased by all investors. In contrast, commercial paper issued under section 4(2) of the act specifies a different set of restrictions in order for the issuer to qualify for exemption from registration; such issues may be sold only to certain investors, they may not be publicly offered, and they may not be purchased by investors with intent to resell.

Under section 3(a)(2) of the act, letter of credit (LOC) backed commercial paper may be issued with exemption from registration. Such issues are guaranteed by U.S. commercial bank. The LOC is issued to protect investors by substituting the credit reputation of the issuer of the LOC for the credit reputation of the issuer of the CP. For the LOC, the issuer pays a fee.

How important are these ratings? There is evidence that suggests that the initial ratings of commercial paper affects common stock returns. Nayar and Rozeff (1994) show that highly rated CP issues made by industrial users (without letter of credit) are often accompanied by significant positive returns. Rating downgrades, notably those that result in an exit from the CP market, are accompanied by significant negative returns. There is some evidence that the initial rating and subsequent rating changes convey important information to investors.

Corporate Bonds

In the corporate bond market, corporations issue securities to raise long-term capital. The investor in the corporate bond market is a creditor to the corporation and has a prior claim to the assets of the corporation, over the equity holders. For example, interest payments to corporate debt must be paid before dividends are paid to equity holders. As we will see later, in the event of financial distress, bondholders have certain rights over how the assets of the firm are distributed. For these reasons, corporate bonds are referred to as senior securities.

Similar to commercial paper issues, the corporate bond issues are regulated by the Securities Act of 1933. The issuer of corporate bonds must comply with the registration requirements of SEC prior to the public offering of bonds. In addition, corporate debt securities also come under the Trust Indenture Act of 1939. Under the provisions of this act, a trustee must be appointed to represent the bondholders. Typically, a bank or a trust company will act as the trustee. Moreover, all contractual provisions between the issuer of corporate bonds and the trustee must be presented in a written form. This is known as the indenture provisions and is filed along with the registration documents.

A Classification of Corporate Debt

Corporate debt securities may be grouped along several dimensions. One category that is used is to classify them according to different sectors of the economy. These sectors are

- finance companies,
- industry,
- telephones,
- utilities,
- Yankee issues, and
- noninvestment-grade or junk issues.

In Table 8-6, we provide the share of these segments during the period January 1993–August 1994. Several noteworthy patterns appear. First, a total of 1,398 issues were made. In all, these issues amounted to $267 billion. The fact that interest rates were low during this period clearly accounts for this large issue of debt. This is also evident in

TABLE 8-6   *Distribution of Credit Risks in the Corporate Bond Market 1993–1994*

	Finance	*Industry*	*Telephone*	*Utilities*	*Yankee*	*Junk*	*Total*	*Percent*
Total								
Number of issues	423	340	78	402	155	160	1,398	
Dollar size	82,200	67,145	16,444	49,409	52,109	20,213	267,307	
AAA								
Number of issues	2	5	14	2	20		43	3.08%
Dollar size	325	1,250	3,075	275	5,390		10,315	3.86%
AA+								
Number of issues	24	3	4	12	1		44	3.15%
Dollar size	2,775	197	390	815	500		4,677	1.75%
AA								
Number of issues	14	29	9	19	14		85	6.08%
Dollar size	3,050	7,713	2,620	1,325	12,216		26,924	10.07%
AA−								
Number of issues	30	16	16	54	26		142	10.16%
Dollar size	6,600	4,660	5,434	5,757	7,926		30,367	11.36%
A+								
Number of issues	84	29	13	52	23		201	14.38%
Dollar size	14,980	4,885	2,575	6,941	10,224		39,605	14.82%
A								
Number of issues	113	59	13	109	9		303	21.67%
Dollar size	27,375	10,522	2,570	14,334	2,249		57,050	21.34%
A−								
Number of issues	72	32	3	23	7		137	9.80%
Dollar size	13,530	5,371	950	2,715	1,625		24,191	9.05%
BBB+								
Number of issues	36	51	3	42	12		144	10.30%
Dollar size	6,390	7,604	650	5,158	2,560		22,362	8.37%
BBB								
Number of issues	35	63	3	70	14		185	13.23%
Dollar size	5,610	11,147	640	9,112	3,000		29,509	11.04%
BBB−								
Number of issues	9	48		19	5		81	5.79%
Dollar size	1,305	12,355		2,987	975		17,622	6.59%

Dollar size is in millions of dollars.

Figure 8-1. Note that the finance companies issued the most debt both in terms of the number of issues (423) and in terms of the dollar amount raised (82.2 billion). It is also significant that only about 3% of the issues were rates AAA. About 72% of the dollar value of the issues were rated A– or better. The rest (28%) were in the noninvestment-grade category.

Credit Risk Distribution. Figures 8-2 through 8-6 show the distribution of credit risks in different sectors of the corporate debt market. Note how scarce the supply of AAA

FIGURE 8-2   *Distribution of Credit Risk in the Finance Sector*

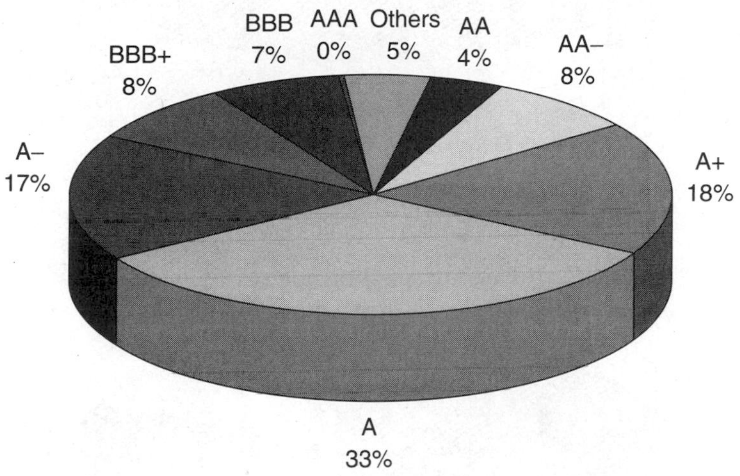

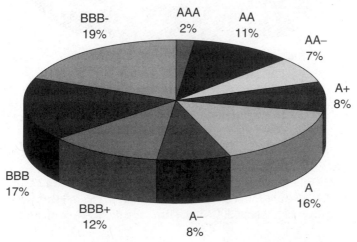

FIGURE 8-3   *Distribution of Credit Risk in the Industry Sector*

FIGURE 8-4   *Distribution of Credit Risk in the Telephone Sector*

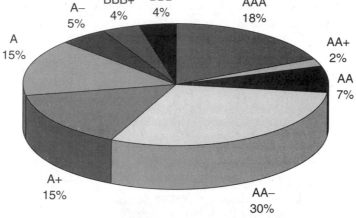

FIGURE 8-5   *Distribution of Credit Risk in the Utilities Sector*

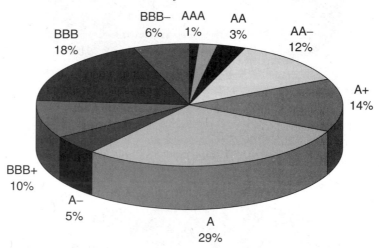

credit is. This is in sharp contrast to the agency market, where virtually all securities enjoy this status.

In the finance sector, AA– or better credit risk accounts for just 12% of the market. Firms in A– to A+ account for nearly 70% of the issues. The industry sector probably reflects the most diversity: About 20% of the firms are rated AA– or better and 32% fell

FIGURE 8-6   *Distribution of Credit Risk in the Yankee Sector*

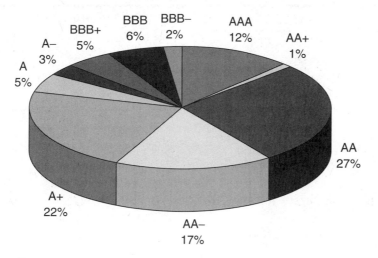

in the range A- to A+. Nearly half of this sector is rated BBB+ or lower. Utilities, Telephone, and Yankee issues have a better proportion of firms enjoying a higher credit reputation. For example, nearly 60% of the telephone, utility, and Yankee issues are rated AA- or better.

Risk Premiums in Corporate Bonds. Table 8-7 summarizes the risk premiums in the corporate bond market during the period January 1993–August 1994. At-issue yields and at-issue risk premiums over comparable Treasuries are used in constructing this table.

Note that during this period 100-year bonds were issued (Coca Cola and Walt Disney were the issuers). The risk-premium behavior is consistent with intuition: As the maturity increases, the risk premiums tend to increase; as the credit reputation declines, risk premiums tend to increase as well. Later, we will present theories of corporate-bond pricing, which attempt to explain the levels of risk premiums that we observe in real world.

Most of the investment-grade bonds issued during the period 1993–1994 did not have any call features. Some of the contractual provisions used in corporate debt contracts are shown in Table 8-8. The article from Forbes (March 1995) shows that some bonds are issued with a put feature which gives investors the right to put the bond back to issues. This can give some protection against an increase in interest rates or an increase in default risk or both. We will show later that junk bonds are issued with call features in a vast majority of or both cases.

TABLE 8-7   *Risk Premiums in the Corporate Bond Market (in basis points)*

Years to Maturity	Finance		Industry		Telephone		Utilities		Yankees	
	AA	BBB	AA	BBB	AA	BBB	AA	BBB	AA	BBB
2	15.00		38.00					57.00	35.00	84.00
3	33.20	95.67	36.67	120.33	35.00		26.50	65.60		
4	51.00						38.50	70.00		
5	39.75	114.00	37.00	133.75	41.33		37.38	83.81	58.25	144.33
6	39.00				50.00		56.50			
7	50.75	113.33	41.50	99.13		80.00	50.56	99.36	63.40	153.33
8				14.00			40.00	91.25		
9							46.00	135.00		195.00
10	53.22	102.06	53.75	101.79	53.57	90.00	43.89	112.21	59.69	103.31
11							42.00	105.00		
12	73.00	101.50	69.00	97.50	32.50		42.75	69.33		
13										
14								60.00		
15	68.20	95.50	69.33	105.00			46.67	59.50	70.75	81.00
16										
17								95.00		
18										
19				95.00						
20	75.00	113.00	69.40	112.00			37.50	68.00	77.00	128.00
21								59.00		
22								83.00		
23							37.00			
24				186.00						
25				176.00			35.00			
26										
27										
28										
29										
30	78.00		41.50	158.21	38.00	86.00	60.75	104.10	61.67	131.50
31				175.00	70.00	93.00	67.50	124.33		
32			40.00	94.00	65.00		76.50	153.83		
33					73.00					
40			49.33		67.50		70.00			
41					72.00					
50			72.50		78.00		85.00			
100			80.67							

TABLE 8-8   *Contractual Provisions of Corporate Debt Contracts*

Provision	*Description*
Call features	Enable issuers to call after a call protection period. The call price is typically at a premium to par and it declines with time.
Refunding provisions	Enable issuers to refund using cheaper sources of debt finance. Refunding restrictions mean that cheaper sources of debt may not be used to refund debt, although the debt may be callable.
Sinking fund provisions	Require investors to retire an outstanding debt issue periodically. The bonds may be retired at par (on a pro-rata basis). Some bonds may be either retired at par or through open market purchases.
Putable bonds	Provide investors with the right to put the debt back to the issuer.
Convertible bonds	Provide investors with the right to convert bonds into a specified number of shares of common stock.
Bonds with warrants	The buyer of debt is also provided with warrants that give the right to buy the issuer's shares of common stock.

Power to the Creditors

By Eric S. Hardy

The traditional corporate bond is rigged against investors. When interest rates rise, it falls in value, just like a Treasury bond. But, unlike Treasury bonds, many corporate bonds don't rise much when interest rates fall. That's because corporate issuers of these bonds reserve the right to call them in early, at only a slight premium over the issue price. Heads you lose, tails you break even.

You can grab back some of this power by buying a bond with a built-in put option. This put gives you the right, but not the obligation, to sell the bond back to the issuer prior to maturity. The put exercise price is usually at par value. Puttable bonds are also generally noncallable—that is, the issuer does not have the right to force you to redeem early.

Nothing is free on Wall Street. You pay for this put feature in the form of reduced yield. Dennis Adler, a corporate bond stategist at Salomon Brothers, says the yield sacrifice on a noncallable 30-year A-rated corporate bond that can be put to the issuer at five par five years out is perhaps 20 basis points (a fifth of a percentage point).

Giving up some yield makes sense for someone who is nervous about his principal. If worry about a coming spike in interest rates has kept you from buying long bonds at all, then puttables are definitely worth a look.

One important caveat here: Almost all bond puts are "European-style," meaning they can be exercised only for a very short time—perhaps on one specific day. Still, having only one day to redeem a bond is better than having none at all.

Source: Reprinted by permission of FORBES Magazine © Forbes Inc., 1995

Redeeming Virtue

Issuer	Coupon	Maturity	Moody's Rating	Amount Issued ($mil)	Recent Price	Yield to Put	Yield to Maturity	Date of First Put	Yield Sacrifice*
Columbia/ HCA Healthcare	8.360	4/15/24	A3	$150	$101.21	7.46%	8.25%	4/15/04	0.41%
Corning	7.625	8/1/24	A2	100	99.36	7.72	7.68	8/1/04	0.62
Eastman Chemical	7.625	6/15/24	Baa1	200	96.90	8.05	7.90	6/15/06	0.42
Eaton	8.000	8/15/06	A2	100	102.56	6.10	7.66	8/15/96	0.33
NBD Bank	8.250	11/1/24	Aa3	250	102.20	7.92	8.07	11/1/04	0.50
New England Telephone	7.875	11/15/29	Aa2	350	102.77	6.11	7.65	11/15/96	0.91
New Jersey Bell	7.850	11/15/29	Aaa	150	103.66	6.92	7.55	11/15/99	0.61
Pennsylvania Power & Light	7.700	10/1/09	A2	200	101.86	7.21	7.49	10/1/99	0.48
RJR Nabisco	6.800	9/1/01	Baa3	100	97.83	7.79	7.23	9/2/97	1.19
Torchmark	8.250	8/15/09	A3	100	101.27	7.28	8.10	8/15/96	0.34

These corporate bonds feature a built-in put option: You get at least one chance to cash in the bond early at par value. You exercise this right if interest rates rise or if the issuer's credit quality deteriorates.

*Yield forfeited by favoring puttable bond over nonputtable bond of comparable maturity and credit quality.

Sources: Bloomberg Financial Markets, Salomon Brothers Fixed Income Research

A few municipal bonds and about 900 corporate issues have some kind of put feature. But note that for many of the corporate issues, the put becomes exercisable only after a change in corporate control. These are called poison puts and are seldom of value to the investor. They are installed to protect the management.

The table lists ten noncallable corporate bonds that can be put back to the issuer no matter who controls the company. In evaluating bonds like these, don't look at the maturity with your usual frame of reference. Often it's better to think of the put exercise date as the maturity.

To illustrate, look at the NBD Bank 8.25s of 2024. The Aa3-rated bond currently sells for 102 to yield 8.1% to maturity. But because the bond can be sold back to NBD at par on Nov. 1, 2004, it is easier to think of this as a ten-year bond yielding 7.9% to maturity. You'll redeem the bond in 2004 if interest rates have climbed or NBD's credit quality has deteriorated.

Alternatively, if rates have fallen and NBD still looks like a good bank, then you will hang on to the paper. At that point you will have, in effect, a new 20-year bond yielding 8.25% to maturity. In this light, your 30-year bond with a 10-year put becomes a 10-year bond with an attached call option on a 20-year bond. With bonds like this one the creditor is in the driver's seat.

Let us review the corporate bonds that were issued during the period 1977–1990, listed in Table 8-9 (derived from Crabbe (1991)). Note that the number and the percentage of corporate bonds that are issued with call features has fallen steadily since 1977. As of 1990, only about 20% of the bonds are callable. In addition, the average maturity of debt has also fallen over time. In a perfect capital market, call features should be of no consequence; the gains to the firm are exactly offset by the discount in the sale price imposed by bondholders to compensate them for potential losses. But in reality, in most corporations there are what are known as "agency problems." These problems arise because corporations are run by managers who should act as agents of stock holders. But, managers will act in their own interests and, unless suitable compensation contracts are put in place, the actions of managers may not necessarily be in the best interest of the stock holders. Some of these agency problems are:

Asymmetric Information. If the firm has favorable information about future cash flows that it is unable to communicate credibly at the time of debt issuance, then it has an incentive to issue debt with call features. Once the favorable information gets released, the firm can call the debt back. Often insiders (managers) know more about the firm and its future prospects than do creditors. This means that the creditors will want to design the debt contract in such a way as to minimize any potential costs that the managers might impose. Another consequence of asymmetric information is that the issuance of new equity typically results in a fall in the company's stock price. Thus, the equity issues tend to have "informational costs."

Under-Investment. If, after financing with noncallable debt, favorable projects arrive, then part of the gains will accrue to the bondholders. Then the managers of

TABLE 8-9   *Investment Grade New Issues 1977–1990*

Year	Total Value	Percentage Noncallable	Number of Issues	Percentage Noncallable	Mean Maturity
1977	16.22	1	182	1	25.71
1978	13.64	1	138	1	25.28
1979	17.53	2	144	2	23.64
1980	27.29	6	248	5	19.28
1981	24.30	2	190	3	16.89
1982	23.80	18	252	21	14.28
1983	18.62	17	195	21	17.70
1984	24.77	31	212	34	11.66
1985	46.74	24	346	25	14.94
1986	94.11	34	641	32	16.98
1987	65.97	51	447	49	13.35
1988	51.51	47	343	45	12.09
1989	57.95	69	342	63	13.06
1990	55.99	85	319	78	12.78

Source: Crabbe (1991)

the firm might forego attractive projects. This under-investment problem can also be mitigated through the issuance of callable debt.

Risk-Shifting. The firm has incentives to take on projects with greater risk when the debt is noncallable. If the risks pay off, the firm gets all the benefits and the bondholders only get the contracted amount. On the other hand, if the risks do not pay off, the firm can appeal to its limited liability and walk away from its obligations. Including a conversion feature helps to mitigate this problem.

EVIDENCE ON DEFAULTS AND FINANCIAL DISTRESS

Moody's defines default as a situation where an issuer misses or delays a contracted interest or principal payment. This definition includes circumstances where:

- the issuer offers a package of new securities that has a diminished financial obligation. This may occur in distressed exchange offers.
- the exchange has the purpose of helping the issuer to avoid default.
- delays in payments within the grace period provided in the indenture are also considered default.

A comprehensive study of defaults during the period 1970–1993 is provided in Moody's Investors Service (1994). Major highlights of this study serve as a useful frame of reference for the modeling of corporate bonds. During a 24-year period of the study,

- 614 issuers defaulted on corporate debt securities valued at over $93 billion.
- highly rated firms had much less of a chance of defaulting than poorly rated firms, given the data on defaults across rating categories.
- senior debt securities had a much higher recovery rate than did junior debt securities.

Table 8-10 lists the yearly default rates across different rating categories. In Figure 8-7 we provide the information for investment-grade and speculative-grade debt securities.

FIGURE 8-7   *Default Rates of Investment-Grade and Speculative-Grade Corporate Debt*

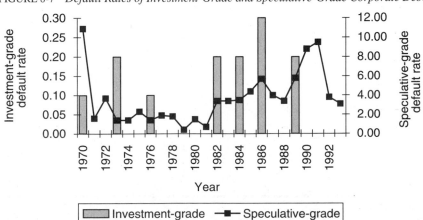

TABLE 8-10   *Default Data, One-Year Default Rates by Year and Rating*

Year	Aaa	Aa	A	Baa	Ba	B	Investment Grade	Speculative Grade
1970	0.00	0.00	0.00	0.30	8.40	21.60	0.10	10.90
1971	0.00	0.00	0.00	0.00	1.50	0.00	0.00	1.60
1972	0.00	0.00	0.00	0.00	0.50	11.80	0.00	3.70
1973	0.00	0.00	0.00	0.50	0.50	3.40	0.20	1.40
1974	0.00	0.00	0.00	0.00	0.00	6.90	0.00	1.40
1975	0.00	0.00	0.00	0.00	1.60	3.00	0.00	2.30
1976	0.00	0.00	0.00	0.00	1.10	0.00	0.10	1.40
1977	0.00	0.00	0.00	0.30	0.60	8.80	0.00	1.90
1978	0.00	0.00	0.00	0.00	1.10	5.30	0.00	1.80
1979	0.00	0.00	0.00	0.00	0.50	0.00	0.00	0.40
1980	0.00	0.00	0.00	0.00	0.00	4.40	0.00	1.50
1981	0.00	0.00	0.00	0.00	0.00	4.10	0.00	0.70
1982	0.00	0.00	0.20	0.30	2.60	2.20	0.20	3.40
1983	0.00	0.00	0.00	0.00	1.00	6.00	0.00	3.40
1984	0.00	0.00	0.00	0.60	0.50	7.30	0.20	3.50
1985	0.00	0.00	0.00	0.00	2.00	8.70	0.00	4.40
1986	0.00	0.00	0.00	1.10	1.90	11.60	0.30	5.70
1987	0.00	0.00	0.00	0.00	2.60	5.30	0.00	4.00
1988	0.00	0.00	0.00	0.00	1.50	5.70	0.00	3.40
1989	0.00	0.30	0.00	0.50	2.70	8.60	0.20	5.80
1990	0.00	0.00	0.00	0.00	3.30	12.90	0.00	8.80
1991	0.00	0.00	0.00	0.20	5.10	13.10	0.00	9.50
1992	0.00	0.00	0.00	0.00	0.20	6.40	0.00	3.80
1993	0.00	0.00	0.00	0.00	0.50	5.20	0.00	3.10

Source: Moody's Investors Services (1994)

The probability of default and the likely recovery rates in the event of default play an important role in the valuation of corporate debt securities. In the models of pricing corporate bonds, these factors are given much prominence. We shall review the corporate debt pricing models after a treatment of the junk bond market and the private placement market next.

High-Yield Bonds

An important segment of the corporate debt market is the high-yield or junk bond market. Table 8-11 summarizes the new issuance activity in the junk bond market during the period 1977 to 1993. After a tentative initial period (1977–1982), this market became quite active in the period 1983 to 1989. Much of the new issuance during this period can be attributed to leveraged buy-out (LBO) activities. The market collapsed subsequently, with the new issues accounting for less than 2% of the market in 1990. The market appears to have stabilized with the new issues of around 20% of the market in 1993.

TABLE 8-11   *New Issues of High-Yield Bonds*

Year	Total Number of Issues	Par Amount in Millions	Total Corporates in Millions	High-Yields as a Percentage of Corporates
1977	61	1,040.2	26,314.2	3.95%
1978	82	1,578.5	21,557.2	7.32%
1979	56	1,399.8	25,831.0	5.42%
1980	45	1,429.3	36,907.2	3.87%
1981	34	1,536.3	40,783.8	3.77%
1982	52	2,691.5	47,208.9	5.70%
1983	95	7,765.2	38,372.9	20.24%
1984	131	15,238.9	82,491.5	18.47%
1985	175	15,684.8	80,476.9	19.49%
1986	226	33,261.8	156,061.3	21.31%
1987	190	30,522.2	126,134.3	24.20%
1988	160	31,095.2	134,791.9	23.07%
1989	130	28,753.2	142,790.7	20.14%
1990	10	1,397.0	109,284.4	1.28%
1991	48	9,967.0	207,300.9	4.81%
1992	245	39,785.2	317,605.7	12.52%
1993	341	57,163.7	313,897.8	18.21%

Source: *This Year in High Yield—The Journal of Global High Yield Bond Research* (1994), Merrill Lynch and Co., New York

Altman (1992) classifies junk bonds into three categories:

1. Bonds that were originally issued as investment-grade debt and that subsequently were downgraded to below the investment-grade status. Such issues are referred to as "fallen angels." Altman (1992) estimates that such issues account for 25% of the market.
2. Bonds that were rated as noninvestment-grade at the time of issuance. The proceeds of such debt issues were allocated primarily for normal business activity. Such issues account for another 25% of the market.
3. The remaining 50% of the junk bond issues that are outstanding were primarily issued for large corporate restructuring. They were issued during the active LBO period 1986–1989.

High-yield debt provides an alternative for issuers who would otherwise rely on commercial bank debt. Borrowers in the commercial bank debt market may be subject to restrictive covenants. In the junk bond market, issuers typically are subject to one or more of the following covenants.

- **Aggregate debt limitations** specify a bound below which the issuer must maintain the total level of debt.

- **Restrictions on dividend payments** ensure that profits are not diverted to stockholders to the detriment of debtholders.
- **Restrictions on mergers, consolidations, and the sale of assets** by the issuing firm.
- **Credible third party guarantees and credit enhancements.**
- **Minimum standards on working capital levels.**

Altman and Nammacher (1987) point out that the high-yield debt market subjects issuers to less restrictive covenants than does private placement. Junk bonds are typically issued in on deferred-payment basis. The idea here is to initially offer a lower coupon and progressively increase the coupons as the firm is able to shed its excessive debt and regain its vitality. Such issues are known as *step up* issues. Another structure that helps in mitigating the temporary liquidity problems is the pay-in-kind (PIK) bonds that do not pay cash coupons but instead pay additional bonds in lieu of coupons.

In striking contrast to investment-grade debt issues, we find from Table 8-12 that most junk bonds are issued with call features. The junk bonds are currently held by large financial institutions. But a number of factors have served to limit the attractiveness of junk bonds to major institutions. Risk-based capital standards have encouraged insurance companies and banks to invest in better quality assets than junk bonds. Credit-rating agencies have become concerned with the lack of liquidity in the junk bond market. Mutual Benefit Life Insurance Company in 1991 was unable to meet the redemptions, at least in part, of the junk-bond investments. In addition, life insurance companies have suffered losses in this market. The insurance subsidiary of the First Executive Corporation suffered significant losses in this market. These observations

TABLE 8-12   *Summary of Junk Bond Issues, January 1993 to August 1994)*

	Maturity	BB+ to BBB	B+ to CCC	Number of Issues	Callable
	5	9.59%	10.88%	4	0
	7	10.39%	11.40%	24	18
	8	9.98%	9.58%	24	21
	9	11.63%	10.31%	6	5
	10	10.45%	10.81%	83	75
	11	9.75%		1	1
	12	9.25%	10.02%	11	10
	15		9.03%	2	2
	20	9.65%		1	1
	30	8.41%		1	1
Amount (in millions)		6,995	18,803		
Total number of bonds		45	112	157	
Total number of bonds callable		29	105		134

notwithstanding, junk bond market appears to have stabilized into a relatively tenacious segment of the debt market.

Private Placements

Historically, private placements of debt issues tend to complement the public issues. This market, in which the issuers are not required to disclose any information to public, tends to place debt with a few large reputable institutions. Such issues are exempt from registration with the SEC. There have been significant changes in the privately placed debt market since 1990, when the Securities and Exchange Commission (SEC) adopted the Rule 144A. This rule allows large institutions that are relatively sophisticated to trade privately placed debt freely among themselves. Such institutions are referred to as qualified institutional buyers (QIBs). QIBs have a discretionary investment of $100 million or more in such debt securities. This definition automatically includes life insurance companies, pension funds, commercial banks, and finance companies. Many of the debt offerings in this market are underwritten and offer several features of the public debt market without the disclosure requirements.

In a recent paper, Carey, Prowse, Rea, and Udell (1993) analyze this market in considerable detail. To get an idea of the increasing importance of this debt market, review the information in Table 8-13. The private placement of debt is about 75% of the public issues of debt. But by and large, privately placed debt tends to have a much shorter average maturity than public issues. The borrowers in the private debt market are small- and medium-sized issuers with over 65% of the issues falling in the 10–100 million-issue size category with a median issue size of 34 million. In contrast, the median issue size in the public debt market is 150 million. In the privately placed debt issues, there are no registration costs, and for smaller issues there are no underwriting expenses; an important lack of expense for small- and medium-sized issuers.

The lenders in this market are typically life insurance companies. They find private-debt issues to be more attractive from a risk-return standpoint and they impose restrictive covenants to better manage the risk. It is also possible for lenders to, for example, customize sinking-fund schedules to manage their risk better. Other covenants may include call protection, minimum net worth requirements, and debt ceilings. In addition to life insurance companies, pension funds and finance companies also are big lenders in this market.

The privately placed debt market, since the advent of Rule 144A, has tended to become more liquid. It has also attracted foreign issuers.

Type of Issue	1975–80	1981–85	1986–91
Public	21.00	35.60	87.60
Private	14.70	19.80	64.80

TABLE 8-13

Gross Issuance by Nonfinancial Companies, in Billions of Dollars

Source: Carey, Prowse, Rea, and Udell (1993)

THEORIES OF CORPORATE-DEBT PRICING

Black and Scholes (1973) recognize that the insights of options-pricing theory can be applied to a variety of problems in corporate finance. Options-pricing models have been applied to corporate finance problems, such as the valuation of corporate debt, warrants, capital budgeting, and executive stock options. The pricing models developed in Chapter 7 can now be applied to value corporate debt securities.

In the pricing of corporate debt securities, options-pricing insights have been used extensively. The design of corporate debt contracts as well as their valuation must account for the fact that the managers have the option of "walking away" from the debtholders. This walk-away option is potent by virtue of the limited liability that owners (stockholders) enjoy. In addition, the fact that financial distress is costly provides opportunities for stockholders to blackmail the creditors and thus engage in "strategic debt service." These ideas will be developed later in this chapter.

Consider a simplified situation in which firm XYZ has a simple capital structure with n shares of common stock and zero coupon bonds with a face value of F. Assume that the bonds are due to mature on date T. The current date is t. Let us assume that the markets are frictionless, with no taxes at corporate or personal level. If we were to assume that financial distress and bankruptcy are costless, then we have the value conservation requirement:

$$V = S + B \qquad (8.4)$$

where V is the total value of the firm, S is the value of equity, and B is the market value of corporate debt. In this situation, equity can be thought of as a call option on the assets of the firm, with a strike price of F and a maturity of $T - t$. This is best understood in the context of the arbitrage argument shown in Table 8-14. Note that the payoff of the equity may be written as

$$\max (0, V^* - F)$$

where V^* is the value of the assets of the firm at date T and F is the face value of debt. If σ is the volatility of the assets of the firm, then the value of equity can be written (using Black and Scholes pricing model developed in Chapter 7) as

$$S = VN(d_1) - Fe^{-r(T-t)}N(d_2) \qquad (8.5)$$

Transaction at Date t	Cashflow at Date t	$V^* \leq F$	$V^* > F$
Buy Equity of the Firm	$-S$	0	$V^* - F$
Buy Bonds of the Firm	$-B$	V^*	F

TABLE 8-14
Corporate Debt Pricing

where $N(d_1)$ is the cumulative normal density evaluated at d_1 and $N(d_2)$ is the cumulative normal density evaluated at d_2. Furthermore,

$$d_1 = \frac{\ln\left(\frac{V}{F}\right) + \left(r + \frac{\sigma^2}{2}\right)(T - t)}{\sigma\sqrt{T - t}}$$

and

$$d_2 = d_1 - \sigma\sqrt{T - t}$$

The value of debt B is

$$V - S$$

Substituting for S from Equation (8.5) and simplifying we get the value of corporate debt to be

$$B = V[1 - N(d_1)] + Fe^{-r(T-t)}N(d_2)$$

Simplifying,

$$B = Fe^{-r(T-t)}\left[N(d_2) + \frac{V}{Fe^{-r(T-t)}}N(-d_1)\right]$$

where we have used the fact that $1 - N(d_1) = N(-d_1)$ by the symmetry of normal distribution.

We can think about the value of corporate debt in the following way. The payoffs of the corporate bond may be written as

$$\min(V^*, F).$$

Rewriting this, we get

$$F - \max(0, F - V^*) \qquad (8.6)$$

Note that the payoff of the risky corporate bond consists of two parts. The first part is F, which is exactly what the buyer of a default-free discount bond will get. The second part is the value of a put option on the assets of the firm with a strike price equal to the face value of corporate debt. Who owns this put option? The equity holders do, which gives them the right to sell the assets of the firm with a strike price equal to the face value of debt. This put option arises by virtue of the limited liability privilege that equity holders enjoy.

Merton (1974) carries this analysis further and computes the default spread between corporate and Treasury discount securities. Let us define the yield to maturity $y_t(T)$ of the corporate discount bond at date t as

$$y_t(T) = -\frac{\ln\left\{\frac{B}{F}\right\}}{T - t}. \qquad (8.7)$$

If r is the default-free riskless rate, then the default spread π_t may be defined as

$$\pi_t = y_t(T) - r. \qquad (8.8)$$

Substituting for B and simplifying, we get the default spread

$$\pi_t = y_t(T) - r = -\frac{1}{T - t}\ln\left[N(d_2) + \frac{V}{Fe^{-r(T-t)}}N(-d_1)\right]. \qquad (8.9)$$

The default spread can be computed exactly as a function of such important factors as (i) the level of debt F, (ii) the volatility of the underlying assets, and (iii) the maturity T of the corporate debt. In fact, using binomial methods such default premiums are easily calculated in spread sheets. Two illustrative examples of default spreads that are obtainable using the model in Merton (1974) appear in Tables 8-15 and 8-16. (These tables are drawn from Anderson and Sundaresan (1996), which provides simple binomial approximations of Merton (1974).) In Tables 8-15 and 8-16 the leverage factor is denoted by $d = \frac{Fe^{-r(T-t)}}{V}$.

Note in these examples that the default spread is increasing in the leverage d and in the volatility of the underlying asset σ^2. The effect with respect to time to maturity depends crucially on the degree of the firm's leverage. For example, for $d = .5$ the premiums for $T = 2$ are less than those for $T = 10$; the reverse holds true for $d = 1.5$. The

σ^2	d	π
0.030	0.200	0.000
0.030	0.500	0.012
0.030	1.000	5.129
0.030	1.500	20.578
0.100	0.200	0.002
0.100	0.500	0.817
0.100	1.000	9.738
0.100	1.500	23.022
0.200	0.200	0.118
0.200	0.500	3.087
0.200	1.000	14.266
0.200	1.500	26.601

TABLE 8-15
Corporate Discount Debt, Two-Year Maturity

Time to maturity $(T - t) = 2.00$ years, $V = 1$, $r = 1.05$

σ^2	d	π
0.030	0.200	0.004
0.030	0.500	0.376
0.030	1.000	2.430
0.030	1.500	4.969
0.100	0.200	0.474
0.100	0.500	2.113
0.100	1.000	4.826
0.100	1.500	7.116
0.200	0.200	1.872
0.200	0.500	4.379
0.200	1.000	7.351
0.200	1.500	9.546

TABLE 8-16
Corporate Discount Debt, Ten-Year Maturity

Time to maturity $(T - t) = 10.00$ years, $V = 1$, $r = 1.05$

reasoning is that, for firms with a low degree of leverage, default will occur only if the firm value declines substantially, a prospect that is more likely for long maturities than for short maturities. For highly leveraged firms, default will be avoided only if the firm value improves significantly, a prospect that is more likely for higher maturities. Sarig and Warga (1989a) use zero coupons issued by the government and corporations of different credit ratings to study the risk structure of interest rates. They conclude that the shape of the default-risk premiums are strikingly similar to the theoretical predictions of Merton (1974). Their figure as reproduced in Figure 8-8 suggests that the model of Merton (1974) is consistent with the shape of the default-premium structure. Their table (see Table 8-17) provides the default evidence for various rating categories.

Now let us review Tables 8-15 and 8-16 to see how the process of financial distress and bankruptcy is modeled. The contractual provisions of the debt contract are specified

FIGURE 8-8   *The Term Structure of Risk Premia*

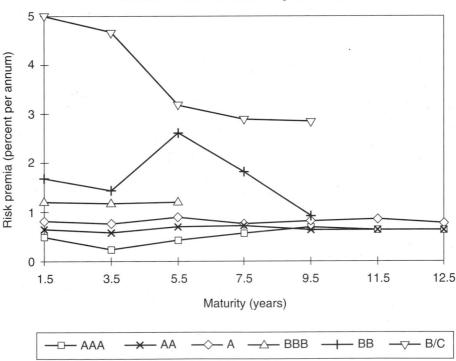

Yield spreads for corporate zero coupon bonds, February 1985 through September 1987. Maturity numbers (horizontal axis) correspond to the average maturity of each cell in Table 8-17. Average yield spreads are calculated as follows: in each month the yield to an individual corporate bond has subtracted from it the yield to a zero coupon government "strip" with identical maturity. If no government strip with identical maturity existed, the yields on the two "strips" with maturities most closely bounding the corporate bond were interpolated to obtain the appropriate risk-free zero coupon yield. These yield differences were then averaged across bonds in a given month and then across time to produce the results.

TABLE 8-17   *Yield Spreads for Corporate Zero Coupon Bonds*

Average yield spreads are calculated over the period February 1985 through September 1987 as follows: in each month the yield to an individual corporate bond has subtracted from it the yield to a zero coupon government "strip" with identical maturity. If no government strip with identical maturity existed, the yield on the two "strips" with maturities most closely bounding the corporate bond were interpolated to obtain the appropriate risk-free zero coupon yield. These yield differences were then averaged across bonds in a given month and then across time to produce the results reported for each cell. The unrated column contains bonds from a mixture of ratings and should not be taken to be the lowest rating group. The figures are in percent per annum, and the number of observations is reported below the yield.

Maturity	AAA	AA	A	BBB	BB	B/C	Unrated
0.5–2.5 Years	0.410	0.621	0.775	1.326	1.670	4.996	3.081
	21	74	123	48	64	41	38
2.5–4.5 Years	0.232	0.562	0.736	1.275	1.495	4.650	3.232
	11	99	251	152	79	117	96
4.5–6.5 Years	NA	0.620	0.778	1.405	2.730	3.365	3.197
		114	221	59	58	125	119
6.5–8.5 Years	NA	0.620	0.660	NA	1.878	2.959	3.443
		96	138		51	80	119
8.5–10.5 Years	0.626	0.575	0.816	NA	0.989	2.912	3.099
	24	69	97		10	10	88
10.5–12.5 Years	NA	0.566	0.854	NA	NA	NA	2.478
		64	110				64
12.5 Plus Years	0.544	0.544	0.740	NA	NA	NA	2.516
	64	501	510				278

Source: Sarig, O., and Warga, A., *Journal of Finance*

exogenously. In Merton (1974), for example, two key contractual provisions are specified exogenously. First, the **lower reorganization boundary** is specified. This is the threshold value of the firm at which the control of the firm transfers from the stockholders to the bondholders. In the context of Table 8-16, bondholders have the right to take over the firm when the value of the firm V^* at maturity date T reaches a level that is less than or equal to F, the promised face amount. Second, the compensation to be received by creditors upon reaching the lower reorganization boundary is specified. The bondholders will receive min (V^*, F) at date T, once they take over.

There are several difficulties with this approach:

- Over the 1926–86 period, the yield spreads on high-grade corporates (AAA-rated) ranged from 15 to 215 basis points and averaged 77 basis points; and the yield spreads on BAAs (also investment-grade) ranged from 51 to 787 basis points and averaged 198 basis points. It is clear from Tables 8-15 and 8-16 that such spreads can only be accounted for within the Merton (1974) model by resorting to implausibly large values of d and σ. This observation appears in Kim, Ramaswamy, and Sundaresan (1993).

- Most corporate securities promise coupon payments; indeed, zero coupon corporate securities are relatively rare, and for good reason. After all, when an investor buys a long-term bond from a corporation, he or she would like to have a periodic credible signal that the corporation is doing well and generating sufficient cash flows to honor its promised coupon obligations; coupons represent such a credible signal. Sinking-fund provisions further enhance the value of the signal by requiring that the balloon payments be periodically reduced.

- Note that Table 8-15 places the burden of bankruptcy on the principal payment at maturity and not on the coupon obligations along the way. We can think of situations where the firm is illiquid and unable to meet a promised coupon. To keep the bondholders from taking over the firm, it may sell additional equity or resort to selling assets.

- The values of Treasury and corporate bonds are influenced significantly by interest-rate risk. For investment-grade corporate bonds, the bulk of the risk is interest-rate related and not due to credit-related factors. Jones, Mason, and Rosenfeld (1984) conclude that the introduction of stochastic interest rates might improve the performance of models such as Merton (1974). Kim, Ramaswamy, and Sundaresan (1993) confirm that the modeling of stochastic interest rates and cash-flow-triggered financial distress can explain the spreads between corporate and Treasury yields better.

- The model implicit in Table 8-15 does not take into account the process by which bankruptcies are resolved. Bankruptcies and financial distress are costly. Such costs have broad ramifications that have been ignored thus far. We will review the empirical evidence later and attempt to incorporate some of these facts into the corporate-pricing model.

Before we take some of the preceding features into account, let us examine how the framework should be modified in order to take into account additional debt claims that may be present in the firm's capital structure.

Subordinated Corporate Debt

In an insightful paper, Black and Cox (1976) have examined the problems associated with the pricing of subordinated debt claims. We will review the basics here. Consider the XYZ company in Table 8-18 and assume that it has two zero coupon issues due to mature at date T. Assume that one issue is senior with a promised face amount F_1 and another is a junior issue with a promised face amount F_2. We will continue to assume that the process of financial distress and bankruptcy is costless. If we were to denote the value at date t of the equity by S, the senior bonds by B_1, and the junior bonds by B_2, then the value conservation requires that

$$V_t = S + B_1 + B_2.$$

We will also assume that the bondholders have no recourse until date T when their face amount becomes due. (This unrealistic assumption will be removed later and the pricing implications will become clearer.)

TABLE 8-18   *Subordinated Corporate Debt*

Transaction at Date t	Cashflow at Date t	$V^* \leq F_1$	$F_1 < V^* \leq (F_1 + F_2)$	$V^* > (F_1 + F_2)$
1. Buy the equity of the firm	$-S$	0	0	$V^* - (F_1 + F_2)$
2. Buy the senior bonds of the firm	$-B_1$	V^*	F_1	F_1
3. Buy the junior bonds of the firm	$-B_2$	0	$V^* - F_1$	F_2

Table 8-18 illustrates the ideas in the pricing of subordinated debt. Note that the payoffs to the senior bondholders may be thought of as a covered call (see Chapter 7 if this is not clear); the senior bondholders own the firm, but they have sold a call on the firm with a strike price equal to the face value F_1 of their debt security. The equity is simply a call on the assets of the firm with a strike price equal to the combined value of the face amount $F_1 + F_2$. By value conservation, we can write the junior debt's value as a portfolio of calls; the subordinated debt is equivalent to a long position in a call with a strike price of F_1 and a short position in a call with a strike price of $F_1 + F_2$. Both calls are on the assets of the firm with a maturity date T.

Safety Covenants

Typically, bond covenanting may specify some net-worth constraints or safety covenants. For example, if at any time l, where $t \leq l \leq T$, the value of the firm V_l were to drop to a level X, then the bondholders have the right to take over the firm and obtain a prespecified compensation—the actual amount may be written down by a certain amount from the originally promised payments to reflect the costliness of financial distress.

Consider Table 8-19, where there is a single issue of a zero coupon debt. Let us modify the covenants so that the lower reorganization boundary is X. If this boundary is

TABLE 8-19   *Safety Covenants*

Transaction at Date t	Cashflow at Date t	First date l (when $V_l \leq X$)	Maturity Date ($V_i > X$ for all i)	Maturity Date ($V_i > X$ for all i)
1. Buy the equity of the firm	$-S$	$\max[X - Y, 0]$	0	$V^* - F$
2. Buy the bonds of the firm	$-B$	Y	V^*	F

reached by the firm's value before T, then the bondholders get an amount Y. In this case, the stockholders have a down-and-out option. A down-and-out call option is very similar to a regular call option (discussed in chapter 7). Unlike a regular call option, however, a down-and-out option automatically expires when the underlying asset reaches a prespecified low value. In the context of the corporate bond pricing problem, stockholders have a call option (as valued in Equation (8.5)) but with a safety covenant, the call becomes a down-and-out option: when the value of the firm reaches a low level X, the firm is taken over. Bond holders get Y and equity holders get $X - Y$ or 0, whichever is higher. Consequently, the bondholders may be thought of as owning the firm, but as having sold a down-and-out option to the stockholders. It is clear from this table that the safety covenant allows the bondholders to take over the firm sooner.

So far, financial distress has not been explicitly modeled in the pricing of corporate debt. It is useful to review the empirical evidence on financial distress before we examine corporate debt pricing models which incorporate financial distress.

Financial Distress

Central to the understanding of corporate debt is the process by which financial distress is managed. This is especially important for poorly rated debt which are subjected to a higher probability of incurring financial distress. John (1993) surveys and synthesizes the factors pertaining to financial distress. He proposes that financial distress happens when the liquid assets of the firm are not sufficient to meet the obligations of the firm's debt contracts. Thus, financial distress can be thought of as a mismatch between the firm's current assets and its current obligations.

It can be handled in a number of ways:

1. The existing assets can be partially liquidated. This will improve the liquidity of the firm and stave off financial distress. The disadvantage of this approach is that there are also liquidation costs (both direct and indirect).
2. The firm can enter into a process of negotiation with the debtholders and reconfigure the debt obligations. This may entail a reduction in the liabilities of the firm or a deferment of the payments. Such debt restructuring will involve
    *   reducing the coupons and/or the principal obligations,
    *   increasing the maturity of the debt, and
    *   accepting the equity of the company in lieu of some of the outstanding obligations.
3. The firm can issue additional claims in order to achieve the liquidity necessary to avoid financial distress.

Note that the process of managing financial distress involves financial reorganization either on the asset side or on the liability side or both. It can be accomplished either out of court or within the formal bankruptcy codes that are applicable. The traditional approach to managing financial distress is for either the debtor or the creditor of the distressed firm to file for bankruptcy protection under Chapter 11. The debtor will then have the right to propose a reorganization within 120 days from the filing date. The process of financial reorganization may involve the creditors and the 120-day period may be extended by the court, if it is deemed necessary. The plan is then evaluated by the debtholders who may either accept or reject it. Chapter 7 of the bankruptcy code is used to liquidate the firm if the reorganization plan is not accepted. The liquidation costs associated with court-supervised procedures can be quite high both in terms of the resources and in terms of the time it takes to complete the process.

The key empirical regularities associated with financial reorganizations in the 1980s are well-documented. [This section and the next one are drawn heavily from Anderson and Sundaresan (1996).] Franks and Torous (1989; 1993) find that:

- Bankruptcies are costly both because of direct costs and because of disruptions in the firm's activities.
- Bankruptcy procedures give considerable scope for opportunistic behavior by the various parties involved.
- Deviations from the absolute priority of claims are common.

All of this suggests that the lower reorganization boundary of the firm used in Merton (1974) and in Black and Cox (1976) misrepresents real-life reorganizations in many important respects. In an important recent study Franks and Torous (1993) point out that the costliness of the formal bankruptcy process creates an incentive for renegotiation of the distressed firm's claims. They report that renegotiations result in substantial deviations from absolute priority that are net favorable to equity. In the renegotiations some or all holders of the firm's securities agree to restructure their claims. However, despite the incentives to do so, in practice it often proves impossible to renegotiate claims, resulting in formal bankruptcy and liquidation (Asquith, Gertner, and Scharfstein (1994)).

Corporate-Debt Pricing with Distress

Kim, Ramaswamy, and Sundaresan (1993) consider a model much like that in Merton (1974) but with several important changes. We will call this the KRS model.

- In the KRS model, financial distress arises out of cash-flow constraints. If the cash flows are insufficient to meet the contractual coupon, the bondholders take over the firm. This definition is the same as the one used by Moody's Investor Service (1994) in defining default.
- The payoffs to the bondholders when a default occurs are affected by the liquidation costs. The payoffs are

$$\min [\delta(t)B_t, \, V^*]$$

where V^* is the value of the firm when default occurred, B_t is the value of an otherwise identical riskless bond, and $\delta(t)$ is a positive fraction. The idea here is that the bondholders will get something less than the riskless bond's value or the value of the firm upon default, whichever is lower.
- In addition, the KRS model allows for stochastic interest rates. The model proposed by Cox, Ingersoll, and Ross (1985) (discussed in chapter 6) is used by KRS.

In KRS, the cash flow process is modeled as follows. The present value of current and expected future cash flows is V_t, which follows a two-state branching process:

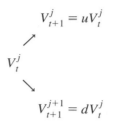

$$V_{t+1}^{j} = uV_t^{j}$$

$$V_t^{j}$$

$$V_{t+1}^{j+1} = dV_t^{j}$$

V_t may be interpreted as the cumulative dividend value of the firm were it to be financed entirely by equity. The cash flows (f_t) of the project are then given by the general two-state branching process:

$$f_{t+1}^{j} = \beta V_{t+1}^{j+1} = \beta u V_t^{j}$$

$$f_t^{j} = \beta V_t^{j}$$

$$f_{t+1}^{j+1} = \beta V_{t+1}^{j+1} = \beta d V_t^{j}$$

The probabilities of transition are specified in a general way as q and $1 - q$. At each node, the conditions of financial distress can be applied and the cash flows to the bondholders can be computed. Using the approach outlined in Chapter 6, we compute the values of debt and equity.

According to KRS, cash-flow-induced bankruptcy is better able to explain the observed spreads between corporate and Treasury yields and is an important consideration in the modeling of corporate debt. Modeling the term structure allows KRS to value callable corporate and Treasury debt.

Anderson and Sundaresan (1996) consider a model similar to Merton (1974). We will call this the AS model. Like KRS, this model admits liquidation costs; it is costly for the creditors to take over the firm. The model is summarized below.

- In the AS model, cash flows are treated in exactly the same way as in KRS.
- In the AS model, liquidation costs are fixed at K for each node.
- The AS model permits a simplified mechanism for the firm to make take-it-or-leave-it offers to debt holders at each node of the lattice. This allows for opportunistic debt service and deviations from absolute priority.
- Thus, the debtholders will get an amount equal to $V - K$, where V is the value of the firm at the time of takeover. But it may be in their best interests to instead entertain a take-it-or-leave-it offer (which is bounded by the cash flows generated by the firm) made by the firm to the debtholders. If the amount offered is equal to or greater than the contracted amount, the creditors will accept it and continue to the next period. If it is less than the contracted amount, the creditors have the choice of either accepting the service or rejecting the debt service. If the debt service is

accepted, the project continues to the next date. If the debt service is rejected, the project is liquidated.

- By formulating the valuation problem in this manner, the firm has the option of choosing to underperform the debt contract even when the health of the project would enable it to fully meet the obligations. This option arises from the costliness of liquidation.

The AS model explicitly accounts for interactions between creditors and equity holders and the lower reorganization boundary; the sharing of cash flows (and values) by the stakeholders is obtained endogenously. This model generates spreads of corporate debt over Treasuries that are consistent with the observed spreads in the market, even at very low levels of debt and liquidation costs. In the United States, yield spreads on long-term corporate bonds of firms rated AAA or AA have averaged approximately 125 basis points in recent years. The AS model reproduces these levels of yield spreads with a liquidation cost as low as $K = 0.047$. In addition, the model allows the exploration of the impact of alternate contractual provisions on the pricing of corporate debt.

Several other papers have modified and extended the insights of Merton (1974) and of Black and Cox (1976). Longstaff and Schwartz (1993) allow deviations from absolute priority in a standard options-pricing framework; however, they assume that the allocation of the value of the bankrupt firm amongst the various stakeholders is specified exogenously rather than being the outcome of an endogenous process of negotiation. Leland (1994) uses the Merton's framework but allows an endogenous lower reorganization boundary; in this model the promised cash flows to creditors are met by issuing new shares until the value of equity is driven to zero. This approach generates default premiums that are closer to what one observes in real life. Attention is confined to perpetual debt in order to get closed form solutions. Another paper that is very close to the spirit of the AS model, Mella-Barral and Perraudin (1993), explicitly considers opportunistic behavior by equity holders when firms are in financial distress. They show that the default premium is increased by the presence of opportunistic behavior. In addition, they show that such behavior may minimize the under-investment problem.

HYBRIDS

A number of fixed-income securities have been issued with a significant exposure to other segments of the capital markets. For example, convertible bonds have been issued by corporations for a long time. Such bonds provide the investors with the option to convert the bond into a prespecified number of shares of the issuing firm. Often, convertible bonds are issued with a call feature. The call option, which is held by the issuer, is used to force conversion, if necessary. More recently, corporations have issued a security known as PERCS. This is the *p*referred *e*quity *r*edemption *c*umulative *s*tock. Such securities are issued for a fixed-term as bonds with a prespecified coupon, but the issuer typically has the right to call in the PERCS by paying cash or common stock at any time. If the issue is not called before the stated maturity, then the PERCS are converted into a prespecified number of shares of common stock on a mandatory basis. In addition, there are a number of fixed-income securities, such as dual currency bonds, currency option bonds, and commodity-linked bonds, that are made by corporations and other institutions. This section describes some of the important products in this market and provides an overview of the theory and empirical evidence regarding the pricing of these products. These products may have exposures to one or more of the following markets: fixed-income, equity, foreign exchange, and commodity. They are referred to as *hybrid securities*.

Convertible Bonds

Perhaps the most common type of hybrid debt instrument that combines equity features with debt features is the convertible bond. Like straight debt, convertible debt pays coupons and principal to investors, and it is senior to equity claims issued by the firm. But the owners of convertible debt have the right to exchange their claim for prespecified number of shares of common stock of the company. Most of the convertible debt is issued with a call feature. This hybrid security has a very long history in the United States and has been studied extensively by researchers.

Convertible bonds account for a significant percentage of the total outstanding corporate debt. According to some studies, convertible debt accounted for nearly a third of the corporate debt of companies in Compustat during 1963–1984. As a rule, convertible debt is issued as a subordinated debt. Typically, issuers have a moderate to low credit rating. Firms with high volatility in earnings, relatively high leverage, and a larger percentage of intangible assets tend to issue convertible securities.

Table 8-20 summarizes some features of two recent issues of convertible debt securities. Note that the credit ratings of these two issuers were poor. In fact of the 27 issues of convertible debt from January 1993 to October 1994, only 4 issues were rated.

The academic research on convertible debt can be divided into (a) studies of the rationale behind this kind of debt and (b) studies of the valuation.

TABLE 8-20   *Two Convertible Debt Issues*

Issuer	Issue Date	Standard & Poors Rating	Amount (in millions)	Offer Price	Coupon
INCO Ltd.	5/7/94	BBB–	150	115.00	5.75%
Swift Energy	1/2/93	B+	100	114.00	6.50%

Rationale for Convertible Debt. Several papers explore the rationale for the use of convertible debt securities. Equity holders have an incentive to prefer riskier projects; this enables them to get the upside if the project does well, and avoid the downside by invoking limited liability if the project does not do well. This line of reasoning also suggests that after issuing regular debt, equity holders may resort to risk shifting. The use of convertible debt solves this problem, as Green (1984) shows. In an influential paper Myers and Majluf (1984) show that when managers have more information about projects than the suppliers of capital, the issuance of traditional capital is not optimal. Constantinides and Grundy (1989b) and Stein (1992) show that the use of convertible debt resolves some of the problems associated with asymmetric information. Stein argues that convertible securities may represent a desirable middleground between the pure-equity financing alternative and the pure-debt financing alternative. Issuance of pure equity has informational costs, as pointed out earlier; issuance of debt may subject the firm to costly financial distress. By issuing a convertible bond and placing a call provision which enables the issuing firm to force conversion when necessary, the firm may be able to optimize its proceeds.

Valuation of Convertible Debt. The structure of the convertible bond is probably better understood in the context of the terms of the issue.

*   The bond has a stated coupon. This is 6.5% for the Swift issue (see Table 8-20).
*   The bond has a stated maturity. The Swift convertibles (see Table 8-20) mature in the year 2003. Thus, their stated life is approximately 10 years.
*   The current market price for the Swift convertibles of 114 is at a premium.

Each convertible bond specifies a conversion ratio which is the number of shares into which bond may be converted at any time. Let us assume that the conversion ratio for this company is 50 shares per bond. If the stock is selling at a price of $22.00 per share, then the value of conversion is $22 \times 50 = 1,100$. This provides one lower bound for the value of convertible. If the bond sold for a lesser price, we can buy it and convert it immediately.

The valuation of the convertible bond requires the identification of an optimal conversion policy. We can provide a simple valuation framework much like that of other interest rate sensitive securities.

Let N be the number of shares of common stock of the firm outstanding. Let there be M the number of convertible bonds outstanding. Let each bond be convertible into n shares of common stock. Each bond is entitled to a coupon payment of c and a principal amount of F. Let us examine the payoffs of the convertible debt at the maturity date T of the bond. If V_T is the value of the firm at date T, then the convertible debt, if still outstanding, is worth the maximum of its value as a straight bond and its value upon conversion. Its conversion value is given by

$$\lambda V_T$$

where,

$$\lambda = \frac{M}{N + M}$$

is the dilution factor associated with the conversion. Then the value of the convertible bond at T is the maximum of either its value as a straight bond or its conversion value as shown:

$$\max (\min [F + c, V_T], \lambda V_T).$$

What is the optimal conversion policy at date T? If the straight bond value ever falls below the conversion value, it is rational for the holder to convert. Similarly, if the straight debt value of the convertible exceeds the conversion value, it is optimal not to convert. Hence, the optimal conversion strategy is to convert when the straight debt value is equal to its conversion value. This means that the value of the convertible debt under the optimal conversion strategy at date $s < T$ is

$$\max (\lambda V_s, P_s + c)$$

where $P_s + c$ is the value of not converting at date s and proceeding optimally forward. Using the recursive valuation techniques developed in Chapters 6 and 7 we can compute the value of convertible debt.

This analysis obviously does not examine call features that are typically present in convertible debt. With a call, either voluntary or involuntary conversion could occur. Clearly, if the conversion value exceeds the straight debt value in the absence of a call, then voluntary conversion should occur. If the conversion value is less than the straight debt value (in the absence of calls) but more than the call price, then the issuer will use the call to force conversion. In general, the valuation of a callable convertible bond requires a fairly elaborate pricing procedure which is beyond the scope of this book. Major papers in this area are Ingersoll (1977) and Brennan and Schwartz (1977; 1980), which focus on the valuation of convertible securities and characterize optimal conversion policies.

The empirical evidence on call policies associated with convertible debt is somewhat mixed. Ingersoll (1977) shows that during the period 1968–1975 more than 95% of the sample of convertible debt was called after considerable delays. The median firm in the sample waited until the conversion value exceeded the call value by more than 40%. The valuation of options requires the modeling of the firm's value process as well as of uncertain interest rates. The call option held by the issuer and the conversion option held by the investors are dual options: The optimal exercise policy of one is contingent on the strategy of the other.

In addition, there are studies of call policies of convertible and non-convertible securities. Most of the convertible bonds are issued with call features that enable the issuers of convertible bonds to better control the conversion policies of investors. Harris and Raviv (1985), Mikkelson (1981), Jaffee and Shleiffer (1990), Asquith and Mullins (1991), and Vu (1986) are examples of this research. Other studies examine the stock-price reactions to the issuance of convertible securities, notably Dann and Mikkelson (1984), Eckbo (1986) and Mikkelson and Partch (1986).

Debt with Warrants

A financing arrangement somewhat similar to convertible debt is a debt issue with attached warrants on the common stock of issuer. Such warrants represent rights to buy prespecified number of shares of common stock at a specified strike price before their expiration date. Superficially, warrants resemble call options. But there are important differences between warrants and call options. Calls are traded in organized exchanges with clearing-house guarantees. Warrants are issued by the firm raising capital. Typically, such warrants are offered as a part of a bond issue by the firm. Secondly, when call options are exercised no new shares are issued by the firm. On the other hand, when warrants are exercised, the firm will issue additional shares of common stock. In return, the investor who exercises the warrants pays the strike price to the firm. Typically, warrants have a life 2 to 5 years, whereas listed options tend to have a much shorter maturity (although LEAPS have maturity comparable to that of warrants).

Cox and Rubinstein (1985) provides a simple analysis of warrants. Their analysis is briefly summarized in Table 8-21. Consider a firm that has N shares of common stock and M warrants that can only be exercised at date T. Let the market price of each warrant be denoted by W. Then the total value of the firm may be denoted as

$$V = NS + MW$$

where S is the price of a share of common stock. As in the analysis of convertible debt, let us consider the payoffs at date T. Assume that the strike price is K. When the warrant is exercised, the payoffs are

$$MW_T = \frac{M}{N + M}(V_T + MK) - MK.$$

The payoffs simply reflect the fact that the warrant holders get their share of the value of the firm, including the strike price paid by the warrant holders. From this payoff, we subtract the strike price that was paid. The above expression may be simplified as

$$MW_T = \frac{M}{N + M}(V_T - NK).$$

The value of the warrant prior to T has to be solved by using the recursive valuation approach presented in Chapters 6 and 7.

Security	Transaction at Date t	$V_T \leq NK$	$V_T > NK$
Buy stock	NS	V_T	$\frac{N}{N + M}(V_T + MK)$
Buy warrants	MW		$\frac{M}{N + M}(V_T - NK)$

TABLE 8-21
Warrant Valuation

PERCS

Preferred equity redemption cumulative stock, or PERCS, are securities that have the following features.

- A life of three to four years.
- The same price as the underlying common stock price at issue date.

- A mandatory conversion feature at the end of their life, and the possibility of conversion by the investor prior to the maturity date of the PERCS.
- Callability by the issuers. The call price is set at a premium to the stock price at issue, but declines eventually to a lesser premium at the end of its life.
- Rules of conversion that are specified at issue. If PERCS are called, they are redeemable into prespecified number of shares of common stock of the issuing company.

In Table 8-22, we list some PERCS issues and their characteristics.

In many ways, PERCS are similar to convertible securities and the framework that is used for pricing convertible debt can also be used, with some modifications, for pricing PERCS.

TABLE 8-22   *PERCS Issues*

Issuer	Issue Date	Redemption Date	Amount (in millions)	Offer Price	Dividend Yield
GM	6/25/91	7/01/94	641.30	41.375	3.31%
Kmart	8/15/91	9/16/94	1,012.00	44.000	3.41%
Sears	2/20/92	4/01/95	1,075.00	43.000	3.75%
Citicorp	10/14/92	1/30/95	1,003.00	14.750	1.21%

PERLS

Principal exchange rate linked securities (PERLS) are debt securities whose principal payments are denominated in a foreign currency, and are linked to a specified exchange rate for U.S. dollars and the currencies of other countries. These debt securities have been issued by agencies and corporations in the United States; the coupon is in U.S. dollars. Essentially, this security provides investors with a currency play on the principal payment. Table 8-23 provides a list of PERLS issues.

The motivation for issuing PERLS can be traced to the asset-liability profile of the issuing company. Consider a company that is expecting a known revenue in Japanese yen five years from now and that requires an amount in U.S. dollars now. It may issue

TABLE 8-23   *PERLS Issues*

Issuer	Issue Date	Coupon	Amount (in millions)	Maturity	Indexed Principal
Sallie Mae	3/12/87	12.125%	100.00	3/20/90	Australian $145.20
Fannie Mae	3/22/89	14.625%	75.00	4/6/94	$75+ Australian $90.9075 − JY9.84375*bn*
Ford Credit	5/6/87	11.00%	100.00	5/19/92	$200 − JY13.920*bn*

PERLS with a maturity of five years that specify that the principal is to be repaid in Japanese yen, but that pay coupons in U.S. dollars. These instruments may be thought of as a way to structure the liabilities of the firm so that they are better aligned with the assets.

CONCLUSION

This chapter described the agency and corporate debt markets. The institutional features of these debt markets were described, and empirical evidence on the maturity composition, the risk premiums, and the sizes of different sectors of these markets were presented. We also reviewed the available theory and empirical evidence on financial distress and corporate-debt valuation. A brief study of hybrid instruments such as convertible debt was also provided.

PROBLEMS

8.1   What are agency debt securities? Identify the eight major federally sponsored agencies.

8.2   Explain the role of Resolution Trust Corporation (RTC).

8.3   Briefly describe the roles of the agencies FHLB, SLMA, and FFCB.

8.4   Table 8-1 indicates that most agency securities are callable. What are the reasons for this?

8.5   Who are the major rating agencies? Describe the rating conventions. Identify the rating ranges for investment- and noninvestment-grade corporate debt.

8.6   Explain why many investment-grade corporate bonds issued during late 1980s and early 1990s do not have call features, whereas bonds issued prior to these periods do have call features.

8.7   Explain why junk bonds have call features.

8.8 (a)   What is the motivation for providing sinking-fund provisions in bonds?

(b)   Consider the Eurobond in the table below that will repay a total of 75 million in three equal payments beginning in year 4.

Sinking Period	Principal Amount Repaid	Years to Repayment
1	25 million	4 years
2	25 million	5 years
3	25 million	6 years

Assume that the holder of this bond will receive an annual coupon of 10%. (i) Write out the cash flow pattern of this bond. (ii) Assume that the sinking-fund requirements are met by buying the bond back at par. How will you go about computing the yield to maturity of the bond?

8.9   What are the key reasons for an issuer to use the commercial paper market for short-term funds?

8.10   What are the different sectors of the corporate bond market? Briefly describe each sector.

8.11 (a)   What are the procedures that are available for managing financial distress?

    (b)   Explain the following terms: (i) Chapter 7, (ii) Chapter 11, (iii) prepacks, (iv) exchange offers, (v) workouts.

8.12   Identify the key differences between junk bonds and investment-grade bonds.

8.13   What is Rule 144A? How has it affected the corporate debt market?

8.14   Describe briefly the privately placed corporate debt market. Who are the typical lenders? What are the pros and cons of borrowing in this market?

8.15   Describe the model used by Merton (1974) to value corporate debt. What are his major conclusions? Critique the model.

8.16   Briefly explain how you will incorporate (i) costly liquidations, (ii) opportunistic debt service, and (iii) deviations from absolute priority in a model of valuing corporate debt.

REFERENCES

Altman, E. 1992. "Revisiting the High-Yield Bond Market." *Financial Management* 21(2):78–92.

Altman, E., and S. Nammachar 1987. *Investing in Junk Bonds: Inside the High Yield Debt Market.* New York: John Wiley & Sons.

Anderson, R. W., and S. M. Sundaresan 1996. "Design and Valuation of Debt Contracts." *Review of Financial Studies* 9(1):37–68.

Asquith, P., R. Gertner, and D. Scharfstein 1994. "Anatomy of Financial Distress: An Examination of Junk-bond Issues." *Quarterly Journal of Economics* 109(3):625–658.

Asquith, P., and D. Mullins, Jr. 1991. "Convertible Debt, Corporate Call Policy and Voluntary Conversion." *Journal of Finance* 46(4):1270–1289.

Baumol, W. J., B. G. Malkiel, and R. E. Quandt 1966. "The Valuation of Convertible Securities." *Quarterly Journal of Economics* 65:48–59.

Black, F., and J. C. Cox 1976. "Valuing Corporate Securities: Some Effects of Bond Indenture Provisions." *Journal of Finance* 31:351–368.

Black, F., and M. Scholes 1973. "The Pricing of Options and Corporate Liabilities." *Journal of Political Economy* 81:637–654.

Brennan, M. J., and E. Schwartz 1977. "Convertible Bonds: Valuation and Optimal Strategies for Call and Conversion." *Journal of Finance* 32:1699–1715.

Brennan, M. J., and E. S. Schwartz 1980. "Analyzing Convertible Bonds." *Journal of Financial and Quantitative Analysis* 15(4):907–929.

Campbell, C. J., L. Ederington, and P. Vankudre 1991. "Tax Shields, Sample Selection Bias and the Information Content of Convertible Bond Calls." *Journal of Finance* 46(4):1291–1324.

Carey, M. S., S. D. Prowse, S. D. Rea, and G. F. Udell 1993. "Recent Developments in the Market for Privately Placed Debt." *Federal Reserve Bulletin* 79(2):77–92.

Constantinides, G., and B. Grundy 1989a. Call and Conversion of Convertible Bonds: Theory and Evidence. University of Chicago Working Paper.

Constantinides, G., and B. Grundy 1989b. "Optimal Investment with Stock Repurchase and Financing as Signals." *Review of Financial Studies* 2:445–465.

Cowan, A. R., N. Nayar, and A. K. Singh 1990. "Stock Returns before and after Calls of Convertible Bonds." *Journal of Financial and Quantitative Analysis* 25:549–554.

Cox, J. C., J. Ingersoll, and S. A. Ross 1985. "A Theory of the Term Structure of Interest Rates." *Econometrica* 53:385–407.

Cox, J. C., and M. Rubinstein 1985. "Options Markets." Englewood Cliffs, New Jersey: Prentice-Hall, Inc.

Crabbe, L. 1991. *Callable Corporate Bonds: A Vanishing Breed.* Washington, D.C.: Board of Governors of the Federal Reserve System.

Crabbe, L., and J. Helwege 1993. *Alternative Tests of Agency Theories of Callable Corporate Bonds.* Washington, D.C.: Board of Governors of the Federal Reserve System.

Dann, L., and W. Mikkelson 1984. "Convertible Debt Issuance, Capital Structure Changes and Financing-Related Information: Some New Evidence." *Journal of Financial Economics* 13(2):157–186.

Diament, P. 1993. "Semi-Empirical Smooth Fit to the Treasury Yield Curve." *The Journal of Fixed-Income* 3(1):55–70.

Dunn, K., and K. Eades 1989. "Voluntary Conversion of Convertible Securities and The Optimal Call Strategy." *Journal of Financial Economics* 23:273–301.

Eckbo, E. 1986. "Valuation Effects of Corporate Debt Offerings." *Journal of Financial Economics* 15:119–151.

Franks, J., and W. Torous 1989. "An Empirical Investigation of Firms in Reorganization." *Journal of Finance* 44:747–779.

Franks, J., and W. Torous 1993. A Comparison of Financial Recontracting in Workouts and Chapter 11 Reorganizations. ESF Finance Network Working Paper 26.

Green, R. C. 1984. "Investment Incentives, Debt and Warrants" *Journal of Financial Economics* 13(1):115–136.

Hardy, E. 1995. "Power to the Creditors." *Forbes* (March 27): 148.

Harris M., and A. Raviv 1985. "A Sequential Signalling Model of Convertible Debt Call Policy." *Journal of Finance* 41:815–830.

Helwege, J. 1994. How Long Do Junk Bonds Spend in Default? Washington, D.C.: Board of Governors of the Federal Reserve System.

Horwood, C. 1995. "Global Bond Markets, Tough Call for U.S. Agencies." *Euromoney* (March): 14, 16.

Ingersoll, J. E. 1977. "An Examination of Corporate Call Policies on Convertible Securities." *Journal of Finance* 32(2):463–478.

Jaffee, D., and A. Shleifer 1990. "Costs of Financial Distress, Delayed Calls of Convertible Bonds and the Role of Investment Banks." *Journal of Business* 63:107–124.

John, K. 1993. "Managing Financial Distress and Valuing Distressed Securities: A Survey and a Research Agenda." *Financial Management* (Special issue on financial distress) 22(3):60–78.

Jones, E. P., S. P. Mason, and E. Rosenfeld 1984. "Contingent Claims Analysis of Corporate Capital Structures: An Empirical Analysis." *Journal of Finance* 39:611–625.

Kim, I. J., K. Ramaswamy, and S. M. Sundaresan 1993. "Valuation of Corporate Fixed-Income Securities." *Financial Management* (Special issue on financial distress) 22(3):60–78.

Leland, H. 1994. "Risky Debt, Bond Covenants and Optimal Capital Structure." *Journal of Finance* 49:1213–1252.

Longstaff, F. A., and E. S. Schwartz 1993. Valuing Risky Debt: A New Approach. Anderson Graduate School of Management at UCLA Working Paper.

Mella-Barral, P., and W. R. M. Perraudin 1993. Strategic Debt Service. CEPR/European Science Foundation Working Paper 39.

Merton, R. C. 1974. "On the Pricing of Corporate Debt: The Risk Structure of Interest Rates." *Journal of Finance* 29:449–470.

Mikkelson, W. H. 1981. "Convertible Calls and Security Returns." *Journal of Financial Economics* 9(3):237–264.

Mikkelson, W. H., and M. M. Partch 1986. "Valuation Effects of Security Offerings and the Issuance Process." *Journal of Financial Economics* 15(1/2):31–60.

Moody's Investor Service 1994. *Corporate Bond Defaults and Default Rates, 1970–1993.* Moody's Investor Service, Global Credit Research.

Myers, S. 1977. "Determinants of Corporate Borrowing." *Journal of Financial Economics:* 5:147–175.

Myers, S., and N. Majluf 1984. "Corporate Financing and Investment Decisions When Firms Have Information That Investors Do not Have." *Journal of Financial Economics* 13:187–221.

Nayar, N., and M. S. Rozeff 1994. "Ratings, Commercial Paper and Equity Returns." *Journal of Finance* 49:1431–1449.

Ofer, A., and A. Natarajan 1987. "Convertible Call Policies." *Journal of Financial Economics* 19:91–108.

Sarig, O., and A. Warga 1989a. "Some Empirical Estimates of the Risk Structure of Interest Rates." *Journal of Finance* 44(5):1351–1360.

Sarig, O., and A. Warga 1989b. "Bond Price Data and Bond Market Liquidity." *Journal of Financial and Quantitative Analysis* 24(3):367–378.

Stein, J. 1992. "Convertible Bonds as Backdoor Financing." *Journal of Financial Economics* 32:1–21.

Townsend, R. 1979. "Optimal Contracts and Competitive Markets with Costly State Verification." *Journal of Economic Theory* 265–293.

Vu, J. 1986. "An Empirical Investigation of Non-Convertible Bonds." *Journal of Financial Economics* 16(2):235–265.

Warga, A. 1992. "Bond Returns, Liquidity and Missing Data." *Journal of Financial and Quantitative Analysis* 27(4):605–617.

Chapter 9

Securitization and Mortgage-Backed Securities

Chapter Objectives

This chapter introduces the concepts of securitization, mortgages, and mortgage-backed securities. A concise description of the primary mortgage market is provided. The mortgage contract and the right to prepay are analyzed in detail. The following questions are addressed.

- What are fixed-rate and adjustable rate mortgages?
- What factors influence prepayments?
- How are prepayments measured?
- What are mortgage-backed securities and how they are priced?
- What are collateralized mortgage obligations (CMOs) and how are they structured?
- What is an option-adjusted spread (OAS)?

INTRODUCTION

In this chapter, we will first investigate in detail the process of securitization. Its application to mortgage-backed securities markets will be discussed. We will then address the primary focus of this chapter, mortgage-backed securities. We describe the underlying mortgage market and the types of mortgage loans. Next, we evaluate prepayments, which are critical to the understanding of mortgages and mortgage-backed securities. The factors that determine prepayments and various measures of prepayments are described. We then describe the process by which mortgage-backed securities are created and illustrate the valuation principles that are used for pricing mortgage-backed securities.

SECURITIZATION

One of the most exciting developments in securities markets in recent times has been securitization. Stated simply, it is a framework in which some illiquid assets of a corporation or a financial institution are transformed into a package of securities backed by these assets, through careful packaging, credit enhancements, liquidity enhancements, and structuring. For example, the accounts receivables constitute an important asset of most corporations. Yet, this asset has credit risk stemming from the varying credit reputations of the counterparties. The terms of the accounts receivables could also differ from one counterparty to another counterparty, depending on the transactions. In effect, the combination of credit risk and the idiosyncratic nature of each component in the account receivables makes them illiquid. The basic steps that are involved in securitization are outlined in Chapter 1.

Motivations for Securitization

Securitization was briefly explored in Chapter 1. Some of the major factors which motivate securitization follow.

Many financial institutions find it desirable to reduce the size of their balance sheet. By carving out certain items in their balance sheet via securitization and selling them to investors, the size of the balance sheet can be reduced. For example, the accounts receivables of a corporation may be used to back the issue of commercial paper known as asset-backed commercial paper. The motivation for downsizing the balance sheet is simple. If the revenues remain the same and the size of the balance sheet goes down, then the return on equity will increase; moreover, less capital is needed to meet the capital-requirements standards that have been mandated by regulatory authorities.

The process of securitization permits poorly rated corporations to participate in certain segments of the capital markets that are otherwise unavailable to them. For example, the commercial paper market, where typically only highly rated corporations participate, is now increasingly attracting poorly rated issuers who are able to use the process of securitization to leverage segments of their balance sheet.

Securitization also enables the firm to transfer some risk to investors and reduce the size of the firm. In the process, firms are able to prepare the ground for major capital structure changes.

The Players in Securitization

There are several players who are involved in the process of securitization. The assets originate with some firm. Often, the firm whose assets back the security is referred to as the **originator.** These assets are then acquired from the originator by the issuer. The issuer typically achieves a bankruptcy remote status by creating a **special purpose vehicle (SPV).** The SPV assures that the pool of assets is held distinct from the originator, so that the bankruptcy or insolvency of the originator will have no consequences on the status of the pool of assets held by the SPV.

Often, a **trustee** will be appointed to ensure this. The trustee's job is to ensure that the issuer complies with all the stated obligations. The collection and disbursement of cash flows is yet another responsibility. Often, this requires prudent reinvestment decisions.

The steps involved in the securitization process and the players are shown in Figure 9-1 (see also Chapter 1). The originators pool their assets according to certain standards.

FIGURE 9-1   *The Process of Securitization*

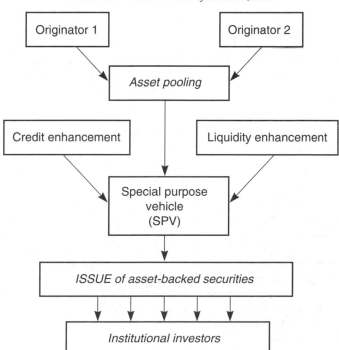

The asset pool is then held in an SPV within an appropriate legal framework so that the originator's financial status is of no consequence to the investors. The process also typically involves **credit and liquidity enhancements.** This is a process in which third parties guarantee to investors the credit-worthiness and timely payments of contractual obligations. The concept of securitization has been applied extensively in the mortgage market to which we turn now.

MORTGAGES

Homeownership in most countries is achieved through a mortgage that is, in essence, a secured loan. The family that wishes to own a home will typically pledge the home as collateral and borrow money from the lender, who is typically a bank or a financial institution. Every month, the home owner will pay an amount, which is credited towards the payment of interest and the outstanding principal amount that has been borrowed. In the event of a default, the lender has the right to take over the home and dispose of it in the market to recover the outstanding balance.

Although this example deals with home ownership, it applies to commercial properties as well. The terms residential property and nonresidential property are used in the real estate market to distinguish the type of property that is used as a collateral. A schematic classification is shown in Figure 9-2.

Primary Mortgage Market

To understand the risks and incentives that are present in the mortgage market, it is useful to begin with the primary mortgage market, where lenders and borrowers interact to

FIGURE 9-2   *Properties Used as Collateral in Mortgages*

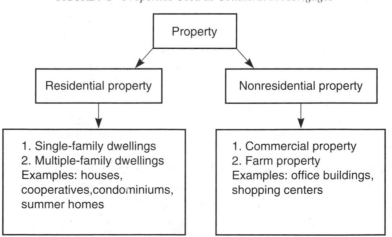

consummate their transactions. The lender (typically a mortgage banker, commercial bank, or other financial institution) reviews applications for mortgage loans from different potential and present homeowners. The original lender is referred to as the originator. The mortgage originator underwrites the loan, processes the necessary documents, and provides the funds to the homeowner (borrower). While homeowners are the principal mortgage borrowers, farmers and commercial institutions also use mortgage financing. Homeowners are classified into single-family and multi-family units by the lenders. More than 95% of the loans in the residential market are originated by thrifts, commercial banks, and mortgage bankers. The lending institution collects a fee for its services. This fee, known as the **origination fee,** is a small percentage of the loan. On a $200,000 loan, such a fee may be 1 point, or 1% of $200,000 = $2000. Lenders also charge processing fees for carrying out certain activities that are discussed later.

The borrowers are typically homeowners. The lender collects a fair amount of information from the potential borrowers to minimize the risk of default. Typically, before a loan is approved, the following data are gathered.

- Information about the borrower's credit history and about other loans and liabilities that the borrower has. The basic motivation here is to compare the loan amount and the resulting mortgage payments with the net income of the borrower less payments towards prior obligations. A rule of thumb used by many lenders requires that the mortgage payments are less than 28% of the borrower's pretax monthly income. This puts an upper bound on the loan that can be taken by the borrower.
- Information about the borrower's net worth and liquidity.
- An assessment of the value of the property. A policy limit is then set on the **loan-to-value (LTV) ratio** and the downpayments that are expected from borrowers. LTV ratios depend on a number of factors, such as the nature of the property, the levels of interest rates, and the credit conditions. For instance, lenders may require that the borrowers make a downpayment of 5% to 25% of the appraised property value. Loans extended in this manner are known as conventional mortgages. Such loans are not insured by government agencies.

Several forms of insurance programs exist in the primary mortgage market to ensure orderly payments on the loans. If the LTV is greater than 80%, then lenders will typically require the borrowers to purchase private mortgage insurance. Usually, the uninsured portion of the loan will be less than 70%–75% of the value of the home. Government agencies such as the Federal Housing Administration (FHA) and the Veterans Administration (VA) provide mortgage insurance which is intended to cover low-income and middle-income families. FHA and VA mortgages tend to require smaller down payments than do conventional mortgages. FHA and VA also impose limits on the amount of mortgages they provide; Table 9-1 illustrates how these limits have changed over the 1980–1994 period.

When private insurance is taken by the lender, the cost is passed on to the borrower through a higher borrowing rate. Borrowers can also obtain insurance in the market from insurance companies.

After a scrutiny of these factors the lender accepts a pool of applications and extends loans to acceptable borrowers. Note that such a loan portfolio, an asset in the

Year	Conventional	FHA	VA	TABLE 9-1
1980	$93,751	$90,000	$100,000	*Government Mortgage*
1981	$98,500	$90,000	$110,000	*Limits 1980–1994*
1982	$107,000	$90,000	$110,000	
1983	$108,300	$90,000	$110,000	
1984	$114,000	$90,000	$110,000	
1985	$115,300	$90,000	$110,000	
1986	$133,250	$90,000	$110,000	
1987	$153,100	$90,000	$110,000	
1988	$168,700	$101,250	$144,000	
1989	$187,600	$101,250	$144,000	
1990	$187,450	$124,875	$184,000	
1991	$191,250	$124,875	$184,000	
1992	$202,300	$124,875	$184,000	
1993	$203,150	$151,725	$184,000	
1994	$203,150	$151,725	$184,000	

Source: Mortgage Product Analysis, Merrill Lynch, December 1994, New York

bank's balance sheet, has a market value that is highly sensitive to the levels of interest rates. This arises from the fact that the borrowers (homeowners) have the option to refinance their loans by prepaying their loans and taking on new loans when mortgage interest rates fall. In addition, most of the bank's liabilities are CDs, FRNs and other short-term instruments. This means that the cost of funds to most financial institutions is tied to the levels of short-term interest rates. On the other hand, the revenues from assets such as mortgage-loan portfolios are tied to longer-term interest rates, as typically the mortgage rates on fifteen-year and thirty-year FRMs tend to be at a spread over respective Treasury counterparts. Thus, the banks have a duration mismatch and therefore have a natural yield-curve risk. If the yield curve were to invert, then the cost of funding the loan exceeds the revenues, unless other asset-liability management techniques are used. These techniques include securitization, issuing adjustable-rate mortgages, and matching the duration of assets and liabilities using the derivative markets. Lenders are subject to the risk of default; this is less of a problem to the extent that the value of the property is greater than the loan at the time of default.

After extending several loans, the originator ends up with a loan portfolio. If he decides to sell this portfolio (to book a profit), then there are well-established institutions in the market to help accomplish this task in an efficient manner. There are organizations such as the Federal Home Loan Mortgage Corporation and the Federal National Mortgage Association, which buy loan portfolios and pool them to make them sufficiently attractive for institutional investors. For a loan portfolio to be purchased by these agencies (see Chapter 8), they must be **conforming loans** meeting certain standards. Loans not satisfying these standards are called **nonconforming loans.** The government agencies play a critical role in enhancing mortgage credit. In addition, there are private entities that also buy nonconforming loans. Together the government agencies and these private entities play the role of conduits. Most commercial and investment banks have subsidiaries that act as private conduits.

Loans (whether they are pooled or not) must be serviced. A number of activities must be performed in servicing loans. These activities include:

- maintaining the status of individual loans in terms of outstanding principal, prepayments, and delinquency records;
- collecting scheduled interest payments, principal payments, and prepayments;
- handling delinquencies, defaults, and foreclosures;
- making payments to owners of the loan portfolio.

There is a servicing fee charged by the financial institutions that provide these services.

One of the choices that the household makes in the mortgage market is the type of the loan it takes. In the following sections, we will focus on residential mortgage loans. The conventional residential mortgage loan falls under two categories, fixed-rate mortgages (FRM) and adjustable-rate mortgages (ARM).

Fixed-Rate Mortgages (FRMs)

FRMs differ from other fixed-income securities with promised common coupon payments. Typically, Treasuries, corporates, agencies, and Eurobonds pay semi-annual or annual coupon payments. Mortgages typically pay **monthly cash flows.** In addition, mortgages are **amortizing** with payments assigned toward both interest and principal.

FRMs have level pay structures, but there are other structures, such as graduated-payment mortgages (**GPMs**), that are also issued from time to time. In GPMs, the initial monthly payments are set somewhat low; then the monthly payments are steadily increased to a prespecified level within five years or so. After this period, the monthly payments are set at that level for the remaining period of the mortgage. In GPMs, because the initial payments are low, the outstanding balance might actually increase leading to **negative amortization** during the first few years of the mortgage.

The traditional mortgage is the thirty-year fixed-rate mortgage with level monthly scheduled payments. This is an amortizing loan, wherein level monthly payments are scheduled over 360 months so that the loan is retired at the end of 360 months. Although thirty-year FRMs are common, there have also been active originations of fifteen-year FRMs in the market.

We illustrate the calculation of monthly payments, interest components, and principal components for a standard thirty-year FRM next. Let F_0 be the face value of the loan that was taken, let n be the original term of the loan in months, and let R be the annualized interest that is specified in the FRM. Then, the monthly payments x are computed as shown in Equation (9.1), where $r = \frac{R}{12}$.

$$x = F_0 \times \frac{r(1 + r)^n}{[(1 + r)^n - 1]} \tag{9.1}$$

These monthly scheduled payments are applied towards both interest and principal. In Table 9-2, we illustrate the effect of R, the annualized interest rate on the monthly payments. As R increases from 5% to 10%, note that the monthly payments increase significantly, from \$536.82 to \$877.57 for thirty-year FRMs.

TABLE 9-2   *Effect of Interest Rates on Scheduled Monthly Payments for Two Terms of Fixed-Rate Mortgages (Original Loan: \$100,000)*

Interest Rate	5.00%	5.50%	6.00%	6.50%	7.00%	7.50%	8.00%	8.50%	9.00%	9.50%	10.00%
Thirty-Year FRM	536.82	567.79	599.55	632.07	665.30	699.21	733.76	768.91	804.62	840.85	877.57
Fifteen-Year FRM	790.79	817.08	843.86	871.11	898.83	927.01	955.65	984.74	1014.27	1044.22	1074.61

If we denote F_t as the outstanding balance at the end of month t after that month's payments have been made, then,

$$F_t = F_{t-1} + \left(\frac{R}{12} \times F_{t-1} \right) - x. \tag{9.2}$$

Then the principal payments will be simply

$$F_{t-1} - F_t \tag{9.3}$$

The interest payments for the month t are given by

$$\frac{R}{12} \times F_{t-1}. \tag{9.4}$$

Figure 9-3 shows the pattern of scheduled interest and principal payments over the life of the mortgage. Note that in the early part of the life of the mortgage, most of the monthly payments x are applied towards repaying the interest component of the loan. It is toward the end of the life of the mortgage that the payments toward principal constitute a major part of the monthly payments. As the mortgage gets older, the outstanding principal balance declines and, as a consequence, the interest payments decline. Since the monthly scheduled payments are fixed, this means that the scheduled principal payments will increase.

The fifteen-year FRM has higher monthly scheduled payments than a thirty-year FRM. To compare these payments, we provide the monthly payments with the interest and principal components for both FRMs in Table 9-2.

FIGURE 9-3   *Scheduled Interest and Principal Payments on a $100,000 Thirty-Year Fixed Rate Mortgage at 8%*

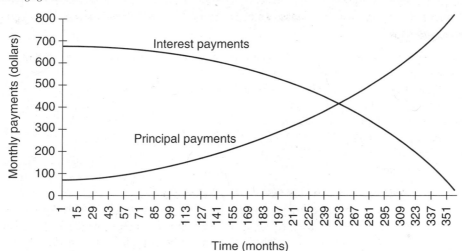

Adjustable-Rate Mortgages (ARMs)

ARMs permit the interest payments to be reset at periodic intervals to prespecified short-term interest rates. The most commonly used short-term indexes are the constant maturity one-year Treasury rate and the Cost-of-Funds Index (COFI), which is the weighted-average cost of funds for the thrift-institution members of the Federal Home Loan Bank of San Francisco.

Since ARMs shift fluctuations in interest rates to the borrowers, the asset-liability management problems of lenders that we alluded to in our general discussion are mitigated. The only exposure that the lender has with a plain-vanilla ARM without caps is the exposure to interest rates during the period between the resets. To the extent the interest-rate risk to the lender is reduced, any resulting benefits will, at least in part, be passed on to the homeowners as a lower cost of borrowing. As we saw in Chapter 5, short-term interest rates are more volatile and, as such, ARMs can subject borrowers to a significant amount of risk if the rates increase unexpectedly. If the homeowners are unable to meet the increased monthly payments resulting from such increases in short-term interest rates, defaults can occur.

It is rarely the case that ARMs are issued without additional contractual features. Typically, ARMs include prespecified interest-rate caps. These caps limit the maximum interest rate that the borrower will pay in case the index rates increase dramatically. Often, ARMs carry caps on reset dates as well as a cap rate applicable throughout the life of the ARM. ARMs also have payment caps.

When the payment cap becomes binding (due to an increase in the short-term rates), the borrower pays the specified capped amount. During this period, the principal amount of the loan may actually increase. This is referred to as negative amortization. Initially when the ARM is offered to the borrowers, a below-market initial rate is specified in the contract. This is known as the teaser rate. To summarize, ARM has the following contractual features:

- A reference rate or an index. This can be the one-year constant maturity T-bill or the eleventh district COFI, etc.
- Reset frequency: monthly, semi-annual or annual.
- Spread over the reference rate.
- Lifetime cap on rates.
- Periodic cap on rates.
- Payment caps.
- Teaser rate.

Currently ARMs account for over 50% of the market share.

ARMs allowed more families to qualify for mortgages. In mid 1984, ARMs accounted for approximately two thirds of the conventional mortgage loans. ARM market share has fluctuated over time, from about 40% in 1981 to a high of 66% in 1984. It has become an established part of the mortgage market. ARM portfolios are more often held by the originators as investments. In 1984 government agencies such as GNMA and FNMA began the securitization of ARMs. Despite these programs, ARMs are not securitized to the same extent as FRMs.

PREPAYMENTS

Mortgages permit the homeowners to prepay their loans. This prepayment provision introduces timing uncertainty into the originating bank's cash flows from its loan portfolio. For example, if the bank originates a pool of mortgages with a weighted-average rate of 8% and six months later the mortgage rates drop significantly below 8%, say to 7%, then the loan portfolio is certain to experience significant prepayments as borrowers rush to refinance their mortgages with less-costly loans. The lender has a long position in the mortgage loan that entitles him to monthly scheduled payments, but has also sold an option to the homeowners that gives them the right to prepay the loan when the circumstances demand it. This means that the bank cannot predict the future cash flows from its loan portfolio with certainty. Clearly, the option to prepay will be priced into the loan by the bank and the borrower will pay a higher interest rate on the loan as a consequence.

Factors Affecting Prepayments

Prepayments of mortgages are driven by a number of factors, each of which merits further elaboration (see also Chapter 1).

Refinancing Incentive. Perhaps the most important reason for prepayments is the refinancing incentive. If the market rates for mortgage loans drop significantly below the rate that a borrower is paying, then the borrower has a very strong reason to prepay as long as the borrower is able to qualify for a new loan. This incentive means that the prepayments accelerate in periods of falling interest rates, especially when there is a belief in the market that the rates have bottomed out.

Seasonality Factor. Families typically do not move during the school year. Things remaining equal, families will move during the period from the middle of June through the first week of September; this results in increased prepayments during this part of the year. This can be thought of as the seasonality factor or the school-year factor.

Age of the Mortgage. During the early part of the mortgage loan, interest payments far exceed the principal component. This, in part, means that the interest savings associated with refinancing are greater during the earlier part of the mortgage loan. We expect the prepayments to be greater during the earlier part of the life of the loan and then stabilize afterwards; indeed, prepayments are higher when the life of the loan is in the range 2 to 8 years. In addition, when a mortgage is more than 25 years old, there may be an incentive to pay it off in order to secure the property's title. The speed of prepayments slows for loans in the age range 10 to 25 years.

Family Circumstances. A number of factors pertaining to family circumstances lead to the prepayment. These factors include marital status (often divorce decisions lead to prepayment) and job switching.

Sometimes, the inability of a household to make the monthly payment (due to job loss or disability) leads to default; under some circumstances, this can precipitate a prepayment. As noted earlier, there are two forms of mortgage insurance. In one form, the lender initiates the insurance and the policy guarantees that the insurance company will pay some or all of the loan in the event the homeowner defaults. In the other form, initiated by the homeowner, the insurance company will pay off the loan obligations in the event of a death of the insured person.

Further, if a family moves (due to factors such as increasing family size, job switches, etc.) and if the loan is assumable, then when the family moves, the next family that moves into the home can assume the mortgage. If the loan is not assumable, it has to be paid in full, which results in prepayments.

Housing Prices. The price of the home is yet another factor in prepayment. The housing price affects the LTV ratio, which in turn affects the ability of the household to qualify for refinancing. When the housing prices increase, the LTV decreases. This enhances the ability of the homeowner to refinance if the going interest rates and family circumstances warrant refinancing. On the other hand, when the housing prices drop, the LTV ratio increases; this diminishes the ability of the homeowner to qualify for refinancing, even if other factors favor refinancing.

The relationship between the asset value of the mortgage and the value of the house thus affects the prepayment incentives.

Asset Value of Mortgage =
Current Face Value of Mortgage − Current Market Value of Mortgage

Mortgage Status (Premium Burnout). The relationship between the contractual interest rate in a mortgage loan and the going mortgage interest rates is a major determinant of the value of the loan. If the contractual interest rate r is greater than the going interest rate R, then the loan is a prime candidate for prepayment. Such mortgages are referred to as **premium mortgages.** If $r < R$, then the mortgage is said to be a **discount mortgage.** We would expect premium mortgages to prepay faster. There is some empirical evidence indicating that the premium mortgages, after some prepayments, tend to stabilize. An initial drop in rates leads to significant prepayments. A subsequent drop does not produce a similar level of prepayments. Hence, a number of premium mortgages remain outstanding. This is referred to as **premium burnout.** We have already hinted at some reasons why this might happen.

Mortgage Term. Evidence suggests that the rate of prepayments depends on other factors as well. For example, the rate of prepayment of FRMs with a maturity of 15 years differs from the rate of prepayment of FRMs with a maturity of 30 years. Waldman, Schwalb, and Feigenberg (1993) present evidence that

- For current coupon and discount coupon securities, prepayments from fifteen-year mortgages have been 11% faster than thirty-year mortgages during the period 1983–1992.
- For high-coupon securities, prepayments from fifteen-year mortgages have been 5% slower than thirty-year mortgages during the period 1986–1992. The seasoning of the mortgage appears to have a significant impact on the speed of prepayment.

Measures of Prepayments

There are different measures of prepayments that are used in the industry to determine the rate of prepayment. These measures are grounded in certain assumptions that must be understood by investors in the mortgage markets. We will discuss each of these measures in turn. All these measures have been developed in the context of mortgage-backed securities. But they are useful even at the level of individual loans.

Twelve-Year Retirement. This is perhaps the simplest and the least important measure of prepayment. It assumes that the mortgage is prepaid exactly after 12 years. If this assumption is made, we can add the prepayments at the end of 12 years to the scheduled payments. The cash flows of the mortgage loan in the absence of default can then be determined for all future months. This measure is clearly inconsistent with what we know about the factors that determine prepayments.

Constant Monthly Mortality. This measure assumes that there is a constant probability that the mortgage will be prepaid following the next month's scheduled payments. For instance, consider the assumption that there is a 0.50% probability that the mortgage will be prepaid following the first month.

This 0.50% probability is referred to as the single monthly mortality rate, or SMM. Using the SMM we can compute the probability that the mortgage will be retired in the next month. It depends on two factors: (a) the probability that the mortgage will survive the first month, $1 - 0.50\% = 99.50\%$, and (b) the mortality rate for month 2 (given that it survived the first month), which is 0.50%. So, the probability that the mortgage will be retired in month 2 is: $0.50\% \times 99.50\% = 0.4975\%$. Using this, we can say that the probability that the mortgage will be retired in month 3 is: $(1 - 0.4975\%) \times 0.50\% = 0.4975\%$ and so on.

Usually an annual prepayment rate known as the conditional prepayments rate (CPR) is used to measure the speed of prepayments. Given an annual CPR we can estimate the SMM. Remember that the probability the mortgage will survive a month is $(1 - SMM)$. For a period of one year, the probability of survival is $(1 - SMM)^{12}$. This is set equal to $(1 - CPR)$. So, we get:

$$(1 - SMM)^{12} = 1 - CPR,$$

or

$$CPR = 1 - (1 - SMM)^{12}.$$

If SMM = 1% (per month), then CPR is 11.36%. In our example, SMM = 1% implies that 1% of the outstanding principal is paid down each month. This measure (CPR) is used widely in the industry to measure prepayments.

As the constant of monthly mortality increases, the probability that the mortgage will be retired early increases; this is useful for computing the prepayments associated with a loan portfolio.

Note that this approach is inconsistent with the fact that the prepayment increases during the first few years, then stays at a relatively low level, and increases again towards the end of the loan period.

FHA Experience. The Federal Home Administration has a large database on actual prepayments of mortgages of different vintages. This data forms the basis for computing the probability that a loan will be retired during any given year.

The probability is computed as follows. The FHA data is organized as a series, giving the probability that the new mortgage will survive to the end of any given year where years are indexed from 1 to 30. Let x_t be this probability. Then, the probability that the mortgage will be retired during any given year t is

$$p_t \equiv x_{t-1} - x_t.$$

The conditional probability that the mortgage will survive through the year t, given that it has survived until the year $t - 1$ is denoted by y_t, and is computed as

$$y_t = 1 - \frac{p_t}{x_{t-1}} = \frac{x_t}{x_{t-1}}.$$

Once we have the conditional probability y_t of a mortgage surviving through the year t given that it has already survived through year $t - 1$, we can use that information to derive the conditional monthly survival probabilities by invoking additional assumptions about the monthly probabilities. For instance, if we assume that the conditional monthly probabilities within each year are constant (say, z_i for year i) then we must have

$$z_i^{12} = y_i \Rightarrow z_i = y_i^{\frac{1}{12}}.$$

These derived monthly probabilities are referred to as the 100% FHA experience. Unlike the CPRs, 100% FHA experience does not decline with the age of the mortgage.

Example 9-1

> 58% of the mortgage pool is expected to survive 10 years and 54% of the pool is expected to survive 11 years. Using this estimate, we may conclude that the prepayment in the 11th year will be 4%, assuming the 100% FHA experience.

Investors use this information and adjust it for different speeds (i.e. 50% FHA experience, 200% FHA experience).

Prepayments measured on the basis of FHA experience, while useful, nonetheless present some problems. Since FHA mortgages are assumable, the speed of prepayments tends to be underestimated.

PSA Experience. The Public Securities Association (PSA) convention assumes that 0.2% of the principal is paid in the first month and will increase by 0.2% in each of the following months, finally leveling out at 6% until the maturity. This convention is referred to as the 100% PSA. By scaling up or down, one can construct different PSA measures. Figure 9-4 shows the prepayment rates for 100% PSA, 150% PSA, and 200% PSA.

The PSA standard benchmark was introduced in July 1985. *It is not a model of prepayments but used as a benchmark in the industry.* Mathematically, 100% PSA benchmark can be expressed as follows:

$$\text{Months 1 to 30: CPR} = 6\% \times \frac{t}{30}$$

where t is the number of months since the origination of the loan, or

$$\text{Months} > 30: \text{CPR} = 6\%.$$

Basically, the seasoning effect of mortgages is incorporated through a linear increase in prepayments and is based on FHA 30-year FRMs.

Mortgage Cash Flows with Prepayments

With the basics of the mortgage contract in place, we can now see how the monthly cash flows of the mortgage loan contract can be projected into the future. In Table 9-3 we construct future cash flows from a single loan with a face value of $100,000 and a rate of 9%. The mortgage loan has a life of 30 years. Prepayments are assumed to occur at a rate of 100% PSA. We detail the calculations of this table next:

FIGURE 9-4   *PSA Prepayment Conventions*

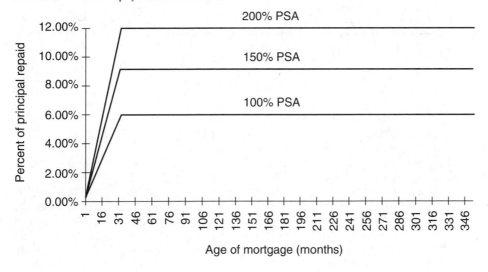

- First, using the prepayment rate assumption, we can compute the SMM for month $t = 1$ as follows.

$$\text{CPR} = 6\% \times \frac{1}{30} = \frac{0.06}{30} = 0.002$$

$$\text{SMM} = 1 - (1 - \text{CPR})^{\frac{1}{12}} = 1 - (1 - 0.002)^{\frac{1}{12}} = 0.00167$$

  This is highlighted in the table corresponding to month 1. As noted earlier, the method of calculating SMM is the same until $t = 30$. After $t = 30$, CPR $= 6\%$ until the loan is retired. Note that SMM $= 0.005143$ after $t = 30$ until the end.

- Second, total mortgage payments at $t = 1$ are obtained by applying Equation (9.1) with $F_0 = 100{,}000$, $n = 360$ and $r = \frac{0.09}{12}$. We get the payment x at $t = 1$ to be 804.62. We calculate the interest payment by multiplying the outstanding balance with the monthly interest rate. For $t = 1$, we get $100{,}000 \times \frac{0.09}{12} = 750$.

- The scheduled principal payment at $t = 1$ is obtained by subtracting the interest payments from the total mortgage payments: $804.62 - 750 = 54.62$.

- Finally, prepayments at $t = 1$ are computed by applying SMM to the remaining principal:

$$= 0.000167 \times [100{,}000 - 54.62]$$

$$= 16.67$$

- Total principal outstanding at $t = 2$ is obtained by subtracting the total principal payments at $t = 1$ from 100,000 to get:

$$100{,}000 - [54.62 + 16.67] = 99{,}928.70.$$

- We then apply the procedure at each time to get the projected future cash flows of the mortgage loan.

TABLE 9-3   *Monthly Cash Flow from a Single Mortgage Loan*
　　　　　　Interest rate: 9%　　　　*Prepayments: 100% PSA*
　　　　　　Annual rate: 9.00%　　　*Monthly: 0.75%*

Months	Life in Months	Mortgage Loan Outstanding	SMM	Mortgage Payment	Interest Payment	Scheduled Principal	Prepayment	Total Principal Paid	Total Cash Flows
1	360	100,000.00	**0.000167**	**804.62**	750.00	54.62	16.67	71.30	821.30
2	359	99,928.70	0.000334	804.49	749.47	55.02	33.35	88.38	837.84
3	358	99,840.33	0.000501	804.22	748.80	55.42	50.03	105.45	854.25
4	357	99,734.88	0.000669	803.82	748.01	55.80	66.70	122.50	870.51
5	356	99,612.38	0.000837	803.28	747.09	56.19	83.35	139.53	886.62
6	355	99,472.85	0.001006	802.61	746.05	56.56	99.97	156.53	902.57
7	354	99,316.32	0.001174	801.80	744.87	56.93	116.55	173.48	918.35
8	353	99,142.84	0.001343	800.86	743.57	57.29	133.09	190.38	933.95
9	352	98,952.46	0.001513	799.78	742.14	57.64	149.58	207.22	949.36
10	351	98,745.24	0.001682	798.57	740.59	57.98	166.01	223.99	964.58
11	350	98,521.25	0.001852	797.23	738.91	58.32	182.36	240.68	979.59
12	349	98,280.57	0.002022	795.75	737.10	58.65	198.64	257.29	994.39
13	348	98,023.29	0.002193	794.14	735.17	58.97	214.83	273.80	1008.97
14	347	97,749.49	0.002364	792.40	733.12	59.28	230.92	290.20	1023.32
15	346	97,459.29	0.002535	790.53	730.94	59.58	246.91	306.50	1037.44
16	345	97,152.79	0.002707	788.52	728.65	59.88	262.79	322.67	1051.32
17	344	96,830.12	0.002878	786.39	726.23	60.16	278.55	338.71	1064.94
18	343	96,491.41	0.003051	784.13	723.69	60.44	294.18	354.62	1078.31
19	342	96,136.79	0.003223	781.73	721.03	60.71	309.67	370.38	1091.41
20	341	95,766.41	0.003396	779.21	718.25	60.97	325.02	385.99	1104.24
21	340	95,380.42	0.003569	776.57	715.35	61.22	340.22	401.43	1116.79
22	339	94,978.99	0.003743	773.80	712.34	61.45	355.25	416.71	1129.05
23	338	94,562.28	0.003917	770.90	709.22	61.68	370.12	431.81	1141.02
24	337	94,130.47	0.004091	767.88	705.98	61.90	384.82	446.72	1152.70
25	336	93,683.75	0.004265	764.74	702.63	62.11	399.33	461.44	1164.07
26	335	93,222.32	0.004440	761.48	699.17	62.31	413.65	475.96	1175.13
27	334	92,746.36	0.004615	758.10	695.60	62.50	427.77	490.27	1185.87
28	333	92,256.09	0.004791	754.60	691.92	62.68	441.69	504.37	1196.29
29	332	91,751.72	0.004967	750.98	688.14	62.85	455.40	518.24	1206.38
30	331	91,233.47	0.005143	747.25	684.25	63.00	468.89	531.89	1216.14
31	330	90,701.58	0.005143	743.41	680.26	63.15	466.15	529.30	1209.56
32	329	90,172.28	0.005143	739.59	676.29	63.29	463.43	526.73	1203.02
33	328	89,645.55	0.005143	735.78	672.34	63.44	460.72	524.16	1196.50
34	327	89,121.39	0.005143	732.00	668.41	63.59	458.03	521.61	1190.02
35	326	88,599.78	0.005143	728.23	664.50	63.74	455.34	519.08	1183.58
36	325	88,080.70	0.005143	724.49	660.61	63.88	452.67	516.56	1177.16
37	324	87,564.14	0.005143	720.76	656.73	64.03	450.01	514.05	1170.78
38	323	87,050.10	0.005143	717.06	652.88	64.18	447.37	511.55	1164.43
39	322	86,538.55	0.005143	713.37	649.04	64.33	444.74	509.07	1158.11
40	321	86,029.48	0.005143	709.70	645.22	64.48	442.12	506.60	1151.82
41	320	85,522.88	0.005143	706.05	641.42	64.63	439.51	504.14	1145.56
42	319	85,018.74	0.005143	702.42	637.64	64.78	436.92	501.70	1139.34
43	318	84,517.05	0.005143	698.81	633.88	64.93	434.34	499.27	1133.14

TABLE 9-3   *Continued*

Months	Life in Months	Mortgage Loan Outstanding	SMM	Mortgage Payment	Interest Payment	Scheduled Principal	Prepayment	Total Principal Paid	Total Cash Flows
44	317	84,017.78	0.005143	695.21	630.13	65.08	431.77	496.85	1126.98
45	316	83,520.93	0.005143	691.64	626.41	65.23	429.21	494.44	1120.85
46	315	83,026.49	0.005143	688.08	622.70	65.38	426.67	492.05	1114.75
47	314	82,534.44	0.005143	684.54	619.01	65.53	424.14	489.67	1108.68
48	313	82,044.77	0.005143	681.02	615.34	65.68	421.62	487.30	1102.64
49	312	81,557.47	0.005143	677.52	611.68	65.84	419.11	484.95	1096.63
50	311	81,072.52	0.005143	674.03	608.04	65.99	416.62	482.61	1090.65
51	310	80,589.91	0.005143	670.57	604.42	66.14	414.13	480.28	1084.70
52	309	80,109.63	0.005143	667.12	600.82	66.29	411.66	477.96	1078.78
53	308	79,631.68	0.005143	663.69	597.24	66.45	409.20	475.65	1072.89
54	307	79,156.02	0.005143	660.27	593.67	66.60	406.76	473.36	1067.03
55	306	78,682.66	0.005143	656.88	590.12	66.76	404.32	471.08	1061.20
56	305	78,211.58	0.005143	653.50	586.59	66.91	401.90	468.81	1055.40
57	304	77,742.77	0.005143	650.14	583.07	67.07	399.49	466.55	1049.62
58	303	77,276.22	0.005143	646.79	579.57	67.22	397.09	464.31	1043.88
59	302	76,811.91	0.005143	643.47	576.09	67.38	394.70	462.08	1038.17
60	301	76,349.83	0.005143	640.16	572.62	67.53	392.32	459.86	1032.48
61	300	75,889.98	0.005143	636.87	569.17	67.69	389.95	457.65	1026.82
62	299	75,432.33	0.005143	633.59	565.74	67.85	387.60	455.45	1021.19
63	298	74,976.88	0.005143	630.33	562.33	68.01	385.26	453.26	1015.59
64	297	74,523.62	0.005143	627.09	558.93	68.16	382.93	451.09	1010.02
65	296	74,072.53	0.005143	623.87	555.54	68.32	380.60	448.93	1004.47
66	295	73,623.60	0.005143	620.66	552.18	68.48	378.29	446.77	998.95
67	294	73,176.83	0.005143	617.46	548.83	68.64	376.00	444.63	993.46
68	293	72,732.20	0.005143	614.29	545.49	68.80	373.71	442.51	988.00
69	292	72,289.69	0.005143	611.13	542.17	68.96	371.43	440.39	982.56
70	291	71,849.30	0.005143	607.99	538.87	69.12	369.17	438.28	977.15
71	290	71,411.02	0.005143	604.86	535.58	69.28	366.91	436.19	971.77
72	289	70,974.83	0.005143	601.75	532.31	69.44	364.67	434.10	966.42
73	288	70,540.72	0.005143	598.65	529.06	69.60	362.43	432.03	961.09
74	287	70,108.69	0.005143	595.58	525.82	69.76	360.21	429.97	955.79
75	286	69,678.72	0.005143	592.51	522.59	69.92	358.00	427.92	950.51
76	285	69,250.80	0.005143	589.46	519.38	70.08	355.80	425.88	945.26
77	284	68,824.92	0.005143	586.43	516.19	70.25	353.61	423.85	940.04
78	283	68,401.07	0.005143	583.42	513.01	70.41	351.43	421.83	934.84
79	282	67,979.23	0.005143	580.42	509.84	70.57	349.26	419.83	929.67
80	281	67,559.40	0.005143	577.43	506.70	70.74	347.10	417.83	924.53
81	280	67,141.57	0.005143	574.46	503.56	70.90	344.95	415.85	919.41
82	279	66,725.73	0.005143	571.51	500.44	71.06	342.81	413.87	914.31
83	278	66,311.86	0.005143	568.57	497.34	71.23	340.68	411.91	909.24
84	277	65,899.95	0.005143	565.64	494.25	71.39	338.56	409.95	904.20
85	276	65,490.00	0.005143	562.73	491.18	71.56	336.45	408.01	899.18
86	275	65,081.99	0.005143	559.84	488.11	71.73	334.35	406.07	894.19
87	274	64,675.92	0.005143	556.96	485.07	71.89	332.26	404.15	889.22
88	273	64,271.77	0.005143	554.10	482.04	72.06	330.18	402.24	884.28

(Continued)

TABLE 9-3   *Continued*

Months	Life in Months	Mortgage Loan Outstanding	SMM	Mortgage Payment	Interest Payment	Scheduled Principal	Prepayment	Total Principal Paid	Total Cash Flows
89	272	63,869.53	0.005143	551.25	479.02	72.23	328.11	400.34	879.36
90	271	63,469.19	0.005143	548.41	476.02	72.39	326.05	398.44	874.46
91	270	63,070.75	0.005143	545.59	473.03	72.56	324.00	396.56	869.59
92	269	62,674.19	0.005143	542.79	470.06	72.73	321.96	394.69	864.75
93	268	62,279.50	0.005143	539.99	467.10	72.90	319.93	392.83	859.92
94	267	61,886.67	0.005143	537.22	464.15	73.07	317.91	390.97	855.12
95	266	61,495.70	0.005143	534.45	461.22	73.24	315.90	389.13	850.35
96	265	61,106.56	0.005143	531.71	458.30	73.41	313.89	387.30	845.60
97	264	60,719.26	0.005143	528.97	455.39	73.58	311.90	385.48	840.87
98	263	60,333.79	0.005143	526.25	452.50	73.75	309.92	383.66	836.17
99	262	59,950.12	0.005143	523.54	449.63	73.92	307.94	381.86	831.49
100	261	59,568.26	0.005143	520.85	446.76	74.09	305.98	380.07	826.83
101	260	59,188.19	0.005143	518.17	443.91	74.26	304.02	378.28	822.20
102	259	58,809.91	0.005143	515.51	441.07	74.43	302.08	376.51	817.58
103	258	58,433.40	0.005143	512.86	438.25	74.61	300.14	374.75	813.00
104	257	58,058.65	0.005143	510.22	435.44	74.78	298.21	372.99	808.43
105	256	57,685.66	0.005143	507.59	432.64	74.95	296.29	371.24	803.89
106	255	57,314.42	0.005143	504.98	429.86	75.13	294.38	369.51	799.37
107	254	56,944.91	0.005143	502.39	427.09	75.30	292.48	367.78	794.87
108	253	56,577.13	0.005143	499.80	424.33	75.47	290.59	366.06	790.39
109	252	56,211.06	0.005143	497.23	421.58	75.65	288.71	364.35	785.94
110	251	55,846.71	0.005143	494.68	418.85	75.82	286.83	362.66	781.51
111	250	55,484.05	0.005143	492.13	416.13	76.00	284.96	360.96	777.10
112	249	55,123.09	0.005143	489.60	413.42	76.18	283.11	359.28	772.71
113	248	54,763.81	0.005143	487.08	410.73	76.35	281.26	357.61	768.34
114	247	54,406.19	0.005143	484.58	408.05	76.53	279.42	355.95	764.00
115	246	54,050.25	0.005143	482.08	405.38	76.71	277.59	354.29	759.67
116	245	53,695.95	0.005143	479.61	402.72	76.89	275.76	352.65	755.37
117	244	53,343.30	0.005143	477.14	400.07	77.06	273.95	351.01	751.09
118	243	52,992.29	0.005143	474.68	397.44	77.24	272.14	349.39	746.83
119	242	52,642.90	0.005143	472.24	394.82	77.42	270.34	347.77	742.59
120	241	52,295.14	0.005143	469.81	392.21	77.60	268.56	346.16	738.37
121	240	51,948.98	0.005143	467.40	389.62	77.78	266.77	344.56	734.17
122	239	51,604.42	0.005143	464.99	387.03	77.96	265.00	342.96	730.00
123	238	51,261.46	0.005143	462.60	384.46	78.14	263.24	341.38	725.84
124	237	50,920.08	0.005143	460.22	381.90	78.32	261.48	339.80	721.70
125	236	50,580.28	0.005143	457.86	379.35	78.50	259.73	338.24	717.59
126	235	50,242.04	0.005143	455.50	376.82	78.69	257.99	336.68	713.49
127	234	49,905.37	0.005143	453.16	374.29	78.87	256.26	335.13	709.42
128	233	49,570.24	0.005143	450.83	371.78	79.05	254.53	333.59	705.36
129	232	49,236.65	0.005143	448.51	369.27	79.24	252.82	332.05	701.33
130	231	48,904.60	0.005143	446.20	366.78	79.42	251.11	330.53	697.31
131	230	48,574.07	0.005143	443.91	364.31	79.60	249.41	329.01	693.32
132	229	48,245.06	0.005143	441.63	361.84	79.79	247.71	327.50	689.34
133	228	47,917.56	0.005143	439.35	359.38	79.97	246.03	326.00	685.38
134	227	47,591.56	0.005143	437.09	356.94	80.16	244.35	324.51	681.45

TABLE 9-3   *Continued*

Months	Life in Months	Mortgage Loan Outstanding	SMM	Mortgage Payment	Interest Payment	Scheduled Principal	Prepayment	Total Principal Paid	Total Cash Flows
135	226	47,267.05	0.005143	434.85	354.50	80.34	242.68	323.03	677.53
136	225	46,944.02	0.005143	432.61	352.08	80.53	241.02	321.55	673.63
137	224	46,622.47	0.005143	430.39	349.67	80.72	239.36	320.08	669.75
138	223	46,302.39	0.005143	428.17	347.27	80.90	237.72	318.62	665.89
139	222	45,983.77	0.005143	425.97	344.88	81.09	236.08	317.17	662.05
140	221	45,666.60	0.005143	423.78	342.50	81.28	234.45	315.73	658.23
141	220	45,350.87	0.005143	421.60	340.13	81.47	232.82	314.29	654.42
142	219	45,036.58	0.005143	419.43	337.77	81.66	231.20	312.86	650.64
143	218	44,723.72	0.005143	417.27	335.43	81.85	229.59	311.44	646.87
144	217	44,412.28	0.005143	415.13	333.09	82.04	227.99	310.03	643.12
145	216	44,102.25	0.005143	412.99	330.77	82.23	226.40	308.62	639.39
146	215	43,793.63	0.005143	410.87	328.45	82.42	224.81	307.22	635.68
147	214	43,486.41	0.005143	408.76	326.15	82.61	223.23	305.83	631.98
148	213	43,180.57	0.005143	406.65	323.85	82.80	221.65	304.45	628.31
149	212	42,876.12	0.005143	404.56	321.57	82.99	220.09	303.08	624.65
150	211	42,573.04	0.005143	402.48	319.30	83.18	218.53	301.71	621.01
151	210	42,271.33	0.005143	400.41	317.04	83.38	216.97	300.35	617.39
152	209	41,970.98	0.005143	398.35	314.78	83.57	215.43	299.00	613.78
153	208	41,671.99	0.005143	396.30	312.54	83.76	213.89	297.65	610.19
154	207	41,374.33	0.005143	394.27	310.31	83.96	212.36	296.32	606.62
155	206	41,078.02	0.005143	392.24	308.09	84.15	210.83	294.98	603.07
156	205	40,783.03	0.005143	390.22	305.87	84.35	209.31	293.66	599.53
157	204	40,489.37	0.005143	388.21	303.67	84.54	207.80	292.35	596.02
158	203	40,197.03	0.005143	386.22	301.48	84.74	206.30	291.04	592.52
159	202	39,905.99	0.005143	384.23	299.29	84.94	204.80	289.74	589.03
160	201	39,616.25	0.005143	382.25	297.12	85.13	203.31	288.44	585.56
161	200	39,327.81	0.005143	380.29	294.96	85.33	201.82	287.15	582.11
162	199	39,040.66	0.005143	378.33	292.80	85.53	200.35	285.87	578.68
163	198	38,754.78	0.005143	376.39	290.66	85.73	198.88	284.60	575.26
164	197	38,470.18	0.005143	374.45	288.53	85.93	197.41	283.34	571.86
165	196	38,186.84	0.005143	372.53	286.40	86.12	195.95	282.08	568.48
166	195	37,904.77	0.005143	370.61	284.29	86.32	194.50	280.82	565.11
167	194	37,623.94	0.005143	368.70	282.18	86.52	193.06	279.58	561.76
168	193	37,344.36	0.005143	366.81	280.08	86.72	191.62	278.34	558.42
169	192	37,066.02	0.005143	364.92	278.00	86.93	190.18	277.11	555.10
170	191	36,788.91	0.005143	363.04	275.92	87.13	188.76	275.88	551.80
171	190	36,513.03	0.005143	361.18	273.85	87.33	187.34	274.67	548.51
172	189	36,238.36	0.005143	359.32	271.79	87.53	185.92	273.46	545.24
173	188	35,964.90	0.005143	357.47	269.74	87.73	184.52	272.25	541.99
174	187	35,692.65	0.005143	355.63	267.69	87.94	183.12	271.05	538.75
175	186	35,421.60	0.005143	353.80	265.66	88.14	181.72	269.86	535.52
176	185	35,151.74	0.005143	351.98	263.64	88.35	180.33	268.68	532.32
177	184	34,883.06	0.005143	350.17	261.62	88.55	178.95	267.50	529.12
178	183	34,615.56	0.005143	348.37	259.62	88.76	177.57	266.33	525.94
179	182	34,349.23	0.005143	346.58	257.62	88.96	176.20	265.16	522.78
180	181	34,084.07	0.005143	344.80	255.63	89.17	174.84	264.00	519.64

(Continued)

TABLE 9-3 *Continued*

Months	Life in Months	Mortgage Loan Outstanding	SMM	Mortgage Payment	Interest Payment	Scheduled Principal	Prepayment	Total Principal Paid	Total Cash Flows
181	180	33,820.06	0.005143	343.03	253.65	89.38	173.48	262.85	516.50
182	179	33,557.21	0.005143	341.26	251.68	89.58	172.12	261.71	513.39
183	178	33,295.50	0.005143	339.51	249.72	89.79	170.78	260.57	510.28
184	177	33,034.94	0.005143	337.76	247.76	90.00	169.44	259.43	507.20
185	176	32,775.50	0.005143	336.02	245.82	90.21	168.10	258.31	504.12
186	175	32,517.20	0.005143	334.29	243.88	90.42	166.77	257.19	501.07
187	174	32,260.01	0.005143	332.58	241.95	90.63	165.45	256.07	498.02
188	173	32,003.93	0.005143	330.87	240.03	90.84	164.13	254.97	494.99
189	172	31,748.97	0.005143	329.16	238.12	91.05	162.82	253.86	491.98
190	171	31,495.11	0.005143	327.47	236.21	91.26	161.51	252.77	488.98
191	170	31,242.34	0.005143	325.79	234.32	91.47	160.21	251.68	486.00
192	169	30,990.66	0.005143	324.11	232.43	91.68	158.91	250.59	483.02
193	168	30,740.07	0.005143	322.44	230.55	91.89	157.62	249.52	480.07
194	167	30,490.55	0.005143	320.79	228.68	92.11	156.34	248.45	477.13
195	166	30,242.10	0.005143	319.14	226.82	92.32	155.06	247.38	474.20
196	165	29,994.72	0.005143	317.49	224.96	92.53	153.79	246.32	471.28
197	164	29,748.40	0.005143	315.86	223.11	92.75	152.52	245.27	468.38
198	163	29,503.13	0.005143	314.24	221.27	92.96	151.26	244.22	465.49
199	162	29,258.91	0.005143	312.62	219.44	93.18	150.00	243.18	462.62
200	161	29,015.73	0.005143	311.01	217.62	93.40	148.75	242.14	459.76
201	160	28,773.59	0.005143	309.41	215.80	93.61	147.50	241.11	456.92
202	159	28,532.47	0.005143	307.82	213.99	93.83	146.26	240.09	454.08
203	158	28,292.39	0.005143	306.24	212.19	94.05	145.02	239.07	451.26
204	157	28,053.31	0.005143	304.66	210.40	94.26	143.79	238.06	448.46
205	156	27,815.26	0.005143	303.10	208.61	94.48	142.57	237.05	445.67
206	155	27,578.21	0.005143	301.54	206.84	94.70	141.35	236.05	442.89
207	154	27,342.15	0.005143	299.99	205.07	94.92	140.13	235.05	440.12
208	153	27,107.10	0.005143	298.44	203.30	95.14	138.92	234.06	437.37
209	152	26,873.04	0.005143	296.91	201.55	95.36	137.72	233.08	434.63
210	151	26,639.96	0.005143	295.38	199.80	95.58	136.52	232.10	431.90
211	150	26,407.85	0.005143	293.86	198.06	95.80	135.32	231.13	429.19
212	149	26,176.73	0.005143	292.35	196.33	96.03	134.13	230.16	426.49
213	148	25,946.57	0.005143	290.85	194.60	96.25	132.95	229.20	423.80
214	147	25,717.37	0.005143	289.35	192.88	96.47	131.77	228.24	421.12
215	146	25,489.13	0.005143	287.86	191.17	96.70	130.59	227.29	418.46
216	145	25,261.84	0.005143	286.38	189.46	96.92	129.42	226.34	415.81
217	144	25,035.49	0.005143	284.91	187.77	97.15	128.26	225.40	413.17
218	143	24,810.09	0.005143	283.45	186.08	97.37	127.10	224.47	410.54
219	142	24,585.62	0.005143	281.99	184.39	97.60	125.94	223.54	407.93
220	141	24,362.08	0.005143	280.54	182.72	97.82	124.79	222.61	405.33
221	140	24,139.47	0.005143	279.10	181.05	98.05	123.65	221.69	402.74
222	139	23,917.77	0.005143	277.66	179.38	98.28	122.50	220.78	400.16
223	138	23,696.99	0.005143	276.23	177.73	98.50	121.37	219.87	397.60
224	137	23,477.12	0.005143	274.81	176.08	98.73	120.24	218.97	395.05
225	136	23,258.15	0.005143	273.40	174.44	98.96	119.11	218.07	392.51

TABLE 9-3   *Continued*

Months	Life in Months	Mortgage Loan Outstanding	SMM	Mortgage Payment	Interest Payment	Scheduled Principal	Prepayment	Total Principal Paid	Total Cash Flows
226	135	23,040.08	0.005143	271.99	172.80	99.19	117.99	217.18	389.98
227	134	22,822.91	0.005143	270.59	171.17	99.42	116.87	216.29	387.46
228	133	22,606.62	0.005143	269.20	169.55	99.65	115.75	215.41	384.96
229	132	22,391.21	0.005143	267.82	167.93	99.88	114.64	214.53	382.46
230	131	22,176.68	0.005143	266.44	166.33	100.11	113.54	213.65	379.98
231	130	21,963.03	0.005143	265.07	164.72	100.35	112.44	212.79	377.51
232	129	21,750.24	0.005143	263.71	163.13	100.58	111.34	211.92	375.05
233	128	21,538.32	0.005143	262.35	161.54	100.81	110.25	211.07	372.60
234	127	21,327.25	0.005143	261.00	159.95	101.05	109.17	210.21	370.17
235	126	21,117.04	0.005143	259.66	158.38	101.28	108.08	209.36	367.74
236	125	20,907.68	0.005143	258.32	156.81	101.52	107.01	208.52	365.33
237	124	20,699.15	0.005143	256.99	155.24	101.75	105.93	207.68	362.93
238	123	20,491.47	0.005143	255.67	153.69	101.99	104.86	206.85	360.54
239	122	20,284.62	0.005143	254.36	152.13	102.22	103.80	206.02	358.16
240	121	20,078.60	0.005143	253.05	150.59	102.46	102.74	205.20	355.79
241	120	19,873.40	0.005143	251.75	149.05	102.70	101.68	204.38	353.43
242	119	19,669.02	0.005143	250.45	147.52	102.94	100.63	203.56	351.08
243	118	19,465.46	0.005143	249.17	145.99	103.17	99.58	202.75	348.75
244	117	19,262.71	0.005143	247.88	144.47	103.41	98.54	201.95	346.42
245	116	19,060.76	0.005143	246.61	142.96	103.65	97.50	201.15	344.11
246	115	18,859.61	0.005143	245.34	141.45	103.89	96.46	200.35	341.80
247	114	18,659.25	0.005143	244.08	139.94	104.13	95.43	199.56	339.51
248	113	18,459.69	0.005143	242.82	138.45	104.38	94.40	198.78	337.22
249	112	18,260.91	0.005143	241.57	136.96	104.62	93.38	198.00	334.95
250	111	18,062.92	0.005143	240.33	135.47	104.86	92.36	197.22	332.69
251	110	17,865.70	0.005143	239.10	133.99	105.10	91.34	196.45	330.44
252	109	17,669.25	0.005143	237.87	132.52	105.35	90.33	195.68	328.20
253	108	17,473.57	0.005143	236.64	131.05	105.59	89.32	194.91	325.97
254	107	17,278.66	0.005143	235.43	129.59	105.84	88.32	194.16	323.75
255	106	17,084.50	0.005143	234.22	128.13	106.08	87.32	193.40	321.54
256	105	16,891.10	0.005143	233.01	126.68	106.33	86.32	192.65	319.33
257	104	16,698.45	0.005143	231.81	125.24	106.57	85.33	191.91	317.14
258	103	16,506.54	0.005143	230.62	123.80	106.82	84.34	191.16	314.96
259	102	16,315.38	0.005143	229.43	122.37	107.07	83.36	190.43	312.79
260	101	16,124.95	0.005143	228.25	120.94	107.32	82.38	189.70	310.63
261	100	15,935.25	0.005143	227.08	119.51	107.57	81.40	188.97	308.48
262	99	15,746.29	0.005143	225.91	118.10	107.81	80.43	188.24	306.34
263	98	15,558.04	0.005143	224.75	116.69	108.06	79.46	187.52	304.21
264	97	15,370.52	0.005143	223.59	115.28	108.32	78.49	186.81	302.09
265	96	15,183.71	0.005143	222.44	113.88	108.57	77.53	186.10	299.98
266	95	14,997.61	0.005143	221.30	112.48	108.82	76.57	185.39	297.87
267	94	14,812.22	0.005143	220.16	111.09	109.07	75.62	184.69	295.78
268	93	14,627.53	0.005143	219.03	109.71	109.32	74.67	183.99	293.70
269	92	14,443.54	0.005143	217.90	108.33	109.58	73.72	183.30	291.62
270	91	14,260.24	0.005143	216.78	106.95	109.83	72.78	182.61	289.56

(Continued)

TABLE 9-3   *Continued*

Months	Life in Months	Mortgage Loan Outstanding	SMM	Mortgage Payment	Interest Payment	Scheduled Principal	Prepayment	Total Principal Paid	Total Cash Flows
271	90	14,077.64	0.005143	215.67	105.58	110.09	71.84	181.92	287.50
272	89	13,895.71	0.005143	214.56	104.22	110.34	70.90	181.24	285.46
273	88	13,714.48	0.005143	213.46	102.86	110.60	69.96	180.56	283.42
274	87	13,533.91	0.005143	212.36	101.50	110.85	69.03	179.89	281.39
275	86	13,354.03	0.005143	211.27	100.16	111.11	68.11	179.22	279.37
276	85	13,174.81	0.005143	210.18	98.81	111.37	67.19	178.55	277.36
277	84	12,996.25	0.005143	209.10	97.47	111.63	66.27	177.89	275.36
278	83	12,818.36	0.005143	208.02	96.14	111.88	65.35	177.23	273.37
279	82	12,641.13	0.005143	206.95	94.81	112.14	64.44	176.58	271.39
280	81	12,464.55	0.005143	205.89	93.48	112.40	63.53	175.93	269.42
281	80	12,288.62	0.005143	204.83	92.16	112.66	62.62	175.29	267.45
282	79	12,113.33	0.005143	203.78	90.85	112.93	61.72	174.64	265.49
283	78	11,938.69	0.005143	202.73	89.54	113.19	60.82	174.01	263.55
284	77	11,764.68	0.005143	201.69	88.24	113.45	59.92	173.37	261.61
285	76	11,591.31	0.005143	200.65	86.93	113.71	59.03	172.74	259.68
286	75	11,418.57	0.005143	199.62	85.64	113.98	58.14	172.12	257.76
287	74	11,246.45	0.005143	198.59	84.35	114.24	57.25	171.49	255.84
288	73	11,074.96	0.005143	197.57	83.06	114.51	56.37	170.88	253.94
289	72	10,904.08	0.005143	196.55	81.78	114.77	55.49	170.26	252.04
290	71	10,733.82	0.005143	195.54	80.50	115.04	54.61	169.65	250.15
291	70	10,564.17	0.005143	194.54	79.23	115.30	53.74	169.04	248.27
292	69	10,395.13	0.005143	193.53	77.96	115.57	52.87	168.44	246.40
293	68	10,226.69	0.005143	192.54	76.70	115.84	52.00	167.84	244.54
294	67	10,058.85	0.005143	191.55	75.44	116.11	51.14	167.24	242.68
295	66	9,891.60	0.005143	190.56	74.19	116.38	50.27	166.65	240.84
296	65	9,724.95	0.005143	189.58	72.94	116.65	49.42	166.06	239.00
297	64	9,558.89	0.005143	188.61	71.69	116.92	48.56	165.48	237.17
298	63	9,393.41	0.005143	187.64	70.45	117.19	47.71	164.90	235.35
299	62	9,228.52	0.005143	186.67	69.21	117.46	46.86	164.32	233.53
300	61	9,064.20	0.005143	185.71	67.98	117.73	46.01	163.74	231.73
301	60	8,900.45	0.005143	184.76	66.75	118.01	45.17	163.17	229.93
302	59	8,737.28	0.005143	183.81	65.53	118.28	44.33	162.61	228.14
303	58	8,574.67	0.005143	182.86	64.31	118.55	43.49	162.04	226.35
304	57	8,412.63	0.005143	181.92	63.09	118.83	42.66	161.48	224.58
305	56	8,251.15	0.005143	180.99	61.88	119.10	41.82	160.93	222.81
306	55	8,090.22	0.005143	180.06	60.68	119.38	40.99	160.37	221.05
307	54	7,929.85	0.005143	179.13	59.47	119.66	40.17	159.82	219.30
308	53	7,770.02	0.005143	178.21	58.28	119.93	39.34	159.28	217.55
309	52	7,610.74	0.005143	177.29	57.08	120.21	38.52	158.74	215.82
310	51	7,452.01	0.005143	176.38	55.89	120.49	37.71	158.20	214.09
311	50	7,293.81	0.005143	175.47	54.70	120.77	36.89	157.66	212.36
312	49	7,136.15	0.005143	174.57	53.52	121.05	36.08	157.13	210.65
313	48	6,979.02	0.005143	173.67	52.34	121.33	35.27	156.60	208.94
314	47	6,822.42	0.005143	172.78	51.17	121.61	34.46	156.07	207.24
315	46	6,666.35	0.005143	171.89	50.00	121.89	33.66	155.55	205.55

TABLE 9-3   *Continued*

Months	Life in Months	Mortgage Loan Outstanding	SMM	Mortgage Payment	Interest Payment	Scheduled Principal	Prepayment	Total Principal Paid	Total Cash Flows
316	45	6,510.80	0.005143	171.01	48.83	122.18	32.86	155.03	203.86
317	44	6,355.76	0.005143	170.13	47.67	122.46	32.06	154.52	202.19
318	43	6,201.24	0.005143	169.25	46.51	122.74	31.26	154.01	200.51
319	42	6,047.24	0.005143	168.38	45.35	123.03	30.47	153.50	198.85
320	41	5,893.74	0.005143	167.52	44.20	123.31	29.68	152.99	197.19
321	40	5,740.75	0.005143	166.65	43.06	123.60	28.89	152.49	195.54
322	39	5,588.26	0.005143	165.80	41.91	123.89	28.10	151.99	193.90
323	38	5,436.27	0.005143	164.95	40.77	124.17	27.32	151.49	192.27
324	37	5,284.78	0.005143	164.10	39.64	124.46	26.54	151.00	190.64
325	36	5,133.78	0.005143	163.25	38.50	124.75	25.76	150.51	189.01
326	35	4,983.27	0.005143	162.41	37.37	125.04	24.99	150.02	187.40
327	34	4,833.25	0.005143	161.58	36.25	125.33	24.21	149.54	185.79
328	33	4,683.70	0.005143	160.75	35.13	125.62	23.44	149.06	184.19
329	32	4,534.64	0.005143	159.92	34.01	125.91	22.67	148.58	182.59
330	31	4,386.06	0.005143	159.10	32.90	126.20	21.91	148.11	181.01
331	30	4,237.95	0.005143	158.28	31.78	126.49	21.15	147.64	179.42
332	29	4,090.31	0.005143	157.47	30.68	126.79	20.38	147.17	177.85
333	28	3,943.13	0.005143	156.66	29.57	127.08	19.63	146.71	176.28
334	27	3,796.43	0.005143	155.85	28.47	127.38	18.87	146.25	174.72
335	26	3,650.18	0.005143	155.05	27.38	127.67	18.12	145.79	173.16
336	25	3,504.39	0.005143	154.25	26.28	127.97	17.36	145.33	171.62
337	24	3,359.06	0.005143	153.46	25.19	128.26	16.62	144.88	170.07
338	23	3,214.18	0.005143	152.67	24.11	128.56	15.87	144.43	168.54
339	22	3,069.75	0.005143	151.88	23.02	128.86	15.13	143.99	167.01
340	21	2,925.76	0.005143	151.10	21.94	129.16	14.38	143.54	165.49
341	20	2,782.22	0.005143	150.33	20.87	129.46	13.64	143.10	163.97
342	19	2,639.12	0.005143	149.55	19.79	129.76	12.91	142.66	162.46
343	18	2,496.45	0.005143	148.78	18.72	130.06	12.17	142.23	160.95
344	17	2,354.22	0.005143	148.02	17.66	130.36	11.44	141.80	159.45
345	16	2,212.42	0.005143	147.26	16.59	130.66	10.71	141.37	157.96
346	15	2,071.06	0.005143	146.50	15.53	130.97	9.98	140.94	156.48
347	14	1,930.11	0.005143	145.75	14.48	131.27	9.25	140.52	155.00
348	13	1,789.59	0.005143	145.00	13.42	131.57	8.53	140.10	153.52
349	12	1,649.49	0.005143	144.25	12.37	131.88	7.81	139.68	152.06
350	11	1,509.80	0.005143	143.51	11.32	132.18	7.09	139.27	150.59
351	10	1,370.53	0.005143	142.77	10.28	132.49	6.37	138.86	149.14
352	9	1,231.68	0.005143	142.04	9.24	132.80	5.65	138.45	147.69
353	8	1,093.23	0.005143	141.31	8.20	133.11	4.94	138.04	146.24
354	7	955.18	0.005143	140.58	7.16	133.41	4.23	137.64	144.81
355	6	817.54	0.005143	139.86	6.13	133.72	3.52	137.24	143.37
356	5	680.30	0.005143	139.14	5.10	134.03	2.81	136.84	141.95
357	4	543.46	0.005143	138.42	4.08	134.35	2.10	136.45	140.52
358	3	407.01	0.005143	137.71	3.05	134.66	1.40	136.06	139.11
359	2	270.95	0.005143	137.00	2.03	134.97	0.70	135.67	137.70
360	1	135.28	0.005143	136.30	1.01	135.28	0.00	135.28	136.30

Figure 9-5 plots the prepayments of this loan with the 100% PSA assumption.

It is important to understand the effect of prepayments on the loan value. The value of the loan with prepayments is compressed to the outstanding balance as interest rates fall. In comparison, the value of a non-callable loan increases as the rates fall.

FIGURE 9-5   *Prepayments of a Single Loan at 100% PSA*

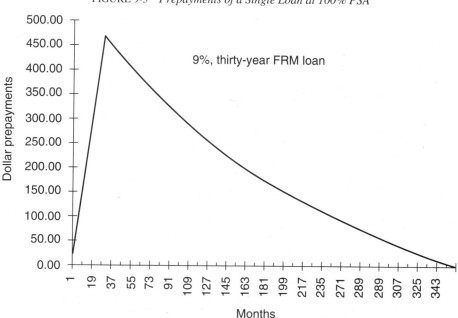

MORTGAGE-BACKED SECURITIES (MBS)

Historical Overview

We begin our discussion of the mortgage-backed securities markets by first providing a summary of how they developed.

In traditional mortgages, prior to securitization, home buyers obtain loans (via borrowing) from mortgage originators. Typically, originators (mortgage banks, thrifts, etc.) lend to many home buyers and thus end up with a loan portfolio. Such loan portfolios may either be held by the originator or sold to other investors. The demand for credit, therefore, comes from home buyers, and the mortgage originators supply the necessary credit. When the demand exceeds the supply in a region, thrifts will sell their loan portfolio (which they originated) in order to supply additional credit. When the supply exceeds the demand in a region, thrifts will buy loan portfolios from other regions. Often, redistribution of mortgage credit from capital-surplus to capital-deficit regions is necessary and to accomplish this, usually the loans are sold and bought by thrifts and mortgage banks around the country. When the overall demand for credit grows at a rate that cannot be sustained by suppliers of credit, the deposit base of lenders may simply be unable to support the demand for credit. For a liquid secondary market in mortgage loans to develop, it is necessary that some conditions are met.

- The originators must continue to service the loans.
- The loans must be standardized with respect to maturity, coupons, and so on.
- There must be a credible guarantee regarding the performance of home buyers in paying the loan back.

The strong demand for mortgage credit precipitated the following sequence of events. In 1934 the Federal Housing Administration (FHA) was set up to insure home loans. In 1938 the Federal National Mortgage Association (Fannie Mae) was created; its mission was to provide a secondary market for FHA and Veterans Administration (VA) mortgage loans, provide additional liquidity to the mortgage market, and improve the distribution of investment capital. Fannie Mae was set up as a wholly-owned government corporation. In 1944, the Veterans Administration (VA) loan guarantee program was set up.

By 1954, Fannie Mae was partly owned by private shareholders and partly by government. In 1968, it was split into the Government National Mortgage Association (GNMA or Ginnie Mae) and Fannie Mae. At present, Fannie Mae is a private corporation whose shares are listed on the New York Stock Exchange. The U.S. Treasury, at its discretion, may buy up to $2.25 billion worth of Fannie Mae's debt. GNMA is wholly government-owned. All of its operations are financed by Treasury borrowings, interest on holdings, guarantee fees, and other fees. The mission of GNMA is to supply and stimulate credit for mortgages through its secondary market activities. GNMA guarantees FHA- and VA-based mortgage-backed securities (MBS).

In 1970 the Federal Home Loan Mortgage Corporation (Freddie Mac) was created by Congress. Freddie Mac provides a link between mortgage lenders and capital markets. It buys from savings and loans institutions, mortgage bankers, and commercial banks, and sells mortgage pass-through securities. It began with an initial capital of $100 million funded by 12 Federal Home Loan Banks through nonvoting common stock.

A comparison of the agencies and their pass-throughs is presented next.

Agency and Private Pass-through Securities: A Comparison

1. **GNMA:** GNMA finances FHA and VA loans. Typically the loans are from single-family, low-income households. GNMA pass-through securities are guaranteed by GNMA and are issued by GNMA-approved originators and servicers. The loans are packaged in sizes of one million or more and placed with a trustee. Upon acceptance of loan documentation, GNMA assigns a pool number which identifies the security

to be issued. The originator or the servicer then issues pass-through securities which are sold to investment bankers for distribution.

GNMA tends to require a greater degree of homogeneity of the mortgages within a given pool. Pools tend to have a single type (single-family, thirty-year fixed, for example) and the mortgages carry the same interest rate. For single family pools the mortgage interest is 50 basis points higher than the pass-through rate: the 50 basis points covers the servicing fee and the guarantee fees. In the GNMA II program, there is more diversity in the underlying loans. Also under the GNMA II program, a central paying and transfer agent consolidates all the payments to the security holders in one monthly check. But there is a delay associated with this process.

The GNMA guarantee of full and timely payment of interest and principal is backed by the full faith and credit of the U.S. Government. GNMA covers low-income (house price less than $152,000) homes. Historically, prepayments are less volatile relative to other agency pass-throughs.

2. FNMA: This agency's stocks trade in NYSE. FNMA buys conventional mortgages and operates a swap program whereby loans of any age can be swapped into FNMA-issued participation securities. Such a swap can be beneficial to the lenders in the sense that the lenders can use the FNMA-issued securities as collaterals in reverse repurchase agreements.

FNMA also provides the guarantee of full and timely payment of interest and principal, but this guarantee is not backed by the full faith and credit of the U.S. Government. However, FNMA does have a $2.25 billion credit with the U.S. Treasury. FNMA pools are much more heterogeneous when compared to the pools in the GNMA. FNMA pools may have mortgages with rates that vary by more than 200 basis points and the loans may be new or seasoned. FNMA covers both FHA and VA loans as well as conventional loans which have a much higher value. Due to this and due to the greater diversity of loans, prepayments are much more volatile.

3. FHLMC: This agency also buys FHA, VA, and conventional mortgages, and operates a swap program whereby loans of any age can be swapped into Freddie Mac-issued participation securities. As noted earlier, such a swap can be beneficial to the lenders in the sense that the lenders can use the Freddie Mac-issued securities as collaterals in reverse repurchase agreements.

FHLMC also provides the guarantee of full and timely payment of interest and principal. But this guarantee is not backed by the full faith and credit of the U.S. Government. But Freddie Mac has a $2.25 billion credit with the U.S. Treasury. Freddie Mac pools are much more heterogeneous when compared to the pools in the GNMA. Freddie Mac pools may have mortgages with rates that vary by more than 200 basis points and the loans may be new or seasoned. FHLMC buys FHA and VA, as well as conventional loans which have a much higher value. Due to this and due to the greater diversity of loans, prepayments are much more volatile.

4. Private Labels: These are nonagency pass-through securities which create a secondary market for nonconforming loans, which are conventional loans that fail to meet the size limits and other requirements placed by the agencies. Private pass-throughs trade at a spread over the agency pass-throughs.

Creation of MBS

Only FHA and VA loans qualify for conversion to GNMA pass-through MBS. The loan pool must have some standard features in terms of coupon, single-family or multifamily, maturity, and so on. The minimum size of the pool is $1 million for single-family loans. GNMA II permits mortgages with different interest rates to be included in the same pool.

The following steps are taken in issuing mortgage-backed securities.

1.   The originators forward the loan portfolio to GNMA with the appropriate documentation, requesting GNMA's commitment to guarantee the securities to be backed by the pooled mortgage portfolio.
2.   GNMA reviews the application. If the review is favorable, then a pool number is assigned and the commitment is issued.
3.   The originators transfer the mortgage documents to custodial agents and send the required pool documents to GNMA.
4.   Anticipating the issuance of the GNMA guarantee, the originators solicit advance commitments from dealers, investment banks, and so on, to sell a specified amount of the securities at a set price and yield.
5.   GNMA reviews the documentation and issues the guarantee.

The originators continue to service the loans: collecting the monthly interest and principal payments, remitting the net amount of the servicing fee to the security holders, and issuing monthly account statements.

GNMAs are not debt obligations of the issuers. They represent real estate assets. The servicers collect 50 basis points per annum of the outstanding principal balance of each mortgage for servicing and the GNMA guarantee. GNMA gets 6 basis points per annum of 50 for its guarantee. Figure 9-6 illustrates the basics of creating an MBS.

FIGURE 9-6   *Creating Mortgage-Backed Securities (an Example)*

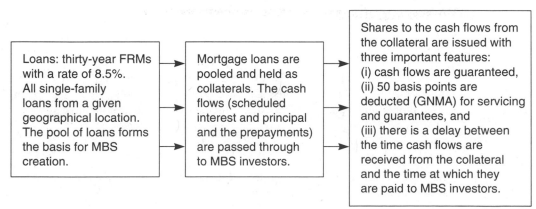

Cash Flows and Market Conventions

Amount of Cash Flow. In principle the cash flows (scheduled interest, principal and pre-payments) from the underlying pool of mortgages are passed through to the investors in the mortgage-backed security with the exception of fees. Servicing fees and guarantee fees will be subtracted from the cash flows generated by the loan portfolio that is back-ing the mortgage-backed security. These fees vary from one agency security to another. For GNMAs, the fees are as follows.

- 44 basis points are retained by the servicer for servicing the loans and guarantees.
- GNMA will get 6 basis points for its guarantee. The issuer essentially guarantees GNMA against any defaults by homeowners. GNMA guarantees against defaults by the issuer.
- These fees mean that the investors in the mortgage-backed security will get 50 basis points less than the coupon of the loan portfolio.

Timing of Cash Flow. Homeowners tend to make their scheduled payments during the first half of each month. The payments to the investors in mortgage-backed securities occur on the 15th of the next month. Market participants refer to this as a 45-day delay. This delay varies from one agency security to another. In reality, the actual delay is a good deal less than that.

Market Conventions. Investors buying an agency security such as a GNMA must un-derstand the market conventions. GNMAs are quoted in $\frac{1}{32}$, similar to Treasury securi-ties. The prices quoted refer to percentages of the outstanding principal balance in the underlying pool. This requires the calculation of the outstanding balance, which in turn requires compilation of the scheduled interest and principal payments as well as any pre-payments. For these computations, the servicing institutions calculate a pool factor. The definition of **pool factor** $p_f(t)$ is

$$p_f(t) = \frac{B_t}{P} \tag{9.5}$$

where B_t is the balance at date t and P is the original balance.

Example 9-2

Consider a $100 million par value of GNMA issued some time ago. Currently it has a pool factor of 0.9 and is quoted at a price of $93\frac{16}{32}$. To an investor who is holding 20 million original par of this GNMA, its market value can be computed as

Par value remaining $= 20 \times 0.9 = 18$ million

Market value $= 18 \times 0.9350 = 16.83$ million.

As in the Treasury markets, this price is the flat price to which the accrued interest is added to determine the invoice price.

The usual settlement practice is to settle two days following the trade date. The first settlement date for any month occurs around the middle of the month. The reason for this is simple: It takes that long to compute and distribute the pool factors. The procedure for computing accrued interest is as follows. The accrued interest ai_t is

$$ai_t = \frac{SD - M}{30} \times c \times \frac{1}{12} \times B$$

where SD is the settlement date, M is the first day of the month within which t falls, B is the principal balance, and c is the coupon rate.

Example 9-3

In Example 9-2, let us assume that the coupon rate $c = 9\%$ and that $SD - M$ is 20 days. Then, the accrued interest is

$$ai_t = \frac{20}{30} \times 9 \times \frac{1}{12} \times 18 = 90,000.$$

Note that the accrued interest calculations differ from Treasuries in important ways. First, interest accrues from the first day of the month; in Treasury markets, the last coupon date is the relevant date from which interest accrues. In the case of GNMA the convention is actual over 360, as the example illustrates. Note that this means that an investor buying a GNMA in April for settlement in the middle of April (say, April 15) is buying a pro-rata share in the outstanding principal balance of a mortgage pool as of the end of March. This investor will expect to receive on May 15 the interest on the balance, computed as of the end of March, plus any prepayments during the month of April.

When agency pass-through securities are traded, they are identified with some key characteristics of the underlying pool. A pool number is assigned that enables investors to learn about the features of the underlying pool, such as whether the pool is fixed or adjustable, the issuer, and the weighted-average coupon. Sometimes trades in securities occur before key features of the underlying pool become available. Such trades are referred to as TBA (to be announced) trades. In TBA trades, investors do not know the pool numbers on the trade date, but will know them before the settlement date.

Prepayment Evidence. GNMA prepayment history is reported in Table 9-4 for two sub-sample periods: 1979–1984 and 1989–1991. Note the decline in prepayments after the peak in 1979. The increase in the levels of interest rates accounted for this decline until 1982. During the 1987–1991 period, prepayments were stable, although at a much higher level relative to the 1980–1984 period. The steep increase in 1991 is due to the decline in refinancing rates. This trend continued on into the 1992–1993 period (not reported here) as well. For the same reason, higher-coupon GNMAs have faster prepayments, as seen during the 1987–1991 period: the $9\frac{1}{2}\%$ GNMA has faster prepayments relative to the 9% GNMA.

| | 1979–1984 | | | | | |
| Year | Coupon $7\frac{1}{2}\%$ (1977) | | Coupon 8% (1977) | | Coupon $9\frac{1}{2}\%$ (1979) | |
	CPR	PSA	CPR	PSA	CPR	PSA
1979	7.5	141	6.7	149	—	—
1980	3.1	51	3.0	51	1.0	46
1981	1.1	18	1.3	21	1.4	30
1982	0.8	13	0.9	15	1.3	21
1983	2.7	46	2.8	46	2.5	41
1984	2.5	42	2.4	41	2.4	39
	1987–1991					
Year	Coupon 9% (1986)		Coupon $9\frac{1}{2}\%$ (1986)		Coupon 8% (1987)	
	CPR	PSA	CPR	PSA	CPR	PSA
1987	1.6	74	2.6	117	—	—
1988	3.5	78	5.0	107	1.6	52
1989	4.7	79	6.2	105	2.7	52
1990	5.3	89	6.8	114	3.6	59
1991	6.4	107	8.7	145	4.2	70

TABLE 9-4
GNMA Prepayment History

Source: Mortgage Product Analysis, Merrill Lynch (December 9, 1994)

Institutional Investors and MBS. MBS comprise a sector in which a number of institutional investors participate. Since MBS are backed by mortgage loans and are guaranteed, credit risk is not a major factor. Investors pay more attention to the nature of the collateral, structure of the issue and the extent to which there is overcollateralization. For the agency-backed pass-throughs, the main risk is the prepayment risk. The investor buys a pro-rata share of the cash flows. If there is a drop in interest rates, prepayments will occur and will be passed through. Figure 9-7 shows the prepayment history for 1988–1995. Note the extraordinary increase in prepayments in 1993–1994. Despite the prepayment risks, MBS have become an important part of portfolios of institutional investors as the article from *Pension World* (September 1993) illustrates.

Managers Breathing Easier After Attacks

By Ray Wise

Emerging from their bunkers after three massive prepayment attacks, managers of mortgage portfolios are breathing easier. They see interest rates nudging higher in the months ahead, and a flat-to-slightly-rising rate environment would give Ginnie Mae's an edge over comparable Treasury bonds.

FIGURE 9-7   *Prepayment History (1988–1995)*

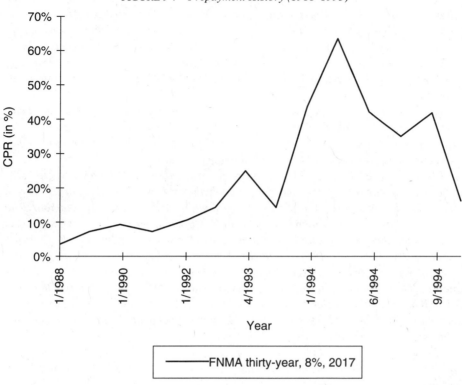

The Treasury Department is curtailing auctions of 30-year bonds in favor of short-to-intermediate maturities. This augurs pressure on the shorter-term Treasuries, causing better relative performance by Ginnie Mae's later this year, says portfolio manager Garitt Kono of the New York-based Dreyfus Corporation.

True, interest rates recently extended their protracted decline, chasing yields on 30-year Treasuries to record lows. "Eventually, though, the rate decline is going to end. Once you get a reversal, you will see more investors coming into the mortgage-backed market," predicts portfolio manager Mike Kennedy of Chicago-based Stein Roe & Farnham.

Technically, the market in mortgage-backed securities looks pretty solid, notes managing director Kay Willcox of Prudential Investment Corp., Newark, N.J. There is a dearth of attractive alternatives; high-grade corporates, for example, are burdened by tight yield spreads. Moreover, reflecting prepayment, underweighting of MBS is widespread. Having recently turned positive on this asset class, fixed-income manager Francis H. Trainer of New York-based Sanford C. Bernstein & Co. has a 23% weighting in MBS; that's up sharply from the 13% he carried last September, but well below a market weighting of 29%.

Yet roaring bulls abound. "Ginnie Mae's yield 20% more than Treasuries, with the same credit quality. I think this is a terrific time for the mortgage-backed market," says *managing director David H. Glen of Scudder, Stevens & Clark, Boston. "We are trying to load up mortgages. You've got an opportunity here." "The mortgage market is an attractive long-term place to put money, despite the interest-rate declines," adds portfolio manager Amy Swanson of Boston-based State Street Research & Management, Inc.*

Falling rates encourage home owners to refinance their mortgages, minimally causing return of principal and reinvestment risk to MBS holders; in the case of a premium coupon, capital loss also results.

The likelihood that prepayment may remain at a high level for months doesn't deter Swanson from being bullish on mortgage securities. "They have good value relative to corporates and Treasuries. It's okay to incur prepayment. You are still earning a handsome return over Treasuries," the money manager notes.

Prepayment risk is managed by Swanson in three ways: applying a worst-case scenario to a mortgage certificate and deciding whether it is worth owning at its current price; trying to anticipate interest-rate changes, and focusing on current coupons. The portfolio of Chris Ray of Putnam Management Co., Boston, who worries less about rate declines than about the possibility that rates may rise sharply, is barbell-shaped; it is focused on 7%–7.5% and 9.5%–10% coupons.

Until fairly recently, conventional wisdom held that widespread mortgage refinancings required fueling by an interest-rate drop of 150 to 200 basis points. That rule-of-thumb has been rendered totally obsolete by the proliferation of refinancing options. Seeking to capitalize on the new environment, mortgage bankers beating the bushes for business have sweetened the deals considerably.

The disparities between interest-rate-sensitive mortgage refinancings on one hand, and all the rest, on the other, have widened. The latter category is secular, fairly predictable and reflects the housing industry cycle.

Example: A young couple living in an apartment with a one-year-old child buys a house from a family needing a bigger spread.

Refinancings driven mainly by steeply falling home loan costs can come so swiftly and unpredictably as to seem like a capital-market manifestation of chaos theory. Prepayment risk can be managed but not eliminated. On the other hand, without that risk, there would be no reason for Ginnie Mae's to out-yield Treasuries.

High-yielding alternatives to mortgage securities are "few and far between," says vice president Leslie Finnemore of Colonial Management Associates, Boston.

In order to better serve investors, the cash flows from mortgage loans are packaged differently in collateralized mortgage obligations (CMOs). This is taken up next.

COLLATERALIZED MORTGAGE OBLIGATIONS (CMOS)

CMOs represent an innovative way to redistribute the cash flows from a pool of mortgages or mortgage-backed securities to various investor classes. Recall that investors in mortgage-backed securities get a pro-rata share of the cash flows of the security including prepayments. CMOs, through careful structuring, can offer varying levels of protection against prepayment.

CMOs were first issued in June 1983 when the FHLMC issued a $1 billion security. The CMO issuance is backed by pools of residential mortgages or mortgage-backed securities such as GNMAs, which serve as the collateral. The collateral is guaranteed by the GNMA, the FNMA, or the FHLMC.

CMO Structure

CMOs tend to be rated AAA or Aaa by the rating agencies. The key to this high credit reputation is the basic requirement that the cash flows generated by the underlying mortgages or the agency securities are more than sufficient to meet the obligations of all tranches even under the most extreme prepayment assumptions. Let us review some of the characteristics of general CMO structures.

- The credit risk is minimized by having a credible third party (such as a Federal agency or a AAA insurance company) guarantee the cash flows.
- The amount of collateral is set such that even under the most pessimistic prepayment assumptions, the total value of the bonds issued will be less than the value of the collateral. The typical worst-case assumption requires that all premium mortgages be immediately prepaid and all discount mortgages have zero prepayments.
- CMOs pay semi-annual or quarterly payments, but the underlying collateral or mortgages make monthly payments. This means that there is some reinvestment of the cash flows from the underlying collateral. Typically, conservative assumptions about the reinvestment rates are made by the rating agencies. Sometimes, the rates that the issuer can get on guaranteed investment contracts (GICs) are used as indicators of possible reinvestment rates.
- The CMO must be heavily over-collateralized. The purpose of this over-collateralizing is to create an insurance cushion that helps to offset any cash flow shortages that may result due to a fall in reinvestment income from the underlying monthly cash flows.

The cash flows from the collateral are divided and allocated to several classes or tranches of bonds. Currently there are two basic CMO structures, sequential structure and planned amortization class (PAC) structure.

CMO Sequential Structure. A typical generic CMO sequential structure (see Table 9-5) has four tranches. Specific rules dictate how the cash flows (including prepayments) from the collateral are allocated to each tranche. The total cash payment to each tranche is also set ahead of time. The first tranche is allotted a stated coupon. In addition to this coupon, the first tranche will also be allotted any prepayments that are made.

Until the first tranche is fully retired, no payments are made to the other tranches, except that the second and third tranches will receive the predetermined coupon amounts. The prepayments are passed through to the second tranche only after the first is fully retired. In this sense, each tranche successively receives prepayments as soon as its immediate predecessor is retired. The last (here the 4th) tranche is called the **Z bond** and receives no cash flows until all earlier tranches are fully retired. The face amount, however, accrues at the stated coupon. After all tranches have been retired, the Z bond receives the coupon on its current face amount plus all the prepayments. Trustees ensure that the remaining collateral is large enough at all times so that all tranches get their promised cash flows. Most of the CMOs are rated AAA by the usual rating agencies. To provide the AAA rating, these agencies require that the present value of zero-prepayment cash flows from the collateral at a discount rate equal to the maximum coupon of the bond determines the maximum amount of bonds that will be issued. The difference between the required bond payments and the cash flow received from the collateral is called the residual and is retained by the issuer of CMOs. Figure 9-8 illustrates a sequential CMO deal.

Tranche	Principal (in millions)	Coupon	Average Life (in years)	Yield
A	150	9.00%	2.50	2 yr T + 100
B	70	9.00%	6.00	5 yr T + 120
C	100	9.00%	10.00	10 yr T + 125
Z	30	9.00%	18.90	30 yr T + 175

TABLE 9-5

Generic Sequential CMO Structure

Agency collateral: FNMA
Weighted-average coupon (net): 9.00%
Weighted-average coupon (gross): 9.70%
Pricing speed: 200% PSA

CMO Planned Amortization Class Structure. In a PAC CMO structure, the tranches are created to provide varying levels of protection from prepayment. In this structure, the collateral's principal is divided into two categories. The first category is designated PAC bonds and the second category is the companion group.

- The amortization schedule for the PAC bonds remains fixed over a range of prepayment rates measured by a range of PSAs. The more stable amortization schedule of the PAC group is at the expense of the companion group.
- The structure therefore allows for many PAC bonds with stable average lives. The companion bonds, on the other hand, have much less stable lives than otherwise similar sequential bonds.
- PAC bonds, because of their more stable amortization schedules, tend to be priced tightly to respective Treasuries. By the same token, bonds in the companion group are priced at much wider spreads relative to Treasuries.

FIGURE 9-8   *Cash Flows to a Sequential CMO Structure*

CMO generic sequential structure
(an example)

Pools of mortgage loans or agency pass-throughs are placed as collaterals. Extra collateral is built into the structure together with other enhancements.

Monthly cash flows (scheduled interest, principal and prepayments) are reinvested. Out of these, semi-annual coupon payments to tranches are made. Prepayments are used to retire the tranches in a sequential manner. The difference in the cash flows between the collateral and the tranches is the CMO equity or CMO residuals.

Properties of tranches

Tranche A: It has the shortest duration and is usually invested in by commercial banks and money managers.

Tranche B: This tranche has a moderate duration and is of interest to banks, retail, and money managers.

Tranche C: It has a longer duration and is invested in by insurance companies, pension funds, etc.

Tranche Z: This has the longest duration and is invested in by pension funds and insurance companies.

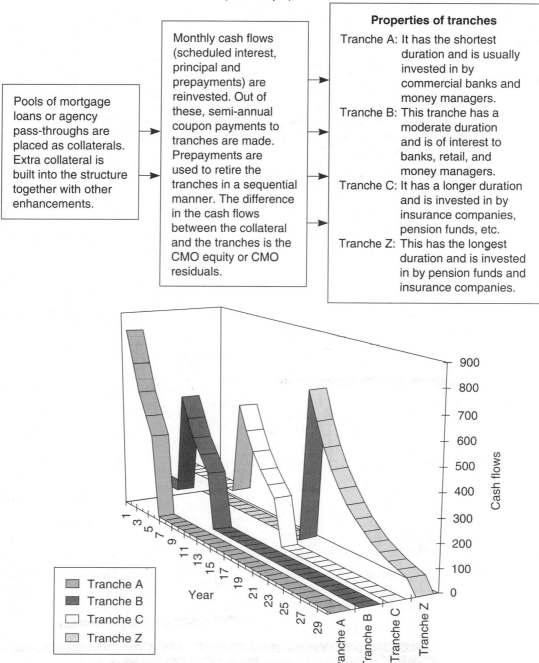

A generic PAC CMO structure is provided in Table 9-6.

TABLE 9-6

PAC CMO Structure

Tranche	Principal (in millions)	Coupon	Average Life (in years)	Yield
PAC-A	60	9.00%	3.50	3 yr T + 70
PAC-B	90	9.00%	8.00	7 yr T + 90
PAC-C	10	9.00%	12.50	10 yr T + 90
PAC-D	30	9.00%	17.00	30 yr T + 100
COMP	100	9.00%	3.00	3 yr T + 250
Z	25	9.00%	18.25	30 yr T + 200

Agency collateral: FNMA
Weighted-average coupon (net): 9.00%
Weighted-average coupon (gross): 9.70%
Pricing speed: 200% PSA

As seen in the table, CMOs can be set up for designing securities that may meet the special needs of different investor groups. A number of CMOs have been issued with tranches that pay coupons at levels tied to the London Interbank Offered Rates (LIBOR). These floating rate CMOs have been popular with commercial banks and foreign institutional investors.

Another type of CMO, known as the targeted amortization class (TAC) CMO, are very similar to PAC CMOs; they also enjoy a specified redemption schedule backed by support tranches in the CMO structure. Unlike PACs, TACs have a longer average maturity when interest rates fall and the prepayments are slower than expected.

VALUATION FRAMEWORK

The basic insight into the valuation of mortgage-backed securities is to recognize that default-free assumable mortgage-backed securities consist of an annuity and a call option that gives the homeowners the right to buy the annuity at a strike price equal to the remaining par amount at any time prior to maturity (from 15 to 30 years). Thus the factors that determine the value of a fixed-rate mortgage are:

- its coupon,
- time to maturity,
- amortization schedule and
- interest rates on comparable mortgages at the time of valuation.

The models for valuing mortgage-backed securities such as Dunn and McConnell (1981) apply the principles of options pricing. More recent models, notably Buser, Hendershott, and Sanders (1990), have extended the basic insights, but the principles of valuation have remained the same. Such valuation models assume the following.

1. The expected instantaneous holding-period return on any mortgage is equal to the instantaneous riskless rate plus an instantaneous risk premium. Mathematically, the

expected return on the mortgage-backed security $E_t\left[\frac{dV(c,\,R_t,\,t)}{V(c,\,R_t,\,t)}\right]$ is equal to the riskless rate R_t plus the risk premium π_t. This leads to

$$E_t\left[\frac{dV(c,\,R_t,\,t)}{V(c,\,R_t,\,t)}\right] = R_t + \pi_t.$$

The rate on the mortgage is denoted by c.

2. Mortgage-backed securities are assumed to obey certain boundary conditions. For example, the value of the mortgage-backed security must satisfy two conditions:

    •   As the mortgage-backed security approaches its maturity date T, its value will go to zero

$$V(c,\,R_T,\,T) = 0. \tag{9.6}$$

    •   As the interest rates approach ∞ the value of the mortgage-backed security approaches zero.

$$\lim_{R_t \to \infty} V(c,\,R_t,\,t) = 0. \tag{9.7}$$

The intuition here is that the mortgage loans are worthless at very high interest rates. Absent the call feature, it is clear that the value of the mortgage-backed security is convex to the origin, as shown in Figure 9-9.

3. The fact that mortgage-backed securities are sold on mortgages that can be prepaid means that we need to impose a condition on the optimal exercise of this prepayment option. We know that the homeowners will tend to prepay the loans when interest rates decrease to a critical low level R^*. We can capture this condition as

$$\lim_{R_t \downarrow R^*} V(c,\,R_t,\,t) = \text{par}. \tag{9.8}$$

The existence of the prepayment feature means that the value of the mortgage-backed securities behave differently at low interest rates. This behavior is sometimes

FIGURE 9-9   *Value of Mortgage-Backed Securities, Effect of Interest Rate*

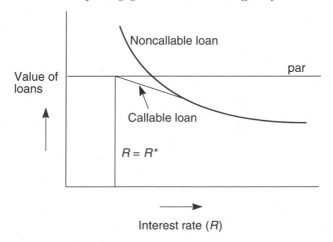

referred to as **compression to par or negative convexity.** When interest rates are close to the coupon of the mortgage-backed security and the volatility of the rates increases, the probability that the call will be exercised increases as well. This may produce a reduction in the price of the mortgage-backed securities.

In the valuation of mortgage-backed securities, we have thus far treated interest rates as the only variable affecting the value of the security and assumed that the mortgage-backed security is default-free. In reality, the fact that some homeowners might default affects the pricing of mortgage-backed securities. If the mortgage-backed security is fully insured and assumable (such as GNMAs), then upon default the guarantor will pay off the mortgage. Thus, the cash flows to mortgage-backed securities are affected by default. For example, defaults that occur during periods of very high interest rates tend to produce a gain for the security holders. When rates are high, the mortgage-backed securities sell below par, but default produces a cash flow equal to par, leading to a windfall gain.

It is also useful to recognize the incentives to voluntary default that the homeowner might have. If the value of the house is relatively high as compared to the value of the mortgage, then the homeowner may not wish to default. But, if the value of the house is well below the value of the mortgage, the incentive to default is high. This may be thought of as a put option or a walk-away option. The effect of this walk-away option is illustrated in Figure 9-10. Note that when the price of the house drops to a critical value H^* it is optimal for the homeowner to default on the mortgage.

More recent models of valuing mortgage-backed securities incorporate the house price as a second factor influencing the value. In such models, the value of the mortgage-backed security will be written as a function of both interest rates and house prices, as $V(c, R_t, H_t, t)$.

As $H_t \rightarrow \infty$, the value of the loan approaches that of the default-free loan. It is useful to examine some of the real-life features of mortgages in the context of this formulation. In a recent work, Wang (1995) analyzes mortgage-backed securities in a two-factor setting. The framework used by Wang (1995) for both the one- and two-factor models is presented in Figure 9-11. Note that when the house prices are low, even though the inter-

FIGURE 9-10   *Value of Mortgage-Backed Securities, House Price, and Default*

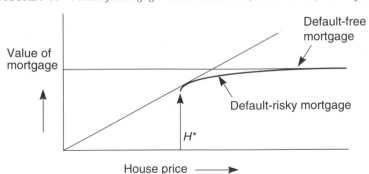

FIGURE 9-11   *Two Models for Valuing Mortgage-Backed Securities*

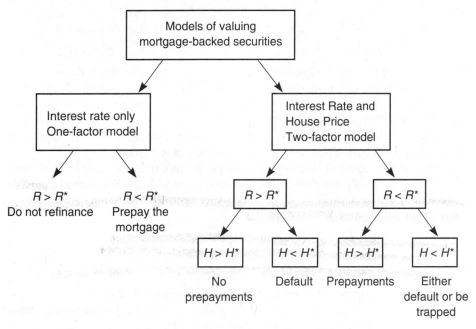

H^* = Critical House Price

est rates may be low, there is less of an incentive to prepay the mortgage; the mortgage value may exceed the house value by such a significant amount that the homeowner finds it suboptimal to exercise the option. This suggests that in periods of falling housing prices, the level of prepayments ought to go down. Our argument suggests that housing prices affect the valuation in two distinct ways:

1. At low housing prices, there is a greater incentive to default.
2. At low housing prices, the incentive to refinance also goes down.

In addition, housing prices enable us to model situations where depressed house prices, while not inducing immediate default, diminish the incentives to refinance.

Transactions costs in a given pool is yet another feature that we need to incorporate in the valuation framework. Homeowners spend time and resources in their refinancing decisions. Title fees, appraisal fees, and so on, constitute direct costs. There are significant indirect costs as well, which include the time spent in the choice of the mortgage loan and its analysis. It is possible that such transactions costs are dependent on the household and its circumstances. Thus, if the pool has a diverse set of homeowners and their transactions costs are distinct, then the prepayments from such a pool may not be easy to estimate. Note also that transactions costs are incurred by the households but are not received by the investors of mortgage-backed securities. If x_t is the transactions cost faced by the homeowner at date t, then the valuation function should exhibit the following property:

$$V(c, R_t, H_t, t) = \text{par} \qquad\qquad \text{if} \quad V(c, R_{t+}, H_{t+}, t+) \geq \text{par} + x_t$$

$$V(c, R_t, H_t, t) = V(c, R_{t+}, H_{t+}, t+) \quad \text{if} \quad V(c, R_{t+}, H_{t+}, t+) < \text{par} + x_t$$

Essentially, these conditions state that the homeowner should refinance if the value (taking into account the transactions costs) associated with that strategy exceeds the value associated with not refinancing. (At each time t, the value of the mortgage is compared with the value associated with prepayments. At an instant after t which is denoted by $t+$, we examine whether the value of the mortgage is higher than the value associated with prepayments net of transactions costs. We choose the optimal strategy.)

Although the conditions that we have laid out are intuitive, they do not necessarily account for values and prepayments that one observes in real-life. For example, the following empirical regularities have been reported with respect to mortgage prepayments but are not accounted for in our framework.

- Prepayment rates for deep discount securities increase over time.
- Prepayment rates for aged premium securities decline over time.
- Prepayment rates on newly originated mortgages increase at first and then decline.

Furthermore, prepayments, as noted earlier, depend on many factors.

It is necessary to modify the framework to obtain a model of valuation which admits these regularities and the richness that prepayments exhibit.

A VALUATION MODEL

The framework that we have provided in the previous section may be specialized to calculate quantitative answers for the valuation of various mortgage-backed securities. First, a choice must be made between a single-factor or a two-factor model. Second, an empirical model of prepayments must be chosen. In addition, several specific modelling choices must be made even within this setting; for example, a specific process must be chosen for the interest-rate process.

The procedure that is used to value most mortgage-backed securities comprises the following steps.

1. An interest-rate process is specified.
2. An empirical model of prepayments is specified and estimated to determine the level of prepayments as a function of three or more factors, including the interest rate as a factor.
3. Monte Carlo simulation procedures are then used to simulate interest-rate paths from the interest-rate process chosen in (1). (See Chapter 7 for a discussion of Monte Carlo Simulation.)
4. Each path is subdivided into 360 monthly intervals for a pool consisting of 30-year mortgages.
5. For each month along each path, three cash flows are identified:
   (a) scheduled interest payments,

(b) scheduled principal payments and

(c) prepayments, which are fed from the empirical model of prepayments.

6. The total cash flows along a given path are discounted back using the appropriate zero coupon rates that are applicable to that path.

7. This process is repeated for a number of paths (usually thousands of paths), and for each path the price (sum of discounted cash flows) is determined.

8. The average of all the prices is computed; suitable variance-reduction procedures are then applied. (See Chapter 7 for a discussion of variance-reduction procedures.)

We will illustrate the steps in a specific example later. Let us first examine a few of the basic issues involved. Notice that a simulation approach which is forward-looking is more or less mandatory in this situation. There are several reasons for this. First of all, the cash flows of a mortgage are path-dependent. Current and future prepayments depend on past interest rates. If interest rates were high in the past, then there is a greater likelihood of higher prepayments in future. Adjustable-rate mortgages are subject to a cap that depends on the previous year's rates. The cash flows of such mortgages are also path-dependent. Finally, complicated CMO structures with intricate priority rules on the allocation of cash flows from an underlying collateral to various tranches require the computation of historical prepayments until the valuation date. Again, in such situations, Monte Carlo simulation is the easiest way to proceed. In step 1 above, we may use any model such as the Black, Derman and Toy model which was developed in detail in Chapter 6.

Example 9-4

Consider the problem of valuing a newly issued thirty-year (360-month) fixed-rate mortgage-backed security. We need to generate the 360 monthly cash flows of this security. These cash flows depend on future interest rates.

We first specify a model of interest rates. Consider a three-period tree, with each period representing a month:

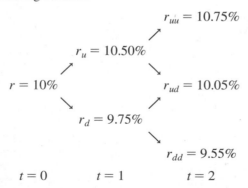

$$r_{uu} = 10.75\%$$
$$r_u = 10.50\%$$
$$r = 10\%$$
$$r_{ud} = 10.05\%$$
$$r_d = 9.75\%$$
$$r_{dd} = 9.55\%$$

$$t = 0 \qquad t = 1 \qquad t = 2$$

As was shown in Chapter 6, this tree can be calibrated to the Treasury yield curve. Note that the construction of the tree requires market data on Treasury yields and the volatilities of yields. The estimates of volatilities are important—they affect the imbedded call option in a significant way. For illustrative purposes Table 9-7 simulates one-period interest rates for the 360-month period.

TABLE 9-7   *Simulated One-period and Zero Rates*

Month	Path 1 One-period	Path 1 Zero Rates	Path 2 One-period	Path 2 Zero Rates	Month	Path 1 One-period	Path 1 Zero Rates	Path 2 One-period	Path 2 Zero Rates
1	4.1%	4.1%	9.7%	9.7%	46	7.9%	12.0%	6.2%	12.0%
2	11.3%	7.6%	11.2%	10.4%	47	19.9%	12.1%	4.7%	11.8%
3	17.8%	10.9%	6.5%	9.1%	48	17.4%	12.2%	14.8%	11.9%
4	4.9%	9.4%	10.6%	9.5%	49	18.9%	12.4%	6.1%	11.7%
5	11.6%	9.8%	10.9%	9.7%	50	6.8%	12.3%	18.7%	11.9%
6	20.0%	11.4%	18.6%	11.2%	51	6.2%	12.1%	10.7%	11.8%
7	5.0%	10.5%	7.3%	10.6%	52	11.5%	12.1%	5.2%	11.7%
8	15.5%	11.1%	14.4%	11.1%	53	6.0%	12.0%	12.0%	11.7%
9	4.2%	10.3%	8.7%	10.8%	54	19.1%	12.1%	17.9%	11.8%
10	9.2%	10.2%	6.6%	10.4%	55	18.5%	12.2%	7.5%	11.8%
11	13.2%	10.5%	17.9%	11.1%	56	4.4%	12.1%	15.7%	11.8%
12	19.8%	11.2%	9.7%	10.9%	57	14.0%	12.1%	8.8%	11.8%
13	10.2%	11.1%	12.6%	11.1%	58	12.2%	12.1%	16.8%	11.9%
14	18.3%	11.6%	6.9%	10.8%	59	14.9%	12.2%	14.5%	11.9%
15	11.9%	11.7%	17.9%	11.2%	60	16.5%	12.2%	4.8%	11.8%
16	15.8%	11.9%	17.1%	11.6%	61	10.8%	12.2%	19.4%	11.9%
17	4.5%	11.5%	19.4%	12.0%	62	8.4%	12.2%	9.8%	11.9%
18	6.5%	11.2%	4.5%	11.6%	63	5.3%	12.0%	10.3%	11.8%
19	7.7%	11.0%	5.4%	11.3%	64	8.8%	12.0%	16.3%	11.9%
20	19.5%	11.4%	4.7%	10.9%	65	6.3%	11.9%	7.1%	11.8%
21	18.2%	11.7%	18.1%	11.3%	66	12.0%	11.9%	15.2%	11.9%
22	14.3%	11.8%	15.8%	11.5%	67	16.3%	12.0%	4.7%	11.8%
23	19.5%	12.2%	7.1%	11.3%	68	18.2%	12.1%	11.6%	11.8%
24	19.2%	12.4%	10.2%	11.2%	69	10.7%	12.0%	16.0%	11.8%
25	11.5%	12.4%	5.2%	11.0%	70	18.0%	12.1%	17.4%	11.9%
26	5.7%	12.1%	16.0%	11.2%	71	10.6%	12.1%	9.0%	11.9%
27	8.1%	12.0%	18.6%	11.4%	72	7.4%	12.0%	16.9%	11.9%
28	10.9%	12.0%	17.3%	11.6%	73	11.0%	12.0%	18.4%	12.0%
29	19.6%	12.2%	9.6%	11.6%	74	6.9%	12.0%	14.4%	12.0%
30	17.3%	12.4%	4.3%	11.3%	75	16.8%	12.0%	15.9%	12.1%
31	15.4%	12.5%	18.1%	11.5%	76	4.8%	11.9%	7.3%	12.0%
32	4.6%	12.2%	19.0%	11.8%	77	12.7%	11.9%	12.0%	12.0%
33	13.3%	12.2%	16.0%	11.9%	78	5.4%	11.8%	11.0%	12.0%
34	5.1%	12.0%	16.2%	12.0%	79	19.9%	11.9%	5.7%	11.9%
35	17.7%	12.2%	6.6%	11.8%	80	6.3%	11.9%	9.5%	11.9%
36	15.6%	12.3%	9.3%	11.8%	81	4.8%	11.8%	14.6%	11.9%
37	17.2%	12.4%	9.3%	11.7%	82	5.5%	11.7%	7.0%	11.9%
38	13.4%	12.4%	16.2%	11.8%	83	15.4%	11.7%	10.1%	11.9%
39	4.8%	12.2%	10.1%	11.8%	84	7.0%	11.7%	6.4%	11.8%
40	10.6%	12.2%	18.4%	11.9%	85	6.0%	11.6%	5.5%	11.7%
41	5.9%	12.0%	14.5%	12.0%	86	13.0%	11.6%	9.9%	11.7%
42	9.3%	12.0%	10.1%	12.0%	87	15.9%	11.7%	10.6%	11.7%
43	13.8%	12.0%	11.5%	11.9%	88	19.2%	11.8%	11.5%	11.7%
44	15.6%	12.1%	13.0%	12.0%	89	16.5%	11.8%	4.3%	11.6%
45	10.5%	12.1%	17.0%	12.1%	90	18.5%	11.9%	11.4%	11.6%

TABLE 9-7   *Continued*

Month	Path 1 One-period	Path 1 Zero Rates	Path 2 One-period	Path 2 Zero Rates	Month	Path 1 One-period	Path 1 Zero Rates	Path 2 One-period	Path 2 Zero Rate
91	13.1%	11.9%	6.4%	11.5%	136	6.2%	11.8%	11.2%	11.7%
92	12.1%	11.9%	9.6%	11.5%	137	4.8%	11.7%	19.4%	11.8%
93	5.0%	11.8%	16.2%	11.6%	138	13.1%	11.8%	17.1%	11.8%
94	18.2%	11.9%	4.3%	11.5%	139	5.8%	11.7%	17.9%	11.9%
95	4.6%	11.8%	12.3%	11.5%	140	15.9%	11.7%	18.8%	11.9%
96	13.5%	11.8%	19.4%	11.6%	141	16.1%	11.8%	8.8%	11.9%
97	8.4%	11.8%	18.9%	11.6%	142	14.6%	11.8%	17.4%	11.9%
98	4.6%	11.7%	10.1%	11.6%	143	7.6%	11.8%	14.9%	12.0%
99	7.5%	11.7%	19.0%	11.7%	144	18.8%	11.8%	12.3%	12.0%
100	5.8%	11.6%	5.9%	11.6%	145	16.6%	11.8%	7.9%	11.9%
101	10.7%	11.6%	7.5%	11.6%	146	8.6%	11.8%	17.5%	12.0%
102	7.5%	11.6%	5.1%	11.5%	147	17.4%	11.9%	8.2%	11.9%
103	9.4%	11.5%	11.1%	11.5%	148	4.8%	11.8%	5.4%	11.9%
104	15.8%	11.6%	11.3%	11.5%	149	12.1%	11.8%	18.2%	11.9%
105	14.8%	11.6%	18.1%	11.6%	150	14.4%	11.8%	16.3%	12.0%
106	8.6%	11.6%	15.3%	11.6%	151	9.9%	11.8%	13.9%	12.0%
107	18.2%	11.6%	11.3%	11.6%	152	10.4%	11.8%	19.7%	12.0%
108	14.5%	11.7%	7.1%	11.6%	153	11.4%	11.8%	18.4%	12.1%
109	5.0%	11.6%	16.3%	11.6%	154	17.1%	11.8%	6.0%	12.0%
110	18.4%	11.7%	14.4%	11.6%	155	7.4%	11.8%	18.8%	12.1%
111	16.8%	11.7%	6.0%	11.6%	156	9.7%	11.8%	8.7%	12.1%
112	10.7%	11.7%	12.9%	11.6%	157	12.2%	11.8%	5.9%	12.0%
113	7.6%	11.7%	4.6%	11.5%	158	4.5%	11.7%	4.6%	12.0%
114	11.2%	11.7%	7.2%	11.5%	159	11.4%	11.7%	10.5%	12.0%
115	17.1%	11.7%	9.8%	11.5%	160	16.7%	11.8%	17.1%	12.0%
116	19.0%	11.8%	17.0%	11.5%	161	5.8%	11.7%	15.4%	12.0%
117	8.5%	11.7%	11.3%	11.5%	162	5.6%	11.7%	4.2%	12.0%
118	5.5%	11.7%	11.1%	11.5%	163	15.5%	11.7%	17.3%	12.0%
119	18.8%	11.7%	11.6%	11.5%	164	12.7%	11.7%	13.0%	12.0%
120	13.8%	11.8%	18.9%	11.6%	165	15.5%	11.7%	4.5%	11.9%
121	18.5%	11.8%	9.6%	11.6%	166	19.6%	11.8%	8.4%	11.9%
122	19.3%	11.9%	15.8%	11.6%	167	5.5%	11.8%	14.4%	11.9%
123	18.7%	11.9%	10.4%	11.6%	168	4.6%	11.7%	18.1%	12.0%
124	12.8%	11.9%	18.0%	11.6%	169	8.4%	11.7%	4.1%	11.9%
125	10.6%	11.9%	6.8%	11.6%	170	11.0%	11.7%	15.7%	12.0%
126	10.3%	11.9%	16.9%	11.6%	171	7.7%	11.7%	16.2%	12.0%
127	6.4%	11.9%	13.2%	11.7%	172	4.3%	11.6%	9.1%	12.0%
128	18.7%	11.9%	11.8%	11.7%	173	18.2%	11.7%	8.2%	11.9%
129	5.1%	11.9%	15.1%	11.7%	174	17.6%	11.7%	13.1%	11.9%
130	11.6%	11.9%	11.1%	11.7%	175	13.1%	11.7%	17.8%	12.0%
131	9.3%	11.8%	11.7%	11.7%	176	10.7%	11.7%	19.4%	12.0%
132	11.6%	11.8%	4.9%	11.6%	177	13.3%	11.7%	16.3%	12.0%
133	11.5%	11.8%	16.8%	11.7%	178	6.3%	11.7%	11.8%	12.0%
134	11.5%	11.8%	18.4%	11.7%	179	14.1%	11.7%	11.5%	12.0%
135	12.1%	11.8%	15.9%	11.7%	180	9.5%	11.7%	12.3%	12.0%

(Continued)

TABLE 9-7   *Continued*

Month	Path 1 One-period	Path 1 Zero Rates	Path 2 One-period	Path 2 Zero Rates	Month	Path 1 One-period	Path 1 Zero Rates	Path 2 One-period	Path 2 Zero Rate
181	7.1%	11.6%	7.0%	12.0%	226	13.3%	11.7%	14.6%	12.2%
182	17.2%	11.7%	12.7%	12.0%	227	9.0%	11.7%	19.7%	12.2%
183	12.3%	11.7%	12.6%	12.0%	228	13.5%	11.7%	18.7%	12.2%
184	7.1%	11.7%	19.2%	12.1%	229	18.7%	11.7%	6.5%	12.2%
185	10.5%	11.6%	16.5%	12.1%	230	15.1%	11.7%	18.3%	12.2%
186	6.7%	11.6%	14.0%	12.1%	231	16.2%	11.7%	14.3%	12.2%
187	11.3%	11.6%	16.0%	12.1%	232	10.1%	11.7%	19.2%	12.3%
188	18.2%	11.7%	16.2%	12.1%	233	13.9%	11.7%	18.9%	12.3%
189	18.0%	11.7%	4.3%	12.1%	234	5.7%	11.7%	11.4%	12.3%
190	12.3%	11.7%	12.4%	12.1%	235	13.5%	11.7%	12.6%	12.3%
191	12.6%	11.7%	9.3%	12.1%	236	10.1%	11.7%	7.3%	12.3%
192	7.6%	11.7%	18.9%	12.1%	237	5.2%	11.7%	15.0%	12.3%
193	11.9%	11.7%	15.8%	12.1%	238	18.8%	11.7%	10.4%	12.3%
194	15.2%	11.7%	15.3%	12.1%	239	15.8%	11.7%	18.5%	12.3%
195	12.1%	11.7%	13.8%	12.2%	240	18.6%	11.8%	14.7%	12.3%
196	10.3%	11.7%	10.7%	12.1%	241	15.4%	11.8%	7.5%	12.3%
197	17.1%	11.7%	19.5%	12.2%	242	13.5%	11.8%	16.8%	12.3%
198	13.6%	11.7%	14.0%	12.2%	243	12.3%	11.8%	17.8%	12.3%
199	16.5%	11.7%	6.2%	12.2%	244	8.3%	11.8%	11.4%	12.3%
200	13.1%	11.8%	9.6%	12.1%	245	5.0%	11.7%	5.3%	12.3%
201	13.0%	11.8%	10.0%	12.1%	246	19.6%	11.8%	15.1%	12.3%
202	17.0%	11.8%	15.1%	12.1%	247	6.3%	11.7%	4.8%	12.3%
203	11.6%	11.8%	10.3%	12.1%	248	17.5%	11.8%	12.6%	12.3%
204	14.6%	11.8%	16.4%	12.2%	249	17.3%	11.8%	11.7%	12.3%
205	7.8%	11.8%	9.3%	12.1%	250	11.9%	11.8%	11.6%	12.3%
206	11.1%	11.8%	18.4%	12.2%	251	8.2%	11.8%	17.6%	12.3%
207	14.2%	11.8%	7.9%	12.2%	252	10.0%	11.8%	19.6%	12.3%
208	6.6%	11.8%	5.7%	12.1%	253	20.0%	11.8%	18.3%	12.4%
209	19.1%	11.8%	13.6%	12.1%	254	11.5%	11.8%	4.6%	12.3%
210	5.1%	11.8%	4.3%	12.1%	255	15.1%	11.8%	8.8%	12.3%
211	13.1%	11.8%	17.9%	12.1%	256	8.7%	11.8%	17.8%	12.3%
212	6.3%	11.7%	6.1%	12.1%	257	5.8%	11.8%	7.6%	12.3%
213	8.0%	11.7%	14.4%	12.1%	258	12.2%	11.8%	12.0%	12.3%
214	15.8%	11.7%	11.3%	12.1%	259	8.1%	11.8%	13.3%	12.3%
215	8.8%	11.7%	11.2%	12.1%	260	7.5%	11.7%	17.4%	12.3%
216	10.1%	11.7%	15.0%	12.1%	261	14.8%	11.8%	14.4%	12.3%
217	7.4%	11.7%	13.7%	12.1%	262	5.7%	11.7%	12.3%	12.3%
218	6.8%	11.7%	15.8%	12.1%	263	15.2%	11.7%	6.2%	12.3%
219	6.3%	11.6%	10.1%	12.1%	264	13.5%	11.8%	8.3%	12.3%
220	13.2%	11.7%	19.0%	12.1%	265	14.7%	11.8%	4.5%	12.3%
221	12.4%	11.7%	16.9%	12.2%	266	7.9%	11.7%	8.6%	12.3%
222	5.4%	11.6%	13.4%	12.2%	267	17.4%	11.8%	11.3%	12.3%
223	10.8%	11.6%	7.0%	12.2%	268	9.9%	11.8%	4.4%	12.2%
224	15.5%	11.6%	8.6%	12.1%	269	7.0%	11.7%	19.9%	12.2%
225	16.8%	11.7%	19.9%	12.2%	270	8.3%	11.7%	6.1%	12.2%

TABLE 9-7   *Continued*

Month	Path 1 One-period	Path 1 Zero Rates	Path 2 One-period	Path 2 Zero Rates	Month	Path 1 One-period	Path 1 Zero Rates	Path 2 One-period	Path 2 Zero Rate
271	15.0%	11.7%	10.8%	12.2%	316	13.4%	11.9%	16.6%	12.2%
272	18.9%	11.8%	17.9%	12.2%	317	19.9%	11.9%	6.9%	12.2%
273	7.5%	11.8%	13.9%	12.2%	318	5.2%	11.9%	17.9%	12.2%
274	16.3%	11.8%	15.6%	12.3%	319	5.2%	11.9%	6.0%	12.2%
275	17.7%	11.8%	9.5%	12.2%	320	7.2%	11.9%	4.6%	12.2%
276	4.7%	11.8%	12.6%	12.2%	321	14.1%	11.9%	4.7%	12.2%
277	12.7%	11.8%	16.4%	12.3%	322	7.8%	11.9%	17.4%	12.2%
278	14.4%	11.8%	19.1%	12.3%	323	12.3%	11.9%	12.2%	12.2%
279	19.7%	11.8%	12.7%	12.3%	324	12.6%	11.9%	13.1%	12.2%
280	19.5%	11.8%	9.7%	12.3%	325	7.9%	11.8%	7.8%	12.2%
281	15.7%	11.8%	4.3%	12.3%	326	16.9%	11.9%	5.6%	12.1%
282	8.8%	11.8%	9.2%	12.2%	327	15.5%	11.9%	10.2%	12.1%
283	8.9%	11.8%	14.6%	12.2%	328	8.5%	11.9%	19.6%	12.2%
284	15.7%	11.8%	12.6%	12.2%	329	5.2%	11.8%	17.0%	12.2%
285	9.0%	11.8%	7.3%	12.2%	330	7.1%	11.8%	13.9%	12.2%
286	18.2%	11.8%	7.1%	12.2%	331	6.3%	11.8%	7.2%	12.2%
287	10.3%	11.8%	12.0%	12.2%	332	11.3%	11.8%	18.9%	12.2%
288	11.2%	11.8%	5.9%	12.2%	333	16.9%	11.8%	14.6%	12.2%
289	4.4%	11.8%	14.6%	12.2%	334	19.2%	11.8%	4.8%	12.2%
290	16.9%	11.8%	9.6%	12.2%	335	17.1%	11.9%	18.0%	12.2%
291	19.2%	11.9%	12.7%	12.2%	336	9.1%	11.9%	13.3%	12.2%
292	17.5%	11.9%	11.3%	12.2%	337	9.2%	11.8%	7.1%	12.2%
293	7.7%	11.9%	19.9%	12.2%	338	15.3%	11.9%	19.7%	12.2%
294	7.1%	11.8%	11.0%	12.2%	339	14.4%	11.9%	17.2%	12.2%
295	16.7%	11.9%	5.1%	12.2%	340	9.1%	11.9%	13.2%	12.2%
296	17.6%	11.9%	10.6%	12.2%	341	13.6%	11.9%	14.3%	12.2%
297	10.6%	11.9%	12.6%	12.2%	342	7.5%	11.8%	15.9%	12.2%
298	14.1%	11.9%	18.7%	12.2%	343	17.9%	11.9%	12.8%	12.2%
299	19.0%	11.9%	18.8%	12.2%	344	7.8%	11.9%	16.0%	12.2%
300	9.3%	11.9%	6.0%	12.2%	345	15.7%	11.9%	4.6%	12.2%
301	17.4%	11.9%	10.8%	12.2%	346	12.3%	11.9%	18.5%	12.2%
302	19.2%	11.9%	14.6%	12.2%	347	14.5%	11.9%	18.5%	12.3%
303	16.4%	11.9%	18.3%	12.2%	348	10.4%	11.9%	9.9%	12.2%
304	19.7%	12.0%	10.9%	12.2%	349	5.2%	11.8%	15.6%	12.3%
305	9.0%	12.0%	8.5%	12.2%	350	8.2%	11.8%	9.9%	12.2%
306	6.0%	11.9%	6.5%	12.2%	351	16.9%	11.9%	19.9%	12.3%
307	11.1%	11.9%	15.2%	12.2%	352	5.0%	11.8%	5.4%	12.2%
308	8.6%	11.9%	18.4%	12.2%	353	12.2%	11.8%	13.7%	12.3%
309	5.4%	11.9%	12.4%	12.2%	354	5.7%	11.8%	5.5%	12.2%
310	9.8%	11.9%	10.3%	12.2%	355	13.3%	11.8%	14.3%	12.2%
311	8.0%	11.9%	14.3%	12.2%	356	18.0%	11.8%	11.2%	12.2%
312	14.2%	11.9%	11.6%	12.2%	357	17.7%	11.9%	18.9%	12.3%
313	18.1%	11.9%	9.3%	12.2%	358	8.9%	11.8%	10.9%	12.3%
314	8.0%	11.9%	8.9%	12.2%	359	14.4%	11.8%	12.9%	12.3%
315	8.4%	11.9%	17.5%	12.2%	360	12.3%	11.9%	4.7%	12.2%

To price a 30-year mortgage-backed security, we need in actuality to extend the tree to 360 months. However, the basic concepts are easily illustrated without any loss of generality using the three-period tree above. For each month (each node of the tree), we can compute the monthly scheduled interest and principal payments using Equations (9.3) and (9.4).

The cash-flow component for each node that needs to be estimated is the pre-payment. To do this, we need a prepayment model. Many models of prepayments have been employed in the literature and in practice. In a model proposed by Richard and Roll (1989), prepayments are modelled as a function of four variables:

$$CPR = x_1 \times x_2 \times x_3 \times x_4 \qquad (9.9)$$

where x_1 is the refinancing factor, x_2 is the seasoning factor, x_3 is the month factor and x_4 is the pool-burnout factor. Each factor may have a specific functional relationship with the current and past values of other variables. For example, x_1 itself may be a function of the weighted-average coupon rate of the pool, the current refinancing rate, the refinancing costs, and the loan-servicing rate. Homeowners may face delays in refinancing when attempting to get a new mortgage. Such lags may also be modelled. The seasoning factor x_2 reflects the fact that the prepayment rates are very low for new mortgages; they tend to increase as the mortgage becomes more seasoned. Full seasoning may take two to three years. The month factor x_3 reflects seasonality in prepayments. This is a school year effect: families tend to move in summer and, with a delay, this affects the MBS prepayments. The burnout factor refers to the fact that even premium mortgages never get completely paid out for many reasons, including

- Borrower's job status. If the borrower does not have a job, he or she may simply be ineligible for a new mortgage.
- Decline in property value. If the house value has declined significantly relative to the loan value, there will be less of an incentive to prepay. On the other hand, the borrower, as noted earlier, has the option to walk away from the loan. The reputational costs of this may be high enough to preclude this from occurring.
- Nonrational or interest-rate insensitive behavior. This is a possibility as well.

The prepayment models, once estimated, provide the prepayment cash flows as a function of observable or estimated factors. This can then be used to obtain the prepayments for each node of the tree.

The first step is to obtain random draws from an arbitrage-free model of interest rates. We can use any of the models which we developed in Chapter 6 and calibrate it with the Treasury zero curve. This will give us a tree of interest rates where, at each node, we will have the monthly interest rate. In addition, as noted in Chapter 6, at each node we can compute the entire Treasury yield curve. Two paths are illustrated in Table 9-7. We compute the refinancing rates at each node through a spread relationship of the following type.

$$RF_t = a + b \times y_t$$

where a and b are estimated parameters and y_t is the yield on a Treasury security with a duration of five to seven years, which approximates the duration of thirty-year FRM loans. RF_t is the refinancing rate. Remember that RF_t is needed to estimate prepayments.

We now can compute the cash flows at each node. These cash flows include scheduled interest payments, scheduled principal payments, and prepayments. This allows us to generate 360 monthly cash flows in each simulated path. We then discount the cash flows at the zero coupon interest rates $z_t(i)$ that is relevant for each month t along path i as shown next. The zero rates for two paths are also shown in Table 9-7.

Given the one-period (monthly) rates, the relevant zero rates are easily computed. The zero rate for n periods in path i is denoted by $z_n(i)$ and is equal to

$$z_n(i) = \sqrt[n]{[1 + r_1(i)][1 + r_2(i)] \cdots [1 + r_n(i)]}$$

where $r_j(i)$ is the one-period rate at month j in path i.

$$P_{\text{model}} = \frac{1}{N}\sum_{i=1}^{N}\left[\frac{C_1(i)}{1 + z_1(i)} + \frac{C_2(i)}{\{1 + z_2(i)\}^2} + \cdots + \frac{C_N(i)}{\{1 + z_N(i)\}^N}\right]$$

where for any month j, $C_j(i)$ is the cash flow in month j associated with path i. We have 360 monthly cash flows for each path i. When a prepayment occurs retiring the pool in month $i = 300$, the cash flows for subsequent months $C_j(i)$ where $j > 300$ will be equal to zero.

We then discount these cash flows at the relevant zero rate $z_j(i)$. We do this for each path i for a total of N paths and average the discounted values.

We vary z until the model value P_{model} is equal to the market value V of the security. We compute the difference

$$\pi_t = P_{\text{model}} - V$$

If $\pi_t > 0$, the model price is higher than the market value. This indicates that the security is cheap, according to the model. In order to make the model produce a value equal to V we need to increase the discount factor. So, we select a $z > 0$ such that the model produces a price equal to the market value. This factor z is referred to as the option-adjusted spread (OAS). A positive OAS indicates that the security is cheap. Conversely, if the OAS is negative, then the security is rich.

$$V = P_{\text{model}} = \frac{1}{N}\sum_{i=1}^{N}\left[\frac{C_1(i)}{1 + z_1(i) + z} + \frac{C_2(i)}{\{1 + z_2(i) + z\}^2} \right.$$
$$\left. + \cdots + \frac{C_N(i)}{\{1 + z_N(i) + z\}^N}\right]$$

The OAS is used extensively in the industry for determining the relative values of mortgage-backed securities.

MORTGAGE DERIVATIVES

A number of mortgage derivatives are currently offered to institutional investors. We will review some of these derivatives.

Strips

Mortgage strips are obtained by dividing the cash flows from an underlying pool of mortgages or mortgage-backed securities through specified allocation of interest and principal to each strip. For example, we can take a 9% GNMA and create a 5% strip and a 12% strip by allocating more of the underlying collateral to the high-coupon strip. An important feature of such strips is that the rate of prepayments is qualitatively influenced by the weighted-average coupon of the underlying pool. For example, a strip with a coupon of 5% will have a much lower prepayment when the underlying pool has a coupon of 9% than when the underlying pool has a coupon of 12%.

The most basic strips in the mortgage market are the Interest Only (IO) strip and the Principal Only (PO) strip.

Interest-Only (IO) Strip. IO strips receive all of the interest payments from the underlying collateral and none from the principal. The price movements of IOs are highly sensitive to interest-rate changes. As interest rates drop, prepayments increase as an increasing number of the households begin to buy new homes or refinance existing loans. Since prepayments are allocated to principal, IOs tend to lose their value in periods of falling interest rates. This is in sharp contrast to many fixed-income securities, which tend to appreciate in value as interest rates fall. Conversely, when interest rates increase, prepayments decrease and the IOs increase in value.

Principal-Only (PO) Strip. PO strips receive all of the principal payments from the underlying collateral and none from the interest. The price movements of POs are also highly sensitive to interest-rate changes. As interest rates drop, prepayments increase as an increasing number of the households begin to buy new homes or refinance existing loans. Since prepayments are allocated to principal, POs tend to increase in their value in periods of falling interest rates. When interest rates increase, prepayments decrease and the POs decrease in value.

REMICs

REMICs are real estate mortgage investment conduits, introduced in the Tax Reform Act of 1986. Prior to the Tax Reform Act, CMOs were issued as debt obligations of the issuer. Thus such issues appeared in a balance sheet as a liability. REMICs, on the other hand, are a legal framework within which mortgage-backed securities are treated as asset sales for tax purposes. REMICs can be structured in a senior-subordinated format. This allows for credit enhancements for mortgage-backed securities with multiple tranches.

CMO Residuals or Equity

As noted earlier, CMO residuals or CMO equity refers to the excess cash flows from the underlying mortgage or collaterals. The excess cash flows are computed over the total cash flows that are paid out to the CMO tranches and the operating expenses. We noted earlier how conservative collateral and reinvestment assumptions are made in structuring CMOs. This means that the actual reinvestment rates and prepayment rates are likely to be more favorable, on average. While CMO residuals are volatile and illiquid, they tend to provide rather unique cash flow properties. CMO equity from a fixed-rate CMO tends to increase when interest rates increase and decrease when interest rates fall.

CONCLUSION

The concept of securitization was further developed in this chapter. We then presented a brief description of mortgage contracts. Both fixed-rate and adjustable-rate mortgage contracts were considered. In mortgage contracts, one of the important features is the ability to prepay. Among the most important factors that influence prepayments are the refinancing rates, age of the mortgage, seasonality, and housing prices. We also discussed measures of prepayments such as PSAs and CPRs. The concept of mortgage-backed securities such as GNMAs and CMOs was then introduced. A valuation framework was presented, which we developed into a simple model of valuing mortgage-backed securities. The concept of option-adjusted spreads (OAS) was developed to identify relatively rich and cheap securities. Mortgage derivatives such as strips, IOs, and POs were then described.

PROBLEMS

9.1   Define securitization. Then explain the role of the following in securitization.
  (a) Special purpose vehicle
  (b) Credit enhancement
  (c) Bankruptcy remoteness

9.2   Define negative convexity. How does this feature affect the spread between mortgage-backed securities and Treasuries in periods of falling interest rates?

9.3   Define CMO.

9.4 **(a)** What factors influence prepayments in mortgage-backed securities markets? How do they affect the pricing of mortgage-backed securities such as GNMAs?
  (b) Compare the prepayment risk of a GNMA with that of a Z tranche in a CMO. Which investors will prefer the Z tranche? Which investors will prefer the GNMA? Why?

9.5   Explain the link between mortgage credit and the capital markets. How has the process of securitization affected the availability of credit and liquidity in the mortgage market?

9.6   In a recent CMO deal, an investment bank issued a CMO with four tranches of bonds: bond A, bond B, bond C, and the Z bond. This deal was rated AAA by the rating agencies. The issuer also kept the CMO residual (or the extra collateral).

(a) Explain briefly the risk properties of the Z bond and the CMO residual.

(b) If you are an investor who wishes to buy a security whose performance will be superior in a high interest rate setting, which of these securities will you buy? Why?

(c) If you had the choice of investing in a Z bond or in a AAA strip with the same maturity as the Z bond, under what circumstances will you prefer the Z bond? Why?

9.7   In the financial press, you note that the GNMA yields are about 200 basis points higher than Treasuries with comparable maturities.

(a) On this basis can we conclude that GNMAs are better investments than Treasuries? Explain your conclusion.

(b) As the interest rates drop, will you expect the yields of GNMA to pick up or drop? Why? Explain your conclusions for premium and discount sectors of GNMA.

9.8 (a) Explain the major differences between PAC, TAC, and sequential CMO structures.

(b) In this context, explain the role of the following terms: (i) companion class, (ii) support class.

9.9   Explain the considerations that lead to a AAA-rating for CMO structures.

REFERENCES

Anderson, G. A., J. R. Barber, and C. H. Chang 1993. "Prepayment Risk and the Duration of Default-Free Mortgage-Backed Securities." *Journal of Financial Research* 16:1–9.

Bartlett, W. W. 1989. Mortgage Backed Securities: Products, Analysis, Trading. New York: New York Institute of Finance.

Becketti, S. 1989. "The Prepayment Risk of Mortgage-Backed Securities." In *Economic Review of the Federal Reserve Bank of Kansas City,* pp. 43–57, Kansas City: Federal Reserve Bank.

Bhattacharya, A., and H. Chin 1992. "Synthetic Mortgage Backed Securities." *Journal of Portfolio Management* 18(3):44–55.

Black, F., E. Derman, and W. Toy 1990. "A One-Factor Model of Interest Rates and Its Application to Treasury Bond Options." *Financial Analysts Journal* 46(1):33–39.

Buser, S. A., P. H. Hendershott, and A. B. Sanders 1990. "Determinants of the Value of Call Options on Default-free Bonds." *Journal of Business* 63(1):533–550.

Carron, A. S. 1992. "Understanding CMOs, REMICs and other Mortgage Derivatives." *Journal of Fixed-Income* 2:25–43.

Doherty, N. A. 1985. *Corporate Risk Management.* New York: McGraw-Hill, Inc.

Donaldson, T. H. 1989. "Credit Risk and Exposure in Securitization and Transactions." New York: St. Martins Press.

Dunn, K., and J. McConnell 1981. "Valuation of GNMA Mortgage-Backed Securities." *Journal of Finance* 36(3):599–616.

Fabozzi, F. J. 1992. *The Handbook of Mortgage-Backed Securities.* Chicago: Probus Publishing.

Garbade, K. D. 1984. "GNMA Pass-Throughs—What Do They Pass Through and What do They Yield?" *Topics in Money and Securities Markets.* New York City: Bankers Trust Company.

Hendershott, P. H., and R. Van Order 1987. "Pricing Mortgages: An Interpretation of the Models and Results." *Journal of Financial Services Research:* 19–55.

Kusy, M. I., and W. T. Ziemba 1986. "A Bank Asset and Liability Management Model." *Operations Research* 34(3):356–376.

Lederman, J. 1990. *The Handbook of Asset Backed Securities.* New York: New York Institute of Finance.

Merrill Lynch 1994. Mortgage Product Analysis. New York: Merrill Lynch.

Morris, D. V. 1990. *Asset Securitization: Principles and Practices.* Executive Enterprise Publications.

Norton, J. J., and P. R. Spellman 1991. "Asset Securitization: International Financial and Legal Perspectives." Oxford: Basil Blackwell.

Richard, S. F., and R. Roll 1989. "Prepayments on Fixed Rate Mortgage Backed Securities." *Journal of Portfolio Management:* 15(3):73–83.

Schwartz, E., and W. Torous 1992. "Prepayment and the Valuation of Mortgage Pass-Through Securities." *Journal of Business:* 15(2):221–240.

Waldman, M., A. Schwalb, and A. K. Feignberg 1993. "Prepayments of Fifteen-Year Mortgages." *Journal of Fixed Income* 2(4):37–44.

Wang, W. 1995. Analysis of Mortgage-backed Securities. Unpublished Ph.D. Dissertation, Columbia University.

Wise, R. 1993. "Managers Breathing Easier After Attacks." *Pension World* 8.

Zweig, P. L. 1989. *The Asset Securitization Handbook.* Homewood, IL: Dow Jones Irwin.

Chapter 10

Tax-Exempt
Debt Securities

Chapter Objectives

This chapter describes the municipal debt market and municipal debt securities. The goal of the chapter is to provide an overview of this important market. In addition, the following questions are addressed in the chapter.

- What have been the historical spreads between municipal securities, Treasuries, and corporate securities?
- What has been the impact of Tax Reform Acts?
- To what degree are municipal securities tax-advantaged?
- What are general obligation bonds?
- What are revenue bonds?

INTRODUCTION

States, municipalities, and counties raise the capital that they need by issuing debt securities which are referred to as municipal debt securities. Such securities tend to have a special tax status: The interest income from municipal debt securities are exempt from federal, state, and, where applicable, city taxes; the capital gains or losses may still be subject to the normal taxation rules that are applicable. This chapter is devoted to the study of municipal debt securities. We begin by describing some of the major municipal debt securities. This is followed by a discussion of the investor base in the municipal securities market. The investor base in this market has changed significantly in the last 20 years. The shapes of the municipal yield curve and the Treasury curve are then discussed. We present evidence that the Tax Reform Act of 1986 and, to a lesser extent, the Tax Act of 1990 account for both the shifts in the investor base and for the change in the slope of the municipal yield curve relative to the Treasury yield curve. Then, the primary and the secondary municipal debt markets are presented.

MUNICIPAL DEBT SECURITIES

There are several major categories of municipal securities.

General Obligation Bond (GO)

A general obligation bond is a security which is backed by the full faith, credit, and taxation powers of the issuer. For example, New York State GO bonds are backed by the various taxes that the state levies. These taxes include income taxes, sales taxes, and excise taxes. Counties and cities tend to rely on property taxes for their GO bonds. Depending on the legal limits on the tax rates that the issuing entity is subjected to, the issue may be either an unlimited tax bond or a limited tax bond. Clearly, unlimited tax issues are made by issuers who may levy taxes at an unlimited rate.

　　　The tax base of the issuing entity and its discretion are important factors in determining the pricing of GO bonds. For example, school districts tend to have a limit on the tax rates that they may charge. The tax base of the issuing city, growth rate of the local economy, and property values are important factors. In addition, the existing level of municipal debt is also a very important consideration in the valuation of GO bonds. Per-capita debt is one of the indicators used to judge the financial soundness of GO bonds.

Revenue Bond

Revenue bonds are issued to fund specific projects; or they are bonds that are protected by the pledge of net revenues from specified projects. The bond issuer will use the revenues generated by the project to service the revenue bond issues. Typical projects funded by revenue bonds are bridges, turnpikes, and airports. Revenue sources from such projects will include tolls and user fees.

Revenue bonds are issued for specific sectoral activities, some of which are listed next.

- *Housing revenue bonds.* These bonds are issued to promote the construction of housing for low- and moderate-income families. The proceeds of the bond issue are typically lent to real estate developers.
- *Utility revenue bonds.* These bonds are issued to support the local utilities, such as gas, water, and electric power systems.
- *Health care revenue bonds.* These bonds are used to raise money for the construction of hospital and health care facilities.
- *Double-barrelled bonds.* These bonds are backed by two distinct sources of revenues. Part of the cash flows of the debt service come from specified projects and the rest from taxation.

In the valuation of revenue bonds, it is important to examine the net revenue of the project. The operating and maintenance expenses are deducted from the revenues before the money is used to service the revenue bonds. The ratio of the net revenue to the debt-service payments, known as the debt-service coverage, is one of the factors often used to judge the financial soundness of revenue bonds. Often, restrictive covenants are specified to ensure effective debt service.

Municipal Notes

Short-term obligations of municipalities are known as municipal notes. They are interest-bearing securities. The following are some categories of municipal notes.

- **Tax anticipation notes (TAN).** TANs are issued in anticipation of future tax receipts from real estate taxes. Typically, the proceeds are used to finance the operations of the municipality.
- **Bond anticipation notes (BAN).** BANs are issued in anticipation of future sale of long-term bonds. The proceeds are used to finance projects.
- **Grant anticipation notes (GAN).** GANs are issued in anticipation of future federal grants.
- **Revenue anticipation notes (RAN).** RANs are issued in anticipation of future revenues.
- **Construction loan notes (CLN).** CLNs are issued for a specific construction project.

In addition to these municipal notes, there are also tax-exempt commercial paper and variable-rate demand notes. Typically, commercial paper has a maturity of 270 days or less. As in the case of corporate commercial paper, CPs are backed by a line of credit from a bank. Municipal markets also have variable-rate notes and zero coupon bonds. In addition, municipal bonds are also refunded. Typically, refunding occurs to circumvent restrictive bond covenants or to take advantage of low interest rates. For example, revenue bonds (as we noted earlier) that have restrictive covenants may be refunded by issuing new bonds and using the proceeds to buy Treasury securities to create an escrow fund. Many municipal bonds are issued in a serial form. In such serial issues, level payments are achieved with orderly amortization of principal.

TAX REFORM ACT 1986

The interest income from municipal securities are exempt from federal and state taxes. For residents of the municipality, there is also exemption at the local level. With the Tax Reform Act of 1986, significant restrictions have been placed on the tax advantages of several municipal securities. The pricing of municipal securities tends to depend a great deal on their current and expected tax status. The Tax Reform Act of 1986 significantly reduced the tax benefits enjoyed by holders of certain municipal securities. Municipal securities issued for traditional governmental purposes, such as highways and utilities, still enjoy the special tax status. Other municipal issues are now called private-activity bonds and under the Tax Reform Act, these do not qualify for special tax status unless they are defined as qualified private-activity bonds. Private-activity bonds are those in which 10% or more of the proceeds are used by private entities and 10% or more of the proceeds are secured by the property used in the private entity's activity. For example, a sports facility could fall into this category. A qualified private-activity bond is one which is issued for prespecified purposes such as airports or student loans.

The Tax Reform Act lead to a reduction in the maximum personal tax rate from 50% to 28%. However, it also subjected municipal bonds to increased taxes. If a municipal bond issue is not qualified, then it will be subject to alternative minimum tax (AMT). These developments reduced the attractiveness of municipal securities. In 1990, the maximum personal tax rate increased to 33%. This served to increase the value of municipal securities to high-income individuals.

AN OVERVIEW OF MUNICIPAL DEBT MARKET

In Tables 10-1 and 10-2, we summarize the activities in the municipal debt market from 1982 to 1991. Table 10-1 shows the activity in the municipal bond market and Table 10-2 provides the corresponding information for municipal notes market. In this 10-year period, the total dollar amount issued increased from $77 million in 1982 to about $172 million in 1991. The total number of issues increased from 6,079 in 1982 to nearly 11,000 issues in 1991. In general, the dollar amount of issues of revenue bonds exceed the dollar amount issues of general obligation bonds. Fixed-rate bonds far exceed variable-rate bonds. In Table 10-2, note that the issues of municipal notes, which amounted to 43.8 million in 1991, is just 25% of the municipal bond market. But, interestingly, the revenue issues were less than general obligations issues in the notes market. Almost all the issues of municipal notes market represented new money in the municipal notes market. On the other hand, in the municipal bond market nearly 25% of the issues constituted refunding.

TABLE 10-1 *Municipal Bond Market (1982–1991)*

	1982	1983	1984	1985	1986	1987	1988	1989	1990	1991
Dollar amount issued (in thousands)	77,179	83,347	101,881	206,991	151,258	105,438	117,789	124,954	127,938	172,576
Number of issues	6,079	6,290	6,392	10,062	7,721	7,089	8,325	9,361	8,831	10,939
Tax-exempt	77,179	83,347	101,881	206,665	138,291	88,957	93,656	105,100	105,648	155,050
Minimum-tax	0	0	0	0	8,932	13,265	21,712	16,693	19,318	13,136
Taxable	0	0	0	326	4,035	3,216	2,422	3,161	2,972	4,390
Negotiated	51,615	59,479	74,760	173,552	115,134	78,269	88,725	91,616	95,203	128,501
Competitive	24,575	21,733	22,892	27,895	30,030	23,171	26,774	29,928	30,315	40,838
Private placements	989	2,134	4,230	5,544	6,093	3,999	2,291	3,411	2,420	3,236
Revenue	53,903	60,765	74,760	166,571	105,481	74,620	86,276	86,339	87,687	114,146
General obligations	23,276	22,582	27,122	40,420	45,777	30,818	31,513	38,615	40,251	58,430
New money	73,135	67,830	85,201	136,225	86,111	59,334	80,679	90,400	104,660	126,450
Refundings	4,044	15,517	16,680	70,767	65,147	46,105	37,110	34,554	23,278	46,127
Fixed-rate	74,900	78,388	79,511	149,321	125,908	91,898	100,229	112,641	115,141	160,156
Variable-rate	2,279	4,959	22,370	57,670	25,350	13,540	17,560	12,313	12,798	12,421

Source: Bond Buyer (1992)

TABLE 10-2 *Municipal Note Market (1982–1991)*

	1982	1983	1984	1985	1986	1987	1988	1989	1990	1991
Dollar amount issued (in thousands)	43,547	37,955	33,577	21,809	21,523	20,272	22,849	29,500	34,693	43,809
Number of issues	6,079	6,290	6,392	10,062	7,721	7,089	8,325	9,361	8,831	10,939
Tax-exempt	43,547	37,955	33,577	21,809	21,116	19,125	21,084	29,107	33,969	42,692
Minimum-tax	0	0	0	0	289	83	291	117	98	326
Taxable	0	0	0	0	119	1,065	1,475	276	627	792
Negotiated	9,066	13,516	14,663	14,835	14,048	12,510	12,845	15,942	21,065	26,158
Competitive	33,567	24,013	18,000	6,316	7,086	7,243	9,549	12,903	13,257	16,889
Private placements	914	426	914	659	390	520	456	656	371	763
Revenue	3,884	5,363	5,033	3,049	1,033	3,278	2,769	3,123	1,978	3,052
General obligations	39,663	32,592	28,544	18,759	20,490	16,994	20,080	26,377	32,715	40,757
New money	43,522	37,781	33,486	21,740	21,508	20,087	22,786	29,450	34,454	43,475
Refundings	25	174	90	69	15	184	64	50	239	334
Fixed-rate	43,425	37,688	32,735	21,452	21,279	20,258	22,225	29,140	34,096	41,636
Variable-rate	123	267	842	356	244	14	625	360	597	2,173

Source: Bond Buyer (1992)

Investors in the Tax-Exempt Market

The tax status of the municipal securities attracts a certain clientele. Individuals with very high tax brackets tend to gravitate to municipal securities when alternative tax shelters are scarce. In a similar way, institutions that pay taxes at rates that are close to their maximum levels will find municipal securities attractive. Commercial banks, and fire and casualty insurance companies fall into this category. By the same token, some institutions tend to stay away from the municipal securities market. For example, tax-exempt institutions (that do not pay taxes) have little incentive to hold municipal securities. Pension funds whose earnings are tax-exempt will invest in corporate and Treasury debt securities as opposed to municipal securities.

The incentives to hold municipal debt securities have changed over time for some institutions. Prior to the Tax Reform Act of 1986, commercial banks were permitted to deduct interest expenses associated with the purchase of municipal securities and the interest income from municipal securities were tax-exempt as well. This double advantage was removed after the Tax Reform Act of 1986. In 1983, Congress disallowed the commercial banks from deducting 15% of the municipal carrying costs associated with the purchases of municipal securities. In 1985, the lost deduction increased to 20%. The 1986 tax reform created two classes of municipal securities, bank-qualified municipals and nonqualified municipals. For nonqualified municipal securities, banks are not allowed to deduct interest expenses associated with the purchase. For an issue to be bank-qualified, no more than $10 million may be issued per year and the proceeds must be used for an essential public purpose. In the case of bank-qualified issues, banks can deduct 80% of the interest paid to the depositors from taxes, provided such funds are used to invest in bank-qualified issues.

Commercial banks that used to hold a large fraction of the short-term municipal debt are no longer such a dominant force in the municipal securities market, but they still are one of the important players. Prior to 1986, it was estimated that households (presumably those in the high tax bracket), commercial banks, and fire and casualty insurance companies accounted for 80% of the investments made in the municipal securities market.

To get a better idea of the nature of investors in this market and how it has changed over time, review Table 10-3 (Farinella and Koch 1994). Two noteworthy patterns may

TABLE 10-3   *Net Purchases of Municipals as a Fraction of Net New Issues*

Investor	1960–69	1970–79	1980–86(II)	1986(III)–92
Commercial banks	62%	36%	19%	-33%
Property-casualty insurers	12%	28%	6%	11%
Individuals	28%	29%	71%	119%
Others	-2%	7%	4%	3%
Net issues (in millions)	67,952	207,088	429,220	361,253

Source: Farinella and Koch (1994)

be seen in the table. Commercial banks, the dominant buyers in the period 1960–1979, have become net sellers in the post-tax-reform-act-of-1986 period. Also, individuals have become the dominant buyers, replacing the commercial banks.

MUNICIPAL YIELD SPREADS

The tax-exempt status of the municipal securities suggests that the yields of municipal securities should be below the yields of comparable corporate securities and Treasury securities. To a taxable investor, the before-tax return on a corporate security should be high enough that its after-tax return is the same as that of a municipal security that is comparable in its risk characteristics.

Often, this is loosely interpreted as the relationship

$$R_{mT} = R_{cT} \times (1 - \tau) \tag{10.1}$$

where R_{mT} is the municipal yield, R_{cT} is the corporate yield, τ is interpreted as the marginal tax rate of the marginal investor, and T is the time to maturity. Since we can observe R_{mT} and R_{cT}, it is possible for us to treat τ as the implied tax bracket of the marginal investor. One of the assumptions of this simple relationship is that the implied tax bracket should be the same regardless of the maturity T of the corporate and municipal securities. Stated differently, it is assumed here that the spread between the corporate and municipal sectors is the same for all maturities. Even though the relation derived in Equation (10.1) ignores these important considerations, it has one important empirical prediction: As the tax rates fall (increase), the spread between corporates and municipals should narrow (widen) further. Indeed, during the early 1980s when the federal income tax was cut by a significant amount, the spreads narrowed, as can be seen from the evidence presented in Table 10-6.

Table 10-4 identifies the factors that influence the spreads between municipals on one hand, and corporates and Treasuries on the other. Note that the spread is a function of current and expected tax status; contractual provisions, such as calls, serial features, and puts; liquidity; default risk; and so on. These factors tend to have a differential effect on the spread between Treasuries and municipals depending on the maturity of the

Factors	Treasuries	Corporates	Municipal
Credit risk	Absent	Very low	Varies
Interest risk	Varies	Varies	Varies
Liquidity risk	Very low	Moderate	High
Timing risk	None	Low	High
Tax risk	Only federal taxes	Fully taxable	Tax-exempt; future tax changes

TABLE 10-4
Factors Affecting Municipal Spreads

securities. For example, the call feature is liable to have a greater effect on a municipal with a longer maturity than on a municipal with a shorter maturity. This suggests that the spread between Treasury and municipals should increase with maturity, holding other factors constant.

Credit risk in the municipal market varies over time and with regions. To get an idea of the incidence of defaults, review Table 10-5. In terms of the number of issues that defaulted, the trend has been toward increasing defaults. The number of defaults peaked in 1987 and, after a drop in 1988–1989, they increased again in 1990–1991. In terms of the dollar value of defaults, the peak occurred in 1983 but fell back to a narrow range of 1 to 2 million in 1986–1990; however, there was another peak of nearly 5 million in 1991.

To get a perspective on these issues, examine the empirical evidence on the spreads between municipal and corporate securities for the period January 1978 to March 1991 in Figure 10-1. The data is presented in Table 10-6.

Year	Number of Issues	Volume (in thousands)
1981	7	97
1982	16	50
1983	24	2,270
1984	42	482
1985	55	373
1986	142	1,195
1987	155	1,635
1988	144	1,063
1989	98	1,077
1990	150	1,919
1991	236	4,734

TABLE 10-5
Municipal Bond Defaults

FIGURE 10-1   *Yields of Treasury, Corporates and Municipal*

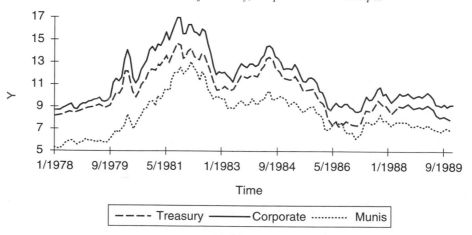

TABLE 10-6   *Spreads and Implied Tax Brackets, 1978–1991*

| Date | Yields (Daily or Weekly) | | | Spreads (in bpts) (C − T) | Spreads (in bpts) (T − M) | Implied Tax Rate |
	Treasury (T)	Aa Corporate (C)	Aa Municipal (M)			
1/1978	8.18	8.70	5.36	52	282	34.47%
2/1978	8.25	8.70	5.23	45	302	36.61%
3/1978	8.23	8.70	5.25	47	298	36.21%
4/1978	8.34	8.88	5.33	54	301	36.09%
5/1978	8.43	9.00	5.75	57	268	31.79%
6/1978	8.50	9.15	5.91	65	259	30.47%
7/1978	8.65	9.27	5.97	62	268	30.98%
8/1978	8.47	8.83	5.81	36	266	31.40%
9/1978	8.47	8.78	5.61	31	286	33.77%
10/1978	8.67	9.14	5.76	47	291	33.56%
11/1978	8.75	9.30	5.81	55	294	33.60%
12/1978	8.85	9.30	6.08	45	277	31.30%
1/1979	8.94	9.47	5.95	53	299	33.45%
2/1979	9.00	9.52	5.93	52	307	34.11%
3/1979	9.03	9.65	5.96	62	307	34.00%
4/1979	9.08	9.69	5.85	61	323	35.57%
5/1979	9.19	9.82	5.95	63	324	35.26%
6/1979	8.92	9.51	5.84	59	308	34.53%
7/1979	8.93	9.47	5.82	54	311	34.83%
8/1979	8.98	9.57	5.87	59	311	34.63%
9/1979	9.17	9.87	6.16	70	301	32.82%
10/1979	9.85	11.17	6.71	132	314	31.88%
11/1979	10.30	11.52	6.84	122	346	33.59%
12/1979	10.12	11.30	6.67	118	345	34.09%
1/1980	10.60	11.65	6.98	105	362	34.15%
2/1980	12.13	13.23	7.35	110	478	39.41%
3/1980	12.34	14.08	8.30	174	404	32.74%
4/1980	11.40	13.36	7.85	196	355	31.14%
5/1980	10.35	11.61	6.96	126	339	32.75%
6/1980	9.81	11.12	7.30	131	251	25.59%
7/1980	10.24	11.48	7.91	124	233	22.75%
8/1980	11.00	12.31	8.33	131	267	24.27%
9/1980	11.34	12.74	8.80	140	254	22.40%
10/1980	11.59	13.17	8.93	158	266	22.95%
11/1980	12.37	14.10	9.46	173	291	23.52%
12/1980	12.40	14.38	9.53	198	287	23.15%
1/1981	12.14	14.01	9.12	187	302	24.88%
2/1981	12.80	14.60	9.94	180	286	22.34%
3/1981	12.69	14.49	9.55	180	314	24.74%
4/1981	13.20	15.00	10.38	180	282	21.36%
5/1981	13.60	15.68	10.68	208	292	21.47%
6/1981	12.96	14.97	10.53	201	243	18.75%
7/1981	13.59	15.67	11.50	208	209	15.38%
8/1981	14.17	16.34	12.11	217	206	14.54%
9/1981	14.67	16.97	12.00	230	267	18.20%
10/1981	14.68	16.96	12.63	228	205	13.96%
11/1981	13.35	15.53	11.94	218	141	10.56%
12/1981	13.45	15.55	12.30	210	115	8.55%
1/1982	14.22	16.34	12.30	212	192	13.50%
2/1982	14.22	16.35	13.09	213	113	7.95%

417

(Continued)

TABLE 10-6 *Continued*

	Yields (Daily or Weekly)					
Date	Treasury (T)	Aa Corporate (C)	Aa Municipal (M)	Spreads (in bpts) (C − T)	Spreads (in bpts) (T − M)	Implied Tax Rate
3/1982	13.53	15.72	12.51	219	102	7.54%
4/1982	13.37	15.62	12.17	225	120	8.98%
5/1982	13.24	15.37	11.36	213	188	14.20%
6/1982	13.92	15.96	12.14	204	178	12.79%
7/1982	13.55	15.75	11.70	220	185	13.65%
8/1982	12.77	14.64	10.56	187	221	17.31%
9/1982	12.07	13.78	10.16	171	191	15.82%
10/1982	11.17	12.63	9.75	146	142	12.71%
11/1982	10.54	11.89	9.99	135	55	5.22%
12/1982	10.54	12.15	9.84	161	70	6.64%
1/1983	10.63	12.04	9.75	141	88	8.28%
2/1983	10.88	12.11	9.75	123	113	10.39%
3/1983	10.63	11.81	8.86	118	177	16.65%
4/1983	10.48	11.58	8.94	110	154	14.69%
5/1983	10.53	11.24	8.78	71	175	16.62%
6/1983	10.93	11.90	9.08	97	185	16.93%
7/1983	11.40	12.46	9.35	106	205	17.98%
8/1983	11.82	12.89	9.70	107	212	17.94%
9/1983	11.63	12.68	9.23	105	240	20.64%
10/1983	11.58	12.54	9.16	96	242	20.90%
11/1983	11.75	12.86	9.39	111	236	20.09%
12/1983	11.88	12.87	9.77	99	211	17.76%
1/1984	11.75	12.65	9.18	90	257	21.87%
2/1984	11.95	12.80	9.30	85	265	22.18%
3/1984	12.38	13.36	9.68	98	270	21.81%
4/1984	12.65	13.64	9.69	99	296	23.40%
5/1984	13.43	14.41	10.28	98	315	23.45%
6/1984	13.44	14.49	10.44	105	300	22.32%
7/1984	13.21	14.25	9.65	104	356	26.95%
8/1984	12.54	13.54	9.68	100	286	22.81%
9/1984	12.29	13.37	9.93	108	236	19.20%
10/1984	11.98	13.02	9.97	104	201	16.78%
11/1984	11.56	12.40	9.79	84	177	15.31%
12/1984	11.52	12.47	9.65	95	187	16.23%
1/1985	11.45	12.46	9.11	101	234	20.44%
2/1985	11.47	12.39	9.26	92	221	19.27%
3/1985	11.81	12.85	9.52	104	229	19.39%
4/1985	11.47	12.45	9.16	98	231	20.14%
5/1985	11.05	11.85	8.79	80	226	20.45%
6/1985	10.45	11.33	8.46	88	199	19.04%
7/1985	10.50	11.28	8.73	78	177	16.86%
8/1985	10.56	11.61	8.96	105	160	15.15%
9/1985	10.61	11.66	9.04	105	157	14.80%
10/1985	10.50	11.51	9.00	101	150	14.29%
11/1985	10.06	11.19	8.45	113	161	16.00%
12/1985	9.54	10.42	8.44	88	110	11.53%
1/1986	9.40	10.33	8.02	93	138	14.68%
2/1986	8.93	9.76	6.93	83	200	22.40%
3/1986	7.96	8.95	6.93	99	103	12.94%

TABLE 10-6 *Continued*

Date	Yields (Daily or Weekly)			Spreads (in bpts) (C − T)	Spreads (in bpts) (T − M)	Implied Tax Rate
	Treasury (T)	Aa Corporate (C)	Aa Municipal (M)			
4/1986	7.39	8.71	7.14	132	25	3.38%
5/1986	7.52	9.09	7.50	157	7	0.27%
6/1986	7.57	9.39	7.75	182	−18	−2.38%
7/1986	7.27	9.11	7.34	184	−7	−0.96%
8/1986	7.33	9.03	7.66	170	−33	−4.50%
9/1986	7.62	9.28	6.94	166	68	8.92%
10/1986	7.70	9.29	6.59	159	111	14.42%
11/1986	7.52	8.99	6.72	147	80	10.64%
12/1986	7.37	8.87	6.70	150	67	9.09%
1/1987	7.39	8.59	6.18	120	121	16.37%
2/1987	7.54	8.58	6.34	104	120	15.92%
3/1987	7.55	8.68	6.47	113	108	14.30%
4/1987	8.25	9.36	7.43	111	82	9.94%
5/1987	8.78	9.95	7.71	117	107	12.19%
6/1987	8.57	9.64	7.69	107	88	10.27%
7/1987	8.64	9.70	7.48	106	116	13.43%
8/1987	8.97	10.09	7.59	112	138	15.38%
9/1987	9.59	10.63	7.90	104	169	17.62%
10/1987	9.61	10.80	8.33	119	128	13.32%
11/1987	8.95	10.09	7.76	114	119	13.30%
12/1987	9.12	10.22	7.83	110	129	14.14%
1/1988	8.83	9.81	7.46	98	137	15.52%
2/1988	8.43	9.43	7.34	100	109	12.93%
3/1988	8.63	9.68	7.55	105	108	12.51%
4/1988	8.95	9.92	7.69	97	126	14.08%
5/1988	9.23	10.25	7.63	102	160	17.33%
6/1988	9.00	10.08	7.67	108	133	14.78%
7/1988	9.14	10.12	7.63	98	151	16.52%
8/1988	9.32	10.27	7.62	95	170	18.24%
9/1988	9.06	10.03	7.30	97	176	19.43%
10/1988	8.89	9.86	7.27	97	162	18.22%
11/1988	9.02	9.98	7.39	96	163	18.07%
12/1988	9.01	10.05	7.40	104	161	17.87%
1/1989	8.93	9.92	7.18	99	175	19.60%
2/1989	9.01	10.11	7.18	110	183	20.31%
3/1989	9.17	10.33	7.42	116	175	19.08%
4/1989	9.03	10.11	7.30	108	173	19.16%
5/1989	8.83	9.82	7.05	99	178	20.16%
6/1989	8.27	9.24	6.94	97	133	16.08%
7/1989	8.08	9.20	6.89	112	119	14.73%
8/1989	8.12	9.09	6.73	97	139	17.12%
9/1989	8.15	9.29	7.10	114	105	12.88%
10/1989	8.00	9.04	7.13	104	87	10.88%
11/1989	7.90	9.20	6.95	130	95	12.03%
12/1989	7.90	9.23	6.76	133	114	14.43%
1/1990	8.26	9.56	6.95	130	131	15.86%
2/1990	8.50	9.68	7.03	118	147	17.29%
3/1990	8.56	9.79	7.09	123	147	17.17%
4/1990	8.76	10.02	7.26	126	150	17.12%

(Continued)

TABLE 10-6 *Continued*

Date	Yields (Daily or Weekly)			Spreads (in bpts) (C − T)	Spreads (in bpts) (T − M)	Implied Tax Rate
	Treasury (T)	Aa Corporate (C)	Aa Municipal (M)			
5/1990	8.73	9.97	7.14	124	159	18.21%
6/1990	8.46	9.69	6.98	123	148	17.49%
7/1990	8.50	9.72	7.03	122	147	17.29%
8/1990	8.86	10.05	7.13	119	173	19.53%
9/1990	9.03	10.17	7.15	114	188	20.82%
10/1990	8.86	10.09	7.24	123	162	18.28%
11/1990	8.54	9.79	6.87	125	167	19.56%
12/1990	8.24	9.55	6.85	131	139	16.87%
1/1991	8.27	9.60	7.00	133	127	15.36%
2/1991	8.03	9.14	6.61	111	142	17.68%
3/1991	8.29	9.15	6.88	86	141	17.01%
4/1991	8.21	9.07	6.81	86	140	17.05%
5/1991	8.27	9.13	6.78	86	149	18.02%
6/1991	8.47	9.37	6.90	90	157	18.54%
7/1991	8.45	9.38	6.89	93	156	18.46%
8/1991	8.14	8.88	6.66	74	148	18.18%
9/1991	7.95	8.79	6.58	84	137	17.23%
10/1991	7.93	8.81	6.44	88	149	18.79%
11/1991	7.92	8.72	6.37	80	155	19.57%
12/1991	7.70	8.55	6.43	85	127	16.49%
1/1992	7.58	8.36	6.29	78	129	17.02%
2/1992	7.85	8.63	6.42	78	143	18.22%
3/1992	7.97	8.62	6.59	65	138	17.31%
4/1992	7.96	8.59	6.54	63	142	17.84%
5/1992	7.89	8.57	6.39	68	150	19.01%
6/1992	7.84	8.45	6.32	61	152	19.39%
7/1992	7.60	8.19	5.90	59	170	22.37%
8/1992	7.39	7.96	5.81	57	158	21.38%
9/1992	7.34	7.99	6.05	65	129	17.57%
10/1992	7.53	8.17	6.18	64	135	17.93%
11/1992	7.61	8.25	6.22	64	139	18.27%
12/1992	7.44	8.12	6.02	68	142	19.09%
1/1993	7.34	7.91	6.05	57	129	17.57%
2/1993	7.09	7.73	5.74	64	135	19.04%
3/1993	6.82	7.39	5.54	57	128	18.77%
4/1993	6.85	7.48	5.64	63	121	17.66%
5/1993	6.92	7.52	5.61	60	131	18.93%
6/1993	6.81	7.48	5.54	67	127	18.65%
7/1993	6.63	7.35	5.40	72	123	18.55%
8/1993	6.32	7.04	5.50	72	82	12.97%
9/1993	6.00	6.88	5.44	88	56	9.33%
10/1993	5.94	6.88	5.23	94	71	11.95%
11/1993	6.21	7.17	5.19	96	102	16.43%
12/1993	6.25	7.22	5.27	97	98	15.68%
1/1994	6.29	7.16	5.19	87	110	17.49%
2/1994	6.49	7.27	5.16	78	133	20.49%
3/1994	6.91	7.64	5.47	73	144	20.84%

Source: Treasury Bulletin

Note from Figure 10-1 that the spreads between Treasuries and municipals have varied a great deal, ranging from a low of -33 basis points in 1986 around the tax-reform-act period to a high of 478 basis points in February 1980. To understand the relationship between the spreads and the levels of the interest rates, we have also plotted the Treasury yields. It seems clear that the municipal spreads tend to widen as the levels of interest rates increase. The implied tax bracket, from Equation (10.1), has been plotted for the same sample period in Figure 10-2.

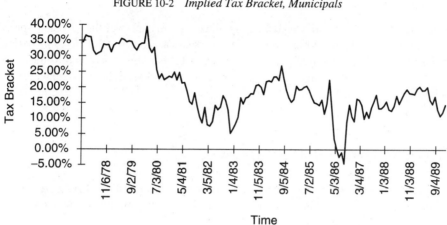

FIGURE 10-2   *Implied Tax Bracket, Municipals*

In the figure, the implied tax brackets ranged from a low of 0% to a high of 44%. Clearly, the level of interest rates and the uncertainty about the tax status, which leads to significant supply adjustments, accounts for this spread behavior.

The data that we have presented in Figures 10-1 and 10-2 give little insight into how the risk structure of spreads have behaved over time. Peek and Wilcox (1986) examine this question. They analyze the behavior of the implied tax brackets for three distinct maturity sectors: one-year, five-year, and ten-year. Their analysis covers 1955 through 1985. For these maturity sectors, they estimate the implied tax rates τ_1, τ_5, and τ_{10} and they find the regularity that $\tau_1 > \tau_5 > \tau_{10}$. Their evidence points to the facts that the municipal yield curve is steeper than the Treasury yield curve and that the municipal yield curve is upward sloping.

In a more recent study, Farinella and Koch (1994) have suggested that the steep upward-sloping nature of the municipal securities yield curve is no longer descriptive of the market conditions after the Tax Reform Act of 1986. Table 10-7 (taken from their work) indicates that the municipal curve is no longer steeply upward-sloping relative to the Treasury. Note in the table that the spread between the twenty-year and one-year Treasuries was 39 basis points compared to the municipal spread of 136 basis points during the period 1960(I)–1979(IV) period. Clearly, the municipal curve was much steeper than the Treasury yield curve during this period. During the 1980(I)–1986(II)

Spread (twenty-year minus one-year)	1960(I)–1979(IV)	1980(I)–1986(II)	1986(III)–1992(IV)
Municipal	1.36%	3.16%	2.11%
Treasury	0.39%	0.84%	1.65%

TABLE 10-7
Slopes of Yield Curves: Municipal vs Treasury

Source: Farinella and Koch (1994)

period, the municipal spread was 316 basis points, well in excess of the Treasury spread of 84 basis points. Note, however, that in the post-Tax Reform-Act-of-1986 period, 1986(III)–1992(IV), the municipal spread was 211 basis points compared to the Treasury spread of 165 basis points. Clearly, the relative steepness of the municipal curve is much less in this period.

ISSUANCE AND PRIMARY MARKET

Most municipal notes (both fixed and variable rate notes) are rated by rating agencies. The rating terminology is shown in Table 10-8. Recall that municipal bonds are also rated, as described in Chapter 7.

Closely linked to the credit reputation of municipal securities is the municipal bonds insurance. There are several large municipal bond insurers: American Municipal Bond Assurance Corporation (AMBAC), Municipal Bond Investors Assurance Corpo-

Security	Moody's	Standard & Poor
Fixed	MIG1	SP-1
Variable	VMIG1	Strong capacity to
Description	Best quality	service debt
Fixed	MIG2	SP-2
Variable	VMIG2	Satisfactory capacity
Description	High quality	to service debt
Fixed	MIG3	SP-3
Variable	VMIG3	Speculative capacity
Description	Favorable quality	to service debt
Fixed	MIG4	
	Adequate quality	
Variable	VMIG4	

TABLE 10-8
Rating Conventions for Municipal Notes

ration (MBIAC), Financial Guarantee Insurance Company (FGIC), and Bond Investors Guaranty Insurance Company (BIG). Rating agencies tend to rate insured municipal bonds at the highest category (Aaa or AAA).

Issuance of municipal securities takes several distinct steps. First, it is important to note that municipal securities do not come under the filing provisions of Securities Act of 1933; thus they are not registered with the SEC. Second, the issuance of GO bonds typically require the approval of the voters since taxes collected from the voters are used to service GO bonds. GO bonds are subject to debt ceilings to electoral supervision either via statutes or via referendum.

Issuance of revenue bonds requires feasibility studies by professionals and may carry restrictive covenants. Such covenants may cover many areas. For example, the municipality may have to set the prices and rates at a level sufficient to ensure a surplus over the maintenance expenses in order to provide debt service. The covenants may also specify maintenance standards, insurance requirements, and restrictions on additional issues of debt.

Typically, covenants require the setting up of specific funds into which revenues are placed. This is done to control the priority of distributing revenues. For example, a debt service fund may be set up to ensure that enough money is deposited into it for debt service. Similarly, a debt service reserve fund may be set up to ensure that a surplus of pre-specified amount is set up. Sinking funds may be set up to retire the issue in an orderly fashion and to avoid a large balloon payment at maturity.

Underwriting

New issues of GO and revenue bonds are effected by the issuing municipalities through the primary market which employs dealers, either through competitive bids or through negotiated sale. Underwriters are dealers who provide a number of functions including pricing of the issue, distribution (reoffer) of the issue, maintenance of a secondary market for the issue, and help in the structuring of the issue to best suit the needs of the issuer.

An important part of underwriting is the official statement, which contains the details about the new issue and about the issuer. One of the roles of the underwriter is to help the issuer prepare this official statement. Underwriters have a major responsibility for verifying the accuracy and truthfulness of the information that is disclosed. The underwriter of an issue makes an implicit recommendation to the investor and there must be a "reasonable basis" for doing so. The Securities and Exchange Commission has a rule, SEC Rule 15c2-12, that governs the information disclosure. In order to establish a reasonable basis, underwriters will review the official statement, inform customers about any official statements, enter into a binding contract with the issuer to distribute the securities to buy, and reoffer the securities to the public. Underwriters, in addition, use their own research staff, secondary market information, and their past experience with the issuers and other issues of similar characteristics to help form their structuring, pricing, and distribution decisions.

SECONDARY MARKET

Much like the Treasury market, the municipal secondary markets are OTC or dealer markets. Interdealer brokers deal exclusively with dealers. They do not deal with public customers, carry positions, or underwrite positions. J. J. Kenny and Chapdelaine are two of the biggest interdealer brokers. Such interdealer brokers provide wire services showing the securities that are available for trades. They do this much like the interdealer brokers in the Treasury markets, concealing the identities of the dealers who wish to make those trades. In addition to the interdealer brokers, dealers also have access to Blue list, which is published daily by Standard and Poor. The **Blue list** contains the interdealer offerings of municipal securities and is a very good indicator of the daily supply in the municipal market. Many dealers subscribe to the Blue list ticker, which enables the dealers to access a specified list of securities. In addition to these sources, Munifacts, a wire service, is provided by *Bond Buyer,* a publication that is active in the municipal market.

Market Conventions

Municipal securities are quoted in terms of yields. The liquidity in this market is poor and hence the bid-offer spreads can be wide, especially for seasoned issues. The convention in the market is such that a bond selling at a discount is priced relative to its maturity. A bond selling at a premium is priced to its call date, provided it is callable at par. Municipal securities pay semi-annual coupons and accrued interest is computed based on a 360-day year basis.

CONCLUSION

There has been a general erosion in the tax advantages of municipal securities. Still, for investors in the high federal tax bracket, municipal securities still offer attractive returns. The article that appeared in *Fortune* (April 1995) is illustrative of this point.

Muni Bonds Still Keep the Taxman at Bay

By ANTONY J. MICHELS

Poor you. You got soaked as the municipal bond market tanked last year. Disgusted, you abandoned ship, deep-sixing your munis and muni funds. But that move too, as it turned out, was all wet. It made you miss the November-to-February rally that boosted the Lehman Brothers Municipal Bond Index to a dazzling 6.2% return.

No use kicking yourself: It's time to think about getting back onboard. Even at today's higher prices and lower yields, tax-exempt muni bonds and the mutual funds that buy them make sense for investors in high tax brackets.

There's no denying that the rally has rendered munis less attractive than during the past few years. For a while, prices went so low relative to U.S. Treasury securities that munis made investment sense even for ordinary Americans, not just rich people. Last March a AAA ten-year muni yielded 5%, vs. 6.4% for a ten-year Treasury note. For an investor in the 28% federal income tax bracket, the muni earned a taxable equivalent yield of almost 7%, handily beating the Treasury.

That sort of deal is no more. Today a ten-year T-note yields 7.3%; a comparable muni yields 5.4%, or a taxable equivalent of 7.5% for an investor in the 28% bracket. The extra smidgen of yield doesn't justify giving up the Treasury, which is easier to trade and has Uncle Sam's rock-solid backing.

If you earn a lot of money, though, munis still measure up. For an investor in the 31% federal income tax bracket, that same ten-year muni's yield is equivalent to a taxable investment that pays 7.8%, beating the Treasury by a healthy margin (see chart). The margin is even healthier if you're in the top tax brackets and if munis issued in your home state exempt you from state and local taxes.

HOW MUNIS BEAT TREASURIES

Muni taxable equivalent yield

U.S. Treasury

AAA munis

2-Year 5   10   15   20   25   30

FORTUNE CHART / SOURCE: STOEVER GLASS & CO.

As the white line shows, investors in the 31% tax bracket earn more after taxes from AAA munis with intermediate or long maturities than from comparable Treasuries.

Want an added incentive to buy munis now? According to James Cooner, head of the muni bond department at Bank of New York, the muni market should hold up better than the Treasury market if the Federal Reserve raises rates again. Reason: the sharp reduction in the number of bonds issued or refinanced by municipalities. Last year the issuance of long-term munis fell 44% from its 1993 peak; this year it is projected to drop still more. "The drop in supply is going to prop up the value of munis compared with other fixed-income investments like Treasuries," Cooner says. He adds that many bonds issued a decade ago are expiring or being called; investors seeking to reinvest the money will fuel demand.

Where can you find the best muni deals? The experts agree that unless you're in the 36% or 39.6% tax brackets, avoid munis with maturities of five years or less. Yields are simply too low compared with Treasuries to make the investment worthwhile.

If you're in the 28% bracket, you've got to buy bonds or bond funds with maturities of 15 years or more before the tax advantage justifies giving up the safety and liquidity of Treasuries. A high-quality 20-year muni has a 6% yield, or a taxable equivalent yield of 8.3%. That's hard to resist—if you can stomach the risk. Twenty years is a long time to hold a bond, and munis are volatile in price: If interest rates rise and you need to sell before the bond matures, you won't get back what you paid. Says Jay Chitnis, a muni bond trader at Stoever Glass & Co. in New York City: "I don't think earning 6% for 20 years is as attractive as 5.4% for ten years."

The usual principles of bond investing apply when you buy munis: Invest some of your money now and some later in case rates do move higher. Ask your financial adviser to explain exactly what security you're buying, its credit rating (bonds rated AAA or higher and insured bonds are best), its maturity, and whether it can be called by the issuer before the maturity date.

*Most pros say you should have at least $50,000 to invest before you start buying individual bonds, which sell in denominations of $5,000. If you don't have the money or want to avoid the bond-buying hassle, invest in a tax-exempt mutual fund. Expenses and sales loads sap a fund's return, so look for no-load funds with very low expenses. Robert Klosterman, a certified financial planner in Minneapolis, recommends **Vanguard Municipal Intermediate-Term,** a no-load fund that has very low annual expenses of 0.20% of assets. The fund recently yielded 5.2%. Klosterman also likes **Strong Municipal Bond** fund, which invests in intermediate-term bonds. It carries no sales load, has annual expenses of 0.80%, and boasts a 5.4% yield.*

PROBLEMS

10.1   Explain the difference between the general obligation bonds and revenue bonds.

10.2   Discuss why the municipal yield curve is steeper than the Treasury yield curve, in general.

10.3   What are the reasons for the relative fall in the steepness of the municipal yield curve relative to the Treasury yield curve after the Tax Reform Act of 1986?

10.4   Discuss why the three major investors in the municipal market are commercial banks, wealthy individuals, and fire and casualty insurers.

10.5   How will changes in future tax policies affect the pricing of municipal bonds?

10.6   Discuss the concept of advanced refunding in the municipal bond markets.

10.7   Why are municipal bonds insured? Who are the major insurers in the municipal bond market?

10.8   The implied tax rate τ is found using the equation

$$R_m = R_T \times (1 - \tau)$$

where R_m is the municipal yield, R_T is the Treasury yield, and τ is the implied tax rate. What are the limitations of this approach? Is it correct to assume that as τ increases, municipal bonds become less attractive investments?

REFERENCES

Ang, J., D. Peterson, and P. Peterson 1985. "Marginal Tax Rates: Evidence from Nontaxable Corporate Bonds: A Note." *Journal of Finance* 40:327–332.

Black, F. 1971. Taxes and Capital Market Equilibrium. Working Paper.

Benson, E. 1981. "Systematic Variation in Yield Spreads for Tax Exempt General Obligation Bonds." *Journal of Financial and Quantitative Analysis* 16:685–702.

Brick, I., and B. Wallingford 1985. "The Relative Tax Benefits of Alternative Call Features in Corporate Debt." *Journal of Financial and Quantitative Analysis* 20:95–105.

Buser, S. A., and P. J. Hess 1985. Corporate Finance and the Relative Yields on Taxable and Tax Exempt Securities. University of Chicago Working Paper #125.

Buser, S. A., and P. J. Hess 1986. "Empirical Determinants of the Relative Yields on Taxable and Tax Exempt Securities." *Journal of Financial Economics* 17:335–355.

Campbell, T. 1980. "On the Extent of Segmentation in the Municipal Securities Market." *Journal of Money, Credit, and Banking* 12:71–83.

Cook, T. Q., and P. H. Hendershott, 1978. "The Impact of Taxes, Risk and Relative Security Supplies on Interest Rate Differentials." *Journal of Finance* 33:173–186.

Farinella, J. A., and T. W. Koch 1994. "Who Took the Slope out of the Municipal Yield Curve?" *Journal of Fixed-Income* 4(2):59–65.

Green, R. C. 1990. A Simple Model of the Taxable and Tax-Exempt Yield Curves. Working Paper.

Hendershott, P. H., and T. Koch 1977. *An Empirical Analysis of the Market for Tax-Exempt Securities: Estimates and Forecasts.* Monograph Series in Finance and Economics. New York: New York University.

Jordan, B. D., and S. D. Jordan 1990. Tax-Timing Options and the Relative Yields on Municipal and Taxable Bonds. Working Paper.

Kidwell, D., and T. W. Koch 1982. "The Behavior of the Interest Rate Differential between Tax Exempt Revenue and General Obligation Bonds." *Journal of Finance* 37:73–85.

Livingston, M. 1979. "Bond Taxation and the Shape of the Yield to Maturity Curve." *Journal of Finance* 34:189–196.

McCulloch, J. H. 1975. "The Tax Adjusted Yield Curve." *Journal of Finance* 30:811–830.

Mussa, M., and R. Kormendi 1979. *The Taxation of Municipal Bonds.* Washington, D.C.: American Enterprise Institute.

Peek, J., and J. A. Wilcox 1986. "Tax Rates and Interest Rates on Tax-Exempt Securities." *New England Economic Review* 29–41.

Skelton, J. L. 1983a. "Relative Risk in Municipal and Corporate Debt." *Journal of Finance* 38: 625–634.

Skelton, J. L. 1983b. "Banks, Firms and the Relative Pricing of Tax Exempt and Taxable Bonds." *Journal of Financial Economics* 12:343–356.

Trzcinka, C. 1982. "The Pricing of Tax-Exempt Bonds and the Miller Hypothesis." *Journal of Finance* 37:907–923.

Van Horne, J. C. 1984. *Financial Market Rates and Flows.* Englewood Cliffs, NJ: Prentice Hall.

Chapter 11

Portfolio-Management Techniques

Chapter Objectives

This chapter describes the portfolio-management principles that are relevant to pension funds, insurance companies, and portfolio- and asset-management companies. We discuss how the asset-management practices are intertwined with the liability structure of the company. We address the following questions.

- What is the nature of the liabilities of pension plans, insurance companies, and commercial banks? How do they affect their asset-management practices?
- What are matched-funding techniques?
- What is immunization?
- How are portfolios indexed?
- What is the concept of portfolio insurance?

INTRODUCTION

Fixed-income portfolios account for a significant part of the money management sector, which includes mutual funds, pension funds, insurance companies, and other money management firms including hedge funds. A number of issues are in overall portfolio management activity. These issues are best understood in the context of the risks of fixed-income securities, discussed in Chapter 1. The portfolio should be assembled to achieve an appropriate balance between the objectives that have been set out for the portfolio-management firm and the various dimensions of risks that are present in different sectors of the fixed-income markets. For example, if the objective of the portfolio manager is to provide for the safety of capital and liquidity, then the composition of the portfolio should be more heavily weighted towards the Treasury, agency, and high-grade corporate sectors of the fixed-income markets. On the other hand, if the objective of the portfolio manager is to provide high growth, then other sectors such as strips and mortgage-backed securities are more relevant.

Portfolio management is guided to a certain extent by the underlying liabilities, the degree depending on the nature of the underlying business. At one extreme, portfolios are managed to maximize the expected return subject to some constraints on the level of risk—in such portfolio management situations, liabilities do not play a very active part. The sponsor of a pension plan may assign part of the pension assets to a professional money manager for a prespecified period with the expectation that the returns on the assets will be maximized during that period. In such a case the liabilities (pension obligations) do not enter directly in the portfolio-management problem faced by the professional money manager. But if the value of the assets fall, sooner or later the sponsor of the pension plan will exert pressure on the money manager to generate a surplus over the liability. Thus, the liabilities will start to dictate the asset-management problem. At the other extreme, portfolio selection may be entirely dictated by the liabilities. An example of this would be the dedicated portfolio construction, where a minimum-cost portfolio is constructed to meet a defined schedule of liabilities. This is typical of municipalities and local governments that invite bids from dealers for dedicated portfolios to implement bond defeasence and capital expenditures.

NATURE OF THE UNDERLYING BUSINESS AND PORTFOLIO MANAGEMENT

We now investigate how the portfolio management is affected by the nature of the business that needs asset management and the underlying economic function that the portfolio manager has to provide.

Pension Funds

For pension plans, the portfolio manager is one of many managing the pension funds of a firm, and the overriding concern is to make sure that the funds are managed to meet the pension liabilities. The penalty for not meeting the liability should be high and the incentives for building a surplus should be great. Pension liabilities (obligations) are long-term and are reasonably predictable. Factors such as mortality and employee turnover typically influence pension obligations. Actuaries are quite conservative and may value liabilities by using discount rates that are not necessarily reflected in the market yields on fixed-income securities of a similar duration. The implications for such a discrepancy for portfolio management are discussed fully later in the chapter. The liabilities are typically correlated with future wages, which are in turn correlated with the stock market. Liabilities are also long-dated with a high duration. Thus the liability has both interest rate and equity exposure. First, to get an appreciation of the assets that are under the management of pension plans, review Tables 11-1 and 11-2.

Table 11-3 summarizes the key features of the liabilities of pension plans. Remember that the assets are typically managed by a number of professional money managers.

TABLE 11-1   *Growth of Pension Assets (in billions of U.S. dollars)*

Year	1950	1960	1970	1980	1982	1984	1986	1987	1988	1989
Assets of Private Pension Plans	13	57	153	627	787	1,000	1,349	1,464	1,634	1,836
Assets of Public Pension Plans	12	34	88	275	361	487	638	706	814	950

Source: U.S. Federal Reserve Board

Flow of funds accounts and EBRI tabulations based on American Council of Life Insurance data.

	DB Plan		DC Plan	
Year	Assets*	Percent	Assets*	Percent
1950	45	88.24%	6	11.76%
1955	92	85.19%	16	14.81%
1960	153	82.26%	33	17.74%
1965	270	79.18%	71	20.82%
1970	323	76.54%	99	23.46%
1975	360	74.23%	125	25.77%
1981	574	72.20%	221	27.80%
1990**	902	68.02%	424	31.98%
2000**	1,453	65.10%	779	34.90%

TABLE 11-2
Defined Benefits (DB) and Defined Contribution (DC) Plans

Source: EBRI Databook on employee benefits

*In billions of 1984 U.S. dollars

**Projected estimates

TABLE 11-3   *Pension Plan Liabilities*

Plan	Liability
Defined contribution plans	Pay as you go. Money is placed by investors in assets and portfolios of their choice.
Defined benefits plan	Long dated liabilities. Highly interest rate sensitive and correlated with future wages. Asset allocation and funding are regulated. Turnover in the labor market, mortality, etc.

Insurance Companies

Insurance companies have a product mix consisting of guaranteed investment contracts (GICs), insurance policies, annuities, and so on. The proceeds from the sale of such products must then be invested in assets in such a way as to maximize profits. The link between assets and liabilities should be rather tight in the asset-allocation policies used by the insurance companies. If the assets provide a better return than the cost associated with meeting the obligations under GICs, insurance products, and annuities, then the insurance company makes a profit. Sometimes the spread between the return on assets and the cost of meeting the liabilities is boosted by assuming additional credit risk (by investing in junk bonds, for instance) or by assuming illiquidity (by investing in real estate, for example) or by lack of diversification. Table 11-4 summarizes the key features of the liabilities of insurance companies.

The liabilities tend to have a very strong interest-rate exposure. Many of the products sold by insurance companies have several contractual provisions that qualitatively alter the interest-rate exposure. For example, whole-life insurance policies that are offered by insurance companies often extend a line of credit to the insured individual. Such loans also provide a cap on the borrowing costs. The net effect of these provisions is that when the interest rates increase, the policy options increase in value. Another example of an option that an insured individual has is to buy additional insurance at pre-specified rates. Other insurance products such as GICs may also contain specified options. In these cases, insurance companies have sold policy options whose values are extremely sensitive to interest-rate changes.

TABLE 11-4   *Insurance Company Liabilities*

Nature of Insurance	Liability
Life insurance	Annuities, GICs, life-insurance products. Interest-rate sensitive. They also depend on mortality rates and demographic factors. Insurance products have option-like features which affect the interest-rate exposure significantly.
Property insurance	The liabilities are related to industry and project specific risks. Liabilities require very close management and technical knowledge.

Banks and Financial Institutions

Traditionally, banks and financial institutions borrow in the short-term maturity sector. Typically, they issue CDs or floating-rate notes (FRNs) that are indexed to short-term interest rates. The proceeds are then loaned out to projects that have longer maturities. Here the primary source of risk is the possibility that the shape of the yield curve might shift. In particular, the possibility that the curve might become inverted poses a big threat to the profitability of the bank. Advanced techniques such as securitization are used to alleviate this risk, in part. In addition, the nature of the bank's business automatically entails the assumption of credit risk (the experience of U.S. Banks with Latin American loans is an obvious case in point) and illiquidity (such as a real estate portfolio). Table 11-5 summarizes the key features of bank liabilities.

Bank Activity	Liabilities
Domestic loans and deposits	Credit risk, yield-curve risks. Generally illiquid.
Foreign loans and liabilities	Foreign-exchange risks, interest-rate risks.
Investment portfolio	Varying credit and liquidity

TABLE 11-5
Bank Liabilities

Portfolio Management

We have considered three important segments of portfolio management industry. Depending on the segment, the liability of the firm will influence the asset-allocation process to a greater or lesser extent. There are also tax-related incentives for some of these segments not to invest in certain areas of fixed-income markets. For example, pension funds are tax-exempt and as a consequence do not generally invest in tax-exempt municipal bond markets. Similar incentives exist for insurance companies as well.

In addition, there are legal and regulatory restrictions on asset allocation. For example, plan charters tend to impose restrictions on the percentage of assets that may be placed in any one sector of the fixed-income market.

Broadly, we may characterize the important aspects of portfolio management as in Table 11-6.

We will explore next different portfolio management techniques that are extensively used in the industry. First, we will consider matched-funding portfolio-management strategies. In this category are (i) dedicated-portfolio policies, (ii) immunization policies, (iii) horizon matching, and (iv) contingent immunization policies. Then, we will explore other policies such as indexation and portfolio insurance, which are much more dynamic and have greater flexibility in their implementation. These strategies are used extensively in practice. An article from *Pension World* (1993) illustrates the relevance of these strategies to institutional investors.

TABLE 11-6 *Portfolio Management Considerations*

Dimension	*Portfolio Management Implications*
Liability characteristics	If the penalty for not meeting the liability is very high, then portfolio management is pinned down almost entirely by the features of the liabilities. In other extreme cases, assets may be managed as per stated policies, as in certain mutual funds.
Tax status	Special tax incentives may induce certain preferences in portfolio management (e.g., pension funds may prefer corporates and avoid municipals).
Charter and legal restrictions	Diversification across different sectors. Short sale restrictions. Ability to trade in derivatives.
Operating policies	Stated policies may require investment in only certain sectors.

Pension Plan Funding Strategies: Defining Terms

By EMAD A. ZIRKY and ROBERT M. MACKEY
Mitchell Hutchins
New York

Matched funding investment strategies are used to fund pension plan liabilities. There seems to be a degree of confusion, within the Taft-Hartley community, as to the meaning of some of the terms used to describe the process. The following information is offered to give a clearer understanding of each strategy, as well as to explain the appropriate application of each technique.

The amount of future pension fund benefit obligations is typically estimated using actuarial projections of such variables as life expectancies, future salaries, inflation, and time of service. Two factors make the funding status of these liabilities more important today than ever before:

1) The amount of these obligations, which approaches the total net worth of the sponsors for some of the more mature plans; and,

2) The reporting requirements under FASB 87.

The Financial Accounting Standards Boards' (FASB) Statement 87 requires corporations to "mark-to-market" the value of their pension obligations. This means that corporations must use existing market rates of interest to discount the future liabilities and arrive at a present value for these obligations. In addition, FASB 87 requires this present value to be compared with the pension assets to arrive at a funded status (surplus or deficit) of the pension plan. This status must be reported on the balance sheet, and any changes in this status reported on the income statement. Matched-funding strategies are an ideal means of controlling the risk of this funded status.

There are four fixed income investment strategies which are used to help meet the future benefit obligations:

1) Dedication: fixed income portfolio structured so that cash flow (interest + maturities) is available as pre-determined obligations become payable.

2) Horizon-matching: fixed income portfolio constructed to match interest rate sensitivity of the liabilities while at the same time having a dedicated structure for the nearer term obligations.

3) Immunization: fixed income portfolio structured for a fixed period to meet a pre-determined target amount. Matches interest rate sensitivity of the assets to the liabilities.

4) Dollar-duration matching: same as immunization, but does not assume that the value of the assets and liabilities are equal.

In deciding which strategy is most suitable, we must look at the nature of the future obligation. For these purposes, it is useful to distinguish between two categories of pension fund liabilities: retired-lives benefits and active-lives benefits.

Future Retiree Payments

As the name implies, retired-lives benefits consist of the future payments to be made to current retirees. Here, the benefits are set—with the exception of any future cost-of-living adjustments which may be made—and the only estimation to be made is with regard to mortality. Since these obligations can be estimated with a high degree of confidence, dedication that matches these obligations with cash flows from the portfolio is an appropriate strategy.

A flexible, less costly solution is a strategy known as horizon-matching. This technique utilizes a portfolio of assets constructed to match the interest rate sensitivity of the liabilities while cash-matching the nearer term, more predictable obligations. In this way, benefit payments can be made directly from the cash flow of the portfolio, while the elimination of the strict cash-matching in the later years provides greater flexibility in incorporating new or revised liabilities should the need arise. In addition, this more flexible structure is less expensive than strict dedication, and it allows greater opportunity in adding value to the portfolio. Matched funding techniques are somewhat less precise, but still useful when applied to active-lives benefits.

The Projected Payments

Active-lives benefits refer to the projected payments to be made to employees who haven't yet retired. Since benefits typically increase with salary and years of service, these obligations are much more difficult to predict. For this reason, dedication is generally inappropriate for the funding of active-lives benefits, but immunization, which matches the interest rate sensitivity of the assets with that of the liabilities, can be a useful strategy. While immunization, from a total return perspective, is advantageous only when rates are "high," from a risk management perspective, it is always a valuable tool. Regardless of the level of interest rates, a portfolio of assets that matches the interest rate sensitivity of the liabilities represents the riskless posture with respect to the funding status of the pension plan.

In addition, from a total return perspective, we must be careful in our determination of the attractiveness of current interest rate levels. While interest rates have certainly retreated from their highs of the early 80s, current rates are still significantly above their all-time historical averages. Horizon-matching, which again combines dedication and immunization, can also be useful if the sponsor wishes to fund near-term payments from the portfolio.

Finally, a strategy which is appropriate when the liabilities are not fully match-funded (fixed-income assets less than the present value of the liabilities) is known as dollar-duration matching. Typically, a sponsor will wish to allocate some portion of the plan assets to equities or other assets in the hopes of earning higher returns than those which might be available in the fixed-income markets. Dollar-duration matching, like immunization, matches the interest rate sensitivity of the assets to that of the liabilities. However, while classical immunization assumes the values of the assets and liabilities are equal, dollar-duration matching considers the relative values of the assets and liabilities and adjusts for any difference.

For example, if a pension fund has assets equal to its liabilities (i.e., it is fully funded), but wishes to allocate one-half of the assets to equities, a dollar-duration matched portfolio would require assets with an interest rate sensitivity equal to twice that of the liabilities.

Offset by Value Change

While the dollar allocation to fixed-income securities would be only one-half of the present value of the liabilities, a change in the present value of the liabilities due to a change in interest rates would be offset by an equal change in the value of the fixed-income (dollar-duration matched) portfolio.

It should be kept in mind that these strategies have applications regardless of the current funded status of the plan. For overfunded plans, matched-funded strategies can be used to hedge the interest rate risk of the liabilities (i.e., fully match-fund the liabilities).

The sponsor can then invest the surplus as aggressively as desired without fear of endangering the funded status of the plan. With underfunded plans, a dollar-duration matched strategy can be used to match the interest rate sensitivity of the liabilities while the sponsor attempts to make up the deficit.

Horizon-matching can also be used in conjunction with a dollar-duration matching strategy regardless of the plan's funded status, if it is desired that benefit payments be made from the cash flow of the portfolio.

MATCHED FUNDING

Dedicated Portfolios

In a number of situations, corporations, local governments, and other institutions are faced with the task of funding a stream of liabilities in the future. In the case of corporations, the liability could be the obligations associated with the pension plans that are in place. The sponsoring firm may have to fund a stream of projected benefits that are payable to retiring employees. The firm may either buy guaranteed investment contracts (GICs) or fund them by buying a suitable portfolio of assets. GICs are typically offered by insurance companies. For a local government, the problem may be one of funding projected capital expenditures to build a highway or a bridge, for example. Matched-funding techniques are used in such situations.

A dedicated portfolio consists of buying a minimum-cost portfolio from a universe of securities subject to restrictions on callability, credit quality, sectors, and so on. The universe of assets may be defined as in Table 11-7. The choice of admissible securities is based on several considerations. First, the universe should not include any security that has significant uncertainty about the timing of future cash flows or about the magnitude of future cash flows. This consideration rules out floating-rate notes, bonds that are callable before the liabilities are due, and mortgage-backed securities which carry significant prepayment risks. Second, the universe should be chosen to ensure a minimum acceptable level of credit risk. Typically, this means that only investment-grade securities are included in the universe of securities. While Treasuries naturally satisfy this requirement, they are also the most expensive choice. Typically, agency securities and corporates of investment credits may be safely included. To the extent possible, the universe should include securities that minimize reinvestment risks. This feature should call for strips whose maturities come closest to the liability dates. Finally, there is no need to include securities that mature after the last payment date in the liability schedule. Transaction costs, bid-offer spreads, and so on may also be incorporated in the solution procedure.

We will illustrate these basic concepts in the context of simple examples.

Security	Contractual Features	Credit Risk
U.S. Treasury	Noncallable	Negligible
Strips	Noncallable	Negligible
Agency	Noncallable	Low
Investment-grade corporates	May be callable	Moderate
Junk bonds		Risky

TABLE 11-7
Universe of Securities

Example 11-1

Consider the problem of funding a stream of pension liabilities consisting of $100 million per year for the next three years. Consider a liability schedule facing the corporation over the next three years with the cash flows due at the end of every year, as shown in Table 11-8. Typically, such a liability schedule will come from the institutions that need to fund the cash outlays associated with capital expenditures or bond-defeasance activities.

	Year 1	Year 2	Year 3
Liabilities	100	100	100

TABLE 11-8
Liability Schedule
(in millions of dollars)

We will assume that the universe of securities consists of three coupon bonds and three strips, as shown in Table 11-9. The matched-funding strategy then consists of finding the minimum-cost portfolio of assets from the universe specified in Table 11-9, subject to the condition that all the liabilities are met.

TABLE 11-9   *Universe of Securities, Example 11-1*

Security	Price at Year 0	Cash Flow at Year 1	Cash Flow at Year 1	Cash Flow at Year 3
Bond 1	100.6520	10	10	110
Bond 2	95.5480	8	8	108
Bond 3	105.7561	12	12	112
Strip 1	94.3396	100	0	0
Strip 2	85.7339	0	100	0
Strip 3	75.1315	0	0	100

From Table 11-9, we can determine the strip rates as follows: the price of strip 1 should equal its discounted face value.

Hence

$$94.3396 = \frac{100}{(1 + y_1)}$$

or,

$$y_1 = 6\%.$$

Similarly, the price of strip 2 implies that

$$85.7339 = \frac{100}{(1 + y_2)^2}$$

or,

$$y_2 = 8\%.$$

Finally, the price of strip 3 implies a three-year strip rate y_3 such that

$$75.1315 = \frac{100}{(1 + y_3)^3}$$

or,

$$y_3 = 10\%.$$

Using the concepts developed in chapter 5, we can calculate the implied spot rates for years 1, 2 and 3 from the coupon bond prices in Table 11-9. If r_1, r_2 and r_3 are the implied spot rates, then the coupon bond prices must satisfy:

$$100.6520 = \frac{10}{1 + r_1} + \frac{10}{(1 + r_2)^2} + \frac{110}{(1 + r_3)^3} \tag{11.1}$$

$$95.5480 = \frac{8}{1 + r_1} + \frac{8}{(1 + r_2)^2} + \frac{108}{(1 + r_3)^3} \tag{11.2}$$

and

$$105.7561 = \frac{12}{1 + r_1} + \frac{12}{(1 + r_2)^2} + \frac{112}{(1 + r_3)^3} \tag{11.3}$$

Solving Equations (11.1), (11.2) and (11.3) we can verify that $r_1 = y_1$, $r_2 = y_2$ and $r_3 = y_3$.

The simplest strategy is to buy the relevant strips to fully fund the liabilities. In this problem, this strategy will be to buy 100 units of each strip. The total cost of this strategy is

$$94.3396 + 85.7339 + 75.1315 = 255.20.$$

Is there a cheaper alternative? In a world where there are no arbitrage opportunities, the present value of the liabilities should be always equal to the present value of assets that we buy to fund. In Table 11-9, the prices are chosen so that there are no arbitrage opportunities. The spot rates indicated by the three coupon bonds for the maturities 1, 2, and 3 years are precisely the same as the strip rates for those maturities, respectively.

The cash flows from the dedicated portfolio will match the liabilities dollar for dollar under the most conservative reinvestment assumptions. Clearly, as we relax the credit quality and permit more aggressive reinvestment assumptions, we will find a lower-cost portfolio. The true cost, however, may be higher. Portfolios may be rededicated from time to time as spreads change. The problem may then be solved as a linear programming problem, for which efficient algorithms are currently available for computation. Consider the matched-funding strategy posed formally as a linear programming problem next.

Example 11-2

Choose n_i such that:

$$\min_{\{n_1, n_2, \cdots, n_N\}} \sum_{i=1}^{N} n_i P_{i0}$$

subject to the funding constraints shown next:

$$\sum_{i=1}^{N} n_i x_{i1} \geq 100$$

$$\sum_{i=1}^{N} n_i x_{i2} \geq 100$$

and

$$\sum_{i=1}^{N} n_i x_{i3} \geq 100$$

where P_{i0} is the price of security i at date 0, x_{i1} is the cashflow from security i at date 1, etc. We choose n_i, the number of each security to buy at date 0, to fully fund the

Security	Allocation
Bond 1	0.2065
Bond 2	0.2291
Bond 3	0.1839
Strip 1	0.9389
Strip 2	0.9389
Strip 3	0.3194

TABLE 11-10
Optimal Allocation,
Example 11-2

liabilities at all future dates. We might also wish to specify additional constraints $n_i \geq 0$. For Example 11-1, the constraints take the form:

$$n_1 10 + n_2 8 + n_3 12 + n_4 100 + n_5 0 + n_6 0 \geq 100$$

$$n_1 10 + n_2 8 + n_3 12 + n_4 0 + n_5 100 + n_6 0 \geq 100$$

$$n_1 110 + n_2 108 + n_3 112 + n_4 0 + n_5 0 + n_6 100 \geq 100$$

Let

$$x = n_1 100.652 + n_2 95.5479 + n_3 105.7561 + n_4 94.3396$$
$$+ n_5 85.7334 + n_6 75.1315$$

be the total cost. Then, we pick n_i ($i = 1, 2, \cdots, 6$) so that $n_i \geq 0$ and the total cost x is minimized. See Table 11-10 for the optimal allocation.

The solution for this simple linear programming problem is: The total cost of this strategy is the same as the strategy of buying the three strips.

From Table 11-10 and the bond prices in Table 11-9 we can compute the total cost of the dedicated portfolio as follows:

$$0.2065(100.6520) + 0.2291(95.5480) + 0.1839(105.7561) + 0.9389(94.3396)$$
$$+ 0.9389(85.7339) + 0.3194(75.1315) = 255.20$$

Thus the cost of this portfolio is the same as buying the strips.

In Example 11-2 the spot rates and the strip rates are identical and, as a result, there is no improvement in the cost of the dedicated portfolio. In reality, as we have seen in Chapter 5, spot rates differ from strip rates. Factors such as liquidity and taxes introduce the differences. This means that the inclusion of both bonds and strips should produce an improvement in the cost of the dedicated portfolio.

Example 11-3

Consider a slightly different universe, but admit the possibility that the spot rates differ from strip rates (Table 11-11).

For Example 11-3 we note that the strip rates are exactly as before, so that $y_1 = 6\%$, $y_2 = 8\%$, and $y_3 = 10\%$. This is because the strip prices in Table 11-11 are the same as the ones in Table 11-9. The bond universe and their prices in Table

TABLE 11-11   *Universe of Securities, Example 11-3*

Security	Price at Year 0	Cash Flow at Year 1	Cash Flow at Year 1	Cash Flow at Year 3
Bond 1	100.000	10	110	0
Bond 2	95.000	8	8	108
Bond 3	105.0000	12	12	112
Strip 1	94.3396	100	0	0
Strip 2	85.7339	0	100	0
Strip 3	75.1315	0	0	100

11-11 have changed. This will produce different implied spot rates. We use the bond prices in Table 11-11 to set up the following conditions:

$$100 = \frac{10}{1 + r_1} + \frac{110}{(1 + r_2)^2} + \frac{0}{(1 + r_3)^3} \qquad (11.4)$$

$$95 = \frac{8}{1 + r_1} + \frac{8}{(1 + r_2)^2} + \frac{108}{(1 + r_3)^3} \qquad (11.5)$$

$$105 = \frac{12}{1 + r_1} + \frac{12}{(1 + r_2)^2} + \frac{112}{(1 + r_3)^3} \qquad (11.6)$$

Solving Equations (11.4) through (11.6), we get the implied spot rates as: $r_1 = 8.11\%$, $r_2 = 10.10\%$ and $r_3 = 10.06\%$.

Since the implied spot rates are higher than the strip rates, we expect the minimum cost portfolio to consist of more bonds based on our analysis.

The optimal allocation from the linear programming formulation is shown in Table 11-12. Note the reduction in cost that is brought about by the inclusion of bonds in the universe, as compared to the cost of funding using strips alone.

The minimum cost portfolio is valued at $0.8117(100) + 0.8929(105) + 0.8117(94.3396) = 251.49$, which is less than the cost of buying the strips to fund the liabilities.

Example 11-3 is admittedly simple. The complications that typically arise in the context of real-life dedications include reinvestment rates, transaction costs, and subsequent rededications.

TABLE 11-12
Optimal Allocation,
Example 11-3

Security	Allocation
Bond 1	0.8117
Bond 2	0.00
Bond 3	0.8929
Strip 1	0.8117
Strip 2	0.00
Strip 3	0.00

Reinvestment Rates. The formulation so far assumes that the coupon dates and redemption dates coincide with the dates on which cash flows are due to meet the liabilities. It is often the case that the liability payment dates are different from the coupon payment dates. Under these circumstances, we need to forecast the reinvestment rates at which cash flows from bonds will be carried forward until the liabilities become due.

Example 11-4

Let us reformulate Example 11-2 by assuming that the coupon dates and the maturity dates of securities occur at dates 0.5, 1.5, and 2.5, whereas the liabilities are due at dates 1, 2, and 3. The formulation of the linear programming problem is modified as follows:

$$\min_{\{n_1,\, n_2,\, \cdots,\, n_N\}} \sum_{i=1}^{N} n_i P_{i0}$$

subject to the funding constraints:

$$\sum_{i=1}^{N} n_i x_{i1} \times (1 + R)^{0.5} \geq 100$$

$$\sum_{i=1}^{N} n_i x_{i2} \times (1 + R)^{0.5} \geq 100$$

and

$$\sum_{i=1}^{N} n_i x_{i3} \times (1 + R)^{0.5} \geq 100$$

where P_{i0} is the price of security i at date 0, x_{i1} is the cash flow from security i at date 1, etc. We assume that cash flows can be reinvested at a rate R.

It should be clear that the reinvestment-rate assumption will affect the minimum cost of the portfolio as well as its composition in general. Note that as the assumed reinvestment rate increases, the minimum cost of the portfolio decreases. Table 11-13 illustrates the effect of the reinvestment rate on the composition and the

TABLE 11-13 *Effect of Reinvestment-Rate Assumption on Minimum Cost Portfolio*

	Reinvestment Rate					
Security	*1%*	*2%*	*3%*	*4%*	*5%*	*6%*
Bond 1	0.376	0.642	0.572	0.310	0.308	0.307
Bond 2	0.400	0.161	0.068	0.073	0.071	0.070
Bond 3	0.000	0.066	0.252	0.502	0.500	0.498
Strip 1	0.925	0.905	0.892	0.884	0.879	0.875
Strip 2	0.925	0.905	0.892	0.884	0.879	0.875
Strip 3	0.149	0.036	0.000	0.000	0.000	0.000
Minimum cost	253.36	252.1	250.74	249.83	248.52	247.20

cost of the minimum-cost portfolio. Note that the minimum-cost portfolio changes as the reinvestment-rate assumptions change. Strips are an integral part of the dedicated portfolio for all reinvestment rates. Bonds become a part of the dedicated portfolio only at certain reinvestment rates.

Transactions Costs. Another problem that is important in dedicated-portfolio problems is the transactions costs and the bid-offer spreads that are encountered when securities are transacted. Using linear programming formulations, most reasonable transactions-costs specifications are easily incorporated.

Rededication. Once the dedicated portfolio is constructed, the initial optimal-funding policy has been found. This does not mean that the original portfolio will continue to be the optimal portfolio as the levels of interest rates and the spreads across markets and maturities change through time. So, as a practical matter, it is useful to reevaluate the optimality of the original portfolio from time to time. In addition, there may be opportunities for rededication when there are qualitative shifts in yields and the shape of the yield curve, and in intermarket spreads.

Immunization

Note that the dedicated-portfolio technique gives the portfolio manager little room for manipulation. Once the universe is defined and the inputs are prepared, the asset allocation becomes fairly straightforward; the policy has, in general, little upside potential. An alternative portfolio-management technique, that is popular in the fixed-income portfolio sector, is the immunization technique.

Running an immunized portfolio assumes the following.

- The present value of the assets must match the present value of the liabilities.
- The duration (or interest-rate sensitivity) of the assets must match the duration of the liabilities.
- The assets must have a dominance pattern over the liabilities for prescribed changes in yields. This dominance pattern requires that certain second-order effects, such as convexity of assets, exceed those of the liabilities. This issue was discussed in Chapter 5 in detail.

Unlike dedicated portfolios, immunization requires dynamic portfolio rebalancing over time. Also, the possibility of unanticipated deficits is greater in the immunization setting, compared to the dedicated portfolio setting.

We will illustrate the immunization concept, continuing to develop our example.

Example 11-5

In Table 11-9, we assume that the yield to maturity of strip 1 is 6%, of strip 2 is 8%, and of strip 3 is 10%. Let us consider the immunization strategy using strip 3. The duration of liability when the market yields are at 10% is $D = 1.942$. In Table 11-14,

TABLE 11-14   *Present Value of Liabilities and Assets as a Function of Discount Rates*

	0%	1%	2%	3%	4%	5%	6%
Value of liability	300.00	294.10	288.39	282.86	277.51	272.32	267.30
Duration of liability	2.00	1.99	1.99	1.98	1.97	1.97	1.96
Value of bond 1	130.00	126.47	123.07	119.80	116.65	113.62	110.69
Duration of bond 1	2.77	2.77	2.76	2.76	2.76	2.75	2.75
Value of bond 2	124.00	120.59	117.30	114.14	111.10	108.17	105.35
Duration of bond 2	2.81	2.80	2.80	2.80	2.79	2.79	2.79
Value of bond 3	136.00	132.35	128.84	125.46	122.20	119.06	116.04
Duration of bond 3	2.74	2.73	2.73	2.72	2.72	2.72	2.71
Value of Strip 1	100.00	99.01	98.04	97.09	96.15	95.24	94.34
Duration of Strip 1	1.00	1.00	1.00	1.00	1.00	1.00	1.00
Value of Strip 2	100.00	98.03	96.12	94.26	92.46	90.70	89.00
Duration of Strip 2	2.00	2.00	2.00	2.00	2.00	2.00	2.00
Value of Strip 3	100.00	97.06	94.23	91.51	88.90	86.38	83.96
Duration of Strip 3	3.00	3.00	3.00	3.00	3.00	3.00	3.00

	7%	8%	9%	10%	11%	12%
Value of liability	262.43	257.71	253.13	**248.69**	244.37	240.18
Duration of liability	1.95	1.95	1.94	**1.94**	1.93	1.92
Value of bond 1	107.87	105.15	102.53	**100.00**	97.56	95.20
Duration of bond 1	2.75	2.74	2.74	**2.74**	2.73	2.73
Value of bond 2	102.62	100.00	97.47	**95.03**	92.67	90.39
Duration of bond 2	2.79	2.78	2.78	**2.78**	2.77	2.77
Value of bond 3	113.12	110.31	107.59	**104.97**	102.44	100.00
Duration of bond 3	2.71	2.71	2.70	**2.70**	2.69	2.69
Value of Strip 1	93.46	92.59	91.74	**90.91**	90.09	89.29
Duration of Strip 1	1.00	1.00	1.00	**1.00**	1.00	1.00
Value of Strip 2	87.34	85.73	84.17	**82.64**	81.16	79.72
Duration of Strip 2	2.00	2.00	2.00	**2.00**	2.00	2.00
Value of Strip 3	81.63	79.38	77.22	**75.13**	73.12	71.18
Duration of Strip 3	3.00	3.00	3.00	**3.00**	3.00	3.00

	13%	14%	15%	16%	17%	18%
Value of liability	236.12	232.16	228.32	224.59	220.96	217.43
Duration of liability	1.92	1.91	1.91	1.90	1.90	1.89
Value of bond 1	92.92	90.71	88.58	86.52	84.53	82.61
Duration of bond 1	2.73	2.72	2.72	2.71	2.71	2.71
Value of bond 2	88.19	86.07	84.02	82.03	80.11	78.26
Duration of bond 2	2.77	2.77	2.76	2.76	2.76	2.75
Value of bond 3	97.64	95.36	93.15	91.02	88.95	86.95
Duration of bond 3	2.69	2.68	2.68	2.67	2.67	2.67
Value of Strip 1	88.50	87.72	86.96	86.21	85.47	84.75
Duration of Strip 1	1.00	1.00	1.00	1.00	1.00	1.00
Value of Strip 2	78.31	76.95	75.61	74.32	73.05	71.82
Duration of Strip 2	2.00	2.00	2.00	2.00	2.00	2.00
Value of Strip 3	69.31	67.50	65.75	64.07	62.44	60.86
Duration of Strip 3	3.00	3.00	3.00	3.00	3.00	3.00

we show the duration of the liability at yield levels varying from 0% to 18%. Note that the duration of strips is always equal to its remaining time to maturity. In order to immunize the liability, the duration of the liability must be equal to the duration of the strip. In order to do this, we impose the following condition:

$$0 = \frac{n_3 P_3}{V_p} D_3 + \frac{P_L}{V_p} D_L \tag{11.7}$$

where n_3 is the number of strip 3, P_3 is the price of strip 3 ($= 75.1315$), D_3 is the duration of the strip ($= 3$), and P_L is the market value of liabilities ($= 248.69$). The total value of the portfolio is

$$V_p = n_3 P_3 + P_L.$$

Solving for n_3 we get

$$n_3 = -\frac{P_L}{V_p} D_L \times \frac{V_p}{P_3 D_3} \tag{11.8}$$

$$n_3 = -\frac{248.69}{V_p} \times 1.94 \times \frac{V_p}{3 \times 75.1315} = -2.14. \tag{11.9}$$

Note that once we select the number of strips to buy to immunize the liability schedule, the market value of the strip is also automatically determined. This means that while we are able to match the duration of the liability with that of the asset (strip 3), the funding of the liability is still at risk—we have provided a hedge for price risk but not for cash-flow funding. The market values of the liability and the asset are shown in Table 11-14 for different interest rate scenarios. Note that the price risks are hedged reasonably. As time passes, the liabilities will become due. For example, at date 1, a cash outflow of 100 will be required. This should be met by selling the requisite amount of strip 3 and rebalancing the position to immunize the liabilities once again.

Let us summarize the advantages and disadvantages of immunization strategy as compared to the dedicated portfolio strategy:

- Immunization strategy has a much greater flexibility. The portfolio manager has the choice of selecting a wide range of assets to immunize the liability schedule. In Example 11-5, then, although we chose strip 3, any other combination of assets could have been chosen.
- The position must be rebalanced to meet cash outflows, as well as to account for the changes in the duration of the liability schedule due to the passage of time.

Example 11-6

We can combine strip 1 and strip 3 to create an asset portfolio which approximately matches the present value of the liability as well as the duration of the liability as shown in Table 11-15. The analysis that was presented in Chapter 5 showed that this barbell portfolio has a greater convexity and, hence, it will have a dominance pattern over the liability schedule that we have.

TABLE 11-15   *Immunization Using Strips 1 and 3*

	# strip 1 = 1.45		# strip 3 = 1.59				
	0%	*1%*	*2%*	*3%*	*4%*	*5%*	*6%*
Value of liability	300.00	294.10	288.39	282.86	277.51	272.32	267.30
Duration of liability	2.00	1.99	1.99	1.98	1.97	1.97	1.96
Value of Strip 1	145.00	143.56	142.16	140.78	139.42	138.10	136.79
Duration of Strip 1	1.00	1.00	1.00	1.00	1.00	1.00	1.00
Value of Strip 3	159.00	154.32	149.83	145.51	141.35	137.35	133.50
Duration of Strip 3	3.00	3.00	3.00	3.00	3.00	3.00	3.00
Total value of strips	304.00	297.89	291.99	286.28	280.77	275.45	270.29
	7%	*8%*	*9%*	*10%*	*11%*	*12%*	
Value of liability	262.43	257.71	253.13	248.69	244.37	240.18	
Duration of liability	1.95	1.95	1.94	1.94	1.93	1.92	
Value of Strip 1	135.51	134.26	133.03	131.82	130.63	129.46	
Duration of Strip 1	1.00	1.00	1.00	1.00	1.00	1.00	
Value of Strip 3	129.79	126.22	122.78	119.46	116.26	113.17	
Duration of Strip 3	3.00	3.00	3.00	3.00	3.00	3.00	
Total value of strips	265.31	260.48	255.80	251.28	246.89	242.64	
	13%	*14%*	*15%*	*16%*	*17%*	*18%*	
Value of liability	236.12	232.16	228.32	224.59	220.96	217.43	
Duration of liability	1.92	1.91	1.91	1.90	1.90	1.89	
Value of Strip 1	128.32	127.19	126.09	125.00	123.93	122.88	
Duration of Strip 1	1.00	1.00	1.00	1.00	1.00	1.00	
Value of Strip 3	110.19	107.32	104.55	101.86	99.27	96.77	
Duration of Strip 3	3.00	3.00	3.00	3.00	3.00	3.00	
Total value of strips	238.51	234.51	230.63	226.86	223.21	219.65	

HORIZON MATCHING

Thus far, we have presented two approaches to portfolio management. The dedicated-portfolio approach left the portfolio manager little room for manipulation. The major advantage of this approach is that the liabilities will always be met. The immunization approach provided the portfolio manager a great deal more flexibility. But this flexibility comes at a price: There is a greater risk that the cash outflows may not be met. In addition, the underlying assumptions that are implicit in the approach (such as parallel shifts in the yield curve) may not be valid during any given period, leading to variations in performance. Horizon matching combines the portfolio-dedication approach and the immunization approach.

The essential features of horizon matching may be summarized as follows:

• It is a hybrid of matched-funding and immunization techniques.

- The relevant horizon (say, 30 years) is split into two parts. Part 1 may consist of a 10-year horizon and part 2 may consist of the remaining 20 years.
- The first part of the liabilities will be managed via matched funding and the second part will be managed via immunization.

The underlying reasoning behind horizon matching is the belief that liabilities over the short term can be predicted with greater precision than the liabilities over the long term.

Contingent Immunization

In contingent immunization strategies, the manager of pension assets takes more risks. In a 16%-yield setting, he may accept a required return of 14%. This requires a lower market-value of assets.

Example 11-7

Consider a pension plan that has a $100 million portfolio. In five years, assuming a 16% rate, it will grow to be $210 million. But by accepting a 14% return, the target portfolio value after five years is only $192 million. In a 16% yield environment, this is attained by setting aside only $91.50 million for investment. This leaves a cushion of $8.50 million for active management.

Immunized portfolio strategies are quite popular in the industry. The article that follows from *Pension and Investments* (May 16, 1994) illustrates this. The top money managers and the assets under their management are also shown.

Strong Market Boosts Immunized Portfolios

By PAUL G. BARR

Despite a 25% jump in total assets of dedicated and immunized portfolios for managers in the Pensions & Investments *1994 directory of money managers, interest by pension executives continues to be minimal, managers say.*

Total assets among the top 25 dedicated and immunized managers rose 25.1% to $67.12 billion, from $53.66 billion in the previous year's survey.

Metropolitan Life Insurance Co., New York; Prudential Fixed Income Advisors, Short Hills, N.J.; and J.P. Morgan Investment Management, New York, held steady as the three largest managers, managing $13.4 billion, $10.4 billion, and $7 billion, respectively.

Pacific Investment Management Co., Newport Beach, Calif., had a huge increase in dedicated and immunized assets under management, climbing $2.6 billion to $3.1 billion. But James Muzzy, managing director, said PIMCO really doesn't seek that type of business.

The gains in 1993 were a single client in a special situation, he said.

Fidelity Investments, Boston, also showed a big jump, rising to $1.7 billion, from $222 million last year, when it did not rank on the Top 25 chart.

Source: *Pensions & Investments* (May 16, 1994) pp. 16, 96.

Managers among the Top 25 who were interviewed said most of the increase in assets probably resulted from the strong performing fixed-income market in 1993.

Any growth in assets would not have come through new clients, said John Werring, president, Prudential Fixed Income Advisors.

Although Prudential Fixed Income's managers are seeing some interest in strategies that attempt to match the durations of a plan sponsor's assets and liabilities, strictly dedicated and immunized portfolios are receiving very little interest, he said.

Likewise, Thomas Shively, chief investment officer of fixed income for State Street Research & Management Co., Boston, said that, if anything, sponsors are "unwinding" pure dedicated and immunized bond portfolios.

State Street Research ranked 10th this year, with $1.81 billion in dedicated/immunized assets under management.

As interest rates took their recent long trip downward, pension executives saw the asset side of their dedicated and immunized portfolios climb, managers said. Eventually, many sponsors sold off those portfolios to capture those gains.

1993's strong fixed-income market—the Salomon Broad Bond Index rose 9.9%— gave dedicated and immunized portfolios a strong enough boost that they probably rose about 20%, managers estimated.

Because dedicated and immunized portfolios generally have a duration that is longer than the market—to match the duration of a pension plan's liabilities—market movements for immunized portfolios usually are greater. (Duration is a widely used measure of the cash flows from a fixed-income investment).

But a decision last year by the Securities and Exchange Commission that could result in higher valuations of some plan sponsors' liabilities, could raise plan sponsor interest in matching fund assets to liabilities.

Pension executives have been undergoing a "steady learning process" regarding a plan's funding level, and relating their assets to liabilities, said Robert Whalen, managing director, CIGNA Investments, Inc., Hartford, Conn. The late 1993 decision by the SEC to enforce a market-based rate for valuing liabilities might have speeded that some, he said.

Mr. Werring of Prudential Fixed Income said that while strict immunized and dedicated portfolios are not getting much interest, a looser version—duration matching— is. In these portfolios, a manager would build a portfolio that is benchmarked against the duration of the liabilities of the plan sponsor, and try to add value trading against that duration.

There are some instances, though, where immunization strategies are being used in an indirect way among pension executives, managers say.

When a plan sponsor purchases an insurance annuity to cover its pension obligations, the insurance company selling the annuity uses immunized portfolios, State Street Research's Mr. Shively said. For instance, a sponsor shedding a major division may want to get that pension liability off of its books and will purchase an annuity to cover its obligation.

CIGNA offers such annuities, but the firm hasn't seen a lot of activity in that area either, Mr. Whalen said.

Firm	$ millions	Firm	$ millions	Firm	$ millions
1. Fidelity Investments	258,400	43. Massachusetts Financial	34,590	85. Brown Brothers Harriman	21,330
2. Bankers Trust	184,452	44. Mellon Capital	34,570	86. BlackRock Financial	20,860
3. Merrill Lynch Asset	159,900	45. Boatman's Trust	34,043	87. G.T. Capital	20,731
4. State Street Bank & Trust	157,854	46. Templeton Worldwide	34,032	88. Lazard Freres	20,673
5. Wells Fargo Nikko	150,711	47. First Nat'l Bank/ Chicago	34,000	89. CS First Boston	20,570
6. Metropolitan Life	128,200	48. UBS Asset New York	33,600	90. BEA	20,540
7. Alliance Capital	115,276	49. Morgan Stanley Asset	33,401	91. ANB Investment & Trust	20,098
8. J.P. Morgan	109,801	50. Lincoln Nat'l Investment	32,857	92. Fischer Francis Trees	19,741
9. Capital Research	103,363	51. Aetna Life Guaranteed	32,665	93. Society Asset	19,647
10. Scudder, Stevens & Clark	96,264	52. Loomis Sayles	32,325	94. Duff & Phelps	19,608
11. Putnam Investments	90,898	53. U.S. Trust/New York	32,153	95. IDS Advisory	18,746
12. Wellington Mgmt.	82,248	54. Banc One	30,363	96. Seligman Henderson	18,503
13. Vanguard Group	80,300	55. HSBC	30,234	97. Wachovia Investment	17,950
14. Northern Trust	77,125	56. Miller Anderson Sherrerd	30,026	98. Prudential Fixed Income	17,183
15. NBD Bank	75,733	57. National City	29,754	99. Bank of New York	16,745
16. Citibank Global	75,000	58. Neuberger & Berman	29,305	100. Lord Abbott	16,607
17. Dreyfus	74,272	59. Hartford Life	28,970	101. Fiduciary Trust	16,526
18. Kemper Financial	69,310	60. Oppenheimer Capital	28,834	102. Payden & Rygel	16,000
19. NationsBank	61,200	61. Stein Roe & Farnham	28,736	103. Bank of Boston	16,000
20. New York Life	60,567	62. Transamerica	28,223	104. Barrow, Hanley, Mewhinney	15,987
21. CIGNA Investments	59,005	63. Chancellor Capital	27,827	105. Rowe Price-Fleming Int'l	15,435
22. Massachusetts Mutual	58,770	64. Mellon Bond	27,604	106. Woodbridge Capital	15,400
23. John Hancock Financial	58,457	65. AMP	27,208	107. PanAgora Asset	15,175
24. Federated Investors	57,204	66. Lincoln Capital Mgmt.	26,321	108. Nationwide Insurance	15,116
25. PNC Investment Mgmt.	56,000	67. Wilmington Trust	25,784	109. Continental Asset	15,019
26. Prudential Asset	55,700	68. Fleet Investment Advisors	25,518	110. Baillie Gilford Overseas	14,982
27. INVESCO North America	53,450	69. Phoenix Home Life	25,137	111. Ark Asset Mgmt.	14,939
28. Pacific Investment	53,001	70. Fayez Sarofim	25,078	112. First Quadrant	14,682
29. TCW	48,553	71. Twentieth Century	24,938	113. Nikko Capital	14,527
30. Goldman Sachs Asset	47,990	72. Delaware Mgmt. Co.	24,500	114. Weiss, Peck & Greer	13,798
31. First Fidelity Bancorporation	47,916	73. RCM Capital	24,481	115. Independence Investment	13,720
32. Boston Co. Asset	44,420	74. Daiwa Int'l	23,888	116. SunBank Capital	13,700
33. T. Rowe Price	43,870	75. Great-West Life	23,557	117. Investment Advisors	13,480
34. Principal Financial Group	42,959	76. Jennison	23,102	118. Columbia Mgmt.	13,293
35. Travelers Insurance	41,300	77. Sanford C. Bernstein	22,998	119. Grantham Mayo v. Otterloo	13,129
36. Morgan Grenfell	41,174	78. First Union Nat'l Bank	22,800	120. Provident Investment	13,079
37. GE Investments	40,436	79. State Street Research	22,486	121. Smith Breeden	13,055
38. Mitchell Hutchins Asset	38,899	80. Standish, Ayer & Wood	22,253	122. Salomon Brothers	12,936
39. Equitable Real Estate	38,677	81. Aeltus Investment Mgmt.	21,875	123. Piper Capital	12,772
40. Bank of America	36,434	82. First Bank System Trust	21,547	124. Nicholas-Applegate	12,521
41. Capital Guardian Trust	35,454	83. Janus Capital	21,462	125. Firstar Investment	12,376
42. Brinson Partners	35,047	84. Norwest Investment	21,443	126. J&W Seligman	12,208

(Continued)

Firm	$ millions	Firm	$ millions	Firm	$ millions
127. McMorgan	12,120	166. JMB Institutional		211. WorldInvest	5,254
128. Dodge & Cox	11,648	Realty	7,692	212. AMR Investment	
129. Schroder Capital	11,623	167. Back Bay Advisors	7,624	Services	5,247
130. ASB Capital	11,586	168. Public Financial	7,610	213. T. Rowe Price Stable	5,205
131. Barings	11,449	169. General American Life	7,608	214. National Asset	5,202
132. Western Asset	11,204	170. Denver Investment		215. Qualivest Capital	5,119
133. Pacific Mutual Life	11,169	Advisors	7,525	216. Lehman Brothers	
134. Smith Barney Capital	11,037	171. Continental Bank	7,378	Global	5,113
135. Continental		172. Warburg, Pincus	7,000	217. Lynch & Mayer	5,109
Assurance	11,013	173. Fifth Third Bancorp	6,987	218. Harris Associates	5,076
136. Criterion Investment	10,854	174. Dunedin Fund		219. Clay Finlay	5,009
137. MacKay-Shields	10,631	Managers	6,939	220. Prudential Real Estate	4,934
138. Trusco Capital	10,500	175. Lombard Odier Int'l	6,804	221. Luther King Capital	4,924
139. Harris Investment	10,365	176. Van Kampen Merritt	6,700	222. Capital Growth Mgmt.	4,904
140. Allmerica Financial	10,300	177. Mutual of America	6,700	223. David L. Babson	4,831
141. CoreStates		178. Cursitor-Eaton Asset	6,675	224. Avatar Investors	4,821
Investment	10,280	179. Old Kent Financial	6,500	225. Value Line Asset	4,813
142. Smith, Barney,		180. Merus Capital	6,495	226. Meridian Investment	4,765
Shearson	9,963	181. Heitmen Advisory	6,421	227. Nicholas	4,757
143. Dimensional Fund		182. Batterymarch Financial	6,386	228. Sit Investment	4,744
Advisors	9,863	183. Martin Currie	6,314	229. NWQ Investment	4,713
144. Columbia Circle		184. Bear Stearns	6,310	230. Certus Financial	4,700
Investors	9,846	185. Mississippi Valley	6,300	231. Union Capital	4,652
145. Midlantic Nat'l Bank	9,800	186. Yarmouth Capital	6,250	232. LaSalle Street Capital	4,604
146. STW Fixed Income	9,681	187. Shawmut	6,226	233. Aldrich, Eastman	
147. Yamaichi Int'l	9,628	188. Voyageur Asset Mgmt.	6,220	& Wallch	4,580
148. First of America		189. Shields Asset	6,204	234. William R. Blair	4,559
Investment	9,446	190. Cooke & Bieler	6,200	235. Kemper Asset	4,505
149. Newbold's Asset	9,411	191. IDS Institutional	6,150	236. Corporate Property	4,500
150. Strong Asset	9,382	192. AON Advisors	6,088	237. Gabelli Asset	4,451
151. Wilshire Associates	9,339	193. OFFITBANK	6,078	238. BSS Asset	4,370
152. Mercantile-Safe		194. Eagle Asset	6,050	239. Sirach Capital	4,368
Deposit	9,313	195. Mellon Equity	5,983	240. Brundage, Story	
153. Invista Capital	9,156	196. Balcor	5,837	& Rose	4,362
154. Copley Real Estate	9,001	197. Morley Capital	5,773	241. Protective Life	
155. Portfolio Group	8,935	198. Hotchkis & Wiley	5,715	Insurance	4,315
156. Provident Life		199. United of Omaha	5,704	242. Commerce Bank	4,297
& Accident	8,783	200. M&I	5,666	243. Wright Investors	
157. UMB Financial		201. Sears Investment	5,661	Service	4,214
Advisors	8,693	202. American United Life	5,478	244. Manning & Napier	4,200
158. MIMLIC Asset	8,678	203. Lowe, Brockenbrough	5,456	245. Atlantic Portfolio	
159. First Interstate/Calif.	8,421	204. Franidin Portfolio	5,422	Analytics	4,147
160. Barnett Banks Trust	8,255	205. Global Advisors	5,416	246. Concert Capital	4,135
161. Integra Trust	8,188	206. RREEF Funds	5,409	247. Public Storage	4,000
162. Capitoline Investment	8,149	207. Oechsle Int'l	5,377	248. Advanced Investment	3,872
163. Glenmede Trust	8,044	208. Washington Square	5,358	249. Commerz Int'l	3,858
164. Munder Capital	8,000	209. Nomura Capital	5,304	250. United Capital	3,801
165. LaSalle Advisors	7,800	210. Chicago Title & Trust	5,288	**Total**	**5,938,130**

INDEXATION

Another portfolio management policy that is extensively used in the industry is the indexation policy. Under this policy, fixed-income portfolio managers will attempt to replicate or outperform the return experience of a chosen index over a prespecified period in future.

In some ways, it is natural to link the performance of the manager of a fixed-income portfolio to the performance of an otherwise identical fixed-income portfolio. If, during a given performance period, the Treasury index with a duration of five years produced a return of, say 5%, then it is reasonable to expect a manager of a fixed-income portfolio with a similar duration to do as well, if not better. The performance evaluation becomes simpler in indexation policies. In addition, by defining a benchmark index to serve as a reference point, the money manager is forced to operate within a broad set of acceptable parameters. For example, if the index used is drawn from domestic Treasuries and investment-grade corporates, then the portfolio manager is expected to operate within these two sectors of the fixed-income markets.

Indexation policy requires the following.

- The choice of a specific index to be used as the performance benchmark.
- The performance period over which the portfolio manager will be managing the indexed portfolio.
- The flexibility level that is acceptable to the money manager and to the investors. This may cover the frequency of transactions, derivatives transactions, repo transactions, security lending, etc.

Indexation Method

Let us define R_I as the index return. We will consider a simple fixed-income portfolio consisting of bullet securities only. Assume that the portfolio consists of N securities. Let R_j be the return on security j. Let x_j be the fraction of security j in the fixed-income portfolio. Note that $\sum_{j=1}^{N} x_j = 1$. Then the portfolio return may be stated as

$$R_p = x_1 R_1 + x_2 R_2 + \cdots + \cdots + x_N R_N. \tag{11.10}$$

Note that all the returns over a future time period are random. Therefore, we have to work with expected returns and the variability of expected returns. Taking expectations from Equation (11.10), we get

$$E[R_p] = x_1 E[R_1] + x_2 E[R_2] + \cdots + \cdots + x_N E[R_N]. \tag{11.11}$$

In an indexation problem, it is the difference between the expected return of the indexed portfolio and that of the index that matters. Therefore, we define $\mu_I = E[R_I]$ and $\pi = R_p - R_I$ as the excess return of the portfolio over the index. Then, we may compute the difference in the expected return as follows. Let $\mu_p = E[\pi]$ and $\mu_j = E[R_j] - E[R_I] \; \forall \; j$. Then,

$$\mu_p = [\mu_p - \mu_I] = x_1 \mu_1 + x_2 \mu_2 + \cdots + \cdots + x_N \mu_N \tag{11.12}$$

In a similar way, we can compute the variance. Let us define

$$\sigma_j^2 = \text{Var}\{R_j - R_I\}$$

and

$$\sigma_{jk} = \text{Cov}\{R_j - R_I, R_k - R_I\}.$$

Then

$$\sigma_p^2 = \text{Var}\{R_p - R_I\} = \text{Var}\left\{\sum_{j=1}^{N} x_j(R_j - R_I)\right\}.$$

It is easy to verify that

$$\sigma_p^2 = \sum_{j=1}^{N} x_j^2 \sigma_j^2 + 2\sum_{j=1}^{N} \sum_{k=1,\,k>j}^{N} x_j x_k \sigma_{jk} \qquad (11.13)$$

Formally, the indexation problem may be stated as a quadratic programming problem in which the variance of the tracing error is minimized subject to the constraints that are normally imposed on security holdings. Formally this is:

$$\min_{x_1, x_2, \cdots, x_N} \sigma_p^2 = \sum_{j=1}^{N} x_j^2 \sigma_j^2 + 2\sum_{j=1}^{N} \sum_{k=1,\,k>j}^{N} x_j x_k \sigma_{jk}$$

subject to the constraints

$$\sum_{j=1}^{N} x_j = 1$$

and

$$x_j \geq 0, \quad \forall\, j = 1, 2, \cdots, N.$$

Index funds are offered as strategies to money that is placed by institutions in defined benefits and defined contribution plans. The article from *Institutional Investor* (September 1994) that follows shows Wells Fargo alone accounted for over $20 billion in assets in the defined contribution plans. A significant part of that was under indexation.

Wells Fargo's Quantum Leap

The bank's special-purpose trust company aims to make structured products a force in 401(k)s.

By JULIE ROHRER

In the 1970s Wells Fargo Bank's money management subsidiary pioneered practical applications of modern portfolio theory to defined-benefit plans, virtually revolutionizing the pension industry. Now Wells is poised to launch a trust company dedicated to defined-contribution plans that could have considerable impact on the 401(k) business.

Currently awaiting final regulatory approval, Wells Fargo Defined Contribution Trust Co. is a joint venture between the bank's 401k Masterworks recordkeeping and administrative services operation and its Wells Fargo Nikko Investment Advisors money management arm, which offers a broad range of structured investment products. By combining the administrative and money management functions in one unit, the new company should bring even greater focus to Wells's rapidly growing defined-contribution effort. Having added close to $4 billion in 401(k) assets to its $15 billion in defined-contribution assets under management in 1993, Wells ranked fifth among the top 401(k) dollar gainers in this magazine's annual Pension Olympics (Institutional Investor, May 1994).

Wells Fargo Nikko is today the largest manager of quant products. Nobody offers more index funds—100-plus varieties (eight in the U.S. equity markets alone)—or tactical-asset-allocation strategies. Wells's latest version of the latter features five diversified Stagecoach LifePath funds that are geared to particular 401(k) participants' planned retirement dates. Index funds and tactical-asset-allocation strategies total some $136 billion of the bank's $165 billion in tax-exempt assets.

What's good for defined-benefit plans, reason Wells officials, should be good for 401(k) participants. Says Donald Luskin, Wells Fargo Nikko managing director: "The defined-contribution market is in some ways like the defined-benefit market of the 1970s. It's searching for its identity and professionalism."

What do 401(k) plan participants need? "Fundamental building blocks of investing, with enough markets represented to provide legitimate asset allocation choices—index funds are quite natural to do that," contends Wells Fargo Nikko chief executive officer Frederick Grauer. Take that a step further to encompass plan participants who don't feel comfortable determining their own investment mix and you have tactical-asset-allocation strategies popping up as a logical solution.

Washington apparently agrees with this assessment. The Federal Retirement Thrift Investment Board, formed by the Federal Employers Retirement System Act of 1987, requires that the equity assets of its savings plan be invested in "a portfolio designed to replicate the performance of a commonly recognized index." Since 1988 $7 billion of the plan's $22 billion in assets have been managed in a Wells equity index fund that tracks the Standard & Poor's 500 and in a commingled U.S. debt index fund that tracks the Lehman Brothers Aggregate Bond index. The remainder is in short-term Treasuries issued to the plan.

In the private sector Koch Industries' 401(k) plan has invested all of its $225 million in assets in Wells Fargo funds. They include an S&P 500 index fund, a money market fund, an S&P 400 index fund, a structured guaranteed-investment-contract bond fund and a tactical-asset-allocation strategy. Koch's manager of foundations and investments, Janice Dollman, says the company wanted conservative options for its 401(k), since the plan is a supplement to a defined-benefit fund.

Wells's crucial commitment to the 401(k) market came in 1988 when it began building its own systems to develop an integrated full-service recordkeeping and administrative capability to complement its investment products. Launched in 1989, 401k MasterWorks today provides 140 companies representing plan assets of more than $4 billion (and 175,000 participants) with recordkeeping and trustee services, employee-benefits consulting, employee communications and education services as well as investment *management and investment funds. MasterWorks has yet to lose a client for service reasons, asserts Alan Kizor, the Wells executive vice president who's in charge of the unit.*

Ironically, Wells hadn't been a major defined-benefit recordkeeper, having abandoned the master-trust business in 1984. That was a blessing in disguise, says Kizor: Instead of straining to adapt master-trust systems to 401(k) reporting, Wells based the MasterWorks system on the bank's IRA accounts; that tracking process proved to be ideally adaptable to the needs of individual 401(k) participants. In the mid-1980s, before daily valuation became a buzzword in the industry, Wells was the largest IRA bank in the country, with thousands of "little trust [IRA] accounts" invested in pooled funds managed by Wells Fargo Nikko. "We had to build proprietary systems to enable individuals to move their IRA money on a daily basis from one fund to another," notes Kizor.

MasterWorks' target market is larger plans of at least 500 participants. Wisely, it has not restricted its business to sponsors that also use Wells Fargo Nikko investment funds; this flexibility has helped to add several clients to its roster. Nevertheless, confides Kizor, "we have yet to take on a single situation where the plan sponsor doesn't use at least one [Wells Fargo Nikko] fund."

From day one MasterWorks permitted plan participants to access their accounts 24 hours a day through an automated voice-response system or to talk to a human being by phone from 6:00 a.m. to 6:00 p.m., Pacific time. About 97 percent of calls to reps get answered within 30 seconds, says Kizor. What's more, participants can conduct business in any one of seven languages: English, Spanish, Taiwanese, Cantonese, Russian, French or Hebrew.

Today daily valuation is almost a given for 401(k) service providers, but, as Koch's Dollman testifies, MasterWorks "actually does daily. We have 18 [distinct] payrolls a month." Wells's system accounts for each payroll the day it is made, so plan deductions or contributions are also recorded on the day they're made. That's a flexibility not all providers could offer, Dollman points out. Says Wells's Kizor, "I'd had no idea there were so many definitions of the word 'pay.'"

MasterWorks guarantees that quarterly statements will be back within ten days of the end of a quarter. Otherwise, says Kizor, "we refund your previous quarter's recordkeeping fees." Loans are expedited practically instantaneously. Dollman observes that a loan requested by a participant in Koch's 401(k) was in the person's hands in four working days.

Many 401(k) plan sponsors, of course, are committed to active management. Fidelity Investments is not exactly quaking in its boots yet. What's more, major players have their own line of quant products to offer 401(k) participants, particularly a wide range of tactical-asset-allocation funds. These are already popular among plan sponsors because they take a key decision-making process out of the unsure hands of plan participants.

But if index funds and other structured products invade the defined-contribution market to the extent that they have the defined-benefit market, Wells should have little to complain about. "This is an important business for Wells Fargo," emphasizes vice chairman Clyde Ostler.

The bank's brand recognition can't hurt its marketing pitch either. A recent publication, "World's Greatest Brands: A Review by Interbrand," (published by John Wiley

& Sons), evaluates the world's top-selling brands on a number of criteria. Fidelity Investments and Vanguard Group are nowhere to be found among the top 100 names. Only one bank—Wells Fargo—makes the list.

PORTFOLIO INSURANCE

Portfolio insurance is a dynamic portfolio-management policy in which a floor level is established below which the pension assets will not fall. The strategy provides for some upside potential as well. This strategy is best illustrated in the context of pension funds asset allocation.

The valuation of pension obligations is a nontrivial issue in defined-benefits (DB) plans. The accumulated pension obligation (ABO), a measure used in the industry, provides a lower bound and is the dollar amount that the company will be expected to pay if the plan is terminated immediately. The projected benefits obligation (PBO) takes into account the growth rate of wages for current employees and is therefore greater than the ABO. These measures are, in turn, used to determine whether a plan is underfunded or overfunded. Most pension portfolios are managed by professional money managers. The sponsor of the pension plan is interested in managing the portfolio in order to meet the promised pension obligations (ABOs or PBOs) at any time. The requirement that the assets in the pension plan must always be above the ABO or PBO is illustrated in Figure 11-1. Notice that in the figure the pension assets, for the most part, have been above pension liabilities.

FIGURE 11-1

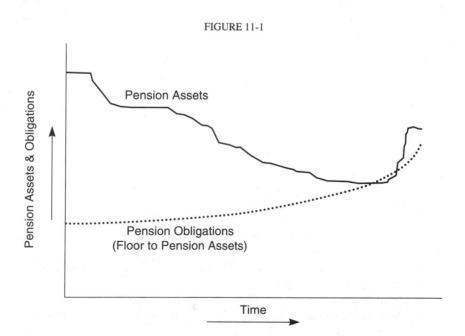

If the penalty for not meeting the liabilities is infinite, then the following portfolio allocation policy is optimal:

- At each point take the surplus of the pension assets over the liability. This surplus can be invested in a mean-variance efficient portfolio without regard for the liabilities of the pension plan.
- The remaining assets will be invested to precisely replicate the liabilities of the pension plan. If the pension liabilities are known with certainty (an unlikely situation), then the remaining assets can be placed in a dedicated portfolio. If, on the other hand, the pension liabilities are correlated with future wages (as is likely to be the case in most defined-benefits plans), then these assets will be placed in a portfolio of equity and fixed-income sectors that is maximally correlated with pension liabilities.

In the fixed-income sector, portfolio insurance strategies are more difficult to implement. The reason for this is the lack of a liquid futures contract on a basket of fixed-income securities. This is not a problem in most equity markets; stock-index futures contracts are traded extensively around the world and are fairly liquid. The development of futures contracts in many benchmark maturities in the Treasury sector and the liquidity in options on futures contracts have made the implementation of portfolio insurance strategies in the fixed-income sector (especially in the Treasury market) less difficult. Currently futures contracts are available on two-year, five-year, ten-year and thirty-year benchmark maturities. In addition, options are traded on ten-year T-note futures as well as on T-bond futures contracts. The lack of comparable futures and options in corporate and mortgage-backed securities areas means that only cross-hedging is possible for these sectors.

How can these contracts be used to implement a synthetic portfolio insurance policy on a diversified fixed-income portfolio? The following steps could lead to a reasonable portfolio insurance policy.

1. The portfolio's risk properties should first be summarized. Summary measures that are typically used include the duration, PVBP, and convexity.
2. The horizon over which the portfolio insurance is in effect must be specified along with the level of protection that is needed.
3. A portfolio of futures contracts should be chosen from each benchmark maturities such that
    (a) the price changes in the futures portfolio are highly correlated with the price changes in the underlying fixed-income portfolio, and
    (b) the risk properties of the fixed-income portfolio are closely matched by the risk properties of the futures portfolio.
    The presence of delivery options in futures contracts makes this a particularly difficult task. (This part of the portfolio insurance is much simpler in equity markets, where stock-index futures contracts tend to be settled in cash.)
4. A strike price of the synthetic put option should be chosen that is consistent with the level of protection that is needed.
5. The replicating portfolio of the synthetic put option on the fixed-income portfolio should then be implemented by trading in the portfolio of futures contracts. This

will require the use of options-pricing models to compute the delta of the synthetic put at each instant in order to implement the futures trades. Steps 4 and 5 should be implemented using the techniques developed in Chapter 7.

CONCLUSION

In this chapter we have developed various portfolio management techniques that are widely used in the fixed-income area. The concepts of dedicated portfolio construction and immunized portfolios were developed in detail. In addition, concepts such as horizon matching, contingent immunization and portfolio insurance were also described. Bond indexes are used to gauge and direct the performances of portfolios. Such strategies known as indexation strategies were also presented in this chapter.

PROBLEMS

11.1 What are GICs? Describe the institutions that are likely to be attracted to GICs.

11.2 When would a dedicated-portfolio strategy be preferred to alternatives such as immunization or indexation? Why?

11.3 A new city municipality is funding a capital project which requires an outlay of $4 million per year for the next five years and an estimated $5 million per year thereafter for another five years. The projections for the next five years are firm, but there is some uncertainty about the projections beyond that. Describe the funding strategies that the city can use. Assume that it can raise capital by issuing general obligations bonds.

11.4 Portfolio insurance provides downside protection as well as upside potential. Explain why, despite these advantages, some investors pursue other strategies such as indexation or immunization.

REFERENCES

Barr, P. G. 1994. "Strong Market Boosts Immunized Portfolios." *Pensions & Investments* (May 16):16, 96.

Bierwag, G., and G. Kaufman 1977. "Coping with the Risk of Interest Rate Fluctuations: A Note." *Journal of Business* 50:364–370.

Bierwag, G. 1977. "Immunization, Duration and the Term Structure of Interest Rates." *Journal of Financial and Quantitative Analysis* 12:725–743.

Fisher, L., and R. Weil 1971. "Coping with the Risk of Interest Rate Fluctuations: Returns to Bondholders from Naive and Optimal Strategies." *Journal of Business* 44:408–431.

Fong, G., and V. Oldrich 1984. "A Risk Minimizing Strategy for Multiple Liability Immunization." *Journal of Finance* 39(5):1541–1546.

Garbade, K. 1985. "Dedicated Bond Portfolios: Construction, Rebalancing, and Swapping." *Topics in Money and Securities Markets*. New York: Bankers Trust Company.

Granito, M. 1987. "The Problem with Bond Index Funds." *Journal of Portfolio Management* 13(4):41–48.

Hiller, R., and C. Schaack 1990. "A Classification of Structured Bond Portfolio Modelling Techniques." *Journal of Portfolio Management* 37–48.

Ingersoll, J. E. 1983. "Is Immunization Feasible? Evidence from CRSP Data." In *Innovations in Bond Portfolio Management: Duration Analysis and Immunization,* G. Kaufman, G. Bierwag, and A. Toevs, eds. JAI Press.

Liebowitz, M. 1987. Matched-Funding Techniques: The Dedicated Bond Portfolio in Pension Funds. Salomon Brothers Inc., Mortgage Research. New York.

Mossaver-Rahamani, S. 1987. "Customizing Benchmarks in Structured Management." *Journal of Portfolio Management* 13(4):65–68.

Rohrer, J. 1994. "Wells Fargo's Quantum Leap." *Institutional Investor* (Sept.):195–196.

Seix, C., and R. Akhoury 1986. "Bond Indexation: The Optimal Quantitative Approach." *Journal of Portfolio Management* 12(3):50–53.

Zirky, E. A., and R. M. Mackey 1993. "Pension Plan Funding Strategies: Defining Terms." *Pension World* (Aug.):40–41.

Part II

Fixed-Income Derivatives

Chapter 12

An Overview of Derivatives Markets

Chapter Objectives

This chapter provides an overview of listed and dealer derivative markets. In addition, specific situations are presented illustrating how such derivatives can be used in practical applications. The following questions are addressed in this chapter.

- What are the differences between listed and OTC derivatives?
- What is the distribution of credit risk in the derivatives market?
- What are Asian options and how are they used in practice?
- What are options on swaps and how can they be used?

INTRODUCTION

During the last twenty-five years, derivative markets have developed in a number of areas of capital markets. Today, managers can trade in derivative products that are customized to manage specific exposures in interest rates, currencies, commodities, and equity markets. Derivative markets reflect varying levels of complexity and customization. At one extreme, there are derivative markets such as the equity stock options listed on the Chicago Board of Options Exchange (CBOE), which are fairly simple and standardized derivative contracts backed by Options Clearing Corporation (OCC) to ensure contract integrity. At the other extreme, dealer derivative contracts, such as interest-rate swaps and OTC options to enter into interest-rate swaps, are also available. Such derivative contracts are highly customized and are backed by the capital allocated by the dealers. Clearly the credit reputation of the dealer is a critical component in ensuring product integrity.

In this chapter, we will provide an overview of derivatives markets in general and of the fixed-income derivatives markets in particular. The purpose of this overview is to get a perspective on the rich variety of derivative markets that are available to the corporate and investment community and how such markets offer improved risk-management capabilities. Our focus will be largely on the derivative markets applied to the financial sector. We shall, however, explore some commodity-related derivatives such as commodity swaps and commodity-linked bonds.

There are two categories of derivative markets, listed derivatives markets and dealer derivative markets. This classification helps in understanding the distinct roles played by these markets and how one complements the other.

LISTED DERIVATIVES MARKETS

Since the advent of futures trading on financial instruments (such as interest rates, stock indices, and foreign currencies) in the early 1970s on the Chicago Board of Trade (CBOT) and the Chicago Mercantile Exchange (CME), listed derivatives have registered an impressive growth in the volume of trading and the breadth of coverage of underlying markets. To get an appreciation of the range of these markets and their size, we first provide some of the largest international exchanges and their average daily trading volume.

As Table 12-1 illustrates, the international exchanges outside the U.S. have begun to challenge the dominance of the U.S. exchanges. The global participation through common clearing arrangements and electronic screen-based trading arrangements such as GLOBEX has significantly enhanced the link between international institutional investors. Although the exchanges in Chicago (CBOT and CME) have maintained their leadership, foreign exchanges, notably LIFFE and MATIF, have made significant strides in recent years.

Exchange	Trading Volume	
Chicago Board of Trade	551,136	
Chicago Mercantile Exchange	427,386	
New York Mercantile Exchange	161,212	
London International Financial Futures Exchange (LIFFE)	150,718	
Marche a Terme International de France (MATIF)	149,718	
Tokyo Stock Exchange (TSE)	66,963	
London Metal Exchange	66,164	
Tokyo International Financial Futures Exchange	61,348	

TABLE 12-1
Large Global Exchanges

Source: Futures Industry Association

In addition, as seen from Table 12-2, it is clear that the most actively traded contracts in the world are truly drawn from all over the globe. For example, the interest-rate futures contracts from around the world clearly dominate the top 10 contracts, as evidenced by the presence of T-bonds, Eurodollars, French government bonds, Bunds, and JGBs.

This is also true for the derivative markets. Note that a number of exchanges, such as LIFFE, MATIF, OSE, and TIFFEE, have become important centers for trading listed derivatives.

Contract	Exchange	Trading Volume
T-bond futures	CBOT	268,330
Eurodollar futures	CME	147,210
NIKKEI 225 futures	OSE	87,980
T-bond futures options	CBOT	86,662
French government bonds	MATIF	84,690
Crude oil	NYMEX	83,027
Euroyen	TIFFE	59,375
JGB futures	TSE	52,124
S & P 500 futures	CME	48,776
NIKKEI 225 options	OSE	48,112
DM futures	CME	43,196
Bund futures	LIFFE	39,500

TABLE 12-2
Most Actively Traded Contracts

Source: Futures Industry Association

Some Listed Derivatives

We now turn to the major exchanges that list derivative products and to the most actively traded products in those exchanges. CBOT and CME, still the premier exchanges, have several actively traded contracts, which we list in Tables 12-3 and 12-4.

The listed derivative markets above span a number of underlying asset markets. In particular, they cover interest rates (long- and short-term), equities, foreign currencies, and commodities. In addition to the products that are listed in Tables 12-3 and 12-4, many options contracts are now traded on broad-based stock indexes. These stock indexes may be relatively broad ones such as the S&P 500 index or the S&P 100 index, or may be more specialized such as the Major Market index (MMI) or National OTC index or NASDAQ index.

Tables 12-5 and 12-6 list some of the major listed derivative contracts. Note that the most popular contracts are on stock indexes. This is not surprising given that most equity assets are managed in diversified portfolios. Such portfolios tend to have a high correlation with broad and narrow stock market indexes. Thus options and futures on such indexes are of value to portfolio managers, who manage diversified (indexed) portfolios or portfolios that reflect specific industry groups. Most listed contracts are standardized: They come with specified maturities and strike prices.

Underlying Asset	Futures	Options
T-bonds	Yes	Yes
T-notes (ten-year)	Yes	Yes
T-notes (five-year)	Yes	Yes
Thirty-day rates	Yes	NA
Zeroes	Yes	Yes
Muni bond index	Yes	Yes
Major Market index	Yes	Yes
MBS	Yes	Yes
Swaps	Yes	Yes

TABLE 12-3
Financial Derivatives at CBOT

Underlying Asset	Futures	Options
T-bills (ninety-day)	Yes	Yes
Eurodollar (ninety-day)	Yes	Yes
LIBOR (thirty-day)	Yes	Yes
S&P 500	Yes	Yes
S&P MidCap 400	Yes	Yes
Nikkei 225	Yes	Yes
All Major foreign exchange	Yes	Yes
Cross foreign exchange	Yes	Yes

TABLE 12-4
Financial Derivatives at CME

TABLE 12-5   *Listed Derivatives*

Contract Option	Features or Underlying Indexes
Stock Index	Major Market index (XMI)
	European options at AMEX
	Institutional index (XII)
	European options at AMEX
	Japan index (JPN)
	European options at AMEX
	S&P 100 index (OEX)
	American options at CBOE
	S&P 500 index (SPX)
	European options at CBOE
S&P 100 reduced-value long-term options (LEAPS)	American options at CBOE
S&P 500 reduced-value long-term options (LEAPS)	European options at CBOE
Common stock LEAPS	CBOE has been trading these options since 1973. Long-term options traded at CBOE for selected stocks.
Capped options on stock indexes	CBOE trades these options. OEX and SPX capped options will be automatically exercised at certain triggers. For calls, the exercise will occur when the cap price is less than or equal to the closing index value.

TABLE 12-6
Listed International Derivatives

Contract Options	Features
Nikkei index warrants	AMEX. Cash-settled. Obligations of issuers.
TOPIX index options	CBOE. Settled in Japanese currency
FT-SE 100 index warrants	AMEX, CBOE, NYSE
CAC-40 index warrants	AMEX, CBOE, NYSE
DAX index warrants	AMEX, CBOE, NYSE

DEALER DERIVATIVES MARKETS

Table 12-7 compares listed derivatives and dealer derivatives. By and large, dealer derivatives are less liquid, more customized and are subject to extensive credit screening by the counterparties involved in the derivatives transactions.

TABLE 12-7   *Listed Derivatives versus Dealer Derivatives*

Dimension of the Contract	*Listed Derivatives*	*Dealer Derivatives*
Liquidity	Typically excellent for nearby contracts. Domestic contracts have greater liquidity.	Typically not as liquid as listed contracts but can be good in certain markets.
Size	Fixed by exchange rules.	Can be customized.
Credit risk	Clearing house guarantees.	Dealer capital coupled with credit enhancements.
Contractual provisions (maturities, exercise, etc.)	Standardized	Customized

An idea of the growth of derivatives in the dealer market can be gained by reviewing Table 12-8. Note that the dominant part of the dealer derivatives market is in interest rates or the fixed-income area. Interest-rate options, swaps, forward-rate agreements, caps, floors, and collars are used extensively by institutional investors for coping with interest-rate risk. In addition to the fact that interest-rate derivatives are the biggest segment of the dealer derivatives market, it also had the biggest growth during the period 1989–1992, a growth rate of 153% during this period. Foreign exchange is the second segment in terms of size and growth rate, while equities and commodities form a distant third.

Table 12-9 lists the dealer derivatives by product. The forwards sector is the biggest segment of the market. The forwards category includes forward-rate agreements (FRAs) and foreign exchange (FX) forward transactions. When the FX forwards are excluded as in Table 12-9, swaps become the largest segment of the derivative markets. The fact that nearly $17 trillion of dealer derivatives were outstanding in 1992 bears attention. Clearly, this market has become an integral component of the capital markets.

TABLE 12-8   *Notional Value of OTC Derivatives by Risk, 1989–1992 (in billions of U.S. dollars)*

Underlying Risk	*1989*	*1990*	*1991*	*1992*	*Growth Rate*
Interest rates	4,311	6,087	8,404	10,923	153
Exchange rates	2,779	3,927	5,415	6,475	133
Equity and commodities	108	158	209	245	127
Total	7,198	10,172	14,028	17,643	145

Source: U.S. General Accounting Office (1994)

TABLE 12-9   *Notional Value of OTC Derivatives by Product, 1989–1992*
(in billions of U.S. dollars)

Product	1989	1990	1991	1992	Growth Rate
Forwards	3,034	4,437	6,061	7,515	148
Futures	1,259	1,540	2,254	3,154	151
Options	953	1,305	1,841	2,263	137
Swaps	1,952	2,890	3,872	4,711	145
Total	7,198	10,172	14,028	17,643	145

Source: U.S. General Accounting Office (1994)

Recall that the integrity of the dealer market depends greatly on the credit reputation of the dealers. Table 12-10 provides a distribution of the credit reputation of swap dealers, showing that the swap market is dominated by highly reputable swap dealers who enjoy a high credit rating from Moody's and Standard and Poor. This underscores the importance of excellent credit standing in the derivative markets.

Some Dealer Derivatives

Dealer derivatives vary widely with respect to underlying asset, maturity, style, and contingency provisions. But to illustrate their versatile nature, Tables 12-11 and 12-12 list examples of some of the varied dealer derivative products (drawn from industry publications).

TABLE 12-10   *Credit Reputation of Swap Dealers*

Credit Reputation	Number of Firms	Notional Amount Outstanding	Percent
AAA or Aaa	21	535	9.70%
AA or Aa	34	1,747	31.70%
A	78	2,023	36.70%
A or better	133	4,305	78.20%
BBB or Baa	38	1,066	19.40%
Total investment-grade	171	5,371	97.50%
Speculative	15	30	0.60%
Unrated	14	106	1.90%
Total noninvestment-grade	29	136	2.50%

Source: U.S. General Accounting Office (1994)

TABLE 12-11 *Dealer Derivatives, Options*

Contract or Product	Features
Asian options	Arithmetic average of prices or arithmetic average of strike prices. Value of Asian options depend on the path of the underlying asset price until exercise.
Forward-start options	A standard (call) option is granted at a future date with prespecified strike price and maturity (executive stock options).
Chooser options	The buyer decides after a specified time whether the option is a call or a put.
Barrier options	The option's payoffs depend on whether during its life the underlying asset reached a prespecified value (down-and-out options).
Lookback options	The buyer can look back during the life of the option to select the strike price or the best underlying asset price.

TABLE 12-12 *Dealer Derivatives, Hybrids*

Contract or Product	Features
Bonds with equity kickers	These bonds are issued to provide an upside potential to investors (convertible bonds, warrants, and unit packages of stocks and bonds).
Warrants	Issuing firm sells warrants that the investor may use to buy from the issuer a prespecified number of shares of common stock at specified prices. Life ranges from 2 years to 10 or more years. Although typically issued with bonds, warrants are detachable. OTC dealers make a secondary market.
Index-linked debt	
S&P index notes	These notes pay a fixed interest rate, but their principal is linked to S&P 500 index.
Liquid-yield option notes (LYONs)	Zero coupon notes where the principal is tied to NYSE composite index. Subject to a minimum.
Bonds with imbedded options	
Put bonds	The buyer may put the bond back to the issuer at par at designated times.
Callable bonds and MBS	These bonds may be called by the issuer depending on the state of the economy (interest rates, seasonality, etc.).

MOTIVATIONS FOR DERIVATIVES

In this section, we provide several illustrative examples of the importance of derivatives in the risk-management strategies of corporations.

Asian Options on CP

The first illustration deals with Asian Options on London Interbank offered rates (LIBOR). Consider a AAA-rated corporation that routinely issues commercial paper (CP) every 90 days. Such issues may be made to fund working capital needs and short-term liquidity demands. Given the business operations of the firm, it may be necessary for the firm to schedule periodic issuance over the planning period. As of January 30, 1994, the treasurer of this corporation knows that the firm will be actively in the CP market. To simplify matters, let us assume that, each time, the firm issues a thirty-day CP. The current rate for the firm in the CP market is 30 days LIBOR minus 10 basis points. Let us further assume that the firm's credit standing is not going to change in a qualitative way over the next six months, so that the spread relative to 30 days LIBOR may be assumed to be 10 basis points for the planning period. Under these circumstances, it is clear that the risk faced by the firm is the possibility that 30 days LIBOR may go up over the next six months. The exposure to the possibility of increased rates on the respective issuance dates poses the risk of increased cost of capital.

One strategy is to hedge each issue. This can be done by using Eurodollar futures contracts or options on Eurodollar futures contracts. (Think through how you would use these markets). But as pointed out earlier, these contracts are standardized and may not suit the issue dates that the treasurer has to deal with. Furthermore, liquidity is currently only significant for contracts whose underlying asset is 90 days LIBOR. If a six-month view is taken by the treasurer, then it may make sense to consider buying a call option on the average of the 30 days LIBOR on the issuance dates. The payoff of such an option may be represented as

$$c = \max\left(0, \{w_1 l_1 + w_2 l_2 + w_3 l_3 + w_4 l_4 + w_5 l_5 + w_6 l_6 - k\}\right) \qquad (12.1)$$

where w_i represents the weight attached to the LIBOR on issue date i, and l_i is the LIBOR on that issue date. Using the values given in Table 12-13, l_i can be easily calculated. For example,

$$l_1 = \frac{100}{1000} = 0.10.$$

Issue Date	Amount (in millions of dollars)	LIBOR on Issue Date
2/15/1994	100	l_1
3/15/1994	200	l_2
4/15/1994	200	l_3
5/15/1994	100	l_4
6/15/1994	200	l_5
7/15/1994	200	l_6

TABLE 12-13
Commercial Paper Issue Schedule, January 30, 1994

Naturally, $\sum_{i=1}^{6} w_i = 1$. Let us think of the strike rate k of the option as the current 30 days LIBOR. Furthermore, let us assume that the option expires on the last issue date and is on a notional principal of the aggregate amount of $1,000 million.

This option gives the issuing corporation several choices.

If the weighted-average rate turns out (ex-post) to be, say, 3.5% (annualized) and the strike rate is 3% (annualized), the option pays 50 basis points on the notional principal as shown next:

$$\frac{50}{100} \times \frac{1}{100} \times \frac{30}{360} \times 1,000,000,000 = \$416,666.67. \qquad (12.2)$$

If the option is American-style, it can be exercised on any issue date with the provision that the payoff at exercise will be the difference between the weighted-average of the LIBOR until the exercise date and the strike rate. If the LIBOR goes up for the period until the first three issue dates and then starts to decline, the issuer may exercise early.

The Asian option is extremely valuable as a strategy. Although this example considered an issuer of short-term paper, the strategy is similar in other markets.

Options on Foreign-Exchange Swaps

The second application deals with the use of a derivative known as options on swaps. Options on a swap are referred to as **swaptions** and represent the right to enter into a swap on or before a specified date at currently determined terms. Such options may be either European- or American-style. If the buyer of the swaption has the right to pay a fixed rate in the swap (upon exercise), it is called a **payer's swaption.** If the buyer of the swaption has the right to receive a fixed rate, it is called a **receiver's swaption.** Note that such options may be structured with fixed and floating legs in different currencies. Options on foreign-currency swaps are defined in a similar way.

Consider a U.S. firm that has bid for a government project to build a plant or a highway in a foreign country. This creates a capital-budgeting problem. If the bid is successful, the bidder will be awarded the project. Winning the project will result in a future stream of cash flows denominated in the foreign currency. If the bid fails, nothing happens.

In such a situation, the firm faces a contingent foreign-currency exposure. This rules out the strategy of selling the future foreign currency receipts forward. Buying a swaption, in which the firm has the right to pay the foreign currency and receive the domestic currency, makes a lot of sense. The firm can use the anticipated foreign currency receipts to fund the swap liability and receive the U.S. dollars receipts at currently agreed-upon terms. We expect that this option will only be exercised if the firm wins the bid. Of course, even if the firm loses the bid, the swaption can be exercised as long as it finishes in-the-money.

Quantos—Foreign Equity Investment without Foreign-Exchange Risk

U.S. investors buying (say) German stocks are exposed to two sources of risk, equity risk in the German market and foreign-currency risk due to shifts in the deutsche mark/

dollar relationship. Consider a forward contract that allows U.S. investors to buy German stocks. The future payoffs of these contracts will be translated into U.S. dollars at currently determined exchange rates. Such forward contracts are known as guaranteed exchange-rate contracts or **Quantos.**

Let S be the current German stock price in deutsche marks, X be the predetermined exchange rate of dollars and deutsche marks, K be the forward price in deutsche marks at which the investor can buy the stock, and S^* be the stock price when the forward contract matures at date t. Then, the payoff of the Quanto is

$$f = X \times (S^* - K). \tag{12.3}$$

Note that the payoff at date t is uncertain since the German stock price S^* at date t is unknown. But the exchange rate is fixed now at X deutsche marks per dollar. Obviously, $f \geq 0$ or $f \leq 0$, depending on the stock price at date t in relation to the forward price K.

Quantity adjusting options are also available to institutions. These dealer derivatives function as follows: Quanto options give the buyer the right to foreign assets (stocks or bonds) at predetermined strike prices. The payoffs (if any) from such options are converted from foreign currencies at currently agreed-upon exchange rates. For example, in our example, the payoffs of the quanto option will be

$$c = X \times \max\{(S^* - K), 0\}. \tag{12.4}$$

In Chapter 7 we provide a method for valuing such options.

Listed or OTC Put Options in Portfolio Insurance

One of the most widely used strategies in the derivatives market is portfolio insurance. Simply stated, the idea is to buy or synthesize a put option on a portfolio to insure it.

For example, an investor holding 100 shares of IBM stock wishes to protect himself against the possibility that the stock price may fall over the next month. If the stock is selling at $70 per share, then by buying a one-month put option at a strike price of $70, the investor has assured himself of full protection. To see why this is the case, compare the naked (uninsured) position and the protected (insured) position in Table 12-14. For the protected position, when the stock price after a month, denoted by S^*, is greater than 70, the investor can participate in the upside potential net of the put premium P; when the stock price is below 70, the put can be exercised to ensure that the terminal cash flow is always 70.

Position	Investment	Cash Flow When $S^* \geq 70$	Cash Flow When $S^* < 70$
Naked	−7000	S^*	S^*
Protected	−(7000 + P)	S^*	70

TABLE 12-14
Portfolio Insurance

P = put premium

If full insurance is costly, then out-of-the-money puts can be purchased to get insurance with deductibles. Likewise, bonds can be protected by buying OTC put options of prespecified maturities. Note that the cost of insurance depends on the level of protection as well as the volatility of the underlying asset that is being insured: The greater the volatility, the higher the cost of insurance. This idea is presented in Figure 12-1.

FIGURE 12-1   *Effect of Level of Protection and Volatility in Portfolio Insurance*

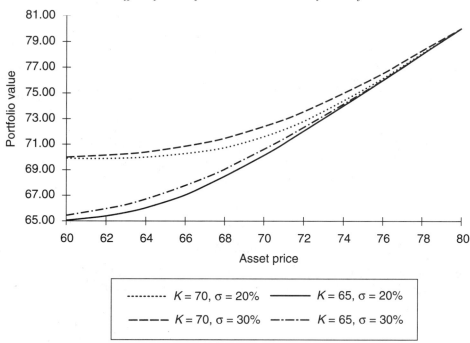

Commodity Swaps in Risk Management

Commodity swaps are a strategy to reduce risk by exchanging cash flows from realized spot rates for cash flows from a predetermined fixed price. Consider the case of the Energy Products Corporation (EPC), which is engaged in the production of crude oil. The projected monthly production of EPC is 10 million barrels per month for the next six months. The crude oil is sold to refiners who process the crude oil to produce refined products such as jet fuel. Most of the crude oil production of EPC is sold in the spot market; forward agreements extend only to small maturities and cover a very small part of the production. The quality of the crude produced is similar to that of West Texas Intermediate (WTI) crude oil, but is not identical. The crude oil prices at which EPC sells its output fluctuate a great deal. The WTI crude oil futures prices on the New York Mercantile Exchange (NYMEX) provide a very good proxy for the price risk experienced by

EPC. The Treasurer of EPC reviews the production schedule on February 8, 1994, and is concerned by the fact that the crude-oil price exposure has led to significant fluctuations in the working capital requirements recently. The investment bankers for EPC have suggested the possible use of dealer derivatives known as commodity swaps. They have also suggested the use of Asian options.

In Figure 12-2, we illustrate a commodity swap by this producer. In this swap transaction, the producer is entering into a swap on a notional principal of 10 million barrels of crude oil. Every month, the producer sells the oil in the spot market. The average price realized in the spot market is paid to the banker through the swap on a notational principal of 10 million barrels per month, and the banker pays the currently agreed-upon fixed price per barrel (in this case $20 per barrel).

FIGURE 12-2   *Commodity Swap*

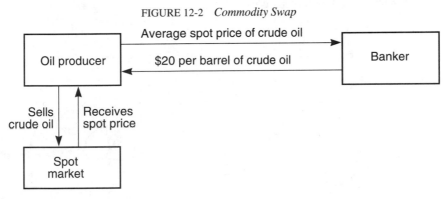

Notes:

1. Every month, the producer sells the oil in the spot market. The average of the spot price in the spot market is paid to the banker through the swap on a notional principal of 10 million barrels every month.

2. The bank pays a fixed price of $20 per barrel.

Another alternative to the producer is an Asian option. For EPC the following features should be present in the Asian option.

- The Asian option will be based on a daily average of NYMEX futures prices. On the exercise date, EPC will get the difference between the average NYMEX futures price (until the exercise date) and the strike price. Note that EPC is interested in an Asian put option that gives the right to sell the output valued at an average price at a currently agreed-upon fixed strike price. This structure is ideal if the daily sales are uniform and there are no seasonal patterns within a month.
- The strike price can be chosen to reflect the risk perceptions of the senior management of EPC. An out-of-the money Asian option is less expensive but provides less of a hedge. It is better to present the cost of several strike-price structures and of the implied hedge protection as measured by the delta of the Asian option.

OTHER CLASSIFICATIONS OF DERIVATIVES

From the standpoint of the relationship between the payoffs of the derivatives and the path taken by an underlying state variable we can classify derivatives into two groups, path-independent dealer derivatives and path-dependent derivatives.

If a standard European call option is priced on the S&P 500 index, then we are only interested in what happened to the S&P 500 index at maturity. It is path-independent. On the other hand, if a lookback call is priced, we need to know the entire path of the S&P 500 index prices. It is path-dependent. Figure 12-3 illustrates the difference. This figure tracks three prices relating to the S&P 500 index:

- the S&P 500 index price,
- the average S&P 500 index price and
- the maximum S&P 500 index price.

FIGURE 12-3   *Stock Price, Average Price and Maximum Price of the S&P 500 Index*

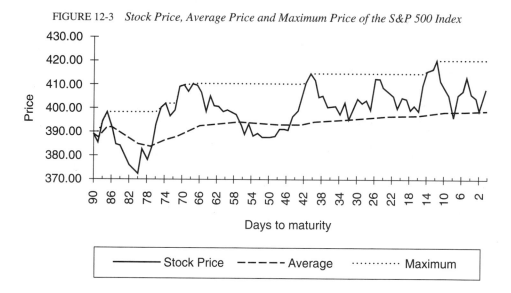

Path-Independent Derivatives

A path-independent security is one whose promised cash flows at any time depend only on the prices and rates at that time. In particular, the promised cash flows do not depend on the history of the prices and rates. Dealer options on bonds, interest-rate swaps, caps, and forward rate agreements fall into this category as do most listed options, forwards, futures, swaps, and dealer derivatives. Path-independent dealer derivatives may be European or American and are easy to price. In Chapter 7, we review the theory behind the pricing of path-independent securities.

Path-Dependent Derivatives

A path-dependent security is one whose promised cash flows at any time depend not only on the prices and rates at that time but also on the history of prices and rates until that date. Asian options and lookback options are examples in this category. Path-dependent dealer derivatives are usually priced using Monte-Carlo simulation techniques.

We list some of the path-dependent derivatives in Table 12-11 and discuss three of them below. The valuation of such exotic options is undertaken in Chapter 7.

Asian Options. This path-dependent option is very popular in the financial community. The payoff of an Asian option depends not only on the underlying asset price on the exercise date but also on the average price of the underlying asset during a prespecified period during the life of the option. The motivation for buying and selling such an option has already been discussed. An Asian call option will have the payoff distribution

$$c_{\text{Asian}} = \max\left(0, \frac{\sum_{i=1}^{n} S_i}{n} - K\right) \tag{12.5}$$

where S_i, $i = 1, 2, \cdots, n$ are the observed prices of the underlying asset at regular intervals (daily, weekly, monthly, etc.). An Asian put will have the payoff distribution:

$$p_{\text{Asian}} = \max\left(0, K - \frac{\sum_{i=1}^{n} S_i}{n}\right) \tag{12.6}$$

Sometimes, average strike-price options, which are conceptually very similar to Asian options, are traded by the dealer community. The strike price is chosen to be the average of the underlying asset price over a prespecified period during the life of the option. This average strike price is then applied to the terminal asset price at exercise date. The average strike-price call will have the payoff distribution

$$c_{\text{average}} = \max\left(0, S_n - \frac{\sum_{i=1}^{n} S_i}{n}\right) \tag{12.7}$$

The average strike-price put will have the payoff distribution

$$P_{\text{average}} = \max\left(0, \frac{\sum_{i=1}^{n} S_i}{n} - S_n\right) \tag{12.8}$$

Barrier Options. We noted that the value of an Asian option depends on the history of underlying asset prices because of the fact that the exercise payoff depends on the historical average. In the case of barrier options, the payoffs depend not only on the terminal price of the underlying asset price but also on whether the underlying asset price reached a certain barrier price, specified exogenously in the contract, during the life of the option. Two examples of such barrier options are given next.

Down-and-out call options. These are options that behave exactly like a standard call option except that the option is automatically extinguished prior to its stated expiry date if the underlying asset price drops below the barrier boundary known as the knock-out boundary. When the boundary is reached, a rebate is paid to the owner of the option. The payoffs can be formally represented as

$$c_{\text{down-and-out}} = \max(0, S^* - K) \quad \text{if} \ \forall \quad \tau \leq T \quad S(\tau) > H.$$

If the knock-out boundary H is hit for the first time prior to the maturity date, then the option is worth $c_{\text{down-and-out}} = R$, where R is the rebate.

Up-and-out call options. These are options which act exactly like standard calls except that when an upper knock-out boundary is reached, the option is automatically extinguished and a rebate R is paid. The payoffs can be formally represented as

$$c_{\text{up-and-out}} = \max(0, S^* - K) \quad \text{if} \ \forall \quad \tau \leq T \quad S(\tau) < H$$

If the knock-out boundary H is hit for the first time prior to the maturity date, then the option is worth $c_{\text{up-and-out}} = R$, where R is the rebate.

In a similar way down-and-in options and up-and-in options can be defined.

Lookback Options. A lookback call option provides the buyer of the option with the right to the difference between the highest underlying asset price that was reached during the life of the option and the prespecified strike price. Similarly, a lookback put option gives the buyer the right to the difference between the strike price and the lowest underlying asset price that was reached during the life of the option.

The payoffs of lookback options may be represented formally as

$$c_{\text{lookback}} = \max[0, \max(S_0, S_1, \cdots, S_n) - K)]$$

$$p_{\text{lookback}} = \max[0, K - \min(S_0, S_1, \cdots, S_n)].$$

In the payoff functions above, $S_1, S_2, \cdots, S_n$ represent the realized underlying asset prices during the life of the option.

DERIVATIVES AND RISK MANAGEMENT

Recent losses in the derivatives market are summarized in this section to provide a perspective on the sources of risk in derivatives transactions. A number of highly reputable banks and investment banks have suffered extensive losses in recent times due to improper risk management and control practices.

MBS Market

- J. P. Morgan in 1992 lost close to $200 million U.S. dollars in the mortgage-backed securities market. It was widely understood that their model of prepayments produced incorrect option-adjusted spreads.
- In 1987, Merrill Lynch lost about $350 million in stripped mortgage-backed securities due to incorrect pricing.

In these two instances, the problem seems to have arisen from proprietary trading activities that used an incorrect model to price the securities. There are two sources of risks here: model risk, and data and validation risk.

Bank Debt

- Westpac, an Australian Bank, lost close to $1 billion U.S. after writing off bad debts.
- Similar write-offs occurred in many U.S. banks after the Latin American countries defaulted.
- Many U.S. and Japanese banks held large amounts of real estate portfolios, which resulted in substantial write-offs when the commercial real estate market soured.
- Barclays in 1992 made a provision of close to $350 million U.S. against a loan that was extended to a British property developer.

There are three sources of risks here: credit risk and lack of contractual control, liquidity and lack-of-diversification risk, and management failure.

Derivatives

- In 1994, Procter and Gamble lost close to $200 million U.S. in interest-rate swap transactions arranged by Bankers Trust Company.
- Recently, Kidder Peabody detected that in the government-bond trading area several fictional trades had been sent to the computer system (for phantom forward reconstitutions), resulting in General Electric taking a write-off totalling nearly $250 million U.S.
- Metallgesellschaft, a German trading firm, lost $1 billion U.S. in commodities and derivatives trading.

There are three sources of risks here: derivatives-risk management and reporting risk, accounting and verification risk, and risk and speculative limits.

Responses to Improper Risk Management

The global value of derivative trading was estimated at around $17 trillion U.S. as shown in Table 12-9. In 1993, the notional value of derivatives held by Bankers Trust was around $2 trillion U.S. To protect against potential defaults large loan reserves are held by international banks. Financial institutions are required to maintain risk-adjusted capital. There is an increased emphasis on disclosure of the true financial health of any company, including the off-balance-sheet liabilities. The clients, auditors, rating agencies, and other constituencies are increasingly looking for detailed and transparent accounting systems based on up-to-date prices. **Chapter 15 is devoted to risk measurement and management. There we will examine the different sources of risk and how it can be measured and managed.**

REGULATION OF DERIVATIVES

A number of agencies are involved in the oversight of the derivative markets. The Commodity Futures Trading Commission (CFTC), The Securities and Exchange Commission (SEC), and the Federal Reserve play important roles in regulating these markets. Given the global links of the dealer and listed derivatives markets, foreign governments and their agencies frequently coordinate regulatory issues that affect the functioning of these markets. The interest-rate and currency swaps markets, futures, and options with multiple global listings are obvious examples.

In the United States, as well as in other countries, listed derivatives are subject to regulatory oversight. In fact, the listing requirements are imposed before a derivative may be listed in an exchange. Such requirements pertain to the number of shares that are traded, number of shareholders, number of shares that are outstanding, compliance with disclosure requirements, and so on. An important ingredient that affects the integrity of derivative instruments is margins. Federal Reserve Board has the authority to review margin requirements. In addition, position and exercise limits may also be set to preclude manipulations. Position limits are limits on the number of derivatives on a given underlying asset that may be held by a single investor or by a group of investors acting in concert. Similarly, exercise limits are the maximum amount that may be exercised within a specified period. In addition, exchanges are subject to certain policies of surveillance. These policies govern the internal audit systems that minimize the potential for manipulation.

Listed futures contracts are marked-to-market daily. The features of markup to market, margins, price limits and position limits serve to protect the integrity of such derivatives markets. In dealer markets, the credit rating of the dealer, the capital assigned to the derivatives business and the contractual provisions (such as up-front collaterals, discretionary marking-to-market, contingency provisions, etc.) serve to protect the integrity of such markets.

CONCLUSION

This chapter provided an overview of listed and dealer derivatives markets. We provided examples of how some exotic derivatives may be used to manage the risks that are encountered in certain financing and business activities. A perspective of the growth of the dealer derivative markets and the distribution of risks in such markets was also provided.

PROBLEMS

12.1   Explain the major differences between the listed derivative and the dealer derivative markets.

12.2   A corporation is planning to issue $100 million par amount of floating rate notes indexed to 180 days LIBOR, one month from now. Its rate on the floater is LIBOR minus 10 basis points, payable every six months. If the corporation wishes to hedge against the possibility of a rise in short-term interest rates, what are the alternatives that are open to it in (i) the listed derivative markets and (ii) the dealer derivative markets? Under what conditions will the corporation choose the dealer markets over listed markets?

12.3   What are the differences between a lookback call and an Asian call option?

12.4   Consider the risk faced by a producer of crude oil.

(a) Articulate the conditions under which such a producer can use the NYMEX crude oil futures contracts to hedge the price risk.

(b) Explain the circumstances under which the producer might use commodity swaps.

(c) When would the producer prefer Asian options?

12.5   Dealers offer caps on interest rates, such as the six-month London Interbank offered rates (LIBOR).

(a) Give examples of institutional investors who are buyers of this derivative.

(b) Characterize the economic conditions under which they will buy such derivatives.

12.6   Options on stock indexes are offered by exchanges and by dealers in the OTC market. Assume that two identical stock index options are available, one in the listed market and one in the OTC market. Are investors indifferent to the choice of these two options? Explain your answer.

12.7   Increasingly, corporate treasurers are confronted with the use of derivatives in their day-to-day activities, as well as in policy matters. Some of the activities of a corporate treasurer are listed below.

Treasury Activity	*Outlook*
CP issue	Bearish on rates
Pension asset allocation	Some upside with a floor equal to
Foreign exchange exposure	accumulated benefits obligations
in a foreign subsidiary	Highly volatile earnings and foreign
	exchange rates

Discuss the use of derivatives in each of these activities.

REFERENCES

Abken, P. 1989. "Interest Rate Caps, Collars, and Floors." *Federal Reserve Bank of Atlanta Economic Review:* 74(6):2–24.

Anderson, T. 1990. *Euromarket Instruments.* New York: New York Institute of Finance.

Anderson, T., and R. Hasan 1989. *Interest Rate Risk Management.* London: IFK Publishing.

Antl, B., ed. 1986. *Swap Finance,* volume 2. London: Euromoney Publications.

Arak, M., L. Goodman, and A. Rones 1989. "Credit Lines for New Instruments: Swaps, Over-the-Counter Options, Forwards and Floor-Ceiling Agreements." In *Proceedings of the Conference on Bank Structure and Competition.* Federal Reserve Bank of Chicago.

Bank for Intentional Settlements 1988. *International Convergence of Capital Measurement and Capital Standards.* Basle, Switzerland.

Becker, B., T. Gira, and J. P. Burns 1991. *Recent Developments in the Derivative Markets.* New York City: American Bar Association.

Cox, J., and M. Rubinstein 1983. *Options Market.* Englewood Cliffs, NJ: Prentice-Hall.

Darby, M. R. 1994. Over-the-Counter Derivatives and Systemic Risk to the Global Financial System. National Bureau of Economic Research Working Paper Series, No. 4801.

Das, S. 1989. *Swap Financing.* Sydney: The Law Book Company.

Davis, K., and I. Harper 1991. *Risk Management in Financial Institutions.* Sydney: Allen and Unwin.

Duffee, G. R. 1994. *On Measuring Credit Risks of Derivative Instruments.* Washington, D.C.: Federal Reserve Board.

Global Derivatives Study Group 1993. *Derivatives; Practices and Principles.* Washington, D.C.: Group of Thirty.

Hull, J. 1989. *Options, Futures and Other Derivative Securities.* Englewood Cliffs, N.J.: Prentice Hall.

Sacks, P., and S. Crawford 1991. *New Products, New Risks.* New York: Harper Business.

Walmsley, J. 1988. *The New Financial Instruments.* New York: John Wiley.

Chapter 13

Treasury Futures Contracts

Chapter Objectives

This chapter introduces the reader to the forward and futures markets. After a concise treatment of these markets, this chapter provides a detailed discussion of the Treasury bond futures contract. The theoretical underpinnings of pricing are presented; Conversion factor, basis, carry, and delivery options are treated in detail. The following questions are addressed.

- What are forward and futures contracts? What are the differences between these contracts?
- What is open interest?
- What is marking-to-market and why is it important?
- What is meant by positive carry or negative carry?
- How can one identify the cheapest deliverable bond to the T-bond futures contract?
- What are delivery options and how are they valued?

INTRODUCTION

The forwards market and the futures market provide a mechanism for dealing with the uncertainty in commodity and asset prices that we encounter in our daily lives. Recall that assets can be bought and sold in the spot market (e.g., the stock market, where we could buy or sell shares of stock almost instantaneously) or in forwards and futures markets in which investors, producers and buyers transact for deferred delivery.

A farmer expecting a crop of oats in a few months faces the possibility of a reduction in the price of oats in the market. If possible, he wants to sell his crop at a price that has been agreed upon at the time of production or at a stage when the size of his crop can be predicted with some accuracy. The farmer typifies a hedger who sells futures or is **short** in the deferred delivery market. Such a participant is sometimes referred to as a **short hedger.**

On the other hand, a corporation such as Quaker Oats, that has to buy oats in futures to meet its production needs, wants to protect itself against the possibility of an increase in the price of oats. Thus, Quaker Oats wants to buy, at a currently established price, the quantity of oats dictated by its production needs. The corporation typifies an investor who buys futures or is **long** in the deferred delivery markets. Such an investor is known as the **long hedger.**

It is easy to see why the producers of oats and the buyers of oats want to reduce, if not eliminate, price uncertainty from their business decisions by engaging in contracts that set prices now but deliver goods later. Forward trading serves precisely this purpose. By selling forward oats at a currently determined price, the farmer eliminates price uncertainty from his business decisions. By buying forward at an agreed-upon price now, Quaker Oats eliminates price uncertainty from its production-planning decisions. Thus forward trading serves to facilitate the coordination of production plans of the various buyers and sellers in various commodity and asset markets. This example is typical of producers of most commodities.

In a similar way, in financial markets, managers and traders face price uncertainty. The manager of a pension-fund portfolio that is fully invested in an equity portfolio is rightfully concerned about the possibility of a drop in equity prices. He may therefore protect the value of his portfolio by selling forward at a price now. Market makers who expect equity prices to go up are willing to buy the equity at a currently determined price. Forward trading enables investors with different expectations about price changes to execute transactions now for settlement later, as specified in the contract.

Although we motivated forward trading from the vantage point of producers of commodities, buyers of commodities, portfolio managers, and traders, there are others who benefit from forward trading. Individuals who have an opinion about the future price movements in an asset market may speculate in forward trading. By providing an avenue for such speculators to express their market view through forward trading, the forward market prices reflect a consensus view of the future price of the asset. This role is sometimes referred to as the **price-discovery role** of forward market. Note that the speculators may not (and typically do not) have any position in the underlying asset. In addition to short hedgers, long hedgers, and speculators, there are **arbitrageurs** who take advantage of any anomalies between spot prices and the prices that are set in the forward market. A market maker in government bonds may also sell or buy forward if he believes that the spot and futures prices enable him to lock in riskless profits.

HISTORY OF FORWARD AND FUTURES TRADING

The concept of deferred delivery agreements is not a recent one. In the latter half of the nineteenth century, the Chicago Board of Trade began trading in futures contracts. Interest in academic literature concerning futures markets dates from the early 1920s. Discussions of forward trading and the desirability of forward markets to improve the efficiency of resource allocation can be found in Keynes (1930) and subsequently in the classic *Value and Capital* (Hicks 1939). The development of this market has been steady since its appearance in the 1860s, but the growth has been phenomenal since the introduction of financial futures contracts. The Chicago Mercantile Exchange introduced foreign currency futures contracts, which may be properly viewed as the first financial futures contracts to be traded. This proved to be the catalyst for the subsequent explosive growth in futures contracts with financial instruments as the underlying assets. A detailed treatment of the development of futures markets is not attempted in this book. The interested reader may consult Carlton (1984) and Silber (1981), as well as the references cited in these papers.

Table 13-1 summarizes the significant developments in the history of the futures markets. The passage, in 1922, of the Grain Futures Act brought futures trading directly under the regulation of the federal government. (See Anderson (1984) for a detailed treatment

Year	Event
1922	Enactment of Grain Futures Act by Congress
1923	Authorized trading in corn, wheat, cotton, coffee, and sugar
1936	Commodity Exchange Act
1965	Live cattle futures contracts
1972	Introduction of foreign currency futures. The first financial futures contracts.
1974	Creation of Commodity Futures Trading Commission (CFTC)
1978	Trading of U.S. Treasury bond futures contracts
1982	Trading in stock index futures contracts and Eurodollar time deposits
1982	Futures Trading Act
1984	Options on futures contracts

TABLE 13-1
Major Developments in the Futures Markets

of regulation of futures contract innovation in the United States.) It also officially authorized the trading of futures in grains, livestock, and oilseeds. Subsequently, several futures contracts covering a variety of underlying goods, such as eggs, cocoa, rubber, and pork, were traded with varying degrees of success. This was followed by some amendments to the Grains Futures Act in 1936. The year 1965 saw the introduction of live cattle futures contracts. In 1972, IMM of the Chicago Mercantile Exchange introduced the first financial futures, a foreign currency futures contract, in which the underlying asset was the spot exchange rate itself. This was followed by several successful innovations in financial futures contracts. In 1978, the Chicago Board of Trade introduced the Treasury bond futures contracts. In 1982, stock index futures contracts were introduced.

From a regulatory perspective, 1974 was an important year. The Commodity Futures Trading Commission (CFTC) was set up in this year to guidelines for contract designation. Although the CFTC was originally intended to be the body responsible for regulating all futures trading, several other agencies have also tended to exercise their power in the regulation of futures trading. The Treasury department, the Securities and Exchange Commission (SEC), and the Federal Reserve have all from time to time influenced the conduct of futures trading in various markets. Anderson (1984) and Kane (1984) provide a discussion of the regulatory structure and the impact of such competition between different agencies.

The futures trading act of 1982 attempted to define the jurisdiction of SEC and CFTC in the matter of futures regulation. At the risk of oversimplification, it can be said that the CFTC was given the jurisdiction over futures contracts on goods and those contracts on securities for which a cash-settlement procedure is used, while the SEC was given the jurisdiction over futures contracts on securities for which a physical delivery system is used. These agencies play a role in many policy issues, such as setting margins and protection against manipulation. In 1984, options were introduced on futures contracts as underlying assets. As of 1987, options were traded actively on stock index futures, foreign currency futures, Treasury futures, and commodity futures contracts.

The impressive growth of futures contracts is evidenced by the diversity of the assets on which futures contracts are currently traded. In addition, exchanges all over the world offer futures contracts on different underlying assets. We have provided in Chapter 12 a summary of the range of the futures contracts that are currently actively traded.

FORWARD CONTRACTS

An investor who buys (sells) a forward contract agrees to buy (sell) one unit of the underlying asset at a specified future time, called the maturity date. The price at which the purchase will be made is called the forward price. The forward price is determined when the contract is written; it is specified in the contract and does not change over the life of the contract. An investor who has agreed to buy is said to be long in the forward market and the investor who has agreed to sell is said to be short in the forward market. The forward price is chosen so that the purchaser of the forward contract, the long position, pays and receives nothing when the contract is written. At the time of maturity, the long position receives one unit of the asset or its cash value, which is delivered by the seller of the forward contract, the short position. On the maturity date the short position receives the forward price specified in the contract.

Cash Flows from Forward Contracts

Let us consider an investor who has established a long position in one forward contract on an asset at time t. Assume that the contract matures at time $s > t$. Let $G_t(s)$ be the forward price at time t, V_j be the cash value of the spot asset at time j and R_j be one plus the riskless rate of interest between time j and time $j + 1$. Table 13-2 presents a summary of the cash flows arising out of the long position in a forward contract.

Date	Forward Price	Cash Price	Interest Rates	Cash Flows from Forward
t	$G_t(s)$	V_t	R_t	0
$t+1$	$G_{t+1}(s)$	V_{t+1}	R_{t+1}	0
$t+2$	$G_{t+2}(s)$	V_{t+2}	R_{t+2}	0
$t+3$	$G_{t+3}(s)$	V_{t+3}	R_{t+3}	0
...	...	...	...	...
...	...	...	...	...
s	$G_s(s)$	V_s	R_s	$G_s(s) - G_t(s)$
Total				

TABLE 13-2
Cash Flows from a
Forward Contract

Example 13-1

A forward contract on crude oil was entered into at date t to buy crude at a price of \$20 per barrel for settlement at date s, which is three days from date t. The forward price and cash price of crude oil are shown in the following table. Also shown are the cash flows from the forward contract.

Date	Forward Price	Cash Price	Cash Flows from Forward
t	20	18	0
$t+1$	21	$19\frac{1}{2}$	0
$t+2$	22	$21\frac{1}{2}$	0
$s = t+3$	$21\frac{1}{2}$	$21\frac{1}{2}$	$21\frac{1}{2} - 20 = 1\frac{1}{2}$

Note that there are no cash flows during t through $t + 2$. As the cash price of oil increases, clearly the forward contract to buy at $20 becomes much more valuable. Its full value is only realized on settlement date. Conversely, if the cash price had fallen below $20, the forward contract to buy at $20 would have become a financial obligation. Once again, all the losses will only be settled on the settlement date.

The value of a forward contract fluctuates between the time it is written and the time it matures. When the contract is written it has no value, but on the maturity date the long realizes a profit or loss equal to the difference between the cash price and the contracted forward price. Between the writing and the maturity, the value of a forward contract will fluctuate because the value of the right to buy at the forward price written in the contract changes as the cash price changes.

Note that on the maturity date s, the forward price $G_s(s)$ must necessarily be equal to the spot price V_s. Were this not the case, it would be possible to make arbitrage profits: if $G_s(s) > V_s$, then we could sell forward, buy spot, and close out by making delivery. These transactions would produce a profit of $G_s(s) - V_s$. In a similar way, if $G_s(s) < V_s$, then we could buy forward, sell spot, and close out by taking delivery. These transactions would produce a profit of $V_s - G_s(s)$.

Example 13-2 illustrates the issues that are involved.

Example 13-2

On March 12 XYZ Corporation agrees to buy 1,000 barrels of crude oil from West Texas Intermediate (WTI) at a price of $19 per barrel with the understanding that the crude oil will be delivered to Cushing, Oklahoma, on May 12, a period of 60 calendar days from March 12. Assume that the financing costs amount to 8.0% annualized. If 30 days later, the crude oil forward price is quoted at $17 per barrel, what is the value of the forward contract to XYZ Corporation? It should be clear that XYZ Corporation has a forward contract (at a forward price of $19) with a negative value. XYZ can dispose of it only by paying compensation to a third party. This can be accomplished by selling forward at a forward price of $17 on April 12. At maturity date, the physical delivery of oil from the original forward contract is used to cover the short position in the second forward contract that was established on April 12. The loss on May 12 is

$$(\$17 - \$19) \times 1000 \equiv \$2000.$$

The present value of the contract as of April 12 is

$$\frac{2000}{\left(1 + \frac{.08 \times 30}{360}\right)} \equiv 1986.75.$$

The fluctuation in the value of a forward contract is due to the fact that forward contracts are not marked to market. The futures contracts, which we describe next, are marked to market, and their value after they are marked to market is always zero.

FUTURES CONTRACTS

An investor who takes a long (short) position in a futures contract agrees to buy (sell) specified units of the underlying asset (or its cash value) on a specified maturity date at a currently specified futures price. The futures price is determined when the contract is written and is specified in the contract. The futures price is set so that no payment is made when the contract is written; that is, at initiation, the futures contract has a zero market value. But as the contract matures, the investor must make or receive daily installment payments toward the eventual purchase of the underlying asset. The total of the daily installments and the payment at maturity will equal the futures price set when the contract was initiated. (This definition is based on Richard and Sundaresan (1981).)

The daily installments are determined by the daily change in the futures price. If the futures price goes up then the investor who is long in the futures contract receives a payment from the investor who is short that equals the change in the daily futures price. This process is called **marking-to-market** on futures exchanges.

The effect of marking-to-market is to rewrite the futures contract each day at the new futures price. Hence the value of the futures contract after the daily settlement will always be zero since the value of a newly written futures contract is zero. When the contract matures, the long will have already paid or received the difference between the initial futures price and the futures price at the maturity time. With these payments to his credit he will have a balance due equal to the futures price at the maturity time. But the value of a futures contract written at the maturity time for immediate delivery must be zero. Therefore, at maturity the futures price must equal the current spot price: The balance due is simply the current spot price at the maturity time.

Cash Flows from Futures

It is useful to consider the cash flows from a futures more formally at this stage. Consider an investor who has established a long position in one futures contract on an asset at time t. Assume that the contract matures at time $s > t$. Let $H_t(s)$ be the futures price at time t, V_j be the cash value of the spot asset at time j and R_j be the one plus the riskless rate of interest between time j and time $j + 1$. In Table 13-3 below, we have presented the cash flows arising out of the long position in a futures contract.

TABLE 13-3

Cash Flows from a
Futures Contract

Date	Futures Price	Cash Price	Interest Rate	Cash Flows from Futures
t	$H_t(s)$	V_t	R_t	0
$t + 1$	$H_{t+1}(s)$	V_{t+1}	R_{t+1}	$H_{t+1}(s) - H_t(s)$
$t + 2$	$H_{t+2}(s)$	V_{t+2}	R_{t+2}	$H_{t+2}(s) - H_{t+1}(s)$
$t + 3$	$H_{t+3}(s)$	V_{t+3}	R_{t+3}	$H_{t+3}(s) - H_{t+2}(s)$
...	...	...	...	...
...	...	...	...	...
s	$H_s(s)$	V_s	R_s	$H_s(s) - H_{s-1}(s)$
Total				$H_s(s) - H_t(s)$

Recall that at maturity date s of a futures contract, the futures price must be exactly equal to the cash price. In other words, $H_s(s) = V_s$. (Note that the sum of the cash flows in the last column of Table 13-3 is $H_s(s) - H_t(s)$, which is the same as $V_s - H_t(s)$.) This means that if the futures price is higher than the cash price at maturity and the investor sells futures and buys cash and effects delivery, the investor can make riskless profits. Similarly if the futures price is less than the cash price and the investor buys futures and sells cash, the investor can make riskless profits.

Exceptions to the rule that the futures price must equal the cash price occur whenever the futures contracts provide either the short or the long with some delivery options. These exceptions are fully treated in the context of specific futures markets later.

The holder of a futures position receives or pays cash on a daily basis. An investor with a long (short) position receives (pays) cash flows when the futures prices increase and pays (receives) cash flows when the futures prices fall. If the future interest rates are random, this introduces a reinvestment risk. If cash is fully invested in interest-bearing securities, then a margin call resulting from unfavorable changes in futures prices will force the investor to liquidate some of the assets to post the additional margin. The opportunity cost of this is unknown at the time the futures position is initiated. Similarly, any receipts of cash due to favorable changes in futures prices will have to be reinvested at rates that are unknown at time t. As a result, we may expect the futures prices at time t to not only embody the expectations about the future cash price V_s at time s but also the path of one-period interest rates between time t and time s.

Example 13-3

Consider a futures contract to buy crude oil entered into at date t for settlement at date s, which is three days from date t. Let us assume for simplicity that the futures settle by cash on date s to the crude oil price at date s. The futures and cash prices as well as the cash flows from futures contracts are shown in the next table.

Date	Futures Price	Cash Price	Cash Flows from Futures
t	20	18	0
$t+1$	21	$19\frac{1}{2}$	1
$t+2$	22	$21\frac{1}{2}$	1
$s = t+3$	$21\frac{1}{2}$	$21\frac{1}{2}$	$-\frac{1}{2}$

Note that as the cash price increases, the futures price increases as well. This coupled with the marking-to-market feature leads to cash inflows at dates $t+1$ and $t+2$. From $t+2$ to $t+3$ future price fell by $\frac{1}{2}$. This resulted in a loss of $\frac{1}{2}$. The sum of the cash flows from futures (in the last column) is the same as in the forward contract in Example 13-1. Only, in the case of futures, it is paid out in installments.

Design Features

The definition of the futures contract and the discussion of the contract presented in Table 13-3 captures the essential features of futures contract. There are, however, several real-life features of such contracts.

Delivery Specifications. The exchanges must decide whether the futures contract calls for physical delivery or cash settlement. In addition, the exchanges must decide on the set of assets that can be used by the investors to satisfy the delivery requirements. The delivery parameters such as location, timing, and quality have to be specified in detail; these issues are resolved on a case-by-case basis. There are also some common considerations that underlie the choice of delivery specifications.

First, the delivery specifications must be such that the deliverable assets are in competitive supply, so that no single economic agent acting alone or a group of dominant agents acting in collusion will be able to corner the supply of deliverable assets. The principal implication of this is the design requirement that, in the case of commodity futures contracts, the deliverable set includes several grades of commodities. For futures contracts on financial assets such as Treasury bonds or Treasury notes, many bonds and notes issued by the Treasury qualify for delivery. While such a design feature serves to mitigate the problem of corners, it introduces a different problem: with so many deliverable assets, the maturity futures price will tend to track the price of cheapest deliverable asset. At the time of contracting, however, investors do not know which asset will be the cheapest when the contract expires. This introduces another element of uncertainty. Exchanges have attempted to deal with this problem by standardizing the assets that may be delivered against a futures contract. For example, in the case of T-bond futures contracts, the Chicago Board of Trade (CBOT) has stipulated that the standard grade is the 8%, twenty-year bond issued by the Treasury. But the deliverable set includes all the bonds issued by the Treasury that have 15 years or more to first call date or maturity. CBOT then standardizes these bonds through a system of conversion factors that attempt to equalize the bond prices and the futures price that has been adjusted by the conversion factor of the bonds. Futures prices track the cheapest deliverable asset's price; as a consequence, the delivery of more expensive bonds is suboptimal. These issues are taken up for detailed analysis later in the book.

The choice between physical delivery and cash settlement is also a nontrivial one. Both types of contracts are popular in the market place. The S&P 500 futures contract are closed out by cash settlement, whereas the T-bond futures contract are closed out by physical delivery. Both are extremely successful contracts. Cash settlement, when coupled with an underlying asset such as the S&P 500 index which is not easily subject to manipulations, ensures complete convergence of the futures price to a competitively determined cash price at maturity. This turns out to be a desirable feature in futures contracts when they are used for hedging. Cash-settlement is characteristic of equity futures contracts and physical settlement is characteristic of debt futures contracts.

It is worth noting that only a tiny percentage of futures contracts are closed by physical delivery and most of them are offset prior to the maturity date. This should come as no surprise, as the diversity of deliverable grades makes taking physical delivery less attractive. A further reduction in incentive to take delivery is attributable to the fact that the short may effect delivery on any business day of the delivery month, typically with short notice. This flexibility is called the timing option implicit in futures contracts.

Many futures contracts permit the short some flexibility in the choice of the location of physical delivery as well. This is referred to as the location option imbedded in futures contracts.

Price Limits. The exchanges may impose price limits. These limits stipulate the range of futures prices within which trading will be sustained in the futures markets. When the futures prices reach the limit, the investor is locked into his or her position and cannot offset. Typically the limits are removed during the delivery months of the futures contract.

Margins. Exchanges set margins to ensure that the investor has sufficient equity to meet any adverse price moves. This, in conjunction with marking-to-market and price limits, serves to minimize the risk of nonperformance by investors who take futures positions. In much of the analysis in the book, we assume that the initial margin requirements to open a futures position can be met by posting interest-bearing securities. This turns out to be a realistic assumption, although in many instances a small percentage of the margin will have to be posted in cash. Once the initial margin level falls to a prespecified level, called the maintenance margin, margin calls will result. This usually happens when the futures prices move in an adverse manner relative to the established futures position for several consecutive days. When this happens, the investor must restore the margin level back to the initial margin level by posting cash.

Here we have merely sketched some of the important design features of futures contracts. A detailed analysis of the design features is taken up on a case by case basis later. Table 13-4 shows an example of the *Wall Street Journal* listings of the futures price quo-

	June	September	December	Total
Prices				
Open	303.20	305.10	307.20	
High	306.10	307.95	310.00	
Low	295.50	297.60	299.50	
Settlement	296.40	298.25	300.15	
Change from previous day	−7.65	−7.75	−7.85	
Lifetime high	306.10	307.95	310.00	
Lifetime low	228.90	229.90	243.20	
Open interest	99,315	2,169	1,743	103,238
Change from previous day				+1,279
Volume				91,721
Volume previous day				67,104

TABLE 13-4
Futures Quotations, S&P 500 Index Futures Prices

Source: *Wall Street Journal,* April 8, 1987

tations for actively traded futures contracts. On April 8, 1987, the open price for the June contract was 303.20; this is the price at which the first transaction was executed. The highest price on April 8 for the June contract was 306.10 and the lowest price on that day was 295.50. In general, the settlement price is a representative price within the range of the market at the end of the day; in the case of S&P 500 futures, it is simply the closing price. The change in the settlement price from the previous day is also reported for each contract. This is useful information, as marking-to-market is based on the settlement prices. In addition, the lifetime-high and lifetime-low prices are reported. Open interest is the number of outstanding contracts on the previous day. For the June contract the open interest stood at 99,315. Note that the open interest falls rapidly as one moves into more distant maturity futures contracts. This is typical of most futures contracts. Total volume is the number of contracts traded on any day. For the S&P 500 index futures on April 8, this was 91,721 contracts. The total open interest across all contracts, as well as the change in this quantity over the previous day are also reported.

Typically a number of maturity dates are available for trading. In the case of S&P 500 index futures, only three maturities were available. The maturities for the Eurodollar time-deposit futures contracts extend up to two years, with one contract maturing every quarter. The size of the S&P 500 futures, also indicated in the Wall Street Journal report, is 500 times the index. By posting an initial margin of $10,000, it is possible to establish a long (short) position in one S&P futures contract. (But by 1995 this had increased to $20,000. Margins can be changed at the discretion of the exchange depending on market conditions.) In effect, this is equivalent to taking a long position in 500 shares of the index, as far as the exposure to S&P 500 index price changes are concerned. Indeed, we will show later that buying futures is equivalent to borrowing and buying the underlying asset.

FORWARD CONTRACTS VS. FUTURES CONTRACTS

Forward contracts differ from futures contracts in a number of ways.

- Forwards are not marked-to-market, as are futures contracts. This alone is sufficient to cause a difference in the forward prices and futures prices in the presence of interest rate uncertainty.
- Forwards are typically entered into by institutions either on a bilateral basis, as in the case of the oil industry, or through extensive OTC markets, as in the case of foreign currency markets. Futures contracts, on the other hand, are traded in centralized open outcry exchanges in which bid-offer prices are established.
- The difference in the market organization, in turn, requires different institutional arrangements for ensuring performance. In the futures markets, anyone with a reasonable amount of capital can participate. Exchanges have clearing houses that monitor the performance of participants through the system of marking-to-market, margins, and margin calls that force the participants to respond quickly to adverse price movements. If any investor is unable to respond, that investor's open position is correspondingly reduced and ultimately extinguished. The clearing houses have capital that they can rely on to meet any residual shortfall. This mechanism is

necessary in order for the open outcry markets to function; there is no time in such a market to conduct extensive credit checks on investors. In forward markets, the situation is quite different. In the bilateral contracts prevalent in the oil industry, for example, the corporations receive sufficient information about the credit risk that they face in forward contracting. This enables them to design the necessary contractual terms to protect themselves from any nonperformance contingencies. In OTC forward markets, high capital requirements and collateral requirements are enforced to screen investors with high credit risks.

- Forward contracts, especially the ones in bilateral settings, specify precise terms concerning the deliverable grades, location, and delivery dates. The goal in such a contracting process is delivery. This aspect differs sharply from the delivery specifications of futures contracts which provide the short with the many imbedded options that we have discussed previously.

Under what circumstances will one prefer forward contracting over futures contracting? When might one expect both markets to coexist, and when might one dominate the other? The answers to these questions depend in good part on the contractual features that we have described above. Economic agents who wish to take delivery of the underlying good at a future date for further processing at some location will prefer the delivery terms associated with forward contracts. The familiarity of such economic agents with one another's credit risks, delivery capabilities, and so on, makes forward contracting viable and indeed preferable to futures contracting. The continued existence of forward contracts in the oil industry is a case in point. The existence of OTC forward markets in foreign currencies is an indication that such markets have a role that cannot be duplicated by futures contracts. As a rule, it is difficult to offset forward contracts in the foreign currency market. Here it is difficult to compare forwards to foreign currency futures markets. In foreign currency markets, forward rates are quoted according to conventions that differ from the futures quotations. The spot quotes are written out to the appropriate number of decimal places. The forward quotes are then expressed in points, by which they sell at a discount or premium. This convention is in contrast with the practice in the futures markets where the futures prices are also written out to the appropriate decimals. It is also worth remembering that forward quotes are given for standard fixed maturities; 30, 60, and 90 days are the most common. Fixed maturities of six months and a year or more are less common. This practice makes the comparison of forwards and futures a bit more difficult, due to the fact that futures contracts have a fixed delivery month and their days to maturity change everyday.

TREASURY FUTURES CONTRACTS

A considerable increase in the volatility in interest rates occurred after the shift in the Fed's policy in October 1979. This was seen earlier in the text. The interest rates have tended to fluctuate a great deal since that shift. This increased volatility has posed significant risks for issuers, financial intermediaries, and investors.

To successfully manage such risks, it is necessary to have hedging vehicles in the marketplace. The introduction of Treasury bill futures contracts in the International Monetary Market in January 1976, Treasury bond futures contracts in the CBT in August 1977, Treasury note (ten-year) futures contracts in the CBT in 1982, and the recent introduction of Treasury note (five-year) futures contracts in CBT and NYCE are, in part, a response to these factors. In this section, the specifications of Treasury futures contracts will be described. T-bond futures contracts and their specifications will be analyzed in detail. Since the Treasury note futures are similar to Treasury bond futures, the analysis for the Treasury bond futures applies to the note contracts as well.

The Treasury bill futures contract listed at the IMM was one of the liquid contracts until the introduction of the Eurodollar futures contract. The Treasury bond (T-bond) futures contract of the Chicago Board of Trade (CBT) continues to be one of the most liquid futures contracts ever traded. CBT also lists a Treasury note futures contract whose specifications are almost identical to the T-bond futures contract, except that the underlying nominal asset is a ten-year note. The margin requirements that are needed to open positions in these contracts are shown in Table 13-5. The margins indicated are exchange-specified minimum amounts; the actual transactions may entail higher margins.

Contract	Initial Margin	Maintenance Margin
Five-year T-note	$1,000	$750
Ten-year T-note	$1,500	$1000
T-bond	$3,000	$2500
T-bill	$1,500	$1200

TABLE 13-5
Margin Requirements for Treasury Futures

Treasury Bill Futures Contracts

The salient features of the T-bill futures contract are provided in Table 13-6. The deliverable asset to the T-bill futures is a $1,000,000 face value Treasury bill that has 90 days to maturity. The invoice price is computed using the formula shown below.

$$P = 1,000,000 \times \left[1 - d \times \left(\frac{\tau}{360} \right) \right] \tag{13.1}$$

where d is the discount rate (expressed in decimals) at the maturity date of the futures, τ is the time to maturity of the T-bill, and P is the invoice price. This convention is based on the fact that U.S. T-bills are sold on a discount basis. The discount rate d is calculated as

$$d = \frac{(100 - P)}{100} \times \frac{360}{\tau} \tag{13.2}$$

where 100 is the face value of the T-bill, P is the market value, and τ is the time to maturity. The settlement prices of futures are quoted as 100 minus the discount rate in percent, which applies to bills delivered on the settlement date. Thus a futures price of 93.50 indicates a discount rate of 6.50%. An investor who is short as of the delivery date in a Treasury bill futures contract may deliver either a ninety-day T-bill, a ninety-one-day

Trading unit	$1,000,000 face value of U.S. Treasury bills deliverable during the months traded.	**TABLE 13-6** *IMM Treasury Bill Futures Contract*
Months traded	March, June, September, December	
Deliverable grade	U.S. Treasury bills with 90 days to maturity.	
Delivery method	Federal Reserve book-entry wire-transfer system.	
Price quote	On a discount basis.	
Minimum price change	$0.01 = \$25$	
Daily price limit	60 basis points or $1,500	
Hours of trade	8:00 AM to 2:00 PM (Chicago time)	
Last trading day	The day before the first delivery day.	
Delivery date	First day of spot month on which the 13-week Treasury bill is issued and the one-year Treasury bill has 13 weeks to maturity.	
Ticker symbol	TB	

T-bill, or a ninety-two-day T-bill. The short will receive upon delivery of a ninety-day T-bill an amount that will be computed using Equation (13.1) as

$$1,000,000 \times \left[1 - 0.065 \times \frac{90}{360} \right] = 983,750.$$

Thus the discount convention in the cash market is also followed in the futures market. But the Eurodollar futures are quoted with an add-on market convention. To make the appropriate comparisons, it is necessary to convert discount yields to add-on yields as shown below:

$$y = \frac{(100 - P)}{P} \times \frac{360}{\tau} \qquad (13.3)$$

where y is the add-on yield equivalent. The discount convention allows the convergence of futures prices on T-bills to converge to the price of the deliverable T-bill at the maturity date of futures contract. Hence the comparison of futures and forward prices is conceptually valid, but the add-on convention used in the Eurodollar futures market makes this comparison much more difficult.

In Table 13-7, the open interest and the quoted prices of T-bill futures contracts are provided, together with the implied discount rates. These prevailed in the market on August 19, 1988. The open interest of the T-bill futures declines rapidly with maturity and beyond the first two contracts, it is difficult to trade sizable quantities without affecting the price. The settlement futures price and the implied discount rate are also provided in the table. An investor can calculate the implied settlement price that he will receive by delivering a Treasury bill with a maturity in the range 90–92 days. An investor who is long in the Treasury bill will receive the Treasury bill in the maturity

TABLE 13-7   *Treasury Bill Futures Prices and Open Interest*

Maturity	Price	Open Interest	Implied Settlement Price of a T-bill	Implied Discount Rate
9/1988	92.68	12628	98.1700	7.32%
12/1988	92.28	5332	98.0700	7.72%
3/1989	92.20	1265	98.0500	7.80%
6/1989	92.10	717	98.0250	7.90%
9/1989	92.01	178	98.0025	7.99%
12/1989	91.92	178	97.9800	8.08%
3/1990	91.87	4	97.9675	8.13%
6/1990	91.83	4	97.9575	8.17%

range 90–92 days depending on what the clearing corporation obtains from the shorts. It is possible to lock in these prices by buying the futures and holding it to maturity. (In the absence of T-bill futures market, it is possible to do this only by entering into the transactions that are shown in Tables 13-8 and 13-9.)

Forward and Futures Rates. The existence of a liquid spot market in bills means that investors can synthetically create forward rates. If the synthetically created forward rates differ from the futures rates, after accounting for transactions costs and risks, then arbitrage profits are possible. To this end, we first illustrate how the Treasury spot markets can be used to borrow and lend at forward rates. Table 13-8 illustrates a strategy to borrow at a future date T_1 at a currently known forward rate, $f_t^b(T_1, T_2)$.

The forward rate is given by the expression below:

$$f_t^b(T_1, T_2) = \frac{b(t, T_1)}{b(t, T_2)}.$$

In the computation of forward rates, bid prices are to be used for the bill maturing on T_2 and ask prices for the bills maturing on T_1. The borrowing is also assumed to take place

TABLE 13-8   *Borrowing at Forward Rate*

Transaction on Current Date	Investment on Current Date t	Maturity Date, First Bill T_1	Maturity Date, Second Bill
Buy the bill that matures on T_1	$-b(t, T_1)$	1	0
Sell the bill that matures on T_2	$b(t, T_2)$		-1
Borrow the difference until T_2	$b(t, T_1) - b(t, T_2)$		$-\dfrac{b(t, T_1) - b(t, T_2)}{b(t, T_2)}$
Total investment	0		
Total cash flow		1	$-\dfrac{b(t, T_1)}{b(t, T_2)}$

at the offer rate. Using the concept of spot rates of interest, let R_1 be the spot rate of interest between t and T_1 and let R_2 be the spot rate of interest between t and T_2. Then,

$$b(t, T_1) = \frac{1}{(1 + R_1)^{T_1 - t}}$$

and

$$b(t, T_2) = \frac{1}{(1 + R_2)^{T_2 - t}}.$$

Hence the rate that we have locked in is

$$f_t^b(T_1, T_2) = \frac{b(t, T_1)}{b(t, T_2)} = \frac{\dfrac{1}{(1 + R_1)^{T_1 - t}}}{\dfrac{1}{(1 + R_2)^{T_2 - t}}}$$

Simplifying, we get

$$f_t^b(T_1, T_2) = \frac{(1 + R_2)^{T_2 - t}}{(1 + R_1)^{T_1 - t}}.$$

Example 13-4

The prices of two T-bills and their maturities are shown below. What is the forward rate that can be locked in for the purposes of borrowing between July 25, 1996 and April 3, 1997?

The bill prices in the table are obtained using the formula in Equation (13.1). The borrowing rate between July 25, 1996 and April 3, 1997 is 4.022%.

Settlement May 2, 1996

Security	Maturity	Bid (Discount)	Offer (Discount)
T-bill	July 25, 1996	4.96%	4.94%
T-bill	April 3, 1997	5.33%	5.31%

Transaction on May 2, 1996	Investment on May 2, 1996	July 25, 1996 Cash Flows	April 3, 1997 Cash Flows
Buy the bill maturing on July 25, 1996 @ 4.94%	-0.98847	1	0
Sell the bill maturing on April 3, 1997 @ 5.33%	0.95025		-1
Borrow the difference until April 3, 1997	0.03822		-0.04022
Total	0	1	-1.04022

In a similar manner, Table 13-9 illustrates a strategy for lending at a future date T_1 at a forward rate, $f_t^l(T_1, T_2)$.

TABLE 13-9   *Lending at Forward Rate*

Transaction on Current Date	Investment on Current Date T_1	Maturity Date, First Bill T_2	Maturity Date, Second Bill
Sell the bill that matures on T_1	$b(t, T_1)$	-1	0
Buy the bill that matures on T_2	$-b(t, T_1)$		1
Lend the difference until T_2	$-[b(t, T_1) - b(t, T_2)]$		$\dfrac{b(t, T_1) - b(t, T_2)}{b(t, T_2)}$
Total investment	0		
Total cash flow		-1	$\dfrac{b(t, T_1)}{b(t, T_2)}$

Example 13-5

For the T-bills provided in the previous example what is the forward rate that can be locked in between July 25, 1996 and April 3, 1997 for lending purposes?

The idea is essentially similar to the previous example, except that we will sell the T-bill maturing on July 25, 1996 at 4.96% and buy the T-bill maturing on April 3, 1997 at 5.31% and lend the difference as shown next.

Transaction on May 2, 1997	Investment on May 2, 1997	July 25, 1996 Cash Flows	April 3, 1997 Cash Flows
Sell the bill maturing on July 25, 1996 @ 4.96%	0.98843	-1	0
Buy the bill maturing on April 3, 1997 @ 5.31%	-0.95044		1
Lend the difference until April 3, 1997	-0.03799		0.03997
Total	0	-1	1.03997

The appropriate lending rate that can be locked in between July 25, 1996 and April 3, 1997 is 3.997%.

In the computation of forward rates, ask prices are used for the bill maturing on T_2 and bid prices for the bills maturing on T_1. The lending is also assumed to take place at the bid rate. In the absence of bid-offer spreads and transactions costs, the two forward rates will coincide. Note that for someone who already has long positions in the bills some of these transactions are easy to enter into.

The existence of the T-bill futures market allows one to perform these transactions with relative ease. Note that these transactions are not necessary if the objective is to simply lock in a forward rate; by selling futures contracts on T-bills, an investor could lock in his borrowing cost. In a similar way by buying the T-bill futures, an investor could lock in his lending costs. If the futures rates differ significantly from the forward rates, then arbitrage profits are possible.

Applications of T-bill Futures. T-bill futures may be used in a variety of risk management situations. Dealers who make a market in T-bills, CDs, and commercial paper may find it desirable to hedge their inventory positions by selling T-bill futures. Alternatively, they may buy T-bill futures to lock in their acquisition cost of future purchases of T-bills. In addition, T-bill futures allows dealers to effectively arbitrage between forward rates and futures rates. In this context, underwriters of short-term money market securities may find T-bill futures to be an attractive vehicle for protecting their price risk until the securities are distributed. For commercial banks and savings and loan associations, T-bill futures provide a tool for asset-liability management. For individual investors and institutional investors, such as pension funds and mutual funds, T-bill futures provide a way to better manage their risk positions.

Treasury Bond and Treasury Note Futures Contracts

The salient features of the T-bond futures contract and the T-note futures (five-year and ten-year) are provided next. In Table 13-10, contractual provisions for Treasury bond futures are indicated. Table 13-11 provides the specifications for the ten-year Treasury note futures contract and Table 13-12 contains the corresponding details for the five-year Treasury note futures contracts. The T-bond futures contract and its design has been extensively copied and adopted by a number of exchanges. The gilt futures contract at LIFFE, the French government bond contract at MATIF, the Bund futures contract on the German government bond, and the Japanese government bond contract have used the design specifications of CBT's U.S. T-bond futures contract extensively.

The contracts in Tables 13-10 to 13-12 have a par value of $100,000 U.S. The contracts also permit the delivery of many eligible underlying securities. The reason why several securities are eligible for delivery is easy to explain—if only one security were permitted for delivery, it would be easy for one or two institutions to corner the supply of that security and create a scarcity that then would lead to the manipulation of the market. But there is a drawback to permitting many securities to be delivered. Each security will have a different coupon and maturity and the compensation upon the delivery of a security depends on the conversion factor of that security—the price (per dollar par) at which the security will provide a yield to maturity or call of 8%. This is a rough way to equalize the relative desirability of delivering any one eligible security. As we will show later, this procedure leads to certain biases in the delivery strategies.

Table 13-13 contains the open interest and prices of the Treasury bond and the ten-year Treasury note contracts. Note that the open interest declines rapidly as the maturity date of futures increases. The depth of the market is typically concentrated in the first two

Trading unit	$100,000 face value of U.S. Treasury bonds deliverable during the months traded.	TABLE 13-10 *CBT Treasury Bond Futures Contract*
Months traded	March, June, September, December	
Deliverable grade	U.S. Treasury bonds with a nominal 8% coupon maturing at least 15 years from delivery date if not callable; or not callable for 15 years from delivery date if callable.	
Delivery method	Federal Reserve book-entry wire-transfer system. Invoice price on delivery is adjusted by conversion factor system to adjust for coupon rates apart from 8% and for varying maturity or call dates.	
Price quote	In percentage of par in minimum increments of $\frac{1}{32}$ of a point or $31.25 per tick (e.g., 74–01 or 74–01/32).	
Daily price limit	$\frac{64}{32}$ or $2,000 per contract above or below the previous day's settlement price.	
Hours of trade	8:00 AM to 2:00 PM (Chicago time)	
Last trading day	Seven business days prior to the last business day of the month.	
Last delivery day	Last business day of the month.	
Ticker symbol	US	

Trading unit	$100,000 face value of U.S. Treasury bonds deliverable during the months traded.	TABLE 13-11 *CBT Ten-year Treasury Note Futures Contract*
Months traded	March, June, September, December	
Deliverable grade	U.S. Treasury notes with a nominal 8% coupon with a maturity of 6.5 to 10 years from delivery date.	
Delivery method	Federal Reserve book-entry wire-transfer system. Invoice price on delivery is adjusted by conversion factor system to adjust for coupon rates apart from 8% and for varying maturity or call dates.	
Price quote	In percentage of par in minimum increments of $\frac{1}{32}$ of a point or $31.25 per tick (e.g., 74–01 or 74–01/32).	
Daily price limit	$\frac{64}{32}$ or $2,000 per contract above or below the previous day's settlement price.	
Hours of trade	8:00 AM to 2:00 PM (Chicago time)	
Last trading day	Seven business days prior to the last business day of the month.	
Last delivery day	Last business day of the month.	
Ticker symbol	TY	

			TABLE 13-12
Trading unit	$100,000 face value of U.S. Treasury notes deliverable during the months traded.		*CBT Five-year Treasury Note Futures Contract*
Months traded	March, June, September, December		
Deliverable grade	Any of the five-year U.S. Treasury notes that have been most recently auctioned with an original maturity of not more than 5 years and 3 months, and a remaining maturity of not less than 4 years and 3 months, as of the first day of the delivery month.		
Delivery method	Federal Reserve book-entry wire-transfer system.		
Price quote	In percentage of par in minimum increments of $\frac{1}{64}$ of a point or $15.625 per tick (e.g., 84–01 or 84–01/64).		
Daily price limit	$\frac{192}{64}$ or $3,000 per contract above or below the previous day's settlement price. (Expandable to 4.50 points or $4,500 per contract.)		
Hours of trade	8:00 AM to 2:00 PM (Chicago time)		
Last trading day	The eighth to last business day of the delivery month.		
Last delivery day	Last business day of the month.		
Ticker symbol	FV		

Contract	Maturity	Price	Open Interest	TABLE 13-13
Treasury bond	9/1988	84.28	228040	*Treasury Bonds and Ten-Year Treasury Notes Futures Prices and Open Interest*
	12/1988	84.08	147337	
	3/1989	83.20	57563	
	6/1989	83.01	38743	
	9/1989	82.15	13485	
	12/1989	81.31	5263	
	3/1990	81.16	577	
	6/1990	81.02	94	
	9/1990	80.21	67	
	12/1990	80.09	13	
	3/1991	79.30	16	
Treasury note	9/1988	84.28	72314	
	12/1988	84.08	30879	
	3/1989	83.20	1424	
	6/1989	83.01	154	
	9/1989	82.15	55	

maturity months. The September 1988 T-bond contract had an open interest of about $22 billion U.S., indicating an extraordinary amount of liquidity. Notice also that the futures prices tend to fall as the maturity date increases. This pattern is typical in an upward-sloping term structure or a positive carry market. We will explain this in some detail later.

Delivery Options in Treasury Bond Futures. It is important to fully understand the T-bond futures contract specification in order to determine the relationship between the futures prices and Treasury bond prices. A seller of a T-bond futures contract has a great deal of flexibility or many delivery options during the delivery month.

The short may deliver any bundle of prespecified Treasury bonds sometime during the delivery month, so long as the investor has not offset his short position.

The Treasury bond futures contract closes for the day at 2:00 PM Chicago time. The Treasury bond market, however, is a dealers' market. Indeed, as long as bond dealers are willing to execute orders, the bond market may be considered to be open. The clearing house of the CBOT accepts delivery during the delivery month until 8:00 PM Chicago time. These observations mean that an investor who has an open short position in T-bond futures as of 2:00 PM Chicago time during the delivery month has the option to deliver any combination of the deliverable issues until 8:00 PM Chicago time. If the deliverable issues were to experience a significant price decline during the 2:00 PM to 8:00 PM period, this option will be of considerable value to the investor who is short. This option is known as the "wild-card" delivery option in T-bond futures contracts. The key is that the invoice price is fixed at 2:00 PM and does not change until the next day of trading. The investor may elect to delay delivery by waiting. This strategy permits the investor to participate in any potential price declines in the 2:00 PM to 8:00 PM period next day. In essence, the investor who is short on the first day of the delivery month has a sequence of six-hour put options during each day of the delivery month until the last day of futures trading. Each put provides the right to sell a bundle of deliverable issues until 8:00 PM at an invoice price set at 2:00 PM. Upon expiration, the investor gets another put at a different invoice (strike) price the next day at 2:00 PM. The T-bond futures ceases trading seven business days prior to the last business day of the contract month. Thus the wild-card option provides the short with a sequence of approximately 15 daily put options.

It is easy to see the directional impact of the wild-card option on T-bond futures price. Since the short has the flexibility associated with the wild-card feature, the long will enter into the futures transaction only if the futures price is discounted by the value of the sequence of put options represented by the wild-card feature. Thus the effect of wild-card option, in a rational setting, is to reduce the futures price by the fair value of the option.

The T-bond futures contract ceases trading seven business days prior to the last business day of the contract month. The clearing house, however, accepts delivery until the last business day of the month. Between the last day of futures trading and the last delivery date, bond prices fluctuate in the marketplace but the futures price stays fixed at its closing level as of the last trading day. This feature of the Treasury bond futures contract is called the end-of-the-month option. The holder of a short position in Treasury bond futures has considerable flexibility during this period. He has a timing option that permits him to select any day during this period to effect delivery. Furthermore, he has a quality option that permits him to select any bundle of deliverable bonds from among approximately 30 deliverable issues.

Note that the design of T-bond futures contract provides several implicit options to the short. This is typical of many futures contracts, as we have seen. These delivery options have important effects on the relationship between futures prices and cash prices.

Empirical Evidence on Deliveries. In this section, we present some evidence on actual deliveries that were made to the T-bond and T-note futures contracts during the period 1977–1987 based on the data provided by Commodity Futures Trading Commission (CFTC). (This section draws heavily from Broadie and Sundaresan (1992).)

Although more than 90% of the open interest is settled by offset in both Treasury bond and Treasury note futures markets, the actual deliveries made in these markets are nevertheless economically significant. Figure 13-1 depicts the actual deliveries made in each contract month traded since the inception of the Treasury bond futures contract. In Figure 13-2, the actual deliveries for the Treasury note contract are plotted. In Table 13-14, we provide some summary statistics for these figures.

FIGURE 13-1   *Deliveries to T-bond Futures Contract (December 1977–March 1991)*

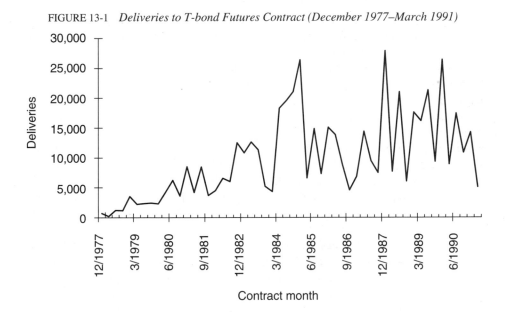

Statistic	Treasury Bonds	Treasury Notes	
Sample period	Dec 1977 to June 1987	June 1982 to June 1987	TABLE 13-14 *Deliveries of Bonds and Notes*
Number of contract months	39	20	
Average face delivered	$7.62 billion	$4.84 billion	
Maximum face delivered	$26.38 billion	$10.77 billion	
Minimum face delivered	$0.20 billion	$1.06 billion	

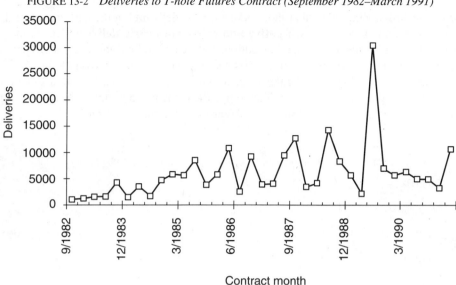

FIGURE 13-2   *Deliveries to T-note Futures Contract (September 1982–March 1991)*

In Figure 13-3, the distribution of deliveries in the Treasury bond futures market has been aggregated across all contracts during the normal yield-curve parts of the sample period, December 1977 to June 1987. The striking fact apparent in the distribution is that deliveries are almost always delayed until the last few days of the delivery month; in this sample period, about 90% of the deliveries were made during the last five days of the delivery month. A significant volume of deliveries also occurred around the last day of futures trading. This is due to **positive carry.**

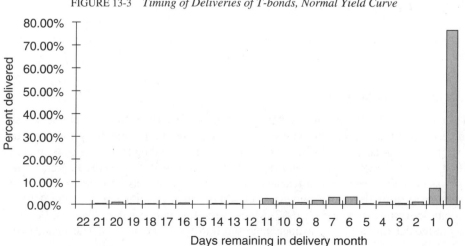

FIGURE 13-3   *Timing of Deliveries of T-bonds, Normal Yield Curve*

Figure 13-4 provides the distribution of deliveries when the yield curve is inverted or downward-sloping. Note that more percentage is delivered in the earlier part of the delivery month. **The carry is negative and this favors early delivery.** On the other hand, the availability of the quality option, wild-card option, and end-of-the-month option favors later delivery. The trade-offs determine the optimal delivery strategy.

The pattern of deliveries for the Treasury note futures contract is similar to that of the Treasury bond futures contract. If anything, the tendency to postpone deliveries until the last delivery date is even stronger for Treasury note futures contracts.

FIGURE 13-4 *Timing of Deliveries of T-bonds, Inverted Yield Curve*

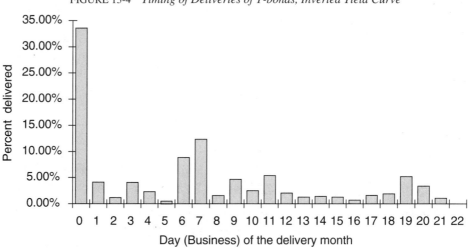

ANALYSIS OF A SPECIFIC CONTRACT: MARCH 1987 T-BOND CONTRACT

To better understand the pricing and delivery strategies, we analyze here a specific T-bond futures contract that expired on March 1987.

Open Interest and Volume

The March 1987 T-bond contract started trading in early 1986. But the volume of trading and open interest only became significant only about three months prior to the delivery month, as shown in Table 13-15. The volume of trading reached a peak of about 300,000 contracts on February 10, 1987, and then started to decline as the delivery month approached. The open interest reached about 225,000 contracts on February 17, 1987, and then steadily declined as investors closed out their positions prior to the delivery month. Indeed, as of March 2, 1987, which is the first delivery date (the first business day of the delivery month), the open interest fell to 108,873 contracts! This is due to the

Date	Settlement Futures Price	Volume of Trading	Open Interest
02/06/87	100.53	186,274	221,782
02/09/87	99.59	237,856	226,794
02/10/87	98.78	307,943	225,296
02/11/87	98.44	280,595	221,616
02/12/87	99.34	221,258	221,424
02/13/87	99.50	184,918	211,828
02/17/87	99.34	165,685	200,041
02/18/87	99.88	208,246	195,679
02/19/87	100.25	252,698	194,212
02/20/87	100.31	138,873	171,404
02/23/87	100.66	173,520	166,627
02/24/87	101.25	227,697	165,163
02/25/87	100.97	192,703	147,248
02/26/87	101.09	230,384	130,078
02/27/87	101.44	180,816	123,287
03/02/87	101.80	32,159	108,873
03/03/87	101.34	37,912	89,677
03/04/87	102.50	28,967	79,103
03/05/87	102.30	28,804	67,579
03/06/87	101.40	23,865	60,048
03/09/87	101.34	19,361	54,634
03/10/87	101.25	11,370	48,580
03/11/87	101.22	14,660	43,389
03/12/87	101.50	9,077	39,279
03/13/87	101.84	10,430	33,970
03/16/87	101.66	9,940	29,829
03/17/87	102.03	12,268	23,793
03/18/87	101.91	7,803	20,817
03/19/87	102.03	7,803	18,524
03/20/87	102.25	9,352	14,759
03/23/87	0.00	9	14,468
03/24/87	0.00	40	14,427
03/25/87	0.00	0	14,425
03/26/87	0.00	0	12,324
03/27/87	0.00	0	10,114
03/30/87	0.00	0	0
03/31/87	0.00	0	0

TABLE 13-15
*March 1987 T-bond
Futures*

fact that most investors who take positions in T-bond futures do so not to make or take delivery but either to hedge their interest-rate risk or to speculate. Given the extraordinary liquidity of the T-bond futures market, hedging is easily done in this market. For example, the peak volume of trading, which was about 300,000 contracts, indicates a dollar trading of 300,000 × 100,000 = $30 billion.

The positions of the sellers and buyers are marked-to-market everyday. Table 13-16 illustrates the profits or losses from selling 100 futures contracts.

Date	Settlement Futures Price	Mark-to Market Cash Flow	Cumulative Profits
02/05/87	100.62500	0.00	0.00
02/06/87	100.53125	9,375.00	9,375.00
02/09/87	99.59375	93,750.00	103,125.00
02/10/87	98.78125	81,250.00	184,375.00
02/11/87	98.43750	34,375.00	218,750.00
02/12/87	99.34375	-90,625.00	128,125.00
02/13/87	99.50000	-15,625.00	112,500.00
02/17/87	99.34375	15,625.00	128,125.00
02/18/87	99.87500	-53,125.00	75,000.00
02/19/87	100.25000	-37,500.00	37,500.00
02/20/87	100.31250	-6,250.00	31,250.00
02/23/87	100.65625	-34,375.00	-3,125.00
02/24/87	101.25000	-59,375.00	-62,500.00
02/25/87	100.96875	28,125.00	-34,375.00
02/26/87	101.09375	-12,500.00	-46,875.00
02/27/87	101.43750	-34,375.00	-81,250.00
03/02/87	101.78125	-34,375.00	-115,625.00
03/03/87	101.34375	43,750.00	-71,875.00
03/04/87	102.50000	-115,625.00	-187,500.00
03/05/87	102.31250	18,750.00	-168,750.00
03/06/87	101.40625	90,625.00	-78,125.00
03/09/87	101.34375	6,250.00	-71,875.00
03/10/87	101.25000	9,375.00	-62,500.00
03/11/87	101.21875	3,125.00	-59,375.00
03/12/87	101.50000	-28,125.00	-87,500.00
03/13/87	101.84375	-34,375.00	-121,875.00
03/16/87	101.65625	18,750.00	-103,125.00
03/17/87	102.03125	-37,500.00	-140,625.00
03/18/87	101.90625	12,500.00	-128,125.00
03/19/87	102.03125	-12,500.00	-140,625.00
03/20/87	102.25000	-21,875.00	-162,500.00

TABLE 13-16
Profits (Losses) from Selling 100 T-bond Contracts

Seller's Option in the March 1987 Contract

The seller of a contract has a timing option. For the March 1987 contract, the first delivery date was March 2, 1987, and the last delivery date was March 31, 1987. The contract expired on March 20, 1987. Table 13-17 provides the actual delivery pattern. Note that

Delivery Days	Amount Delivered
03/02/87	0
03/03/87	0
03/04/87	0
03/05/87	0
03/06/87	0
03/09/87	0
03/10/87	0
03/11/87	0
03/12/87	0
03/13/87	0
03/16/87	0
03/17/87	0
03/18/87	0
03/19/87	0
03/20/87	0
03/23/87	0
03/24/87	1
03/25/87	2
03/26/87	2,101
03/27/87	2,210
03/30/87	10,114
Total	14,428

TABLE 13-17
Timing of Deliveries for the March 1987 Contract

bulk of the deliveries took place on March 30, 1987, which is nearly the last delivery date.

As noted in Table 13-10, any T-bond that has a minimum of 15 years to its maturity date or (if callable) to its first call date is eligible for delivery. There are many T-bonds that satisfy this broad requirement and the seller of the T-bond futures has the option of deciding which combination of eligible T-bonds should be delivered. This is the quality option.

The delivery of a specific deliverable bond into the futures market results in the payment of an invoice price. The option of selecting a specific bundle of deliverable bonds is with the short. Note from Table 13-17 that bulk of the actual deliveries to the March 1987 contract tended to occur at the end of the delivery month. The aggregate face value of the T-bonds must be equal to $100,000 for each futures contract. Although the CBT standard par deliverable bond is an 8% T-bond with 20 years to maturity, typically T-bonds with different maturities and coupons get delivered. This is due to the fact that a par bond is usually unavailable and more importantly, as we will show later, it is economically optimal to deliver other bonds for most yield curves. Note from Table 13-21 that only six T-bonds were used in delivery.

On March 2, 1987, if the par bond were available and delivered, a short would have received $101,800 (plus accrued interest on that date) for the delivery of $100,000 face value of par T-bond. This is calculated from the futures price on that day, 101.80.

Invoicing Deliveries

A key delivery parameter is the conversion factor. The underlying premise is that the futures price must be adjusted upwards if the T-bond that is delivered has a coupon in excess of 8% and adjusted downwards if the delivered T-bond has a coupon of less than 8%.

The exact formula for the computation of the conversion factor is provided below:

$$CF = \frac{1}{\left(1 + \frac{y}{2}\right)^{\frac{x}{6}}} \left[\frac{c}{2} + \left(\frac{c}{0.08} \left[1 - \frac{1}{\left(1 + \frac{0.08}{2}\right)^{2N}} \right] + \frac{1}{\left(1 + \frac{0.08}{2}\right)^{2N}} \right) \right] - \frac{c}{2} \frac{6 - x}{6}$$

where CF is the conversion factor, c is the coupon expressed in decimals, N is the full number of years to maturity or first call date, and x is the number of months by which maturity exceeds N rounded down to the nearest quarter. Clearly, $x = 0, 3, 6,$ or 9. The formula provides CF directly when $x = 0, 3,$ or 6. When $x = 9$ the formula becomes

$$CF = \frac{1}{\left(1 + \frac{y}{2}\right)^{\frac{1}{2}}} \left[\frac{c}{2} + \left[\frac{c}{0.08} \left[1 - \frac{1}{\left(1 + \frac{0.08}{2}\right)^{2N+1}} \right] + \frac{1}{\left(1 + \frac{0.08}{2}\right)^{2N+1}} \right] \right] - \frac{c}{4}$$

We illustrate the computation of the conversion factor in two specific examples.

Example 13-6   14% callable T-bond: 11/15/2006–11

1. As of the first delivery date (March 1, 1987) compute the time to the first call date of the bond and round it down to the nearest quarter.
2. For the 14% T-bond, the relevant maturity is 19 years and 6 months. There are 18 full years for the period 1988 to 2005. There are 10 full months in 1987 starting March 1, 1987, and we stop at August 31, 2006, giving 8 full months in 2006. So, the total is 19 years and 6 months.
3. Compute the value of a 14% T-bond with 19 years and six months to maturity such that it will yield 8.0% to maturity. This is 1.5875 for the 14% T-bond.

Example 13-7   7.25% noncallable T-bond: 5/15/2016

1. As of the first delivery date (March 1, 1987) compute the time to the maturity date of the bond and round it down to the nearest quarter.
2. For the 7.25% T-bond, the relevant maturity is 29 years. There is a total of 28 full years for the period 1988 to 2015. There are 10 full months in 1987 starting March 1, 1987, and we stop at February 28, 2016, giving 2 full months in 2006. So, the total is 29 years.
3. Compute the value of a 7.25% T-bond with 29 years such that it will yield 8.0% to maturity. This is 0.9159 for the 7.25% T-bond.

The conversion factor is used to determine the invoice price, which is the compensation paid for delivering a contract-grade bond. First the futures price is multiplied by the conversion factor of the bond. Then the accrued interest is added to determine the invoice price.

To calculate the invoice price that will be paid in the futures market, let us assume that the delivery occurs on March 20, 1987. Recall from Table 13-15 that the futures price is 102.25.

Example 13-8

Table 13-18 illustrates the factors involved in the calculation of the invoice price for the 14% T-bond. The invoice price is

$$102.25 \times 1.5875 + 4.8343 = 167.156.$$

Futures Price	102.25
Coupon	14%
Maturity	11/15/2011
Conversion factor	1.5875
Accrued interest	4.8343
Invoice price	167.156

TABLE 13-18
*March 1987 14% T-bond
Futures, Invoice Price
Calculations*

Example 13-9

In a similar way, Table 13-19 illustrates the factors for calculating the invoice price for the 7.25% T-bond.

$$102.25 \times 0.9159 + 2.5035 = 96.154$$

Futures Price	102.25
Coupon	7.25%
Maturity	5/15/2016
Conversion factor	0.9159
Accrued interest	2.5035
Invoice price	96.154

TABLE 13-19
*March 1987 7.2570
T-bond Futures, Invoice
Price Calculations*

The conversion factors and the invoice prices of all the deliverable bonds in these examples are shown in Table 13-20.

TABLE 13-20 Cheapest Deliverable Treasury Bond Analysis, March 1987 Futures

Coupon	Maturity	Price (Flat)	Accrued Interest	YTM/YTC	PVBP (dollars per million par)	Modified Duration (in years)	Conversion Factor	Basis (in ticks; $\frac{1}{32}$)	Repo Rate	Basis after Carry ($\frac{1}{32}$)
11.625%	11/15/02	133.750	3.0186	7.850%	1108	8.10	1.3188	87.83	6.05%	75.57
10.750%	2/15/03	126.156	0.0594	7.850%	1069	8.47	1.2436	83.88	6.05%	72.48
10.750%	5/15/03	126.313	2.7914	7.853%	1079	8.36	1.2457	81.96	6.05%	71.21
11.125%	8/15/03	130.000	0.0615	7.850%	1112	8.55	1.2811	87.41	6.05%	75.48
11.875%	11/15/03	136.938	3.0836	7.866%	1166	8.33	1.3516	85.50	6.05%	73.04
12.375%	5/15/04	142.000	3.2134	7.877%	1218	8.39	1.4027	84.96	6.05%	71.82
13.750%	8/15/04	155.531	0.0760	7.856%	1320	8.48	1.5326	104.98	6.05%	89.07
11.625%	11/15/04	135.438	3.0186	7.880%	1191	8.60	1.3383	79.82	6.05%	67.93
12.000%	5/15/05	139.333	3.1160	7.893%	1234	8.66	1.3781	77.75	6.05%	65.37
10.750%	8/15/05	127.375	0.0594	7.908%	1156	9.07	1.2613	66.37	6.05%	55.24
9.375%	2/15/06	115.625	0.0518	7.786%	1096	9.47	1.1321	101.03	6.05%	92.36
7.875%c	11/15/07	101.813	2.0449	7.697%	1042	10.03	0.9890	114.08	6.05%	108.30
8.375%c	8/15/08	105.688	0.0463	7.824%	1076	10.18	1.0336	96.42	6.05%	89.21
8.750%c	11/15/08	108.719	2.2721	7.902%	1099	9.90	1.0680	83.82	6.05%	76.40
9.125%c	5/15/09	112.000	2.3695	7.963%	1130	9.88	1.1035	75.95	6.05%	67.90
10.375%c	11/15/09	123.281	2.6941	8.113%	1217	9.66	1.2216	61.62	6.05%	51.55
11.750%c	2/15/10	135.938	0.0649	8.240%	1312	9.65	1.3520	52.30	6.05%	39.39
10.000%c	5/15/10	120.688	2.5967	8.021%	1215	9.86	1.1891	82.11	6.05%	72.83
12.750%c	11/15/10	145.656	3.3108	8.311%	1402	9.41	1.4546	37.00	6.05%	23.31
13.875%c	5/15/11	156.938	3.6029	8.356%	1502	9.36	1.5689	34.69	6.05%	19.44
14.000%c	**11/15/11**	**158.625**	**3.6354**	**8.354%**	**1529**	**9.42**	**1.5875**	**29.55**	**6.05%**	**14.23**
10.375%c	11/15/12	124.781	2.6941	8.072%	1292	10.13	1.2374	59.46	6.05%	49.73
12.000%c	8/15/15	140.938	0.0663	8.248%	1462	10.37	1.4053	42.82	6.05%	30.12
13.250%c	**5/15/14**	**153.813**	**3.4406**	**8.254%**	**1554**	**9.88**	**1.5394**	**28.51**	**6.05%**	**14.84**
12.500%c	8/15/14	146.500	0.0691	8.212%	1499	10.22	1.4640	34.23	6.05%	20.92
11.750%c	11/15/14	140.125	3.0511	8.095%	1461	10.20	1.3885	70.20	6.05%	58.91
11.250%	2/15/15	138.625	0.0662	7.828%	1484	10.70	1.3599	113.07	6.05%	102.62
10.625%	8/15/15	131.719	0.0587	7.828%	1428	10.84	1.2921	107.65	6.05%	97.96
9.875%	11/15/15	123.250	2.5642	7.828%	1354	10.76	1.2093	99.77	6.05%	91.53
9.250%	2/15/16	117.000	0.0511	7.767%	1305	11.15	1.1396	121.23	6.05%	113.33
7.250%	5/15/16	95.000	1.8826	7.680%	1110	11.46	0.9159	128.50	6.05%	123.47
7.500%	11/15/16	98.625	1.9475	7.616%	1157	11.50	0.9437	156.17	6.05%	151.04

Settlement date: 2/17/87
Final Delivery Date: 03/31/87
cindicates a callable bond

Basis in T-Bond Futures

A concept that is widely used in the analysis of the T-bond contract is the basis. Let P_t be the flat price of the deliverable T-bond, CF be its conversion factor, and $H_t(s)$ be the futures price at date t for maturity at date s. Recognizing that futures contracts permit delivery on any business day of the delivery month, we will interpret s as the last business day of the delivery month in a positive-carry market and interpret s as the first business day of the month in a negative-carry market. The **basis** B_t is defined as

$$B_t = P_t - CF \times H_t(s).$$

If t happens to be in the delivery month, then by the no arbitrage principal, we must have $B_t > 0$. If this were not the case, by simultaneously selling the futures and immediately delivering, one could lock in riskless profits. For reasons that we will present shortly, the basis must be positive even on other days.

Figures 13-5 and 13-6 track the basis of these two deliverable T-bonds to the March 1987 futures contract. Note that the basis of the low-coupon bond decreases as the maturity date approaches but does not converge to zero. On the other hand, the basis of the high-coupon bond is converging closer to zero. Intuitively, this indicates that the futures price is tracking more closely the price behavior of the high-coupon bond. Thus the existence of a *coupon bias* for delivery is illustrated by these figures.

Determination of Delivery

We now analyze the optimal delivery strategies for the March 1987 futures contract. Let us say that in February 1987 we wish to determine the optimal delivery strategy for the

FIGURE 13-5   *Basis Behavior for the 14% Long Bond*

Days on delivery month

FIGURE 13-6   *Basis Behavior for the 7.25% Long Bond*

March 1987 futures contract. From the contractual specifications laid out in our discussion thus far, we have the following conclusions:

- Eligible Treasury bonds can be delivered on any day from March 1, 1987, to March 31, 1987.
- The last day of futures trading will be March 20, 1987, leaving seven business days (23, 24, 25, 26, 27, 30 and 31) for the completion of the delivery process.
- As noted in Table 13-10, T-bonds that are eligible for delivery to the March futures must have 15 years or more to maturity as of March 1, 1987, if they are noncallable. If callable, they must have at least 15 years to the first call date.

Table 13-20 lists all deliverable T-bonds to the March 1987 futures contract as of February 1987. In addition, this table indicates the characteristics of all the eligible Treasury bonds, such as PVBP, duration, and so on. The total bonds delivered amounted to $1.4 billion face value as seen in Tables 13-20 and 13-21. It is of interest to note from Table 13-21 that bulk of the deliveries were effected using low duration bonds. We will explain why this was the case later.

To better understand the pricing of Treasury futures contract, we now develop the concept of cash-and-carry arbitrage.

Cash-and-Carry Arbitrage Principle. The cash-and-carry principle is a pricing principle that is widely used in the industry. The logic behind this principle works as follows: if the price at which an investor can sell a bond in the forward market (at the maturity date of the forward contract) is higher than the cost of financing the bond, then the investor should sell forward and finance the bond. Otherwise, the investor should buy forward and sell the bond in a repurchase transaction.

Coupon	Maturity Date	Deliveries	
11.625	11/15/2002		**TABLE 13-21**
10.750	02/15/2003		*Deliverable T-bonds to*
10.750	05/15/2003		*the March 1987 Futures*
11.125	08/15/2003		*Contract*
11.875	11/15/2003		
12.375	05/15/2004		
13.750	08/15/2004		
11.625	11/15/2004		
12.000	05/15/2005		
10.750	08/15/2005		
9.375	02/15/2006		
7.875	11/15/2007		
8.375	08/15/2008		
8.750	11/15/2008		
9.125	05/15/2009		
10.375	11/15/2009		
11.759	02/15/2010		
10.000	05/15/2010		
12.750	11/15/2010	3,935	
13.875	05/15/2011	1,555	
14.000	11/15/2011	4,736	
10.375	11/15/2012		
12.000	08/15/2013	2,695	
13.250	05/15/2014	1,505	
12.500	08/15/2014	2	
11.750	11/15/2014		
11.250	02/15/2015		
10.625	08/15/2015		
9.875	11/15/2015		
9.250	02/15/2016		
7.250	05/15/2016		
7.500	11/15/2016		
Total deliveries:		14,428	

In order to effect such a trade, a bond trader first gathers information about the following aspects of the trade:

- The price of the bond, its accrued interest, and its coupon dates. These factors are crucial to the profitability of the trade. The accrued interest is what the trader gets if the trader is long in the bond.
- The status of the bond in the market for repurchase agreements. If the bond trades special in the repo market, the financing cost of that bond may be substantial. Once again, this is central to the profitability of the trade.

- The futures price is obviously the major determinant of the compensation that the trader may expect to receive should the trader decide to deliver or offset.

If we make several key assumptions, we can regard the futures contract as a forward contract.

- Markets are frictionless and there are no taxes.
- Each bond is priced to reflect the present value of its future cash flows.
- Only one T-bond is eligible for delivery and is available in plentiful supply.
- The financing rate is a constant; overnight repos and term repos may be entered into at the same rate.

Let the forward price at date t for settlement at date T be $G_t(T)$. The analysis is summarized in Table 13-22. Note that the total cash flows at T will be zero because the forward price converges to the cash price: $G_T(T) = P_T$. Equivalently, the basis at maturity is zero. Then, to preclude arbitrage, it must follow that the investment at t must be zero as well. But the investment at t is equal to

$$-(P_t + ai_t) + PV_t(G_t(T)) + PV_t(ai_T) + PV_t(c) = 0.$$

If the financing rate is assumed to be constant at a level r, then the expression may be written as

$$G_t(T) = (P_t + ai_t) \times \left(1 + r \times \frac{T-t}{360}\right) - ai_T - c \times \left(1 + r \times \frac{T-s}{360}\right).$$

Quite often, the quantity on the right-hand side of the expression is referred to as the forward price, reflecting the fact that the cash-and-carry arbitrage ignores the marking-to-market feature and the fact that the seller's delivery options are ignored.

Let

$$G_t(T) \equiv (P_t + ai_t) \times \left(1 + r \times \frac{T-t}{360}\right) - ai_T - c \times \left(1 + r \times \frac{T-s}{360}\right).$$

TABLE 13-22   *Cash-and-Carry Arbitrage*

Transaction at t	Cash Flow at t	Coupon Date s	Maturity Date T
1. Sell Forward	0		$(G_t(T) - G_T(T))$
2. Buy the Bond	$-(P_t + ai_t)$		
Receive coupon		c	
Receive market value of bond at T			$P_T + ai_T$
3. Borrow $PV_t(c)$	$PV_t(c)$	$-c$	
4. Borrow $PV_t(ai_T)$	$PV_t(ai_T)$		$-ai_T$
5. Borrow	$PV_t(G_t(T))$		$-G_t(T)$
Total cash flow at s and T		0	0

The forward price is computed under the assumption that there is only one deliverable bond and that the bond has to be delivered on the last day of futures trading. As we know from the discussion of T-bond futures specifications, these assumptions are restrictive; many bonds are deliverable and there are significant flexibilities in the timing of deliveries. As a result of ignoring these options that the short has in the futures market, the computed forward price tends to be higher than the futures price. In other words, because of the options that the short has in the futures market, he is willing to sell bonds for deferred delivery at a lower (futures) price than he would in the forward market, which assumes that the short has no flexibility.

Note that the transactions in Table 13-22 demonstrate how a short position in a forward contract can be hedged by borrowing and buying the underlying deliverable bond. In fact, the hedging strategy is a fully financed position in the underlying bond. This implies that a long position in a T-bond forward contract is equivalent to borrowing and buying the underlying T-bond. Likewise, a short position in the T-bond forward contract is equivalent to shorting the T-bond and placing the proceeds in a riskless asset. Note that such transactions will be executed in the repo markets which were discussed earlier in the text.

For T-bond futures contracts similar arguments can be made. We must use the cheapest deliverable bond to execute the equivalent transactions. A short position in T-bond futures can be hedged by borrowing and buying the cheapest deliverable bond (say, bond X). All the delivery options belong to the seller and, as such, the short position carries little risk. If some other T-bond (say, bond Y) becomes cheap to deliver, the existing T-bond X can be sold and bond Y can be purchased. Since Y is cheaper than X, the short position will make money.

On the other hand, a long position in T-bond futures has many risks. Since all delivery options are with the seller, the long position will not know which bond might be delivered and when.

In addition, the delivery in the futures market will produce a revenue equal to the invoice price (excluding accrued interest), which is

$$CF \times H_t(T)$$

The forward price represents the price at which the bond can be sold forward to break even. The invoice price represents the actual revenue by willing the bond in the futures market. Therefore, the difference between the forward price of the bond and the invoice price measures the profit or loss associated with the strategy of selling futures and borrowing and buying the bond. This difference is what is known as the **basis after carry** (BAC). This concept is widely used by bond traders who study the spread between futures and forward prices. The basis after carry measures the net cost of carrying the bond in a repurchase transaction, and delivering it into the futures market and receiving the invoice price. If the basis and basis after carry are negative, then profits are realized by this arbitrage strategy. But typically the basis and basis after carry are positive, as Table 13-20 illustrates. This table corresponds to the deliverable bonds to the March 1987 futures contract as of February 17, 1987. As may be noted from Table 13-16, the futures price on this day stood at 99.34375. The basis after carry is also positive for all deliverable bonds.

Note that the basis after carry can be split into two components, the basis and the carry.

$$\text{BAC}_i = (P_t + ai_t) \times \left(1 + r \times \frac{T-t}{360}\right) - ai_T - c \times \left(1 + r \times \frac{T-s}{360}\right)$$
$$- \text{CF}_i \times H_t(T).$$

Intuitively, we can write BAC as

$$\text{BAC}_i = [P_t - \text{CF}_i \times H_t(T)] - \left[ai_T - ai_t + c \times \left(1 + r \times \frac{T-s}{360}\right)\right]$$
$$+ (P_t + ai_t) \times r \times \frac{T-t}{360}$$

which says that

$$\text{BAC} = \text{Basis} - \text{reinvested cash inflows} + \text{financing costs}$$

When the carry is positive, BAC is less than the basis; otherwise, it is greater than the basis. Traders can minimize their losses by delaying delivery in a positive carry market if there are no adverse price movements.

It is worth remembering that when BAC < 0 there will be arbitrage opportunities. This requires selling futures, and borrowing and buying the cheapest bond for delivery. The bond transaction will be positioned through a repo desk. On the other hand, if BAC > 0, there is no riskless arbitrage opportunity; if we try to buy futures and short the cheapest bond, there is always the risk that on the delivery month some other bond might become cheaper to deliver. If this were to happen, that bond will be delivered and the short position will have to be covered, perhaps at a considerable cost.

Usually the traders use the basis after carry of a deliverable bond to determine which bond is cheapest to deliverable issue (CDI). On a daily basis, the basis after carry is calculated for each deliverable issue and the issue that has the lowest basis after carry is identified as the CDI. In the computations of basis after carry, a financing rate of 6.05% is assumed for all T-bonds.

A related concept is the implied repo rate. This concept computes the internal rate of return associated with the strategy of selling T-bond futures, and borrowing and buying an eligible T-bond and delivering it to the futures market at maturity. In the expression that we derived for the basis after carry, we set BAC $= 0$ and solve for $r = r^*$ as the implied repo rate. The resulting expression for the implied repo rate is

$$r^* = \frac{[\text{CF}_i \times H_t(T) - P_{it} + ai_T + c - ai_t]}{\left[(P_{it} + ai_t) \times \frac{T-t}{360} - c \times \frac{T-s}{360}\right]} \tag{13.4}$$

Equation (13.4) is valid when there is a coupon payment at date s prior to the maturity date T of the futures contract. If there is no coupon payment, then the equation can be simplified by setting $c = 0$ to get the implied repo rate as:

$$r^* = \frac{[\text{CF}_i \times H_t(T) - ai_T - (P_{it} + ai_t)]}{[P_{it} + ai_t]} \times \frac{360}{T-t}$$

FIGURE 13-7a   *Basis and Basis After Carry for 14%, 11/15/2011 T-bond*

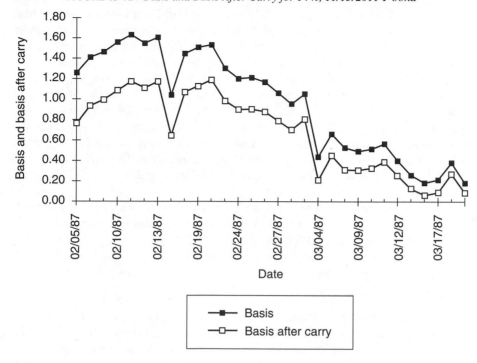

FIGURE 13-7b   *Basis and Basis After Carry for 7.25%, 5/15/2016 T-bond*

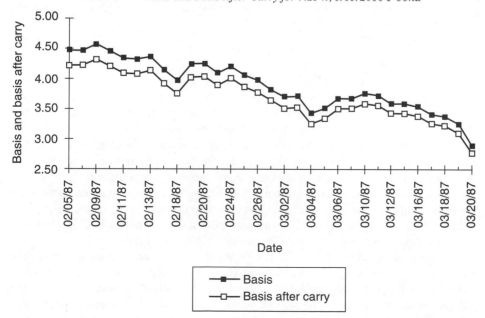

We plot next the behavior of the basis and the basis after carry for the 14% T-bond and the 7.25% T-bond. (See Figures 13-7a and 13-7b.) Note that the basis and the basis after carry converge to zero for the 14% T-bond whereas there is no sense of convergence as far as the 7.25% T-bond is concerned. Note also that the basis after carry for the high-coupon bond approaches closer to zero as the maturity date approaches.

From Table 13-20 it should be clear that the 14% T-bond maturing on November 15, 2011 has a basis after carry of 14 ticks and is the CDI. For the March 1987 contract, quite a few T-bonds were cheap. For instance, 13.875%, 5-15-2011 had a basis after carry of 19 ticks, and 13.25%, 5-15-2014 had a basis after carry of 15 ticks. Note that these T-bonds were delivered in large amounts as was indicated in Table 13-21. T-bonds with a large basis after carry were never delivered. As a result of the positive carry, most of the deliveries took place around the last possible delivery date. This is indicated in Table 13-17.

In this section, it was assumed that the financing rates are known and that there are no timing options to the short. The ability of the short to deliver any one or a combination of T-bonds was accounted for only indirectly by the basis after carry, which considers T-bonds, one at a time, for delivery consideration. These assumptions are relaxed by using interest rate models such as the Black, Derman and Toy model discussed in Chapter 6.

Coupon Bias in Deliveries. We have shown that for the March 1987 T-bond contract, high-coupon bonds were cheaper to deliver. Is there a general coupon bias? To address this question, we examine the circumstances under which low-coupon bonds may be cheaper to deliver. To do this, we vary the yield from 6.78% to 10.58%. This is done in Tables 13-23a and 13-23b.

We compute the ratio of price to the conversion factor for the high-coupon and the low-coupon bonds. Consider the ratio

$$\frac{P_i}{CF_i} \ \forall \ i.$$

Note that at yield levels (indicated by boldface in Tables 13-23a and 13-23b) above 8.03%, this ratio is smaller for low-coupon bonds. On the other hand, at yield levels below 7.93% we find that the high-coupon bond has a lower ratio. This suggests that at higher yields, low-coupon long-maturity bonds are cheaper to deliver. Conversely, at low yields, high-coupon, short-maturity bonds are cheaper to deliver. The economic reasoning behind this is the following. As rates fall, all bonds appreciate in price, but low-coupon, long-maturity bonds tend to become relatively more expensive; hence it is cheaper to deliver high-coupon, short-maturity bonds. In a similar manner, as the rates go up all bonds become cheap, but the low-coupon, long-maturity bonds tend to become cheaper than the high-coupon, short-maturity bonds. As a consequence, low-coupon, long-maturity bonds are delivered during periods of high interest rates.

Broadie and Sundaresan (1992) examine whether futures prices are bid down by the value of the options present in futures contracts. Using a single-factor model, they conclude that delivery options are important and that they affect the futures price. If the delivery options implicit in the futures market have economic value, then a rational agent will assume a long position in the futures contract only if the investor sells at a dis-

YTM	Flat Price	Full Price	Flat Price/CF
7.13%	172.19	175.82	108.46
7.23%	170.59	174.23	107.46
7.33%	169.02	172.66	106.47
7.43%	167.48	171.11	105.50
7.53%	165.95	169.58	104.54
7.63%	164.44	168.08	103.59
7.73%	162.96	166.59	102.65
7.83%	161.49	165.13	101.73
7.93%	**160.05**	**163.68**	**100.82**
8.03%	**158.63**	**162.26**	**99.92**
8.13%	157.22	160.86	99.04
8.23%	155.83	159.47	98.16
8.33%	154.47	158.10	97.30
8.43%	153.12	156.75	96.45
8.53%	151.79	155.42	95.61
8.63%	150.47	154.11	94.79
8.73%	149.18	152.81	93.97
8.83%	147.90	151.54	93.17
8.93%	146.64	150.28	92.37
9.03%	145.40	149.03	91.59
9.13%	144.17	147.81	90.82
9.23%	142.96	146.59	90.05
9.33%	141.76	145.40	89.30
9.43%	140.58	144.22	88.56
9.53%	139.42	143.06	87.82
9.63%	138.27	141.91	87.10
9.73%	137.14	140.77	86.39
9.83%	136.02	139.66	85.68
9.93%	134.92	138.55	84.99
10.03%	133.83	137.46	84.30
10.13%	132.75	136.38	83.62
10.23%	131.69	135.32	82.95
10.33%	130.64	134.27	82.29
10.43%	129.60	133.24	81.64
10.53%	128.58	132.22	81.00
10.63%	127.57	131.21	80.36
10.73%	126.58	130.21	79.73
10.83%	125.59	129.23	79.11
10.93%	124.62	128.26	78.50

TABLE 13-23a

Conversion Factor Bias, 14%, 11/15/2006 T-bond

Note: Flat price/conversion factor is the conversion factor bias

count relative to the forward price where there are no such options. From an empirical standpoint, the difference between the cash price and the adjusted futures price (invoice price) as of the first delivery date gives us the market value of the wild-card and end-of-the-month options.

YTM	Flat Price	Full Price	Flat Price/CF
6.78%	105.93	107.81	115.66
6.88%	104.62	106.50	114.22
6.98%	103.33	105.21	112.82
7.08%	102.07	103.95	111.44
7.18%	100.83	102.72	110.09
7.28%	99.62	101.50	108.77
7.38%	98.43	100.31	107.47
7.48%	97.27	99.15	106.20
7.58%	96.12	98.00	104.95
7.68%	95.00	96.88	103.72
7.78%	93.90	95.78	102.52
7.88%	92.82	94.70	101.34
7.98%	91.76	93.64	100.19
8.08%	90.72	92.60	99.05
8.18%	89.70	91.58	97.94
8.28%	88.70	90.58	96.85
8.38%	87.72	89.60	95.77
8.48%	86.75	88.63	94.72
8.58%	85.81	87.69	93.69
8.68%	84.88	86.76	92.67
8.78%	83.97	85.85	91.68
8.88%	83.07	84.95	90.70
8.98%	82.19	84.07	89.74
9.08%	81.33	83.21	88.80
9.18%	80.48	82.36	87.87
9.28%	79.64	81.53	86.96
9.38%	78.83	80.71	86.07
9.48%	78.02	79.90	85.19
9.58%	77.23	79.11	84.33
9.68%	76.46	78.34	83.48
9.78%	75.69	77.58	82.65
9.88%	74.94	76.83	81.83
9.98%	74.21	76.09	81.02
10.08%	73.48	75.37	80.23
10.18%	72.77	74.66	79.46
10.28%	72.07	73.96	78.69
10.38%	71.39	73.27	77.94
10.48%	70.71	72.59	77.20
10.58%	70.05	71.93	76.48

TABLE 13-23b

Conversion Factor Bias, 7.25%, 5/15/2016 T-bond

Note: Flat price/conversion factor is the conversion factor bias

They find that the discounts are of the order of 9 to 16 ticks for Treasury bonds and 13 ticks for Treasury notes on the first delivery date. For the expiry date of futures, the discounts for Treasury bonds average about 6 to 9 ticks and for Treasury notes about 6 ticks.

CONCLUSION

In this chapter, we have defined futures and forward contracts and identified some important differences between these two deferred delivery agreements. This chapter also provided some conditions under which both markets may play useful functions. A historical perspective of the markets was provided, leading to their current configuration. We then examined in detail the Treasury futures contracts and the delivery options that are contained in them.

PROBLEMS

13.1   Define the following terms: (i) open interest, (ii) volume of trading, (iii) clearing house, (iv) price limits.

13.2   What are the differences between cash settlement and physical deliveries in the futures markets? Why do we observe physical deliveries in the Treasury futures and cash settlement in the equity index futures?

13.3   Define: (i) basis and (ii) basis after carry. What do these concepts attempt to capture?

13.4   Describe the seller's options in a Treasury futures contract. How do these options affect the basis after carry? What would be the basis after carry in the absence of the seller's options? Why?

13.5 (a)   Generally, we find that the Treasury futures prices decline with maturity in an upward-sloping yield curve. Why?

  (b)   Usually, under the same circumstances, equity index futures tend to increase with maturity. Why?

13.6   The market price of a thirty-year T-bond (6.25% coupon, August 15, 2023, maturity) is quoted at $103\frac{14}{32}$ for settlement on September 24, 1993.

  (a)   Calculate the yield to maturity (compounded semi-annually) and (ii) the value of an 0.01 per $1 million par amount.

  (b)   Determine the conversion factor for this bond to the December 1993 T-bond futures contract.

13.7   For the T-bond in Problem 13.6, the financing costs (term repo to the end of December) are relatively stable at 3.0% (annualized) in the repo market.

  (a)   A bond trader wishes to carry a 25 million face amount of this bond until December 31, 1993. What is the minimum price at which he will be able to sell this security on December 31, 1993 to break even? Why?

  (b)   On September 24, 1993, the December T-bond futures was quoted at $120\frac{2}{32}$. Compute (i) the basis and (ii) the basis after carry. Is there an opportunity for arbitrage? If there is an arbitrage possibility, set up the trade that will enable you to reap arbitrage gains.

13.8   Present the term structure of futures prices (futures prices versus delivery month) for (i) the crude oil futures markets and (ii) the T-bond futures markets. Explain the pattern that you observe.

REFERENCES

Anderson, R. 1984. "The Regulation of Futures Contracts Innovations in the United States." *Journal of Futures Markets* 4:297–332.

Black, F. 1976. "The Pricing of Commodity Contracts." *Journal of Financial Economics* 3:167–179.

Broadie, M., and S. Sundaresan 1992. "The Pricing of Timing and Quality Options: An Application to Treasury Bond and Treasury Note Futures Market." Columbia University Working Paper.

Carlton, D. 1984. "Futures Markets: Their Purpose, Their History, Their Growth, Their Successes and Failures." *Journal of Futures Markets* 4:237–271.

Cox, J., J. Ingersoll, and S. Ross 1981. "The Relation between Forward Prices and Futures Prices." *Journal of Financial Economics* 9(4):321–346.

Garbade, K. D., and W. L. Silber 1983. "Futures Contracts on Commodities with Multiple Varieties: An Analysis of Premiums and Discounts." *Journal of Business* 56:249–271.

Gay, G. D., and S. Manaster 1984. "The Quality Option Implicit in Futures Contracts." *Journal of Financial Economics* 13:353–370.

Gay, G. D., and S. Manaster 1986. "Implicit Delivery Options and Optimal Delivery Strategies for Financial Futures Contracts." *Journal of Financial Economics* 16:41–72.

Hicks, J. 1939. *Value and Capital: An Enquiry into Some Fundamental Principles of Economic Theory.* 2d ed. Oxford: Oxford University Press.

Jarrow, R., and G. Oldfield 1981. "Forward Contracts and Futures Contracts." *Journal of Financial Economics* 9(4):373–382.

Kane, E. 1984. "Regulatory Structure in Futures Markets: Jurisdictional Competition between the SEC, the CFTC and Other Agencies." *Journal of Futures Markets* 4:367–384.

Keynes, J. 1930. *A Treatise on Money.* New York: Harcourt Brace and Company.

Kilcollin, T. E. 1982. "Difference Systems in Financial Futures Markets." *Journal of Finance* 37:1183–1197.

Livingston, M. 1984. "The Cheapest Deliverable Bond for the CBT Treasury Bond Futures Contract." *Journal of Futures Markets* 4:161–172.

Richard, S., and M. Sundaresan 1981. "A Continuous Time Model of Forward Prices and Futures Prices in a Multigood Economy." *Journal of Financial Economics* 9(4):347–371.

Silber, W. 1981. "Innovation, Competition and New Contract Design in Futures Markets." *Journal of Futures Markets* 1(2):123–155.

Chapter 14

Eurodollar Futures and Swaps

Chapter Objectives

This chapter describes the Eurodollar futures markets and the interest-rate swap markets. These two markets are shown to be tightly aligned. The Eurodollar contract, its specifications, and its applications are illustrated with specific examples. In addition, the following questions are addressed.

- What are Eurodollar futures contracts and where are they traded?
- How can Eurodollar futures contracts be used to swap from floating-rate liabilities into fixed-rate liabilities?
- What are TED spreads?
- What is an interest-rate swap? How is it priced?
- What is the impact of the swap dealer's credit reputation on the swap bid-offer spreads?
- How can swaps be used to manage risk?

INTRODUCTION

In this chapter we provide a description of the Eurodollar time deposits and the Eurodollar futures contracts. The cash settlement feature of Eurodollar futures is described and its implications for swapping from floating to fixed-rate liabilities are investigated. This is followed by a discussion of the spread between Eurodollar futures contracts and Treasury bill futures contracts. This spread, known as the TED spread, is used by investors in their trading strategies. Options on Eurodollar futures contracts are discussed next. The use of such options to create caps, floors and collars on Libor is illustrated through examples. We then define interest rate swaps and describe the evolution of the swap market and swap-related derivatives. Risk characteristics of interest rate swaps are then examined. Two approaches for the valuation of swaps are presented: the first approach uses forward rates and the second approach uses the par bond curve concept. Risk management of swaps and the credit risk of swaps are investigated next. Finally, the chapter analyzes the swap spreads and presents some empirical evidence on spreads.

EURODOLLAR FUTURES CONTRACTS

Eurodollar deposits are dollar deposits that are maintained outside the United States. Generally, they are exempt from the Federal Reserve regulations that apply to the domestic deposits markets. The rates that apply to Eurodollar deposits in interbank transactions are known as the London Interbank Offered Rates (LIBOR). The LIBOR spot market is active in maturities ranging from a few days to 10 years. The depth of the market is especially great in the three-month and six-month maturity sectors.

The market for Eurodollar deposits is among the largest financial markets with many participating institutions. In fact, many other financial markets such as the swap markets and the commercial paper markets, to name just two, regard LIBOR as benchmarks in setting their relevant rates.

The Eurodollar futures contract introduced by the Chicago Mercantile Exchange is currently one of the most actively traded futures contracts in the United States and in the world. This contract settles to 90-day London Interbank Offered Rate (LIBOR), which is the yield derived from the underlying asset that is the 90-day Eurodollar time deposit. This method of computing the futures price is unique and is a departure from the futures-pricing formulations in the literature. Since the price-to-yield transformation is not linear, the pricing of futures contracts on yields does not follow directly from the pricing of the corresponding futures. More importantly, it also renders the standard implied forward rates calculations from the LIBOR term structure different from the futures price; such forward rates apply only to situations where the forward and futures contracts are on asset prices and not to situations where the contracts are on yields.

Currently Eurodollar futures contracts with virtually identical specifications are traded at the International Monetary Market (IMM) in Chicago, the Singapore International Monetary Exchange (SIMEX), and the London International Financial Futures Exchange (LIFFE). Proposals are currently well under way to list Eurodollar futures contracts in Tokyo as well. IMM and SIMEX also have common clearing systems whereby Eurodollar futures positions that are established in one exchange can be offset in the other.

Table 14-1 gives a sample of Eurodollar futures contracts.

Maturity	Price	Implied Interest	Open Interest	
				TABLE 14-1
12/1994	93.80	6.20	366,565	*Eurodollar Futures*
3/1995	93.11	6.89	465,930	*Contracts, November 28,*
6/1995	92.49	7.51	330,946	*1994*
9/1995	92.11	7.89	259,957	
12/1995	91.85	8.15	189,708	
3/1996	91.81	8.19	183,087	
6/1996	91.74	8.26	143,724	
9/1996	91.68	8.32	142,058	
12/1996	91.64	8.36	106,181	
3/1997	91.67	8.33	99,762	
6/1997	91.65	8.35	78,133	
9/1997	91.64	8.36	60,754	
12/1997	91.62	8.38	51,071	
3/1998	91.64	8.36	45,930	
6/1998	91.62	8.38	36,559	
9/1998	91.60	8.40	29,466	
12/1998	91.58	8.42	28,246	
3/1999	91.60	8.40	23,790	
6/1999	91.58	8.42	19,063	
9/1999	91.55	8.45	13,254	
12/1999	91.50	8.50	9,675	
3/2000	91.52	8.48	8,653	
6/2000	91.50	8.50	5,949	
9/2000	91.47	8.53	7,263	
12/2000	91.41	8.59	6,860	
3/2001	91.44	8.56	6,704	
6/2001	91.42	8.58	5,608	
9/2001	91.39	8.61	5,595	
12/2001	91.34	8.66	4,057	
3/2002	91.39	8.61	2,989	
6/2002	91.37	8.63	2,785	
9/2002	91.35	8.65	2,104	

We describe the underlying cash market next.

Calculating Yields in the Cash Market

In the Eurodollar time deposit market, deposits are traded between participating banks for maturities ranging from a few days to several years. On the trade date, the banks negotiate on principal, interest and maturity. The settlement date is typically two London business days after the trade date. On the settlement date, the principal amount is sent by the lender to the borrower. On the maturity date, principal plus the interest is sent by the borrower to the lender. Interest on Eurodollar time deposits is calculated on actual/360 basis as Example 14-1 illustrates.

Example 14-1

One million dollars is borrowed for 45 days in the Eurodollar time deposit market at a quoted rate of 5.25% (annualized). What is the interest due after 45 days?

$$\text{Interest} = \$1,000,000 \times 0.0525 \times \frac{45}{360}$$
$$= \$6,562.50$$

We can generalize from this example so that τ is the time to maturity in days between the settlement date t and the maturity date s. Let $l_t(\tau)$ be the LIBOR quoted on a principal amount $b(t, s)$ at date t. We will choose $b(t, s)$ so that it grows to $1 at date s. Then, the dollar interest earned (using Example 14-1) is:

$$I = b(t, s) \times l_t(\tau) \times \frac{\tau}{360}. \tag{14.1}$$

Rearranging

$$l_t(\tau) = \frac{360}{\tau}\left[\frac{I}{b(t, s)}\right] \tag{14.2}$$

Remember that the principal $b(t, s)$ borrowed is chosen at t such that

$$1 = b(t, s) + I. \tag{14.3}$$

Using Equation (14.3) to eliminate I in Equation (14.2) we get

$$l_t(\tau) = \frac{360}{\tau}\left[\frac{1}{b(t, s)} - 1\right]. \tag{14.4}$$

To compare the return on Eurodollar time deposits with the return on other securities, it is useful to construct the continuously compounded return as well.

Example 14-2

What is the continuously compounded return on the Eurodollar time deposit in Example 14-1?

The continuously compounded yield, denoted by y, is

$$y = \frac{365}{\tau}\ln\left[\frac{P + I}{P}\right],$$

where P is the principal borrowed, I is the dollar interest earned and τ is the time to maturity in days.

$$y = \frac{365}{45} \ln \left[\frac{1,000,000 + 6,562.50}{1,000,000} \right]$$
$$= 5.306\%$$

Note that cash market yield is higher than the quoted LIBOR.

Having examined the yield calculations in the Eurodollar cash (deposit) market, we turn to the Eurodollar futures settlement next.

Eurodollar Futures Settlement to Yields

A key feature of Eurodollar futures contract is the manner in which they are settled at maturity. The futures contract settles by cash on its maturity date with no delivery or timing flexibilities to either the investor who is short or to the investor who is long. On the expiration date, which is the second London business day before the third Wednesday of the maturity month, the contract settles by cash to LIBOR using the following procedure.

On the expiration date, the clearing house determines the LIBOR for three-month Eurodollar deposits on two different times, the time of termination of trading and at a randomly selected time within 90 minutes of the termination of trading. The determination of the LIBOR is done via a sampling procedure. The clearing house selects, at random, 12 reference banks from a list of no less than 20 participating banks. Each bank provides a quotation to the clearing house on the LIBOR applied to three-month Eurodollar time deposits. The clearing house eliminates the highest two quotes and the lowest two quotes and computes an arithmetic average of the remaining eight quotes of the LIBOR. This is regarded by the clearing house as the LIBOR for that time. The final settlement price of the Eurodollar futures contract is obtained by performing this LIBOR computation at the two times indicated above and then subtracting the arithmetic mean of the computed LIBOR (rounded to the nearest basis point) from 100.

Thus, at maturity, futures price (by design) converges to $100 \times (1 - \text{LIBOR})$ where the LIBOR is expressed in decimals with a resolution of a basis point. For example, an 8.01% (annualized) LIBOR will be expressed as 0.0801. Equivalently, 100 minus the Eurodollar futures price will converge to the three-month LIBOR. Figure 14-1 illustrates the convergence process for the December 1988 futures contract. A summary of Eurodollar futures features is in Table 14-2.

Several factors about the Eurodollar futures contracts in Table 14-1 deserve special attention. First, Eurodollar futures extend until 2002, more than seven years from November 1994. The contract is heavily used for hedging and synthesizing interest-rate swaps, FRAs, and other swap-related derivatives. We will explore such uses later. Second, note that the open interest in the December 1994 maturity is 366,000 contracts, each with a par amount of $1 million. This represents a tremendous amount of liquidity for institutional investors. In fact, liquidity until 1999 is fairly good. The total volume of

FIGURE 14-1   *Eurodollar Futures Rates and the Three-Month LIBOR*

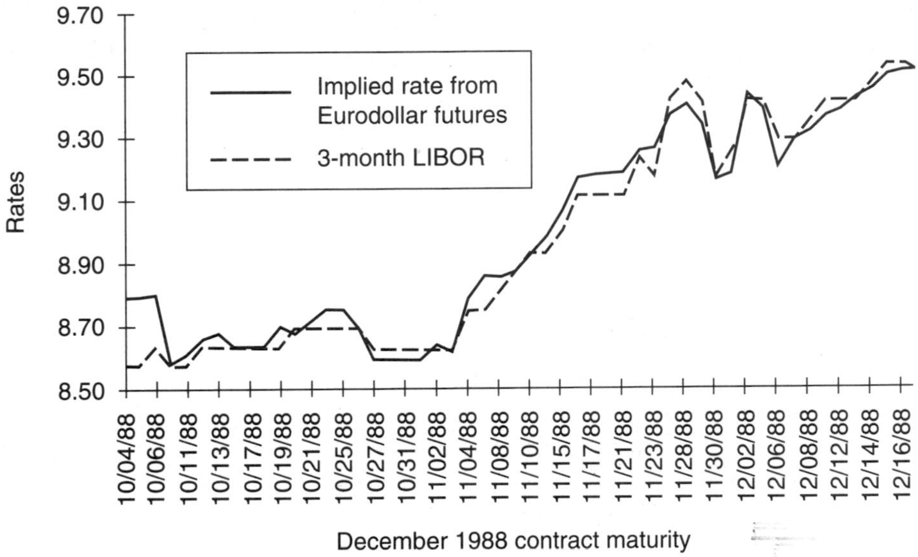

December 1988 contract maturity

		TABLE 14-2
Underlying instrument	Three-month Eurodollar time deposits	*Eurodollar Futures*
Contract size	$1,000,000 U.S. face value	*Contracts*
Contract months	March, June, September, December	
Minimum price change	0.01 = $25	
Trading hours	8:20 AM to 3:00 PM (EST)	
Delivery terms	Cash settlement on last trading day; settlement based on LIBOR	
Last day of trading	Two London business days before third Wednesday of delivery month	

trading in this futures market was nearly 750,000, representing a par amount of $750 billion. We have also computed the quantity called the **implied interest rate** in Table 14-1; this is 100 minus the futures price. For example, corresponding to the December 1994 futures price of 93.80, the implied interest rate is $100 - 93.80 = 6.20$.

We now relate the Eurodollar futures settlement price to the 90-day LIBOR on the settlement (maturity) date of the futures contract. As in the cash market calculations, we will standardize the principal amount $b(t, s)$ at date t so that at maturity we get a total (principal + interest) of $1. Note that for the Eurodollar futures contract maturing on date s, the relevant principal is $b(s, s + 90)$ since the contract settles to 90-day LIBOR at date s.

Let $l_s(90)$ denote the three-month LIBOR (annualized) at date s. LIBOR on a Euro-dollar time deposit with a maturity of τ days is defined using a money-market convention according to the formula:

$$l_s(\tau) = \frac{360}{\tau} \times \left(\frac{1}{b(s, s + \tau)} - 1 \right).$$ (14.5)

The Eurodollar futures price $H_s(s)$ at maturity date s is

$$H_s(s) \equiv 100 \times [1 - l_s(90)].$$ (14.6)

This follows from the add on settlement feature of the Eurodollar futures contract that was described earlier. The resulting Eurodollar futures price is in percentages of a one million face amount of a 90-day time deposit. The market resolution is a basis point worth $1,000,000 \times \frac{1}{100} \times \frac{1}{100} \times \frac{90}{360} = \$25$.

We will illustrate the use of Eurodollar futures in synthesizing LIBOR-based swaps through a simple example. Remember that the Eurodollar futures price settles to 90-day LIBOR, $l_s(90)$, at maturity date s, as in Equation (14.6).

Example 14-3

Consider the case of a December 1987 Eurodollar futures contract. This contract matured on December 14, 1987, at a settlement price of 91.62. The 90-day LIBOR on that day stood at 8.38%. The maturity price was $100 - 8.38 = 91.62$.

This settlement feature of Eurodollar futures is unique and is known as the **add on settlement** feature. Contrast this with the discount settlement feature used in the Treasury bill futures market (see Chapter 13).

Example 14-4 Market Resolution

The Eurodollar futures prices are in percentages of a one-million face amount of a 90-day time deposit. The market resolution is a basis point that is worth $1,000,000 \times \frac{1}{100} \times \frac{1}{100} \times \frac{90}{360} = \$25$. Thus if the Eurodollar futures price moves from 92.58 to 92.62 in one day, the dollar value of that move of 4 basis points is $4 \times 25 = \$100$ per contract.

Example 14-5

Consider a firm that has floating-rate liabilities indexed off a 90-day LIBOR on a face amount of $100 million. The firm would like to swap these into a stream of fixed-rate liabilities. Assume that the liability schedule facing the firm as of January 2, 1987, is as shown in Table 14-3. Liabilities are assumed to fall due each quarter on the maturity dates of Eurodollar futures contracts.

t	s_1	s_2	s_3	s_4
1/2/1987	3/16/1987	6/15/1987	9/14/1987	12/14/1987

TABLE 14-3
Schedule of Floating Liabilities

The schedule of the Eurodollar futures prices as of January 2, 1987, is shown in Table 14-4. The ex-post settlement prices of these futures contracts on their respective maturity dates is shown in Table 14-5. The implied rate of interest $r_t(s_i) = 100 - H_t(s_i)$ is also indicated for each futures contract. Note that the implied rate of interest for each contract is known as of date t, January 2, 1987.

$H_t(s_1)$	$H_t(s_2)$	$H_t(s_3)$	$H_t(s_4)$
93.95	93.95	93.86	93.68
6.05%	6.05%	6.14%	6.32%

TABLE 14-4
Schedule of Eurodollar Futures Prices, January 2, 1987

$H_{s_1}(s_1)$	$H_{s_2}(s_2)$	$H_{s_3}(s_3)$	$H_{s_4}(s_4)$
93.50	93.77	92.50	91.62
6.50%	6.23%	7.50%	8.38%

TABLE 14-5
Eurodollar Futures Prices at Maturity

By selling a portfolio of futures contracts (called a **strip of futures**) on date t it is possible for the firm to convert its floating liabilities into a stream of currently known liabilities as given by the implied rates of interest. To see this clearly, review Table 14-6 where the firm has sold a strip of 100 futures contracts.

The firm at date t sells a strip of Eurodollar futures contracts maturing on dates s_i ($i = 1, \cdots, 4$). The payoffs from futures contracts (ignoring marking-to-market) will be the date t futures price minus the settlement futures price. For example, the payoff from the March 1987 contract on date s_1 will be $[H_t(s_1) - H_{s_1}(s_1)] \times 2500 \times 100$. On March 16, 1987, the Eurodollar futures price settled at 93.50. Therefore the payoff is $(93.95 - 93.50) \times 2500 \times 100 = \$112,500$. From Table 14-5, it is clear that the LIBOR increased during this period and, as a result, the futures prices fell. The profits from futures prices enabled the firm to lock in the rates that were determined at date t. The Eurodollar futures market permitted the firm to lock in, at date t, the known rates as shown in the bottom cell of Table 14-6.

TABLE 14-6 *Swap Execution*

Transaction	t 1/2/1987	s_1 3/16/1987	s_2 6/15/1987	s_3 9/14/1987	s_4 12/14/1987
	Sell 100 of each futures				
Cash flow from futures		$6.50 - 6.05$ $\times 250,000$ $= 112,500$	$6.23 - 6.05$ $\times 250,000$ $= 45,000$	$7.50 - 6.14$ $\times 250,000$ $= 340,000$	$8.38 - 6.32$ $\times 250,000$ $= 515,000$
Liabilities		$-6.50 \times 250,000$ $= -1,625,000$	$-6.23 \times 250,000$ $= -1,557,500$	$-7.50 \times 250,000$ $= -1,875,000$	$-8.38 \times 250,000$ $= -2,095,000$
Total		$-6.05 \times 250,000$ $= -1,512,500$	$-6.05 \times 250,000$ $= -1,512,500$	$-6.14 \times 250,000$ $= -1,535,000$	$-6.32 \times 250,000$ $= -1,580,000$

Swap Rate Calculations

The effective rate that is locked in by the firm is the swap rate and is computed as follows. Intuitively, the swap rate is the fixed rate that is paid on the same dates as the floating payments with a present value equal to that of the floating payments. From Tables 14-4 and 14-6 we see that the rates locked in as of date t were 6.05 for s_1, 6.05 for s_2, 6.14 for s_3 and 6.32 for s_4. These rates were known at date t, as seen from Table 14-4. Intuitively, we will expect that the effective fixed rate (swap rate) locked in at date t will be a weighted average of these rates implied by Eurodollar futures contracts. We proceed to compute this next.

Let $b(t, j)$, $(j = 1, \ldots, 4)$ be the discount functions quoted at date t for various future dates j. Then the swap rate x payable at each date s_i must satisfy the equality

$$x[b(t, s_1) + b(t, s_2) + b(t, s_3) + b(t, s_4)]$$
$$= r_t(s_1)b(t, s_1) + r_t(s_2)b(t, s_2) + r_t(s_3)b(t, s_3) + r_t(s_4)b(t, s_4). \tag{14.7}$$

The left-hand side of the previous equation calculates the present value of paying $x\%$ at dates s_1, s_2, s_3 and s_4. The right-hand side calculates the present value of paying the implied interest rates from Eurodollar futures contracts set at t but paid at the reset dates s_1, s_2, s_3 and s_4. The implied interest rates at date t are known from Table 14-4 as: $r_t(s_1) = 6.05\%$, $r_t(s_2) = 6.05\%$, $r_t(s_3) = 6.14\%$ and $r_t(s_4) = 6.32\%$. Once we calculate the discount factors $b(t, s_1)$, $b(t, s_2)$, $b(t, s_3)$ and $b(t, s_4)$ we can solve for the effective swap rate x from the previous equation. We write out explicitly the effective swap rate x in the next equation. Note that Equation (14.8) may be regarded as a swap valuation model. Once we plug in the implied interest rates and discount rates, the swap rate is readily obtained. The actual calculation of the discount rates is computationally more involved but we illustrate a simple procedure next.

The swap rate x is

$$x = \frac{r_t(s_1)b(t, s_1) + r_t(s_2)b(t, s_2) + r_t(s_3)b(t, s_3) + r_t(s_4)b(t, s_4)}{[b(t, s_1) + b(t, s_2) + b(t, s_3) + b(t, s_4)]}. \tag{14.8}$$

Equation (14.8) simply requires that in a swap, the fixed rate x must have the same present value (shown on the left-hand side) as the floating payments (which, by virtue of Eurodollar futures settlement feature, is given by the right-hand side).

Example 14-6

In the context of Example 14-5, the swap rate is easily calculated. On January 2, 1987, the LIBOR of different maturities were as shown in Table 14-7a. The discount factors are calculated using the formula:

$$b(t, j) = \frac{1}{1 + \text{LIBOR} \times \frac{y}{360}} \tag{14.9}$$

where y is the maturity in days of LIBOR.

At date t we obtain LIBOR quotes for settlement at the reset dates s_1, s_2, s_3 and s_4. Using this information, which is reported in Table 14-7a, we can calculate the discount factors for each reset date. We illustrate the discount rate calculations for date s_1.

$$y = \# \text{ days between } t \text{ and } s_1$$
$$= \text{Difference between March 16, 1987 and January 2, 1987}$$
$$= 73 \text{ days}$$

LIBOR at date t for settlement at date s_1 is 6.3125%.

Using Equation (14.9), we get the discount factor as:

$$b(t, s_1) = \frac{1}{1 + 0.063125 \times \frac{73}{360}} = 0.9874.$$

This information as well as the discount factors for reset dates s_2, s_3 and s_4 are provided in Table 14-7a. The LIBOR data upon which our calculations are based is also given.

Alternatively, the discount rates can be calculated using Eurodollar futures prices. This approach is shown in Table 14-7b.

The zero price for the maturity 3/16/1987 is calculated exactly as shown earlier. To calculate the zero price for maturity 6/15/1987, we need to calculate the implied futures rate between 3/16/1987 and 6/15/1987. This is 6.05%. This rate applies to loans starting at 3/16/1987 and maturing at 6/15/1987 for a loan maturity of 91 days. The relevant zero price for maturity at 6/15/1987 is obtained as follows:

$$\frac{1}{1 + 0.063125 \cdot \frac{73}{360}} \times \frac{1}{1 + 0.06050 \cdot \frac{91}{360}} = 0.972489.$$

TABLE 14-7a
Schedule of LIBOR and Discount Functions, January 2, 1987

	Three-Month s_1	Six-Month s_2	Nine-Month s_3	Twelve-Month s_4
LIBOR	6.3125%	6.25%	6.25%	6.25%
Days	73	164	255	346
Discount	0.9874	0.9723	0.9576	0.9433

TABLE 14-7b   Schedule of Eurodollar Futures Prices and Discount Rates, on January 2, 1987

Eurodollar Futures or Spot LIBOR	Implied Futures Rate or Spot LIBOR	Maturity Date of Futures or LIBOR	Number of Days from the Settlement	Zero Price	Days between Futures Settlement
	6.3125%	3/16/87	73	0.9874	
93.95	6.0500%	3/16/87	73	0.9725	91
93.95	6.0500%	6/15/87	164	0.9578	91
93.86	6.1400%	9/14/87	255	0.9432	91
93.68	6.3200%	12/14/87	346		

In a similar manner, the relevant zero price for maturity 9/14/1987 is:

$$\frac{1}{1 + 0.063125 \cdot \frac{73}{360}} \times \frac{1}{1 + 0.06050 \cdot \frac{91}{360}} \times \frac{1}{1 + 0.06050 \cdot \frac{91}{360}} = 0.957841.$$

Proceeding in this manner, we can compute the relevant discount factors. Using these discount functions, the swap rate x is

$$= \frac{6.05\% \times 0.9874 + 6.05\% \times 0.9723 + 6.14\% \times 0.9578 + 6.32\% \times 0.9433}{0.9874 + 0.9723 + 0.9578 + 0.9433}$$

$$= \frac{23.69749}{3.8606} = 6.1383\%.$$

The swap rate x is 6.1383%, based on the discount functions and the implied rates of interest at date t.

Eurodollar Futures vs. Swap Markets

While Eurodollar futures contracts may be used to execute swaps and they contain information about swap rates, institutions find it much easier to execute swaps by contacting swap intermediaries. There are good reasons as to why this is the case. With Eurodollar futures, the convergence to LIBOR is on the maturity date. This is ideal if the reset date and payment date coincide with the maturity date. For other swap structures, Eurodollar futures can not be used in so direct a manner. On the other hand, the swap market is well organized and the transactions are easily arranged. The credit risks are more easily factored into the contract. It is also easy to customize the swap contract to suit the needs of contracting parties: arbitrary indices, reset frequencies, and payment dates may be easily fitted into the swap contract.

However, the existence of Eurodollar futures markets and the swap rates implicit in Eurodollar futures force a tight link between swap rates and Eurodollar rates. The arbitrage possibilities between the two markets ensures a greater efficiency in the swap market. Since most swap intermediaries hedge their risks in the Eurodollar market, the rates in these markets are linked closely. It should also be noted that Eurodollar futures on 30-day LIBOR is traded at IMM, though this contract is less active compared to the 90-day LIBOR contract.

Intermarket Spreads

In this section, we will explore intermarket spread strategies using Eurodollar futures and T-bill futures contracts. These strategies are referred to as **TED spreads.** Consider the data presented in Table 14-8.

The TED spread and the prices of Eurodollar and T-bill futures are shown for December 1987 maturity in Figures 14-2 and 14-3, respectively. These contracts move parallel to each other, for the most part. The T-bill contract tracks the prices of deliverable T-bills. Such bills are free from default risk. The Eurodollar futures contracts track the LIBOR and when the banking industry undergoes a downturn, then LIBOR rates will

TABLE 14-8   *T-bill and Eurodollar Futures*

Date	T-bill Futures	Euro-dollar Futures	TED Spread	Date	T-bill Futures	Euro-dollar Futures	TED Spread	Date	T-bill Futures	Euro-dollar Futures	TED Spread
06/01/87	91.90	93.10	120.00	08/05/87	92.32	93.66	134.00	10/09/87	90.85	92.33	148.00
06/02/87	91.55	92.82	127.00	08/06/87	92.30	93.64	134.00	10/12/87	90.84	92.34	150.00
06/03/87	91.74	92.97	123.00	08/07/87	92.31	93.64	133.00	10/13/87	90.94	92.41	147.00
06/04/87	91.78	93.01	123.00	08/10/87	92.33	93.66	133.00	10/14/87	90.65	92.11	146.00
06/05/87	91.88	93.17	129.00	08/11/87	92.39	93.71	132.00	10/15/87	90.54	92.05	151.00
06/08/87	91.87	93.20	133.00	08/12/87	92.44	93.75	131.00	10/16/87	90.44	92.05	161.00
06/09/87	91.81	93.19	138.00	08/13/87	92.58	93.82	124.00	10/19/87	90.64	92.50	186.00
06/10/87	91.86	93.24	138.00	08/14/87	92.59	93.85	126.00	10/20/87	91.80	93.80	200.00
06/11/87	91.94	93.26	132.00	08/17/87	92.55	93.84	129.00	10/21/87	92.06	93.93	187.00
06/12/87	92.23	93.50	127.00	08/18/87	92.41	93.73	132.00	10/22/87	92.40	94.19	179.00
06/15/87	92.24	93.59	135.00	08/19/87	92.35	93.67	132.00	10/23/87	92.23	93.97	174.00
06/16/87	92.23	93.59	136.00	08/20/87	92.39	93.66	127.00	10/26/87	92.54	94.28	174.00
06/17/87	92.33	93.67	134.00	08/21/87	92.33	93.59	126.00	10/27/87	92.36	94.08	172.00
06/18/87	92.28	93.63	135.00	08/24/87	92.31	93.51	120.00	10/28/87	92.34	94.15	181.00
06/19/87	92.28	93.66	138.00	08/25/87	92.36	93.53	117.00	10/29/87	92.47	94.23	176.00
06/22/87	92.41	93.75	134.00	08/26/87	92.32	93.47	115.00	10/30/87	92.42	94.12	170.00
06/23/87	92.39	93.68	129.00	08/27/87	92.16	93.32	116.00	11/02/87	92.29	93.98	169.00
06/24/87	92.26	93.59	133.00	08/28/87	92.07	93.25	118.00	11/03/87	92.42	94.13	171.00
06/25/87	92.35	93.68	133.00	08/31/87	92.07	93.31	124.00	11/04/87	92.50	94.18	168.00
06/26/87	92.22	93.62	140.00	09/01/87	92.01	93.26	125.00	11/05/87	92.69	94.24	155.00
06/29/87	92.28	93.69	141.00	09/02/87	91.84	93.13	129.00	11/06/87	92.63	94.13	150.00
06/30/87	92.31	93.69	138.00	09/03/87	91.84	93.14	130.00	11/09/87	92.56	94.01	145.00
07/01/87	92.40	93.78	138.00	09/04/87	91.65	92.97	132.00	11/10/87	92.54	94.02	148.00
07/02/87	92.51	93.88	137.00	09/08/87	91.47	92.83	136.00	11/11/87	92.48	94.00	152.00
07/06/87	92.51	93.89	138.00	09/09/87	91.53	92.89	136.00	11/12/87	92.50	93.96	146.00
07/07/87	92.56	93.90	134.00	09/10/87	91.62	92.98	136.00	11/13/87	92.42	93.77	135.00
07/08/87	92.56	93.90	134.00	09/11/87	91.71	93.03	132.00	11/16/87	92.37	93.80	143.00
07/09/87	92.46	93.86	140.00	09/14/87	91.69	92.94	125.00	11/17/87	92.43	93.93	150.00
07/10/87	92.60	93.95	135.00	09/15/87	91.59	92.91	132.00	11/18/87	92.45	94.04	159.00
07/13/87	92.55	93.93	138.00	09/16/87	91.61	92.91	130.00	11/19/87	92.53	94.17	164.00
07/14/87	92.66	94.00	134.00	09/17/87	91.62	92.94	132.00	11/20/87	92.49	94.12	163.00
07/15/87	92.51	93.87	136.00	09/18/87	91.73	93.03	130.00	11/23/87	92.45	94.06	161.00
07/16/87	92.54	93.93	139.00	09/21/87	91.69	93.02	133.00	11/24/87	92.41	93.99	158.00
07/17/87	92.60	93.97	137.00	09/22/87	91.79	93.09	130.00	11/25/87	92.37	94.00	163.00
07/20/87	92.58	93.96	138.00	09/23/87	91.78	93.08	130.00	11/27/87	92.19	93.99	180.00
07/21/87	92.49	93.82	133.00	09/24/87	91.64	92.92	128.00	11/30/87	92.32	94.17	185.00
07/22/87	92.43	93.76	133.00	09/25/87	91.59	92.84	125.00	12/01/87	92.27	94.12	185.00
07/23/87	92.36	93.70	134.00	09/28/87	91.58	92.81	123.00	12/02/87	92.24	94.24	200.00
07/24/87	92.30	93.64	134.00	09/29/87	91.42	92.70	128.00	12/03/87	92.25	94.32	207.00
07/27/87	92.29	93.63	134.00	09/30/87	91.40	92.69	129.00	12/04/87	92.25	94.36	211.00
07/28/87	92.28	93.55	127.00	10/01/87	91.39	92.72	133.00	12/07/87	92.12	94.07	195.00
07/29/87	92.29	93.56	127.00	10/02/87	91.45	92.77	132.00	12/08/87	92.07	94.03	196.00
07/30/87	92.34	93.62	128.00	10/05/87	91.35	92.64	129.00	12/09/87	92.05	94.07	202.00
07/31/87	92.31	93.59	128.00	10/06/87	91.26	92.60	134.00	12/10/87	91.91	94.03	212.00
08/03/87	92.17	93.51	134.00	10/07/87	91.16	92.58	142.00	12/11/87	91.79	94.05	226.00
08/04/87	92.17	93.54	137.00	10/08/87	90.95	92.38	143.00	12/14/87	91.62	94.04	242.00

FIGURE 14-2   *TED Spread During 1986–1987*

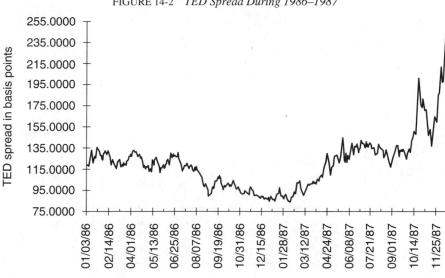

FIGURE 14-3   *Eurodollar and T-bill Futures Prices*

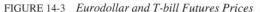

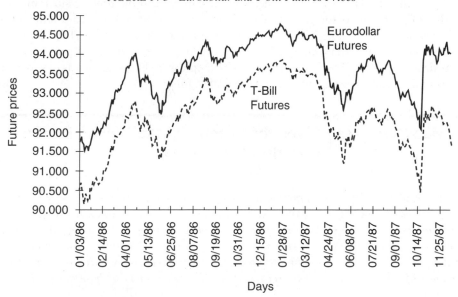

increase significantly. Generally, any shock to the economy that significantly affects the banking sector will affect the LIBOR and hence the Eurodollar futures prices. These arguments are best illustrated by reviewing the TED spread around the stock market crash of 1987, as shown in Figure 14-4.

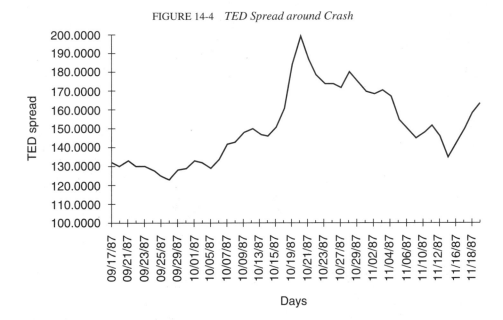

FIGURE 14-4   *TED Spread around Crash*

Note that the TED spread widened significantly around the time of stock market crash. In fact, market participants tend to use the TED spread as a mechanism to incorporate some of their market views. As the enclosed article from Barrons (Feb. 27, 1995 p. MW9) by Andrew Bary suggests, market participants bet on the yield gaps between bank deposits and risk-free Treasuries using TED spreads. This spread tends to widen in times of financial crisis and tighten in periods of stability.

Has Greenspan Given the Green Light to Buying Bonds With Borrowed Money?

By Andrew Bary

The leveraged bond trade may be returning with a vengeance. From 1991 through 1993, buying bonds with gobs of borrowed money became one of the most lucrative games in financial history as the Federal Reserve kept short-term rates at the lowest levels in a generation. During that long period of easy money, formerly unknown Wall Street bond traders and hedge-fund operators became grotesquely wealthy by purchasing massive amounts of 4% and 5% Treasury securities and financing them with money borrowed at 3%.

That game came to an abrupt halt a year ago when the Fed began raising short-term rates. But with Fed Chairman Alan Greenspan signaling Wednesday that the cen-

tral bank may be done tightening, the leveraged bond trade started to look a lot more appealing.

The two-year Treasury note, long the security of choice with the speculative set, surged on Wednesday after Greenspan's comments, as its yield fell nearly 20 basis points to 6.85%. And at the market peak Thursday, the two-year yielded just 6.73%, 30 basis points below its closing level on the prior Friday and off nearly a full percentage point since the start of the year. The two-year note ended the week at 6.84%

Speculation ran through the market Wednesday and Thursday that hedge funds and other speculators were putting back their old leveraged positions. "I think the trade is coming back," says Jim Bianco, director of research at Arbor Trading Group in Barrington, Ill.

He detects signs of increased two-year note speculation in the sharply narrowing yield gap between the two-year and the three-month T-bill. Bianco notes that since the end of December, the two-year note yield has fallen dramatically while the rate on the three-month T-bill has actually increased, to 5.72%. "This is one of the largest divergences in history," Bianco says, noting that the two securities usually move in the same direction. Bianco ventures that the two-year note has moved so much because speculators can finance it profitably with 6% short-term money, while the T-bill can't be leveraged profitably at today's rates.

Some wags said Greenspan's comments amounted to a hedge-fund bailout. "The macro guys got killed in the carry trade last year. They need some help," said one hedge-fund manager.

Positive Carry

It's not hard to see why the two-year note appeals to a leveraged speculator right now. It yields nearly a point above the 6% Fed funds rate, providing the holder with a spread known as positive carry. Until recently, there was plenty of positive carry in this trade, but also a lot of risk because the Fed was ratcheting up short rates. But if the Fed is just one tightening step away from being finished, the danger in the two-year is greatly reduced.

It's difficult for small investors to emulate the big boys because bond dealers normally won't sell Treasuries to individuals with just 5% down. But risk-taking investors can traffic in the highly liquid Eurodollar futures market in Chicago. Eurodollars offer the same play as the two-year note. Bullish investors can buy Eurodollar futures, particularly the December 1995 and March 1996 contracts, while bears can sell them.

The TED Spread

Betting on the yield gap between bank deposits and risk-free Treasuries has been popular with speculators for over a decade. The spread tends to widen in times of financial crisis, and tighten in periods of calm. The usual way to play this relationship is through the "TED," a reference to the spread between Treasury bill futures and Eurodollar futures.

Since the start of the year, there has been a dramatic narrowing in the TED of about ¼-percentage-point, as the Orange County bond liquidations ended and as the credit markets rallied. In the past week alone, two-year swap spreads, a proxy for the TED, tightened nearly 10 basis points to 22 basis points, a big move in a usually stable spread.

At mid-week, when the TED spread hit its narrowest point, some Wall Street dealers and others supposedly put on massive arbitrage trades, betting the spread would eventually reverse. These traders bought two-year Treasury notes and sold "strips" of Eurodollar futures extending out two years, or they bought two-year notes and sold the fixed side of interest-rate swaps. One sign of huge arbitrage activity was a big jump of nearly 100,000 contracts in Eurodollar open interest on Wednesday and Thursday. That rise in open interest is equivalent to $100 billion of Eurodollar futures.

"This is a great risk-reward trade," one bond dealer said Friday. He figures the trade works under several scenarios: If Mexico's financial troubles deepen, if the U.S. economy slows, or if the U.S. bond market moves sharply lower. It probably loses, however, if the Fed can engineer a soft landing for the economy.

With the bond rally of 1995 has come a marked improvement in the derivative mortgage securities market. Institutional investors who wouldn't go near volatile stuff like inverse floaters and principal-only strips have been nibbling lately because these instruments offer a leveraged bet on lower rates.

For bullish individuals with a stomach for risk, there are three closed-end bond funds that provide a nearly pure play on mortgage derivatives. The TWC/Dean Witter Term Trust 2000, TWC/Dean Witter Term Trust 2002 and TWC/Dean Witter Term Trust 2003 all had a lousy 1994. And their share prices got walloped after dividend cuts last month.

These derivative-laden funds, sold by Dean Witter and managed by Trust Co. of the West, have come under so much pressure because angry brokers have been getting their clients out.

The selling, however, may present an opportunity because the funds trade at discounts of about 15% to their net asset values, versus premiums of 10% a year ago. "The TCW funds are among the few closed-end bond funds I've been buying lately," says Thomas Herzfeld, head of Thomas Herzfeld Advisors, a closed-end fund specialist. The TWC/Dean Witter Term Trusts 2000 and 2003 finished Friday at $6\frac{5}{8}$, while the TWC/Dean Witter Term Trust 2002 ended at 7.

Given their current discounts and portfolio composition, these funds could reward patient investors with double-digit returns in a benign market. But, as the original investors, who paid $10 a share, learned, the trio do carry more risk than the typical mortgage mutual fund.

Options on Eurodollar Futures Contracts

Calls and puts are traded on Eurodollar futures contracts. These contracts are listed at the IMM in the Chicago Mercantile Exchange. The settlement feature of the Eurodollar futures implies that a call option on Eurodollar futures is equivalent to a put option on LIBOR. Likewise, a put option on Eurodollar futures is equivalent to a call option on LIBOR.

To see this clearly, let us consider the data in Table 14-9. On May 9, 1996, the Eurodollar futures price is 94.48. Several calls and puts are available on the June Eurodollar futures contract. It is important to note that these options settle by cash at maturity and they expire on the same day as the underlying futures contract. Let us examine the call with a strike price of 94.25. At maturity, this call will pay an amount equal to:

$$\max[0, H - 94.25]$$

where H is the Eurodollar futures price at maturity. We know that $H = 100 - \text{LIBOR}$ from Equation 14.6. Using this, we get the payoff of the call option on Eurodollar futures to be

$$\max[0, 5.75 - \text{LIBOR}].$$

This is also the payoff of a put option on LIBOR with a strike rate of 5.75%. From Table 14-9 we find that this call costs 24 basis points. Each basis point costs $25 so that the value of this option is $24 \times 25 = \$600$.

Strike	Call	Put
93.75	0.73	r
94.00	0.48	r
94.25	**0.24**	0.01
94.50	0.04	0.06
94.75	0.01	**0.27**
95.00	r	0.52

TABLE 14-9
*Options On
Eurodollar Futures
Trade Date: 5/9/96
Eurodollar Futures
(June 96) 94.48*

In a similar way, the put with a strike price of 94.75 will pay at maturity an amount equal to:

$$\max[0, 94.75 - H]$$

where H is the Eurodollar futures price at maturity. Since at maturity, the Eurodollar futures price settles to LIBOR by the condition $H = 100 - \text{LIBOR}$, we can rewrite the payoff of the put at maturity as

$$\max[0, \text{LIBOR} - 5.25].$$

This is the payoff of a call option on LIBOR with a strike rate of 5.25%. From Table 14-9 we find that this put option costs 27 basis points. Its cost is $27 \times 25 = \$675$.

Caps, Floors and Collars on LIBOR

Eurodollar futures and options on Eurodollar futures can be used to customize different return-risk profiles for investors who have assets or liabilities denominated in LIBOR. Consider Table 14-10 in which we examine scenarios at the maturity of Eurodollar

TABLE 14-10   *Payoffs of Options on Maturity Date Under Different Scenarios*

LIBOR	3.0%	3.5%	4.0%	4.5%	5.0%	5.5%	6.0%	6.5%	7.0%	7.5%	8.0%
Futures Price	97.00	96.50	96.00	95.50	95.00	94.50	94.00	93.50	93.00	92.50	92.00
Call (Strike=94.25)	2.51	2.01	1.51	1.01	0.51	0.01	-0.24	-0.24	-0.24	-0.24	-0.24
Put (Strike=94.75)	-0.27	-0.27	-0.27	-0.27	-0.27	-0.02	0.48	0.98	1.48	1.98	2.48
Long Futures @ 94.48	2.52	2.02	1.52	1.02	0.52	0.02	-0.48	-0.98	-1.48	-1.98	-2.48
Short Futures @ 94.48	-2.52	-2.02	-1.52	-1.02	-0.52	-0.02	0.48	0.98	1.48	1.98	2.48

futures contract where LIBOR can vary from a low of 3% to a high of 8%. Note that the Eurodollar futures price, as a consequence of its settlement to LIBOR, varies from a high of 97.00 to a low of 92.00. In Table 14-10, we have described the net payoffs of a long position in call initiated at a cost of 0.24; a long position in put initiated at a cost of 0.27; a long position in futures initiated at a futures price of 94.48; and a short position in futures initiated at a futures price of 94.48. For example, when the futures price is 97.00, the put ends up out-of-the-money, leading to a loss of 0.27, whereas a long position in futures yields $(97.00 - 94.48) = 2.52$.

Example 14-7

How can investors use these contracts to synthesize different return-risk profiles? Consider an issuer who has liabilities denominated in LIBOR. The cost per million dollars par amount of the liability is directly proportional to LIBOR for this issuer. For example, when LIBOR is 6%, the cost will be

$$1,000,000 \times 0.06 \times \frac{90}{360} = 15,000.$$

Suppose the issuer believes that LIBOR has a good chance of going above 5.25%. Then the issuer can buy a put option on Eurodollar futures at a strike price of 94.75. The total costs with and without the put are shown in Table 14-11. Note that for LIBOR levels above 5.25%, the cost is capped out at

$$= 1,000,000 \times 0.0525 \times \frac{90}{360} + 27 \times 25$$
$$= \$13,800.$$

This establishes a **cap** on the total cost.

TABLE 14-11   *Constructing Caps, Floors and Collars on LIBOR*

LIBOR	-3.0%	-3.5%	-4.0%	-4.5%	-5.0%	-5.5%
Total cost (per million)	-7,500.00	-8,750.00	-10,000.00	-11,250.00	-12,500.00	-13,750.00
Buy a put (Strike=94.75)	-675.00	-675.00	-675.00	-675.00	-675.00	-50.00
Total cost (with the put)	-8,175.00	-9,425.00	-10,675.00	-11,925.00	-13,175.00	-13,800.00
Write a call	-6,275.00	-5,025.00	-3,775.00	-2,525.00	-1,275.00	-25.00
Total cost	-13,775.00	-13,775.00	-13,775.00	-13,775.00	-13,775.00	-13,775.00
Buy a put & write a call	-6,950.00	-5,700.00	-4,450.00	-3,200.00	-1,950.00	-75.00
Total cost	-14,450.00	-14,450.00	-14,450.00	-14,450.00	-14,450.00	-13,825.00

LIBOR	-6.0%	-6.5%	-7.0%	-7.5%	-8.0%
Total cost (per million)	-15,000.00	-16,250.00	-17,500.00	-18,750.00	-20,000.00
Buy a put (Strike=94.75)	1,200.00	2,450.00	3,700.00	4,950.00	6,200.00
Total cost (with the put)	-13,800.00	-13,800.00	-13,800.00	-13,800.00	-13,800.00
Write a call	600.00	600.00	600.00	600.00	600.00
Total cost	-14,400.00	-15,650.00	-16,900.00	-18,150.00	-19,400.00
Buy a put & write a call	1,800.00	3,050.00	4,300.00	5,550.00	6,800
Total cost	-13,200.00	-13,200.00	-13,200.00	-13,200.00	-13,200.00

If LIBOR goes below 5.25%, the issuer is able to take advantage of the falling LIBOR although the cost of the put option diminishes the advantage of falling rates. The payoffs of the positions are shown in Figure 14-5.

Example 14-8

What if the issuer believes that the LIBOR is likely to go up by a moderate amount but is willing to bet that it is unlikely to go down below 5.75%? The strategy of writing a call at a strike of 94.25 will produce an income of $24 \times 25 = \$600$ per million par. If LIBOR goes up, the issuer ends up keeping the call premium as the call finishes out-of-the-money. This cushions the cost of the liability. If LIBOR goes down, the call ends up in-the-money. For example, if LIBOR = 5%, we can

FIGURE 14-5   *Constructing a Cap on LIBOR*

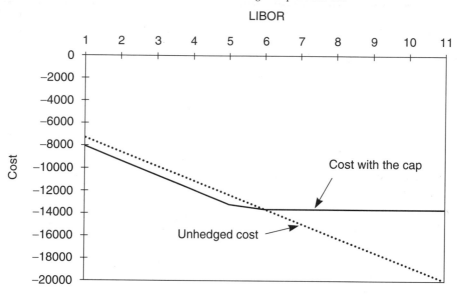

see from Table 14-11 that the cost is $1,000,000 \times .05 \times \frac{90}{360} = \$12,500$. But the call is worth $[5.75 - 5.00] = 0.75$ or 75 basis points. This is equal to $75 \times 25 = \$1275$. Hence the total cost becomes $12,500 + 1,275 = 13,775$. In fact, for all levels of LIBOR below 5%, the cost is 13,775. The payoffs are shown in Figure 14-6. This establishes a **floor** on the cost.

Let us say that the issuer would like to cap LIBOR by buying a put option on Eurodollar futures but would like to finance a part of this purchase by selling a call option on Eurodollar futures. In this case, the issuer would like to get a cap if LIBOR were to go up but is willing to give up some of the gains if LIBOR were to go down. This is known as a **collar** on LIBOR. Note from Table 14-11 that this strategy locks in a total cost of 13,200 when LIBOR goes above 5.75% and a total cost of 14,450 when LIBOR goes below 5.25%. This is illustrated in Figure 14-7.

We can thus use Eurodollar futures and options on Eurodollar futures to create swaps, caps, floors and collars on LIBOR. Since futures and options on Eurodollars are listed in exchanges, they tend to be standardized with a limited set of maturities, strike prices and so on. Also, they are mostly indexed to 90-day LIBOR. In order to get better customization, it is necessary to go to the dealer markets. So, we examine the interest rate swap market next.

FIGURE 14-6   *Constructing a Floor on LIBOR*

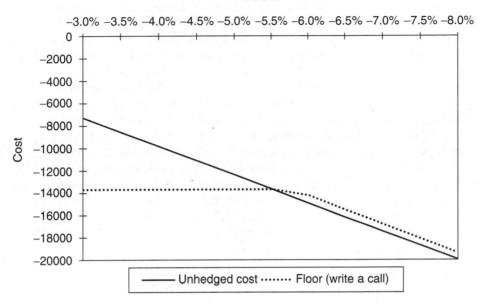

FIGURE 14-7   *Constructing a Collar on LIBOR*

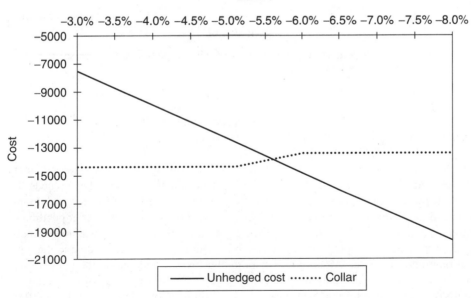

INTEREST-RATE SWAPS

Transactions in which two parties agree to make periodic payments to one another computed on the basis of specific interest rates on a notional principal amount are known as interest-rate swaps. In most interest-rate swaps, there are two legs or payments; the payment made by one counterparty is based on a floating rate of interest such as the LIBOR, while the payment made by the other counterparty is based on a fixed rate of interest or a different floating interest rate. Participants in the swap market use interest-rate swaps to transform one type of interest liability into another. The swap transaction is used as a tool to manage their interest-rate exposure or to lock in a predetermined profit level.

In Figure 14-8, the basic structure of interest-rate swap is depicted. The counterparty Y borrows in the floating-rate market by issuing a five-year floater (say, at the LIBOR plus 1%), which is reset every six months; and counterparty X borrows in the fixed-rate market by issuing a five-year note (say, at 12%). They then enter into a swap transaction with a AAA swap dealer. The swap allows Y to receive a six-month LIBOR every six months. In turn, Y will pay a fixed rate of the five-year Treasury plus 25 basis points. Let us assume that the five-year Treasury is yielding 11%. Then the cost to Y will be 11.25% + 1% = 12.25%.

FIGURE 14-8   *A Five-Year Intermediate Interest-Rate Swap*

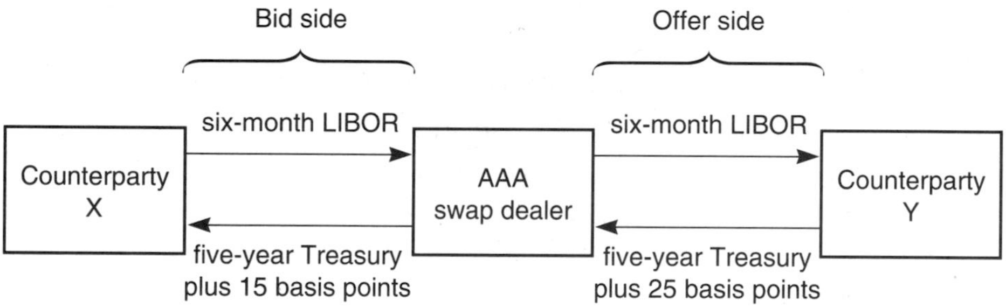

Counterparty X pays floating-rate swap payments of the six-month LIBOR and receives from the swap dealer the five-year Treasury plus 15 basis points. The total cost for X is 12% − 11.15% + LIBOR or LIBOR + 75 basis points.

The swap will turn out to be beneficial if Y's borrowing cost in the fixed-rate market exceeds 12.25% and X's borrowing cost in the floating-rate market exceeds the LIBOR plus 75 basis points. Usually, the floating-rate borrower (X) will be a corporation and the fixed-rate borrower (Y) will be a bank. If the bank is in a better position to monitor and manage the risks of X, then a bilateral contract such as swap may benefit both parties. For example, Y may have an informational advantage relative to the typical floating-rate lender. Moreover, Y is in the business of evaluating the risks of borrowers and, as a result, may have acquired greater monitoring and risk-management skills over time. In addition, Y also has an equilibrium supply of borrowers with differing borrowing requirements. As a result, Y's search costs are lower in terms of identifying and matching two counterparties with complementary borrowing needs. For this service, Y typically gets a fee. The advantages of better information and lower transactions costs (of monitoring, for instance) are reflected in the swap transaction.

The foregoing observations suggest that it is necessary to admit differential information and the costs of monitoring and searching to rationalize a swap transaction.

Swaps can also be arranged to manage the risk of specific asset or liability exposures. An **asset swap,** for example, combines an existing asset such as a bond or a note with a swap to create a different risk-return profile. Consider an investor who owns a fixed-rate asset. He can engage in an interest rate swap as shown in Figure 14-9.

FIGURE 14-9

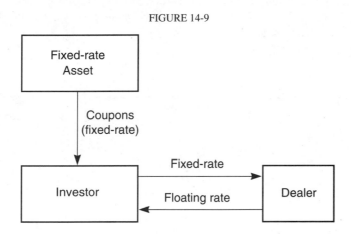

The investor swaps the coupons with the swap dealer for floating rate revenues. If the fixed-rate asset held by the investor is highly illiquid, then the swap may allow the investor to "trade" the cashflows of this illiquid asset at a competitive floating rate.

The underlying asset used in an asset swap can be a zero coupon bond, CMO or a premium or a discount bond. This implies that the swap payments and netting of cashflows between the counterparties can vary to suit the needs of the counterparties. If the asset is a mortgage-backed security, then it will be paying monthly cashflows that go toward interest and amortizing principal payments. Such assets can be combined with **Index Amortizing Swaps** where the notional principal is amortized to precisely mirror the asset's remaining principal amount. Index amortizing swaps use the following terms:

- *Notional principal amount* is the original amount at the beginning of the swap.
- *Lock-Out Period* is the period during which there is no amortization of the notional amount. This is specified on the trade date of the swap.
- *Stated final maturity* is the expiry date of the swap. The swap may amortize to zero before this date.

- *Amortization Schedule* applies to the notional principal after the lock-out period and is specified in the index amortization swap. It typically depends on the levels of some chosen interest rate index.

The amortization rate is computed at the beginning of each reset period (after the lock-out period) based on the level of the interest rate index. The interest rate index used can be chosen from LIBOR (3 months or 6 months), or any benchmark Treasury rates (2, 3, 5, 10 or 30). Table 14-12 is an illustration of the amortization schedule in an index amortizing swap.

Some swaps have a **clean up call** whereby the swap can be called away if the remaining notional amount drops to about 5% of the original amount.

As the swap structure in Figure 14-10 shows, the investor has hedged the position in the asset through the swap. As rates drop, the asset prepays, but the swap also increases the amortization rate.

TABLE 14-12
Amortization Schedule

Notional Amount:	$500,000,000
Lock-out period:	3 years
Final maturity:	6 years
Reset:	Quarterly
Index:	3-month LIBOR

Three-Month LIBOR	Amortization/Period
4.50%	100%
5.50%	15%
6.50%	5%
7.50%	0%

FIGURE 14-10   *Index Amortizing Swaps*

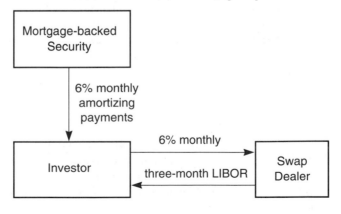

Size of Swap Markets

The swap market is currently estimated at about $6 trillion. The size of the market reported above is based on the notional principal of the swaps outstanding. In a survey, the ISDA (International Swap Dealers Association) has provided some indication of the distribution of the size of currency and interest rate swap markets. A summary is provided in Table 14-13. The figures pertain to the period ending December 1987. As Table 14-13 indicates, the total outstanding volume is close to $1.1 trillion, with roughly 80% of the transactions accounted for by the notional principal of interest-rate swaps and the remaining by currency swaps. U.S. dollar-denominated swaps dominated the marketplace in 1987.

Currency	Interest-Rate Swap	Currency Swap
U.S. dollars	$703,154	$98,015
	79.05%	44.72%
Yen	$59,988	$37,025
	6.74%	16.89%
Sterling	$40,142	$6,327
	4.51%	2.89%
Deutsche mark	$39,583	$12,281
	4.45%	5.60%
Others	$46,662	$65,542
	5.25%	29.90%
Total	$889,529	$219,190
	80.23%	19.77%

TABLE 14-13

Outstanding Swap Transactions, December 1987 (in Millions of Dollars)

To get another perspective of the swap market, we reproduce from Alworth (1993) below the activities in the swap market during the period 1987–1991.

Note from Table 14-14 that the transactions between intermediaries have grown during 1987–1991 much more than the transactions of end users. In addition, the share of U.S. dollar-denominated swaps fell during this period.

Diversity of Swap Contracts

In addition to the size of the swap markets, the diversity of contracts that are structured in the market bears some attention. Swaps are structured on different underlying instruments with different maturity dates. To gain a perspective on the diversity of this market, examine Table 14-15. There are five basic types of swaps. Fixed-to-floating in the

TABLE 14-14   *Main Features of the Interest Rate Swap Market 1987–1991*
Notional Principal in Billions of U.S. Dollars

	New Swaps Arranged					Amount Outstanding	
	1987	*1988*	*1989*	*1990*	*1991*	*End of 1987*	*End of 1991*
End-user transactions	261.9	375.0	515.5	779.7	860.1	476.2	1,722.8
U.S. dollar	192.6	237.9	331.4	415.2	476.4	379.9	831.0
Other currencies	69.3	137.1	184.1	364.5	383.6	96.3	891.8
Interbank transactions							
(between ISDA members)	125.9	193.1	318.0	484.5	761.8	206.7	1,342.3
U.S. dollar	94.1	128.4	213.8	261.1	450.0	161.6	675.0
Other currencies	31.8	64.7	104.2	223.4	311.8	45.1	667.3
Total	387.8	568.1	833.5	1,264.2	1,621.8	682.9	3,065.1
U.S. dollar	286.7	366.3	545.2	676.3	926.4	541.5	1,506.0
Other currencies	101.1	201.8	288.3	587.9	695.4	141.4	1,559.1

TABLE 14-15   *Diversity of Swaps Market*

Type of Swap	*Term of Swap*	*Remarks*
Interest-rate swaps	2 to 10 years	Same currency, one party pays fixed and the other pays floating.
Basis swaps	2 to 7 years	Same currency, parties pay floating cash flows keyed to different indices.
Currency swaps, fixed-to-fixed	2 to 10 years	Different currencies, both pay fixed-interest payments.
Currency swaps, fixed-to-floating	2 to 10 years	Different currencies, one pays fixed and the other floating.
Currency swaps, floating-to-floating	2 to 10 years	Different currencies, both pay floating interest payments.

same currency, floating-to-floating in the same currency, their counterparts across two currencies, and currency swaps that are fixed-to-fixed. In addition, there are markets that are closely related to swap markets.

- Interest-rate caps. This agreement caps the interest obligations at a predetermined rate for a prespecified period of time. For example, firm A agrees to sell a cap on a three-month LIBOR at 6.5% for every quarter for the next two years. In return, firm B pays firm A an agreed-upon compensation.
- Swaptions. Bank A may sell an option to bank B whereby bank B will have the option to enter into a swap any time before a predetermined date at predetermined terms of exchange.
- Floor. An investor holding a portfolio of floating rate notes whose coupons are indexed to LIBOR might wish to buy a floor on LIBOR. If the floor rate is 6% and LIBOR falls below 6%, then the difference is paid to the investor on the agree-upon notional principal.

The swap-related products such as caps, floors and swaptions are dealer market products. Since they are highly customized, they differ from the caps and floors discussed earlier in the context of options on Eurodollar futures contracts. These Eurodollar futures options are standardized (90-day LIBOR, fixed strike prices and maturities) and are not liquid beyond six months.

Risk Characteristics of Swaps

In general, swaps are subject to three distinct sources of risk: interest-rate risk, default risk, and foreign currency risk. (See also the discussion in Chapter 12.) These components of risk interplay in subtle ways that must be understood to manage the total risk of swaps. To put these risk characteristics of swaps into proper perspective, consider some broad risk questions for the matched swap transaction in Figure 14-8. In a matched swap transaction, the intermediary has brokered the swap. In this case, the intermediary faces no interest-rate risk in the absence of default by either of the two parties. The floating-rate borrower ends up with a fixed-rate obligation, which means that his risk is the same as a fixed-rate note with a coupon of 12.25% with the same term and liquidity features (so long as there is no default). In a similar way, the fixed-rate borrower ends up with floating obligations at a cost of the LIBOR plus 75 basis points. His risk is the same as that of a floating-rate borrower with the reset dates and payment dates as specified in the swap contract (so long as there is no default).

There is a positive probability of default in swaps, but the impact of default is drastically different for the three players in Figure 14-8. For the intermediary, default by one counterparty moves the transaction from a matched book to a forward contract. To see this, let us assume that the floating-rate borrower defaults. Then the intermediary will have to pay 11.15% and accept a payment of the LIBOR from the solvent counterparty. This is obviously a forward purchase of the LIBOR, which may either have a positive or negative value at the time of default. For the counterparty that defaulted, the effect of default is to move the transaction from a forward contract to a straight floating-rate debt contract. Of course, the precise outcome will depend on the contingency provisions that were written into the swap contract. For the solvent counterparty, the effect should have no consequences, as the financial intermediary performs the role of a clearing house.

The default risk in a swap can be quite important and can arise due to a number of factors. A swap defect by Hammersmith and Fulham in the late 1980s occured when the swap agreement was declared unlawful. As the enclosed article by Cohen (1989) shows, the default risk can be quite significant.

When Fingers Get Burned

NORMA COHEN reports on the implications of local councils' interest rate swaps

When the London borough of Hammersmith was finally barred last February by the Department of the Environment from making payments due under its interest rate swap and options contracts, it opened up a legal Pandora's box that it has since been unable to close.

Source: *Financial Times* (September 6, 1989). Reprinted by permission.

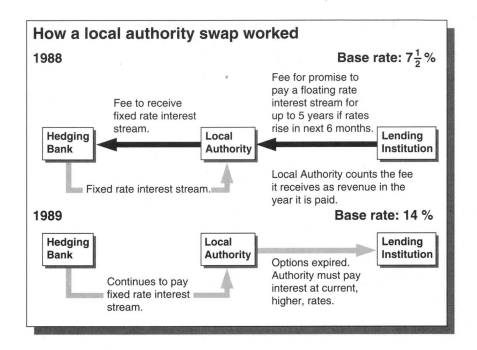

How a local authority swap worked

1988   **Base rate: $7\frac{1}{2}$%**

Fee to receive fixed rate interest stream.

Fee for promise to pay a floating rate interest stream for up to 5 years if rates rise in next 6 months.

Hedging Bank ← Local Authority ← Lending Institution

Fixed rate interest stream.

Local Authority counts the fee it receives as revenue in the year it is paid.

1989   **Base rate: 14 %**

Hedging Bank   Local Authority → Lending Institution

Continues to pay fixed rate interest stream.

Options expired. Authority must pay interest at current, higher, rates.

The immediate issue is over the right of local authorities to conduct capital markets operations—whether the purpose is for reducing interest rate risk or for raising revenues.

Initially, the consideration appeared to be a political one. The Conservative Government objected to authorities using fee income from the capital markets to escape from Whitehall's restrictions on local council spending.

However, in the process of making a political point, the DoE has unleashed the spectre of a series of lawsuits between banks, local government, central government and money brokers that could swamp the courts for years to come. It has also called into question the legality of swaps with all non-corporate entities, such as UK building societies, which have only recently begun to use the swap markets to reduce their own exposure to volatile interest rates.

Larger building societies are specifically permitted under current UK law to conduct capital markets operations aimed at reducing risk. But when they agree to a swap, bankers have no way of knowing what its actual purpose is. Therefore, any transaction with a building society could be at risk.

The Corporations Act of 1988 affirms that swap agreements entered into in good faith with corporate borrowers are sound. But there is no such safe harbour for non-corporate entities. This category includes any mutually-owned organisation such as a friendly society or charitable trust or any quasi-governmental body which uses capital market instruments.

"This is the most significant legal question for the swaps market since it began in the early 1980s," said Mr Michael Canby, a partner at Linklaters and Paines and a spe-

cialist in capital markets transactions. The total market in interest rate swaps was the equivalent of $1,010 billion at the end of 1988, according to the International Swap Dealers Association. Of that, $52.27bn were interest rate swaps in sterling.

At the height of its activities in interest rate swaps, Hammersmith alone accounted for nearly 10 per cent of the sterling market. While swaps with local authorities account for only a small portion of overall swaps business, the market has been badly shaken by the realisation that contracts are not inviolate after all. This has caused bankers in the UK and abroad to reassess all their swap counterparties in an effort to plug the legal loopholes.

On October 4, the High Court will consider a request by the District Auditor to rule all of Hammersmith's interest rate swap and options contracts ultra vires—*outside its legal jurisdiction. The auditor will argue that the council never had the legal authority to enter into contracts that at one time had a notional principal value of about £5bn, and will ask the court to rule all of them void. Such a ruling would mean that payments to bank counterparties, estimated at about £186m over the next five years if interest rates remain stable, will not need to be paid. Hammersmith, a Labour-controlled council, has already said it does not intend to contest the auditor's case.*

However, the banks to whom the fees are owed have mounted a vigorous legal challenge to the auditor's charges, enlisting the services of the most expensive legal advice in the City of London to defend the right of Labour-controlled Hammersmith to engage in capital markets activities.

But whatever the High Court decides, the matter will not be laid to rest.

If the swaps are ruled legal, it will force local authorities to pay huge sums to bankers. This could spell financial ruin for several local authorities, raising the question of whether local governments can go bankrupt and whether the central government has any obligation to stand behind them if they do.

If the swaps are all ruled illegal, as the Audit Commission insists, bankers stand to lose hundreds of millions of pounds, not just from Hammersmith but from every authority which has arranged similar transactions. It will hobble local authorities—and potentially all non-corporate entities—in their efforts to use the capital markets to raise funds and reduce risk.

If the court rules that some of the transactions are legal—a view that many bankers privately believe is the most likely—it will leave the judge to decide which of the banks must be paid and which need not. This will leave the banks, which have presented a united front on the matter up until now, to fight it out among themselves over which transactions are the legal ones. The court proceedings are likely to make public some unwelcome details about how each bank does business, possibly exposing some sloppy lending practices.

Bankers and their legal advisers agree that it is unlikely that the DoE, when it provoked the crisis last February by refusing to sanction payments by Hammersmith to its bankers, understood the far-reaching consequences of its actions.

While some cynical bankers argue that the DoE intended to punish the banking community for its tacit assistance in local authorities' fund-raising efforts, it is more likely that the Department simply did not have the technical expertise to allow it to foresee all the problems which would unfold.

In February, Mr Nicholas Ridley, the Environment Secretary at the time, declined a request by Hammersmith to be allowed to make payments without its councillors becoming subject to fines or disqualification. The action provoked a crisis, forcing Hammersmith and four other local councils to hold up millions of pounds in payments to banks.

The action did not come out of the blue. In July 1988, the District Auditor for Hammersmith—Deloitte Haskins and Sells—told Hammersmith that it believed its activities in the swaps and options markets were probably illegal and that it should begin winding down its position and seek further legal advice. While Hammersmith did seek legal advice in July 1988 and wind down its portfolio, it continued to make payments under existing contracts.

In 1988, the Audit Commission circulated legal opinions it had sought with respect to interest rate swap and option agreements. While the Commission's leading counsel felt that those swaps entered into for purposes of managing debt were probably legal, he took the view that those entered into for the purpose of raising fee income were probably not. The Commission's junior counsel took the view that all local authority swap and options agreements were probably illegal.

In presenting the case to the High Court, the Audit Commission and Deloitte Haskins & Sells are taking the view of the Commission's junior counsel and asking that all of Hammersmith's transactions be ruled ultra vires. *This position is likely to be the starting point for a series of legal battles:*

- *If the High Court rules in favour of the District Auditor, the lenders will continue to appeal until all avenues are exhausted.*
- *Bankers have already begun to comb through their local authority swap and options portfolios for those transactions in which the local authority was the net beneficiary—in other words, the bank made a net payment instead of receiving one in return. The banks will then sue the local authorities for return of these proceeds, arguing that those contracts were* ultra vires *as well.*
- *Banks are also considering whether to proceed against the money brokers which arranged the transactions on their behalf.*

The role of the money brokers is somewhat complex since they only acted as middlemen. Banks habitually demanded to know the name of the local authority they were matched with, with many refusing transactions linked to rate-capped boroughs. But bankers still argue that they dealt with the brokers in good faith, believing brokers would not match them to illegal transactions.

What the banks knew and when they knew it remains a central issue in the whole case. The banks' affidavit before the High Court argues that the Audit Commission never specifically told them that the transactions were illegal and they had no reason to believe they were. Therefore, even if swaps and options are deemed to be off limits for councils in the future, it is unfair to punish banks retrospectively.

Furthermore, the bankers say, the Local Government Act of 1972 does not require them to ask local councils in advance whether the transaction is legal. But several banks did wonder whether the transactions were legal. Several banks and securities houses had sought counsel's advice in 1987 and 1988 about the advisability of entering into swap and options transactions with local authorities. Linklaters and Paines, for instance, had come to the conclusion several years ago that the authorities might be exceeding their competence by entering into those transactions and advised clients accordingly.

The integrity of the clearing process is a function of the capital adequacy of the intermediary and its credit-worthiness. It is in this context that the rules pertaining to the capital adequacy of swap market makers proposed by Federal Reserve and the Bank for International Settlements (BIS) have some important implications. We examine them later in this chapter.

In a foreign currency swap, there is a foreign currency risk exposure, as well. In the absence of default, the intermediary has a matched position; when there is default, the transaction moves into an open forward contract on foreign currency, in addition to the intermediary assuming the interest-rate risk. For the solvent counterparty, there is no change in the transaction when there is default. For example, a U.S. company pays £1 million sterling and receives $2 million U.S. at an exchange rate of two dollars per pound sterling. This transaction will be reversed at a later date that is specified in the contract now.

The risk characteristics associated with reset dates, payment dates, index maturity, and cash flows are less easy to characterize without formal arguments. If the floating leg of the swap resets frequently and does not have many option-like features, then the risk of the swap may be shown to be essentially that of the fixed side plus the face amount outstanding under some simplifying assumptions. We show that this is the case later in the chapter.

Valuation of Swaps

In this section, a framework is developed for the valuation of swaps. Although the discussion will primarily focus on interest-rate swaps, the insights are applicable to other swap contracts.

The valuation of floating-rate payments in swaps has received some attention recently in the academic literature. Cox, Ingersoll, and Ross (1980) and Ramaswamy and Sundaresan (1986) have developed arbitrage-free models of pricing floating-rate payments. Ramaswamy and Sundaresan (1986) develop a continuous-time model of pricing floaters that are subject to default risk. The model accommodates collars, drop lock, and conversion features, but requires continuous resets and payments. Interest-rate swaps have also begun to attract formal analyses; see Bicksler and Chen (1986), Smith, Smithson, and Wakeman (1986, 1988), Turnbull (1987), and Sundaresan (1991). In a recent paper, Cooper and Mello (1991) study the default risk of swaps. They study, in a partial equilibrium setting, the default risk of swaps, the spreads due to default, and the possible wealth transfers due to swaps.

The valuation of swaps requires precise specification of the timing of resets and payments. In addition, we need to specify the index maturity to which floating payments are linked. As before, let s_i be the ith reset date. Let τ be the index (LIBOR) maturity.

Furthermore, let $t_p(s_i)$ be the payment date associated with the reset date s_i. Most interest rate swaps are known as generic interest rate swaps. In such swaps, typically the floating index is six-month LIBOR so that $\tau = 6$ months. Also in these swaps, the reset date (s_i) precedes the payment date $t_p(s_i)$ by exactly the index maturity τ (six months). Generic interest rate swaps are particularly easy to value. The settlement date in such swaps are typically the first reset dates. We illustrate the general principles of valuing generic interest rate swaps with a simple example next.

Example 14-9

Table 14-16 shows the prices of zero coupon bonds (strips) and their yields as of August 25, 1995. What is the swap rate on a two-year generic interest rate swap? Assume that the floating rates reset every six months. The first reset occurs on August 25, 1995. The credit risk of the counterparties can be ignored.

	Zero yields on 8-25-1995 Settlement Date 8/25/95			TABLE 14-16 *Valuation of Swaps*
Maturity (in months)	*Yield*	*Zero Prices*	*Forward Rates*	
6	5.50%	0.9732	5.5000%	
12	5.70%	0.9453	5.9002%	
18	5.90%	0.9165	6.3006%	
24	6.20%	0.8850	7.1026%	
30	6.50%	0.8522	7.7044%	

In the first approach, we will calculate the six-month forward rates for every reset date. Then, we will calculate the present value of all these forward rates. The fixed-rate which has the same present value is the swap rate. We will illustrate these calculations now.

As of August 25, 1995 the six-month spot rate is 5.50%. This is the rate to which the floating leg is reset. At date $t = 6$, the floating leg will pay 5.50%. This should be discounted back to $t = 0$ by using the six-month zero price at $t = 0$, which is 0.9732. The discounted value is $0.0550 \times 0.9732 = 0.0535$. This is shown in Table 14-17.

At date $t = 0$, we can calculate the six-month forward rate that will prevail from $t = 6$ to $t = 12$. This rate, $f_o(6, 12)$ is given by:

$$\left[1 + \frac{0.0550}{2}\right]\left[1 + \frac{f_o(6, 12)}{2}\right] = \left[1 + \frac{0.0570}{2}\right]^2.$$

Thus, $f_o(6, 12) = 5.90\%$. The floating leg will reset to this rate at $t = 6$ but will actually pay this amount at $t = 12$. So, the present value at $t = 0$ of receiving 5.90% at $t = 12$ is:

$$0.059 \times 0.9453 = 0.0558.$$

This is shown in Table 14-17.

TABLE 14-17   *Pricing a Two-Year Swap*
Method 1: Set PV of Floating Equal to PV of Fixed

	0	6	12	18	24	Time
		$t = 6$	$t = 12$	$t = 18$	$t = 24$	*Sum*
Floating payments		5.50%	5.90%	6.30%	7.10%	
Zero prices		0.9732	0.9453	0.9165	0.8850	3.7201
PV(float)		0.0535	0.0558	0.0577	0.0629	0.2299
Total:		0.2299				

Swap rate: $(0.22991)/3.7201 = 6.1802\%$

We can also calculate the relevant forward rates to which the floating leg will reset at $t = 12$ and $t = 18$ for payments at $t = 18$ and $t = 24$ respectively. The present value of all floating payments is 0.2299 as shown in Table 14-17. Suppose that the fixed-leg of the swap pays x (in decimals) at dates $t = 6, 12, 18$ and 24. Then the present value of these fixed-payments is

$$x[0.9732 + 0.9453 + 0.9165 + 0.8850] = 3.7201x.$$

Setting the present value of floating leg equal to the present value of fixed-leg, we get

$$3.7201x = 0.2299$$

or,
$$x = 0.061802.$$

Hence, the effective swap rate is $x = 6.1802\%$.

Another approach to pricing interest rate swaps is to replicate the cash flows of the swap. Consider the two-year generic interest rate swap in the example. Every six months, the floating leg of this swap pays the six-month rate that prevailed on the last reset date. The floating leg can be replicated as follows: take $1 at date $t = 0$ and invest it into the prevailing six-month rate. At date $t = 6$, we get $1 plus the six-month rate. The six-month rate that we receive at $t = 6$ exactly replicates what we would have received in the floating leg of the swap at $t = 6$. Next, with the $1 remaining at $t = 6$, we can invest in the six-month rate at $t = 6$. At $t = 12$, this strategy will produce a cashflow of $1 plus the six-month interest rate that prevailed at $t = 6$. We can keep this interest at

$t = 12$ (which exactly replicates the cash flow of the floating leg at $t = 12$) and roll $1 at $t = 12$ into the then prevailing six-month rate. Proceeding this way we will get the cash flows described in Table 14-18. Let i_6, i_{12} and i_{18} be the six-month interest rates at dates $t = 6$, 12 and 18 respectively.

TABLE 14-18

$t = 0$	$t = 6$	$t = 12$	$t = 18$	$t = 24$
1. Invest $1 in six-month rate	Receive $(1 + 0.055)$			
2.	Keep 0.055 as interest and roll $1 into six-month rate at $t = 6$	Receive $(1 + i_6)$		
3.		Keep i_6 as interest and roll $1 into six-month rate at $t = 12$	Receive $(1 + i_{12})$	
4.			Keep i_{12} as interest and roll $1 into six-month rate at $t = 18$	Receive $(1 + i_{18})$
Cash flows received	$i_0 = 5.5\%$	i_6	i_{12}	$1 + i_{18}$

Note that our strategy cost us $1 at $t = 0$ and produced cash flows of i_0 at $t = 6$, i_6 at $t = 12$, i_{12} at $t = 18$ and $1 + i_{18}$ at $t = 24$. This is exactly what the floating leg of the swap would have paid except that at $t = 24$, the floating leg will not pay the balloon of $1. In order to account for this, we issue a zero coupon bond at $t = 0$ maturing at $t = 24$. This produces a cash inflow equal to the price of the zero coupon bond at $t = 0$ but produces an outflow of $1 at $t = 24$ (to pay the balloon). We summarize these transactions in Table 14-19. If the fixed-leg pays x at each date, then its present value is

$$x[b(0, 6) + b(0, 12) + b(0, 18) + b(0, 24)].$$

Since the present value of floating cash flows must equal the present value of fixed cash flows, we get

$$1 - b(0, 24) = x[b(0, 6) + b(0, 12) + b(0, 18) + b(0, 24)]$$

or,

$$1 = x[b(0, 6) + b(0, 12) + b(0, 18) + b(0, 24)] + b(0, 24). \qquad (14.10)$$

TABLE 14-19

$t = 0$	$t = 6$	$t = 12$	$t = 18$	$t = 24$
Cost: $1 (from Table 14-18)				
Cash flows (from Table 14-18)	i_0	i_6	i_{12}	$1 + i_{18}$
Issue a zero-coupon bond maturing at $t = 24$				
Proceeds: $b(0, 24)$				-1
Net cash flows $1 - b(0, 24)$	i_0	i_6	i_{12}	i_{18}

Note in Equation (14.10) that the right-hand side is the present value of all the fixed (coupon) payments plus the present value of the balloon payments. Equation (14.10) says that the present value is equal to 1. In other words, the swap rate, x, is the two-year par bond yield. This provides us with another approach to valuing swaps. We illustrate this approach for the swap example next. In Table 14-20, we have tried a coupon of 5% (annualized). The present value of this bond is

$$2.5 \times 0.9732 + 2.5 \times 0.9453 + 2.5 \times 0.9165 + 102.5 \times 0.8850$$

which is equal to 97.80. The bond sells at a discount. When the coupon is set at 6.1802%, it sells at par. Clearly, this is the swap rate. Both approaches led us to the same conclusion.

TABLE 14-20   *Pricing a Two-Year Swap*
Method 2: Valuing by the Par Bond Yield

			Settlement Date	8/25/95		
			Coupon Bond Prices			
			$c = 5\%$		$c = 6.1802\%$	
Maturity (in months)	*Yield*	*Zero Prices*	*Cash Flows*	*PV*	*Cash Flows*	*PV*
6	5.50%	0.9732	2.5	2.43309	3.0901	3.007397
12	5.70%	0.9453	2.5	2.3633684	3.0901	2.921218
18	5.90%	0.9165	2.5	2.2911892	3.0901	2.832002
24	6.20%	0.8850	102.5	90.71711	103.0901	91.23937
			Sum	97.80		100.00

RISK MANAGEMENT OF SWAPS

Commercial banks and investment banks act as intermediaries in many swap transactions. The swap books of intermediaries present unique risk-management problems. Until a suitable counterparty is found, an intermediary "warehouses" the swap without having arranged an offsetting swap, and thereby assumes the position of a counterparty. In addition to acting as an intermediary to match two counterparties, intermediaries usually assume the credit risks of both counterparties. The credit risks of the counterparties make the swaps somewhat idiosyncratic and make it difficult to organize a liquid secondary market.

The size of the swap book in many cases runs into hundreds of millions or even billions of dollars. The diversity of indices used and such contractual features as options to extend or cancel, caps, and floors make risk measurement and management a difficult task. The Federal Reserve and BIS guidelines issued recently impart a sense of urgency to the tasks of risk measurement and risk management. We provide some highlights of the guidelines next to provide a perspective on the issue of risk management of swaps.

Federal Reserve-BIS Guidelines for Swaps

The Federal Reserve and the Bank for International Settlements have proposed sweeping guidelines for the risk measurement of swaps. These guidelines require the calculation of the marked-to-market value of all interest-rate swaps. In order to perform this task, it is necessary to have a theoretically sound model of swap valuation.

A key concept in the proposed guidelines is the replacement cost of swaps. This is computed by adding only the positive marked-to-market values. To this replacement cost is added a measure of the future potential increases in credit exposure. This future potential exposure measure is calculated by multiplying the total notional value of the contracts by one of the credit conversion factors in Table 14-21.

Remaining Maturity	Interest-Rate Swaps	Foreign Currency Swaps
One year or less	0.0%	1.0%
Over one year	0.5%	5.0%

TABLE 14-21
Credit Conversion Factors

No potential exposure is calculated for single-currency interest-rate swaps in which payments are made based on two floating-rate indices, that is, floating/floating or basis swaps. The credit exposure on these contracts is evaluated solely on the basis of their marked-to-market value. Exchange-rate contracts with an original maturity of 14 days or less are excluded. Instruments traded on exchanges that require daily payment of variation margin are also excluded. The only form of netting recognized is netting by novation. **Netting by novation** is a contract between two counterparties under which any obligation to each other to deliver a given currency on a given date is automatically amalgamated with all the other obligations for the same currency and value date, legally substituting one single-net amount for the previous gross obligations.

In a market that is liquid, bid-offer spreads are small and the task of marking-to-market is simple. But swap contracts that are illiquid do not always have a liquid secondary market and the determination of their value requires two important considerations. First, an appropriately tested swap-valuation model is necessary to perform the task of valuation. Second, the valuation should be done by an agent who has no vested interest in either overstating or understating the value of the swap positions. For example, if the swap desk finds that marking-to-market results in a substantial charge to its profits, it may not report it, fearing adverse senior management action.

Management of the Credit Risk of Swaps

The credit risk associated with swaps is an important component of the overall risk of swaps. The management of credit risk proceeds along two distinct lines:

1. Contractual provisions, contingencies, documentation, and collaterals.
2. Diversification of the swap book across industry segments and market segments.

Much of credit-risk management rests with the structuring of the swap agreements, contingency provisions, termination provisions, and collateral requirements. Usually collateral in the form of readily marketable securities are demanded from the participant with weaker credit to guard against potential credit risk.

In setting aside the capital that is needed to support swap activities, it is first necessary to mark the swaps to market, so as to correctly determine the replacement cost of swaps. This requires a properly calibrated model for valuing swaps in general.

Once this is done and the interest-rate exposure is properly hedged, as indicated in the previous section, the credit risk of the book has to be aggregated. For this it is useful to subdivide the swaps into two groups: one in which the intermediary is paying fixed and the other in which the intermediary is paying floating. Within each of these groups, swaps must be further classified across different credit-risk categories, and then marked-to-market and aggregated within those credit-risk classifications. This will enable the management of the swap book to identify which of the swap agreements have significant replacement costs due to deteriorating credit risk and to what extent the swap book is reasonably matched. Marking-to-market will effectively indicate the health of the swap book upon the termination of each swap agreement (voluntary or involuntary) in the book. If there is a net loss, then the capital that is set aside should be sufficient to meet those losses.

Just how important is the credit risk? ISDA conducted a study over the ten-year period 1981–1991 in which they found that the losses amounted to about $358 million. As a fraction of the notional principal, this is 0.0115%, a small amount. This is not a proper way to estimate the credit loss. The notional principal of a swap often significantly overestimates the true value of the swap. On a mark-to-market basis, the loss percentage was 0.46%. We enclose an article by Liebowitz from *Investment Dealers Digest* (August 3, 1992) to illustrate some issues concerning default risk in swaps.

Will the ISDA Default Study Impress the Regulators?

Losses are low, but conclusion may miss the point

By Michael Liebowitz

The International Swap Dealers Association's valiant attempt last week to depict the swaps business as a relatively danger-free zone provoked more questions than it actually answered.

The results of a quick-and-dirty survey, commissioned last spring by ISDA, executed by the group's chief accountants, Arthur Andersen & Co., and unveiled at a conference at the Plaza Hotel in New York, elicited a certain smug feeling among the conferees that swaps are indeed safe and represent a better risk than, say, bank loans.

While the accuracy and fairness of the study are not in dispute, some observers noted that it did not go far enough. In particular, it did not address the concerns of regulators who want to know what would happen during a collapse of large portfolios where counterparties took major hits.

Based on a survey of swap dealers representing over 70% of the $4.34 trillion swap market, the study found that cumulative losses over a ten-year period ending last year amounted to only $358.36 million, or 0.0115% of the total notional amount. At the urging of several ISDA members, the true number against which to reflect these loss figures is the gross mark-to-market value of the swaps. This number came to $77.49 billion, so the loss percentage came to 0.46%.

"The losses were relatively small," said Malcolm Basing, chairman of ISDA and a managing director at Swiss Bank Corp., in an interview. "It fits in with our day-to-day observations [that] the swaps business is well managed and credit exposure is well controlled."

The study concluded that gross claims on a mark-to-market value amounted to $539.29 million, of which $126.49 million was recovered from sales, transfers, settlements and liquidation of collateral.

Hammersmith & Fulham

The largest percentage of the loss predictably resulted from swaps involving UK local authorities, which backed out of certain swap agreements last year, claiming they were void after the House of Lords ruled that such financial transactions were illegal. Total losses emanating from UK councils ran up to $177.74 million, or nearly 50% of the total losses.

To many who remember the first days of the Hammersmith & Fulham dispute, the numbers presented in the survey seemed a trifle low. Early estimates of the losses sustained by counterparties to the UK authorities reached as high as £600 million. But Basing was quick to defend the survey's figure, stating that those estimates were only the replacement value of the portfolios, "not necessarily the losses.

"There have been a lot of out-of-court settlements, and so clearly the numbers would be reduced by that," he said. "Secondly, it is difficult to say whether the press estimates were accurate. The survey does underline that [the UK authorities loss] was a problem, but the message is the same. Even if the total writeoffs [from the UK] were 50% bigger, it would still be negligible."

Failures Managed Easily

The remaining large losses were broken down as follows: corporations, $94.53 million (or 26.38%); non-dealer financial institutions, $60.14 million (or 16.78%); and savings and loans, $20.28 million (or 5.66%).

The moral behind the default study was that whatever large-scale failures have occured, they were easily managed and barely caused a ripple in the huge market. The swap community enjoys discussing the ease with which the portfolios of Drexel Burnham Lambert, Development Finance Corp. of New Zealand, Bank of New England and British and Commonwealth Merchant Bank were dismantled.

In each case, none of the defaults was caused by problems in their swaps books, but rather wholly external events unrelated to swaps. For the most part, these institutions had relatively well managed and balanced books, and did not really test the market's ability to sustain a collapse of a large portfolio. As Basing put it: "We are not surprised by the number. If you think about it, defaults like DFC at the end of the day were handled fairly. The losses were modest in size."

Undoubtedly, the study was intended to impress the regulators, including Federal Reserve Board officials, who were present at last week's conference. It is not clear in the end whether the study will appease the regulators at all, since it doesn't address the sort of "what-if" questions they are posing.

The Fed, the Securities and Exchange Commission and the Government Accounting Office are all preparing studies of the derivatives markets in one form or another. The SEC last month passed a new rule that requires hitherto unregulated affiliates and holding companies of brokerage companies to file quarterly financial reports with the agency on positions in futures, real estate and derivatives.

When reached for comment, SEC commissioner Mary Schapiro said she had not yet read the study, but reiterated her earlier claims that derivative instruments still represent a "big worry."

However, she added, "I think I have always tried to say that the concern is we don't really know how big the risk is.

"It could be the biggest risk [in the financial system] or not such a big one. The regulators need to get a handle on it."

The credit risk and interest-rate risk interact in subtle ways. In order to examine this further, it is useful to examine the marked-to-market value of the swap book for different term structure scenarios and credit-risk assumptions. Monte Carlo simulation techniques and a two-state variables (credit risk and interest-rate risk) approach grounded in a contingent claims pricing framework can be used to accomplish this task.

SWAP SPREADS

The swap spreads of a AAA dealer are plotted in Figure 14-11 for the period 1988–1991, for two-year and ten-year swaps. Also plotted is the spread between the ten-year and two-year Treasury on-the-run securities for the same period. Note that during November 1988–May 1989, this spread was negative and the Treasury yield curve was inverted. The swap spreads corresponding to the ten-year swaps were below the swap spreads for the two-year swaps during this period of inverted yield curve. Generally, the Treasury yield curve was upward-sloping for the rest of the period and the ten-year swap spreads were well in excess of the two-year swap spreads.

FIGURE 14-11   *Swap Spreads Versus Shape of the Yield Curve*

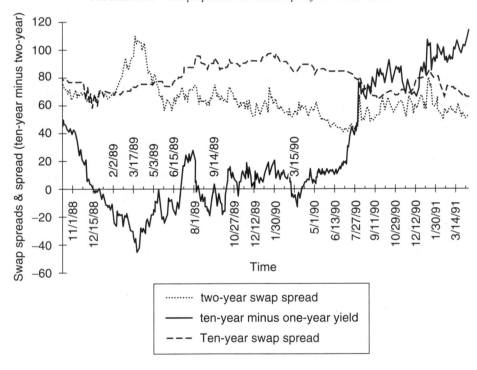

The difference in the swap spreads significantly narrowed again during the August 1990—April 1991 period, even though the Treasury yield curve was strongly upward sloping. This suggests that there are other factors that may be at work. Recent papers by Grinblatt (1994) and Duffie and Singleton (1995) have examined the swap spreads. Grinblatt has argued that a big factor in the swap spread is liquidity. Duffie and Singleton (1995) provide a framework for valuing swaps with default risk. They report evidence that both default and liquidity are important factors in the determination of swap spreads.

Sun, Sundaresan, and Wang (1993) examines the effect of the dealer's credit reputation on the bid-offer spreads of swap quotations. Much of this section is drawn from
this study.

Table 14-22a and 14-22b document the swap spreads and the term structure of the
swap spreads. These are based on the spreads between swap-offer rates quoted by an
AAA-rated swap dealer and the Treasury yields for 605 daily observations in the period
October 11, 1988, to April 15, 1991. The spreads and term premiums are measured in
basis points. The term premiums of the spread are defined as the spread relative to a
two-year spread. Note that the spreads are generally increasing with maturity irrespec-

TABLE 14-22a   *Swap Spreads, October 11, 1988–April 15, 1991*

	Maturity					
Statistic	*Two-year*	*Three-year*	*Four-year*	*Five-year*	*Seven-year*	*Ten-year*
Full sample period (N = 605)						
Mean	64.33	70.84	72.78	76.54	77.49	81.60
SD	12.35	7.65	6.84	8.32	8.20	9.10
t-value	128.05**	227.74**	261.58**	226.16**	232.38**	220.27**
Inverted-yield-curve sample period, (N = 200), December 14, 1988–October 11, 1989						
Mean	74.89	75.56	74.15	76.59	77.34	79.87
SD	13.25	7.78	7.51	9.23	8.78	8.91
t-value	79.71**	137.00**	139.22**	117.10**	124.30**	126.53**

TABLE 14-22b   *Term Premium of Swap Spread, October 11, 1988–April 15, 1991*

	Maturity				
Statistic	*Three-year*	*Four-year*	*Five-year*	*Seven-year*	*Ten-year*
Full sample period (N = 605)					
Mean	6.52	8.45	12.21	13.16	17.27
SD	7.74	11.76	14.18	14.29	16.44
t-value	23.75**	17.66**	21.16**	22.63**	25.81**
T^2 $(F_{5,600})$		1,605.25 (318.92**)			
Inverted-yield-curve sample period, (N = 200), December 14, 1988–October 11, 1989					
Mean	0.67	−0.74	1.70	2.45	4.98
SD	7.29	14.56	16.77	16.87	17.85
t-value	1.30	−0.72	1.43	2.05**	3.94**
T^2 $(F_{5,195})$		318.19 (62.36**)			

**Rejections at the 1% significance level are indicated by two asterisks.

The yield curve is defined as inverted when the ten-year Treasury yield is less than the two-year Treasury yield.

Source: Sun, Sundaresan, and Wang (1993)

tive of the shape of the yield curve. Table 14-23 documents the AAA and A swap-offer rates and bid-offer spreads for the same period. The bid-offer spreads for the AAA swap dealer are always 10 basis points, while the bid-offer spreads for the A swap dealer vary around 4.75 basis points.

TABLE 14-23   *Summary Statistics for Swap-Offer Rates and Bid-Offer Spreads, October 11, 1988–April 15, 1991*

		Maturity					
	Statistic	*Two-year*	*Three-year*	*Four-year*	*Five-year*	*Seven-year*	*Ten-year*
AAA							
Swap-offer rates	Mean	8.881%	9.004%	9.082%	9.140%	9.251%	9.316%
	SD	0.790%	0.670%	0.580%	0.517%	0.450%	0.416%
Bid-offer spreads (in basis points)	Mean	10	10	10	10	10	10
A							
Swap-offer rates	Mean	8.837%	8.955%	9.052%	9.114%	9.227%	9.290%
	SD	0.778%	0.659%	0.585%	0.518%	0.455%	0.421%
Bid-offer spreads (in basis points)	Mean	4.73	4.74	4.65	4.67	4.79	4.77
	SD	1.19	1.12	1.06	0.90	1.05	0.93

Bid-offer spreads are always 10 basis points for a AAA swap dealer.

$N = 605$.

Source: Sun, Sundaresan, and Wang (1993)

Assume that the credit quality of the counterparties is the same for different swap dealers, and that the swap contracts do not differ in other dimensions, such as the upfront fee and collaterals. Then, intuitively, the swap-offer rates of AAA-rated dealers should be higher than those of A-rated dealers, while the swap-bid rates of AAA-rated dealers should be lower than those of A-rated dealers. (See Table 14-24.)

Table 14-25 presents the differences between AAA and A swap rates as frequencies.

Reputation of the Investor

Most swap dealers offer swap quotations that are the same irrespective of the credit standing of clients. Usually, an upfront fee is assessed, depending upon the maturity and the notional amount of the swap contract. This fee might vary with the credit standing of clients. Marking-to-market and the posting of marketable collateral may be required of clients whose credit quality decline with time. Clearly, these provisions are integral parts of swap contracts.

In this context it is useful to note that swap dealers tend to work with an approved list of clients who have been cleared by the credit committee of the swap dealer. For example, the AAA dealer may require that the average credit rating of any counterpar-

TABLE 14-24 *Differences in Swap Rates, October 11, 1988–April 15, 1991 (in basis points)*

Statistic	Maturity					
	Two-year	Three-year	Four-year	Five-year	Seven-year	Ten-year
AAA *offer rates minus* A *offer rates*						
Mean	4.33	4.96	3.03	2.59	2.68	2.62
SD	5.84	3.63	6.34	4.21	4.09	4.74
t-value	18.22**	33.57**	11.77**	15.13**	16.10**	13.58**
$T^2 (F_{6,599})$			1,497.66 (247.54**)			
A *bid rates minus* AAA *bid rates*						
Mean	0.94	0.31	2.31	2.75	2.54	2.62
SD	6.03	3.91	6.34	4.21	4.12	4.77
t-value	3.83**	1.94*	8.96**	16.06**	15.17**	13.50**
$T^2 (F_{6,599})$			482.56 (79.76**)			
AAA *mid-market rates minus* A *mid-market rates*						
Mean	1.69	2.32	0.36	-0.08	0.07	0.00
SD	5.91	3.73	6.32	4.18	4.07	4.73
t-value	7.05**	15.33**	1.41	-0.47	0.42	0.00
$T^2 (F_{6,599})$			240.53 (39.76**)			

$N = 605$.

**Rejections at 5% and 1% significance levels are indicated by one and two asterisks.

Source: Sun, Sundaresan, and Wang (1993)

TABLE 14-25 *Frequencies of the Spreads between AAA and A Swap Rates, October 11, 1988–April 15, 1991*

AAA *offer rates over* A *offer rates*

Basis Points	Maturity					
	Two-year	Three-year	Four-year	Five-year	Seven-year	Ten-year
above 10	7.11%	5.45%	1.65%	1.16%	0.99%	0.99%
5 to 10	34.21%	45.29%	21.49%	11.90%	12.89%	6.94%
0 to 5	52.89%	45.29%	67.77%	77.85%	75.21%	82.81%
−5 to 0	4.79%	3.47%	8.10%	8.10%	9.59%	9.09%
−10 to −5	0.33%	0.17%	0.50%	0.33%	0.83%	0.17%
below −10	0.66%	0.33%	0.50%	0.66%	0.50%	0.00%

A *bid rates over* AAA *bid rates*

Basis Points	Maturity					
	Two-year	Three-year	Four-year	Five-year	Seven-year	Ten-year
above 10	1.16%	0.66%	0.99%	0.99%	1.16%	0.00%
5 to 10	6.45%	3.97%	9.42%	10.91%	10.08%	10.41%
0 to 5	58.86%	54.05%	72.07%	78.02%	76.36%	82.31%
−5 to 0	26.61%	33.22%	15.37%	8.76%	10.74%	6.12%
−10 to −5	7.93%	6.78%	1.49%	0.83%	1.49%	0.83%
below −10	0.99%	1.32%	0.66%	0.50%	0.17%	0.33%

$N = 605$.

Source: Sun, Sundaresan, and Wang (1993)

ties be AA or better; the minimum acceptable credit rating is A. In this case, it seems reasonable to assume that the credit quality of the counterparties is relatively better for the AAA dealer, which will counteract the AAA dealer's advantage in charging higher bid-offered spreads. Hence the empirical finding that the AAA swap rates bracket the A swap rates lends stronger support to our hypothesis about the impact of credit ratings on bid-offered spreads.

CONCLUSION

We showed several ways in which interest-rate swaps are priced. Eurodollar futures provide one avenue. Another avenue is to extract the zero prices from the market and work with them. We showed that the spreads between swap rates and Treasury yields, overall, increase significantly with maturities, while the increase is much smaller when the Treasury yield curve is inverted. The bid-offer spreads of market makers are sensitive to their credit reputations. It is interesting to note that Merrill Lynch and several other firms have formed new subsidiaries to engage in the swap business with large clients; these separately capitalized, credit-enhanced subsidiaries have been structured to get a AAA rating. Several other investment banks, including Lehman Brothers and Salomon Brothers, have launched such credit-enhanced subsidiaries. In the equity derivatives market, a self-funded AAA vehicle has been formed by Goldman Sachs.

PROBLEMS

14.1 The Treasurer of XYZ corporation examines the liability structure of the company on November 1, 1988. He notices that the rollover of commercial paper has been very expensive to the company, as the rates have increased from a low of about 7% in January 1988 to a high of about 8.25% in October 31, 1988. See Figure 14-12. At the same time, the spread between AAA rates (long term) and P1 + six-month CP rates has declined from a high of 310 basis points in January 1, 1988, to 110 basis points in October 31, 1988. See Figure 14-13.

About $200 million worth of floating rate notes are outstanding in XYZ corporation's balance sheet. These floaters are plain-vanilla floaters maturing on November 1, 2015, and paying a coupon of six months LIBOR plus a fixed spread of 25 basis points. In fact, November 1, 1988, was a reset date for these floaters. Historically, CP rates and LIBOR are highly correlated; in fact, most CP rates are indexed to the LIBOR.

Concerned by the increase in short-term interest rates, the treasurer of P&G Corporation explores with the company's investment banker, BG, some derivatives-based strategies. BG proposes a five-year interest-rate swap as detailed in Figure 14-14. Essentially, BG proposes that XYZ pay a fixed (swap) rate of a five-year Treasury (T) plus 100 basis points. In turn, every six months BG will pay XYZ a six-month LIBOR. XYZ is keen to first examine the implications of this swap on the funding costs associated with the floating-rate notes. BG suggests that the notional principal of the swap should be $200 million.

(a) Summarize the advantages and disadvantages of the interest-rate swap from XYZ Corporation's standpoint.

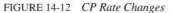

FIGURE 14-12   *CP Rate Changes*

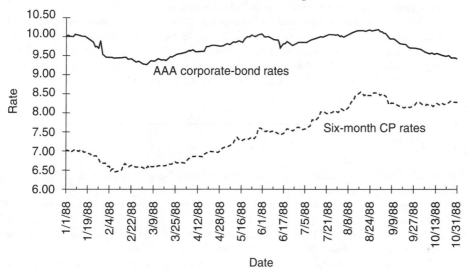

FIGURE 14-13   *Spreads—AAA Bond Rates Minuts Six-Month CP Rates*

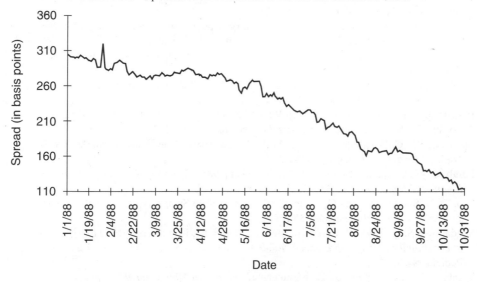

FIGURE 14-14

(b) Based on the data, extract the zero rates from LIBOR par bond yields. Using these zero rates, price the interest-rate swap. Are BG's quotes reasonable?

(c) XYZ Corporation did the swap on November 1, 1988. Six months later, on May 1, 1989, it decided to reevaluate the swap. As seen in Figure 14-11, the yield curve has become inverted and XYZ had the option of doing a four-and-a-half-year swap with BG to offset the original swap. On May 1, 1989, after the reset and the payment, determine the marked-to-market value of the swap to XYZ Corporation. Explain your answer.

REFERENCES

Alworth, J. 1993. "The Valuation of US Dollar Interest Rate Swaps." *BIS Economic Papers.* 35: January. Basle, Switzerland.

Bicksler, J., and A. H. Chen 1986. "An Economic Analysis of Interest Rate Swaps." *Journal of Finance* 41:645–655.

Burghardt, G., T. Belton, M. Lane, G. Luce, and R. McVey 1991. *Eurodollar Futures and Options: Controlling Money Market Risk.* Chicago, IL: Probus Publishing Co.

Cooper, I., and A. S. Mello 1991. "The Default Risk of Swaps." *Journal of Finance* 48:597–620.

Cox, J. C., J. E. Ingersoll, Jr., and S. A. Ross 1980. "An Analysis of Variable Rate Loan Contracts." *Journal of Finance* 35:389–403.

1988. "Capital Adequacy: The BIS Framework and Its Portfolio Implications." *The Journal of International Securities Markets*: 191–218.

Duffie, D. and K. Singleton 1995. "An Econometric Model of the Term Structure of Interest Rate Swap Yields." Graduate School of Business, Stanford University.

Federal Reserve System 1987. "Capital Maintenance: Revision to Capital Adequacy Guidelines." Regulation Y: Docket No. R-0567.

Grinblatt, M. 1994. "An Analytic Solution for Interest Rate Swap Spreads." Working paper, UCLA, Andersen School of Management.

Ramaswamy, K., and S. M. Sundaresan 1986. "The Valuation of Floating-Rate Instruments: Theory and Evidence." *Journal of Financial Economics* 17:251–272.

Smith, C. W., C. W. Smithson, and L. M. Wakeman 1986. "The Evolving Market for Swaps." *Midland Corporate Finance Journal* 3:20–32.

Smith, C. W., C. W. Smithson, and L. M. Wakeman 1988. "The Market for Interest Rate Swaps." *Financial Management* 17:34–44.

Sun, T., S. Sundaresan, and C. Wang 1993. "Interest Rate Swaps: An Empirical Investigation." *Journal of Financial Economics* 36:77–99.

Sundaresan, S. M. 1991. "Valuation of Swaps." In Sarkis J. Khoury, ed., *Recent Developments in International Banking and Finance,* vol. 5, S. J. Khoury, ed., pp. New York: Elsevier Science Publishers.

Turnbull, S. M. 1987. "Swaps: Zero sum game?" *Financial Management* 16:15–21.

Whittaker, J. G. 1987. "Interest Rate Swaps: Risk and Regulation." *Economic Review of the Federal Reserve Bank of Kansas City*: 3–13.

Chapter 15

Risk Management

Chapter Objectives

This chapter integrates the concepts of risk developed in the text to provide a framework for measuring and managing risk. The focus of this chapter is to define risk, measure risk and manage risk in a portfolio context. Such portfolios may be trading portfolios which are typically held for a short period of time (such as a few days or weeks) or investment portfolios which may be held for months. The following issues are addressed in the chapter.

- What is risk?
- What are different sources of risk?
- How can the risk of a portfolio be measured?
- What is the effect of correlation of returns of securities on the risk of a portfolio?
- How does holding period affect risk?
- What is the concept of benchmark equivalents and how are they used to aggregate risk?
- What is the concept of Value-at-Risk (VAR)?

INTRODUCTION

The concept of risk is central to players in capital markets. In this text, we have addressed the issue of risk in each chapter as it applies to the market segment discussed in that chapter. For example, in Part I of the text, we looked at the risk of specific segments of fixed-income markets such as Treasury, options, corporate and mortgage-backed securities. In Part II of the text, we explored the risk of derivative securities such as futures and swaps. Chapter 4 addressed the question of measuring the risk of Treasury securities using concepts such as $DV01$, duration and convexity. Chapter 7 provided measures of risk that are commonly used for options. We noted there that to measure the risk of options we need options pricing models which allow us to calculate the exposure or the risk of the option for a given change in the price of the underlying security. These measures include the concepts of delta, gamma and vega. In the context of Chapter 12, we discussed the use of derivatives in risk management situations. Also, in Chapter 14, we explored the risk management issues in the context of interest rate swaps. Treating risk at the level of specific markets as we did in the earlier chapters is extremely useful to managers and traders who take big positions in those markets. They need to understand the risk that they are exposed to in order to manage it properly.

For senior managers it is the overall risk of the firm that matters the most. The risks that are taken by managers at various levels (such as divisions or trading desks) must be aggregated in a way so that senior managers are able to assess the following questions.

- Where are concentrations of risk? This needs to be split further into specific categories of concentrations such as market risk and credit risk.
- Are returns of divisions commensurate with the risk taken by the divisions?
- What is the capital requirement of each division, given its risk exposure?
- Are compensation levels commensurate with the risk-adjusted performance?

This chapter will provide an integrated framework for defining risk, measuring risk and managing risk. The task of risk management has now become a paramount consideration with the advent of derivative markets and globalization of product and financial markets. To get a perspective on risk management, we examine the fixed-income part of the capital markets.

Note that the fixed-income division is divided into several profit centers. Each profit center has its own risk-return profile. For the senior management, the fixed-income division is just one (perhaps the most important) unit. In addition to fixed-income there may be other units such as FX, Equity, Commodities, Syndication, Investment Banking and so on. The key issue facing the senior management is the ability to understand and react to the overall riskiness of the firm without being swamped by too much information from various reporting divisions. We explore the issues using the fixed-income unit as an example. The logic of our analysis carries over to other units as well.

Each subdivision of the fixed-income unit is reporting in Figure 15-1 some key information pertaining to risk and return. For example, the Treasury and Agency desk is reporting its marked-to-market position value, profit and loss, its overall position in some benchmark equivalents (its position in terms of a benchmark security such as

FIGURE 15-1 *A Framework for Risk Management*

The Risk Distribution in Fixed-income Markets

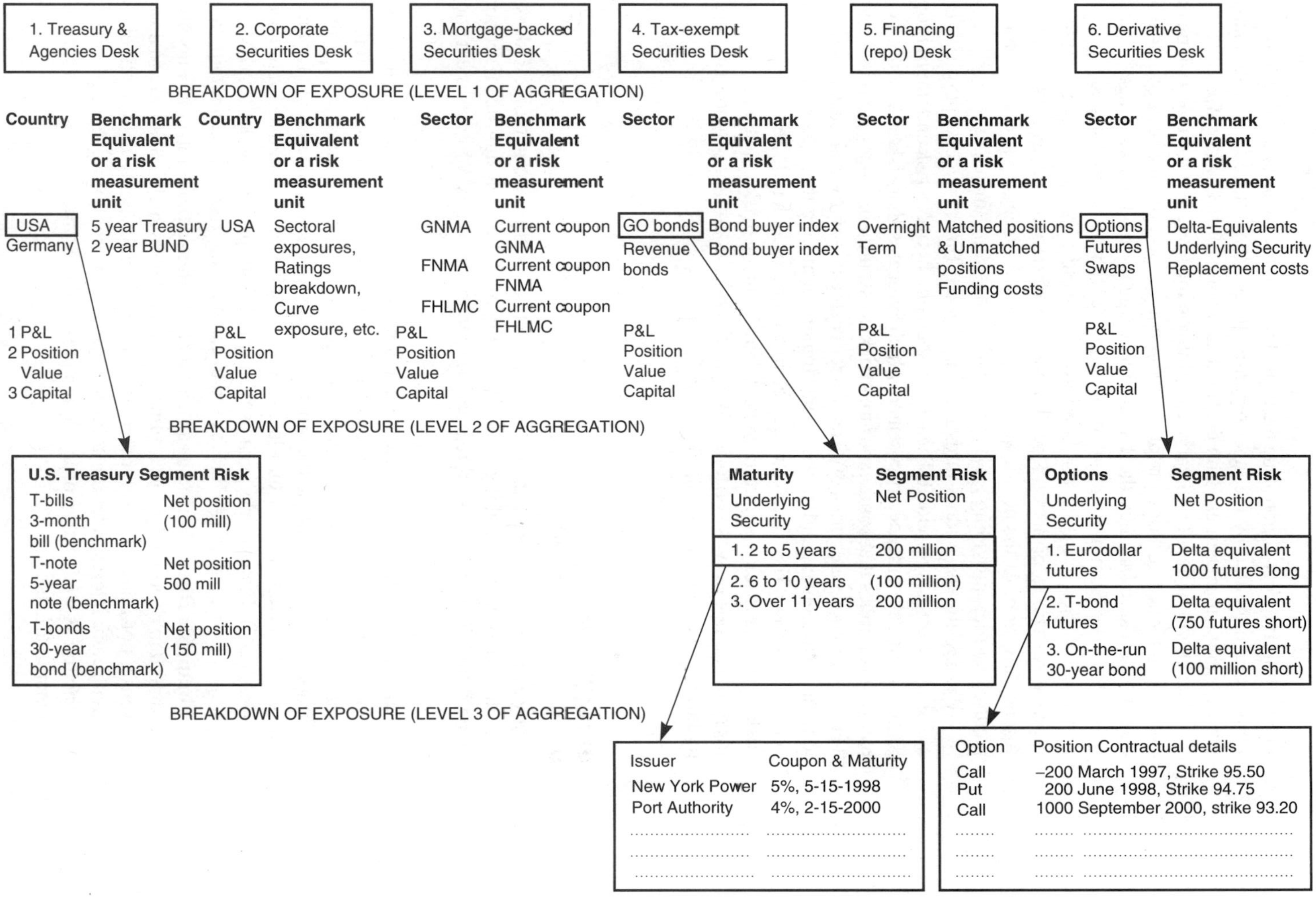

1. Treasury & Agencies Desk	2. Corporate Securities Desk	3. Mortgage-backed Securities Desk	4. Tax-exempt Securities Desk	5. Financing (repo) Desk	6. Derivative Securities Desk

BREAKDOWN OF EXPOSURE (LEVEL 1 OF AGGREGATION)

Country	Benchmark Equivalent or a risk measurement unit	Country	Benchmark Equivalent or a risk measurement unit	Sector	Benchmark Equivalent or a risk measurement unit	Sector	Benchmark Equivalent or a risk measurement unit	Sector	Benchmark Equivalent or a risk measurement unit	Sector	Benchmark Equivalent or a risk measurement unit
USA Germany	5 year Treasury 2 year BUND	USA	Sectoral exposures, Ratings breakdown, Curve	GNMA FNMA FHLMC	Current coupon GNMA Current coupon FNMA Current coupon FHLMC	GO bonds Revenue bonds	Bond buyer index Bond buyer index	Overnight Term	Matched positions & Unmatched positions Funding costs	Options Futures Swaps	Delta-Equivalents Underlying Security Replacement costs
1 P&L 2 Position 3 Capital			P&L exposure, etc. Position Value Capital		P&L Position Value Capital		P&L Position Value Capital		P&L Position Value Capital		P&L Position Value Capital

BREAKDOWN OF EXPOSURE (LEVEL 2 OF AGGREGATION)

U.S. Treasury Segment Risk

	Segment Risk
T-bills 3-month bill (benchmark)	Net position (100 mill)
T-note 5-year note (benchmark)	Net position 500 mill
T-bonds 30-year bond (benchmark)	Net position (150 mill)

Maturity Underlying Security	Segment Risk Net Position
1. 2 to 5 years	200 million
2. 6 to 10 years	(100 million)
3. Over 11 years	200 million

Options Underlying Security	Segment Risk Net Position
1. Eurodollar futures	Delta equivalent 1000 futures long
2. T-bond futures	Delta equivalent (750 futures short)
3. On-the-run 30-year bond	Delta equivalent (100 million short)

BREAKDOWN OF EXPOSURE (LEVEL 3 OF AGGREGATION)

Issuer	Coupon & Maturity
New York Power	5%, 5-15-1998
Port Authority	4%, 2-15-2000

Option	Position	Contractual details
Call	–200	March 1997, Strike 95.50
Put	200	June 1998, Strike 94.75
Call	1000	September 2000, strike 93.20

on-the-run five-year T-note) and the capital needed to cover its credit exposure. Similar reports are submitted by the other reporting units. In a nutshell, such summary reports present senior management with the financial health of its key divisions.

The extent of detail will vary depending on the level at which the risk management problem is looked at. For example, the summary report discussed above does not indicate the exposure faced by the Treasury and Agency desk for a change in the shape of the yield curve. Summary information on the curve risk is presented at a lower level in Figure 15-1 wherein the net position across the yield curve for specific maturity sectors is provided. This information is perhaps more critical to the manager of the Treasury and Agency division. At the next lower level, the risk is disaggregated and a more detailed picture emerges, providing greater detail to the operating manager.

We develop these ideas further in this chapter. First, the concept of risk is defined and some examples provided. Then, the association between risk and return is discussed. Some empirical evidence is presented which indicates that risk and return go hand in hand. This implies that some exposure to risk is essential in order to obtain higher return. Then we provide categories of risks. Under each category, we discuss issues pertaining to their measurement and management. Important among these categories are the market risk and credit risk. These are treated in considerable detail. The concept of Value at Risk (VAR) is discussed in this context. The Value-at-Risk calculations are illustrated for cash and derivatives portfolios. We conclude by examining some market responses to the risk management problems.

WHAT IS RISK?

In any economic undertaking there is uncertainty about future outcomes. Risk associated with an economic undertaking is the possibility of suffering a significant economic loss in the future. This definition of risk can be seen in the context of investment and financing as shown next.

Investment Risk   An investment in a project results in future cash flows that are uncertain. The uncertainties in cash flows arise from one's inability to forecast future events (sales growth, defaults, product price, product liabilities, etc.) perfectly. This implies that the return on the project should provide a compensation for the risk that is being taken. This in turn leads to the concept of risk-adjusted return on capital (RAROC). Frameworks such as the capital asset pricing model (CAPM) and arbitrage pricing theory (APT) are used to calculate the risk-adjusted return on capital.

Financing Risk   Financing an activity by issuing a fixed-rate loan may produce an uncertain opportunity cost if future interest rates on such loans were to drop. In this sense, not issuing a fixed-rate loan now (an inaction) may be thought of as a view that future interest rates are going to fall. It is thus possible to encounter risk through inaction as well: action or inaction represents a certain view of the future in the relevant markets.

Since risky actions produce uncertain future outcomes, one of the major consequences of risk is the potential for economic loss of profits and/or capital. The main theme is that risk translates to variability in future cash flows and value which may lead to potential economic losses. The following factors influence the risk of a portfolio or a trading position.

1. The volatility of each security in the portfolio.
2. The position in each security. Here we have to look at the weight of a security as a fraction of the overall portfolio as well as whether the position is long or short.
3. The correlation structure of securities in the portfolio. The correlation structure interacts with the position (long or short) to significantly influence the risk.
4. The implied or the explicit holding period. In some cases, the holding period may be explicit where the portfolio is held in order to meet a liability (possibly random) at a future point in time. There may be other situations where the assets (such as real estate or emerging market debt) are sufficiently illiquid that the time needed to unwind the position places an implicit holding period that may vary from a few days to several weeks.

Let us address the relationship between risk and the variability of returns in the context of two examples.

Example 15-1   Long-Term Bond

An investor purchases a zero coupon bond with a maturity of 30 years. The bond pays no coupons but promises to pay $1000 at the end of 30 years. At the time of purchase, the yield to maturity of the zero coupon was 8%. The price of the bond is

$$\frac{1000}{1.08^{30}} = 99.38.$$

This investment action is risky. If the yield to maturity were to fluctuate between 6% and 10%, the value of this bond will fluctuate from a high of 174.11 to a low of 57.31, as shown next in Table 15-1.

The return of the asset varies from a high of 75.20% to a low of -42.33%.

| | Yield | | | | | TABLE 15-1 |
	6%	7%	8%	9%	10%	*Investment Risk of a Thirty-Year Bond*
Price	174.11	131.37	99.38	75.37	57.31	
Return	75.20%	32.19%	0.00%	-24.16%	-42.33%	

As this example illustrates, risk often translates to variability of return. In this sense, a higher variability of returns may be thought of as a greater exposure to risk.

Example 15-2 Short-Term Bond

Let us consider an alternative investment action in which the investor purchases a zero coupon bond with a maturity of one year. This bond also pays no coupons but promises to pay $1000 at the end of one year. At the time of purchase, the yield to maturity of the one year zero coupon was 8%. The price of the bond is

$$\frac{1000}{1.08^1} = 925.93.$$

This investment action is also risky. If the yield to maturity were to fluctuate between 6% and 10%, the value of this bond will fluctuate from a high of 943.40 to a low of 909.09 as shown in Table 15-2. The return of the asset varies from a high of 4.85% to a low of -1.82%.

TABLE 15-2
Investment Risk of a One-Year Bond

	Yield					
	3%	*4%*	*5%*	*6%*	*8%*	*10%*
Price	970.87	961.54	952.38	943.40	934.58	909.09
Return	4.85%	3.85%	2.86%	1.89%	0%	-1.82%

Inspection of the price fluctuations in Tables 15-1 and 15-2 immediately suggest that the thirty-year bond is riskier than the one-year bond. The returns vary from +75.20% to -42.33%. By contrast, the one-year bond returns are fairly stable.

Of course, in the analysis we have assumed that the yields of the short-term bond and the long-term bonds move in parallel. In reality, as we have seen in Chapter 5, this will not be the case. These examples are used to motivate the idea that the variability of returns and risk go hand in hand.

It is also clear that large changes in yields (of the order of +2% to -2%) tend to occur over a period of several months, in general. Therefore, generally, the longer the holding period, the greater the risk for many transactions.

Normal Distribution

Since risk is about the possibility of suffering a significant economic loss in the future, it is essential to estimate the probability of encountering extreme outcomes in the future. In addition, it is useful to be able to assign some probability that a significant loss can result in any given holding period.

As shown in Chapter 5, based on historical returns, it is possible to estimate the volatility and the average return. Using these sample estimates, and assuming that the returns are normally distributed, we can assign probabilities regarding future returns.

Normal distribution is a symmetric distribution of returns which can be constructed once the average and the volatility of the returns are specified.

The distribution of returns under the assumption of normality is shown in Figure 15-2. In Figure 15-2, we have assumed that the long-term bond has a mean return of 7% and a volatility of 15%. The short-term bond is assumed to have a mean return of 5% and a volatility of 10%. The relative variability of return for the two bonds is shown in Figure 15-2. Note that the long-term bond has a much greater variation compared to the short-term bond and hence is riskier.

How reasonable is the normality assumption? The evidence appears to suggest that it is at best an approximation of the future behavior of portfolio returns in the equity market. The returns behavior in other markets may deviate from normality. As noted, normal distribution requires us to specify the mean returns of the portfolio and the volatility of the returns of the portfolio. In Figure 15-2, note that when the volatility is higher, more extreme outcomes are realized. This indicates greater risk. Hence for the long-term bond the curve is flatter. For the short-term bond, the volatility is lower and hence the curve is narrower resulting in a more pronounced peak.

FIGURE 15-2   *Risk of Long-Term and Short-Term Bonds*

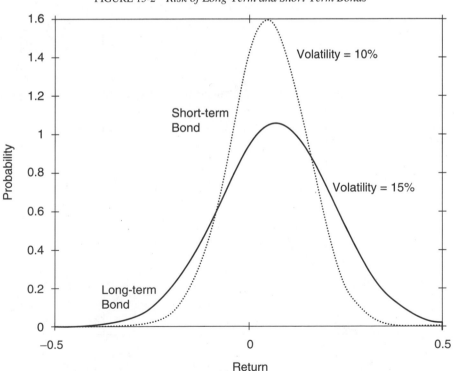

Mathematically, the probability density function $\phi(x)$ of a normal distribution describes the probability that the returns will fall within a very narrow band around x and is given below:

$$\phi(x) = \frac{1}{\sqrt{2\pi}\sigma} e^{-\frac{1}{2}\frac{(x-\mu)^2}{\sigma^2}}. \tag{15.1}$$

Given the mean μ and the volatility σ of the return variable x we can define the standard normal variable $z = \frac{x-\mu}{\sigma}$. The standard normal variable has a mean of zero and a volatility of one. The area under the standard normal density function is one. The standard normal density denoted by $n(z)$ is given by

$$n(z) = \frac{1}{\sqrt{2\pi}} e^{\frac{-z^2}{2}}. \tag{15.2}$$

The probability density function can then be integrated to determine the probability that the returns will lie in a certain range. Usually, the range of returns are measured in units of volatility. For example, the probability that the returns will fall within -2.33 units of volatility and +2.33 units of volatility around the mean is 99% in the case of normal distribution. This is shown in Figure 15-3.

FIGURE 15-3   *Standard Normal Distribution*

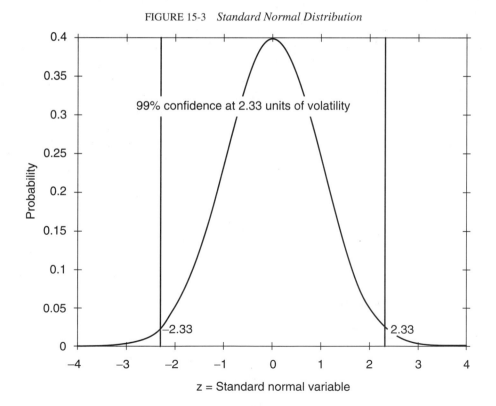

The probabilities can be calculated as follows:

$$\text{Probability } (\mu - 2.33\sigma < x < \mu + 2.33\sigma) = \int_{\mu-2.33}^{\mu+2.33\sigma} \frac{1}{\sqrt{2\pi}\sigma} e^{-\frac{1}{2}\frac{(x-\mu)^2}{\sigma^2}} \, dx \qquad (15.3)$$
$$= 0.99.$$

As seen from Equation (15.3), confidence intervals represent the range within which the future returns (or dollar values) are expected to lie with a prespecified probability. For example, x is expected to lie 99% of the time between $\mu - 2\sigma$ and $\mu + 2\sigma$. Given an estimate of μ and σ we are able to construct these confidence intervals under the assumption of normality.

Example 15-3

For the long-term bond, the mean return is 7% and the volatility is 15%. What is the 99% confidence interval? Assume that these are annualized estimates and that the bond will be held for a period of one year.

Since $\mu = 7\%$ and $\sigma = 15\%$ the confidence intervals are $\mu - 2.33\sigma = 7\% - 2.33 \times 15\% = -27.95\%$ and $\mu + 2.33\sigma = 7\% + 2.33 \times 15\% = 41.95\%$. So, we conclude that the returns will lie 99% of the time between -27.95% and 41.95% in one year's time into the future. Stated slightly differently, we can say that there is only a ½% chance that the returns will be below -27.95%.

Can this confidence interval be translated to dollar terms? We explore this in the next example.

Example 15-4

An investor has $1 million invested in the long-term bond. What is the 99% confidence interval for this investor for a one year horizon?

The confidence intervals for dollar values are obtained by simply multiplying the confidence intervals for returns by the market value of the security.

The lower limit is -27.95% × 1 million = 279,500. The upper limit is 41.95% × 1 million = 419,500. One important implication is that the losses can exceed 279,500 only ½% of the time. This measure of risk is called the Value-at-Risk (VAR) in the industry. VAR can be calculated for any specified holding periods.

Holding Period. Normal distribution allows us to estimate the potential losses on a portfolio in a given holding period with some degree of confidence. It turns out that for a holding period of τ years, we can compute the volatility of returns using the formula

$$\sigma(\tau) = \sigma \times \sqrt{\tau}.$$

This allows us to calculate the confidence intervals for any holding period. Implicit in all these calculations is the assumption that our estimated volatility is correct and is representative of the volatility into the future holding periods.

Example 15-5

An investor has \$1 million invested in the long-term bond. What is the 99% confidence interval for this investor for a horizon of 30 days?

Assuming that a year has 252 trading days, we can calculate the relevant volatility for a one-month holding period as

$$\sigma(\tau) = 15\% \times \sqrt{\frac{30}{252}} = 5.175\%.$$

The expected return for this holding period is

$$\mu(\tau) = 7\% \times \frac{30}{252} = 0.833\%.$$

The confidence intervals corresponding to 99% level are: $\mu - 2.33\sigma = 0.833\%$ $- 2.33 \times 5.175\% = -11.224\%$ and $\mu + 2.33\sigma = 0.833\% + 2.33 \times 5.175\% = 12.90$. Given that the market value of the investment is \$1 million, the intervals corresponding to the value are computed next. The lower limit is $-11.224\% \times$ 1 million $= 112,400$. The upper limit is $12.90\% \times 1$ million$= 129,000$.

We have presented some basic concepts in risk measurement. Before we continue these ideas further, it is important to have a perspective on the relationship between risk and return in different segments of the capital markets.

RISK AND RETURN

It is possible to minimize risk by selecting prudent investments such as Treasury bills in the fixed-income markets. But such a strategy also sharply reduces the return that one might expect to receive. Thus risk and return are two sides of any portfolio or trading strategy, as we have seen in Chapter 4. For example, we defined concepts such as bond equivalent yields, current yields, yield to maturity and rates of return (daily, monthly, annual and continuous compounding). In addition, as we showed in Chapter 4 and in the earlier sections of this chapter, volatility of security returns may be thought of as a quantitative measure of risk. Based on historical data, we can then construct measures of risk (volatility) and return. To get the perspective that risk and return go hand in hand, let us review some empirical evidence.

This relationship was documented by Ibbotson and Sinqfield (1994). Note in Table 15-3 how the long-term of return of different asset classes bears a direct relation to their riskiness as measured by the volatility. This relationship is based on long-term holding periods and simple buy and hold policies with reinvestment of dividends and coupons. For short-term holding periods with more dynamic trading the results will obviously differ. But the notion that higher expected return requires higher risk-taking is

Sector	Mean	Volatility	
1. Common stocks	12.0%	21.10%	**TABLE 15-3**
2. Small company stocks	17.70%	35.90%	*Risk Return (40-Year Average)*
3. Long-term corporate bonds	5.20%	8.50%	
4. Long-term government bonds	4.60%	8.50%	
5. Intermediate-term government bonds	4.90%	5.50%	
6. T-bills	3.50%	3.40%	
Inflation	3.20%	4.80%	

a very general one. The task of risk measurement becomes considerably more complicated when trading is more dynamic.

The time series properties of the returns and risks associated with different asset classes also brings home the point that, on balance, asset classes which provide better return are also subjected to greater variations. This is shown in Figure 15-4.

FIGURE 15-4   *Equity versus T-bill Returns*

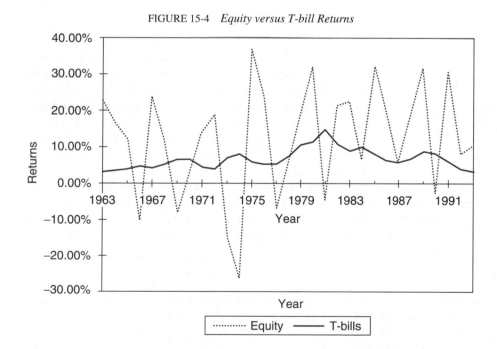

Note that the equity sector has on average provided better returns than the Treasury bill sector. But this has come at the expense of significant fluctuations over time. The Treasury bill sector has provided low returns but has been subjected to much lower variations. With the exception of the period 1979–1983, T-bills have been remarkably stable. As noted in Chapters 2 and 3, 1979–1983 was a particularly volatile period in the interest rate markets.

SOURCES OF RISK

Risk arises from a number of sources. These are interdependent and ultimately the risks manifest themselves in the price or the value of the portfolio (or the transaction) at which the portfolio (or the transaction) can be liquidated. We address the following important categories of risk:

- Market risk
- Credit risk
- Operational risk
- Liquidity risk
- Systemic risk

This way of isolating the sources of risk is useful from a conceptual standpoint. Each source of risk requires careful attention, monitoring and management.

Market Risk

Perhaps the most central source of risk is the market risk. The market risk of a security or a transaction is the component that is attributable to fluctuations in the price of the security or the value of transaction due to underlying market exposure. Such an exposure can stem from equity markets, interest rates, commodity prices and foreign exchange markets. For derivatives, risk can arise from more than one of these sources. For example, a listed option on the S&P 100 index carries with it a significant market risk associated with the U.S. equity market. On the other hand, a hybrid instrument such as a convertible bond has both equity and interest-rate risks.

Market risk can also be dependent on the asset-liability structure. A financial institution whose assets have a longer duration than its liabilities may have a significant interest rate exposure. This is sometimes referred to as the gap risk. In order to clarify issues, we will begin by examining the cash market risks before examining the risk of derivatives.

Cash Market. The concept is probably illustrated best with simple examples in equity and fixed-income markets. Consider simple stock, fixed-income and derivatives portfolios set up in Tables 15-4, 15-5 and 15-6 respectively. We will first focus on the cash market and later take up the derivatives portfolio for further analysis.

Security	Number of Shares	Share Price	Position Value
Stock A	100,000	50	5,000,000
Stock B	200,000	25	5,000,000

TABLE 15-4
Equity Portfolio

Security	Maturity in years	Par Amount in millions	Position Value in millions
Bond 1	5	100	120
Bond 2	10	50	60

TABLE 15-5
Treasury Portfolio

Security	Maturity in years	Contract Details	Position Value
Call on Stock A	0.5	Delta = 0.5	2000 options Each option is on 100 shares
Swap (Generic)	2	Fixed = 6% Leg Floating=LIBOR Notional Principal = 100 million	2,598,100

TABLE 15-6
Derivatives Portfolio

Note that the position risk can be summarized in many ways.

Position Value. One simple way is to simply report the notional amount of the equity and fixed-income positions of the dealer. Thus, we can say that the equity desk has a position value of $10 million and the fixed-income desk has a position value of $180 million. This measure has obvious drawbacks: (i) it does not take into account the relative market exposures of different securities in the portfolio, and (ii) it is silent on the reinvestment and funding risks that may be present in the portfolio. For example, it is not clear whether the positions have been financed in repo markets. It does capture the obvious fact that the fixed-income market is the dominant part of the book for this dealer measured in terms of the position size. Even for this measure to make sense, it is necessary to ensure that the prices used to compute the position value are not stale. In markets where prices change rapidly, it may even be necessary to mark the position value using real-time prices. Clearly, the systems requirements to do this for dealers who routinely transact in many markets around the world requires careful attention. This is especially a problem in the derivatives book since the position values may depend on assumptions made about the volatility of the underlying securities and on the zero prices that have been extracted to value swaps.

Value-at-Risk (VAR)

Earlier we indicated how the VAR of a security can be measured. Suppose we decide to incorporate some additional features of the securities to refine the measure of risk so that it can be applied to a portfolio. For the equity and fixed-income portfolio, let us incorporate information about variance and covariance of security returns. The variance and covariance information is annualized and presented in Tables 15-7 and 15-8.

Security	Stock A	Stock B
Stock A	0.06250	0.00375
Stock B	0.00375	0.02250

TABLE 15-7
Variance-Covariance
Matrix of Returns
Equity Sector

Security	Bond 1	Bond 2
Bond 1	0.02560	0.01536
Bond 2	0.01536	0.01440

TABLE 15-8
Variance-Covariance
Matrix of Returns
Fixed-Income Sector

VAR of Equity Sector. The total risk of the equity position might be summarized in terms of the variance of the returns of the equity portfolio. This variance, σ_p^2 may be explicitly computed in the following steps. First, the value of the portfolio (position value) is computed as V_p

$$V_p = n_A V_A + n_B V_B \tag{15.4}$$

where n_A is the number of shares of security A and V_A is the market price of security A and so on. Then the change in the value of the portfolio ΔV_p may be calculated as

$$\Delta V_p = n_A \Delta V_A + n_B \Delta V_B. \tag{15.5}$$

The return of the portfolio R_p is $\frac{\Delta V_p}{V_p}$; this is given by

$$R_p = \frac{\Delta V_p}{V_p} = x_A R_A + x_B R_B \tag{15.6}$$

where R_A is the return on security A and R_B is the return on security B. In addition, x_A is the fraction of the market value of the portfolio represented by security A and x_B is the fraction of the market value of the portfolio represented by security B.

As we showed earlier the risk of this portfolio depends on its volatility. So, we first proceed to calculate the volatility of returns. Now the variance of the portfolio return may be computed as

$$\sigma_p^2 = x_A^2 \sigma_A^2 + x_B^2 \sigma_B^2 + 2 x_A x_B \text{cov}(R_A, R_B). \tag{15.7}$$

For the data given in Table 15-4, we can compute $x_A = x_B = 0.5$.

Note in Table 15-7, that the variance of stock A, $\sigma_A^2 = 0.06250$. This implies that the volatility of stock A $\sigma_A = \sqrt{0.0625} = 0.25$. Also note from Table 15-7 that the variance of stock B, $\sigma_B^2 = 0.02250$. This implies that the volatility of stock B $\sigma_B = \sqrt{0.0225} =$

0.15. Finally, note that the covariance of returns from stock A and stock B, $\sigma_{AB} = 0.00375$. But the covariance is related to the correlation coefficient ρ by the formula

$$\sigma_{AB} = \rho\sigma_A\sigma_B.$$

Using this we can solve for the correlation coefficient ρ as

$$\rho = \frac{\sigma_{AB}}{\sigma_A\sigma_B} = \frac{0.00375}{0.25 \times 0.15} = 0.10.$$

Using these data we can compute the portfolio variability as

$$\sigma_p^2 = 0.5^2 \times 0.25^2 + 0.5^2 \times 0.15^2 + 2 \times 0.5 \times 0.5 \times 0.10 \times 0.15 \times 0.25$$
$$= 0.023125. \tag{15.8}$$

The volatility of the portfolio return is $\sigma_p = \sqrt{0.023125} = 0.1521$.

The dollar value at risk is expressed in units of standard deviations as

$$\sigma_V = V_p\sigma_p = 10,000,000 \times 0.1521 \times \sqrt{\frac{1}{252}} = \$95,795. \tag{15.9}$$

For a 99% confidence interval, we multiply this by 2.33 to get

$$2.33 \times 95,795 = 223,201.$$

The dollar value that is at risk is 223,201 in the sense that there is only a half a percent chance that the losses will exceed 223,201 in one day in the equity portfolio. What is the effect of correlation on the overall risk of the equity portfolio? As the correlation increases, the portfolio gets to be riskier. The reason is simple: with a positive correlation, both securities tend to do well at the same time and they tend to have poor returns at the same time. This increases the overall riskiness of the portfolio, if the portfolio is long in both the securities. Table 15-9 illustrates the effect of correlation between securities A and B on the overall riskiness of the portfolio. Note how the diversification effect reduces the risk of the portfolio. The confidence levels are shown for 68% (one unit of volatility) and 99% (2.33 units of volatility).

Do VARs Add? Is it possible for us to simply compute the VAR of security A and the VAR of security B and add them together to get the VAR of the portfolio? If not, what is the bias that we would have introduced by adding the VARs of individual securities to estimate the portfolio VAR?

Let us address these questions by first determining the VAR of individual securities. VAR of stock A is

$$VAR_A = 2.33 \times 0.25 \times 5,000,000 \times \sqrt{\frac{1}{252}} = 183,470.$$

VAR of stock B is

$$VAR_B = 2.33 \times 0.15 \times 5,000,000 \times \sqrt{\frac{1}{252}} = 110,082.$$

Note that the sum of the VARs for 99% confidence over a one day holding period is

$$VAR_A + VAR_B = 293,552.$$

The portfolio VAR is only 223,201. So, we conclude that the VARs are not additive in general. The reason is that the securities are less than perfectly correlated. Note for Table 15-9 that as the correlation increases, the portfolio VAR is approaching the sum of the VARs of the individual securities. This clearly illustrates the benefits of diversification.

But by adding the individual VARs we are overstating the VAR of the overall portfolio. This observation applies to Figure 15-1 as well. We can compute the VAR for each division in the fixed-income sector. The VAR for each division should be subject to some risk limits. By adding the VARs of all divisions, we will be significantly overstating the overall riskiness of the fixed-income unit. This arises because the correlation benefits across different divisions of the fixed-income unit are ignored. In a sense, such a calculation will show that the overall risk limit is binding when in fact the overall VAR may be a lot less.

Value-at-Risk of Fixed-Income Sector. In a similar way, we can compute the risk of fixed-income portfolio as well. However, we will approach this problem in two stages. First we will ignore the information in Table 15-8 which contains the correlation information between the two bonds. Instead, we will just use the information concerning the dollar value of an 0.01 of each fixed-income security.

TABLE 15-9

Correlation	Variance	Volatility of Equity Portfolio	Dollar Value of Equity at Risk Confidence Levels	
			68%	99%
-0.70	0.008	9.01%	56,782	132,302
-0.60	0.010	10.00%	62,994	146,776
-0.50	0.012	10.90%	68,646	159,946
-0.40	0.014	11.73%	73,867	172,110
-0.30	0.016	12.50%	78,743	183,470
-0.20	0.018	13.23%	83,333	194,167
-0.10	0.019	13.92%	87,684	204,304
0.00	0.021	14.58%	91,829	213,961
0.10	0.023	15.21%	95,795	223,201
0.20	0.025	15.81%	99,602	232,074
0.30	0.027	16.39%	103,270	240,619
0.40	0.029	16.96%	106,812	248,871
0.50	0.031	17.50%	110,240	256,858
0.60	0.033	18.03%	113,564	264,605
0.70	0.034	18.54%	116,794	272,130
VAR of Stock A			78,743	183,470
VAR of Stock B			47,246	110,082

As shown in Table 15-10, the five-year bond has a $DV01$ of \$500 per million and the ten-year bond has a $DV01$ of 700 dollars per million. The dollar value that is at risk in the fixed-income portfolio is calculated as follows.

$$DV01_p = n_1 DV01_1 + n_2 DV02 \tag{15.10}$$

Then, the $DV01_p$ is computed as follows.

$$DV01_p = 100 \times 500 + 50 \times 700 = \$85,000 \tag{15.11}$$

<table>
<tr><td>Security</td><td>DV01</td></tr>
<tr><td>Bond 1</td><td>500</td></tr>
<tr><td>Bond 2</td><td>700</td></tr>
</table>

TABLE 15-10
$DV01$ of Securities

Note that the $DV01$ may be used to construct benchmark or risk equivalents. For example, it is possible to express the risk of the fixed-income portfolio in five-year equivalents as follows: In the example, the \$50 million par value of the ten-year bond may be restated in five-year equivalents as $50 \times \frac{700}{500} = 70$ million. Thus the five-year equivalents for this fixed-income portfolio is $100 + 70 = 170$ million par amount. Often, risk limits are set for fixed-income positions in such equivalents. Such risk limits may give the portfolio manager or the trader some latitude in the choice of securities. This measure, however, assumes that when the five-year rates move by one basis point, the ten-year rates also move by one basis point. In other words, we assume that the yields move in parallel.

Thus the dollar value of an 0.01 of the portfolio does not take into account the information about the variances and covariances of the securities which is provided in Table 15-8. We proceed to do this next. In addition, it must be remembered that the $DV01$ is valid only for a basis point (or a very small) change in yield and does not easily generalize to arbitrary holding periods over which changes can be significant.

As we noted earlier, long-term interest rates tend to be less volatile than short-term interest rates. They are generally positively correlated. In Table 15-8, note that the returns have a strong positive correlation.

For the data given in Table 15-5, we can compute $x_1 = \frac{120}{180} = \frac{2}{3}$ and $x_2 = \frac{60}{180} = \frac{1}{3}$.

Note in Table 15-8 that the variance of bond 1, $\sigma_1^2 = 0.02560$. This implies that the volatility of bond 1, $\sigma_1 = \sqrt{0.0256} = 0.16$. Also note from Table 15-8 that the variance of bond 2, $\sigma_2^2 = 0.01440$. This implies that the volatility of bond 2, $\sigma_2 = \sqrt{0.0144} = 0.12$. Finally, note that the covariance of returns from bond 1 and bond 2, $\sigma_{12} = 0.01536$. But the covariance is given by the formula

$$\sigma_{12} = \rho \sigma_1 \sigma_2.$$

Using this we can solve for the correlation coefficient ρ as

$$\rho = \frac{\sigma_{12}}{\sigma_1 \sigma_2} = \frac{0.01536}{0.16 \times 0.12} = 0.80.$$

Now we are in a position to consider the fixed-income portfolio's risk as measured by the variance of the portfolio return. It may be computed as

$$\sigma_p^2 = x_1^2\sigma_1^2 + x_2^2\sigma_2^2 + 2x_1x_2\text{cov}(R_1, R_2). \tag{15.12}$$

We can compute the portfolio variability as

$$\sigma_p^2 = \left[\frac{2}{3}\right]^2 \times 0.16^2 + \left[\frac{1}{3}\right]^2 \times 0.12^2 + 2 \times \frac{2}{3} \times \frac{1}{3} \times 0.80 \times 0.16 \times 0.12 \tag{15.13}$$

$$= 0.01980.$$

This implies a portfolio volatility of $\sigma_p = 0.1407$. We now explicitly recognize that the securities may have changes in yields that are less than perfect. We now compute the VAR of the fixed-income portfolio for a one day holding period (for a 99% confidence level) as follows.

$$\text{Var}(\Delta V_p) = V_p \times \sigma_p = 180,000,000 \times 0.1407 \times 2.33 \times \sqrt{\frac{1}{252}} \tag{15.14}$$

$$= 3,718,001.$$

This is precisely the measure of risk that we have used for the equity portfolio.

VAR for Derivatives

The approach that we have presented for the measurement of risk for the cash market (equity and fixed-income markets) may be easily extended to derivatives as well. But derivative securities (such as options which have a nonlinear payoff in their underlying security's prices) present some problems. To illustrate the ideas, turn to the information presented in Table 15-6.

In Table 15-6, we list a book consisting of the option on stock A and a generic interest rate swap with five years to maturity. What is the appropriate way to measure the risk of such a book? The first thing to note is that the measurement of risk of this book requires an appropriate model of pricing options. In addition, there must be a satisfactory estimation procedure by which the volatility of the underlying asset is estimated. Using inappropriate models or estimation procedures can lead to significant errors in the measurement of risk. For swaps, as seen in Chapter 14, it is essential to estimate the zero prices to be able to determine their replacement costs and their VAR. This implies that we must rely on models for estimating zero prices such as the ones discussed in Chapter 5. Let us begin with the VAR calculations of options next.

VAR of Options. First we focus on measuring the risk of the call option whose price we denote by C. For the option we can compute the return as

$$R = \frac{dC}{C}.$$

The return can be slightly rearranged as

$$R = \frac{dC}{dP_A}\frac{dP_A}{P_A} \times \frac{P_A}{C}.$$

By writing the option's return in this manner, it is expressed in terms of the return (R_A) of the underlying security and the delta (δ) of the option. Note that we can now write the option's return as

$$R = \delta \times R_A \times \frac{P_A}{C}.$$

The volatility of the returns is then,

$$\sigma_R = \delta \times \sigma_A \times \frac{P_A}{C}.$$

Just as we did for cash market securities, we need to find the VAR in terms of dollar amounts rather than returns. To do this we simply multiply σ_R by the market value of the option C and then apply the relevant confidence interval factor L. The VAR for specified confidence level L and a holding period τ years is

$$VAR = L\delta\sigma_A\sqrt{\tau}P_A.$$

Obviously, $L = 2.33$ if the confidence level required is 99%. The VAR of the option (per contract) assuming that each option is on 100 shares (from Table 15-6) is

$$VAR = 2.33 \times 0.5 \times 0.25 \times \sqrt{\frac{1}{252}} \times 100 \times 50 = 91.735.$$

Since the book has 2000 options, its VAR is $2000 \times 91.735 = 183,470$. Note that the VAR of the option is simply the VAR of the underlying asset multiplied by the delta of the option. Of course, the delta of the option will depend on the options pricing model that is used. The VAR analysis for the option assumes that the delta of the option stays at 0.5, which is reasonable for a small holding period. For longer holding periods, such as 30 days, this assumption is unrealistic. The VAR measure for a thirty-day holding period is

$$VAR = 2.33 \times 0.5 \times 0.25 \times \sqrt{\frac{30}{252}} \times 100 \times 50 \times 2000 = 1,004,908.$$

A more reasonable approach is to simulate the underlying asset value for the holding period by determining the value of the option at the end of each scenario, and estimating the average across all possible paths. Such an approach will correctly capture the changes in the delta of the derivative instrument. We illustrate this approach for options next.

Monte Carlo Simulation. In the simulation approach, we generate several paths for stock A. For each path we calculate the value of the option at the end of the holding period (30 days). This way we correctly account for the passage of time as well as for the fact that in some paths, option will be out-of-the-money and in others, the option will be in-the-money. Clearly, this procedure reflects the changes in delta into the calculations. In order to simulate the prices of stock A, we use the procedure developed in Chapter 7.

The risk-neutral price process for A is generated such that the price at a future date T is given by the equation below.

$$\ln P_T = \ln P_0 + \left\{ \left(r - \tfrac{1}{2}\sigma^2 \right) \Delta t + \sigma \sqrt{\Delta t} \tilde{z} \right\} \qquad (15.15)$$

In this equation, P_0 is the price of stock A now ($50), r is the riskless rate (assumed to be 5%) and σ is the volatility of the returns of stock A (assumed to be 25% from Table 15-7). The variable $\tilde{z}$ is a standard normal variable with a mean of one and variance of one.

We can write this equation as

$$P_T = P_0 \times e^{\{(r - \frac{1}{2}\sigma^2)\Delta t + \sigma \sqrt{\Delta t}\tilde{z}\}}.$$

Next, we repeat this procedure to generate 300 paths by drawing 300 values of $\tilde{z}$. For each path we determine P_T. For each path at the end of 30 days, we use the Black-Scholes options pricing model to value the call option. In pricing the option, we assume $r = 5\%$ and $\sigma = 25\%$. The call values are determined for each path. The resulting frequency distribution of call prices is shown in Figure 15-5.

FIGURE 15-5   *Distribution of Call on Stock A*

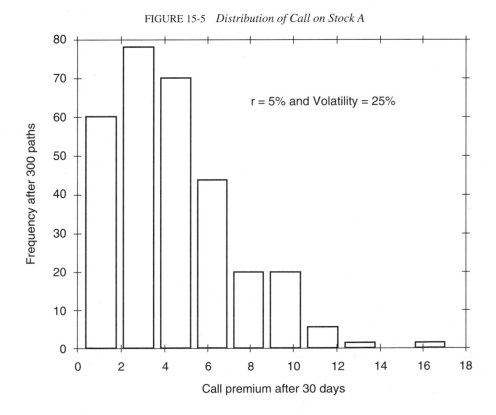

In Table 15-11 we indicate the outcome along each path. The change in the value of the option has been sorted from the lowest realization to the highest realization.

Based on the frequency distribution, we can construct the 99% confidence level. In fact, the simulation results show that the probability that the option will lose value by more than 734,417 is only $1%. The results are shown in Figure 15-6.

Note that the VAR determined using the current delta of the option was 1,004,908, which is significantly higher than the VAR obtained by simulation. This suggests that the VAR procedure used for the cash market (in which payoffs are typically linear) is generally inappropriate for securities such as options (where the payoffs are nonlinear). We now turn to the measurement of VAR for the swap contract in the derivatives book shown in Table 15-6.

VAR of Swaps. The VAR of a swap contract depends on the zero coupon bond prices that are needed to calculate the value of the swap. A full-blown treatment of calculating the VAR of a swap is not presented here. We show how the swap can be valued and how the volatility of the swap value depends on the variance-covariance structure of the zero prices.

The generic interest rate swap shown in Table 15-6 has two years to maturity. As discussed in Chapter 14, the valuation of swaps requires the estimation of the zero

FIGURE 15-6   *VAR of Call Option by Simulation*

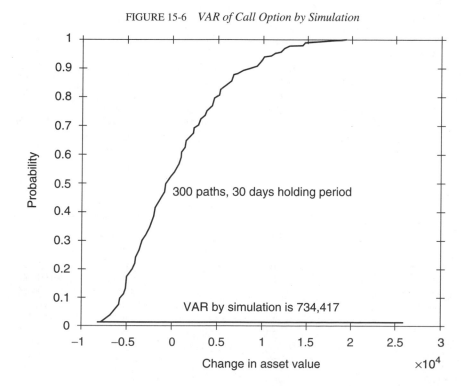

300 paths, 30 days holding period

VAR by simulation is 734,417

TABLE 15-11

Cumulative Probability	Change in Call Value	Cumulative Probability	Change in Call Value	Cumulative Probability	Change in Call Value
0.003	-788,648	0.170	-472,256	0.337	-287,190
0.007	-755,242	0.173	-470,432	0.340	-285,631
0.010	-734,417	0.177	-463,423	0.343	-279,724
0.013	-718,293	0.180	-459,714	0.347	-271,396
0.017	-707,706	0.183	-456,591	0.350	-270,575
0.020	-704,838	0.187	-451,662	0.353	-269,789
0.023	-696,716	0.190	-450,943	0.357	-269,163
0.027	-695,567	0.193	-448,283	0.360	-267,848
0.030	-681,464	0.197	-442,876	0.363	-263,229
0.033	-677,586	0.200	-437,221	0.367	-260,084
0.037	-676,145	0.203	-429,595	0.370	-258,502
0.040	-676,131	0.207	-421,681	0.373	-254,887
0.043	-672,192	0.210	-419,528	0.377	-248,799
0.047	-671,523	0.213	-418,615	0.380	-248,317
0.050	-667,335	0.217	-414,310	0.383	-240,393
0.053	-665,901	0.220	-402,878	0.387	-240,061
0.057	-638,185	0.223	-402,736	0.390	-239,076
0.060	-632,861	0.227	-400,557	0.393	-237,998
0.063	-629,562	0.230	-398,450	0.397	-234,687
0.067	-617,120	0.233	-397,446	0.400	-232,542
0.070	-614,818	0.237	-392,164	0.403	-215,235
0.073	-613,787	0.240	-392,138	0.407	-195,883
0.077	-608,065	0.243	-387,325	0.410	-192,920
0.080	-593,360	0.247	-383,467	0.413	-191,661
0.083	-589,536	0.250	-379,010	0.417	-188,367
0.087	-576,826	0.253	-377,742	0.420	-187,240
0.090	-576,470	0.257	-377,709	0.423	-182,533
0.093	-570,473	0.260	-375,504	0.427	-181,276
0.097	-570,408	0.263	-373,163	0.430	-176,065
0.100	-569,241	0.267	-371,823	0.433	-175,337
0.103	-565,283	0.270	-371,106	0.437	-172,245
0.107	-558,877	0.273	-367,141	0.440	-163,386
0.110	-553,233	0.277	-358,861	0.443	-152,260
0.113	-548,144	0.280	-355,294	0.447	-149,969
0.117	-542,865	0.283	-344,398	0.450	-148,684
0.120	-522,893	0.287	-344,224	0.453	-143,958
0.123	-521,254	0.290	-342,861	0.457	-142,130
0.127	-514,941	0.293	-340,306	0.460	-136,763
0.130	-506,929	0.297	-331,354	0.463	-135,990
0.133	-506,422	0.300	-326,630	0.467	-133,455
0.137	-504,399	0.303	-324,120	0.470	-131,398
0.140	-499,511	0.307	-316,196	0.473	-125,222
0.143	-498,052	0.310	-312,816	0.477	-121,844
0.147	-487,136	0.313	-310,981	0.480	-109,724
0.150	-487,081	0.317	-309,430	0.483	-106,841
0.153	-485,679	0.320	-309,404	0.487	-105,348
0.157	-482,118	0.323	-307,760	0.490	-100,229
0.160	-477,031	0.327	-298,602	0.493	-96,273
0.163	-474,980	0.330	-293,081	0.497	-95,466
0.167	-474,791	0.333	-291,257	0.500	-90,005

590

Cumulative Probability	Change in Call Value	Cumulative Probability	Change in Call Value	Cumulative Probability	Change in Call Value
0.503	−88,495	0.670	88,308	0.837	388,540
0.507	−86,038	0.673	88,534	0.840	401,414
0.510	−85,636	0.677	97,192	0.843	420,278
0.513	−83,307	0.680	112,778	0.847	445,363
0.517	−81,006	0.683	115,545	0.850	454,745
0.520	−78,257	0.687	118,241	0.853	473,939
0.523	−74,215	0.690	131,621	0.857	497,352
0.527	−72,969	0.693	132,139	0.860	513,377
0.530	−68,669	0.697	132,618	0.863	520,474
0.533	−64,707	0.700	134,498	0.867	567,697
0.537	−64,130	0.703	137,434	0.870	586,906
0.540	−61,210	0.707	137,666	0.873	592,116
0.543	−61,071	0.710	138,124	0.877	610,500
0.547	−57,722	0.713	161,501	0.880	623,734
0.550	−50,640	0.717	161,905	0.883	651,709
0.553	−45,588	0.720	170,871	0.887	698,338
0.557	−37,624	0.723	174,994	0.890	717,967
0.560	−36,122	0.727	177,421	0.893	736,815
0.563	−28,820	0.730	178,381	0.897	755,654
0.567	−26,476	0.733	180,039	0.900	766,961
0.570	−25,884	0.737	186,817	0.903	767,109
0.573	−25,505	0.740	215,565	0.907	773,485
0.577	−24,787	0.743	223,894	0.910	775,022
0.580	−22,383	0.747	226,225	0.913	781,158
0.583	−16,052	0.750	228,115	0.917	783,367
0.587	−15,517	0.753	228,971	0.920	783,428
0.590	−14,408	0.757	233,118	0.923	785,876
0.593	−14,337	0.760	233,775	0.927	804,115
0.597	−10,002	0.763	234,542	0.930	820,710
0.600	−4,938	0.767	236,508	0.933	824,494
0.603	−2,071	0.770	236,681	0.937	826,131
0.607	17,314	0.773	236,912	0.940	847,632
0.610	17,476	0.777	238,144	0.943	905,558
0.613	18,113	0.780	240,621	0.947	917,425
0.617	23,997	0.783	241,328	0.950	983,559
0.620	26,012	0.787	242,575	0.953	1,005,118
0.623	30,844	0.790	259,471	0.957	1,011,531
0.627	36,691	0.793	293,573	0.960	1,037,453
0.630	40,691	0.797	300,552	0.963	1,051,357
0.633	47,650	0.800	303,290	0.967	1,077,121
0.637	55,099	0.803	318,553	0.970	1,083,652
0.640	62,657	0.807	319,207	0.973	1,087,876
0.643	67,111	0.810	321,648	0.977	1,103,643
0.647	68,904	0.813	323,060	0.980	1,218,367
0.650	70,149	0.817	323,469	0.983	1,307,475
0.653	72,077	0.820	333,545	0.987	1,542,662
0.657	73,994	0.823	336,940	0.990	1,597,125
0.660	79,163	0.827	357,724	0.993	1,899,263
0.663	82,819	0.830	361,002	0.997	2,078,484
0.667	88,155	0.833	376,546	1.000	2,280,702

coupon bond prices. Let us consider the cash flows of the swap to lay out clearly the steps that are needed to compute the VAR of swap. The two-year swap given in Table 15-6 has four cash flows as shown in Table 15-12. The next payment date of the swap is three months from now. Thereafter, there are three additional payment dates, each occurring at six month intervals.

Time	Fixed-Leg	Floating-Leg
$t+3$	$\frac{6\%}{2}$	4%
$t+9$	$\frac{6\%}{2}$	LIBOR
$t+15$	$\frac{6\%}{2}$	LIBOR
$t+21$	$\frac{6\%}{2}$	LIBOR

TABLE 15-12
Cash Flows of Swaps

Note that the value of the swap, as shown in Chapter 14, is found by calculating the present value of each leg and taking the difference between the two values. The fixed-leg pays an amount equal to $3\% \times 100,000,000 = 3,000,000$ every six months. The present value of the fixed-leg is:

$$\text{PV(Fixed)} = 3,000,000 \times [b(t, t+3) + b(t, t+9) + b(t, t+15) + b(t, t+21)]$$

where the zero coupon bond prices at date t for maturities at dates $t+3, t+9, t+15$ and $t+21$ are respectively given by $b(t, t+3)$, $b(t, t+9)$, $b(t, t+15)$ and $b(t, t+21)$. As shown in Table 15-12, the present value of the fixed-leg is

$$\text{PV(Fixed)} = 3,000,000 \times [0.9901 + 0.9690 + 0.9459 + 0.9211] = 11,478,300$$

(The zero prices are reported only up to four decimals. In actual calculations, the zero prices are not approximated to four decimals.)

The value of the floating leg is easy to determine. Note that at date t, the next floating coupon is already known. This is because we are dealing with a generic interest rate swap where the next coupon is reset six months ahead of the payment date. Let us say that the coupon to be paid at $t+3$ was reset six months earlier (at $t-3$) at the then prevailing LIBOR of 4.00% (annualized). As discussed in Chapter 14, the value of the present value of the floating leg can be determined as shown in Table 15-13.

Intuitively, the present value of the floating leg can be obtained as follows: first, we recognize that the next payment at date $t+3$ is already set at 4% (annualized). Its present value is

$$2,000,000 b(t, t+3) = 2,000,000 \times 0.9901 = 1,980,200.$$

The subsequent payments in the floating leg can be replicated by rolling over 100 million at date $t+3$ in a sequence of six-month LIBOR until maturity. The 100 million that is required at $t+3$ has a present value at t of

$$100,000,000 b(t, t+3) = 100,000,000 \times 0.9901 = 99,010,000.$$

	Zero Yields			TABLE 15-13
Maturity (in months)	Yield	Zero Prices	Forward Rates	*Valuation of Swaps*
3	4.00%	0.9901	4.0000%	
9	4.25%	0.9690	4.3751%	
15	4.50%	0.9459	4.8756%	
21	4.75%	0.9211	5.3763%	

Pricing a Two-Year Swap

	3	9	15	21	Time
	$t = 3$	$t = 9$	$t = 15$	$t = 21$	
Fixed payments	6.00%	6.00%	6.00%	6.00%	
Floating payments	4.00%	4.38%	4.88%	5.38%	
Zero prices	0.9901	0.9690	0.9459	0.9211	
PV (float)	0.0198	0.0212	0.0231	0.0248	
Total PV (float)		**8,880,200**			
PV (fixed)	0.0297	0.0291	0.0284	0.0276	
Total PV (fixed)		**11,478,366**			
Value of swap		**2,596,395**			

Since the floating leg does not pay the balloon payment, we subtract from the par amount the present value of the par amount. The present value of this at t of

$$100,000,000 b(t, t + 21) = 100,000,000 \times 0.9211 = 92,110,000.$$

Therefore the present value of the floating leg is

$$PV(\text{Floating}) = 2,000,000 b(t, t + 3) + 100,000,000[b(t, t + 3) - b(t, t + 21)].$$

Or,

$$PV(\text{Floating}) = 8,880,200.$$

The swap value is the difference between the fixed and floating leg, which is $11,478,366 - 8,881,971 = 2,596,395$.

The swap value can be written as a function of the zero coupon bond prices.

$$S = 3,000,000 \times [b(t, t + 3) + b(t, t + 9) + b(t, t + 15) + b(t, t + 21)]$$
$$- [2,000,000 b(t, t + 3) + 100,000,000\{b(t, t + 3) - b(t, t + 21)\}]$$

The volatility of the swap value σ_S clearly depends on the variance-covarince matrix of the zero prices. As a consequence the VAR of the swap will in turn depend on the variance-covariance matrix of the zero prices. Once σ_S is calculated, the procedure for computing the VAR proceeds exactly as we have done earlier for the cash portfolio.

Modelling Correlation

The stock portfolio can also be analyzed using the simulation technique. One advantage of simulation is that we can model different scenarios which we anticipate. A key consideration is the fact that stock A and stock B are correlated. This correlation must be modelled in the simulation. Consider the equity portfolio in Table 15-4. For this portfolio let us introduce some basic notations. Let the (2×2) variance-covariance matrix of returns be denoted as Ω. It is given by

$$\begin{bmatrix} \sigma_A^2 & \sigma_{AB} \\ \sigma_{AB} & \sigma_B^2 \end{bmatrix}.$$

Let the weights of the stocks in the portfolio be denoted by the (2×1) vector x

$$\begin{bmatrix} x_A \\ x_B \end{bmatrix}.$$

Then the variance of the stock portfolio can be compactly denoted by

$$\sigma_p^2 = x'\Omega x.$$

The idea behind denoting the portfolio this way is simple: although we are illustrating the basic ideas with just two securities, the logic goes over even if the portfolio were to contain many securities. We will simply define Ω and x to reflect the characteristics and the number of securities in the portfolio.

The presence of correlation poses a problem in performing simulation. How do we simulate the paths of stock B if we know that its returns are correlated with the returns of stock A? It turns out that this problem can be solved by using a technique known as Cholesky factorization. Simply stated, the Cholesky factorization allows us to simulate each stock's path using standard normal variables after a modification is made to the variance terms. The Cholesky factorization finds a matrix X such that

$$\Omega = X'X.$$

The matrix X turns out to have a nice structure for simulation purposes. In the context of our example X' is

$$\begin{bmatrix} \sigma_A & 0 \\ \rho\sigma_B & \sigma_B\sqrt{1-\rho^2} \end{bmatrix}.$$

Given this factorization, we can implement the simulation as follows:

1. First we generate a set of standard normal variables $\tilde{z}_A$ and $\tilde{z}_B$ for each stock. We will simulate 300 paths by generating 300 draws of $\tilde{z}_A$ and $\tilde{z}_B$ respectively. Note that $\tilde{z}_A$

and $\tilde{z}_B$ are standard normal variates with a mean of zero and a volatility of one. Also, note that $\tilde{z}_A$ and $\tilde{z}_B$ are not correlated with each other.

2. Using these we generate the price paths for stocks A and B. The price of stock A at any date T in the future is

$$P_A(T) = P_A(0)e^{\{(\mu_A - \frac{1}{2}\sigma_A^2)\Delta t + \sigma_A\sqrt{\Delta t}\tilde{z}_A\}}.$$

The expected return of stock A is denoted by μ_A. The price of stock B at any date T in the future will capture the correlation properties as shown next.

$$P_B(T) = P_B(0)e^{\{(\mu_B - \frac{1}{2}\sigma_B^2)\Delta t + (\rho\tilde{z}_A + \sqrt{1-\rho^2}\tilde{z}_B)\sigma_B\sqrt{\Delta t}\}}$$

The expected return of stock B is denoted by μ_B. Note that we have modified the variance of the security B according to the Cholesky factorization. The price processes of A and B can now be simulated as before except that they now capture the correlation structure as well.

3. It is useful to note that the returns R_A and R_B of the stocks are respectively given by

$$R_A = \ln\left(\frac{P_A(T)}{P_A(0)}\right)$$

and

$$R_B = \ln\left(\frac{P_B(T)}{P_B(0)}\right).$$

Using this definition of returns in the price expressions we get

$$R_A = \left(\mu_A - \frac{1}{2}\sigma_A^2\right)\Delta t + \sigma_A\sqrt{\Delta t}\tilde{z}_A$$

and

$$R_B = \left(\mu_B - \frac{1}{2}\sigma_B^2\right)\Delta t + \left(\rho\tilde{z}_A + \sqrt{1-\rho^2}\tilde{z}_B\right)\sigma_B\sqrt{\Delta t}.$$

We can easily verify that the variance of R_A is $\sigma_A^2\Delta t$ and that the variance of R_B is $\sigma_B^2\Delta t$. In addition, we can verify that the covariance between A and B is $\rho\sigma_A\sigma_B\Delta t$. This shows how the Cholesky factorization can help in setting up the simulation for correlated variables. Programs like Mathematica and Matlab have built-in Cholesky factorization codes. Some technical conditions which are necessary for the factorization to work are not discussed here.

4. We have simulated the behavior of the equity portfolio using 300 paths. At the end of 30 days, we computed the value of the portfolio and determined the change in the value of the portfolio (relative to the beginning value of 10 million) for each path. Then the change in the values was sorted and a frequency distribution was created. Based on the frequency distribution, the VAR of the portfolio was calculated for a 99% confidence level. The frequency distribution and the VAR are illustrated in Figures 15-7 and 15-8 respectively.

FIGURE 15-7   *Frequency Distribution of Equity Portfolio*

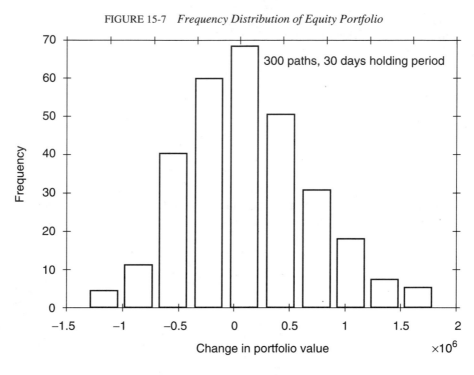

FIGURE 15-8   *VAR of Equity Portfolio by Simulation*

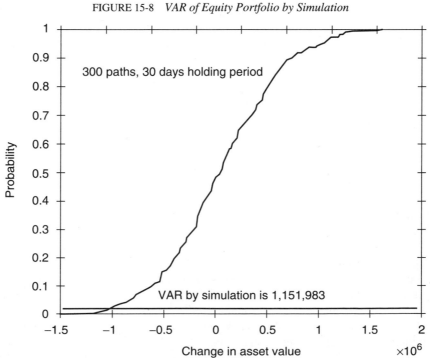

In Figure 15-7, note that the portfolio value changes from a low of about -1.35 million to a high of about 1.75 million in 30 days time. In these simulations, the correlation coefficient was assumed to be 0.10. The implication of this manifests itself into the scatter plot in Figure 15-9 where the prices of stock A are plotted against the returns of stock B.

FIGURE 15-9   *Stock A versus Stock B*

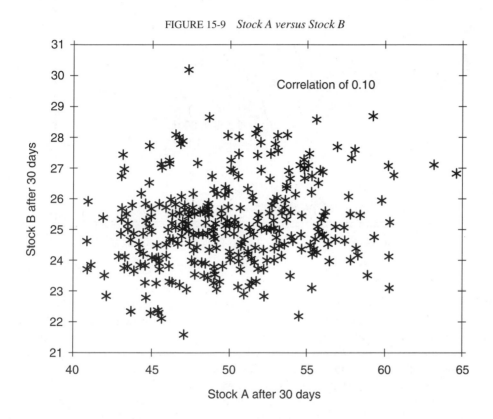

What happens to the VAR when the correlation between stock A and stock B increases to 0.8? Intuition suggests that the VAR should increase. The simulation results are shown in Figures 15-10 and 15-11 under this correlation assumption.

The VAR of the portfolio has increased to a level of 1,387,302, higher than the VAR level of 1,151,963 reached when the correlation was 0.10. Note that with a correlation of 0.8 the future prices (and returns) of stocks A and B are much more closely aligned as shown in Figure 15-11.

Credit Risk

Credit risk arises in practice whenever a counterparty is unable or unwilling to perform in accordance with the prespecified contractual provisions of a transaction, leading to

FIGURE 15-10   *VAR of Equity Portfolio by Simulation*

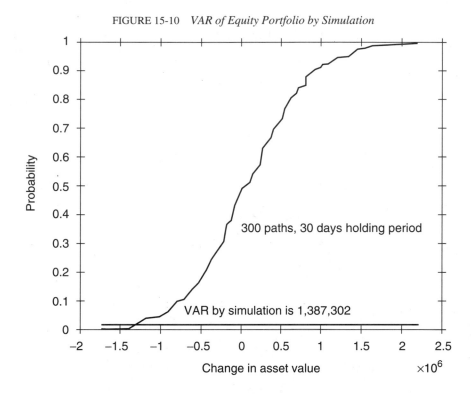

300 paths, 30 days holding period

VAR by simulation is 1,387,302

economic losses to the other party. As a simple example, corporation XYZ has taken a three-month loan of $100 million from Bank A. The loan calls for the payment of interest and principal after one month totalling $102.5 million. At the end of one month, corporation XYZ fails to pay the full amount. This necessitates certain actions by Bank A to recover the amount. These actions are costly and the outcome is uncertain.

Table 15-14 illustrates a hypothetical interest rate swap book of a company. As shown in the table, some of the swaps have a positive marked-to-market value and others have a negative marked-to-market value. Note that the company has engaged in more

Number of Swaps	Swap Maturity	Marked-to-Market Value	Counterparty
1	5	100,000	A
2	4	−200,000	A
3	3	−500,000	X
4	7	1,000,000	Y
5	6	670,000	X

TABLE 15-14
Credit Risk of a Swap Book

FIGURE 15-11   *Prices: Stock A versus Stock B*

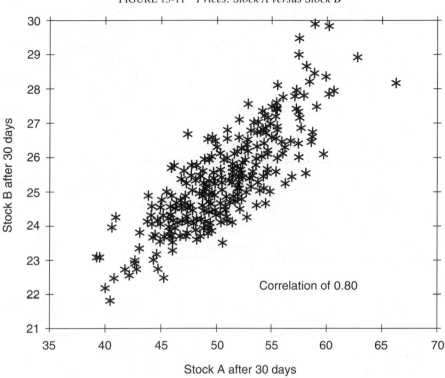

Correlation of 0.80

than one swap with the same counterparty. The notional value of swaps total $500 million. The company has three swaps that have a positive marked-to-market value and two swaps that have a negative marked-to-market value. The total value of positive marked-to-market value swaps is $1,770,000. The total value of the negative marked-to-market value is -$700,000. One way to measure the value of the swap book is 1,770,000 − 700,000 = $1,070,000.

This assumes that there are no defaults by any of the counterparties. In reality one has to worry about this possibility. Default by a counterparty has an asymmetric effect. If, for example, counterparty Y defaults in swap number four, then the firm potentially stands to lose $1 million. Of course, depending on the swap termination provisions, collaterals, and margins, the loss may be less than that. The idea here is that the firm will have to find other counterparties to replace the swaps on which the counterparties have defaulted. This is costly when the swap has a positive marked-to-market value to the firm. This suggests that the credit exposure of the firm is the sum of all positive marked-to-market values, which is $1,770,000.

One innovation that is fast becoming an industry practice in many transactions is the concept of netting. Under netting, instead of counterparty X paying 100 million to counterparty Y and counterparty X receiving 90 million from counterparty Y, the difference of 10 million will be paid by X to Y. Netting allows banks in bilateral transactions to set aside much less capital to support credit risk. The concept of netting has been endorsed by regulatory bodies. In addition, several private sector organizations have attempted to standardize the netting procedures. The Exchange Clearing House Organization (ECHO) initiated by several European banks has introduced multilateral netting of spot and forward transactions. The International Swap Dealers Association (ISDA) has instituted the netting arrangement in swap transactions. Netting may actually enable the firm to reduce the credit exposure. We group the net exposure for each counterparty in Table 15-15.

Counterparty	Marked-to-Market Value
A	-100,000
X	170,000
Y	1,000,000

TABLE 15-15

Net Credit Risk of Swaps

Note that by netting the swap exposures with each counterparty, we find that the firm is able to reduce its exposure further. For the firm, the net exposure with counterparty A is -100,000. The corresponding exposure with counterparty X is 170,000. Thus, the aggregate exposure from credit risk for the firm is $1,170,000.

Typically, firms carry reserves to manage credit exposures. These reserves are a function of the credit quality of the counterparties. Typically, firms may impose a constraint on the average credit quality of the pool of counterparties. For example, some firms require that the average credit rating should be AA or better.

But the credit risk depends not only on the credit quality of the counterparties but also on the diversification (or lack thereof) of counterparties across different industry segments. If a swap dealer has a number of open contracts in one or two industry sectors, then a recession in those sectors can expose the dealer to a greater degree of credit exposure than would otherwise be the case.

The approach behind the measurement of credit risk in our swap example is fairly general. We must price the transactions with each counterparty, utilize netting wherever possible and focus on the transactions that have a positive marked-to-market value. Typically, many transactions may be marked to a model. This situation also represents model risks. For most derivative contracts (such as options), there are many dimensions of risk as noted earlier. Generally, a two-step procedure is used for assessing the credit exposure in derivatives transactions. First, we simulate the underlying variables (such as interest rates or futures prices) to determine the payoffs of the derivative asset. Then, we ascribe certain probabilities of default by counterparties. We combine these two sets of information and arrive at a measure of credit exposure. Often, Monte-Carlo simulation procedures are used for assessing the credit exposure. In implementing this procedure, it is necessary to obtain and process information about factors that determine the probability of default and the recovery rates in the event of a default. That is,

- The distribution of future interest rates or the market values of the derivative asset. This is accomplished by specifying a stochastic process for the underlying state variables which may be stock price, interest rates or volatilities. In a single-state variable model, only one factor will be specified. In two-state variable models, two factors will be specified, and so on.
- The probability of default by the counterparty in the preceding step. This is a function of many factors, such as the overall state of the economy, state of the industry and company specific factors. Typically, the credit reputation of the counterparty and potential changes in credit reputation convey useful information about the probability of defaults. Moodys and Standard and Poor provide statistics on default rates. One-year default rates are computed by dividing the number of rated issuers defaulting over the calendar year by the number of nondefaulted rated issuers in each rating group. This is shown in Table 15-16. Clearly, Table 15-16 shows the association between credit rating and default rates. In modelling credit risk, it is the future default rates that are of interest.

TABLE 15-16
*One-Year Default Rates,
1989–1993*

Credit Reputation	1989	1990	1991	1992	1993
Aaa	0.0	0.0	0.0	0.0	0.0
Aa	0.3	0.0	0.0	0.0	0.02
A	0.0	0.0	0.0	0.0	0.01
Baa	0.5	0.0	0.20	0.0	0.16
Ba	2.7	3.3	5.1	0.2	0.5
B	8.6	12.9	13.1	6.4	5.2

Source: Moody's Investor Service

- The recovery rates associated with defaults. These recovery rates depend on a number of things such as margins, collaterals, termination provisions, covenants, and seniority. Again, recovery rates have to be forecasted to model the credit risk associated with any transactions.

In the context of interest rate swaps, the credit exposure over time depends on two factors. The first factor is the passage of time. This implies that over time the number of remaining cash flows in the swap reduces and as a result the exposure also reduces. The second factor is that at the time of initiation the swap was priced to be zero valued. As time passes, the value of the swap tends to deviate from zero due to changing market conditions. This will in turn cause the swap's credit exposure to increase. The tradeoffs typically imply that the credit exposure of the swap increases for a few years before the first effect starts to dominate. After peaking, the credit exposure reduces over the rest of the life of the swap. Note that this is due to the fact that in interest rate swaps, there is no balloon payment. In contracts with balloon payments, we would not expect to see this pattern of credit exposure over time.

Operational Risk

This risk arises from improper accounting systems and incorrect settlement of transactions and payments. The operating systems include backoffices dealing with clearance, settlement, order processing, computer and accounting systems. Typically, an audit department is responsible for overseeing these activities. Operational risk in listed options sometimes occurs in the clearing house activities. In traditional banking activities where transactions occur in different time zones, there is an operational risk: one leg of the transaction might be done before the other leg can be completed. A bank may end up delivering the securities before the cash gets paid. This poses a big risk, if the transactions run into millions of dollars. Such operational risks are present in large money transfers which are ever-present in financial transactions. In addition, operational risk also results from the absence of adequate position and risk limits. Even where proper risk limits are present it is important that they are enforced: traders and managers who do not live by such risk limits should be taken to task.

Perhaps a telling case in point where the operational risks ultimately resulted in the eventual failure of a firm is the Baring Brothers case. The trading activities of one trader in Singapore were not subject to appropriate risk limits. Eventually, the trader was able to build up sufficient losses by piling up his trading positions to the point where the bank collapsed. The accumulated losses in futures markets amounted to about $1.4 billion. A review of the enclosed article from *Pensions and Investments* (March 20, 1995, page 26) indicates that one key problem in the risk management system was the fact that trading and clearing of trades were under the same manager's authority. Segregation of trading and backoffice operations (clearing) would have mitigated the problem significantly. It was perhaps equally important that huge positions were permitted without periodic and ad hoc reviews by the senior managers. Such reviews should present information about the VAR of the trade and the potential for significant capital commitments.

Risk Management Gets New Respect

By PAUL G. BARR

Investment professionals say risk management controls can be improved across the board at financial institutions, although the situation at Barings PLC, London, probably was an extreme case of lax controls.

Barings' unprecedented $1.4 billion loss in futures contracts has financial executives of all stripes questioning the quality of risk management controls in and outside of their firms.

And consultants say investment losses aren't always the first sign of trouble; investment gains sometimes can be just as big a concern. One consultant says pension funds are among the most vulnerable to problems from hidden, excessive risk.

"It kind of wakes you up and makes you realize this can happen to anybody," said Jeremy Dyer, fund manager for Scottish Amicable Investment Managers Ltd., Glasgow, in reference to Baring's speedy collapse.

Source: *Pensions & Investments* (March 20, 1995). Reprinted with permission.

Likewise, Francis Petrash, senior manager of risk management technology, Coopers & Lybrand, L.L.P., New York, said Barings' losses are "raising the consciousness" of senior managers on risk management controls.

While the bankruptcy of Orange County, Calif., and the collapse of Askin Capital Management raised questions about risk management, those institutions were not viewed to be as sophisticated as Barings, industry participants say.

"Barings was a well-run firm," but apparently didn't have the controls, said William Michaelcheck, who runs Mariner Partners, an investment partnership in New York. "I don't think there's a firm on earth that's not questioning their systems today," he said shortly after Barings' problems came to light.

Based on press reports, consultants say Barings committed some fundamental risk control errors, particularly if both trading and clearance were under the authority of one person.

Segregation of trading and back-office operations is "something an auditor learns in the first week of class," said David Orszulak, a manager for Price Waterhouse L.L.P., in its investment management and securities operations consulting group, Hartford, Conn. Separating the two is done not only to avoid financial disasters—as happened at Barings—but to avoid the temptation to bend the rules, he said.

And one of the first signs of a possible lapse might not be a catastrophe on the scale of what happened at Barings.

"I'm as much concerned with someone taking a big win as much as taking a big loss," said Scott Lummer, managing director, Ibbotson Associates, Chicago. It's "actually a more severe problem given human nature," he said. When a strategy or trader makes a lot of money, the tendency is to think more money should have been devoted to the strategy or trader, Mr. Lummer said.

Mr. Orszulak said it should be an "equally egregious offense" to make money stretching investment guidelines as it is to lose money doing so. "A wrong is a wrong," he said.

And to find the next Barings, one could perhaps look to the investors who profited trading against Barings' futures positions.

All the money Barings lost was won by others, and those winnings create the potential to confuse fortunate market movement with investment skill, Mr. Lummer said. On the other side of that billion dollars or so profit, "somewhere there's a 'damn we're good;' That's the next Barings," Mr. Lummer said.

Once a manager or trader starts making more money, guidelines are stretched or ignored the next time around. In these cases, supervisors start thinking the trader is skillful, not just lucky, he said.

And without downplaying what happened to Barings, Mr. Lummer said bigger dangers still lie with non-financial, investing institutions, such as pension funds and corporations.

Financial companies "are going to be, by their very nature, having to take risk," he said. "Trading companies, they make money, they lose money, that's going to happen."

But "most pension plans are probably underestimating the risk they are taking," he said. "We have a lot of concerns."

The number of losses at institutions in 1994 from derivatives is greater than what is known, including at pension funds, Mr. Lummer said.

Nonetheless, all companies can do a better job of managing their risk, given that firms selling derivatives or derivatives strategies are going to downplay possible bad outcomes. "Companies are taking exposures that are being soft-peddled" by the managers of the assets, Mr. Lummer said.

Some see equity-linked derivatives and derivative strategies as being the next source of unexpected losses. Mr. Michaelcheck of Mariner Partners said the next big test could come with equity-linked derivative products in the United States, where volatility has been very low in recent years. "I think there are a lot of equity derivatives that haven't been tested yet," he said.

To help prevent unexpected positions being taken, consultants said firms have to set various levels of trading limits beginning with each trader all the way up to firmwide limits.

While most firms have set trading limits, too often they are broken when a trader, manager or strategy becomes successful.

Those guidelines should not be broken, Mr. Lummer said. Perhaps guidelines can be changed for experienced traders, but once they are set, "that's the law, no ifs, ands or buts," he said. The key is defining risk, setting guidelines, and not overstepping them.

Moreover, Mr. Petrash of Coopers & Lybrand said traders and their supervisors should meet regularly to discuss the trader's positions and the potential profits and losses, and the risks being taken.

While computer systems can sometimes be cracked, and accounting numbers played with, using personal interaction and tracking cash flows are two simple ways to keep a stronger handle on a firm's market risk.

On a daily basis, a trader's position sheets should be cross-referenced with the day's trading records, consultants say. Both the supervisor and the trader need to sign off on those positions, and discuss the strategies and possible outcomes related to the positions, Mr. Petrash said.

Moreover, there should be a daily trading exceptions report, which would not necessarily limit a trader's ability to trade, but would flag trades of an unusual size or nature, he said. There also should be regular discussions between a trader and supervisor of how particular trades can be unwound if they prove unprofitable, and what will be the costs of unwinding them, Mr. Petrash said.

Tom Ho, president of Global Advanced Technology Corp., a New York-based fixed-income and risk management consultant, said firms now generally rely too much on risk control systems that look backward, and act as more of a report card. Instead the industry should move to surveillance types of systems that are proactive in seeking out potential deviations from a firm's desired risk, he said.

Mr. Petrash noted a risk management system doesn't act only as a control, but also as a means to profit. They can lead to enhanced opportunities in the marketplace.

While industry professionals were close to undivided on their call for strong controls, the cost of implementing controls is less clear.

The cost of an adequate risk control trading system can run as high as the tens of millions to hundreds of millions of dollars, Mr. Petrash said. It depends on what it is worth for an investment firm's employees to sleep well at night, he said.

Robert D. Arnott, chief investment officer for money manager First Quadrant Corp., Pasadena, Calif., said trading systems are widely available, and not expensive. At the most basic level, "Custodial banks can track aggregate positions," he said.

Greg Pond, president of ADS Associates, Calabasas, Calif., a trading systems firm, said costs vary widely depending on the needs of the institution. His firm has installed its systems and trading software at prices from roughly $350,000 to $3 million.

Another case in point is the ability of some trading units to perform trades where the connection between putative profits from certain trades and actual cash (if any) resulting from such transactions is not properly accounted for in a timely fashion. This happened in the case of the Kidder Peabody situation. In this case, the accounting system for handling certain trades in the strips markets and the government bond markets appeared to have a flaw which was exploited to make paper profits on which the compensation appeared to have been determined. As the *Business Week* article (May 2, 1994, page 121) shows, this practice was allowed over a period of two years, reflecting serious lack of operational and management controls.

Why Didn't Kidder Catch On?

Wall Street is skeptical of the "We wuz robbed" explanation

By Leah Nathans Spiro,
with Philip L. Zweig, in New York and Tim Smart in New Haven

Was it simply an isolated incident, a scheme that even the best controls couldn't have detected? Or did it reflect a broad, systemic breakdown?

That is a key issue facing Kidder, Peabody & Co.'s senior managers as they investigate who was behind a two-year, $350 million, phony government bond trading scheme that was disclosed on Apr. 17. Kidder Chief Executive Michael A. Carpenter says he and his top lieutenant, fixed-income head Edward A. Cerullo, were victims of a very sophisticated rogue trader named Joseph Jett, who ran the firm's government bond desk. Jett has been fired, and six other employees were suspended from their jobs. Jett could not be reached for comment.

Carpenter insists that Kidder's controls and risk-management systems are just as good as the rest of the Street's, even though no systems are foolproof: "The altimeter said we were flying at the right altitude, and the compass said we were flying in the right direction, and we banged into the mountain."

Raised Eyebrows

Yet many on Wall Street are skeptical of Carpenter's "We wuz robbed" explanation of what is one of the largest Wall Street losses ever. How could the scheme have gone on undetected since 1991? Why didn't 15-year Kidder veteran Cerullo, who was Jett's boss, have a better handle on how Jett was generating "profits" of $20 million to $40 *million a month? And most important, are Carpenter and Cerullo to blame for building a culture at Kidder that kowtowed to superstar traders?*

John F. Welch Jr., the tough-guy chief executive of General Electric, which owns Kidder, supports Carpenter. "I think, based on everything I know, Carpenter learned of the situation, attacked it vigorously, and has never tried in any way not to get it out," says Welch. "Do I wish he had a nose that had smelled it earlier? Sure. But that's hindsight." GE took a $210 million charge for the Kidder losses on $1.07 billion in first-quarter earnings.

Yet Welch implies that the mess could have been avoided. "Clearly this man [Jett] couldn't do it alone. People either knowingly made errors or didn't see red flags," says Welch. "No question, when Gary Lynch is through with this investigation, there will be findings" that could lead to further action against employees or their supervisors. Welch is referring to the Kidder-commissioned inquiry being conducted by attorney Lynch.

Lynch is likely to have plenty of questions for Cerullo. A fanatical antismoker who is well-liked and respected at Kidder, Cerullo has had other scrapes with problem traders. In 1991, he was fined $5,000 and censured by the National Association of Securities Dealers for failing to supervise a trader who engineered unauthorized bond transactions. Carpenter backs Cerullo. "He's kicking himself. But I am 100% behind him," says Carpenter. Cerullo declined comment.

Massive Positions

Jett's scheme involved arbitrage trades between the value of pieces of Treasury bonds, called strips, and the recombined bonds. Trouble was, says Kidder, Jett was not generating profit from the slightly greater value of the reconstituted bond, as is usually the practice. Instead, using forward contracts in the strips, he could create much larger bogus profits by exploiting flaws in Kidder's accounting system.

That Jett was allowed to carry out this ploy for such a long time, say Wall Street traders and risk managers, reflects major controls lapses. They claim that if Cerullo truly understood the massive positions Jett must have been taking, he would have questioned Jett about how he was generating such profits. Trading Treasury strips is generally a very low margin area of the fixed-income business, say traders.

Carpenter responds that the profits were not out of line with the real trades on the books and that Cerullo and he were unaware of the phony trades because they accumulated gradually over a period of time. Cerullo "did understand his trading strategy," says Carpenter. But "there didn't seem to be anything terribly out of line. We felt we were running a low-risk, high-margin business."

Kidder may have ignored the lesson learned by Salomon Brothers Inc. in the wake of the 1991 Treasury bond bid rigging scandal: Don't give too much power to traders. When asked whether Cerullo knows how Michael W. Vranos, Kidder's star mortgage-backed trader, generates profits, a senior Kidder official says: "Ed doesn't sit him down and say, 'How did you do it this month?'" But you can be sure such conversations with Kidder traders will occur in the future.

Liquidity Risk

This risk is especially important when the asset portfolio that needs to be funded is highly illiquid. Such illiquid assets might be emerging market debt or real estate or long dated OTC options. The risk is the inability to fund these asset portfolios. For example, commercial banks hold reserves based on certain assumptions about the proportion of depositors who are likely to withdraw cash. This provides the basis for extension of credit. If their assumptions prove to be incorrect and more depositors decide to withdraw money, the bank will face a liquidity crisis. An extreme example is the case of a bank run. In a run, a significant percent of depositors decide to withdraw their deposits and the bank runs the risk of a failure precipitated by illiquidity.

Often, firms find that they engage in transactions that are not liquid: in other words, there are no active secondary markets in which such contracts may be freely traded. For example, an oil company may sell its output to its institutional customers using long-term forward contracts.

Consider the situation of a firm that has sold long dated forwards as shown in Table 15-17. As the price of oil fluctuates in the spot market, the value of these long dated forward contracts will fluctuate. For example, if the spot price of oil falls to $17.00 per barrel, these forward contracts will be extremely valuable to the firm. But since these are bilateral forward contracts, they are not liquid. As a consequence, even though the value of these contracts has increased, the firm is unable to liquidate the contracts and realize their value. Conversely, if the spot price of oil were to increase to $25.00 per barrel, then the value of these forward contracts will decline sharply, even though there are no cashflow implications to the firm until the contracts mature. An opportunity cost of selling the oil at a higher price is clearly present.

The firm may wish to hedge its forward positions using the crude oil futures at NYMEX. In choosing this alternative, it must be aware of the liquidity problems that such large hedges might produce. NYMEX futures do extend to several months, but the liquidity beyond a few months is not that great. As a consequence, the firm must hedge its long-term forward commitments with short-term NYMEX futures. The term structure of the futures prices changes its shape from time to time; the market may be in normal backwardation when distant futures prices are higher than short-dated futures prices. Or the term structure may be in contango wherein longer maturity futures prices are lower than shorter maturity futures prices. Besides, futures prices are marked to market. This means that there may be large variation margin calls leading to significant liquidity problems. Suppose that the firm ends up buying 800,000 barrels worth of futures

Counterparty	Forward Maturity	Forward Price per Barrel	Amount Sold in Barrels	TABLE 15-17 Long-Term Forwards in Oil
A	5 years	20.00	100,000	
X	8 years	21.05	200,000	
Y	2 years	22.15	500,000	

and the futures prices moved from $20.00 a barrel to $19.50 in one day. Then, the variation margin call will be $800,000 \times 0.50 = \$400,000$. Of course, the situation can be more problematic if the term structure of the futures prices moves from contango to normal backwardation when the hedge is in place. This will lead to a rise in distant futures prices which the firm cannot take advantage of, as it has already locked in prices in long-term forwards, but it will end up paying huge variation margin calls on short-term futures contracts for which the prices have fallen.

The situation described above is an important one with potentially dire consequences for the financial health of the firm. The case of Metallgesellschaft (MG) is illustrative of this problem. As the enclosed article from *The Economist* (February 4, 1995, page 71) indicates, MG was using short-term crude oil futures contracts at the NYMEX to hedge its long-term forward committments to deliver fuel. The resulting funding risk was further accentuated by the need to "roll over" periodically from one short-term future (as it neared expiration) to the next. According to the auditors, the estimated losses as of December 1993 was a little over $1 billion.

Metallgesellschaft

Germany's Corporate Whodunnit

A report on the Metallgesellschaft affair raises more questions than it answers about who was responsible for one of Germany's biggest business fiascos

BERLIN

Just over a year since the near-collapse of Metallgesellschaft (MG), one of Germany's biggest industrial conglomerates, the leading figures in the affair are still trading blows. On January 20th Heinz Schimmelbusch, the firm's former boss, filed a lawsuit in New York alleging that Deutsche Bank and one of its executives, Ronaldo Schmitz, who is the chairman of MG's supervisory board, were in part responsible for the financial troubles that laid the company low. A week later an auditors' report commissioned by MG's shareholders, which include Deutsche, put the blame squarely on Mr Schimmelbusch and other former MG executives.

Reputations are not the only thing at stake. As they assess the cases, the courts will also, by implication, be judging the fitness of Deutsche and other banks as owners and supervisors of German companies. Doubts about their ability as overseers grew again this week when it emerged that Klöckner-Humboldt-Deutz, an engine maker in which Deutsche has a 36% stake, needs a DM719m ($472m) rescue package. And the Metallgesellschaft affair has become part of the lore about the supposed danger of financial derivatives.

The dispute is about the fuel-trading business of MG Refining & Marketing (MGRM), an American subsidiary of MG, and its huge positions in derivatives (most of which were futures contracts). After it was revealed in December 1993 that the trading arm had run into trouble, Mr Schimmelbusch and other senior MG managers were removed by the supervisory board. Deutsche Bank and MG's new boss, Kajo Neukirchen, claim that MGRM had been recklessly punting on oil futures. They say that closing out these contracts was the only way to avoid further losses.

MG's former managers take a different view. They argue that the intervention of the supervisory board simply made matters worse, an argument that is supported by two American academics, Merton Miller, a Nobel prize-winning economist, and Christopher Culp, one of his colleagues at the University of Chicago. The two Americans have said that Deutsche and MG's new management doomed what would eventually have turned out to be a profitable trading operation by closing out some of MGRM's contracts when oil prices were plummeting.

Both camps can agree on some aspects of the affair. Nobody, for instance, disputes that MGRM's use of short-term energy futures contracts to hedge long-term commitments to deliver fuel meant that it would have to stump up more collateral on its loss-making futures positions if oil prices fell. They also agree that the scheme required MGRM continuously to sell short-term futures contracts, and to buy new ones. This "rollover" meant that the company might one day have to pay more for new contracts than it made from old ones.

Just this nightmare occurred through much of 1993. By December of that year MGRM had long positions in energy derivatives equivalent to 185m barrels of oil. Rolling over the contracts cost the firm a total of $88m in October and November alone. Here, however, explanations of what happened diverge. MG claims that instead of prolonging its subsidiary's losses, it had to close out its positions. The auditors reckon that MGRM's total loss by the end of December 1993 was just over $1 billion.

It was a self-inflicted wound, contend Messrs Miller and Culp. MRGM's futures were hedging long-term contracts to supply products such as petrol and heating oil for up to a decade at fixed prices which were then higher than those in the spot market. As oil prices fell, dragging down the value of MGRM's futures contracts, the value of the long-term contracts surged, in theory offsetting the losses. Had MGRM persevered, it would have made a profit.

The auditors' report attacks this thesis in two ways. First, it suggests that as early as June 1993 Mr Schimmelbusch tried in vain to reduce MGRM's positions. The report quotes a memo from Mr Schimmelbusch dated that month in which MG's former boss asks his chief financial officer, Meinhard Forster, to cut the credit employed by the trading businesses "in a draconian manner if necessary".

Yet MGRM's position jumped from 100m barrels in June to 185m barrels by December. The auditors claim that MGRM was trying to offset losses from its futures positions—a view which Mr Schimmelbusch apparently shared. According to the auditors, in a meeting in December with members of MG's supervisory board, including Mr Schmitz, Mr Schimmelbusch described MGRM's rush to add business as a "double or quits" gamble. He denies that he said this.

Had MG's banks put up more cash, they might have forestalled a forced liquidation. In Mr Miller's view that would have been better than taking a $1 billion loss on a potentially profitable position. The auditors dispute this, too. Their report claims that some 59m barrels-worth of the underlying long-term contracts had a negative value of about $12m. MG counts itself lucky to have escaped these contracts at no cost.

If this claim stands up to scrutiny, then the contracts in question did not gain in value as oil prices fell. That means the futures contracts backing them were hedging nothing. The implication is that they were a pure gamble on energy prices. This is likely to be hotly disputed by those who took the positions. MG's argument will almost certainly not be the last one in this affair. Mr Schimmelbusch and MGRM's former managers are all pressing ahead with lawsuits. Until these are played out, the Metallgesellschaft affair will continue to haunt Germany's mightiest bank.

Systemic Risk

Interbank and interdealer transactions have grown significantly in many markets. In such situations, one bank or one dealer may be a counterparty to a number of transactions with very many banks and dealers. If, due to a crisis, (induced by liquidity, credit or market exposures) that dealer or bank fails in its obligation as a counterparty in various transactions, then a domino effect could result in which several other banks and dealers also end up in a crisis. The ramifications of a systemic failure are extensive. Typically, central banks and regulatory authorities play an active role to try to prevent such calamities. The capital adequacy requirements, government guarantees and audits are examples of some policy actions that serve to lower the probability of a systemic failure. In addition, during such episodes, central banks often play an active role to stem the damage. For example, during the stock market crash of 1987, the Federal Reserve provided liquidity.

SYSTEMS AND DATA REQUIREMENTS

Over the last ten years, risk management has assumed a more important role in money-center banks, investment banks and security-dealing firms. This is one area where some of the most recent developments in valuation theory, computer hardware and software interact to produce integrated multi-market risk measurement and management systems. Let us review the ingredients of a risk management system.

Data: It is necessary to deliver data (preferably real-time) to firms from many markets in order for firms to measure the positions of securities held. In many situations, transactions are so customized that they cannot be valued using the market data alone; models may be needed to value such transactions. Recall the example of a swap transaction which can only be priced by deriving the zero coupon bond prices from a specific segment of the fixed-income market. This indicates that the data have to be processed through some preliminary models and statistical methods to generate inputs to the valuation framework. The firm needs to have reliable and timely access to historical data to estimate volatilities and cross correlations.

Valuation models: The measurement of risk is only as good as the models that have been used to generate the measures. This is not a serious problem where the markets are active and the positions and risk measures do not require models for valuation. But in most cases, models are needed to value positions and assess their risks. Take the example of pricing and measuring the risk of an option on zero coupon bond yields. Several models may be used for this purpose, including Black and Scholes (1973), Ho and Lee (1986), Black, Derman and Toy (1987), Hull and White (1989), Cox, Ingersoll and Ross (1985) and Heath, Jarrow and Morton (1990).

Even in situations where there is a general agreement on what is the single correct model (and usually there is no agreement on this matter), there is the issue of estimating the parameters that go into the model. Firms using the same model may use different procedures for estimation.

Computer technology: With the advent of global 24-hour trading by many institutions, the technology used to support the trading systems has become the focus. Real-time analytics, better integration of front office (sales and trading) and back office (order processing, settlement, clearance and accounting) systems, use of workstations, and so on have become more and more common in the last decade. A number of data vendors such as Reuters, Telerate, Bloomberg, and Quotron, have started to offer live data at widely distributed locations. In fact, typically such data are also supplied with relatively good valuation models, historical information and analytics. Portfolio management software with the ability to perform marked-to-market valuation and performance measurement are also offered in the market.

CONCLUSION

Over the years, capital markets have created innovations to more effectively manage risk. Some of these innovations have come at the instigation of regulators; others have come due to technological advances.

In addition, structured transactions and fully funded subsidiaries have been developed to deal with the issue of credit risk. Asset-backed commercial paper programs have enabled issuers with poor credit reputation to take advantage of some of the better quality assets in their balance sheets to issue highly rated paper at a lower cost. This innovation uses a special purpose vehicle (SPV) as discussed in Chapters 1 and 9 with credit and liquidity enhancements. In a similar way, dealers have created fully funded AAA subsidiaries to engage in swap transactions.

The regulators have responded by focusing on auditing financial institutions to ensure that their internal controls, risk measurement systems and models that are needed to value securities are adequate. The idea that all firms must have satisfactory capital requirements to participate in markets has gained wide acceptance in the regulatory discussions. As noted in Chapter 14, there have been developments in which swap transactions have to be performed with collaterals and discretionary marking to market.

The area of risk management will continue to attract considerable attention from regulators and constituents of financial institutions and dealers. While significant strides have been made in the measurement and management of risk, there are still several open issues. One important issue is the interactions between different sources of risk. When there is a big move in the market, many counterparties become more vulnerable to credit risk. This is also precisely the situation when market liquidity becomes a problem. As a result, we see that the market risk, credit risk and liquidity risk tend to interact. No satisfactory approaches are available currently to deal with this problem.

PROBLEMS

15.1   The table below lists the swap transactions of a dealer.
(a) Determine the credit exposure of this dealer.
(b) Due to a recession, the credit reputation of all counterparties deteriorated. Examine how the firm should go about making loss reserves. Identify the counterparties against whom the firm has maximum exposure.

Question 1

Number	Swap Maturity	Marked to Market Value	Counterparty
1	5	200,000	A
2	4	-40,000	A
3	3	-900,000	X
4	7	1,000,000	Y
5	6	670,000	Y
6	4	800,000	Y
7	2	70,000	X
8	2	170,000	X
9	3	200,000	X
10	4	170,000	A

15.2   What are the ramifications of the Group of 30 recommendations for security dealers? Focus on the data, systems and modelling issues that need to be addressed.
15.3   You have invested $1 million in a security which has a volatility of 15% (annualized). What is the VAR of this security for a holding period of 30 days at 99% confidence level?
15.4   The variance-covariance matrix of two securities is shown next.

Question 4
VAR of a Portfolio

Security	A	B
A	0.0225	0.0120
B		0.0100

The share price of A is 100 and that of B is 80. Determine the VAR of a value-weighted portfolio of these securities at 99% confidence level for a holding period of one day.
15.5   In Problem 15.3, determine the VAR of an equally weighted portfolio at 99% confidence level for a holding period of one day.

REFERENCES

Bank for Intentional Settlements 1988. International Convergence of Capital Measurement and Capital Standards. Basle, Switzerland.

Barr, P. G. 1995. "Risk Management Gets New Respect." *Pensions and Investments* (March 20):26.

Black, F., and M. Scholes 1973. "The Pricing of Options and Corporate Liabilities." *Journal of Political Economy* 81:637–659.

Black, F., E. Derman, and W. Toy 1990. "A One-Factor Model of Interest Rates and Its Applications to Treasury Bond Options." *Financial Analysts Journal* 46(1):33–39.

1993. *Corporate Finance, Derivatives Supplement.* Euromoney Publications.

Cox, J. C., J. Ingersoll and S. A. Ross 1985. "A Theory of the Term Structure of Interest Rates." *Econometrica* 53:385–407.

Davis, K., and I. Harper 1991. *Risk Management in Financial Institutions.* Sydney; Allen and Unwin.

1992. *Derivatives,* Special Issue. *Euromoney.*

1993. Derivatives; Practices and Principles. Global Derivatives Study Group Report. Washington, D.C.: Group of Thirty.

Duffee, G. R. 1994. "On Measuring Credit Risks of Derivative Instruments." Federal Reserve Board.

Edwards, F. R. 1994. "Systemic Risk in OTC Derivatives Markets: Much Ado About Not Too Much." Columbia University.

Edwards, F. R. 1994. "Are Derivatives Hazardous to Your Health." Columbia University.

Heath, D., R. Jarrow, and A. Morton 1990. "Bond Pricing and the Term Structure of Interest Rates: A Discrete Time Approximation." *Journal of Financial and Quantitative Analysis* 25(4):419–440.

Ho, T. S. Y., and S. Lee 1986. "Term Structure Movements and Pricing of Interest Rate Contingent Claims." *The Journal of Finance* XLI(5):1011–1029.

1995. "Metallgesellschaft." *Economist* (February 4):71.

1995. *RiskMetrics™—Technical Document,* J.P. Morgan, Global Research. New York: Morgan Guaranty Trust Company.

Spiro, L. N. 1994. "Why Didn't Kidder Catch On." *Business Week* (May 2):121.

Index